MACROMEDIA

Dreamweaver® 2004

Comprehensive Concepts
and Techniques

Gary B. Shelly
Thomas J. Cashman
Dolores J. Wells

index.htm

THOMSON COURSE TECHNOLOGY

25 THOMSON PLACE

BOSTON MA 02210

THOMSON
COURSE TECHNOLOGY™

SHELLY
CASHMAN
SERIES®

Australia • Canada • Denmark • Japan • Mexico • New Zealand • Philippines • Puerto Rico • Singapore
South Africa • Spain • United Kingdom • United Stat

* 9 5 0 6 3 9 7 0 *

THOMSON

COURSE TECHNOLOGY

Macromedia Dreamweaver MX 2004:
Comprehensive Concepts and Techniques

Gary B. Shelly
Thomas J. Cashman
Dolores J. Wells

Managing Editor:
Alexandra Arnold

Senior Acquisitions Editor:
Dana Merk

Senior Product Manager:
Karen Stevens

Product Manager:
Reed Cotter

Associate Product Manager:
Selena Coppock

Print Buyer:
Laura Astorino

Production Editor:
Pamela Elizian

Copy Editor:
Lori Silfen

Proofreader:
Nancy Lamm

QA Manuscript Reviewers:
Alex White, John Freitas,
Burt LaFountain, Marianne Snow

Cover Artist:
John Still

Composition:
GEX Publishing Services

MACROMEDIA®

Dreamweaver MX 2004

Comprehensive Concepts and Techniques

Contents

Appendix B

Dreamweaver and Accessibility

Appendix C

Publishing to a Web Server

Preface

The Shelly Cashman Series® offers the finest textbooks in computer education. We are proud of the fact that our textbook series has been the most widely used books in education. With each new edition of our Dreamweaver books, we have made significant improvements based on the software and comments made by the instructors and students. *Macromedia® Dreamweaver® MX 2004: Comprehensive Concepts and Techniques* continues with the innovation, quality, and reliability that you have come to expect from the Shelly Cashman Series.

Macromedia Dreamweaver is known as the standard in visual authoring. Macromedia Dreamweaver MX 2004 enhances the work experience for users in the following ways: (1) richer CSS support; (2) dynamic cross-browser validation; (3) built-in graphics editing; (4) secure FTP; (5) seamless integration with external files and code; (6) tighter integration with other Macromedia tools; (7) enhanced coding tools; and (8) an improved user interface.

In this *Macromedia Dreamweaver MX 2004* book, you will find an educationally sound and easy-to-follow pedagogy that combines a step-by-step approach with corresponding screens. All projects and exercises in this book are designed to take full advantage of the Dreamweaver MX 2004 enhancements. The popular Other Ways and More About features offer in-depth knowledge of Dreamweaver MX 2004. The new Q&A feature provides answers to common questions students have about the Web design process. The Learn It Online page presents a wealth of additional exercises to ensure your students have all the reinforcement they need. The project material is developed carefully to ensure that students will see the importance of learning Dreamweaver for future coursework.

Objectives of This Textbook

Macromedia Dreamweaver MX 2004: Comprehensive Concepts and Techniques is intended for a course that offers in-depth instruction in Dreamweaver MX 2004 and the creation of Web sites. No experience with a computer is assumed, and no mathematics beyond the high school freshman level is required. The objectives of this book are:

- To teach students how to use Dreamweaver MX 2004
- To expose students to proper Web site design and management techniques
- To acquaint students with the proper procedures to create Web sites suitable for coursework, professional purposes, and personal use
- To develop an exercise-oriented approach that allows learning by doing
- To encourage independent study and help those who are working alone

The Shelly Cashman Approach

Features of the Shelly Cashman Series *Macromedia Dreamweaver MX 2004* books include:

- **Project Orientation** Each project in the book presents a practical problem and complete solution using an easy-to-understand approach.
- **Step-by-Step, Screen-by-Screen Instructions** Each of the tasks required to complete a project is identified throughout the project. Full-color screens with call outs accompany the steps.

- **Thoroughly Tested Projects**   Unparalleled quality is ensured because every screen in the book is produced by the author only after performing a step, and then each project must pass Thomson Course Technology's award-winning Quality Assurance program.

- **Other Ways Boxes and Quick Reference**   The Other Ways boxes displayed at the end of many of the step-by-step sequences specify the other ways to do the task completed in the steps. Thus, the steps and the Other Ways box make a comprehensive reference unit. The Quick Reference at the back of the book provides a quick reference to common keyboard shortcuts.

- **More About and Q&A Features**   These marginal annotations provide background information, tips, and answers to common questions that complement the topics covered, adding depth and perspective to the learning process.

- **Integration of the World Wide Web**   The World Wide Web is integrated into the Dreamweaver MX 2004 learning experience by (1) More About annotations that send students to Web sites for up-to-date information and alternative approaches to tasks; and (2) the Learn It Online page at the end of each project, which has project reinforcement exercises, learning games, and other types of student activities.

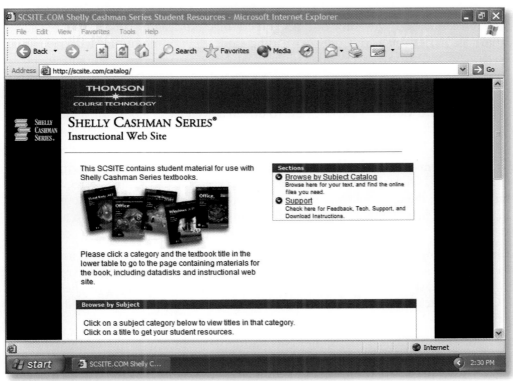

FIGURE 1

Organization of This Textbook

Macromedia Dreamweaver MX 2004: Comprehensive Concepts and Techniques provides detailed instruction on how to use Dreamweaver MX 2004. The material is divided into an introduction chapter, nine projects, three appendices, and a quick reference summary.

Introduction – Web Site Development and Macromedia Dreamweaver MX 2004
In the Introduction, students are presented with the basics of the Internet and World
Wide Web and their associated terms. Topics include differentiating between Web
pages and Web sites and types of Web pages; identifying Web browser features; an
overview of planning, designing, developing, testing, publishing, and maintaining a
Web site; a discussion of HTML; various methods and tools used in Web site creation; and a brief description of the new features in Dreamweaver MX 2004.

Project 1 – Creating a Dreamweaver Web Page and Local Site In Project 1, students
are introduced to the Dreamweaver environment. Students create a local site and the
home page for the Web site that they develop throughout the projects in the book.
Topics include starting and quitting Dreamweaver; an introduction to the
Dreamweaver workspace and panel groups; creating a local site; creating a Web
page, applying a background image, and formatting Web page properties; inserting
line breaks and special characters; inserting a horizontal rule; using the Check
Spelling feature; previewing and printing a page in a Web browser; and an overview
of Dreamweaver Help.

Project 2 – Adding Web Pages, Links, and Images In Project 2, students learn how to
add new pages to an existing Web site and then how to add links and images. Topics
include using Dreamweaver's file browser feature; understanding and modifying
image file formats; adding page images to a Web page; creating relative, absolute, and
e-mail links; changing the color of links and editing and deleting links; using the site
map; displaying the page in Code view; using Code view to modify HTML code; and
an overview of Dreamweaver's accessibility features.

Project 3 – Tables and Page Layout In Project 3, students are introduced to techniques
for using tables in Web site design. Topics include an introduction to page layout using
tables in Standard view and Layout view to design a Web page; modifying a table structure; understanding HTML table tags; adding content to a table and formatting the content; formatting the table; and creating head content.

Project 4 – Forms In Project 4, students are introduced to the concept of forms and
form processing. Topics include client-side versus server-side processing; designing and
creating a form; the different form objects; adding text fields and text areas to a form;
using a table to help with form layout; form accessibility options; and how to add behaviors to a form.

Project 5 – Templates and Style Sheets In Project 5, students learn how to use templates and style sheets. Topics include creating a template; understanding differences
between HTML styles and cascading style sheets; creating a cascading style sheet; applying CSS attributes to a template; creating a Web page from a template; and using the
Assets panel.

Project 6 – Layers, Image Maps, and Navigation Bars In Project 6, students learn
how to add layers and create image maps and navigation bars. Topics include understanding the concept of a layer, and how to resize, name, and align layers; how an image
map works; how to create an image map and how to assign behaviors to manipulate layers within the map; how to insert the Date object; and how to create a navigation bar.

Project 7 – Page Layout with Frames In Project 7, students learn how to use frames to
design the presentation of a Web page. Topics include understanding the advantages and
disadvantages of using frames; creating a frameset and frames; setting and modifying the
properties for a frame and a frameset; adding static content to a frame; and adding Flash
buttons as navigation elements.

Project 8 – Animation and Behaviors In Project 8, students learn the concept of animation using the timeline and how to create linear and nonlinear timelines. Topics
include understanding the concept of a timeline; using the Timelines panel; adding a

layer to a timeline; adding a behavior to a layer; showing and hiding layers; and adding a play button to a timeline.

Project 9 – Media Objects In Project 9, students learn about different media objects and how to add media objects to a Web site. Topics include inserting Flash text and Flash movies into a Web page; adding linked sound and embedded sound to a Web page; inserting video into a Web page; checking for plug-ins; and inserting Shockwave movies and Java applets into a Web page.

Appendices The book includes three appendices. Appendix A presents an introduction to the Macromedia Dreamweaver Help system. Appendix B discusses Dreamweaver and Accessibility features; and Appendix C illustrates how to define and publish a Web site to a remote server.

Quick Reference In Dreamweaver, you can accomplish a task in a number of ways, such as using the mouse, menu, context menu, and keyboard. The Quick Reference provides a quick reference to common keyboard shortcuts.

End-of-Project Student Activities

A notable strength of the Shelly Cashman Series *Macromedia Dreamweaver MX 2004* books is the extensive student activities at the end of each project. Well-structured student activities can make the difference between students merely participating in a class and students retaining the information they learn. The activities in the Shelly Cashman Series *Macromedia Dreamweaver MX 2004* books include the following:

- **What You Should Know** A listing of the tasks completed within a project together with the pages on which the step-by-step, screen-by-screen explanations appear.

- **Learn It Online** Every project features a Learn It Online page comprising ten exercises. These exercises include True/False, Multiple Choice, Short Answer, Flash Cards, Practice Test, Learning Games, Tips and Tricks, Newsgroup usage, Expanding Your Horizons, and Search Sleuth.

- **Apply Your Knowledge** This exercise usually requires students to open and manipulate a file on the Data Disk. To obtain a copy of the Data Disk, follow the instructions on the inside back cover of this textbook.

- **In the Lab** Three in-depth assignments per project require students to utilize the project concepts and techniques to solve problems on a computer.

- **Cases and Places** Five unique real-world case-study situations, including one small-group activity.

Shelly Cashman Series Instructor Resources

The Shelly Cashman Series is dedicated to providing you with all of the tools you need to make your class a success. Information on all supplementary materials is available through your Thomson Course Technology representative or by calling one of the following telephone numbers: Colleges and Universities and Private Career Colleges, 1-800-648-7450; High Schools, 1-800-824-5179; Canada, 1-800-268-2222; Corporations with IT Training Centers, 1-800-648-7450; and Government Agencies, Health-Care Organizations, and Correctional Facilities, 1-800-477-3692.

The Instructor Resources for this textbook include both teaching and testing aids. The contents of each item on the Instructor Resources CD-ROM (ISBN 1-4188-4353-9) are described below.

INSTRUCTOR'S MANUAL The Instructor's Manual is made up of Microsoft Word files, which include detailed lesson plans with page number references, lecture notes, teaching tips, classroom activities, discussion topics, projects to assign, and transparency references. The transparencies are available through the Figure Files described below.

LECTURE SUCCESS SYSTEM The Lecture Success System consists of intermediate files that correspond to certain figures in the book, allowing you to step through the creation of an application in a project during a lecture without entering large amounts of data.

SYLLABUS Sample syllabi, which can be customized easily to a course, are included. The syllabi cover policies, class and lab assignments and exams, and procedural information.

FIGURE FILES Illustrations for every figure in the textbook are available in electronic form. Use this ancillary to present a slide show in lecture or to print transparencies for use in lecture with an overhead projector. If you have a personal computer and LCD device, this ancillary can be an effective tool for presenting lectures.

POWERPOINT PRESENTATIONS PowerPoint Presentations is a multimedia lecture presentation system that provides slides for each project. Presentations are based on project objectives. Use this presentation system to present well-organized lectures that are both interesting and knowledge based. PowerPoint Presentations provides consistent coverage at schools that use multiple lecturers.

SOLUTIONS TO EXERCISES Solutions are included for the end-of-project exercises, as well as the Project Reinforcement exercises.

TEST BANK & TEST ENGINE The ExamView test bank includes 110 questions for every project (25 multiple-choice, 50 true/false, and 35 completion) with page number references, and when appropriate, figure references. A version of the test bank you can print also is included. The test bank comes with a copy of the test engine, ExamView, the ultimate tool for your objective-based testing needs. ExamView is a state-of-the-art test builder that is easy to use. ExamView enables you to create paper-, LAN-, or Web-based tests from test banks designed specifically for your Course Technology textbook. Utilize the ultra-efficient QuickTest Wizard to create tests in less than five minutes by taking advantage of Course Technology's question banks, or customize your own exams from scratch.

DATA FILES FOR STUDENTS All the files that are required by students to complete the exercises are included. You can distribute the files on the Instructor Resources CD-ROM to your students over a network, or you can have them follow the instructions on the inside back cover of this book to obtain a copy of the Data Disk.

ADDITIONAL ACTIVITIES FOR STUDENTS These additional activities consist of Project Reinforcement Exercises, which are true/false, multiple choice, and short answer questions that help students gain confidence in the material learned.

Online Content

Thomson Course Technology offers textbook-based content for Blackboard, WebCT, and MyCourse 2.1.

BLACKBOARD AND WEBCT As the leading provider of IT content for the Blackboard and WebCT platforms, Thomson Course Technology delivers rich content that enhances your textbook to give your students a unique learning experience. Thomson Course Technology has partnered with WebCT and Blackboard to deliver our market-leading content through these state-of-the-art online learning platforms.

MYCOURSE 2.1 MyCourse 2.1 is Thomson Course Technology's powerful online course management and content delivery system. Completely maintained and hosted by Thomson, MyCourse 2.1 delivers an online learning environment that is completely secure and provides superior performance. MyCourse 2.1 allows nontechnical users to create, customize, and deliver World Wide Web-based courses; post content and assignments; manage student enrollment; administer exams; track results in the online gradebook; and more.

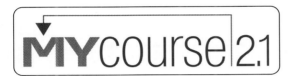

Macromedia Dreamweaver MX 2004 30-Day Trial Edition

A copy of the Dreamweaver MX 2004 30-Day trial edition can be found on the Macromedia Web site (www.macromedia.com). Point to Downloads in the top navigation bar, click Free Trials, and then follow the on-screen instructions. When you activate the software, you will receive a license that allows you to use the software for 30 days. Thomson Course Technology and Macromedia provide no product support for this trial edition. When the trial period ends, you can purchase a copy of Macromedia Dreamweaver MX 2004, or uninstall the trial edition and reinstall your previous version.

The minimum system requirements for the 30-day trial edition is a 600 MHz Intel Pentium III processor or equivalent; Windows XP, Windows 2000, Windows 98 SE (4.10.2222 A), or Windows Server 2003; 128 MB RAM (256 MB recommended); and 275 MB available disk space.

To the Student... Getting the Most Out of Your Book

Welcome to *Macromedia Dreamweaver MX 2004: Comprehensive Concepts and Techniques.* You can save yourself a lot of time and gain a better understanding of Dreamweaver MX 2004 if you spend a few minutes reviewing the figures and callouts in this section.

1 Project Orientation

The project orientation lets you see firsthand how Web development problems are solved from start to finish using Dreamweaver MX 2004. Each project begins by presenting a practical Web page development problem and then shows the Web pages that will be created to solve the problem. The remainder of the project steps through creating the Web pages.

2 Consistent Step-By-Step, Screen-By-Screen Presentation

Project solutions are built using a step-by-step, screen-by-screen approach. This pedagogy allows you to build the solution on a computer as you read through the project. Generally, each step is followed by an italic explanation that indicates the result of the step.

3 More Than Just Step-By-Step

More About and Q&A annotations in the margins of the book and substantive text in the paragraphs provide background information, Web design techniques, and tips that complement the topics covered, adding depth and perspective. When you finish with this book, you will be ready to use Dreamweaver MX 2004 to create sophisticated Web pages on your own.

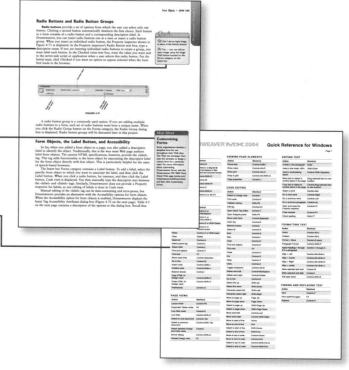

4 Dreamweaver Quick Reference

The Quick Reference provides a listing of keyboard shortcuts to use with Dreamweaver MX 2004.

5 Refer to the Introduction for Guidelines on Planning and Designing a Web Site

In any Web site development project, including the exercises at the end of each project, you should use a systematic methodology to create Web pages to ensure consistency and completness. The Introduction project takes you from the planning stage to the publishing stage.

6 Review

After you successfully step through a project, a section titled What You Should Know summarizes the project tasks with which you should be familiar. Terms you should know for test purposes are bold in the text.

7 Reinforcement and Extension

The Learn It Online page at the end of each project offers reinforcement in the form of review questions, learning games, and practice tests. Also included are Web-based exercises that require you to extend your learning beyond the book.

8 Laboratory Exercises

If you really want to learn how to create Web pages using Dreamweaver, then you must design and implement solutions on your own. Every project concludes with several carefully developed laboratory assignments that increase in complexity. In addition, the Cases and Places exercises at the end of each project are unique real-world situations, including one small-group activity.

Shelly Cashman Series – Traditionally Bound Textbooks

The Shelly Cashman Series presents the following computer subjects in a variety of traditionally bound textbooks. For more information, see your Course Technology representative or call 1-800-648-7450. For Shelly Cashman Series information, visit Shelly Cashman Online at **scseries.com**

COMPUTERS

Computers	Discovering Computers 2006: A Gateway to Information, Complete
	Discovering Computers 2006: A Gateway to Information, Introductory
	Discovering Computers 2006: A Gateway to Information, Brief
	Discovering Computers: Fundamentals, Second Edition
	Teachers Discovering Computers: Integrating Technology in the Classroom, Third Edition
	Essential Introduction to Computers, Sixth Edition (40-page)

WINDOWS APPLICATIONS

Microsoft Office	Microsoft Office 2003: Essential Concepts and Techniques (5 projects)
	Microsoft Office 2003: Brief Concepts and Techniques (9 projects)
	Microsoft Office 2003: Introductory Concepts and Techniques, Second Edition (15 projects)
	Microsoft Office 2003: Advanced Concepts and Techniques (12 projects)
	Microsoft Office 2003: Post Advanced Concepts and Techniques (11 projects)
	Microsoft Office XP: Essential Concepts and Techniques (5 projects)
	Microsoft Office XP: Brief Concepts and Techniques (9 projects)
	Microsoft Office XP: Introductory Concepts and Techniques, Windows XP Edition (15 projects)
	Microsoft Office XP: Introductory Concepts and Techniques, Enhanced Edition (15 projects)
	Microsoft Office XP: Advanced Concepts and Techniques (11 projects)
	Microsoft Office XP: Post Advanced Concepts and Techniques (11 projects)
Integration	Teachers Discovering and Integrating Microsoft Office: Essential Concepts and Techniques, Second Edition
	Integrating Microsoft Office XP Applications and the World Wide Web: Essential Concepts and Techniques
PIM	Microsoft Outlook 2002: Essential Concepts and Techniques • Microsoft Office Outlook 2003: Introductory Concepts and Techniques
Microsoft Works	Microsoft Works 6: Complete Concepts and Techniques[1] • Microsoft Works 2000: Complete Concepts and Techniques[1]
Microsoft Windows	Microsoft Windows XP: Comprehensive Concepts and Techniques, Service Pack 2 Update[2]
	Microsoft Windows XP: Brief Concepts and Techniques
	Microsoft Windows 2000: Comprehensive Concepts and Techniques[2]
	Microsoft Windows 2000: Brief Concepts and Techniques
	Microsoft Windows 98: Comprehensive Concepts and Techniques[2]
	Microsoft Windows 98: Essential Concepts and Techniques
	Introduction to Microsoft Windows NT Workstation 4
Notebook Organizer	Microsoft Office OneNote 2003: Introductory Concepts and Techniques
Word Processing	Microsoft Office Word 2003: Comprehensive Concepts and Techniques[2] • Microsoft Word 2002: Comprehensive Concepts and Techniques[2]
Spreadsheets	Microsoft Office Excel 2003: Comprehensive Concepts and Techniques[2] • Microsoft Excel 2002: Comprehensive Concepts and Techniques[2]
Database	Microsoft Office Access 2003: Comprehensive Concepts and Techniques[2] • Microsoft Access 2002: Comprehensive Concepts and Techniques[2]
Presentation Graphics	Microsoft Office PowerPoint 2003: Comprehensive Concepts and Techniques[2] • Microsoft PowerPoint 2002: Comprehensive Concepts and Techniques[2]
Desktop Publishing	Microsoft Office Publisher 2003: Comprehensive Concepts and Techniques[2] • Microsoft Publisher 2002: Comprehensive Concepts and Techniques[1]

PROGRAMMING

Programming	Microsoft Visual Basic .NET: Comprehensive Concepts and Techniques[2] • Microsoft Visual Basic 6: Complete Concepts and Techniques[1] • Java Programming: Comprehensive Concepts and Techniques, Second Edition[2] • Structured COBOL Programming, Second Edition • Understanding and Troubleshooting Your PC • Programming Fundamentals Using Microsoft Visual Basic .NET

INTERNET

Concepts	Discovering the Internet: Brief Concepts and Techniques • Discovering the Internet: Complete Concepts and Techniques
Browser	Microsoft Internet Explorer 6: Introductory Concepts and Techniques, Windows XP Edition • Microsoft Internet Explorer 5: An Introduction • Netscape Navigator 6: An Introduction
Web Page Creation	Web Design: Introductory Concepts and Techniques • HTML: Comprehensive Concepts and Techniques, Third Edition[2] • Microsoft Office FrontPage 2003: Comprehensive Concepts and Techniques[2] • Microsoft FrontPage 2002: Comprehensive Concepts and Techniques[2] • Microsoft FrontPage 2002: Essential Concepts and Techniques • JavaScript: Complete Concepts and Techniques, Second Edition[1] • Macromedia Dreamweaver MX: Comprehensive Concepts and Techniques[2]

SYSTEMS ANALYSIS

Systems Analysis	Systems Analysis and Design, Sixth Edition

DATA COMMUNICATIONS

Data Communications	Business Data Communications: Introductory Concepts and Techniques, Fourth Edition

[1]Also available as an Introductory Edition, which is a shortened version of the complete book, [2]Also available as an Introductory Edition and as a Complete Edition, which are shortened versions of the comprehensive book.

MACROMEDIA
Dreamweaver MX 2004

Web Site Development and Macromedia Dreamweaver MX 2004

Objectives

You will have mastered the material in this project when you can:

- Describe the significance of the Internet and its associated terms
- Describe the World Wide Web and its associated terms
- Identify the difference between the Internet and the World Wide Web
- Specify the difference between a Web page and a Web site
- Define Web browsers and identify their main features
- Identify the nine types of Web sites
- Discuss how to plan, design, develop, test, publish, and maintain a Web site
- Identify the various methods and tools used to create a Web page and Web site
- Recognize the basic tags within HTML
- Discuss the advantages of using Web page authoring programs such as Dreamweaver

The Internet

The **Internet**, sometimes simply called the **Net**, is a global network, connecting millions of computers. Within this global network, a user who has permission at any one computer can access and obtain information from any other computer within the network. A **network** is a group of computers and associated devices that are connected by communications facilities. A network can span a global area and involve permanent connections, such as cables, or temporary connections made through telephone or other communications links. Within this global network are local, regional, national, and international networks. Each of these networks provides communications, services, and access to information.

The Internet has had a relatively brief, but explosive, history. This network grew out of an experiment begun in the 1960s by the U.S. Department of Defense (DOD). Today, the Internet is a public, cooperative, and self-sustaining facility that is accessible to hundreds of millions of people worldwide.

The World Wide Web and Web Browsers

The **World Wide Web** (**WWW**), also called the **Web**, is the most popular service on the Internet. The Web consists of a system of global **network servers** that supports specially formatted documents and provides a means for sharing these resources with many people at the same time. A network server is known as the **host computer**, and your computer, from which you access the information, is called the **client**. The protocol that enables the transfer of data from the host computer to the client is the **Hypertext Transfer Protocol** (**HTTP**).

Accessing the Web

Users access Web resources, such as text, graphics, sound, video, and multimedia, through a **Web page**. Every Web page is identified by a unique address, or Uniform Resource Locator (URL). The URL provides the global address of the location of the Web page. URLs are discussed later in this Introduction. Viewing data contained on a Web page requires a Web browser. A **Web browser** is a software program that requests a Web page, interprets the code contained within the page, and then displays the contents of the Web page on your computer display device.

Web Browsers

Web browsers contain special buttons and other features to help you navigate through Web sites. The more popular Web browser software programs are **Microsoft Internet Explorer** and **Netscape Navigator**. This book uses Internet Explorer as the primary browser. When you start Internet Explorer, it opens a Web page that has been set as the start, or home, page (Figure I-1). The home page can be any page on the Web and can be designated by the user through the browser's Tools menu. Important features of Internet Explorer are summarized in Table I-1 on the next page.

FIGURE I-1

Table I-1 Internet Explorer Features	
FEATURE	**DEFINITION**
Title bar	Displays the name of the program and the name of the Web page you are viewing
Menu bar	Displays the names of the menus; each menu contains a list of commands you can use to perform tasks such as printing, saving, and editing
Standard Buttons toolbar	Contains buttons, boxes, and menus that allow you to perform tasks more quickly than using the menu bar and related menus
Address bar	Displays the Web site address, or URL, of the Web page you are viewing
Document window	Contains the Web page content

Nearly all Web pages have unique characteristics, but almost every Web page contains the same basic elements. Common elements you find on most Web pages are headings or titles, text, pictures or images, background enhancements, and hyperlinks. A **hyperlink**, or **link**, can link to another place in the same Web page or to an entirely different Web page. Normally, you click the hyperlink to follow the link pathway. Figure I-2 contains a variety of link types with the pointer over one of the links. Clicking a link causes the Web page associated with the link to be displayed in a browser window. The linked object might link to another Web page within the same Web site or might link to a Web page at a different Web site in another city or country. In both instances, the linked page might appear in the same browser window or in a separate browser window, depending on the HTML code associated with the link. HTML is discussed later in this Introduction.

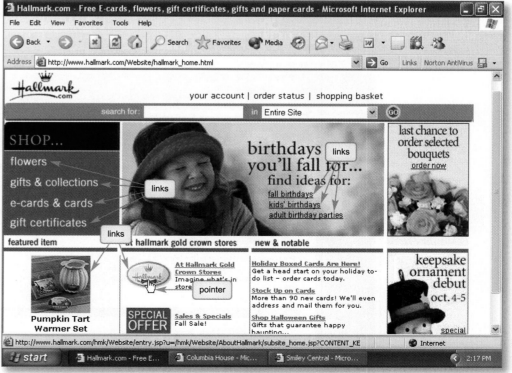

FIGURE I-2

Most Web pages are part of a Web site. A **Web site** is a group of linked Web pages. Most Web sites contains a home page, which generally is the first Web page visitors see when they enter the site. A **home page** (also called an **index page**) typically provides information about the Web site's purpose and content. Most Web sites also contain additional content and pages. An individual, company, or organization owns and manages each Web site.

Accessing the Web requires a connection through a regional or national Internet service provider (ISP), an online service provider (OSP), or a wireless service provider (WSP). Figure I-3 illustrates ways to access the Internet using these service providers. An **Internet service provider** (**ISP**) is a business that has a permanent Internet connection and provides temporary connections to individuals, companies, or other organizations. An **online service provider** (**OSP**) is similar to an ISP, but provides additional member-only services, such as financial data and travel information. America Online is an example of an OSP. A **wireless service provider** (**WSP**) provides Internet access to users with Web-enabled devices or wireless modems. Generally, all of these providers charge a fee for their services.

FIGURE I-3

Types of Web Sites

The nine basic types of Web sites are portal, news, informational, business/marketing, educational, entertainment, advocacy, personal, and blog. A **portal Web site** (Figure I-4a) provides a variety of Internet services from a single, convenient location. Most portals offer free services such as search engines; local, national, and worldwide news; sports; weather; reference tools; maps; stock quotes; newsgroups; chat rooms; and calendars. A **news Web site** (Figure I-4b) contains news articles relating to current events. An **informational Web site** (Figure I-4c) contains factual information, such as research and statistics. Governmental agencies and nonprofit organizations are the primary providers of informational Web pages. A **business/marketing Web site** (Figure I-4d) contains content that promotes or sells products or services. An **educational Web site** (Figure I-4e) provides exciting, challenging avenues for formal and informal teaching and learning. An **entertainment Web site** (Figure I-4f) offers an interactive and engaging environment and contains music, video, sports, games, and other similar features. Within an **advocacy Web site** (Figure I-4g), you will find content that describes a cause, opinion, question, or idea. A **personal Web site** (Figure I-4h) is published by an individual or family and generally is not associated with any organization. A **blog** (Figure I-4i), which is short for Web log, is a Web site that uses a regularly updated journal format to reflect the interests, opinions, and personality of the author and sometimes of site visitors. As you progress through this book, you will have an opportunity to learn more about all these types of Web pages.

(a) Portal

(b) News

(c) Informational

FIGURE I-4

(d) Business/marketing

(e) Educational

(f) Entertainment

(g) Advocacy

(h) Personal

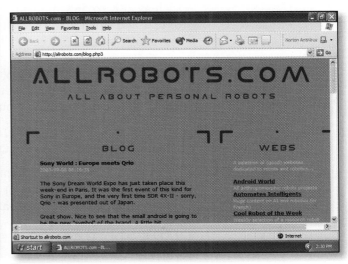

(i) Blog

FIGURE I-4 *(continued)*

Planning a Web Site

Although publishing a Web page and/or a Web site is easy, advanced planning is paramount in ensuring a successful Web site. Publishing a Web site, which makes it available on the Internet, is discussed later in this Introduction. Thousands of individuals create and publish Web pages every day, some using word processing software or markup languages to create their pages. Others use professional design and management editors such as Dreamweaver.

Planning Basics — Purpose

Those who rush into the publishing process without the proper planning tend to design Web sites that are unorganized and difficult to navigate. Visitors to this type of Web site will lose interest quickly and will not return. As you begin planning your Web site, consider the following guidelines to ensure you set and attain realistic goals.

PURPOSE AND GOAL Determine the purpose and goal of your Web site. Create a focus by developing a **purpose statement**, which communicates the intention of the Web site. Consider the nine basic types of Web sites mentioned previously. Will your Web site consist of just one basic type or a combination of two or more types?

TARGET AUDIENCE Identify your audience. The people who visit your Web site will determine whether your Web site is a success. Although you welcome all visitors, you need to know as much as possible about your target audience. To learn more about the visitors to your Web site, determine whether you want to attract people with similar interests, and consider the gender, education, age range, income, profession/job field, and computer proficiency of your target audience.

NEW WEB TECHNOLOGIES Evaluate whether your potential visitors have access to high-speed broadband media or to baseband media, and use this information to determine what elements to include within your Web site. **Broadband** transmits multiple signals simultaneously and includes media and hardware such as **T1 lines, DSL (digital subscriber lines), ISDN (Integrated Services Digital Network), fiber optics**, and **cable modems**. **Baseband** transmits one signal at a time and includes media and hardware such as 28K to 56K modems. Baseband works well with a Web site composed mostly of text and small images. Web sites that contain many images or **multimedia**, such as video and animations, generally require that the visitors have a broadband connection.

WEB SITE COMPARISON Visit other Web sites that are similar to your proposed site. What do you like about these sites? What do you dislike? Look for inspirational ideas. How can you make your Web site better?

Planning Basics — Content

An informative, well-planned Web site is not difficult to create. To ensure a successful Web experience for your visitors, consider the following guidelines to provide appropriate content and other valuable Web page elements.

VALUE-ADDED CONTENT Consider the different types of content to include within your Web site. Use the following questions as guidelines:

- What topics do you want to cover?
- How much information will you present about each topic?
- What will attract your target audience to your Web site?

- What methods will you use to keep your audience returning to your site?
- What changes will you have to make to keep your site updated?

TEXT Because text is the primary component of most Web pages, be brief and incorporate lists whenever possible. Use common words and simple language, and check your spelling and grammar. Create your textual content to accomplish your goals effectively.

IMAGES After text, images are the most commonly included content. Ask yourself these questions with respect to your use of images:

- Will you have a common logo and/or theme on all Web pages?
- Are these images readily available?
- What images will you have to locate?
- What images will you have to create?
- How many images per page will you have?

COLOR PALETTE The color palette you select for your Web site can enhance or detract from your message or goal. Do not think in terms of your favorite colors. Instead, consider how color can support your goal. Ask yourself the following questions:

- Do your selected colors work well with your goal?
- Are the colors part of the universal 216 browser-safe color palette?
- Did you limit the number of colors to a selected few?

MULTIMEDIA Multimedia adds interactivity and action to your Web pages. Animation, audio, and video are types of multimedia. If you plan to add multimedia, determine whether the visitor will require plug-ins. A **plug-in** extends the capability of a Web browser. Some of the more commonly used plug-ins are Shockwave Player, Macromedia Flash, and Windows Media Player. Most plug-ins are free and can be downloaded from the Web.

Web Site Navigation

It is not possible to predict how a visitor will access a Web site or at what point the visitor will enter within the Web site structure. Visitors can arrive at any page within a Web site by a variety of ways: a hyperlink, a search engine, a directory, typing a Web address directly, and so on. On every page of your Web site, you must provide clear answers to the three basic questions your visitors will ask: Where am I? Where do I go from here? How do I get to the home page? A well-organized Web site provides the answers to these questions. Once the visitor is at a Web site, **navigation**, which is the pathway through your site, must be obvious and intuitive. Individual Web pages cannot be isolated from the rest of the site if the site is to be successful. At all times and on all pages in your site, you must give the visitor a sense of place, of context within the site. Most Web designers use a navigation map to visualize the navigation pathway.

Q: I want to develop a Web site. What should I do first?

A: Start with and organize your content. Then create your navigation map.

Design Basics — Navigation Map

A **navigation map** outlines the structure of the entire Web site, showing all of the pages within the site and the connections from one page to others. The navigation map provides the structure, or road map, through the Web site, but does not provide detail as to the content of the individual pages. Web site navigation should be consistent from page to page, so your visitors do not have to guess where they are within the site each time they encounter a new page. All pages in the site should contain a link to the home page. Consider the following for site navigation.

STRUCTURE The goal and the type of a Web site is a major determinant in the type of structure selected for a specific Web site. The navigation map serves as a blueprint for your navigational structure. Consider the following navigational structure types and determine which one best meets your needs:

- In a **linear structure** (Figure I-5a), the user navigates sequentially, moving from one page to the next. This is the simplest way to organize a Web site. Information that flows as a narrative, as a timeline, or in logical order is ideal for sequential treatment. Simple sequential organization, however, usually works only for smaller sites. Many online tutorials use a linear structure.

- A **hierarchical structure** (Figure I-5b) is one of the better ways to organize complex bodies of information. This type of structure is well-suited for Web sites because most visitors are familiar with hierarchical charts. For a hierarchical structure to be effective requires thorough organization of the content.

- A **Web structure** (Figure I-5c), which also is called a **random structure**, places few restrictions on organizational patterns. This type of structure is associated with the free flow of ideas and can be confusing to a user. A random structure is better suited for experienced users looking for further education or enrichment and is not recommended if your goal is to provide a basic understanding of a particular topic. If a Web site is relatively small, however, a random structure could work well.

- If a Web site consists of a number of topics of equal importance, a **grid structure** (Figure I-5d) could be the best navigational choice. Procedural manuals, events, and item lists are examples of content well-suited for this type of structure.

- Large Web sites frequently use a **hybrid structure**, which is a combination of the previous listed structures, to organize information (Figure I-6 on the next page).

(a) **Linear structure**

(b) **Hierarchical structure**

(c) **Web structure**

(d) **Grid structure**

FIGURE I-5

FIGURE I-6

TOOLS Determine the tool to be used to create the navigation map. If your Web site is small, the organizational chart included in the Microsoft Office applications, as shown in Figure I-7 using PowerPoint, is an easy-to-use tool. For larger, more diverse Web sites, Visio Professional, Flow Charting PDQ, FlowCharter Professional, and OrgPlus are some of the programs you can use to chart and organize your Web site. Dreamweaver provides a site map feature. The Dreamweaver site map shows the site structure two levels deep, starting from the home page and is an ideal tool for laying out a site structure.

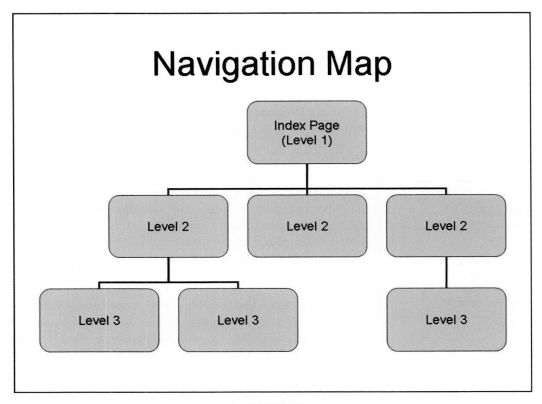

FIGURE I-7

NAVIGATION ELEMENTS The more common types of navigation elements include text, buttons, other images, image maps, a site index, a menu, a search feature, navigation bars, and frames. Depending on the complexity of your Web site, you may want to include some or all of these elements.

Developing a Web Site

Once the structure is complete, the next step is to develop the Web site. Because text and images are a Web site's more common elements, make them your main focus. Then consider page layout and color.

Development Basics — Typography, Images, Page Layout, and Color

The combination of typography, images, page layout, and color comprise the elements of your finished Web site. Correct use of these elements plays an important part in the development process. Consider the following guidelines.

TYPOGRAPHY Good **typography**, which is the appearance and arrangement of the characters that make up your text, is just as important for a Web page as it is for any other medium. A **font** consists of all the characters available in a particular style and weight for a specific design. Selecting fonts for display on a computer screen, however, is different from selecting fonts for a magazine, a book, or another printed medium. That the text displays on a computer screen and not on a piece of paper is immaterial; it still should be easy to read. As a viewer of a Web page, you may never consciously notice the **typeface**, which is the design of the text characters, but the typeface subconsciously affects your reaction to the page.

When selecting a font, determine its purpose on your Web page. Is it to be used for a title? For onscreen reading? Is it likely to be printed? Will the font fit in with the theme of the Web site? Is it a Web-safe font, such as Times New Roman, Courier, or Arial? **Web-safe fonts** are the more popular fonts and the ones that most visitors are likely to have installed on their computers.

Q: Many pages on the Web contain multiple elements and are very "busy." Is this a good practice?

A: Not necessarily. Simple pages download faster and make an immediate impression on the reader.

IMAGES Images can enhance almost any Web page if used appropriately. Without the visual impact of shape, color, and contrast, Web pages can be uninteresting graphically and will not motivate the visitor to investigate their contents. Images and page performance, however, are issues for many visitors. When adding images, consider your potential audience and the technology they have available. Also remember that a background image or a graphical menu increases visitor download time. You may lose visitors who do not have broadband access if your Web page contains an excessive number of graphical items.

PAGE LAYOUT The importance of proper page layout cannot be overemphasized. A suitable design draws visitors to your Web site. Although no single design system is appropriate for all Web pages, a consistent, logical layout allows you to add text and images easily. The Web page layouts shown in Figure I-8 on the next page illustrate two different layouts. The layout on the left (Figure I-8a on the next page) illustrates a plain page with a heading and text. The page layout on the right (Figure I-8b on the next page) presents strong visual contrast by using a variety of layout elements.

Maintaining consistency and updating changes throughout a site are two of the biggest challenges faced by Web designers. A **template** is a special type of HTML document that can help with these challenges. Dreamweaver provides several page layout templates that can be modified easily. In laying out your Web pages, consider the following guidelines to ensure visitors have the best viewing experience:

- Include only one topic per page
- Control the vertical and horizontal size of the page
- Start text on the left to accommodate the majority of individuals, who read from left to right
- Use concise statements and bulleted points to get your point across; studies indicate most people scan the text

COLOR When creating a Web page, use color to add interest and vitality to your site. Color can be used in tables, as backgrounds, and with fonts. Use the right combination of colors to decorate the layout and tie the Web site pages together.

(a) (b)

FIGURE I-8

Reviewing and Testing a Web Site

Some Web site developers argue that reviewing and testing should take place throughout the developmental process. While this may be true, it also is important to review and test the final product. This ongoing process ensures that you identify and correct any problems before publishing to the Web. When reviewing and testing your Web site, ask the following questions:

- Is the Web site free of spelling and/or grammatical errors?
- Is the page layout consistent, and does it generate a sense of balance and order?
- Are any links broken?
- Do multimedia interactivity and forms function correctly?
- Does the Web site display properly in the more widely used browsers?
- Does the Web site function properly in different browsers, including older browser versions?
- Have you initiated a **group test**, in which you have asked other individuals to test your Web site and provide feedback?

Publishing a Web Site

After your Web site has been tested thoroughly, it can be published. **Publishing** a Web site is the process of making it available to your visitors. This step involves the actual uploading of the Web site to a server. After the uploading process is completed, all pages within the Web site should be tested again.

Publishing Basics — Domain Name, Server Space, and Uploading

With your Web site thoroughly tested and any problems corrected, you must make the site available to your audience by obtaining a domain name, acquiring server space, and uploading the site. Consider the following to ensure site availability.

OBTAIN A DOMAIN NAME To allow visitors to access your Web site, you must obtain a domain name. Web sites are accessed by an IP address or a domain name. An **IP address** (**Internet Protocol address**) is a number that uniquely identifies each computer or device connected to the Internet. A **domain name** is the text version of an IP address. The **Domain Name System** (**DNS**) is an Internet service that translates domain names into their corresponding IP addresses. The **Uniform Resource Locator** (**URL**), also called a **Web address**, tells the browser on which server to locate the Web page. A URL consists of a communications standard, such as **Hypertext Transfer Protocol (HTTP)**, the domain name, and sometimes the path to a specific Web page (Figure I-9 on the next page).

Domain names are unique and must be registered. The **Accredited Registrar Directory** provides a listing of **Internet Corporation for Assigned Names and Numbers** (**ICANN**) accredited domain name registrars. Your most difficult task likely will be to find a name that is not already registered. You can locate a name by using a specialized search engine at one of the many accredited domain name registrars listed on the ICANN Web site (icann.org/registrars/accredited-list.html). In addition to registering your business name as a domain name, you may want to register the names of your products, services, and/or other related names. Expect to pay approximately $15 to $35 per year for a domain name.

Consider the following guidelines when selecting a domain name:

- Select a name that is easy to pronounce, spell, and remember.
- Select a name that relates to the Web site content and suggests the nature of your product or service.
- If the Web site is a business, use the business name.
- Select a name that is free and clear of trademark issues.
- Purchase variations and the .org and .net versions of your domain name.
- Some ISPs will obtain a domain name for you if you use their service to host your Web site.

ACQUIRE SERVER SPACE Locate an ISP that will host your Web site. Recall that an ISP is a business that has a permanent Internet connection. ISPs offer temporary connections to individuals and companies free or for a fee.

If you select an ISP that provides free server space, most likely your visitors will be subjected to advertisements and pop-up windows. Other options to explore for free server space include the provider from which you obtain your Internet connection; **online communities**, such as Yahoo!GeoCities (geocities.yahoo.com), Tripod (tripod.lycos.com), and MSN Web Communities (communities.msn.com); and your educational institution's Web server.

More About

Selecting a Domain Name

When selecting a domain name, keep it simple. If possible, avoid hyphens. To learn more about domain name selection, visit the Dreamweaver MX 2004 More About Web page (scsite.com/dreamweavermx04/more.htm) and then click Domain Name Selection.

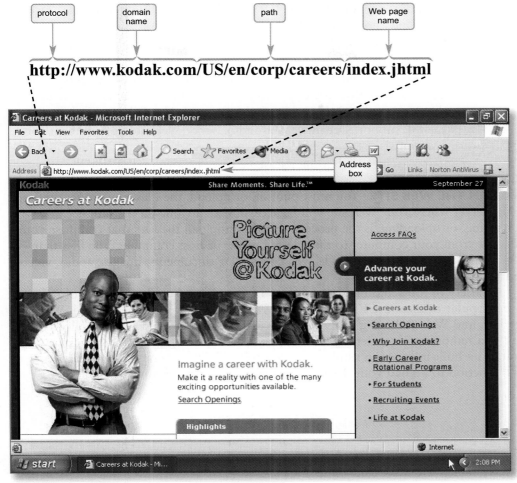

FIGURE I-9

If the purpose of your Web site is to sell a product or service or to promote a professional organization, you should consider a fee-based ISP. Use a search engine such as Google (google.com) and search for Web site hosting, or visit Hosting Repository (hostingrepository.com), where you will find thousands of Web hosting plans, as well as reviews and ratings of Web hosting providers. Selecting a reliable provider requires investigation on your part. Many providers provide multiple hosting plans. When selecting an ISP, consider the following questions and how they apply to your particular situation and Web site:

1. What is the monthly fee? Is a discount available if you sign up for a year? Are setup fees charged?
2. How much server space is provided for the monthly fee? Can you purchase additional space? If so, how much does it cost?
3. What is the average server uptime on a monthly basis? What is the average server downtime?
4. What are the server specifications? Can the server handle many users? Does it have battery backup power?
5. Are **server logs**, which keep track of the number of accesses, available?
6. What is the ISP's form of connectivity — that is, how does it connect to the Internet: OC3, T1, T3, or some other way?
7. Is a money-back guarantee offered?

8. What technical support does the ISP provide and when is it available? Does it have an online knowledge base?

9. Does the server on which the Web site will reside have CGI capabilities and Active Server Page (ASP) support?

10. Does the server on which the Web site will reside support e-commerce, multimedia, and **Secure Sockets Layer** (**SSL**) for encrypting confidential data such as credit card numbers? Are additional fees required for these capabilities?

11. Does the ISP support Dreamweaver and/or other Web site development software programs?

12. Are mailboxes included in the package? If so, how many?

PUBLISH THE WEB SITE You must publish, or upload, the files from your computer to the server where your Web site will be accessible to anyone on the Internet. Publishing, or **uploading**, is the process of transmitting all the files that comprise your Web site from your computer to the selected server or host computer. The files that make up your Web site can include Web pages, PDF documents, images, audio, video, animation, and others.

A variety of tools and methods exist to manage the upload task. Some of the more popular of these are FTP programs, Windows Web Publishing Wizard, Web Folders, and Web authoring programs such as Dreamweaver. These tools allow you to link to a remote server, enter a password, and then upload your files. Dreamweaver contains a built-in function similar to independent FTP programs. The Dreamweaver FTP function to upload your Web site is covered in Project 3 and in Appendix C.

Maintaining a Web Site

Most Web sites require maintenance and updating. Some types of ongoing Web maintenance include the following:

- Changing content, either by adding new text and images or by deleting obsolete ones
- Checking for broken links and adding new links
- Documenting the last change date (even when no revisions have been made)

Use the information from the server logs provided by your ISP to determine what needs to be updated or changed. Statistics contained within these logs generally include the number of visitors trying to access your site at one time, what resources they request, how long they stay at the site, at what point they enter the site, what pages they view, and what errors they encounter. Learning to use and apply the information contained within the server log will help you to make your Web site successful.

After you make updates and/or changes to the site, notify your viewers with a What's New announcement.

Methods and Tools Used to Create Web Pages

Web developers have several options for creating Web pages: a text editor, an HTML editor, software applications, or a WYSIWYG text editor (discussed in detail on page DW 19). Microsoft Notepad and WordPad are examples of a **text editor**. These simple, easy-to-use programs allow the user to enter, edit, save, and print text. An **HTML editor** is a more sophisticated version of a text editor. In addition to basic text-editing functions, more advanced features, such as syntax highlighting, color-coding, and spell checking, are available. **Software applications**, such as Microsoft Word, Excel, and

Publisher, provide a Save as Web Page command on the File menu. This feature converts the application document into an HTML file. Examples of a **WYSIWYG text editor** are programs such as Microsoft FrontPage and Macromedia Dreamweaver. These programs provide an integrated text editor with a graphical user interface that allows the user to view both the code and the document as it is being created.

A Web developer can use any of these options to create Web pages. Regardless of the option selected, however, it still is important to understand the specifics of HTML.

HTML

Web pages are written in plain text and saved in the American Standard Code for Information Interchange format. The **American Standard Code for Information Interchange**, or **ASCII** (pronounced ASK-ee), format is the most widely used coding system to represent data. Using the ASCII format makes Web pages universally readable by different Web browsers regardless of the computer platform on which they reside.

Hypertext Markup Language (**HTML**) is an authoring language that defines the structure and layout of a document so that it displays as a Web page in a Web browser such as Microsoft Internet Explorer or Netscape Navigator. A Web page has two components: source code and document content. The **source code**, which contains tags, is program instructions. The **tags** within the source code control the appearance of the document content. The **document content** is the text and images that the browser displays. The browser interprets the tags contained within the code, and the code instructs the browser how to display the Web page. For instance, if you define a line of text on your Web page as a heading, the browser knows to display this line as a heading.

All HTML tag formats are the same. They start with a left angle bracket (< or less than symbol), followed by the name of the tag, and end with a right angle bracket (> or greater than symbol). Most tags have a start and an end tag and are called **two-sided tags**. The end tags are the same as the start tags except they are preceded by a forward slash (/). Some HTML tags, such as the one used to indicate a line break <br>, do not have an end tag. These are known as **one-sided tags**. Other tags, such as the one to indicate a new paragraph <p>, have an end tag, but the end tag can be omitted. For consistency, it is better with this type of tag to include both the start and end tags.

Some tags can contain an **attribute**, or **property**, which is additional information placed within the angle brackets. Attributes are not repeated or contained in the end tag. Some attributes are used individually, while other attributes can include a value modifier. A **value modifier** specifies conditions within the tag. For example, you can use a value modifier to specify the font type or size or the placement of text on the page. To create and display a centered heading, for instance, you would use the following code:

```
<h1 align=center>This is the largest header tag and the text will be centered</h1>
```

In this example, h1 is the HTML tag, align is the attribute, and center is the value modifier. Notice that the attribute does not appear as part of the end tag, </h1>.

You can use Microsoft Notepad or WordPad (which are text editors) to create HTML documents. Place each tag in a pair around the text or section that you want to define (**mark up**) with that tag. HTML tags are not case-sensitive; therefore, you can enter HTML tags in uppercase or lowercase or a combination of both. To be consistent, however, you should adopt a standard practice when typing tags. The examples in this book use lowercase.

More About

HTML

The World Wide Web Consortium (W3C) develops and updates Web protocols. To learn more about the most recent changes to HTML, visit the Dreamweaver MX 2004 More About Web page (scsite.com/dreamweavermx04/more.htm) and then click W3C.

Q&A

Q: Should I test my Web page in more than one browser?

A: Yes—at a minimum you should test a Web page in the most recent versions of Internet Explorer and Netscape Navigator.

HTML tags also are used to format the hyperlinks that connect information on the World Wide Web. HTML tags number in the hundreds, but some are used more than others. All documents, however, require four basic tags. Figure I-10 illustrates the basic tags required for all HTML documents. Table I-2 summarizes the more commonly used HTML tags.

FIGURE I-10

Table I-2 Commonly Used HTML Tags	
TAG	**STRUCTURE**
\<html\>...\</html\>	Encloses the entire HTML document
\<head\>...\</head\>	Encloses the head of the HTML document
\<body\>...\</body\>	Encloses the body of the HTML document
TAG	**TITLE AND HEADINGS**
\<title\>...\</title\>	Indicates the title of the document
\<h1\>...\</h1\>	Heading level 1
\<h2\>...\</h2\>	Heading level 2
\<h3\>...\</h3\>	Heading level 3
\<h4\>...\</h4\>	Heading level 4
\<h5\>...\</h5\>	Heading level 5
\<h6\>...\</h6\>	Heading level 6
TAG	**PARAGRAPHS, BREAKS, AND SEPARATORS**
\<p\>...\</p\>	Plain paragraph; end tag optional
\<br\>	Line break
\<hr\>	Horizontal rule line
\<ol\>...\</ol\>	Ordered, numbered list
\<ul\>...\</ul\>	Unordered, bulleted list
\<menu\>...\</menu\>	Menu list of items

Table I-2 Commonly Used HTML Tags (continued)

TAG	PARAGRAPHS, BREAKS, AND SEPARATORS
<dir>...</dir>	Directory listing
<li>...</li>	List item, used with <ol>, <ul>, <menu>, and <dir>
<dl>...</dl>	Definition of glossary list
<dt>...</dt>	Definition term; part of a definition list
<dd>...</dd>	Definition corresponding to a definition term
TAG	CHARACTER FORMATTING
...	Bold text
<u>...</u>	Underlined text
<i>...</i>	Italic text
TAG	LINKS
<a>...</a>	Combined with the HREF attribute, creates a link to another document or anchor
<a>...</a>	Combined with the NAME attribute, creates an anchor which can be linked to
TAG	IMAGE
<img>...</img>	Inserts an image into the document

Web Page Authoring Programs

Many of today's Web page authoring programs, including Dreamweaver, are What You See Is What You Get (WYSIWYG) HTML text editors. A WYSIWYG text editor allows a user to view a document as it will appear in the final product and to edit the text, images, or other elements directly within that view. Before programs such as Dreamweaver existed, Web page designers were required to type, or hand-code, Web pages. Educators and Web designers still debate the issue surrounding the necessity of knowing HTML. You do not need to know HTML to create Web pages in Dreamweaver, but an understanding of HTML will help you if you need to alter Dreamweaver-generated code. If you know HTML, then you can make changes to code and Dreamweaver will accept the changes.

Macromedia Dreamweaver MX 2004

Dreamweaver is the standard in visual authoring. Macromedia Dreamweaver MX 2004 is part of the MX 2004 product family, which includes Macromedia Flash MX 2004, ColdFusion MX 2004, and Fireworks MX 2004. Dreamweaver provides features that access these separate products. Some of the new features of Dreamweaver MX 2004 include the following:

- Cross-browser validation for compatibility across all the leading browsers
- More powerful CSS support
- Built-in graphics editing with Macromedia Fireworks
- Secure FTP

- Increased support for a platform-independent development environment
- Better integration with external files and code from such programs as Microsoft Word and Excel
- Enhanced coding and editing tools
- Tighter integration with other Macromedia tools

Dreamweaver makes it easy to get started and provides you with helpful tools to enhance your Web design and development experience. Working in a single environment, you create, build, and manage Web sites and Internet applications. The workspace environment is customizable to fit your particular needs.

Coding tools and features that are included within Dreamweaver are references for HTML, CSS, and JavaScript and code editors that allow you to edit the code directly. **Macromedia Roundtrip HTML technology** imports HTML documents without reformatting the code. Downloadable extensions from the Macromedia Web site make it easy to add functionality to any Web site. Examples of some of these extensions include shopping carts and online payment features.

Instead of writing individual HTML files for every page, use a database to store content and then retrieve the content dynamically in response to a user's request. Implementing and using this feature, you can update the information once, in one place, instead of manually editing many pages.

Dreamweaver provides the tools that help you author accessible content. These accessible pages comply with government guidelines and Section 508 of the Federal Rehabilitation Act. Another key feature is Cascading Style Sheets styles (CSS styles). CSS styles are collections of formatting definitions that affect the appearance of Web page elements. You can use CSS styles to format text, images, headings, tables, and so forth. Implementing and applying this feature, you can update the formatting one time across many Web pages.

Dreamweaver allows you to publish Web sites with relative ease to a local area network, which connects computers in a limited geographical area, or to the Web, for anyone with Internet access to see. The concepts and techniques presented in this book provide the tools you need to plan, develop, and publish professional Web sites, such as the Web sites shown in Figure I-11 and I-12 on the following page.

Summary

The Introduction to Web Site Development and Macromedia Dreamweaver MX 2004 provided an overview of the Internet and the World Wide Web and the key terms associated with those technologies. An overview of the nine basic types of Web pages also was presented. The Introduction furnished information on developing a Web site, including planning basics. The process of designing a Web site and each phase within this process were discussed. Information about testing, publishing, and maintaining a Web site also was presented, including an overview of obtaining a domain name, acquiring server space, and uploading a Web site. Methods and tools used to create Web pages were introduced. A short overview of HTML and some of the more commonly used HTML tags were presented. Finally, the advantages of using Dreamweaver in Web development were discussed. These advantages include a WYSIWYG text editor; a visual, customizable development environment; accessibility compliance; downloadable extensions; database access capabilities; and Cascading Style Sheets.

For an updated list of links, visit the Dreamweaver companion site at http://scsite.com/dreamweavermx04.

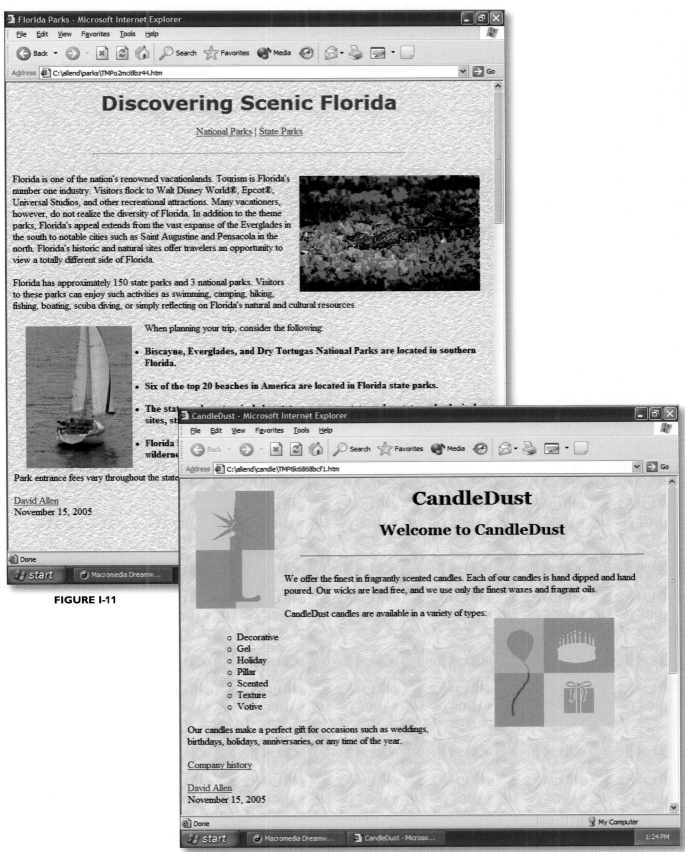

FIGURE I-11

FIGURE I-12

Learn It Online

Instructions: To complete the Learn It Online exercises, start your browser, click the Address bar, and then enter the Web address scsite.com/dreamweavermx2004/learn. When the Dreamweaver MX 2004 Learn It Online page is displayed, follow the instructions in the exercises below. Each exercise has instructions for printing your results, either for your own records or for submission to your instructor.

1 Project Reinforcement TF, MC, and SA

Below Dreamweaver Introduction Project, click the Project Reinforcement link. Print the quiz by clicking Print on the File menu for each page. Answer each question.

2 Flash Cards

Below Dreamweaver Introduction Project, click the Flash Cards link and read the instructions. Type 20 (or a number specified by your instructor) in the Number of playing cards text box, type your name in the Enter your Name text box, and then click the Flip Card button. When the flash card is displayed, read the question and then click the ANSWER box arrow to select an answer. Flip through Flash Cards. If your score is 15 (75%) correct or greater, click Print on the File menu to print your results. If your score is less than 15 (75%) correct, then redo this exercise by clicking the Replay button.

3 Practice Test

Below Dreamweaver Introduction Project, click the Practice Test link. Answer each question, enter your first and last name at the bottom of the page, and then click the Grade Test button. When the graded practice test is displayed on your screen, click Print on the File menu to print a hard copy. Continue to take practice tests until you score 80% or better.

4 Who Wants To Be a Computer Genius?

Below Dreamweaver Introduction Project, click the Computer Genius link. Read the instructions, enter your first and last name at the bottom of the page, and then click the PLAY button. When your score is displayed, click the PRINT RESULTS link to print a hard copy.

5 Wheel of Terms

Below Dreamweaver Introduction Project, click the Wheel of Terms link. Read the instructions, and then enter your first and last name and your school name. Click the PLAY button. When your score is displayed, right-click the score and then click Print on the shortcut menu to print a hard copy.

6 Crossword Puzzle Challenge

Below Dreamweaver Introduction Project, click the Crossword Puzzle Challenge link. Read the instructions, and then enter your first and last name. Click the SUBMIT button. Work the crossword puzzle. When you are finished, click the Submit button. When the crossword puzzle is redisplayed, click the Print Puzzle button to print a hard copy.

7 Tips and Tricks

Below Dreamweaver Introduction Project, click the Tips and Tricks link. Click a topic that pertains to the Introduction Project. Right-click the information and then click Print on the shortcut menu. Construct a brief example of what the information relates to in Dreamweaver to confirm you understand how to use the tip or trick.

8 Newsgroups

Below Dreamweaver Introduction Project, click the Newsgroups link. Click a topic that pertains to the Introduction Project. Print three comments.

9 Expanding Your Horizons

Below Dreamweaver Introduction Project, click the Expanding Your Horizons link. Click a topic that pertains to the Introduction Project. Print the information. Construct a brief example of what the information relates to in Dreamweaver to confirm you understand the contents of the article.

10 Search Sleuth

Below Dreamweaver Introduction Project, click the Search Sleuth link. To search for a term that pertains to this project, select a term below the Introduction Project title and then use the Google search engine at google.com (or any major search engine) to display and print two Web pages that present information on the term.

Apply Your Knowledge

1 Web Site Creation

Instructions: As discussed in this project, creating a Web site involves planning, designing, developing, reviewing and testing, publishing, and maintaining the site. Open the Apply I-1 Web Site Creation file on the Dreamweaver Data Disk. See the inside back cover of this book for instructions for downloading the Data Disk or see your instructor for information on accessing the files required for this book. As shown in Table I-3, the Apply I-1 Web Site Creation file contains information about the Web site creation process. Use the information contained in this table to develop a plan for creating a Web site.

Table I-3 Creating a Web Site	
PLANNING	
Web site name:	What is your Web site name?
Web site type:	What is the Web site type: portal, news, informational, business/marketing, educational, entertainment, advocacy, personal, or blog?
Web site purpose:	What is the purpose of your Web site?
Target audience:	How can you identify your target audience?
Web technologies to be used:	Will you design for broadband or baseband? Explain your selection.
Content:	What topics will you cover? How much information will you present on each topic? How will you attract your audience? What will you do to entice your audience to return to your Web site? How will you keep the Web site updated?
Text, images, and multimedia:	Will your site contain text only? What type of images will you include? Where will you obtain your images? Will you have a common logo? Will plug-ins be required?
DESIGNING	
Navigation map:	What type of structure will you use? What tools will you use to design your navigation map?
Navigational elements:	What navigational elements will you include?
DEVELOPING	
Typography:	What font will you use? How many different fonts will you use on your site?
Images:	How will you use images to enhance your site? Will you use a background image?
Page layout:	What type of layout will you use? How many topics per page? How will text be presented: bulleted or paragraph style? Will the audience need to scroll the page?
Color:	What color combinations will you use for your site? To what elements will you apply the color(s) — fonts, background, tables, other elements?

(continued)

Web Site Creation *(continued)*

Table I-3 Creating a Web Site *(continued)*	
REVIEWING AND TESTING	
Review:	What elements will you review? Will you use a group review?
Testing:	What elements will you test? Will you use self-testing? Will you use group testing?
PUBLISHING	
Domain name:	What is your domain name? Have you registered your domain name? What ISP will host your Web site? What criteria did you use to select the ISP?
MAINTAINING	
Ongoing maintenance:	How often will you update your Web site? What elements will you update? Will you add additional features? Does your ISP provide server logs? Will you use the server logs for maintenance purposes?

Perform the following steps using your word processing program and browser.

1. With the Apply I-1 Web Site Creation file open in your word processing program, select a name for your Web site.
2. Use a specialized search engine at one of the many accredited domain name registrars to verify that your selected Web site name is available.
3. Answer each question in the table. Use complete sentences to answer the questions. Type your answers in column 3.
4. Save the document with the file name, Apply I-1 My Web Site Creation.doc. Submit a copy to your instructor.

1 Using Internet Explorer

Problem: Microsoft's Internet Explorer (IE) has many new features that can make your work on the Internet more efficient. Using the Media feature, for example, you can play music, video, or multimedia files; listen to your favorite Internet radio station; and enhance your browsing experience. You can customize the image toolbar that displays when you point to an image on a Web page. IE also includes other enhancements. Visit the Microsoft Internet Explorer How-to-Articles Web page (Figure I-13) and select three articles concerning topics with which you are not familiar. Read the articles and then create a word processing document detailing what you learned.

FIGURE I-13

Instructions: Perform the following tasks.

1. Start your browser. Open the Microsoft Internet Explorer How-to Articles Web page (microsoft.com/windows/ie/using/howto/default.mspx).
2. Click one of the On This Page links.
3. Select three articles that contain information with which you are not familiar.
4. Click the link for each article and read the article.
5. Start your word processing program.
6. List three important points that you learned from this Web site.
7. Write a summary of what you learned from each article. Include within your summary your opinion of the article and if you will apply what you learned or use it with your Web browser.
8. Save the document with the file name, Lab I-1 How-to.doc. Print a copy of the document.

In the Lab

2 Types of Web Pages

Problem: A Web designer is familiar with different types of Web pages and the sort of information displayed on these types of Web pages. The Introduction describes nine types of Web pages. Search the Internet and locate at least one example of each type of Web page.

Instructions: Perform the following tasks.

1. Start your browser. Open the Google (google.com) search engine Web page (Figure I-14) and search for an example of each of the following types of Web pages: portal, news, informational, business/marketing, educational, entertainment, advocacy, personal, and blog.

FIGURE I-14

2. Start your word processing program.
3. Copy and paste the link from each of these Web page types into your word processing document.
4. Identify the type of Web page for each link.
5. Explain why you selected this Web page and how it fits the definition of the specific type.
6. Save the document with the file name, Lab I-2 Web Page types.doc. Print a copy of the document if instructed to do so.
7. Submit the assignment to your instructor.

In the Lab

3 Web Site Hosting

Problem: Selecting the correct host or ISP for your Web site can be a confusing process. Many Web sites offer this service, but determining which one is best for your particular needs can be somewhat complicated. Assume your Web site will sell a product. Compare several ISPs and select the one that will best meet your needs.

Instructions: Perform the following tasks.

1. Review the information and questions on pages DW 15–16 discussing the guidelines for acquiring active server space to host your Web site.
2. Start your browser. Open the Hosting Repository Web page shown in Figure I-15 (hostingrepository.com).

FIGURE I-15

3. Click the Ecommerce link.
4. Click one of the host server links and review the information relating to the services offered by your selected ISP.
5. Start your word processing program.
6. Read and answer the questions on pages DW 15–16. Use the information provided in the list of services offered by your selected ISP.
7. Write a short summary explaining why you would or would not select this ISP to host your Web site.
8. Save the document with the file name, Lab I-3 Web Site Hosting.doc. If instructed to do so, print a copy of the document and hand it in or e-mail it to your instructor.

Cases and Places

The difficulty of these case studies varies:
■ are the least difficult and ■■ are more difficult. The last exercise is a group exercise.

1 ■ Use a search engine such as Google (google.com) and research information about planning a Web site. Use your word processing program and write a two-page summary of what you learned. Save the document as caseI-1.doc. Print a copy and hand it in or e-mail a copy to your instructor.

2 ■ Your goal is to create a personal Web site navigation map that contains three pages — the home page, a page about your favorite hobbies, and a page about places you like to visit. On a piece of paper, draw a navigation map for your proposed Web site. Write a sentence or two describing the type of structure you used and why you selected that structure.

3 ■■ Plug-ins are used on many Web sites. Start your browser and search for plug-ins. Prepare a list of the plug-ins you found. Create a summary statement describing how and why you could use each plug-in in a Web site. Include the link where you can download each of the plug-ins.

4 ■■ Typography within a Web page is one of its more important elements. Start your browser and search for examples of Web sites that include what you consider appropriate typography and Web sites with inappropriate typography. Write a short summary of why you consider these to be appropriate and inappropriate. Copy and paste the Web site addresses into your document.

5 ■■ **Working Together** Each team member is to search the Internet for Web sites illustrating each of these structures. Each team member then will use word processing software to write a minimum of 100 words describing the Web sites and explaining why they think this is an appropriate or inappropriate structure for that particular Web site. The team then will coordinate its research to complete a final document.

Creating a Dreamweaver Web Page and Local Site

PROJECT

1

CASE PERSPECTIVE

Florida native David Allen worked with you last summer at a state environmental agency. Your job at the agency included Internet communications. Because you both love the outdoors, particularly Florida's state and national parks, you became good friends. David visits several parks every year. During each visit, he discovers something new and exciting. David wants to share his knowledge and to provide a way to make Florida residents and visitors aware of the uniqueness, beauty, and wildlife of the parks.

David knows the far-reaching capabilities of the Internet. He wants to use the Web to communicate to the public about Florida's parks, but he has limited knowledge about Web design and development. David knows that your interest and experience with the Internet could assist him in this endeavor, and he asks for your help. You like the idea and tell him that you can create a Web site using Dreamweaver. You get together to define the Web site and to plan the index page. When you are finished creating the Discovering Scenic Florida Web page, you will show it to David for his feedback.

As you read through this project, you will learn how to use Dreamweaver MX 2004 to define a local site and create a Web page and how to display the Web page in a browser.

Creating a Dreamweaver Web Page and Local Site

P R O J E C T

1

Objectives

You will have mastered the material in this project when you can:

- Describe Dreamweaver and identify its key features
- Start Dreamweaver
- Describe the Dreamweaver window and workspace
- Define a local site
- Add a background image
- Create and save a Web page
- Open and close panels
- Display and describe the Property inspector
- Format and modify text elements on a Web page
- Define and insert a line break and special characters
- Add a horizontal rule
- Change a Web page title
- Check spelling
- Preview a Web page in a Web browser
- Print a Web page
- Define Dreamweaver Help
- Quit Dreamweaver
- Open a new Web page

What Is Macromedia Dreamweaver MX 2004?

Macromedia Dreamweaver MX 2004 is a powerful Web page authoring and Web site management software program and HTML editor used to design, code, and create professional-looking Web pages, Web sites, and Web applications. The visual editing features of Dreamweaver allow you to create pages without writing a line of code. Dreamweaver provides many tools and features, including the following:

- **Automatic Web Page Creation** — Dreamweaver provides tools you can use to develop your Web pages without having to spend hours writing HTML code. Dreamweaver automatically generates the HTML code necessary to publish your Web pages.

- **Web Site Management** — Dreamweaver enables you to view a site, including all local and remote files associated with the selected site. Using Dreamweaver, you can perform standard maintenance operations such as viewing, opening, and moving files; transferring files between local and remote sites; and designing your site navigation with the Site Map.

- **Standard Macromedia Web Authoring Tools** — Dreamweaver includes a user interface that is consistent across all Macromedia authoring tools. This consistency enables easy integration with other Macromedia Web-related programs, such as Macromedia Flash, Director, Shockwave, and ColdFusion.

Other key features include the integrated user interface, the integrated file explorer, panel management, database integration, and standards and accessibility support. Dreamweaver MX 2004 is customizable and can run in operating systems such as Windows XP, Windows 2000, Windows NT, and Mac OS X.

Project One — Florida Parks

To create documents similar to those you will encounter on the Web and in academic, business, and personal environments, you can use Dreamweaver to produce Web pages such as the Discovering Scenic Florida Web page shown in Figure 1-1. The Web page shown in Figure 1-1 is the index page for the Florida Parks Web site. This informational page provides interesting facts about Florida's state and national parks. The page begins with a centered main heading, followed by a horizontal rule. Following the rule are two short informational paragraphs. The first paragraph contains two occurrences of the registered trademark symbol. Following the second paragraph is an introductory sentence for a bulleted list. The list contains four bulleted items. A concluding sentence, the author's name, and current date end the page. A background image is applied to the page.

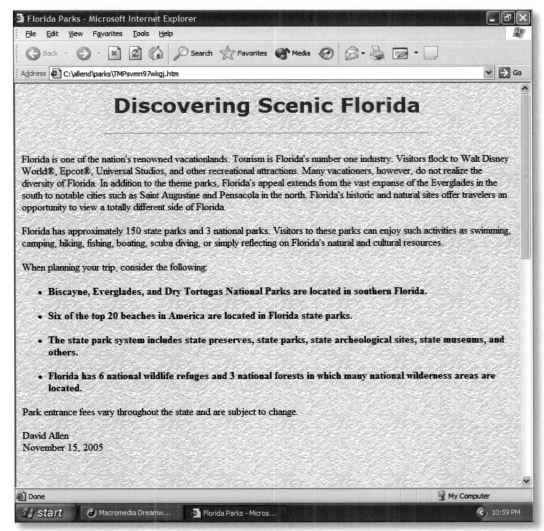

FIGURE 1-1

More About

Dreamweaver Features

For more information about Dreamweaver MX 2004 features, visit the Dreamweaver MX 2004 More About Web page (scsite.com/ dreamweavermx04/more.htm) and then click Dreamweaver MX 2004 Features.

Starting Dreamweaver

If you are stepping through this project on a computer and you want your screen to agree with the Dreamweaver figures in this book, then you should change your screen's resolution to 800 × 600. The browser used to display the Web page figures is Internet Explorer. The browser text size is set to Medium.

Getting started in Dreamweaver is as easy as opening an existing HTML document or creating a new document. The Dreamweaver environment consists of toolbars, windows, objects, panels, inspectors, and tools you use to create your Web pages and to manage your Web site, which is a collection of Web pages. It is important to understand the basic concepts behind the Dreamweaver workspace and how to choose options, use inspectors and panels, and set preferences that best fit your work style.

The first time Dreamweaver MX 2004 is launched after the initial installation, a Workspace Setup dialog box is displayed with two options: Designer or Coder. This Workspace Setup choice is a one-time event. Programmers who work primarily with HTML and other languages generally select the Coder workspace. The Designer workspace contains a visual integrated workspace and is ideal for beginners and non-programmers. For the exercises in this book, select the Designer workspace.

Following the Workspace Setup choice, the Dreamweaver MX 2004 program starts. The settings on your computer determine what displays. By default, the Start page is displayed each time you start Dreamweaver. The Start page's visual representation is a good tool for beginners, but more proficient Dreamweaver users generally disable this feature. You disable the Start page at the end of this project. If you are opening Dreamweaver from a computer at your school, most likely the program is set up and ready to use.

To start Dreamweaver, Windows must be running. The following steps show how to start Dreamweaver or ask your instructor how to start Dreamweaver.

To Start Dreamweaver

1

• **Click the Start button on the Windows taskbar, point to All Programs on the Start menu, point to Macromedia on the All Programs submenu, and then point to Macromedia Dreamweaver MX 2004 on the Macromedia submenu.**

The Start menu, All Programs submenu, and Macromedia submenu are displayed (Figure 1-2). Your Start menu will display different programs than those in Figure 1-2.

FIGURE 1-2

2

• **Click Macromedia Dreamweaver MX 2004.**

The Start page appears (Figure 1-3). A portion of the Start page is hidden by Dreamweaver panels. You disable the Start page at the end of this project.

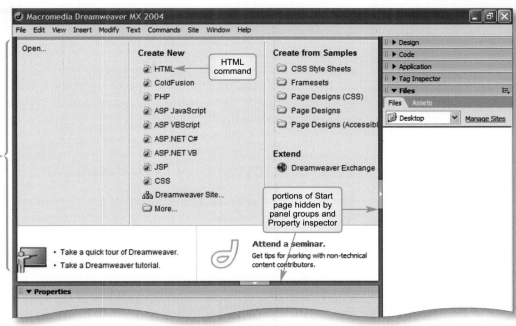

FIGURE 1-3

3

• **Click HTML in the Create New column. If necessary, maximize the Dreamweaver window and the Document window by clicking the Maximize button in the upper-right corner of the windows.**

• **If necessary, click Window on the menu bar and then click Insert.**

The Start page closes, and the Dreamweaver workspace is displayed (Figure 1-4). The Dreamweaver workspace contains menu names, toolbars, and panel groups. The Windows taskbar displays the Macromedia Dreamweaver MX 2004 button, indicating Dreamweaver is running.

FIGURE 1-4

Other Ways

1. Double-click Dreamweaver icon on desktop

The screen in Figure 1-4 on the previous page shows a typical Dreamweaver workspace, with some of the more commonly used components displayed. The **Dreamweaver workspace** is an integrated environment in which the Document window and panels are incorporated into one larger application window. The panel groups are docked, or attached, on the right. The Insert bar is located at the top of the Document window, and the Property inspector is located at the bottom of the Document window. You can move, resize, and/or collapse the panels to accommodate your individual preferences.

The Dreamweaver Workspace

The Dreamweaver workspace consists of a variety of components to make your work more efficient and Web pages appear more professional. This section discusses the following components of the Dreamweaver workspace: title bar, Document window, panels and panel groups, status bar, menu bar, and toolbars.

As you learn to use each of these tools, you will discover some redundancy among these elements. To apply a Font tag, for instance, you can access the command through the Property inspector, through the Text menu, or through the context menu. The different options are available for various user preferences. The projects in this book present the more commonly used methods. The Other Ways boxes at the end of many of the step-by-step sequences give other ways to accomplish a task when they are available. As you become proficient working in the Dreamweaver environment, you will develop a technique for using the tools that best suits your personal preferences.

Title Bar

The **title bar** (Figure 1-4) displays the application name, Macromedia Dreamweaver MX 2004; in brackets, the Web page title; and, in parentheses, the file path and file name of the displayed Web page. In Figure 1-4, the title bar displays [Untitled Document (Untitled-1)]. Untitled Document represents the Web page title, and Untitled-1 represents the file path and file name. Following the file name, Dreamweaver displays an asterisk if you have made changes that have not yet been saved. After you give a Web page a title and save the document, the title bar reflects these changes by displaying the path and title and removing the asterisk.

Document Window

The **Document window** displays the current document, or Web page, including text, tables, graphics, and other items. In Figure 1-4, the Document window is blank. The Document window is similar in appearance to the Internet Explorer or Netscape browser window. You work in the Document window in one of three views: **Design view**, the design environment where you assemble your Web page elements and design your page (Figure 1-4 displays Design view); **Code view**, which is a hand-coding environment for writing and editing code; or **Split view**, which allows you to see both Code view and Design view for the same document in a single window. When you open a new document in Dreamweaver, the default view is Design view. These views are discussed in detail in Project 2.

Panels and Panel Groups

Panel groups are sets of related panels docked together below one heading. Panels provide control over a wide range of Dreamweaver commands and functions. Each panel group can be expanded or collapsed, and can be docked or undocked with other panel groups. Panel groups also can be docked to the integrated Document window. This makes it easy to access the panels you need without cluttering your workspace. Panels within a panel group are displayed as tabs.

Some panels, such as the Property inspector and the Insert bar, are stand-alone panels. The **Insert bar** allows quick access to objects and behaviors. It contains buttons for creating various types of objects, such as images, tables, layers, frames, and tags, and inserting them into a document. Each object is a piece of HTML code that allows you to set various attributes as you insert it. For example, you can insert a table by clicking the Table button on the Insert bar Common category and then set the table attributes through the Property inspector. The buttons on the Insert bar are organized into several categories, which you can switch through a pop-up menu on the left side of the Insert bar. Some categories also have buttons with pop-up menus. When you select an option from a pop-up menu, it becomes the default action for the button. The default position for the Insert bar is at the top of the Document window (Figure 1-4 on page DW 33). When you start Dreamweaver, the category in which you were last working is displayed.

The **Property inspector** (Figure 1-4) displays settings for the selected element's properties or attributes. This panel is context-sensitive, meaning it changes based on the selected element, which can include text, tables, images, and other elements. When Dreamweaver starts, the Property inspector is positioned at the bottom of the Document window and displays text properties if a Document window is open. Otherwise, the Property inspector is blank.

To expand or collapse a panel group, click the expand/collapse arrow to the left of the group's name; to undock and move a panel group, drag the gripper at the left edge of the group's title bar (Figure 1-4). To open panels, use the Window menu. Each panel is explained in detail as it is used in the projects throughout the book.

> ### More About
>
> #### Panel Groups
>
> To drag a floating (undocked) panel group without docking it, drag the panel group by the bar above its title bar. The panel group does not dock as long as it is not dragged by its gripper.

Status Bar

The **status bar** at the bottom of the Document window (Figure 1-4) provides additional information about the document you are creating. The status bar presents the following information:

- **Tag selector:** Displays the hierarchy of tags surrounding the current selection. Click any tag in the hierarchy to select that tag and all its contents.
- **Window Size pop-up menu button:** Displays the Window Size pop-up menu, which includes the window's current dimensions (in pixels).
- **Estimated document size and download time:** Displays the size and estimated download time of the current page. Dreamweaver MX 2004 calculates the size based on the entire contents of the page, including all linked objects such as images and plug-ins.

Vertical Bar

A vertical bar separates the panel groups, and a horizontal bar separates the Property inspector from the Document window. Both bars contain an expand/collapse arrow. Clicking this arrow hides/displays the panel groups and the Property inspector (Figure 1-5 on the next page). If your screen resolution is set to 800 × 600, a portion of the Property inspector does not display when the panel groups are expanded.

Menu Bar

The **menu bar** displays the Dreamweaver menu names (Figure 1-5). Each menu contains a list of commands you can use to perform tasks such as opening, saving, modifying, previewing, and inserting data into your Web page. When you point to a menu name on the menu bar, the area of the menu bar containing the name is highlighted.

FIGURE 1-5

To display a menu, such as the View menu (Figure 1-5), click the menu name on the menu bar. If you point to a menu command that has an arrow at its right edge, a submenu displays another list of commands. Many menus display some commands that appear gray, or dimmed, instead of black, which indicates they are not available for the current selection.

Toolbars

Dreamweaver contains two toolbars: the Document toolbar and the Standard toolbar. You can choose to display or hide the toolbars by clicking View on the menu bar and then clicking Toolbars. If a toolbar name has a check mark next to it, it is displayed in the window. To hide the toolbar, click the name of the toolbar with the check mark, and it no longer displays.

The **Document toolbar** (Figure 1-6 on the next page) is the default toolbar that displays in the Document window. It contains buttons that provide different views of the Document window (e.g., Code, Split, and Design) and some common operations, such as No Browser Check Errors, File Management, Preview/Debug in Browser, Check Cross-Browser Compatibility, Web Page Title, Refresh Design View, and View Options. All View option commands also are available through the View menu.

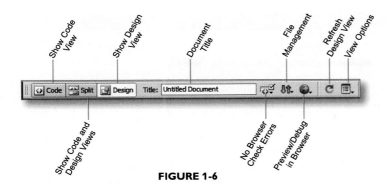

FIGURE 1-6

The **Standard toolbar** (Figure 1-7) contains buttons for common operations from the File and Edit menus: New, Open, Save, Save All, Cut, Copy, Paste, Undo, and Redo. The Standard toolbar does not display by default in the Dreamweaver Document window when you first start Dreamweaver. You can display the Standard toolbar through the Toolbars command on the View menu, or by right-clicking a toolbar anywhere but on a button and then clicking Standard on the context menu. Similar to other toolbars and panels, you can dock/undock and move the Standard toolbar, so it may be displayed in a different location on your screen.

FIGURE 1-7

Opening and Closing Panels

The Dreamweaver workspace accommodates different styles of working and levels of expertise. Through the workspace, you can open and close the panel groups and display/hide other Dreamweaver features as needed. To open a panel group, select and then click the name of a panel on the Window menu. Closing unused panels provides uncluttered workspace in the Document window. To close an individual panel group, click Close panel group on the Options pop-up menu accessed through the panel group's title bar (Figure 1-8 on the next page). To expand/collapse a panel, click the panel's expand/collapse arrow at the left of the group's name.

Opening and closing each panel individually is a time-consuming task. Dreamweaver provides a shortcut to accomplish this job quickly. The F4 key is a toggle key that opens and/or closes all panels and inspectors at one time. The step on the next page illustrates how to close all open panels.

FIGURE 1-8

To Close and Open Panels

1

• **Press the F4 key.**

All the open panels and inspectors close, and the maximum workspace is available in the Document window (Figure 1-9).

2

• **Press the F4 key again to redisplay the panels.**

FIGURE 1-9

Defining a Local Site

Web design and Web site management are two important skills that a builder of Web sites must understand and apply. Dreamweaver MX 2004 is a site creation and management tool. To use Dreamweaver efficiently, you first must define the local site. After defining the local site, you then publish to a remote site. Publishing to a remote site is discussed in Project 3 and Appendix C.

The general definition of a **site**, or Web site, is a set of linked documents with shared attributes, such as related topics, a similar design, or a shared purpose. In Dreamweaver, however, site can refer to any of the following:

- A **Web site**, which is a set of pages on a server that are viewed through a Web browser by a visitor to the site.
- A **remote site**, which are files on the server that make up a Web site, from the author's point of view rather than a visitor's point of view.
- A **local site**, which are files on your local disk that correspond to the files on the remote site. You edit the files on your local disk, and then upload them to the remote site.
- A **Dreamweaver site definition**, which is a set of defining characteristics for a local site, plus information on how the local site corresponds to a remote site.

All Dreamweaver Web sites begin with a local root folder. As you become familiar with Dreamweaver and complete the projects in this book, you will find references to a **local root folder**, a **root folder**, and **root**. These terms are interchangeable. This folder is no different from any other folder on your computer's hard drive or other storage media, except for the way in which Dreamweaver views it. When Dreamweaver looks for Web pages, links, images, and other files, the program defaults to the designated root folder. Any media within the Web site that are outside of the root folder will not display when the Web site is previewed in a Web browser. Within the root folder, you can create additional folders or subfolders to organize images and other elements. A **subfolder** (also called a **nested folder**) is a folder inside another folder.

Dreamweaver provides two options to define a site and create the hierarchy: create the root folder and any subfolders, or create the pages and then create the folders when saving the files. In this book, you create the root folder and subfolders and then create the Web pages.

One of Dreamweaver's more prominent organizational tools is its Files panel. Use the **Files panel** for standard file maintenance operations, such as the following:

- Creating files
- Viewing, opening, and moving files
- Creating folders
- Deleting items
- Managing a site

The Files panel enables you to view a site, including local, remote, and testing server files associated with a selected site. In this project, you view only the local site.

Creating the Local Root Folder and Subfolders

Several options are available to create and manage your local root folder and subfolders: Dreamweaver's Files panel, Dreamweaver's Site Definition feature, or Windows file management. In this book, you use Dreamweaver's Site Definition feature to create the local root folder and subfolders, Dreamweaver's Files panel to manage and edit your files and folders, and Windows file management to download the data files.

To organize and create a Web site and understand how you access Web documents, it is important to understand paths and folders. The term, path, sometimes is confusing for new users of the Web. It is, however, a simple concept: A **path** is the succession of folders that must be navigated to get from one folder to another. In the DOS world, folders are referred to as **directories**. These two terms often are used interchangeably.

A typical path structure has a **master folder**, usually called the root and designated by the symbol "\". This root folder contains within it all of the other subfolders or nested folders. Further, each subfolder may contain additional subfolders or nested folders. These folders contain the Web site files. One of the more commonly used subfolders contains the site's images.

Because many files are required for a Dreamweaver Web site, it is advisable to create the projects using another type of media rather than the floppy drive (A:). Steps in this project instruct you to create the local site on the C:\ drive, on the computer's hard drive. It is suggested, however, that you check with your instructor to verify the location and path you will use to create and save your local Web site. Other options may include a Zip drive, USB flash drive, or a network drive.

For this book, you first create a local root folder using your last name and first initial. Examples in this book use David Allen as the Web site author. Thus, David's local root folder is allend. Next, you create a subfolder and name it parks. Finally, you create another subfolder within parks and name it images. All Florida Parks related files and subfolders are stored within the parks folder. When you navigate through this folder hierarchy, you are navigating along the path. The path and folder within the Florida Parks Web site are C:\allend\parks\. The path to the images folder is C:\allend\parks\images\. When you create your folders, you will use your last name and first initial for the root folder. In all references to allend, substitute your last name and first initial.

Using Site Definition to Create a Local Site

You create a site definition using Dreamweaver's Site Definition dialog box. Two options are available: Basic or Advanced. The Basic method, or **Site Definition Wizard**, guides you through site setup step by step and takes you through a series of six screens. In the Advanced method, all options are contained on one screen. The Advanced method is a more efficient method. Using this view, you set all the same basic information that the Site Wizard collects, plus additional options such as the following:

- **Refresh local file list:** Updates the site list whenever a new file is added to the site folder; checked by default
- **Enable cache:** Allocates memory to store frequently used site data; checked by default
- **Default images folder:** An option feature to specify the location of images in the site
- **HTTP address:** Used to define the URL of a Web site and to verify absolute links

The two main categories in a site definition are **Local Info** (Local Information) and **Remote Info** (Remote Information). In this project, you create the local site definition using the Advanced method. The site definition is stored in the Windows registry and is not part of the site. If you use removable media to store your files and move to another computer, you must recreate the site definition on that computer. Remote site definition is discussed in Project 3.

After you have completed the Site definition, the hierarchy structure displays in Dreamweaver's Files panel. This hierarchy structure is similar to the Windows XP file organization. The Files panel provides a view of the devices and folders on your computer and shows how these devices and folders are organized. A small device icon or folder icon is displayed next to each object in the list. The device icon represents a device such as the Desktop or a disk drive, and the folder icon represents a folder. Many of these icons have a plus or minus sign next to them, which indicates whether the device or folder contains additional folders. The plus and minus signs are controls that you can click to expand or collapse the view of the file hierarchy. In the Files panel, the site folders and files appear in a different color than non-site folders and files so that you easily can distinguish between the two.

You define a local site by telling Dreamweaver where you plan to store local files. Use the Site Definition Advanced approach and the following steps to show how to create a local Web site.

To Use Site Definition to Create a Local Web Site

1

• **Click Site on the menu bar and then point to Manage Sites.**

The Site menu is displayed, and the Manage Sites command is selected (Figure 1-10).

FIGURE 1-10

2

• **Click Manage Sites.**

The Manage Sites dialog box is displayed (Figure 1-11).

FIGURE 1-11

3

• **Click the New button.**

A pop-up menu is displayed (Figure 1-12).

FIGURE 1-12

4

• **Click Site on the pop-up menu.**

• **If necessary, click the Advanced tab. Verify that Local Info is selected in the Category column.**

The Site Definition window is displayed, and the Advanced tab is selected. Unnamed Site 1 is highlighted in the Site name text box (Figure 1-13).

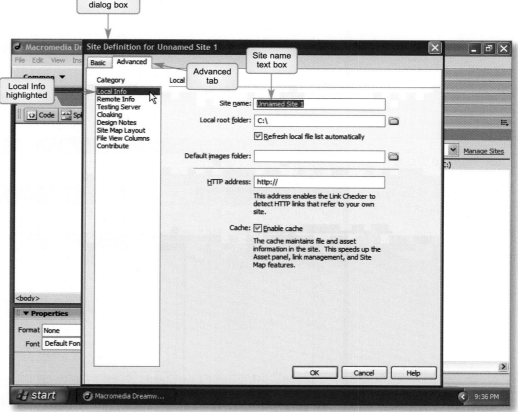

FIGURE 1-13

5

• **Type** Florida Parks **as the site name.**

This name is for your reference only. It is not part of the path and is not visible to viewers of your site (Figure 1-14).

FIGURE 1-14

6

• **Click the folder icon to the right of the Local root folder text box.**

• **If you are creating and saving your sites at another location or on other media, navigate to that location and substitute the location for Local Disk (C):.**

The Choose local root folder for site dialog box is displayed. Local Disk (C): appears in the Select text box (Figure 1-15).

FIGURE 1-15

7

• **Click the Create New Folder icon.**

The New Folder (1) text box is displayed (Figure 1-16). New Folder(1) is highlighted. The folder number on your computer may be different or absent.

FIGURE 1-16

8

• **Type your last name and first initial (with no spaces between your last name and initial) in the folder text box.**

• **Press the ENTER key to select the folder.**

Your last name and first initial are displayed in the folder's text box (Figure 1-17).

FIGURE 1-17

9

• **Double-click the your name folder.**

The author's folder name is displayed in the Select text box (Figure 1-18).

FIGURE 1-18

10

• **Click the Create New Folder icon.**

• **Type** parks **as the name of the new folder and then press the ENTER key.**

• **Double-click the parks folder name.**

The parks subfolder is created, and the folder name is displayed in the Select text box (Figure 1-19).

FIGURE 1-19

• **Click the Select button.**

The Site Definition dialog box is displayed, the Advanced tab is selected, and the Local root folder text box contains the C:\allend\parks\ path (Figure 1-20).

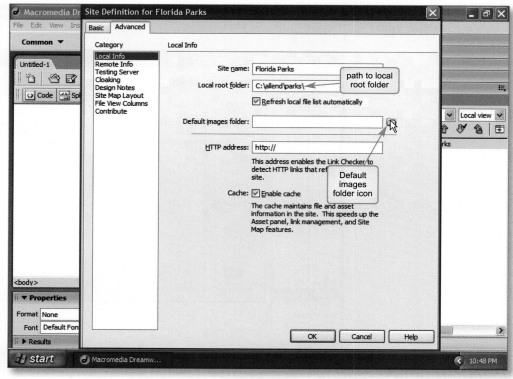

FIGURE 1-20

• **Click the folder icon to the right of the Default images folder text box.**

• **Navigate to the your name\parks folder.**

• **Click the Create New Folder icon.**

• **Type** images **as the name of the new folder and then press the ENTER key. Double-click the images folder name.**

An images subfolder is created, and the folder name is displayed in the Select text box (Figure 1-21).

FIGURE 1-21

• **Click the Select button.**

• **Verify that the Refresh local file list automatically and the Enable cache check boxes are selected in the Site Definition dialog box.**

• **Point to the OK button.**

The Site Definition dialog box is displayed, and the path for the default images folder is displayed in the Default images folder text box (Figure 1-22).

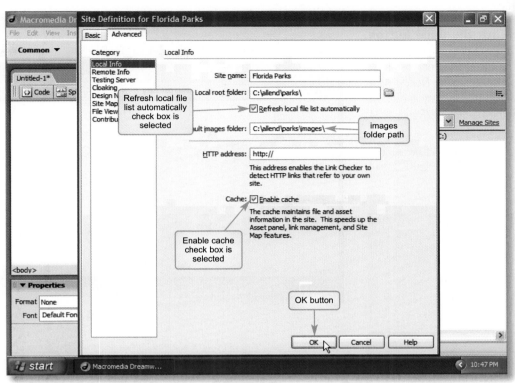

FIGURE 1-22

• **Click the OK button.**

The Manage Sites dialog box is displayed, and the Florida Parks site is added to the dialog box (Figure 1-23).

FIGURE 1-23

15

• **Click the Done button.**

The Dreamweaver workspace is displayed. The Florida Parks Web site hierarchy is displayed in the File panels (Figure 1-24).

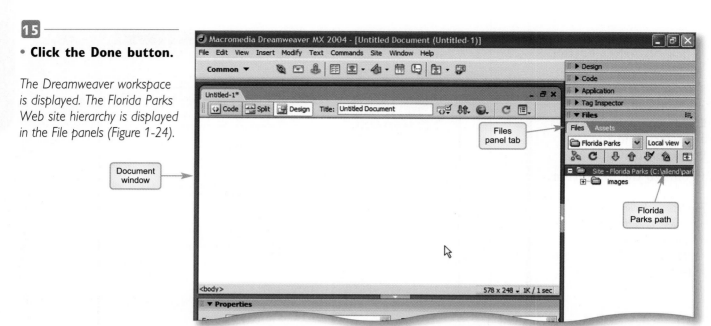

FIGURE 1-24

Copying Data Files to the Florida Parks Folder

Your data disk contains background images for Project 1. You can copy data files one by one through the Dreamweaver Files panel as you progress through this project. Alternatively, using the Windows My Computer option, you can establish the basic framework for the parks Web site by copying all the files and images at one time. Windows provides several ways through the View menu for you to arrange and identify your files when viewing them: Show in Groups, Thumbnails, Tiles, Filmstrip, Icons, List, and Details. The figures in this book use the List view when using the Windows My Computer option to copy the data files. Your computer may use a different view to display the files. The following steps illustrate how to copy data files to the local Web site.

To Copy Data Files to the Local Web Site

1

• **Click the Start button on the Windows taskbar and then click My Computer.**

The My Computer window is displayed (Figure 1-25).

FIGURE 1-25

2

• **Double-click Local Disk (C:) and then navigate to the location of the data files for Project 1.**

If necessary, check with your instructor to verify the location of the data files. In Figure 1-26, the data files are located on Drive C:\.

FIGURE 1-26

3

• **Double-click the DataFiles folder and then double-click the Proj01 folder.**

The Proj01 folder is selected, and the path to Proj01 is displayed in the Address text box (Figure 1-27).

FIGURE 1-27

4

• **Double-click the parks folder and then double-click the images folder.**

The images folder is selected, and the path to the images folder is displayed in the Address text box (Figure 1-28).

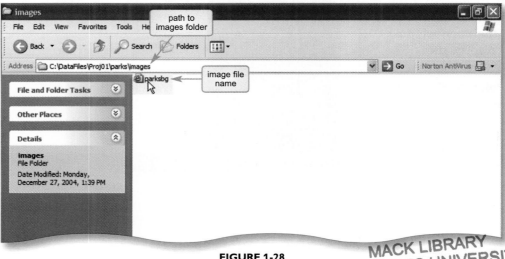

FIGURE 1-28

5

• **Right-click the parksbg image file.**

The context menu is displayed (Figure 1-29).

• **Point to the Copy command.**

FIGURE 1-29

6

• **Click Copy and then click the My Computer Back button the number of times necessary to navigate to the your name folder.**

• **Double-click the your name folder, double-click the parks folder, and then double-click the images folder.**

• **Right-click anywhere in the open window to display the context menu.**

• **Point to the Paste command.**

The context menu is displayed and Paste is highlighted (Figure 1-30).

FIGURE 1-30

7

• **Click the Paste command.**

The parksbg image is pasted into the Florida Parks Web site images folder (Figure 1-31).

8

• **Click the images window Close button.**

The image window closes and Dreamweaver appears. The images folder is displayed in Dreamweaver's Files panel.

FIGURE 1-31

Your site definition and file hierarchy structure is complete, and your data files are copied into the images folder.

Removing or Editing a Web Site

On occasion, you may need to remove or edit a Web site. To remove or edit a Web site, click Site on the menu bar and then click the Manage Sites command. This displays the Manage Sites dialog box. Select the site name and then click the Remove button to remove the site. Dreamweaver displays a Dreamweaver MX 2004 caution box providing you with an opportunity to cancel. Click the No button to cancel. Otherwise, click the Yes button, and Dreamweaver removes the site. To edit a site, click the site name and then click the Edit button. Dreamweaver displays the Site Definition dialog box, and from there, you can change any of the options you selected when you first created the site. Removing a site in Dreamweaver removes the settings for the site. The files and folders remain and must be deleted separately.

Saving a Web Page

With the Florida Parks site defined and the data files copied to the site, the next step is to save the untitled Dreamweaver document. When you defined the site, you designated C:\allend\parks\ as the local root folder. You can copy and paste files into this folder using Windows XP or use Dreamweaver's file management tools to copy and paste. You also can save a Dreamweaver document into this folder. Dreamweaver treats any item placed in the folder as part of the site.

When a document is saved as a Web page, the Web page also remains in the computer's memory and is displayed in the Document window. It is a good practice to save when you first open the document and then save regularly while you are working in Dreamweaver. By doing so, you protect yourself from losing all the work you have done since the last time you saved.

The Standard Toolbar

The Standard toolbar contains buttons for common operations from the File and Edit menus: New, Open, Save, Save All, Cut, Copy, Paste, Undo, and Redo. It is useful to have this toolbar displayed when creating and saving Web pages.

The Index Page

The **home page** is the starting point for the rest of your Web site. For most Web sites, the home page is named index. This name has special significance because most Web servers recognize index.htm (or index.html) as the default home page. When you save your document, Dreamweaver automatically appends the extension .htm to the file name. Documents with the .htm extension display in Web browsers. The home page for your Florida Parks Web site is named index. The following steps show how to display the Standard toolbar and to save the untitled document as index.htm in the parks local root folder.

To Display the Standard Toolbar and Save a Document as a Web Page

1

• **Click View on the menu bar, point to Toolbars, and then point to Standard on the Toolbars submenu.**

Dreamweaver displays the View menu and the Toolbars submenu (Figure 1-32).

FIGURE 1-32

2

• **Click Standard.**

*The Standard toolbar
is displayed in the
Dreamweaver
workspace (Figure 1-33).
Previous settings determine the
location of the Standard
toolbar. The Standard toolbar
on your computer may be
displayed below the Document
toolbar or in another location.*

FIGURE 1-33

3

• **Click the Save button
on the Standard toolbar.**

*The Save As dialog box is
displayed (Figure 1-34). The
parks folder name is displayed
in the Save in text box. The
default file name, Untitled-1,
is highlighted in the File name
text box.*

FIGURE 1-34

4

• **Type** index **as the file name.**

The index file name is displayed in the File name text box (Figure 1-35).

FIGURE 1-35

5

• **Click the Save button.**

The parks index page is saved in the parks local folder and is displayed in the Files panel (Figure 1-36). The path and file name (parks/index.htm) are displayed on the Dreamweaver title bar.

FIGURE 1-36

Web Page Backgrounds

Each new Web page you create displays with a default white or gray background and other default properties. You can modify these default properties using the **Page Properties** dialog box. The Page Properties dialog box lets you specify appearance, links, and many other aspects of page design. You can assign new page properties for each new page you create, and modify those for existing pages. The page properties you select apply only to the active document.

You can change the default and enhance your Web page, for example, by adding a background image and/or background color. If you use both a background image and a background color, the color appears while the image downloads, and then the image covers the color. Additionally, Dreamweaver provides a series of Web-safe color schemes, accessed through the Commands menu. In this project, you add a background image to the Web page.

Adding a Background Image

When you copied the data file earlier in this project, you copied an image file that is the background for the Florida Parks Web site. You use background images to add texture and interesting color to a Web page. Use background images cautiously, however. Web page images displayed on top of a busy background image may not mix well, and text may be difficult to read. Images and image formats are discussed in more detail in Project 2.

The following steps illustrate how to use the Page Properties dialog box to add a background image to the home page.

To Add a Background Image to the Index Page

1

• **Click Modify on the menu bar and then point to Page Properties (Figure 1-37).**

FIGURE 1-37

2

• **Click Page Properties.**

• **Verify that the Appearance category is selected.**

The Page Properties dialog box is displayed, and the Appearance category is highlighted (Figure 1-38).

FIGURE 1-38

3

• **Click the Browse button and then click the images folder.**

Dreamweaver displays the Select Image Source dialog box (Figure 1-39). The parks folder name is displayed in the Look in text box, and the images folder is highlighted.

FIGURE 1-39

4

• **Click the OK button.**

• **Click the parksbg file.**

• **If necessary, click the Preview images check box to select it.**

The images folder is opened and displayed in the Look in text box. The file name, parksbg is displayed in the File name text box. A preview of the image is displayed in the Image preview area. The dimensions of the image, type of image, file size, and download time are listed below the image (Figure 1-40).

FIGURE 1-40

5

• **Click the OK button in the Select Image Source dialog box and then point to the OK button in the Page Properties dialog box.**

The Page Properties dialog box is displayed with the folder and file name in the Background image text box (Figure 1-41).

FIGURE 1-41

6

• **Click the OK button and then click the Save button on the Standard toolbar.**

The background image is applied to the Florida Parks page, and the updated page is saved (Figure 1-42).

FIGURE 1-42

Adding Text to a Web Page

In Dreamweaver, you can create a Web page in several ways: (1) you can type a new document; (2) you can open an existing HTML document, even if it was not created in Dreamweaver; (3) you can copy and paste text; and (4) you can import a Word document.

In this project, you create the index page for Florida Parks Web page by typing the text in the Document window. Entering text into a Dreamweaver document is similar to typing text in a word processing document. You can position the insertion point at the top left of the Document window or within another element, such as a table cell. Pressing the ENTER key creates a new paragraph and inserts a blank line. Web browsers automatically insert a blank line of space between paragraphs. To start a new single line without a blank line between lines of text requires a **line break**. You can insert a line break by holding down the SHIFT key and then pressing the ENTER key or by clicking the Line Break command on the Insert HTML Special Characters submenu.

If you type a wrong letter and notice the error before pressing the ENTER key, press the BACKSPACE key to erase all the characters back to and including the one that is incorrect. If you mistakenly press the ENTER key and then discover the error, simply press the BACKSPACE key to return the insertion point to the previous line. Clicking the **Undo** button on the Standard toolbar reverses the most recent actions. The **Redo** button reverses the last undo action. The Undo and Redo commands also are accessible on the Edit menu.

Organizing Your Workspace

To organize your workspace, you hide the panel groups and collapse the lower portion of the Property inspector. This gives you additional workspace in the Dreamweaver Document window. The following steps show how to organize your workspace by hiding the panel groups.

To Hide the Panel Groups

1

• **Click the expand/ collapse arrow on the panel groups vertical bar.**

• **Click the Property inspector expander arrow.**

The panel group is hidden, and the Property inspector is collapsed (Figure 1-43).

FIGURE 1-43

Adding Text

Table 1-1 includes the text for the Florida Parks Web page. After typing the sections of the document, you will press the ENTER key to insert a blank line.

Table 1-1 Discovering Scenic Florida Web Page Text			
SECTION	HEADING, PART 1, AND PART 2	SECTION	PART 3, ITEMS FOR BULLETED LIST, AND CLOSING
Heading	Discovering Scenic Florida	Part 3	When planning your trip, consider the following:
Part 1	Florida is one of the nation's renowned vacationlands. Tourism is Florida's number one industry. Visitors flock to Walt Disney World, Epcot, Universal Studios, and other recreational attractions. Many vacationers, however, do not realize the diversity of Florida. In addition to the theme parks, Florida's appeal extends from the vast expanse of the Everglades in the south to notable cities such as Saint Augustine and Pensacola in the north. Florida's historic and natural sites offer travelers an opportunity to view a totally different side of Florida.	Items list	Biscayne, Everglades, and Dry Tortugas National Parks are located in southern Florida. <enter>

Six of the top 20 beaches in America are located in Florida state parks. <enter>

The state park system includes state preserves, state parks, state archeological sites, state museums, and others. <enter>

Florida has 6 national wildlife refuges and 3 national forests in which many national wilderness areas are located. <enter> |
| Part 2 | Florida has approximately 150 state parks and 3 national parks. Visitors to these parks can enjoy such activities as swimming, camping, hiking, fishing, boating, scuba diving, or simply reflecting on Florida's natural and cultural resources. | Closing | Park entrance fees vary throughout the state and are subject to change. |

The following steps, show how to add text to the Document window and insert blank lines between sections of text.

To Add Text

1

• **Type the heading** Discovering Scenic Florida **as shown in Table 1-1, and then press the ENTER key.**

The heading is entered in the Document window (Figure 1-44). Pressing the ENTER key creates a new paragraph.

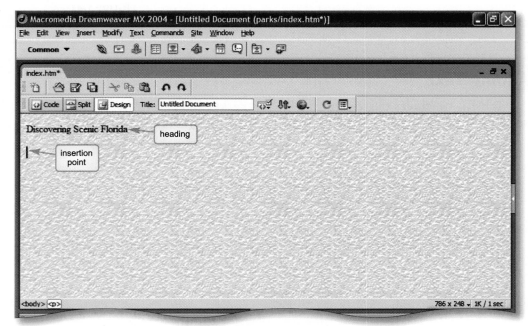

FIGURE 1-44

2

• **Type the text of Part 1 as shown in Table 1-1 on the previous page, and then press the ENTER key.**

The introductory paragraph is entered (Figure 1-45). Pressing the ENTER key creates a new paragraph.

Part 1

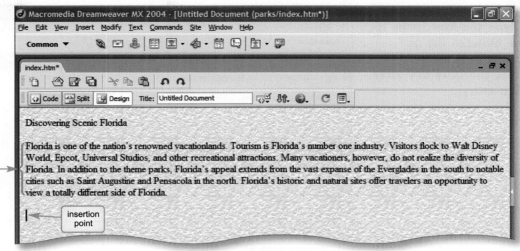

FIGURE 1-45

3

• **Type the text of Part 2 as shown in Table 1-1, and then press the ENTER key.**

The second paragraph is entered (Figure 1-46).

Part 2

FIGURE 1-46

4

• **Type the text of Part 3 as shown in Table 1-1, and then press the ENTER key.**

The third paragraph is entered (Figure 1-47).

Part 3

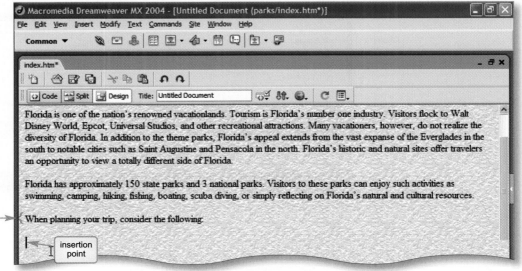

FIGURE 1-47

5

• **Type the four items for the bulleted list as shown in Table 1-1. Press the ENTER key after each entry.**

The items for the bulleted list are entered (Figure 1-48). Later in this project, you will format the list so it becomes a bulleted list.

FIGURE 1-48

6

• **Type the closing paragraph shown in Table 1-1 on page DW 60, and then press the ENTER key.**

• **Click the Save button on the Standard toolbar.**

The paragraph is entered (Figure 1-49).

FIGURE 1-49

If you feel you need to start over for any reason, Dreamweaver makes it easy to delete a Web page or other file. Save and close the page, display the panel groups by clicking the vertical bar expand/collapse arrow, click the name of the page you want to delete, right-click to display the context menu, point to Edit, and then point to and click Delete on the Edit submenu. Click the Yes button in the Dreamweaver caution dialog box to delete the page or the No button to cancel the action.

Formatting Text

The next step is to format the text. Dreamweaver provides three options for formatting text: the Text menu, the Insert bar Text category, and the Property inspector. To format the text for the Discovering Scenic Florida Web page, you use the text-related features of the Property inspector. If the panels group is displayed, a portion of the Property inspector is hidden.

The Property inspector is one of the panels you will use most often when creating and formatting Web pages. The Property inspector initially displays the more commonly used attributes, or properties, of the selected object. The object can be a table, text, an image, or some other item. The Property inspector is context-sensitive, so options within the Property inspector change relative to the selected object.

Property Inspector Features

The Property inspector lets you see the current properties of an element and allows you to alter or edit them. The Property inspector is divided into two sections. Clicking the expander arrow in the lower-right corner of the Property inspector collapses the Property inspector to show only the more commonly used properties for the selected element or expands the Property inspector to show more options. Some objects, such as text, do not contain additional properties within the expanded panel (Figure 1-50 on the next page). The question mark icon opens the Help window.

Collapsing/Hiding the Property Inspector

Having panels such as the Property inspector display in the Dreamweaver window requires considerable window space. If you are finished working with this panel, it generally is better to collapse it, hide it, or close it. **Collapsing** it leaves the title bar in the window, which allows you to expand it easily by clicking the expand/collapse arrow instead of using the Properties command on the Window menu. Pressing CTRL+F3 also collapses/expands the Property inspector. **Hiding** it hides the panel and the title bar. To hide the Property inspector and the Property inspector title bar, click the expand/collapse arrow on the horizontal bar. **Closing** it removes it completely from the Document window. To close the Property inspector, display the context menu by right-clicking on the Properties title bar, and then selecting the Close panel group command or click the Options menu and select the Close panel group command from the pop-up menu.

By default, the Property inspector displays the properties for text on a blank document. Most changes you make to properties are applied immediately in the Document window. For some properties, however, changes are not applied until you click outside the property-editing text fields, press the ENTER key, or press the TAB key to switch to another property. The following section describes the text-related features of the Property inspector (Figure 1-50 and Figure 1-51).

Q: When a change is made in the Property inspector, when is the change applied?

A: Most changes are applied immediately. You can confirm that changes are applied, however, by clicking the TAB or ENTER button.

FIGURE 1-50

FIGURE 1-51

FORMAT The **Format box** allows you to apply a Paragraph, Heading, or Preformatted style to the text. Clicking the Format box displays a pop-up menu from which you can select a style.

The **Paragraph style** is the normal default style for text on a Web page. **Paragraph formatting** is the process of changing the appearance of text. **Heading styles** are used to create divisions and separate one segment of text from another. The Heading numbers range from 1 through 6 and correspond to the HTML elements H1, H2, and so on. The smaller the number of the heading, the bigger the text displayed when viewed in a Web browser. These formats are displayed based on how different browsers interpret the tags, offering little consistency and control over layout and appearance. When you apply a heading tag to a paragraph, Dreamweaver automatically adds the next line of text as a standard paragraph. Use the **Preformatted style** when you do not want a Web browser to change the line of text in any way.

FONT Font combination applies the selected font combination to the text and determines how a browser displays text on your Web page. The browser uses the first font in the combination that is installed on the user's system. If none of the fonts in the combination are installed, the browser displays the text as specified by the user's browser preferences. Most font faces in common usage on the Web are serif, sans-serif, or monospace fonts. The default font used on most Web pages is Times (also called Times New Roman or New Times), which is a serif font. The most commonly used sans-serif fonts are Arial, Helvetica, Geneva, and Verdana, while the most commonly used monospace font is Courier (also called Courier New). Use the Font combination pop-up menu to apply a font combination.

STYLE By default, Dreamweaver uses Cascading Style Sheets (CSS) styles to format text. **Cascading Style Sheets** (**CSS**) are a collection of formatting rules that control the appearance of content in a Web page. The styles that you apply to text using the Property inspector or menu commands create CSS rules that are embedded in the head of the current document. To change the default from CSS tags to HTML tags, click the Edit menu and select the Preferences command. Under the General category, Editing options, deselect the Use CSS instead of HTML tags check box. Styles are discussed in Project 5.

SIZE The **Text Size box** provides options that allow you to apply a font size to a single character or to an entire page of text. Font sizes in HTML range from 1 through 7, with size 7 being the largest. The default HTML font size, or **BASEFONT**, is 3, which equates to 12 points in a word processing document.

TEXT COLOR When you create a new document in Dreamweaver, the default text color is black. The **Text Color** box contains palettes of colors you can apply to emphasize, differentiate, and highlight topics. To display the text in a selected Web-safe color, click the Text Color box to access the different methods of selecting preset colors or creating custom ones. Colors also are represented by a hexadecimal value (for example, #FF0000) in the adjacent text field.

BOLD AND ITALIC The **Bold button** and the **Italic button** allow you to format text using these two font styles in the Property inspector. These are the two more commonly used styles. Dreamweaver also supports a variety of other font styles, which are available through the Text menu. To view these other styles, click Text on the menu bar and then point to Style. The Style submenu contains a list of additional styles, such as Underline, Strikethrough, and Teletype.

ALIGN LEFT, ALIGN CENTER, ALIGN RIGHT, AND JUSTIFY In Dreamweaver, the default alignment for text is left alignment. To change the default alignment, select the text you want to align or simply position the mouse pointer at the beginning of the text. Click an alignment button: Align Center, Align Right, or Justify. You can align and center complete blocks of text, but you cannot align or center part of a heading or part of a paragraph.

LINK The **Link (Hyperlink) box** allows you to make selected text or other objects a hyperlink to a specified URL or Web page. To select the URL or Web page, you can click the Point to File or Browse for File icon to the right of the Link box to browse to a page in your Web site and select the file name, type the URL, or drag a file from the Files panel into the Link box. Links are covered in detail in Project 2.

TARGET In the **Target pop-up menu box**, you specify the frame or window in which the linked page should load. If you are using frames, the names of all the frames in the current document are displayed in the list. If the specified frame does not exist when the current document is opened in a browser, the linked page loads in a new window with the name you specified. Once this window exists, other files can be targeted to it.

UNORDERED LIST Web developers often use a list to structure a page. An unordered list turns the selected paragraph or heading into an item in a bulleted list. If no text is selected before the **Unordered List button** is clicked, a new bulleted list is started.

ORDERED LIST An ordered list is similar to an unordered list. This type of list, however, turns the selected paragraph or heading into an item in a numbered list. If no text is selected before the **Ordered List button** is clicked, a new numbered list is started.

INDENT AND OUTDENT To set off a block quote, you can use the Indent feature. The **Text Indent button** will indent a line or a paragraph from both margins. In HTML, this is the blockquote tag. The **Text Outdent button** removes the indentation from the selected text by removing the blockquote tag. In a list, indenting creates a nested list, and removing the indentation unnests the list. A **nested list** is one list inside another list.

PAGE PROPERTIES Clicking the Page Properties button opens the Page Properties dialog box.

LIST ITEM Clicking the List Items button opens the List Properties dialog box. This button is dimmed until an existing list is created and the insertion point is contained within the list.

Applying Property Inspector Text-Related Features

The text for your Web page displays in the Document window. The next step in creating your Web page is to format this text. **Formatting** means to apply different fonts, change heading styles, insert special characters, and insert other such elements that enhance the appearance of the Web page. You use commands from the Property inspector to format the text.

Within Dreamweaver, you can format text before you type, or you can apply new formats after you type. If you have used word processing software, you will find many of the Dreamweaver formatting commands similar to the commands within a word processing program. At this point, your Web page contains only text, so the Property inspector displays attributes related to text.

To set block formatting, such as formatting a heading or an unordered list, position the insertion point in the line or paragraph and then format the text. To set character formatting, such as choosing a font or font size, however, you first must select the character, word, or words.

Text Headings

Just as in a word processing document, designers use the heading structure in a Web page to set apart document or section titles. The six levels of HTML headings are Heading 1 through Heading 6. **Heading 1 <h1>** produces the largest text and **Heading 6 <h6>** the smallest. By default, browsers will display the six heading levels in the same font, with the point size decreasing as the importance of the heading decreases. The following steps show how to format the heading.

More About

The Property Inspector

The Property inspector initially displays the most commonly used properties of the selected object. Click the expander arrow in the lower-right corner of the Property inspector to see more of the element's properties.

More About

Text Size

You can set the size of the text in your Web page, but viewers of your Web page also can change the size through their browser. When creating a page, use the font size that looks right for the page you are creating.

To Format Text with Heading 1

1

• **If necessary, scroll up and then position the insertion point anywhere in the heading text, Discovering Scenic Florida (Figure 1-52).**

FIGURE 1-52

2

• **Click the Format box arrow in the Property inspector and then point to Heading 1.**

The Format pop-up menu is displayed with a list of formatting styles. Heading 1 is highlighted in the list (Figure 1-53).

FIGURE 1-53

3

• **Click Heading 1.**

The Heading 1 style is applied to the Discovering Scenic Florida heading (Figure 1-54). The <h1> HTML tag displays in the Tag selector, indicating Heading 1 is selected.

FIGURE 1-54

Centering Text

Using the **Align Center button** in the Property inspector allows you to center text. This button is very similar to the Center button in a word processing program. To center a single line or a paragraph, position the mouse pointer in the line or paragraph, and then click the button to center the text. You do not need to select a single line or single paragraph to center it. To center more than one paragraph at a time, however, you must select all paragraphs. The following step illustrates how to center the heading.

To Center the Web Page Heading

1

• **If necessary, click anywhere in the heading, Discovering Scenic Florida. Click the Align Center button in the Property inspector.**

The heading, Discovering Scenic Florida, is centered (Figure 1-55).

FIGURE 1-55

Text is one of the more important elements of most any Web page. How the text displays on a Web page can attract or detract from the overall appearance. Using the appropriate font type can enhance and entice viewers to browse your Web site.

Specifying Font Types

Type is important because it attracts attention, sets the style and tone of a Web page, influences how readers interpret the words, and defines the feeling of the page. The **font type** refers to the basic design of the lettering. Several methods are used to classify fonts. The most common way is to place them in different families based on shared characteristics. The five basic font type families are:

1. Serif, such as Times or Times New Roman
2. Sans-serif, such as Helvetica and Arial
3. Monospace, such as Courier
4. Cursive, such as Brush Script
5. Decorative and fantasy

Two general categories of typefaces are serif and sans-serif. **Sans-serif** typefaces are composed of simple lines, whereas **serif** typefaces use small decorative marks to embellish characters and make them easier to read. Helvetica and Arial are sans-serif types, and Times New Roman is a serif type. A **monospace** font, such as Courier, is

Q&A

Q: Can I add a font to the Font list in the Property inspector?

A: Yes—Click the Edit Font List button in the Font pop-up menu. In the Edit Font List dialog box, select the font(s) from the Available fonts list, and add them to the Chosen fonts box.

More About

Formatting Text

Research shows that people read on-screen text differently than they read the printed word. They are more apt to scan and look for the important concepts. Many changes in formatting could make a site confusing.

one in which every character takes up the same amount of horizontal space. **Cursive** font styles emulate handwritten letterforms. **Decorative and fantasy** is a family for fonts that do not fit any of the other families.

Most Web pages use only the first three families. Dreamweaver provides a font combination feature available in the Property inspector. **Font combinations** determine how a browser displays your Web page's text. In the Property inspector, you can select one of six font combinations. A browser looks for the first font in the combination on the user's computer, then the second, and then the third. If none of the fonts in the combination is installed on the user's computer, the browser displays the text as specified by the user's browser preferences. The following steps show how to change the font type.

To Change the Font Type

1

• **Click to the left of the heading, Discovering Scenic Florida, and then drag through the entire heading.**

The heading is selected (Figure 1-56).

FIGURE 1-56

2

• **Click the Font combination box arrow and then point to Verdana, Arial, Helvetica, sans-serif.**

The Font combination pop-up menu is displayed, and the Verdana, Arial, Helvetica, sans-serif combination is highlighted (Figure 1-57). The menu includes six different font combinations and the default font.

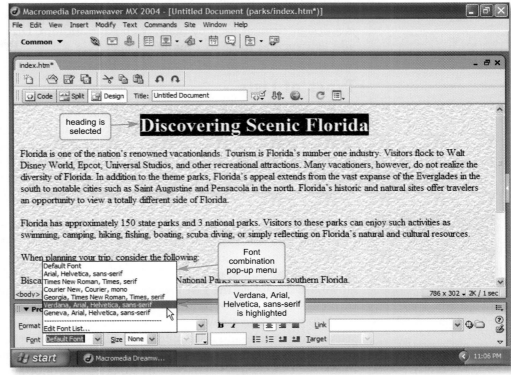

FIGURE 1-57

3

• **Click Verdana, Arial, Helvetica, sans-serif.**

The new font type is applied to the selected heading, and style1 displays in the Style text box (Figure 1-58).

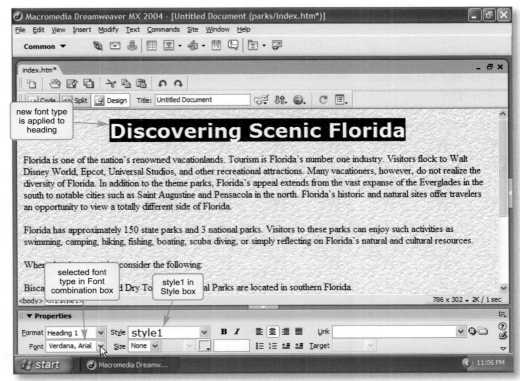

FIGURE 1-58

Other Ways

1. On the Text menu point to Font, click Verdana, Arial, Helvetica, sans-serif
2. Right-click selected text, point to Font on context menu, click Verdana, Arial, Helvetica, sans-serif

In addition to headings and font type attributes, other text design options are available. Presenting information in small chunks, such as bulleted or numbered lists, is a design element used by many Web page authors. Dreamweaver makes it easy to add lists such as these to your Web page.

Types of Lists

One way to group and organize information is by using lists. Web pages can have three types of lists: ordered or numbered, unordered or bulleted, and definition. **Ordered lists** contain text preceded by numbered steps. **Unordered lists** contain text preceded by bullets (dots or other symbols) or image bullets. You use an unordered list if the list items need not be listed in any particular order. **Definition lists** do not use leading characters such as bullet points or numbers. Glossaries and descriptions often use this type of list.

The Unordered List and Ordered List buttons are available in the Property inspector. You access the Definition List command through the Text menu List command submenu. Through the List Properties dialog box, you can set the number style, reset the count, or set the bullet style options for individual list items or for the entire list. To access the List Properties dialog box, click anywhere in the list, and then click the List Item button in the Property inspector.

You can create a new list or you can create a list using existing text. When you select existing text and add bullets, the blank line between the list items is deleted. Later in this project, you add line breaks to reinsert a blank line between each list item. The following steps show how to create an unordered list using existing text.

To Create an Unordered List

1

• **Click to the left of the line, Biscayne, Everglades, and Dry Tortugas National Parks are located in southern Florida (Figure 1-59).**

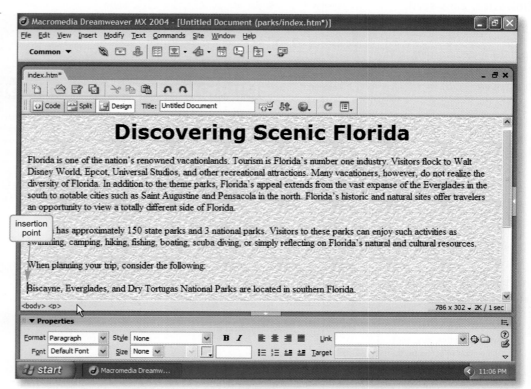

FIGURE 1-59

2

• **Drag to select the text, Biscayne, Everglades, and Dry Tortugas National Parks are located in southern Florida, and the next three lines.**

• **Point to the Unordered List button in the Property inspector.**

The text is selected (Figure 1-60).

list items are selected

FIGURE 1-60

3

• **Click the Unordered List button.**

A bullet is added to each line, the four lines are indented, and the space between each item is deleted (Figure 1-61).

bullets are applied to list items

FIGURE 1-61

Other Ways

1. On Text menu point to List, click Unordered List on List submenu
2. Right-click, point to List, click Unordered List on List submenu

Other text formatting options are applying bold or italic styles to text. **Bold** characters display somewhat thicker and darker than those that are not bold. **Italic** characters slant to the right. The Property inspector contains buttons for both bold and italic font styles.

Bold Formatting

To bold text within Dreamweaver is a simple procedure. If you have used word processing software, you are familiar with this process. The next step illustrates how to emphasize the bullet points by applying bold formatting.

To Bold Text

1

• **If necessary, drag through the bulleted points to select all four lines.**

• **Click the Bold button and then click anywhere in the Document window to deselect the text.**

Bold formatting is applied to the unordered list items (Figure 1-62).

bold formatting is applied to the bulleted items

FIGURE 1-62

More About

HTML

For more information about HTML, visit the Dreamweaver MX 2004 More About Web page (scsite.com/dreamweavermx04/more.htm) and then click HTML.

Understanding Line Breaks

When you added bullets to the items list earlier in this project, the blank line between each item was removed. Removing the blank line between items is a result of how Dreamweaver interprets the HTML code. A blank line between the bulleted items, however, will provide better spacing and readability when the Web page is viewed in a browser. You can add blank lines in several ways. You might assume that pressing the ENTER key at the end of each line would be the quickest way to accomplish this. Pressing the ENTER key, however, adds another bullet. The easiest way to accomplish the task of adding blank lines is to insert line breaks. Recall that the line break starts a new single line without inserting a blank line between lines of text. Inserting two line breaks, however, adds a single blank line.

Dreamweaver provides a Line Break command through the Insert HTML Special Characters submenu. It is easier, however, to use the **SHIFT+ENTER** keyboard shortcut. The following steps show how to add a blank line between each of the bulleted items.

To Add a Line Break

1

• **Click at the end of the first bulleted item.**

• **Press SHIFT+ENTER two times.**

Two line breaks are inserted (Figure 1-63). When the Web page is viewed in Dreamweaver, it appears that two blank lines are inserted. When viewed in a browser, however, only one blank line is displayed between each item. You will view your Web page in a browser later in this project.

FIGURE 1-63

2

• **Press SHIFT+ENTER two times at the end of the second and third bulleted items to insert blank lines between the second and third and the third and fourth bulleted list items.**

The bulleted items are displayed with blank lines between them in the Document window (Figure 1-64).

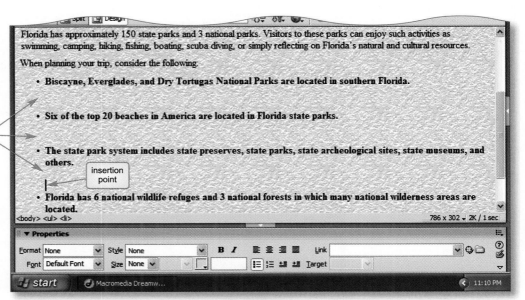

FIGURE 1-64

When creating a Web document, it is a good idea to add your name and date to the document. Insert a single line break between your name and the date. The following steps show how to add this information.

To Add Your Name and Date

1

• **If necessary, scroll down to display the closing paragraph. Click at the end of the closing paragraph.**

• **Press the ENTER key.**

The insertion point moves to the next paragraph (Figure 1-65).

FIGURE 1-65

2

• **Type your name and then press SHIFT+ENTER.**

The insertion point moves to the next line (Figure 1-66). No line space is displayed between the name and the insertion point.

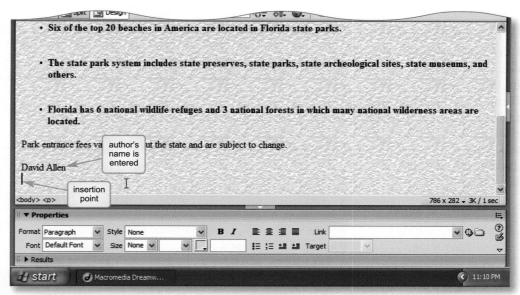

FIGURE 1-66

3

• **Type the current date and then press the ENTER key (Figure 1-67).**

FIGURE 1-67

Special Characters

Sometimes it is necessary to enter non-keyboard characters such as quotes, trademarks, and registrations into a Web page. To have the browser display these special characters requires a character code. Character codes for causing a browser to show special characters generally are called **HTML entities**. HTML represents these codes by a name or a number. HTML includes entity names for characters such as the copyright symbol (©), the ampersand (&), and the registered trademark symbol (®). Each entity has both a name and a numeric equivalent (such as —). Table 1-2 on the next page contains a list of HTML entities supported by Dreamweaver.

Table 1-2 HTML Entities

BUTTON NAME	DESCRIPTION	HTML TAGS AND CHARACTER ENTITIES
Line Break	Places a line break at the insertion point	\
Non-Breaking Space	Places a non-breaking space at the insertion point	
Left Quote	Places opening, curved double quotation marks at the insertion point	&#147;
Right Quote	Places closing, curved double quotation marks at the insertion point	&#148;
Em Dash	Places an em dash at the insertion point	&#151;
Pound	Places a pound (currency) symbol at the insertion point	&pound;
Euro	Places a euro (currency) symbol at the insertion point	&euro;
Yen	Places a yen (currency) symbol at the insertion point	&yen;
Copyright	Places a copyright symbol at the insertion point	&copy;
Registered Trademark	Places a registered trademark symbol at the insertion point	&reg;
Trademark	Places a trademark symbol at the insertion point	&#153;
Other Characters	Provides a set of special characters from which to select	Other ASCII characters

In the Florida Parks Web page, both Walt Disney World® and Epcot® are registered trademarks. The following steps illustrate how to insert the registered trademark symbol next to these names, using the Insert menu and the HTML Special Characters submenu.

To Insert a Registered Trademark Character

1

• If necessary, scroll up to display the first paragraph in the Web page.

• Click to the right of World (in Walt Disney World) and before the comma (Figure 1-68).

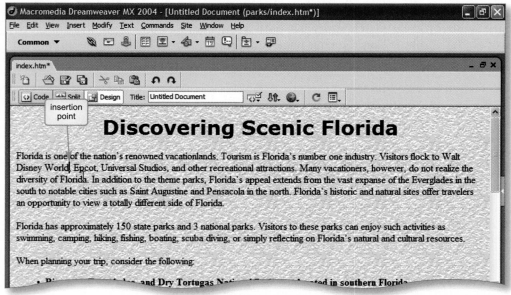

FIGURE 1-68

2

• **Click Insert on the menu bar, point to HTML, point to Special Characters on the HTML submenu, and then point to Registered on the Special Characters submenu.**

Dreamweaver displays the HTML submenu and the Special Characters submenu (Figure 1-69).

FIGURE 1-69

3

• **Click Registered on the Special Characters submenu.**

• **Click to the right of Epcot and before the comma.**

The registered trademark symbol is inserted into the document and the insertion point is to the right of Epcot (Figure 1-70).

FIGURE 1-70

4

• **Click Insert on the menu bar, point to HTML, point to Special Characters, and then click Registered.**

• **Click anywhere in the document to deselect the symbol.**

The registered trademark symbol is inserted into the document (Figure 1-71).

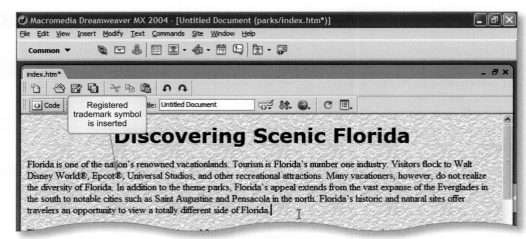

FIGURE 1-71

Web-Safe Colors

Adding color to text can attract attention to important information and emphasize different aspects of a Web page. It is easy to change the color of an individual character, a word, a line, a paragraph, or the text of an entire document. In HTML, colors are expressed either as hexadecimal values (for example, #FF0000) or as color names (such as red).

Use the **color picker** to select the colors for page elements or text. Through the Property inspector, Dreamweaver provides access to five different color palettes: Color Cubes, Continuous Tone, Windows OS, Mac OS, and Grayscale. Color Cubes is the default color palette. Figure 1-72 shows the Color Cubes color palette available on the color palette pop-up menu.

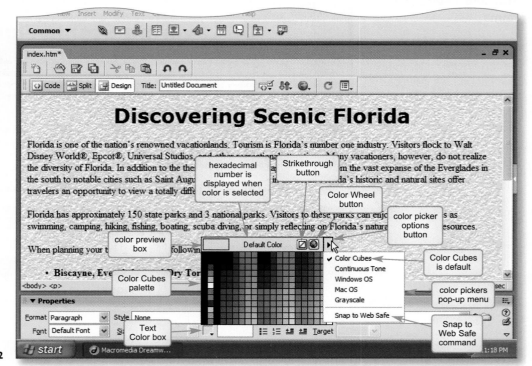

FIGURE 1-72

Two of the color palettes, Color Cubes and Continuous Tone, display Web-safe colors. Web-safe colors are colors that display correctly on the screen when someone is viewing your Web page in a browser. A Web-safe color is one that appears the same in Netscape Navigator and Microsoft Internet Explorer on both Windows and Macintosh systems. Most experts agree that approximately 212 to 216 Web-safe colors exist. Testing by experts, however, suggests that Internet Explorer renders only 212 Web-safe colors. Table 1-3 contains a list of the color picker options.

Table 1-3 Color Picker Options

OPTION	FUNCTION
Color preview box	Provides a preview of the currently selected color or the color picked up by the eyedropper
Hex value area	Displays the hexadecimal value of the current color or the color picked up by the eyedropper
Strikethrough button	Clears the current color and retains the default color
Color Wheel button	Opens the system color pickers via the operating system Color dialog box
Option button	Displays a pop-up menu from which you can select one of five color pickers or the Snap to Web Safe command
Snap to Web Safe command	Automatically changes non-Web-safe colors to the nearest Web-safe values

Q&A

Q: Are there other reasons why I would use Web-safe colors?

A: Another reason to use the Web-safe color palette is if you will be developing for alternative Web devices such as PDA and cell phone displays. Many of these devices offer only black-and-white (1-bit) or 256 color (8-bit) displays.

Dreamweaver has an **eyedropper** feature that lets you select colors and make perfect color matches. When you are working with color palettes, you can use the eyedropper to choose a color from anywhere on the screen, including outside of Dreamweaver, and apply the color to a selected object in the Document window. You place the eyedropper over the color you want to select and then click the mouse button. As soon as you click the mouse button, the color automatically is applied to the selected object. If you move the eyedropper to an object outside of Dreamweaver, the eyedropper changes to the block arrow mouse pointer shape until you move it back into the Dreamweaver window. Clicking the color picker options button and then selecting the Snap to Web Safe command will ensure the selected color is a Web-safe color.

Changing Text Color

The default color for Dreamweaver text is black. The following steps show how to change the text color of the heading to a shade of green.

To Change the Text Color

1

• **Select the heading and then click the Text Color box in the Property inspector.**

The Color Cubes palette is displayed (Figure 1-73). The color palette includes Web-safe colors, the color preview box, and the six-digit hexadecimal number that represents the selected color.

FIGURE 1-73

2

• **Position the eyedropper on the shade of green represented by hexadecimal number #006600 (row 1 and column 6 from the left).**

The selected color is displayed in the color preview box, and the hexadecimal value area displays the number for the color (Figure 1-74).

FIGURE 1-74

3

- **Click the eyedropper to apply the color to the selected text.**
- **Click anywhere in the document to deselect the text.**

The color is applied to the text. The heading is displayed in the selected green color (Figure 1-75). Occasionally you may have to press the ESC key to close the picker.

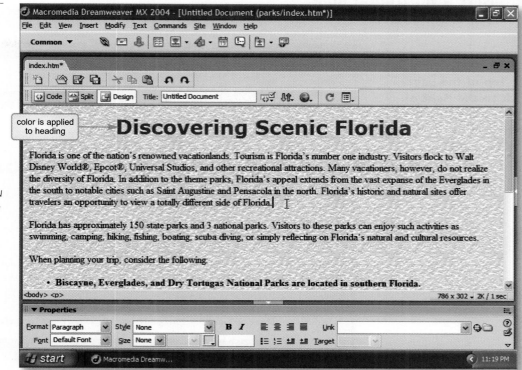

FIGURE 1-75

To add additional details to the Florida Parks Web page, a horizontal rule is inserted below the title. Many Web designers use a horizontal rule to divide a Web page into sections and as a style element.

Horizontal Rules

A horizontal rule (or line) is useful for organizing information and visually separating text and objects. You can specify the width and height of the rule in pixels or as a percentage of the page size. The rule can be aligned to the left, center, or right, and you can add shading or draw the line in a solid color. These attributes are available in the Property inspector. The HTML tag for a horizontal rule is <hr>.

Inserting a Horizontal Rule

On the Discovering Scenic Florida Web page, you insert a horizontal rule between the document heading and text as shown in the following steps. You use the default shaded line, but change the width and the height of the rule and then center the rule.

To Insert a Horizontal Rule

1

• If necessary, scroll to the top of the page. Click to the right of the heading, Discovering Scenic Florida (Figure 1-76).

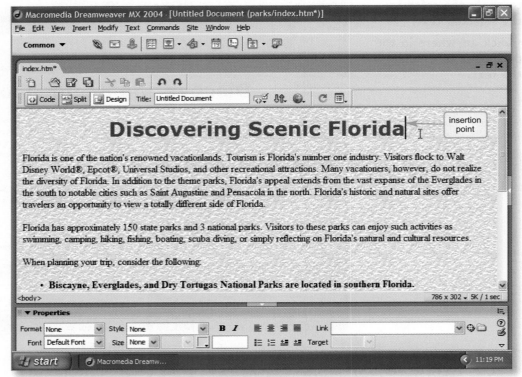

FIGURE 1-76

2

• Click Insert on the menu bar, point to HTML, and then point to Horizontal Rule (Figure 1-77).

FIGURE 1-77

3

• **Click Horizontal Rule.**

The horizontal rule is inserted below the heading (Figure 1-78). The attributes in the Property inspector change to those for the horizontal rule. The horizontal line on your Web page may display somewhat differently than that shown in the figures.

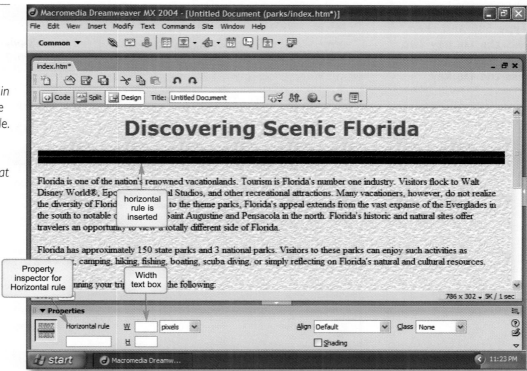

FIGURE 1-78

4

• **Click the Shading check box to select it.**

• **Click the Width text box.**

The attributes in the Property inspector change to those for the horizontal rule. The Shading check box is checked. The insertion point is in the Width text box (Figure 1-79).

FIGURE 1-79

5

• **Type** 500 **and then press the** TAB **key two times. Type** 6 **and then press the** TAB **key.**

The width of the line is decreased, and the height of the line is increased. Default is highlighted in the Align box (Figure 1-80).

FIGURE 1-80

6

• **Click the Align box arrow and then click Center.**

The rule is centered. Even though the rule appeared centered before applying the Center attribute, it would not necessarily appear centered when viewed in all browsers. Adding the Center attribute assures that it always is centered below the heading.

FIGURE 1-81

7

- **Click anywhere in the Document window to deselect the horizontal rule.**

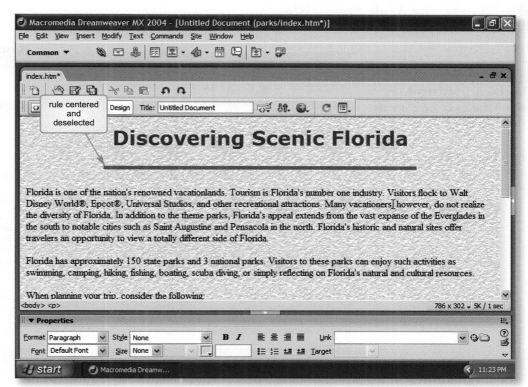

FIGURE 1-82

Web Page Titles

A **Web page title** helps Web site visitors keep track of what they are viewing as they browse. It is important to give your Web page an appropriate title. When visitors to your Web page create bookmarks or add the Web page to their Favorites lists, the title is used for the reference. If you do not title a page, the page will be displayed in the browser window, Favorites lists, and history lists as Untitled Document. Because many search engines use the Web page title, it is important to use a creative and meaningful name. Giving the document a file name by saving it is not the same as giving the page a title.

Changing a Web Page Title

The current title of your Web page is Untitled Document. Unless you change the title of the Web page, this name will be displayed on the browser title bar when the page is opened in a browser window. The following steps show how to change the name of the Web page to Florida Parks.

To Change the Web Page Title

1

• **Drag through the text, Untitled Document, in the Title text box on the Document toolbar.**

The text is highlighted to indicate that it is selected (Figure 1-83).

FIGURE 1-83

2

• **Type** Florida Parks **in the Title text box and then press the ENTER key.**

The new name, Florida Parks, is displayed in the Title text box and on the Dreamweaver title bar (Figure 1-84).

• **Click the Save button on the Standard toolbar.**

The document changes are saved.

FIGURE 1-84

With all the text of the document entered and formatted, you next check the spelling of the document.

Check Spelling

After you create a Web page, you should check it visually for spelling errors. In addition, you can use Dreamweaver's Check Spelling command to identify possible misspellings. The Check Spelling command ignores HTML tags and attributes. Recall from the Introduction that attributes are additional information contained within an HTML tag.

The following steps show how to start the Check Spelling command and check your entire document. Your Web page may contain different misspelled words depending on the accuracy of your typing.

To Check Spelling

1

• **Click Text on the menu bar and then point to Check Spelling.**

Dreamweaver displays the Text menu (Figure 1-85).

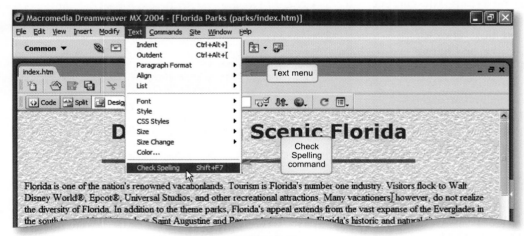

FIGURE 1-85

2

• **Click Check Spelling.**

The Check Spelling dialog box is displayed. The Dreamweaver spelling checker displays the word, Epcot, in the Word not found in dictionary text box. Suggestions for the correct spelling are displayed in the Suggestions list (Figure 1-86).

FIGURE 1-86

3

• **Click the Ignore button.**

The spelling checker ignores the word, Epcot, and continues searching for additional misspelled words. If the spelling checker identifies a word that is spelled correctly, clicking the Ignore button skips the word.

4

• **Correct any misspelled word by accepting the suggested replacement or by typing the correct word in the Change to text box. Click the Change or Change All button.**

When Dreamweaver has checked all text for misspellings it displays a Macromedia Dreamweaver MX 2004 dialog box informing you that the spelling check is complete (Figure 1-87).

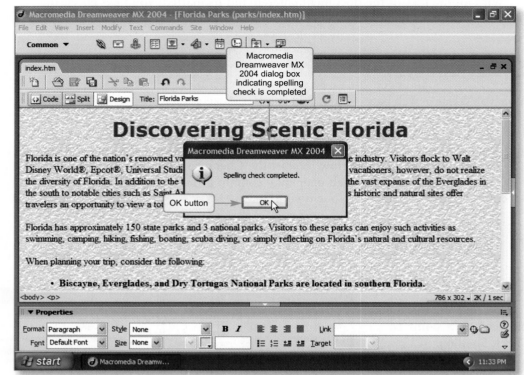

FIGURE 1-87

5

• **Click the OK button and then press CTRL+S to save any changes.**

Dreamweaver closes the Check Spelling dialog box and displays the Document window. The document is saved.

With your Web page ready to share with the world, you next must select browsers to ensure your visitors can view the page properly. The two more popular browsers are Internet Explorer and Netscape.

Previewing a Web Page in a Browser

After you have created a Web page, it is a good practice to test your Web pages by previewing them in Web browsers to ensure they display correctly. Using this strategy helps you catch errors so you will not copy or repeat them.

As you create your Web page, you should be aware of the variety of available Web browsers. More than 25 different Web browsers are in use, most of which have been released in more than one version. Most Web developers target recent versions of Netscape Navigator and Microsoft Internet Explorer, which are used by the majority of Web users. You also should know that visitors viewing your Web page might have earlier versions of these browsers. You can define up to 20 browsers for previewing.

Selecting a Browser

The browser preferences are selected in the Preferences dialog box. This dialog box provides options to select and define the settings for a primary and a secondary browser. Additionally, a Preview using temporary file option is available. When the check box for this option is checked, you can preview a page without first having to save the page. Although it is a good practice to save before previewing in a browser, occasions will arise when you want to view a page before saving it.

The following steps show how to select your target browsers: Microsoft Internet Explorer and Netscape Navigator. To complete these steps requires that you have both Internet Explorer and Netscape Navigator installed on your computer.

More About

Browsers

Just as you can specify a primary and secondary browser, you also can remove a browser from your list. Click Edit on the menu bar, click Preferences, and then click the Preview in Browser category. Select the name of the browser you want to remove and then click the minus (–) button.

To Select Primary and Secondary Target Browsers

1

• **Click Edit on the menu bar and then point to Preferences.**

Dreamweaver displays the Edit menu and Preferences is highlighted (Figure 1-88).

FIGURE 1-88

2

• **Click Preferences and then click the Preview in Browser category.**

The Preferences dialog box is displayed, and the Preview in Browser category is selected (Figure 1-89). The primary browser was selected when Dreamweaver was installed on your computer. In this book, the primary browser is Internet Explorer. The browser name, iexplore, was selected automatically during the Dreamweaver installation.

FIGURE 1-89

3

• **Click the plus (+) button in the Preview in Browser area.**

Dreamweaver displays the Add Browser dialog box (Figure 1-90).

FIGURE 1-90

4

• **Click the Browse button and then locate the Netscp.exe file. Most likely this file is located on Local Drive (C:). Use the following path to locate the file: C:\Program Files\ Netscape\Netscape\ Netscp.exe, and then click the file name.**

The Select Browser dialog box is displayed (Figure 1-91). The Netscp.exe file is selected. Different versions of Netscape may display a different file name or a different path.

FIGURE 1-91

5

• **Click the Open button.**

• **If necessary, click the Secondary browser check box to select it.**

The Name text box displays Netscp.exe. The Application text box displays the path and file name (Figure 1-92). The path and spelling of Netscape on your computer may be different than those shown.

FIGURE 1-92

6

• **Click the OK button.**

Netscape is added as the secondary browser (Figure 1-93).

FIGURE 1-93

7

• **If necessary, click the Preview using temporary file check box to select it.**

• **Click the OK button. If a Dreamweaver MX 2004 dialog box appears, click the OK button.**

The target browsers are selected, and Dreamweaver displays the Document window.

Previewing a Web Page

With the target browsers set up, you can preview your Web pages in the browsers at any time. You do not have to save the document first. The steps on the next page illustrate how to preview a Web page.

To Preview the Web Page

1

• **Click File on the menu bar, point to Preview in Browser, and then point to iexplore.**

The File menu and Preview in Browser submenu are displayed (Figure 1-94). The Preview in Browser submenu includes the names of both your primary and secondary browsers and the Edit Browser List command. Clicking the Edit Browser List command displays the Preferences dialog box.

FIGURE 1-94

2

• **Click iexplore (Internet Explorer).**

• **If necessary, maximize your browser window.**

Internet Explorer starts and displays the Web page in a browser window (Figure 1-95). Your browser name may be different. The file name displayed in the Address bar is a temporary name.

FIGURE 1-95

• **Click Internet Explorer's Close button.**

• **Click File on the menu bar and then point to Preview in Browser.**

• **Click Netscp.exe on the Preview in Browser submenu.**

Netscape opens and displays the Web page in a browser window (Figure 1-96). Your browser name may be different. Compare how the files display in the two browsers.

FIGURE 1-96

4

• **Click Netscape's Close button.**

Your instructor may require that you print a copy of your Web page. The next step illustrates how to print a page.

Printing a Web Page

A variety of reasons exists for why you may want to print a Web page. Interestingly, Dreamweaver provides an option to print code, but does not provide a print option to print the Design view. To print a Web page, you first must preview it in a browser. Printing a page from your browser is similar to printing a word processing document. The steps on the next page illustrate how to print the Web page in a browser.

To Print a Web Page

1

• **Press F12.**

The Web page is displayed in Internet Explorer.

2

• **Click File on the menu bar and point to Print (Figure 1-97).**

3

• **Click Print. If necessary, select an appropriate printer.**

Internet Explorer displays the Print dialog box (Figure 1-98). Your selected printer is likely to be different from the one shown in Figure 1-98.

4

• **Click the Print button.**

The Print dialog box closes, and your Web page is sent to the printer.

5

• **Retrieve the printout and then click Internet Explorer's Close button.**

The browser closes, and Dreamweaver displays the Document window.

FIGURE 1-97

FIGURE 1-98

Dreamweaver Help System

Reference materials and other forms of assistance are available using the Dreamweaver Help system. You can display these documents, print them, or copy them to a word processing document. Table 1-4 summarizes the categories of online Help available. Several methods are available to activate the first four types listed in the table. Appendix A provides detailed instructions on using Dreamweaver Help.

Table 1-4 Dreamweaver Help System

TYPE	DESCRIPTION	HOW TO ACTIVATE
Contents sheet	Use the Contents sheet to view information organized by topic and then by subtopic, as you would in the table of contents of a book.	• Press the F1 key. Click the Contents tab. • Click Help on the menu bar and then click Using Dreamweaver. Click the Contents tab. • Click the options button on the title bar of a panel group and then click Help on the options pop-up menu. Click the Contents tab.
Index sheet	Use the Index sheet to look up specific terms or concepts, as you would in the index of a book.	• Press the F1 key. Click the Index tab. • Click Help on the menu bar and then click Using Dreamweaver. Click the Index tab. • Click the options button on the title bar of a panel group and then click Help on the options pop-up menu. Click the Index tab.
Search sheet	Use the Search sheet to find any character string, anywhere in the text of the Help system.	• Press the F1 key. Click the Search tab. • Click Help on the menu bar and then click Using Dreamweaver. Click the Search tab. • Click the options button on the title bar of a panel group and then click Help on the options pop-up menu. Click the Search tab.
Question Mark button or Help icon	Clicking the Question Mark button provides context-sensitive help in dialog boxes and panels.	• Click a Help button or Question Mark button in a dialog box. • Click the Help icon in an inspector or other kind of window.
Tutorials	Step-by-step lessons that focus on a specific Web design feature or topic.	• Click Help on the menu bar and then click Getting Started and Tutorials.
Dreamweaver online tutorials	Step-by-step online tutorials.	• Access the Dreamweaver tutorial Web site at macromedia.com/desdev/mx/dreamweaver/index.html

Disabling the Start Page and Quitting Dreamweaver

After you create, save, preview, and print the Florida Parks Web page and review how to use Help, Project 1 is complete. The following step shows how to close the Web page, quit Dreamweaver MX 2004, and return control to Windows.

To Disable the Start Page, Close the Web Site, and Quit Dreamweaver

1 Click Edit on the menu bar and then click Preferences.

2 If necessary, click General in the Category column.

3 Click the Show start page check box to deselect it, and then click the OK button.

4 Click the Close button in the right corner of the Dreamweaver title bar.

Other Ways

1. On File menu click Exit
2. Press CTRL+Q

The next time you start Dreamweaver, the Start page will not be displayed. The Document window, the Dreamweaver window, and the Florida Parks Web site all close. If you have unsaved changes, Dreamweaver will prompt you to save the changes. Clicking the Yes button in the Dreamweaver MX 2004 dialog box saves the changes.

Starting Dreamweaver and Opening a New Web Page

Opening an existing Web page in Dreamweaver is much the same as opening an existing document in most other software applications: that is, you use the File menu and Open command. In addition to this common method to open a Web page, Dreamweaver provides other options. The Dreamweaver File menu also contains the Open Recent command. Pointing to this command displays the Open Recent submenu, which contains a list of the 10 most recently opened files. Additionally, if you want the page on which you currently are working to display when you next open Dreamweaver, you can select the Reopen Documents on startup command from the Open Recent submenu.

If the page you want to open is part of a Dreamweaver Web site, you can open the file from the Files panel. To open a Web page from the Files panel, you first must select the appropriate Web site. The Files pop-up menu in the Files panel lists sites you have defined. When you open the site, a list of the pages and subfolders within the site displays. To open the page you want, double-click the file name. After opening the page, you can modify text, images, tables, and any other elements.

Earlier in this project, you disabled the Start page. The next time you open Dreamweaver, therefore, the Start page will not display. Instead, a blank window is displayed, requiring that you open an existing document or open a new document. Dreamweaver provides four options to open a new Document window:

- Click File on the menu bar and then click the New command
- Press CTRL+N
- Select the site's root folder, right-click, and then click New File on the context menu
- Click the Files panel Options menu, click File on the pop-up menu, and then click the New File command

The first two options display the New Document dialog box. From this dialog box, you select the Basic page category and HTML Basic page and then click the Create button. When you select either option three or four, a new untitled document is created and is displayed in the Files panel. You then name the document and double-click the name to open the document from the Files panel.

Project Summary

Project 1 introduced you to starting Dreamweaver, defining a Web site, and creating a Web page. You added an image background and used Dreamweaver's Property inspector to format text, change font color, and center text. You also learned how to apply color to text and use an unordered list to organize information. You added line breaks, special characters, and a horizontal rule. Once your Web page was completed, you learned how to save the Web page and preview it in a browser. You also learned how to print using the browser. To enhance your knowledge of Dreamweaver further, you learned basics about the Dreamweaver Help system.

What You Should Know

Having completed this project, you now should be able to perform the tasks below. The tasks are listed in the same order they were presented in the project. For a list of keyboard commands for topics introduced in this project, see the Quick Reference for Windows at the back of this book and refer to the Shortcut column.

1. Start Dreamweaver (DW 32)
2. Close and Open Panels (DW 38)
3. Use Site Definition to Create a Local Web Site (DW 41)
4. Copy Data Files to the Local Web Site (DW 48)
5. Display the Standard Toolbar and Save a Document as a Web Page (DW 52)
6. Add a Background Image to the Index Page (DW 55)
7. Hide the Panel Groups (DW 59)
8. Add Text (DW 60)
9. Format Text with Heading 1 (DW 67)
10. Center the Web Page Heading (DW 69)
11. Change the Font Type (DW 70)
12. Create an Unordered List (DW 72)
13. Bold Text (DW 74)
14. Add a Line Break (DW 75)
15. Add Your Name and Date (DW 76)
16. Insert a Registered Trademark Character (DW 78)
17. Change the Text Color (DW 82)
18. Insert a Horizontal Rule (DW 84)
19. Change the Web Page Title (DW 88)
20. Check Spelling (DW 89)
21. Select Primary and Secondary Target Browsers (DW 91)
22. Preview the Web Page (DW 95)
23. Print a Web Page (DW 97)
24. Disable the Start Page, Close the Web Site, and Quit Dreamweaver (DW 99)

Learn It Online

Instructions: To complete the Learn It Online exercises, start your browser, click the Address bar, and then enter the Web address scsite.com/dreamweavermx2004/learn. When the Dreamweaver MX 2004 Learn It Online page is displayed, follow the instructions in the exercises below. Each exercise has instructions for printing your results, either for your own records or for submission to your instructor.

1 Project Reinforcement TF, MC, and SA

Below Dreamweaver Project 1, click the Project Reinforcement link. Print the quiz by clicking Print on the File menu for each page. Answer each question.

2 Flash Cards

Below Dreamweaver Project 1, click the Flash Cards link and read the instructions. Type 20 (or a number specified by your instructor) in the Number of playing cards text box, type your name in the Enter your Name text box, and then click the Flip Card button. When the flash card is displayed, read the question and then click the ANSWER box arrow to select an answer. Flip through Flash Cards. If your score is 15 (75%) correct or greater, click Print on the File menu to print your results. If your score is less than 15 (75%) correct, then redo this exercise by clicking the Replay button.

3 Practice Test

Below Dreamweaver Project 1, click the Practice Test link. Answer each question, enter your first and last name at the bottom of the page, and then click the Grade Test button. When the graded practice test is displayed on your screen, click Print on the File menu to print a hard copy. Continue to take practice tests until you score 80% or better.

4 Who Wants To Be a Computer Genius?

Below Dreamweaver Project 1, click the Computer Genius link. Read the instructions, enter your first and last name at the bottom of the page, and then click the PLAY button. When your score is displayed, click the PRINT RESULTS link to print a hard copy.

5 Wheel of Terms

Below Dreamweaver Project 1, click the Wheel of Terms link. Read the instructions, and then enter your first and last name and your school name. Click the PLAY button. When your score is displayed, right-click the score and then click Print on the shortcut menu to print a hard copy.

6 Crossword Puzzle Challenge

Below Dreamweaver Project 1, click the Crossword Puzzle Challenge link. Read the instructions, and then enter your first and last name. Click the SUBMIT button. Work the crossword puzzle. When you are finished, click the Submit button. When the crossword puzzle is redisplayed, click the Print Puzzle button to print a hard copy.

7 Tips and Tricks

Below Dreamweaver Project 1, click the Tips and Tricks link. Click a topic that pertains to Project 1. Right-click the information and then click Print on the shortcut menu. Construct a brief example of what the information relates to in Dreamweaver to confirm you understand how to use the tip or trick.

8 Newsgroups

Below Dreamweaver Project 1, click the Newsgroups link. Click a topic that pertains to Project 1. Print three comments.

9 Expanding Your Horizons

Below Dreamweaver Project 1, click the Expanding Your Horizons link. Click a topic that pertains to Project 1. Print the information. Construct a brief example of what the information relates to in Dreamweaver to confirm you understand the contents of the article.

10 Search Sleuth

Below Dreamweaver Project 1, click the Search Sleuth link. To search for a term that pertains to this project, select a term below the Project 1 title and then use the Google search engine at google.com (or any major search engine) to display and print two Web pages that present information on the term.

1 B & B Lawn Service Web Site

Instructions: Start Dreamweaver. Perform the following tasks to define a Web site and create and format a Web page for B & B Lawn Service. The Web page as it displays in a browser is shown in Figure 1-99. The text for the Web site is shown in Table 1-5 on the next page.

Software and hardware settings determine how a Web page is displayed in a browser. Your Web pages may display differently in your browser than those in the figures.

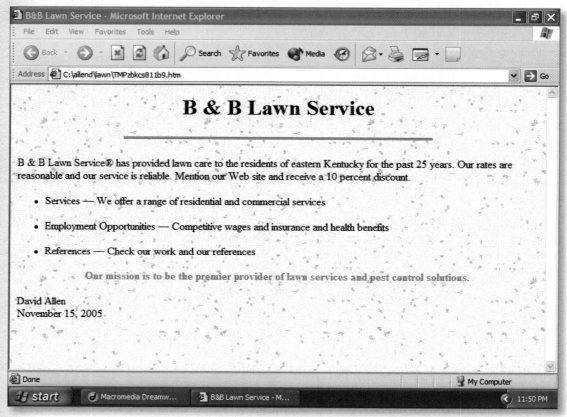

FIGURE 1-99

Apply Your Knowledge

Table 1-5 B & B Lawn Service Web Page

SECTION	WEB PAGE TEXT
Heading	B & B Lawn Service
Introductory Paragraph	B & B Lawn Service® has provided lawn care to the residents of eastern Kentucky for the past 25 years. Our rates are reasonable and our service is reliable. Mention our Web site and receive a 10 percent discount.
List Item 1	Services — We offer a range of residential and commercial services
List Item 2	Employment Opportunities — Competitive wages and insurance and health benefits
List Item 3	References — Check our work and our references
Closing	Our mission is to be the premier provider of lawn services and pest control solutions.

1. Click Site on the menu bar and then click Manage Sites. Use the Site Definition Advanced window option to create a local Web site under the your name folder. In the Site Definition Site name text box, name the site Lawn Service. In the Local root folder text box, create a new subfolder under the your name folder, and name the new subfolder lawn. The path will be C:\yourname\lawn (substitute your name). In the Default images folder text box, create a new subfolder and name the folder images.

2. Click File on the menu bar and then click New. Click Basic Page in the Category column and HTML in the Basic page column in the New Document dialog box and then click Create. If necessary, display the Standard toolbar. Use the Save As command on the File menu to save the page with the name index.

3. Use the Windows My Computer option to copy the data file image to your lawn images folder.

4. Click the Modify menu and then click Page Properties. Apply the background image (located in the images folder) to the index page.

5. Type the Web page text shown in Table 1-5. Press the ENTER key after typing the text in each section and after each one of the list items in the table. The em dash, used in the three list items, is an HTML object. To insert the em dash, click the Insert menu, point to HTML, point to Text Objects, and then click Em.

6. Select the heading text and then apply Heading 1. Click the Align Center button in the Property inspector to center the heading.

7. Select the three list items. Click the Unordered List button in the Property inspector to create a bulleted list with these three items.

8. Select the closing paragraph. Click the Align Center button and then click the Bold button in the Property inspector. Do not deselect the sentence.

9. Click the Text Color box and select hexadecimal color #FF3333. This color swatch is located in the 5th row from bottom and 5th column from the right.

(continued)

B & B Lawn Service Web Site *(continued)*

10. Click at the end of the heading and then press the ENTER key. Click Insert on the menu bar, point to HTML, and then click Horizontal Rule. Specify a width of 450 pixels, a height of 4, center alignment, and no shading.

11. Click to the right of B & B Lawn Service in the first paragraph. Click Insert on the menu bar, click HTML, click Special Characters, and then click the Registered command.

12. Click at the end of the first bulleted item. Insert two line breaks between the first and second bulleted items and then insert two line breaks between the second and third bulleted items.

13. Title the Web page, B&B Lawn Service, using the Title text box on the Document toolbar.

14. Scroll to the bottom of the page. If necessary, click the Align Left button. Type your name, insert a line break. and then type the current date.

15. Click Text on the menu bar and then click Check Spelling. Spell check your document and correct any errors.

16. Click File on the menu bar and then click Save.

17. Press the F12 key to view the Web page in the browser. Print a copy if required and hand it in to your instructor. Click the browser's Close button.

18. Click the Dreamweaver Close button to quit Dreamweaver.

1 CandleDust Web Site

Problem: A friend of yours, Mary Stewart, is starting her own business selling candles. She has asked you to assist her in preparing a Web page to help her advertise her candles (Figure 1-100 on the next page).

Software and hardware settings determine how a Web page is displayed in a browser. Your Web pages may display differently in your browser than those in the figures.

Instructions: Start Dreamweaver. Perform the tasks on the following pages to define a Web site and create and format a Web page for CandleDust. The text for the Web page is shown in Table 1-6 on the next page.

FIGURE 1-100

Table 1-6 CandleDust Web Page	
SECTION	**WEB PAGE TEXT**
Heading	CandleDust
Subheading	Welcome to CandleDust
Introductory Paragraph	We offer the finest in fragrantly scented candles. Each of our candles is hand dipped and handpoured. Our wicks are lead free, and we use only the finest waxes and fragrant oils.
Second Paragraph	CandleDust candles are available in a variety of types:
List Item 1	Decorative
List Item 2	Gel
List Item 3	Holiday
List Item 4	Pillar

(continued)

CandleDust Web Site *(continued)*

Table 1-6 CandleDust Web Page *(continued)*	
SECTION	**WEB PAGE TEXT**
List Item 5	Scented
List Item 6	Texture
List Item 7	Votive
Closing	Our candles make a perfect gift for occasions such as weddings, birthdays, holidays, anniversaries, or any time of the year.

1. Click Site on the menu bar and then click Manage Sites. Use the Site Definition Advanced window option to create a local Web site under the your name folder. In the Site Definition Site name text box, name the site CandleDust. In the Local root folder text box, create a new subfolder under the your name folder, and name the new subfolder candle. The path will be C:\yourname\candle. In the Default images folder text box, create a new subfolder and name the folder images.
2. Click File on the menu bar and then click New. Click Basic Page in the Category column and HTML in the Basic page column in the New Document dialog box and then click Create. Use the Save As command on the File menu to save the page with the name index. If necessary, display the Standard toolbar.
3. Use the Windows My Computer option to copy the data file image to your candle images folder.
4. Click the Modify menu and then click Page Properties. Apply the background image to the index page.
5. Click in the Document window and then type the Web page text shown in Table 1-6 starting on page DW 105. Press the ENTER key after typing each section and after each list item in the table.
6. Select the heading text and apply Heading 1. Select the subheading text and apply Heading 2. Select both headings and then click the Align Center button in the Property inspector to center the titles. Change the font type to Georgia, Times New Roman, Times, serif.
7. Select the list items. Click the Unordered List button in the Property inspector and then click the Text Indent button in the Property inspector.
8. Click at the end of the subheading, Welcome to CandleDust, and then press the ENTER key. Click Insert on the menu bar, point to HTML, and then click Horizontal Rule. Change the width to 550 pixels, and specify no shading and center alignment.
9. Type CandleDust as the title in the Title text box.
10. Click at the end of the closing line and then press the ENTER key. Type your name. Insert a line break and then type the current date.
11. Spell check your document and correct any errors.
12. Click the Save button.
13. View the Web page in your browser. Print a copy, if required, and hand it in to your instructor. Close the browser.
14. Quit Dreamweaver.

2 Credit Protection Web Site

Problem: Marcy Cantu is an intern in a small law practice. She recently lost her wallet, which contained all of her credit cards. She called the credit card companies and canceled her credit cards. One of the attorneys suggested she also call the three credit bureaus to make them aware of this problem. Because searching for the names, telephone numbers, and addresses of the three credit bureaus was quite time-consuming, Marcy decided she wants to have this information readily available for herself in the event she ever needs it again and for others who might find themselves in a similar situation. She has asked you to prepare the Web page shown in Figure 1-101.

Software and hardware settings determine how a Web page is displayed in a browser. Your Web pages may display differently in your browser than those in the figures.

FIGURE 1-101

(continued)

Credit Protection Web Site *(continued)*

Instructions: Start Dreamweaver. Perform the following tasks to define a Web site and create and format an informational Web page on credit protection. The text for the Web page is shown in Table 1-7.

Table 1-7 Credit Protection Web Page

SECTION	WEB PAGE TEXT
Heading	Credit Protection
Introductory Paragraph	A credit card can be a great financial tool, but it also is a big responsibility. Applying for and receiving a credit card generally is an easy procedure. Offers from credit card companies arrive frequently in the regular mail.
Second Paragraph	Many people, particularly first-time users, do not fully understand the implications of a credit card. They may charge more than they can repay. This can damage a credit rating and create credit problems that can be difficult to fix.
Third Paragraph	Before you submit a credit application, obtain a copy of your credit report from one of the three major credit reporting agencies to make sure it is accurate.
List Item 1	Equifax Information Services, LLC P. O. Box 740241 Atlanta, GA 30374
List Item 2	Experian Consumer Opt-Out 701 Experian Parkway Allen, TX 75013
List Item 3	TransUnion LLC's Name Removal Option P.O. Box 97328 Jackson, MS 39288-7328

1. Define a local Web site under the your name folder. Name the site Credit Protection. Create a new subfolder under the your name folder and name the new subfolder credit. Create an images folder and copy the image data file into the images folder.
2. Open a new Document window and use the Save As command to save the page as index. Apply the background image to the index page.
3. Type the heading and first three paragraphs of the Web page text shown in Table 1-7. Press the ENTER key after typing each section of the text in the table.
4. Type list item 1. Insert a line break after the company name and after the address. Press the ENTER key after the city and state. Type list items 2 and 3. Insert a line break after the company name and address and press the ENTER key after the city and state.

In the Lab

5. Select the heading text and apply Heading 1. Align to the left (to ensure the heading is displayed properly in the browser). Insert a horizontal rule following the heading. Align the rule to the left. Use 250 for the width, 7 for the height, and no shading. Deselect the rule.

6. Click Edit on the menu bar and then click Select All. Change the font type to Georgia, Times New Roman, Times, serif for all the text on the Web page.

7. Select the three list items (companies and addresses) and create an unordered (bulleted) list. Insert two line breaks between item 1 and item 2 and between item 2 and item 3.

8. Select the name of the company in the first bulleted list item (Equifax Information Services, LLC) and bold the company name. Apply the bold attribute to the names of the other two companies.

9. Select Untitled Document in the Title text box on the Document toolbar and type Credit Protection as the title of the Web page.

10. Click at the end of the last line of text and then press the ENTER key. If a bullet displays, click the Unordered List button in the Property inspector to remove the bullet. Type your name, add a line break, and then type the current date.

11. Spell check your document, correct any errors, and then save the page.

12. View the Web page in your browser. Print a copy, if required, and hand it in to your instructor. Close the browser and then quit Dreamweaver.

3 Plant City Web Site

Problem: Juan Benito recently moved to Plant City, Florida. He discovered that Plant City has a colorful history and that many consider the city to be the Strawberry Capital of the United States. He has asked you to help prepare a Web page (Figure 1-102 on the next page) so he can share information with friends, relatives, and visitors to Florida about the city's historical facts.

Software and hardware settings determine how a Web page is displayed in a browser. Your Web pages may display differently in your browser than those in the figures.

(continued)

Plant City Web Site *(continued)*

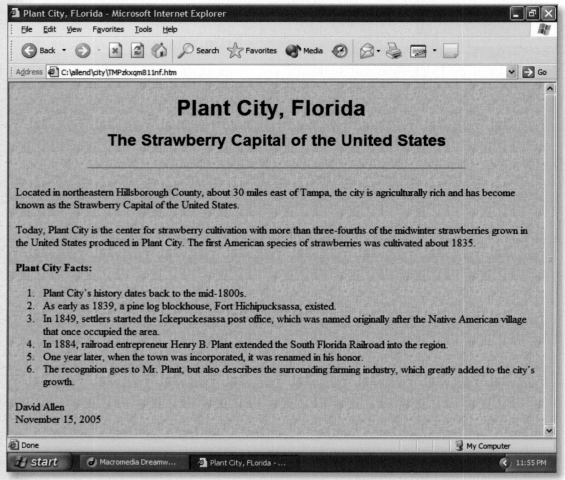

FIGURE 1-102

Instructions: Start Dreamweaver. Perform the tasks on the next page to define a Web site and create and format an informational Web page on Plant City, Florida. The text of the Web page is shown in Table 1-8 on the next page.

In the Lab

Table 1-8 Plant City, Florida Web Site	
SECTION	**WEB PAGE TEXT**
Heading	Plant City, Florida
Subheading	The Strawberry Capital of the United States
Introductory Paragraph	Located in northeastern Hillsborough County, about 30 miles east of Tampa, the city is agriculturally rich and has become known as the Strawberry Capital of the United States.
Second Paragraph	Today, Plant City is the center for strawberry cultivation with more than three-fourths of the midwinter strawberries grown in the United States produced in Plant City. The first American species of strawberries was cultivated about 1835.
Third Paragraph	Plant City Facts:
List Item 1	Plant City's history dates back to the mid-1800s.
List Item 2	As early as 1839, a pine log blockhouse, Fort Hichipucksassa, existed.
List Item 3	In 1849, settlers started the Ickepuckesassa post office, which was named originally after the Native American village that once occupied the area.
List Item 4	In 1884, railroad entrepreneur Henry B. Plant extended the South Florida Railroad into the region.
List Item 5	One year later, when the town was incorporated, it was renamed in his honor.
List Item 6	The recognition goes to Mr. Plant, but also describes the surrounding farming industry, which greatly added to the city's growth.

1. Define a local Web site under the your name folder. Name the site Plant City. Create a subfolder and name it city. Create an images subfolder and copy the image data files into the folder.
2. Open a new Document window and use the Save As command to save the page as index. Apply the background image to the index page.
3. Click in the Document window and then type the Web page text shown in Table 1-8. Press the ENTER key after typing the text in each section in the table.
4. Select the heading text and apply Heading 1. Select the subheading text and apply Heading 2. Center both headings. Change the heading font type to Arial, Helvetica, sans-serif.
5. Insert a centered horizontal line, 550 pixels in width, with no shading, below the subtitle.
6. Select the third paragraph, Plant City Facts:, and then apply bold formatting to the text.
7. Select list items 1 through 6 and apply an ordered list format.
8. Change the Web page title to Plant City, Florida.
9. Insert your name and the current date at the bottom of the Web page.
10. Spell check your document and correct any errors. Save the Web page.
11. View the Web page in the browser. Print a copy, if required, and hand it in to your instructor. Close the browser. Quit Dreamweaver.

Cases and Places

The difficulty of these case studies varies:
■ are the least difficult and ■■ are the most difficult. The last exercise is a group exercise.

1 ■ Define a Web site named Favorite Sports with a subfolder named sports. Prepare a Web page listing your favorite sports and favorite teams. Include a title for your Web page. Bold and center the title, and then apply the Heading 1 style. Include a sentence or two explaining why you like the sport and why you like the teams. Bold and italicize the names of the teams and the sports. Give the Web page a meaningful title. Apply a background image to your Web page. Spell check the document. Use the concepts and techniques presented in the project to format the text. Save the file in the sports folder. For a selection of images and backgrounds, visit the Dreamweaver MX 2004 Media Web page (scsite.com/ dreamweavermx04/media).

2 ■ Your instructor has asked you to create a Web page about one of your hobbies. Define the Web site using Hobbies for the site name and hobby for the subfolder name. Italicize and center the title, and then apply the Heading 2 style. Type a paragraph of three or four sentences explaining why you selected the subject. Select and center the paragraph. Add a list of three items and create an ordered list from the three items. Include line breaks between each numbered item. Title the Web page the name of the hobby you selected. Spell check your document. Use the concepts and techniques presented in the project to format the text. For a selection of images and backgrounds, visit the Dreamweaver MX 2004 Media Web page (scsite.com/dreamweavermx04/media).

3 ■■ Define a Web site and create a Web page that gives a description and information about your favorite type of music. Name the Web site Favorite Music and the subfolder music. Apply a background image to the Web page. Include a left-aligned heading formatted with the Heading 1 style. Include a subheading formatted with Heading 2. Insert a horizontal rule following the subheading. List four facts about why you selected this type of music. Include the names of three of your favorite songs and the names of the artists. Bold and italicize the name of the songs and artists and apply a font color of your choice. Create an ordered list from the four facts. Title the Web page Favorite Music. Save the file as index in the music folder. Use the concepts and techniques presented in the project to format the text. For a selection of images and backgrounds, visit the Dreamweaver MX 2004 Media Web page (scsite.com/dreamweavermx04/media).

Cases and Places

4 ■■ Assume you are running for office in your city's local government. Define a Web site using the name of the city in which you live and a subfolder named government. Include the following information in your Web page: your name, centered, with Heading 1 and a font color of your choice; the name of the office for which you are running, bold and italicized; and a paragraph about the duties of the office in Courier font. Create a bulleted list within your Web page. Change the title of the Web page from Untitled Document to your name. Use the concepts and techniques presented in the project to format the text. For a selection of images and backgrounds, visit the Dreamweaver MX 2004 Media Web page (scsite.com/dreamweavermx04/media).

5 ■■ **Working Together** Your school has a budget for student trips. Your assignment and that of your teammates is to put together a Web site and Web page, that list locations and trips from which the student body can select. Apply an appropriate background image. Include a title, formatted with Heading 1, and a subtitle, formatted with Heading 2. Insert a shaded horizontal line following the subtitle. List three locations. Bold and apply a font color to each location name. Add a bullet to each location name. Include information about each location. Title the page Student Government. Use the concepts and techniques presented in the project to format the text. For a selection of images and backgrounds, visit the Dreamweaver MX 2004 Media Web page (scsite.com/dreamweavermx04/media).

MACROMEDIA
Dreamweaver MX 2004

Adding Web Pages, Links, and Images

PROJECT

2

CASE PERSPECTIVE

A coworker at the state environmental agency, Joan Komisky, who also is interested in Florida's parks, viewed the Web page that you and David created. She has offered some suggestions and asked to help with the design. Both you and David agreed, and the three of you have become a team.

Joan suggests adding images to the home page. David proposes that the Web site include a page for Florida's three national parks and another page with information about his three favorite state parks located in northwest Florida. You explain to David and Joan that the addition of each new page will require hyperlinks from the home page and links from each page back to the home page. You assure them that Dreamweaver includes all the tools they need to add these and other types of links, including e-mail links, to related Web sites. You create a navigation map to illustrate how the links will work among the three pages. All team members agree that these two new pages should be added and that the pages will include images and links. With the addition of these two pages, the Web page you created in Project 1 will become a Web site.

As you read through this project, you will learn how to add pages to a Web site, how to add images to a Web page, and how to insert absolute, relative, and e-mail links.

MACROMEDIA
Dreamweaver MX 2004

Adding Web Pages, Links, and Images

PROJECT

2

Objectives

You will have mastered the material in this project when you can:

- Define and set a home page
- Add pages to a Web site
- Describe Dreamweaver's image accessibility features
- Describe image file formats
- Insert, resize, and align images within a Web page
- Describe the different types of links

- Create a relative, absolute, and e-mail link
- Describe how to change the color of links
- Edit and delete links
- Describe and display the Site Map
- Describe Code view, Split view, and Design view
- View Code view

Introduction

Project 2 introduces the addition of Web pages to the local site created in Project 1 and the integration of links and graphics into the Web pages that make up the site. Recall from Project 1 that a site or a Web site is a set of linked documents with shared attributes, such as related topics, a similar design, or a shared purpose.

The Dreamweaver site structure feature provides a way to maintain and organize your files. A Web page essentially is a text document and a collection of HTML code. The HTML (Hypertext Markup Language) code defines the structure and lay-out of a Web document and is generated automatically by Dreamweaver. Images and other media content are separate files. For example, a page that displays text and three images consists of four separate files — one for the text document and one for each of the three images.

Most Web site builders include images on their Web pages. It is important that you take the time to learn about images, image properties, and the types of images best suited for a particular situation. Image properties, such as alternative text for accessibility issues, alignment, and size adjustment, help you to understand the effects of using images on Web pages.

When a file or image is referenced within the HTML document, a link (or hyper-link) exists within the HTML code to the external file or image. A link (hyperlink) is a Web page element that, when clicked, accesses another Web page, or a different place within the existing Web page. A Web page can contain different types of links: internal, or relative; absolute; e-mail; and named anchors, which are links to a specific place within a document. This project discusses how to create these links.

Project Two — Two New Pages, Links, and Images

In this project, you continue with the creation of the Florida Parks Web site. You add two additional Web pages, add image backgrounds to the two new pages, add images to all three pages, add links to and from the index page, and add absolute links to three state parks (Figures 2-1a, 2-1b, and 2-1c on the next page).

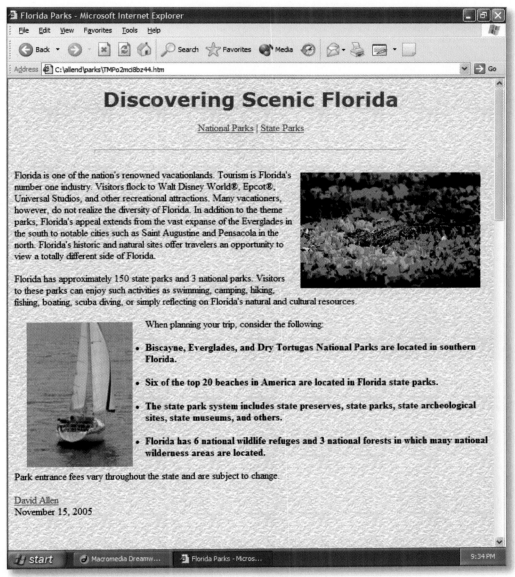

(a) Florida Parks Index (Home) Page

FIGURE 2-1 (continued)

(b) Florida National Parks Web Page

(c) Florida State Parks Web Page

FIGURE 2-1 *(continued)*

In the Introduction project, four types of Web structures were illustrated: linear, hierarchical, web (or random), and grid. This project uses a hierarchical structure (Figure 2-2). The index page is the home page, or entrance to the Web site. From this page, the visitor to this site can link to a page about Florida national parks or to a page about Florida state parks.

FIGURE 2-2

Managing a Web Site

Organization is a key element of Web design. Dreamweaver works best with entire sites rather than individual Web pages and has many built-in tools to make site creation easy, such as checking links and organizing files. You defined the parks Web site in Project 1 and created the index page. You can add pages to your site by creating a new page and saving it as part of the site or by opening an existing page from another source and saving it as part of the site. In this project, you will create two new pages.

Almost all Web sites have a home page. Compare the home page to your front door. Generally, the front door is the first thing guests see when they visit you. The same applies to a Web site's home page. When someone visits a Web site, he or she usually enters through the home page.

The home page normally is named **index.htm** or **index.html**. This file name has special significance. Most Web servers recognize index.htm (or index.html) as the default home page and automatically display this page without requiring that the user type the full Uniform Resource Locator (URL), or Web address. For example, if you type http://www.tipsahoy.com into a Web browser address box and access the Web site, what you see is http://www.tipsahoy.com/index.htm, even though you did not type it that way.

Organizing your Web site and using Dreamweaver's site management features can assure you that the media within your Web page will display correctly. Bringing all of these elements together will start you on your way to becoming a successful Web site developer.

Before you start enhancing your Web site, you copy the data files into the site's folder hierarchy.

Copying Data Files to the Local Web Site

Your Data Disk contains images for Project 2. These images are in an images folder. You use the Windows My Computer option to copy the Project 2 images to your parks images folder. See the inside back cover for instructions for downloading the Data Disk or see your instructor for information about accessing the files required for this book.

The Data Files folder for this project is stored on Local Disk (C:). The location on your computer may be different. If necessary, verify the location of the Data Files folder with your instructor. The following steps show how to copy the files to the parks local root folder.

To Copy Data Files to the Parks Web Site

1 Click the Start button on the Windows taskbar and then click My Computer.

2 Double-click Local Disk (C:) and then navigate to the location of the data files for Project 2.

3 Double-click the DataFiles folder and then double-click the Proj02 folder.

4 Double-click the parks folder and then double-click the images folder.

5 Click the alligator image file or the first file in the list.

6 Hold down the SHIFT key and then click the poncedeleon image file, or the last file in the list.

7 Right-click the selected files to display the context menu.

8 Click the Copy command and then click the My Computer Back button the number of times necessary to navigate to the your name folder.

9 Double-click the your name folder, double-click the parks folder, and then double-click the images folder.

10 Right-click anywhere in the open window to display the context menu.

11 Click the Paste command (Figure 2-3).

12 Click the images window Close button.

The six images are pasted into the Florida Parks Web site images folder, and the folder now contains seven images, including the parksbg image file (Figure 2-3).

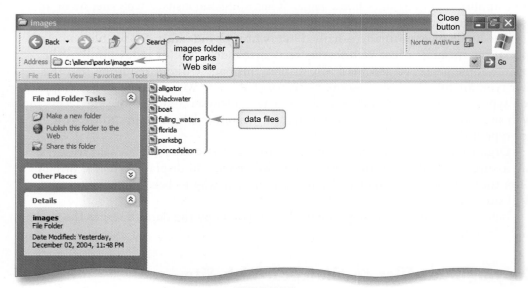

FIGURE 2-3

The data files are copied to the parks Web site file hierarchy. The next step is to start Dreamweaver.

Starting Dreamweaver and Opening a Web Site

Each time you start Dreamweaver, it opens to the last site displayed when you closed the program. It therefore may be necessary for you to open the parks Web site. The **Files pop-up menu** in the Files panel lists sites you have defined. When you open the site, a list of pages and subfolders within the site displays. The following steps illustrate how to start Dreamweaver and open the Florida Parks Web site.

To Start Dreamweaver and Open the Parks Web Site

• **Click the Start button on the Windows taskbar. Point to All Programs on the Start menu, point to Macromedia on the All Programs submenu, and then click Macromedia Dreamweaver MX 2004 on the Macromedia submenu. If necessary, display the panel groups.**

Dreamweaver opens and displays panel groups and an empty Document window. If the Start page displays, click Open in the Open a Recent Item column and then select the parks index.htm file.

FIGURE 2-4

• **Click the Files panel box arrow and point to Florida Parks on the Files pop-up menu (Figure 2-4).**

3

• **Click Florida Parks.**

The Florida Parks Web site hierarchy displays in the Files panel (Figure 2-5).

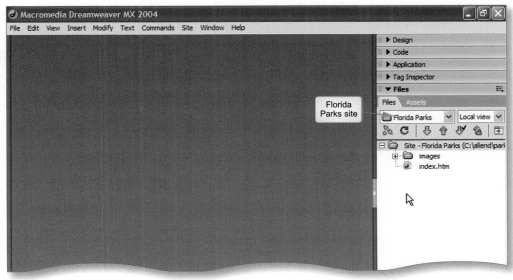

FIGURE 2-5

Opening a Web Page

Once you have created and saved a Web page or copied a Web page to a Web site, you often will have reason to retrieve it from disk. Opening an existing Web page in Dreamweaver is much the same as opening an existing document in most other software applications; that is, you use the File menu and Open command or you can use Dreamweaver's unique File and Open Recent command. If, however, the page is part of a Dreamweaver Web site, you also can open the file from the Files panel.

After opening the page, you can modify text, images, tables, and any other elements. The following step illustrates how to open a Web page from a local site in the Files panel.

To Open a Web Page from a Local Web Site

1

• **Double-click index.htm in the Files panel.**

• **If necessary, click View on the menu bar, point to Toolbars, and then click Standard.**

The Florida Parks index page displays in the Document window, and the name of the page displays on the tab at the top of the window. The Standard toolbar displays (Figure 2-6).

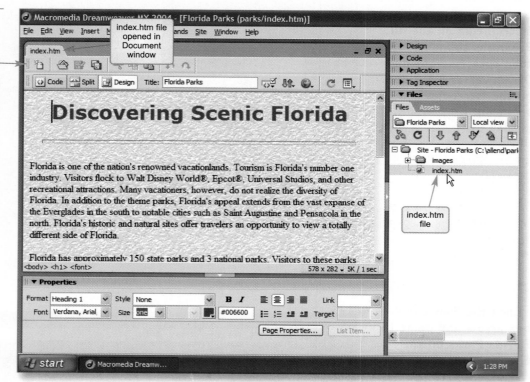

FIGURE 2-6

The Files Panel

Organization is one of the keys to a successful Web site. Creating documents without considering where in the folder hierarchy they should go generally creates a difficult-to-manage Web site. The Dreamweaver **Files panel** provides a view of the devices and folders on your computer and shows how these devices and folders are organized. You can create new folders and files for your site through the Files panel, which is similar to the Windows XP file organization method. You also can use the Files panel to drag or copy and paste files to your Web site.

The main directory of a disk is called the **root directory** or the **top-level directory**. A small device icon or folder icon is displayed next to each object in the list. The **device icon** represents a device such as the Desktop or a disk drive, and the **folder icon** represents a folder. Many of these icons have a plus or minus sign next to them, which indicates whether the device or folder contains additional folders or files. Windows XP arranges all of these objects — root directory, folders, subfolders, and files — in a hierarchy. The plus and minus signs are controls that you can click to expand or collapse the view of the file hierarchy. In the Files panel, Dreamweaver uses the same hierarchy arrangement, but site folders appear in a different color than non-site folders so that you easily can distinguish between the two.

More About

Refreshing the Files Panel

To refresh the Files panel, click the Refresh button on the Files panel toolbar or press the F5 key.

The Home Page and the Site Map

Most Web sites have a starting point, called a home page. In a personal home page within a Web site, for example, you probably would list your name, your e-mail address, some personal information, and links to other information on your Web site. The index page you created in Project 1 is the home page for the parks Web site.

Although you cannot tell which page in a Web site is the home page by viewing the site files, Dreamweaver provides a graphical option to view the home page — the Site Map. You access the Site Map through the Files panel. To create a Site Map requires that you designate one page in the Web site as a home page. You will use the Site Map to view the Web site later in this project. The next section sets the home page.

Setting a Home Page

Each Web site you create within Dreamweaver should have a home page. A **home page** is similar to a table of contents or an index in a book. The home page generally contains links to all the other pages within the Web site. Most home pages are named index.htm or index.html. The steps on the next page show how to define the home page through the Files panel.

To Set a Home Page

1

• **Right-click the index.htm file name in the Files panel.**

• **Point to Set as Home Page.**

The context menu displays (Figure 2-7).

2

• **Click Set as Home Page on the context menu.**

The index.htm file is set as the home page for the parks Web site. In the files list, however, no changes are evident.

FIGURE 2-7

Q: Is it necessary to create a folder for images within the Web site?

A: Critical to Web development is the hierarchy of folders and files in a Web site. Even for the very simplest of sites, you should create a separate folder for the images. The folder name can be any name you choose, but it is best to use a descriptive, meaningful name.

Adding Pages to a Web Site

You copied the files necessary to begin creating your Web site to the parks local root folder in the Files panel, and you set the home page. It is time to start building and enhancing your site. You will add two additional pages to the Web site: Florida National Parks and Florida State Parks. You will add links and page images to the index page and links, a background image, and page images to the two new pages.

Opening a New Document Window

The next step is to open a new Document window. This will become the Florida National Parks page. The following steps illustrate how to open a new document window and save the page as national.htm.

To Open a New Document Window

1

• **Click File on the menu bar and then point to New.**

The File menu is displayed (Figure 2-8).

FIGURE 2-8

2

• **Click New. If necessary, click the General tab and then click Basic page in the Category list.**

• **If necessary, click HTML in the Basic page list.**

The New Document dialog box displays. Basic page is highlighted in the Category list. HTML is the default in the Basic page list (Figure 2-9).

FIGURE 2-9

3

• **Click the Create
button.**

*A new Untitled-2 Document
window displays (Figure 2-10).
The number following Untitled
increases each time you open
a new Document window.
Your computer may display a
different number.*

FIGURE 2-10

4

• **Click the Save button
on the Standard toolbar.**

*The Save As dialog box
displays and Untitled-2 is
highlighted in the File name
text box (Figure 2-11).*

FIGURE 2-11

5

- **Type** national **for the file name.**

The national file name displays in the File name text box (Figure 2-12).

FIGURE 2-12

6

- **Click the Save button.**

The national.htm page is saved in the parks local folder and displays in Dreamweaver's Files panel. The .htm extension is added automatically by Dreamweaver. The path and file name (parks/national.htm) appear on the Dreamweaver title bar (Figure 2-13).

FIGURE 2-13

To organize your workspace, you hide the panel groups and collapse the lower portion of the Property inspector. This gives you additional window space in the Dreamweaver Document window. The following steps show how to organize your workspace by hiding the panel groups.

To Prepare the Workspace

1 Click the expand/collapse arrow on the panel groups vertical bar.

2 Click the Property inspector expander arrow.

The national.htm Document window displays, the Property inspector is collapsed, and the panel groups are hidden (Figure 2-14).

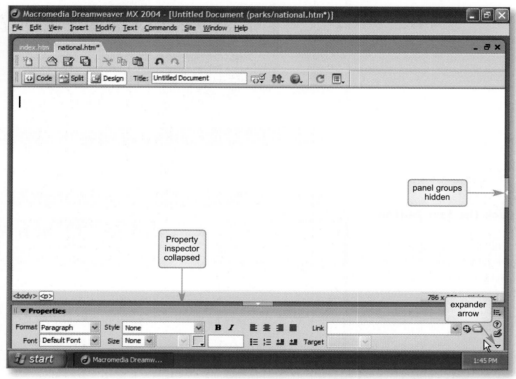

FIGURE 2-14

With the workspace prepared and the Document window displayed, you can begin creating the Web page for Florida National Parks.

Creating the National Parks Web Page

To create the page for Florida National Parks, you type the text in the Document window. Table 2-1 includes the text for the Florida National Parks Web page. Press the ENTER key or insert a line break, or <br>, as indicated in the instructions in Table 2-1 on the next page.

More About

Using the Keyboard Shortcut Editor

For more information about using keyboard shortcuts, visit the Dreamweaver MX 2004 More About Web page (scsite.com/dreamweavermx04/more) and then click Dreamweaver MX 2004 Shortcut Editor.

Table 2-1 Florida National Parks Web Page Text

SECTION	WEB PAGE TEXT
Heading	Florida National Parks<ENTER>
Subheading	Experience the Real Florida!<ENTER>
Part 1	Everglades National Park Everglades National Park is the only subtropical preserve in North America. The park is known for its rich bird life and is the only place in the world where alligators and crocodiles exist side by side.<ENTER>
Part 2	Biscayne National Park Biscayne National Park is a delight for wildlife-watching, snorkeling, diving, boating, and fishing. The park contains the longest stretch of mangrove forest left on Florida's east coast and a spectacular living coral reef.<ENTER>
Part 3	Dry Tortugas National Park About 70 miles west of Key West is the Dry Tortugas National Park, a cluster of seven islands, composed of sand and coral reefs. Located on one of the islands is Ft. Jefferson, the largest of the 19th century American coastal forts. The area also is known for its legends of pirates and sunken ships.<ENTER>
Closing	Home<ENTER>

The following steps show how to create the Web page and insert blank lines and line breaks between sections of text as necessary.

To Create the National Parks Web Page

1

• **Type the heading** Florida National Parks **as shown in Table 2-1. Press the ENTER key.**

The heading is entered in the Document window (Figure 2-15). Pressing the ENTER key creates a new paragraph.

FIGURE 2-15

2

• **Type the subheading** Experience the Real Florida! **as shown in Table 2-1, and then press the ENTER key.**

The subheading is entered in the Document window (Figure 2-16).

FIGURE 2-16

3

• **Type the rest of the text as shown in Table 2-1. Press the ENTER key and insert line breaks as indicated in the instructions.**

The text for the Florida National Parks is entered (Figure 2-17).

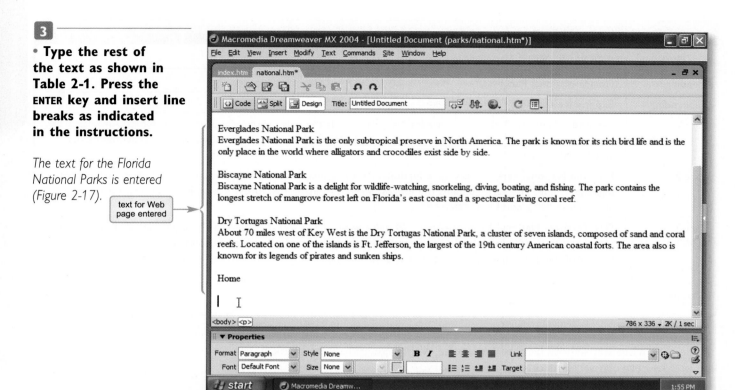

FIGURE 2-17

In Project 1, you formatted the index page by adding headings and bullets, centering, and bolding text. The following steps show how to apply similar formatting to the Florida National Parks page. Recall that SHIFT + ENTER inserts a line break.

To Format the Florida National Parks Page

1 If necessary, expand the Property inspector, scroll up to the top of the Web page, and then apply Heading 1 to the heading text.

2 Apply Heading 2 to the subheading text.

3 Center the heading and subheading.

4 Add bullets to the following three lines: Everglades National Park, Biscayne National Park, and Dry Tortugas National Park.

5 Bold each of these three lines: Everglades National Park, Biscayne National Park, and Dry Tortugas National Park.

6 Add two line breaks after the text describing the Everglades National Park and two line breaks after the text describing the Biscayne National Park.

7 Type Florida National Parks as the Web page title.

8 Save the national.htm Web page.

9 Press F12 to view the page in the browser and to verify that the line spacing is correct, as shown in Figure 2-18. Close the browser.

The Florida National Parks Web page text is entered, formatted, and saved.

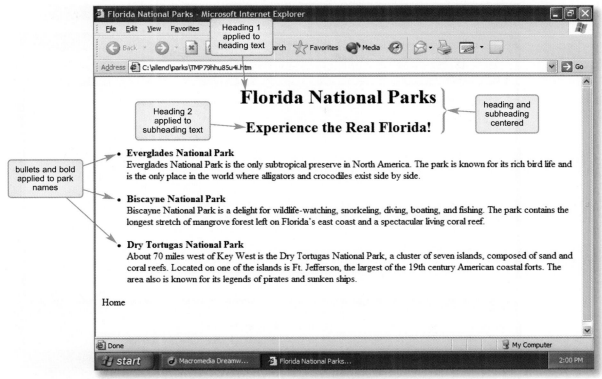

FIGURE 2-18

Creating the State Parks Web Page

You will enter the text for the Florida State Parks Page the same way you entered the text for the Florida National Parks page. Table 2-2 includes all the text for the Florida State Parks Web page.

To Open a New Document Window

1 Click File on the menu bar and then point to New.

2 Click New. If necessary, click the General tab and then click Basic page in the Category list.

3 If necessary, click HTML in the Basic page list.

4 Click the Create button.

5 Save the Web page as state_parks.htm in the parks folder.

A new Document window displays, and the name of the saved page is displayed on the title bar (Figure 2-19).

Type the text for the State Parks Web page using Table 2-2 on the following page and the following step. Press the ENTER key or insert a line break, or <br>, as indicated in the table.

FIGURE 2-19

SECTION	WEB PAGE TEXT
Table 2-2 Florida State Parks Web Page Text	
Heading	Florida State Parks<ENTER>
Subheading	Northwest Region<ENTER>
Part 1	Florida has more than 150 state parks. Three of the more unusual and scenic parks are located in the north-western part of the state.<ENTER>
Part 2	Blackwater River State Park Activities at Blackwater include camping, picnicking, fishing, nature trails, boating, and canoeing. This 590-acre park is located in Holt, Florida. The Blackwater River has one of the purer sand-bottom rivers in the world.<ENTER>
Part 3	Ponce de Leon Spring State Park Activities within this park include fishing, nature trails, picnicking, and swimming. Numerous springs are found within the park.<ENTER>The main spring in the park is created through the merging of two flows from a limestone cavity. These two flows produce more than 14 million gallons of crystal-clear water daily.<ENTER>
Part 4	Falling Waters State Park This park is located in Chipley, Florida. The park derives its name from one of Florida's more notable geological features: a 67-foot waterfall.<ENTER>It also is known for the Falling Waters Sink. The sink is a 100-foot-deep, 20-foot-wide cylindrical pit. Into the pit flows a small stream, which drops 67 feet to the bottom of the sink. The destination of the water is not yet known.<ENTER>
Closing	Home<ENTER>

To Create the State Parks Web Page

1 **Type the text of the Web page as shown in Table 2-2.**

The text for the Florida State Parks Web page is entered (Figure 2-20).

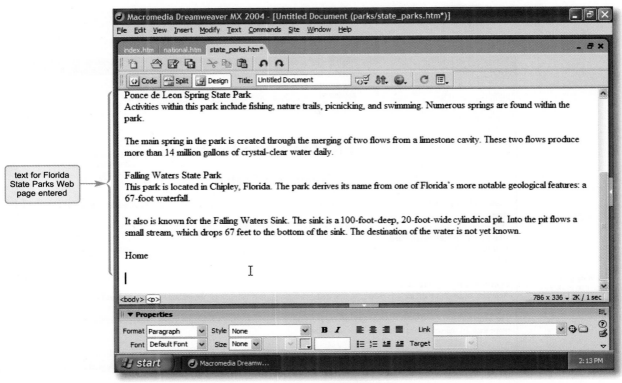

text for Florida State Parks Web page entered

FIGURE 2-20

To Format the Florida State Parks Page

1 If necessary, scroll to the top of the Web page and then apply Heading 1 to the heading.

2 Apply Heading 2 to the subheading.

3 Center the heading and subheading.

4 Bold the names of each of the three parks where they are used as subtitles.

5 Type Florida State Parks - NW as the Web page title.

6 Click the Save button on the Standard toolbar.

7 Press F12 to view the page in the browser and to verify that the line spacing is correct, as shown in Figure 2-21 on the next page.

8 Close the browser.

The text for the Florida State Parks page is entered, formatted, and saved.

You have completed entering and formatting the text for the two new pages and copied the images to the parks local root folder in the Files panel. It is time to add additional enhancements to your site. In Project 1, you added a background image to the index page. In this project, you learn more about images. You will add the same background image to the two new pages, and then add page images and links to all three pages.

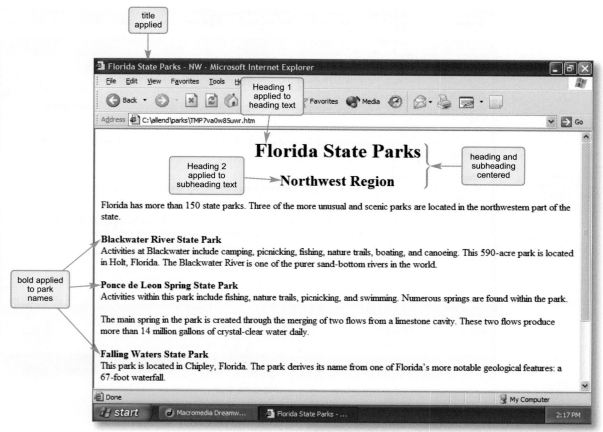

FIGURE 2-21

Images

If used correctly and with an understanding of the Web site audience, images add excitement and interest to a Web page. When you are selecting images for a Web site, it is important to understand that the size and type of image or images used within a Web page affect how fast the Web page downloads and displays in the viewer's Web browser. A Web page that downloads too slowly will turn away visitors.

Image File Formats

Graphical images used on the Web are in one of two broad categories: vector and bitmap. **Vector** images are composed of key points and paths, which define shapes and coloring instructions, such as line and fill colors. The vector file contains a description of the image expressed mathematically. The file describes the image to the computer, and the computer draws it. This type of image generally is associated with Macromedia's Flash or Adobe's LiveMotion animation programs. One of the benefits of vector images is file size, particularly relative to the file size of bitmap images.

Bitmap images are the more common type of image file. A bitmap file maps out or plots an image on a pixel-by-pixel basis. A **pixel**, or **picture element**, is the smallest point in a graphical image. Graphic monitors display images by dividing the display screen into thousands (or millions) of pixels, arranged in a **grid** of rows and columns. The pixels appear connected because they are so close together. This grid of pixels is a **bitmap**. The **bit-resolution** of an image is described by the number of bits used to represent each pixel. An 8-bit image supports up to 256 colors, and a 24- or 32-bit image supports up to 16.7 million colors.

Web browsers currently support three bitmap image file types: GIF, JPEG, and PNG.

GIF GIF (.gif) is an acronym for **Graphics Interchange Format**. The GIF format uses 8-bit resolution, supports up to a maximum of 256 colors, and uses combinations of these 256 colors to simulate colors beyond that range. The GIF format is best for displaying images such as logos, icons, buttons, and other images with even colors and tones. GIF images come in two different versions: GIF87 format and GIF89a format. The GIF89a format contains three features not available in the GIF87 or JPEG formats: transparency, interlacing, and animation. The **transparency** feature allows the user to specify a transparency color, which allows the background color or image to display. The **interlacing** feature lets the browser begin to build a low-resolution version of the full-sized GIF picture on the screen while the file is still downloading. Using an animated GIF editor, GIF89a images can be **animated**. Animated GIF images are simply a number of GIF images saved into a single file and looped, or repeated over and over. A number of shareware GIF editors are available to create animated GIFs. If you do not want to create your own animations, you can find thousands of free animated GIFs on the Internet available for downloading.

JPEG JPEG (.jpg) is an acronym for **Joint Photographic Experts Group**. JPEG files are the best format for photographic images because JPEG files can contain up to 16.7 million colors. **Progressive JPEG** is a new variation of the JPEG image format. This image format supports a gradually built display such as the interlaced GIFs. Older browsers do not support progressive JPEG files.

PNG PNG stands for **Portable Network Graphics**. PNG is the native file format of Macromedia Fireworks. PNG files retain all the original layer, vector, color, and effect information (such as a drop shadow), and all elements are fully editable at all times. Many browsers do not support this format without a special plug-in. Generally, it is better to use GIF or JPEG images in your Web pages.

When developing a Web site that consists of many pages, you should maintain a consistent, professional layout and design throughout all of the pages. The pages in a single site, for example, should use similar features such as background colors or images, margins, and headings.

Background Colors and Background Images

Most Web pages display with a default white or gray background. Generally, the browser used to display the Web page determines the default background. You can enhance your Web page by adding a background image and/or background color or adding one of Dreamweaver's Web-safe color schemes.

If you use a background color, the same cautions apply to background color as they do to text color. You want to use Web-safe colors, such as those in the Dreamweaver color schemes. This means the colors will display correctly on the computer screen when someone is viewing your Web page. To insert an image or color for the page background, you use the Page Properties dialog box.

Background images add texture and interesting color to a Web page and set the overall appearance of the document. Most browsers support background images. A background image can be a large image, but more frequently it is a smaller image. The image tiles to fill the screen in the Dreamweaver Document window and in the browser window. In Project 1, you added a background image to the index page. Now you add the same image to the National Parks Web page and the State Parks page. The following steps illustrate how to add a background image to these two pages.

Q&A

Q: Is it necessary to add a background image to a Web page?

A: No, you do not need to add a background image. If you do add a background image to your Web page, however, select an image that does not clash with the text and other content. The background image should not overwhelm the Web page.

To Add a Background Image to the National Parks Web Page

1 Click the national.htm tab.

2 Click Modify on the menu bar and then click Page Properties.

3 Click the Browse button to the right of the Background image box.

4 If necessary, navigate to the images folder.

5 Click parksbg.gif and then click the OK button in the Select Image Source dialog box.

6 Click the OK button in the Page Properties dialog box.

7 Click the Save button on the Standard toolbar.

The background image is applied to the National Parks page (Figure 2-22).

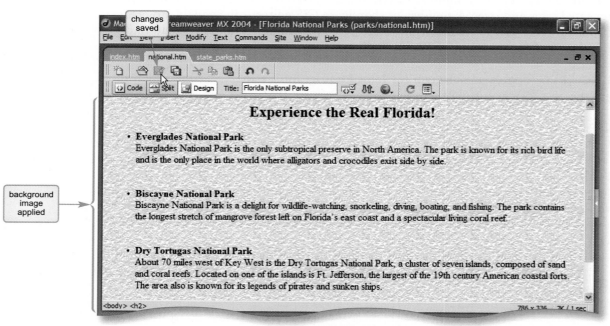

FIGURE 2-22

To Add a Background Image to the State Parks Web Page

1 Click the state_parks.htm tab.

2 Click Modify on the menu bar and then click Page Properties.

3 Click the Browse button to the right of the Background image box.

4 Click parksbg.gif and then click the OK button in the Select Image Source dialog box.

5 Click the OK button in the Page Properties dialog box.

6 Click the Save button on the Standard toolbar.

The background image is applied to the State Parks page (Figure 2-23 on the next page).

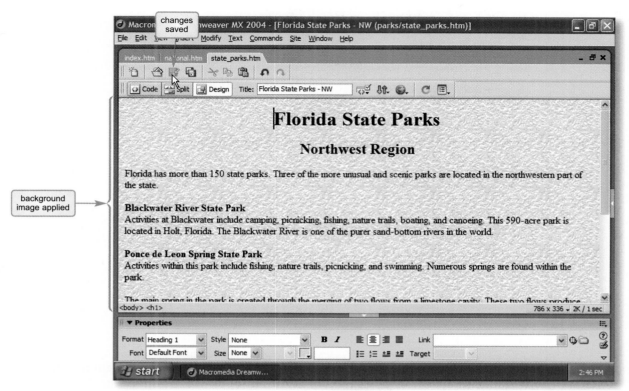

background
image applied

FIGURE 2-23

To enhance your index Web page further, you will add two images. One of the images will display at the top right of the document, and the second image will display at the bottom to the left of the bulleted list. Dreamweaver's Assets panel provides visual cues, and the invisible element feature provides placement control for these images.

Assets Panel

Assets are elements, such as images or Flash files, that you use in building a page or a site. The **Assets panel**, which is grouped with the Files panel, helps you manage and organize your Web site's assets (Figure 2-24 on the next page). This panel contains a list of all the asset types (images, colors, URLs, Flash and Shockwave files, movies, scripts, templates, and library items) within the selected local root folder. The Site list shows all of the assets in your site. The Favorites list shows only the assets you have selected and added to the list. To add an asset to the Favorites list, select the item in the Site list and then click the Add to Favorites button. Remove an item from the list by selecting the item and then clicking the Remove from Favorites button. The Assets panel in Figure 2-24 is resized to show all options. You resize the panels by moving the mouse pointer over the vertical bar until it displays as a two-headed arrow. Then you hold down the mouse button and drag.

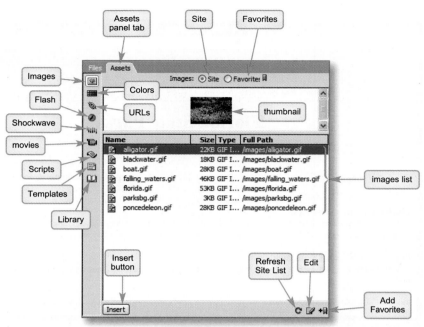

FIGURE 2-24

You can insert most asset types into a document by dragging them into the Document window or by using the Insert button at the bottom of the Assets panel. You also either can insert colors and URLs or apply them to selected text in Design view. Additionally, you can apply URLs to other elements in Design view, such as images. When an image file name is highlighted, a thumbnail of the image displays at the top of the Assets panel. You use the Assets panel to insert the images into the Florida Parks Web pages.

Invisible Elements

Dreamweaver's Document window displays what you would see in a Web browser window. It sometimes is helpful, however, when designing a Web page to see the placement of certain elements. For example, viewing the Line Break code <br> provides a visual cue regarding the layout. Dreamweaver enables you to control the visibility of 13 different codes, including those for image placement, through the Preferences dialog box.

When you insert and align an image into a Document window, Dreamweaver displays an **invisible element marker** that shows the location of the inserted image within the HTML code. This visual aid displays as a small yellow icon. When the icon is selected, it displays as blue and can be used to cut and paste or drag and drop the image. Other aligned elements include tables, ActiveX objects, plug-ins, and applets. To hide all invisible elements temporarily, deselect Visual Aids through the View menu.

The steps on the next page illustrate how to display the invisible element marker for aligned elements such as images and turn on Invisible Elements through the Visual Aids submenu command.

To Set Invisible Element Preferences and Turn on Visual Aids

1

• **Click Edit on the menu bar and then click Preferences.**

• **Click Invisible Elements in the Category list.**

The Preferences dialog box displays, and Invisible Elements is highlighted in the Category list (Figure 2-25).

FIGURE 2-25

2

• **Click the Anchor points for aligned elements check box (Figure 2-26).**

FIGURE 2-26

3

• **Click the OK button.**

The Document window displays with no visible change.

4

• **Click View on the menu bar, point to Visual Aids, and then point to Invisible Elements.**

The View menu and the Visual Aids submenu display. Invisible Elements is highlighted (Figure 2-27). Note: If a check mark already is displayed to the left of the Invisible Elements command, do not complete the next step.

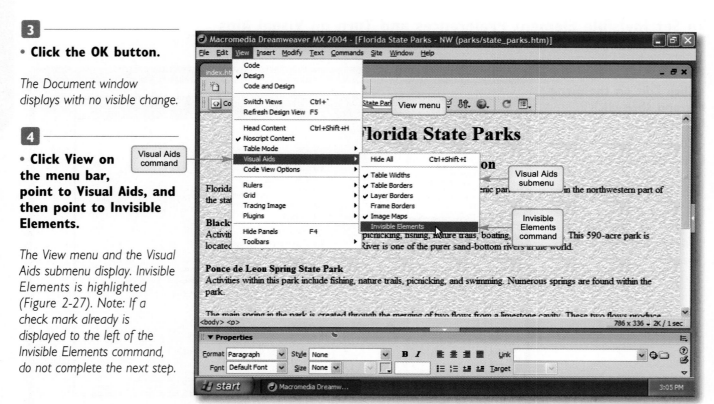

FIGURE 2-27

5

• **Click Invisible Elements.**

A check mark is added to the Invisible Elements command, and the Document window displays with no visible changes.

Inserting an Image into a Web Page

Inserting images into your Web page is easy and quick with Dreamweaver — just drag and drop the image from the Files panel or the Assets panel. Image placement, however, can be more complex. When the Web page is viewed in a browser, the image may display somewhat differently than in the Document window. If the images do not display correctly, you can select and modify the placement of the images in the Document window by dragging the invisible element marker to move the image.

To Insert an Image into the Index Page

1

• **Click the index.htm page tab. If necessary, scroll to the top of the page.**

• **Click the vertical bar expand/collapse arrow to display the panel groups.**

• **If necessary, click the Assets panel tab. Verify that the Images icon is selected.**

• **Click alligator.gif in the Assets panel.**

The index page displays and the Assets panel is selected. The file, alligator.gif is highlighted (Figure 2-28).

FIGURE 2-28

2

• **If necessary, scroll to the top of the page in the index Document window.**

• **Drag alligator.gif from the Assets panel to the left of the first line of the first paragraph. Do not release the mouse button.**

When you start to drag, a page icon displays next to the mouse pointer (Figure 2-29), indicating the image is being dragged.

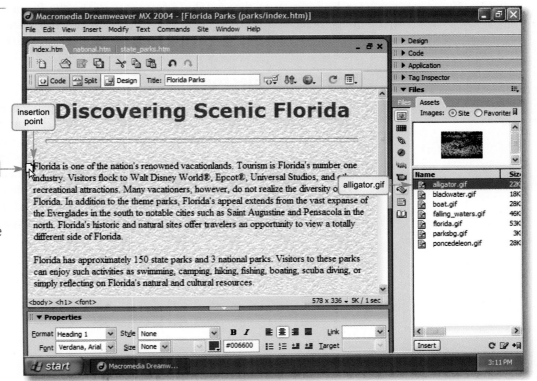

FIGURE 2-29

3

• **Release the mouse button and then click the alligator image to select it if necessary.**

The border and handles around the image indicate it is selected. The attributes change in the Property inspector to reflect the selected object (Figure 2-30).

FIGURE 2-30

In addition to the visual aid feature, you use the Property inspector to help with image placement and add other attributes. When you select an image within the Document window, the Property inspector displays properties specific to that image.

Property Inspector Image Features

The Property inspector lets you see the current properties of the selected element. The Property inspector is divided into two sections. Clicking the expander arrow in the lower-right corner of the Property inspector collapses the Property inspector to show only the most commonly used properties for the selected element or expands the Property inspector to show more options. The Property inspector for images contains several image-related features in the top and lower sections.

The following section describes the image-related features of the Property inspector (Figure 2-31 on the next page). The panel groups are hidden to display a full view of the Property inspector.

FIGURE 2-31

W AND H The **W** and **H** boxes indicate the width and height of the image, in pixels. Dreamweaver automatically displays the dimensions when an image is inserted into a page. You can specify the image size in the following units: pc (picas), pt (points), in (inches), mm (millimeters), cm (centimeters), and combinations, such as 2in+5mm. Dreamweaver converts the values to pixels in the HTML source code.

LINK The **Link** box allows you to make the selected image a hyperlink to a specified URL or Web page. To create a link, you can click the Point to File or Browse for File icon to the right of the Link box to browse to a page in your Web site, or drag a file from the site window into the Link box. For an external link, you can type the URL directly into the Link box or use copy and paste.

ALIGN **Align** sets the alignment of an image in relation to other elements in the same paragraph, table, or line. Align is discussed in more detail later in this project.

ALT **Alt** specifies alternative text that appears in place of the image for text-only browsers or for browsers that have been set to download images manually. For visually impaired users who use speech synthesizers with text-only browsers, the text is spoken aloud. In some browsers, this text also appears when the pointer is over the image.

MAP AND HOTSPOT TOOLS Use the **Map** box and the **Hotspot tools** to label and create an image map.

V SPACE AND H SPACE V Space and H Space add space, in pixels, along the sides of the image. **V Space** adds space along the top and bottom of an image. **H Space** adds space along the left and right of an image.

TARGET **Target** specifies the frame or window in which the linked page should load. This option is not available when the image is linked to another file.

LOW SRC **Low Src** specifies the image that should load before the main image. Many designers use a small black-and-white version of the main image because it loads quickly and gives visitors an idea of what they will see.

BORDER **Border** is the width, in pixels, of the image's border. The default is no border.

EDIT **Edit** provides five different editing option tools: (a) **Optimize in Fireworks**, which opens the Macromedia Fireworks image-editing application; (b) **Crop**, which lets you edit images by reducing the area of the image; (c) **Image resampling**, which adds or subtracts pixels from a resized JPEG or GIF image file to match the appearance of the original image as closely as possible; (d) **Brightness/Contrast**, which modifies the contrast or brightness of pixels in an image; and (e) **Sharpening**, which adjusts the focus of an image by increasing the contrast of edges found within the image. Editing tools (b) through (e) do not require an external image-editing application. These editing functions are discussed in more detail later in this project.

RESET SIZE If an image size is changed, **Reset Size** resets the W and H values to the original size of the image.

LEFT, CENTER, AND RIGHT In Dreamweaver, the default alignment for an image is left alignment. To change the default alignment, select the image you want to align. Click an alignment button: Align Center, Align Right, or Justify.

SRC **Src** specifies the source file for the image.

After you insert the image into the Web page and then select it, the Property inspector displays features specific to images. As discussed earlier, alignment is one of these features. **Alignment** determines where on the page the image displays and if and how text wraps around the image.

Aligning an Image

When you insert an image into a Web page, by default, the text around the image aligns to the bottom of the image. The image alignment options on the Align pop-up menu in the Property inspector let you set the alignment for the image in relation to other page content. Dreamweaver provides 10 alignment options for images. Table 2-3 describes these image alignment options.

Table 2-3 Image Alignment Options

ALIGNMENT OPTION	DESCRIPTION
Default	Aligns the image with the baseline of the text in most browser default settings
Baseline	Aligns the image with the baseline of the text regardless of the browser setting
Top	Aligns the image with the top of the item; item can be text or another object
Middle	Aligns the image with the baseline of the text or object at the vertical middle of the image
Bottom	Aligns the image with the baseline of the text or the bottom of another image regardless of the browser setting
Text Top	Aligns the image with the top of the tallest character in a line of text
Absolute Middle	Aligns the image with the middle of the current line of text
Absolute Bottom	Aligns the image with the bottom of the current line of text or another object
Left	Aligns the image at the left margin
Right	Aligns the image at the right margin

As indicated in Table 2-3, the Align pop-up menu contains 10 alignment options. The more widely used options are left, right, and center. The steps on the next page show how to align the alligator image to the right and create text wrapping to the left of the image.

To Align an Image

1

• **If necessary, click the alligator image to select it and then click the Align box arrow in the Property inspector. Point to Right on the pop-up menu.**

The Align pop-up menu is displayed, and Right is highlighted (Figure 2-32).

FIGURE 2-32

2

• **Click Right.**

The image moves to the right side of the window and is highlighted (Figure 2-33). An element marker displays to indicate the location of the insertion point. The element marker is highlighted because the image is selected.

FIGURE 2-33

Adjusting Space around Images

When aligning an image, by default, only about three pixels of space are inserted between the image and adjacent text. You can adjust the amount of vertical and horizontal space between the image and text through the V Space and H Space settings in the Property inspector. The V Space setting controls the vertical space above or below an image. The H Space setting controls the horizontal space to the left or right side of the image. The following step shows how to add vertical and horizontal spacing.

To Adjust the Horizontal and Vertical Space

1

• **Click the image to remove the highlighting.**

• **Click the V Space text box and type** 6 **as the vertical space.**

• **Press the TAB key and type** 12 **as the horizontal space. Press the TAB key.**

Dreamweaver adds additional horizontal and vertical space between the image and the text (Figure 2-34).

FIGURE 2-34

Another feature within the Property inspector is Alt text. For individuals who are visually impaired, the Alt text can be interpreted by their screen readers. Dreamweaver supports two screen readers — JAWS and Window-Eyes.

Specifying the Alt Text

The **Alt** text is short for **Alternative Text** and provides an alternative source of information about the image. The text typed in the Alt box displays as the image is downloading. This text also appears as a ScreenTip as the mouse pointer is moved over the image when it is displayed in some browsers. The step on the next page illustrates how to add Alt text to the alligator image.

More About

Accessibility Issues

For more information about authoring for accessibility, visit the Dreamweaver MX 2004 More About Web page (scsite.com/dreamweavermx04/more) and then click Dreamweaver MX Accessibility Issues.

To Add Alt Text

1

- **If necessary, click the alligator image to select it. Click the Alt box and then type** Florida alligator **as the alternate text.**

- **Press the TAB key.**

The Alt text is entered in the Alt text box (Figure 2-35).

- **If necessary, click the image to deselect the highlighting.**

FIGURE 2-35

To enhance your Web page further, you will add a sailboat image. This image is displayed on the left side of the page, to the left of the bulleted items. The following steps show how to insert an image of a sailboat in the Web page.

To Insert the Sailboat Image

1

- **Scroll down and position the insertion point so it is to the left of the sentence introducing the bulleted list (Figure 2-36).**

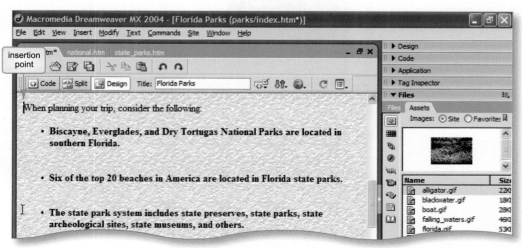

FIGURE 2-36

2

- **Click the boat image in the Assets panel and then drag the boat.gif image to the insertion point.**

The boat image is displayed (Figure 2-37). The border and handles around the image indicate it is selected.

FIGURE 2-37

3

- **Click the Align box arrow and then click Left in the Align pop-up menu.**

The image moves to the left side of the window, and the text adjusts to the right (Figure 2-38). The bullets do not display, and some of the text is hidden by the image. Adjusting the spacing will display the bullets and text.

FIGURE 2-38

4

- **Click the V Space box and type** 6 **as the vertical space.**

- **Click the H Space box and type** 20 **as the horizontal space.**

- **Press the TAB key.**

- **Click anywhere in the Document window to deselect the image.**

Additional horizontal and vertical space is added between the image and the text, and the bullets are displayed (Figure 2-39).

FIGURE 2-39

5

- **Click the image to select it.**

- **Click the Alt box and type** Sailboat **as the alternate text.**

- **Press the ENTER key.**

The Alt text is applied (Figure 2-40).

FIGURE 2-40

6

• **Click the Save button on the Standard toolbar.**

• **Press the F12 key.**

• **Move the mouse point over the alligator and sailboat images to display the Alt text.**

The index page displays in your browser and all changes to the index page are saved (Figure 2-41). Web pages may display differently in your browser. The browser and selected text size affect how a Web page displays. In Figure 2-41, the text size is set to Medium.

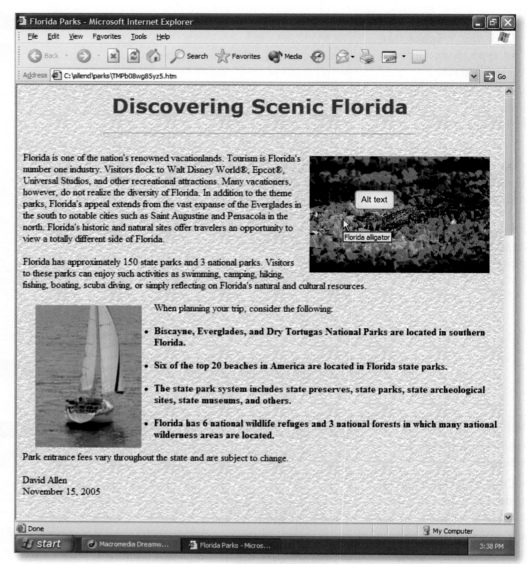

FIGURE 2-41

7

• **Close the browser to return to Dreamweaver.**

The second page in your Web site is the National Parks page. To develop the National Parks page further and add information showing the locations of the three Florida national parks, you will add a Florida map. References to each park are contained on the map. The steps on the next page show how to add the Florida map image to the National Parks Web page.

To Insert and Align an Image in the National Parks Web Page

1

• **Click the national.htm Web page tab.**

• **If necessary, scroll to the top of the page. Position the insertion point between the bullet and the text heading of the second bulleted item (Biscayne National Park).**

The insertion point is positioned to the left of Biscayne National Park and to the right of the bullet (Figure 2-42).

FIGURE 2-42

2

• **Drag the florida.gif file from the Assets panel to the insertion point and then, if necessary, click the image to select it.**

The border and handles around the image indicate it is selected (Figure 2-43). The attributes change in the Property inspector to reflect the selected object.

FIGURE 2-43

3

• **Click the Align box arrow and then click Right.**

The image is aligned to the right in the Document window (Figure 2-44).

FIGURE 2-44

4

• **Click the V Space box and type** 8 **as the vertical space.**

• **Click the H Space box and type** 10 **as the horizontal space.**

• **Click the Alt box and type** Florida Map **as the alternate text.**

• **Press the ENTER key (Figure 2-45).**

FIGURE 2-45

• **Click the Save button on the Standard toolbar.**

The Florida National Parks Web page is saved.

• **Press the F12 key.**

The Florida National Parks Web page is displayed in the browser (Figure 2-46).

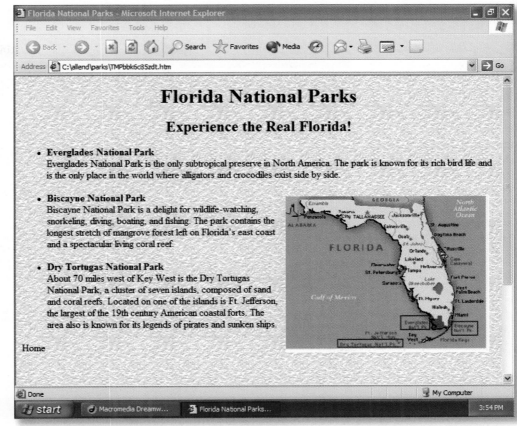

• **Close the browser to return to Dreamweaver.**

FIGURE 2-46

The third page in your Web site is the Florida State Parks page. To add interest to this page, you will add three images. You will align two of the images to the left and one to the right. The steps on the next page illustrate how to add the images to the Florida State Parks Web page.

To Insert and Align Images in the State Parks Web Page

1

• **Click the state_parks. htm Web page tab.**

• **If necessary, scroll to the top of the document. Position the insertion point to the left of Blackwater River State Park.**

The insertion point is to the left of Blackwater River State Park (Figure 2-47).

FIGURE 2-47

2

• **Drag the blackwater.gif file from the Assets panel to the insertion point.**

• **If necessary, click the image to select it and then click the Align box arrow in the Property inspector.**

• **Click Left on the Align pop-up menu.**

The image aligns to the left (Figure 2-48).

FIGURE 2-48

3

• **Click the V Space box and then type** 8 **as the vertical space.**

• **Click the H Space box and then type** 10 **as the horizontal space.**

• **Click the Alt box, type** Blackwater River State Park **as the alternate text, and then press the** ENTER **key.**

The image is highlighted. The Alt text, V Space, and H Space attributes are added for the Blackwater image (Figure 2-49).

FIGURE 2-49

4

• **If necessary, scroll down and then position the insertion point to the right of the word, park, in the last line in the Ponce de Leon Spring State Park paragraph.**

The insertion point is to the right of the last sentence in the third paragraph (Figure 2-50).

FIGURE 2-50

5

• **Drag the poncedeleon. gif image to the insertion point and then, if necessary, select the image.**

The image is selected (Figure 2-51).

FIGURE 2-51

6

• **Click the Align box arrow and then click Right on the Align pop-up menu.**

The poncedeleon.gif image moves to the right side of the window (Figure 2-52).

FIGURE 2-52

7

• **Click the V Space box and then type** 6 **as the vertical space.**

• **Click the H Space box and then type** 12 **as the horizontal space.**

• **Click the Alt box, type** Ponce de Leon Spring State Park **as the alternate text, and then press the ENTER key.**

The image is positioned on the page (Figure 2-53).

FIGURE 2-53

8

• **Position the insertion point to the left of the words, Falling Waters State Park.**

• **Drag the falling_waters. gif image from the Assets panel to the insertion point and then, if necessary, select the image.**

The Falling Waters image is inserted on the page (Figure 2-54).

FIGURE 2-54

9

- **Click the Align box arrow and then click Left on the Align pop-up menu.**

- **Click the V Space box and then type 8 as the vertical space.**

- **Click the H Space box and then type 12 as the horizontal space.**

- **Click the Alt box, type** Falling Waters State Park **as the alternate text, and then press the ENTER key.**

- **Click anywhere on the page to deselect the image.**

- **Click the Save button on the Standard toolbar.**

The image is positioned on the page and the Web page is saved (Figure 2-55).

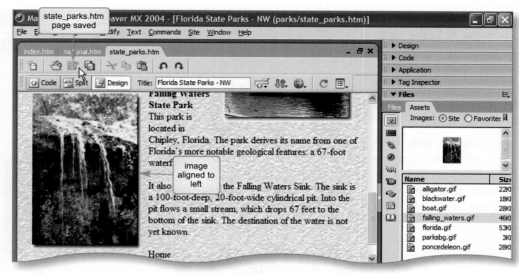

FIGURE 2-55

10

- **Press the F12 key.**

The State Parks page is displayed in the browser (Figure 2-56).

11

- **Close the browser.**

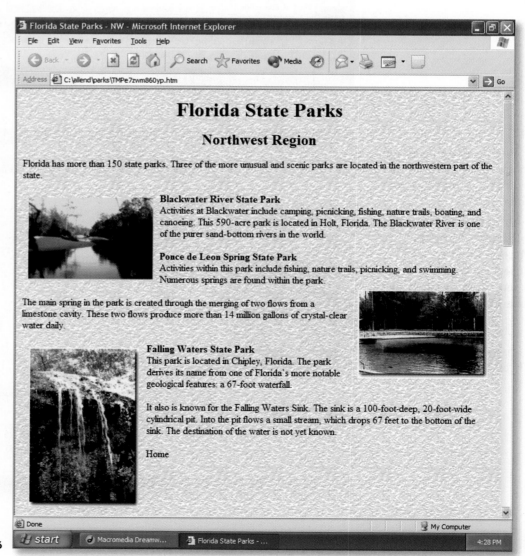

FIGURE 2-56

Image Editing Tools

Dreamweaver makes available several basic image editing tools to modify and enhance an image. You access these functions through the Property inspector.

- Use an external image editor: Macromedia's Fireworks is the default image editor, but you can specify which external editor should start for a specified file type. To select an external editor, click Edit on the menu bar and display the Preferences dialog box. Select File Types/Editors from the Category list to display the Preferences File Types/Editors dialog box. Select the image extension and then browse for the External Code Editor executable file.

- Crop an image: **Cropping** lets you edit an image by reducing the area of the image and allows you to eliminate unwanted or distracting portions of the image. Cropping can be very effective for improving the appearance of a photo by highlighting the main point of interest in an image. When you crop an image and then save the page, the source image file is changed on the disk. To return the image to its original size, click the Undo button on the Standard toolbar. Prior to saving, you may want to keep a backup copy of the image file in the event you need to revert to the original image.

- Brightness/Contrast: The **Brightness/Contrast** tool modifies the contrast or brightness of the pixels in an image. Recall that a pixel is the smallest point in a graphical image. Brightness makes the image lighter or darker overall, while Contrast either emphasizes or de-emphasizes the difference between lighter and darker regions. This affects the highlights, shadows, and midtones of an image. The values for the brightness and contrast settings range from -100 to 100.

- Resampling: The process of **resampling** adds or subtracts pixels from a resized JPEG or GIF image file to match the appearance of the original image as closely as possible. Resampling an image also reduces an image's file size, resulting in improved download performance. When you resize an image in Dreamweaver, you can resample it to accommodate its new dimensions. To resample a resized image, resize the image as previously described and then click the Resample button in the Property inspector.

- Sharpening: **Sharpening** adjusts the focus of an image by increasing the contrast of edges found within the image. The Sharpening icon is hidden when the Panel groups are displayed.

The Falling Waters image in the Florida State Parks page extends somewhat below the last line of the text. Cropping the image and emphasizing the waterfall in the image would enhance the page. The following steps show how to crop the image, and then modify the brightness/contrast.

To Crop and Modify Brightness/Contrast of an Image

1

• **If necessary, select the falling waters image.**

• **Click the Crop Tool icon in the Property inspector. If a Dreamweaver MX 2004 caution dialog box displays, click the OK button.**

A bounding box with crop handles appears around the selected image (Figure 2-57).

FIGURE 2-57

2

• **Click the crop handle in the lower-right corner and adjust the handles until the bounding box surrounds the area of the image similar to that shown in Figure 2-58.**

The area of the image to retain is selected (Figure 2-58).

FIGURE 2-58

3

- **Double-click inside the bounding box.**
- **Click the image.**

The image is cropped and selected (Figure 2-59). If you need to make changes, click the Undo button on the Standard toolbar and repeat steps 1 and 2.

FIGURE 2-59

4

- **Click the Brightness and Contrast tool. If a Dreamweaver MX 2004 caution dialog box displays, click the OK button.**

The Brightness/Contrast dialog box displays (Figure 2-60).

FIGURE 2-60

5

• **Drag the Brightness slider to the left and adjust the setting to -10.**

• **Drag the Contrast slider to the right and adjust the setting to 20.**

The brightness and contrast are changed in the image (Figure 2-61).

FIGURE 2-61

6

• **Click the OK button.**

• **Click the Save button on the Standard toolbar.**

The State Parks page is saved.

• **Press the F12 key to view the cropped image in your browser.**

The Florida State Parks page is displayed in your browser (Figure 2-62).

7

• **Close the browser to return to the Dreamweaver window.**

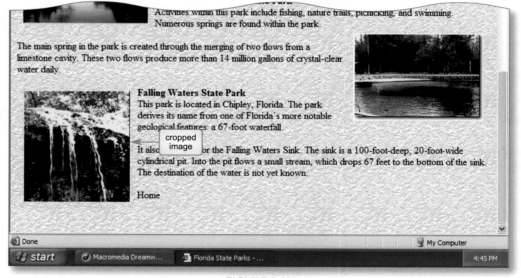

FIGURE 2-62

To connect the pages within the Web site and to display the navigation structure of the pages in the Site Map, you create links. The next section discusses the different types of links.

Understanding Different Types of Links

Links are the distinguishing feature of the World Wide Web. A link, also referred to as a hyperlink, is the path to another document, to another part of the same document, or to other media such as an image or a movie. Most links display as colored and/or underlined text, although you also can link from an image or other object. Clicking a link accesses the corresponding document, other media, or another place within the same document. If you place the mouse pointer over the link, the Web address of the link, or path, usually appears at the bottom of the window, on the status bar.

Three types of link paths are available: absolute, relative, and root-relative. An **absolute link** provides the complete URL of the document. This type of link also is referred to as an **external link**. Absolute links generally contain a protocol (such as http://) and primarily are used to link to documents on other servers.

You use **relative links** for local links. This type of link also is referred to as a **document-relative link**, or an **internal link**. If the linked documents are in the same folder, such as those in your parks folder, this is the best type of link to use. You also can use a relative link to link to a document in another folder, such as the images folder. All the files you see in the Files panel Local View are internal files and are referenced as relative links. You accomplish this by specifying the path through the folder hierarchy from the current document to the linked document. Consider the following examples.

- To link to another file in the same folder, specify the file name. Example: everglades.htm.
- To link to a file in a subfolder of the current Web site folder (such as the images folder), the link path would consist of the name of the subfolder, a forward slash (/), and then the file name. Example: images/gator.jpg.

You use the **root-relative link** primarily when working with a large Web site that requires several servers. Web developers generally use this type of link when they must move HTML files from one folder or server to another folder or server. Root-relative links are beyond the scope of this book.

Two other types of links are named anchor and e-mail links. A **named anchor** lets the user link to a specific location within a document. To create a named anchor, click the Named Anchor command on the Insert menu. An **e-mail link** creates a blank e-mail message containing the recipient's address. Another type of link is a **null**, or **script, link**. This type of link provides for attaching behaviors to an object or executes JavaScript code.

Named Anchor

To create a named anchor, place the insertion point where you want the named anchor. Then click the Named Anchor command on the Insert menu. Type a name for the anchor in the Named Anchor text box.

Relative Links

Another Dreamweaver feature is the variety of ways in which to create a relative link. Three of the more commonly used methods are point to file, drag-and-drop, and browse for file. The point to file and drag-and-drop methods require that the Property inspector and the Files or Assets panels be open. To use the **point to file method**, you drag the Point to File icon to the image in the Files or Assets panel. In the **drag-and-drop method**, you drag the file from the Files or Assets panel to the Link text box in the Property inspector. The **browse for file method** is accomplished through the Select File dialog box. A fourth method is to use the context menu. Select the text for the link, right-click to display the context menu, and then select the Link command.

The next step is to add the text to create the relative links from the home page to the National and State Parks pages. You use the drag-and-drop method to create a relative link from the text to a specific Web page.

More About

Undo Cropping

You can undo the effect of the Crop command and revert to the original image file up until the time that you quit Dreamweaver or edit the file in an external image-editing application. To undo the effects, click Edit on the menu bar and then click the Undo Crop command.

Adding Text for the Relative Links

To create relative links from the index page, you add text to the index page and use the text to create the links to the other two Web pages in your Web site. You will center the text directly below the Discovering Scenic Florida heading. The following steps show how to add the text for the links.

To Add Text for Relative Links

1

• **Click the Files panel tab.**

• **Click the index.htm tab in the Document window. If necessary, scroll to the top of the page and then position the insertion point at the end of the title, Discovering Scenic Florida.**

• **Press the ENTER key.**

• **If necessary, click the Text Color hexadecimal box, select the hexadecimal number, press the DELETE key, and then press the ENTER key.**

The insertion point is centered below the title, and the text color is returned to the default. The Files panel displays (Figure 2-63).

FIGURE 2-63

2

• **Type** National Parks **and then press the SPACEBAR.**

The text for the first link, National Parks, is displayed in the Document window (Figure 2-64).

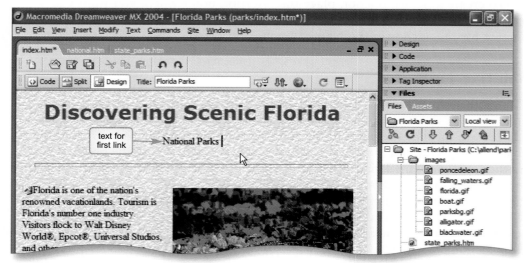

FIGURE 2-64

3

• **Hold down the SHIFT key and then press the vertical line key (|). Press the SPACEBAR and then type** State Parks **as the second link.**

The text for both links is displayed in the Document window (Figure 2-65).

FIGURE 2-65

You will use the text, National Parks, to create a link to the National Parks Web page and the text, State Parks, to create a link to the State Parks page.

Creating a Relative Link Using Drag-and-Drop

A relative link is used to create links between local files or files within one Web site. The drag-and-drop method requires that the Property inspector be displayed and that the site files display in the Files or Assets panel. When you view Dreamweaver with an 800 × 600 resolution, the panel groups hide a portion of the Property inspector. You still can use the drag-and-drop method, however, because the Link text box remains visible in the Property inspector.

The following steps illustrate how to use the drag-and-drop method to create a relative link from the Florida Parks home page to the National Parks Web page.

To Create a Relative Link Using Drag-and-Drop

1

• **Drag to select the text, National Parks.**

The National Parks text is highlighted (Figure 2-66).

FIGURE 2-66

2

• **Drag the national.htm file from the Files panel to the Link box in the Property inspector. Do not release the mouse button.**

When you start to drag, a circle icon with a diagonal line through it displays next to the mouse pointer (Figure 2-67).

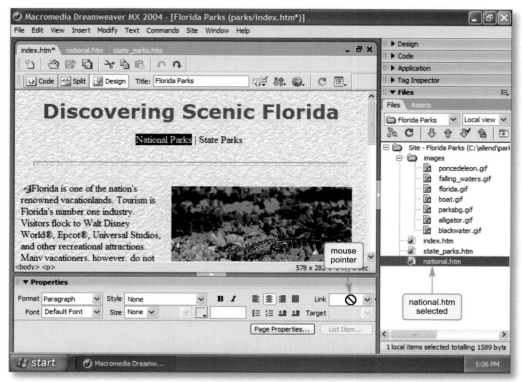

FIGURE 2-67

3

• **Release the mouse button. Click National Parks to display the linked text.**

The linked text displays underlined and in a different color in the Document window, and the link text displays in the Link box (Figure 2-68). If you click anywhere else in the document, the linked document name does not display in the Link box.

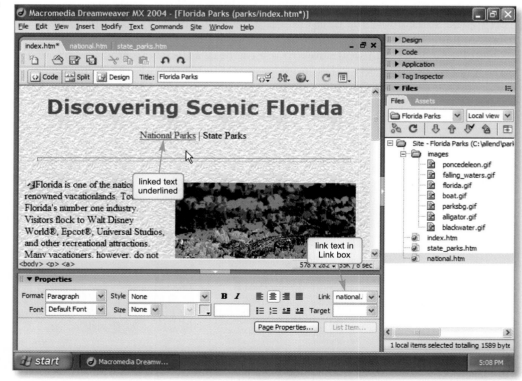

FIGURE 2-68

Creating a Relative Link Using the Context Menu

The context menu is a second way to create a link. Using this method, you select the file name in the Select File dialog box. The following steps illustrate how to use the context menu to create a link to the State Parks page.

To Create a Relative Link Using the Context Menu

1

• **Drag to select the text, State Parks, and right-click to display the context menu. Point to Make Link.**

The text, State Parks, is highlighted, and the context menu is displayed. The Make Link command is highlighted (Figure 2-69).

FIGURE 2-69

2

• **Click the Make Link command and click state_parks.**

The Select File dialog box is displayed and state_parks is highlighted (Figure 2-70).

FIGURE 2-70

3

• **Click the OK button and then click the selected text, State Parks, to display the link.**

• **Click the Save button on the Standard toolbar.**

The linked text displays underlined and in a different color in the Document window, and the link text displays in the Link box (Figure 2-71). If you click anywhere else in the document, the linked document name does not display in the Link box.

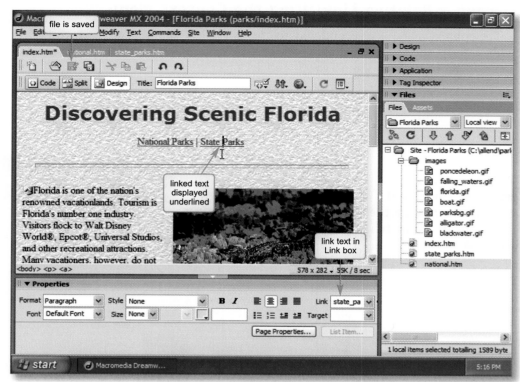

FIGURE 2-71

4

• **Press the F12 key to view the index page in your browser.**

• **Click the National Parks link and then click the browser Back button.**

• **Click the State Parks link.**

• **Close the browser.**

Other Ways

1. Click Link box, type file name
2. Click Point to File icon in Property inspector, drag to file name

Creating a Relative Link to the Home Page

Visitors can enter a Web site at any point, so it is important always to include a link from each page within the site back to the home page. You, therefore, create a relative link to the home page from the National Parks page and from the State Parks page. The following steps show how to create a link from the National Parks page and a link from the State Parks page to the home page.

To Create a Relative Link to the Home Page

1

- **Click the national.htm tab and then scroll to the bottom of the page. Drag to select Home.**

The text, Home, is highlighted (Figure 2-72). This text will become a link.

FIGURE 2-72

2

- **Drag the index.htm file name from the Files panel to the Link box.**
- **Click the text, Home, to display the link.**
- **Click the Save button on the Standard toolbar.**

The link is created (Figure 2-73). The National Parks page is saved.

3

- **Press the F12 key to view the National Parks page in your browser.**
- **Click the Home link.**

The index page displays in the browser.

FIGURE 2-73

4

• **Close the browser.**

The browser is closed, and Dreamweaver displays.

5

• **Click the state_parks. htm tab. If necessary, scroll to the end of the document and then drag to select the text, Home (Figure 2-74).**

FIGURE 2-74

6

• **Drag the index.htm file name from the Files panel to the Link box.**

• **Click the text, Home, to display the link.**

• **Click the Save button on the Standard toolbar.**

The link is created, and index.htm displays in the Link box (Figure 2-75). The State Parks page is saved.

7

• **Press the F12 key to view the State Parks page in your browser.**

• **Click the Home link to verify that it works.**

• **Close the browser.**

FIGURE 2-75

Creating an Absolute Link

Recall that an absolute link (also called an external link) contains the complete Web site address of a document. You create absolute links the same way you create relative links — select the text and drag or type the Web site address. You now will create three absolute links in the State Parks page. These links are from the name of each of the three parks to a Web page about the selected park. The following steps show how to create the three absolute links. Keep in mind that Web site addresses change. If the absolute links do not work, check the Dreamweaver MX 2004 companion site at http://www.scsite.com/dreamweavermx04/ for updates.

To Create an Absolute Link

1 If necessary, scroll to the top of the page. Drag to select the text, **Blackwater River State Park.**

2 Click the Link box and then type `http://www.floridastateparks.org/blackwaterriver/` **as the link.**

3 Drag to select the text, **Ponce de Leon Spring State Park.** Click the Link box and then type `http://www.floridastateparks.org/poncedeleonsprings/` as the link.

4 If necessary, scroll down and then drag to select the text, **Falling Waters State Park.** Click the Link box and then type `http://www.floridastateparks.org/fallingwaters/` **as the link.**

5 Click the Save button on the Standard toolbar.

6 Press the F12 key and then click each link to verify that they work. Click the browser Back button after clicking each link.

The three absolute links to the respective state parks pages are added (Figure 2-76), and the Web page is saved.

7 Close the browser.

FIGURE 2-76

Other Ways

1. Start browser, open Web page, select URL, copy URL, close browser, paste in Link box

E-Mail Links

An **e-mail link** is one of the foundation elements of any successful Web site. It is important for visitors to be able to contact you for additional information or to comment on the Web page or Web site. When visitors click an e-mail link, their default e-mail program opens to a new e-mail message. The e-mail address you specify is inserted automatically in the To box.

Creating an E-Mail Link

The following steps show how to create an e-mail link for your home page using your name as the linked text. You do this through the Insert menu.

To Add an E-Mail Link

1

• **Click the index.htm tab, scroll down, and then drag to select your name. Click Insert on the menu bar and then point to Email Link.**

In this figure, David Allen is highlighted, and the Insert menu is displayed (Figure 2-77). Your name should be highlighted on your screen.

FIGURE 2-77

Dreamweaver Project 2

2

• **Click Email Link.**

The Email Link dialog box is displayed. In this figure, David Allen is highlighted in the Text text box (Figure 2-78). On your computer, your name is displayed in the Text text box.

FIGURE 2-78

3

• **Click the E-Mail text box and then type your e-mail address.**

In this figure, the e-mail address for David Allen is displayed in the E-Mail text box (Figure 2-79). On your computer, Dreamweaver displays your e-mail address.

FIGURE 2-79

4

• **Click the OK button.**

• **Click the expand/ collapse arrow on the vertical bar to hide the panel groups.**

• **Click anywhere in the highlighted text your name.**

• **Click the Save button on the Standard toolbar.**

The selected text for the e-mail link, David Allen, is displayed as linked text and the index page is saved. The Link box displays the e-mail address (Figure 2-80). On your computer, Dreamweaver displays your name as the linked text.

FIGURE 2-80

5

• **Press the F12 key to view the page in your browser. Click your name.**

Your e-mail program opens with your e-mail address in the To text box.

6

• **Close your e-mail program and then close the browser.**

Changing the Color of Links

The Page Properties dialog box provides three options for link colors: Link (the link has not been clicked), Active Link (the link changes color when the user clicks it), and Visited Link (the link has been visited). The default color for the three options is black. It is easy to make changes to these default settings and select colors that complement the background and other colors you are using on your Web pages. This is accomplished through the Page Properties dialog box. You display the Page Properties dialog box by clicking Modify on the menu bar. You then can click the box that corresponds to one of the three types of links and select a color to match your color scheme.

Editing and Deleting Links

Web development is a never-ending process. At some point, it will be necessary to edit or delete a link. For instance, an e-mail address may change, a URL to an external link may change, or an existing link may contain an error.

Dreamweaver makes it easy to edit or delete a link. First, select the link or click within the link you want to change. The linked document name displays in the Link box in the Property inspector. To delete the link without deleting the text on the Web page, delete the text from the Link box in the Property inspector. To edit the link, make the change in the Link box.

A second method to edit or delete a link is to use the context menu. Right-click within the link you want to change and then click Remove Link on the context menu to eliminate the link; click Change Link on the context menu to edit the link. Clicking the URLs icon in the Assets panel displays a list of all absolute and e-mail links within the Web site.

The Site Map

Earlier in this project, you set the index page as the home page. Dreamweaver provides a visual site map for viewing the relationships among files. The **Site Map** is a graphical representation of the structure of a Web site. You visually can design and modify the Web site structure through the Site Map. The home page displays at the top level of the map, and linked pages display at the lower levels. The Site Map view allows you to create, change, display, save, and print a Web site's structure and navigation. As previously discussed, a Web site's structure is the relationships among the pages in the Web site.

Viewing the Site Map

The home page now contains links to other pages in the site, and each page in the site contains links back to the home page. The State Parks page contains a link to three external Web sites, which are outside of the local site and located on a different server.

You created links from the home page to the two other pages in the Web site (National Parks and State Parks) and links from these two pages back to the home page. You can use the Site Map to view a graphical image of these links. In addition to allowing you to view the Site Map, Dreamweaver also has an option that lets you view your file list and Site Map simultaneously.

Displaying the Site Map and Local Files

The Site Map shows the pages as icons and displays links in the order in which they are encountered in the HTML source code. Starting from the home page, the Site Map default displays the site structure two levels deep. The relative links have a plus sign to their left. If you click the plus (+) sign, pages below the second level display. Some pages have a minus sign to their left. If you click the minus (−) sign, pages linked below the second level are hidden. Text displayed in blue and marked with a globe icon indicates a file on another site or a special link such as an e-mail link. Text displayed in red indicates a broken link. You access the Site Map through the Files panel. The following steps show how to display the site map with the newly created links among the pages in the Florida Parks Web site.

To Display the Site Map and Local Files List

1

• **If necessary, click the index.htm tab.**

• **Click the expand/ collapse arrow on the panel groups vertical bar to display the Files panel.**

• **Click the View box arrow and then point to Map view in the View pop-up menu (Figure 2-81).**

FIGURE 2-81

2

• **Click Map view and then point to the Expand/Collapse button on the Files panel toolbar.**

Dreamweaver displays a graphical view of the Web site in the Files panel, including all links from the index page (Figure 2-82).

FIGURE 2-82

3

• **Click the Expand/ Collapse button. Point to the plus sign to the left of the national.htm icon.**

The Site Map expands and displays a graphical structure of the links between the index page and the other two pages and external links (Figure 2-83). The plus signs to the left of the national.htm and state_parks.htm pages indicate that additional files or links are below these pages.

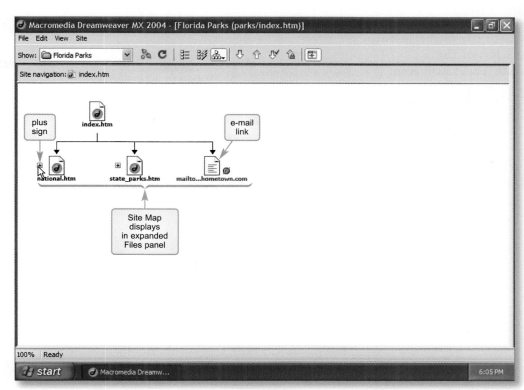

FIGURE 2-83

4

• **Click the plus sign to the left of the national.htm icon.**

The structure further expands and displays the relative link to the index page from the national.htm page (Figure 2-84).

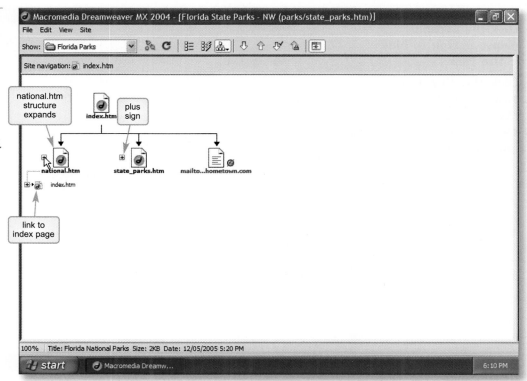

FIGURE 2-84

5

• **Click the plus sign to the left of the state_parks.htm icon.**

The structure further expands and displays the relative link to the index page from the State Parks page and the absolute (external) links to the three state parks (Figure 2-85).

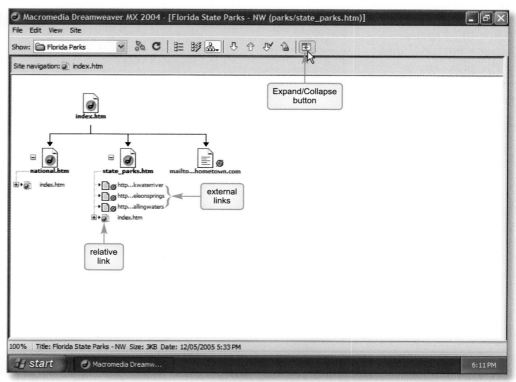

FIGURE 2-85

6

• **Click the Expand/ Collapse button to hide the Site Map.**

• **Click the View box arrow and then point to Local view in the View pop-up menu (Figure 2-86).**

FIGURE 2-86

7

• **Click Local view.**

The Site - Florida Parks file hierarchy displays (Figure 2-87).

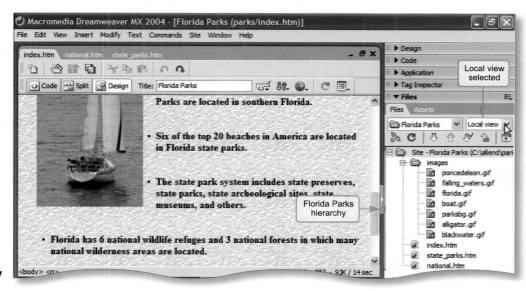

FIGURE 2-87

HTML Code View

Dreamweaver provides two views, or ways, to look at a document: **Design view** and **Code view**. Thus far, you have been working in Design view. As you create and work with documents, Dreamweaver automatically generates the underlying HTML code. Recall that the HTML code defines the structure and layout of a Web document by using a variety of tags and attributes. Even though Dreamweaver generates the code, occasions occur that necessitate the tweaking or modifying of code.

Dreamweaver provides several options for viewing and working with HTML code. You can split the Document window so that it displays both the Code view and the Design view. You can display only the Code view in the Document window, or you can open the Code inspector. The **Code inspector** opens in a separate window, so you can keep the whole Document window reserved for Design view.

Using Code View and Design View

In Split view, you work in a split-screen environment. You can see the design and the code at the same time. Splitting the Document window to view the code makes it easier to view the visual design while you make changes in the HTML code. When you make a change in Design view, the HTML code also is changed but is not visible in the Document window. You can set word wrapping, display line numbers for the code, highlight invalid HTML code, set syntax coloring for code elements, and set indenting through the View menu's Code View Options submenu. Viewing the code at this early stage may not seem important, but the more code you learn, the more productive you will become.

Within the HTML code, tags can be entered in uppercase, lowercase, or a combination of upper- and lowercase. The case of the tags has no effect on how the browser displays the output. When you view the code in Code view in Dreamweaver, some HTML tags display in lowercase letters and some attributes in uppercase letters. This is the Dreamweaver default.

In this book, when describing HTML tags, we use lowercase letters for tags and attributes to make it easier to differentiate them from the other text.

The following steps show how to use the Code View and Design View option to look at the code for the
 (line break) and <p> (paragraph) tags. The paragraph tag has an opening tag, <p>, and a closing tag, </p>. The
 (line break) tag does not have a closing tag.

To View Design View and Code View Simultaneously

1

• **Click the state_parks. htm tab.**

• **Hide the Files panel and collapse the Property inspector.**

• **Position the insertion point to the left of the heading, Florida State Parks. Point to the Split button on the Document toolbar (Figure 2-88).**

FIGURE 2-88

2

• **Click the Split button. If necessary, click the View menu, point to Code View Options, and then click Line Numbers.**

The window splits. The upper window displays Code view and the lower window displays Design view (Figure 2-89). The insertion point is displayed in Code view in the same location as in Design view (to the left of the heading). The lines are numbered in Code view. The HTML code is displayed in color and in lowercase surrounded by < (less than) and > (greater than) symbols. Your window may display Design view in the upper window and Code view in the lower window.

FIGURE 2-89

3

• **Click the Design button.**

The Design view displays.

Modifying HTML Code

One of the more common problems within Dreamweaver and the HTML code relates to line breaks and paragraphs. Occasionally, you inadvertently press the ENTER key or insert a line break and need to remove the tag. Or, you may copy and paste or open a text file that contains unneeded paragraphs or line breaks.

Pressing the BACKSPACE key or DELETE key may return you to the previous line, but does not always delete the line break or paragraph tag within the HTML code. The deletion of these tags is determined by the position of the insertion point when you press the BACKSPACE or DELETE keys. If the insertion point is still inside the HTML code, pressing the BACKSPACE key will not delete these tags and your page will not display correctly. When this occurs, the best solution is to delete the tag through Code view.

Quitting Dreamweaver

After you add pages to your Web site, including images and links, and then verify links using the Site Map, Project 2 is complete. The next step shows how to close the Web site, quit Dreamweaver MX 2004, and return control to Windows.

To Close the Web Site and Quit Dreamweaver

1 **Click the Close button on the right corner of the Dreamweaver title bar.**

The Dreamweaver window, the Document window, and the Florida Parks Web site all close. If you have unsaved changes, Dreamweaver will prompt you to save the changes. Clicking the Yes button in the Dreamweaver MX 2004 dialog box saves the changes.

Project Summary

Project 2 introduced you to images, links, the Site Map, and how to view HTML code. You began the project by using the Windows My Computer option to copy data files to the local site. You added two new pages, one for Florida national parks and one for Florida state parks, to the Web site you created in Project 1. Next, you added page images to the index page. Following that, you added a background image and page images to the National and State Parks pages. Then, you added relative links to all three pages. You added an e-mail link to the home page and absolute links to the State Parks page. You also learned to use the Site Map. Finally, you learned how to view HTML code.

What You Should Know

Having completed this project, you should be able to perform the tasks below. The tasks are listed in the same order they were presented in this project. For a list of keyboard commands for topics introduced in this project, see the Quick Reference for Windows at the back of this book and refer to the Shortcut column.

1. Copy Data Files to the Parks Web Site (DW 120)
2. Start Dreamweaver and Open the Parks Web Site (DW 121)
3. Open a Web Page from a Local Web Site (DW 122)
4. Set a Home Page (DW 124)
5. Open a New Document Window (DW 125)
6. Prepare the Workspace (DW 128)
7. Create the National Parks Web Page (DW 129)
8. Format the Florida National Parks Page (DW 130)
9. Open a New Document Window (DW 131)
10. Create the State Parks Web Page (DW 132)

Learn It Online

Instructions: To complete the Learn It Online exercises, start your browser, click the Address bar, and then enter the Web address scsite.com/dreamweavermx2004/learn. When the Dreamweaver MX 2004 Learn It Online page is displayed, follow the instructions in the exercises below. Each exercise has instructions for printing your results, either for your own records or for submission to your instructor.

1 Project Reinforcement TF, MC, and SA

Below Dreamweaver Project 2, click the Project Reinforcement link. Print the quiz by clicking Print on the File menu for each page. Answer each question.

2 Flash Cards

Below Dreamweaver Project 2, click the Flash Cards link and read the instructions. Type 20 (or a number specified by your instructor) in the Number of playing cards text box, type your name in the Enter your Name text box, and then click the Flip Card button. When the flash card is displayed, read the question and then click the ANSWER box arrow to select an answer. Flip through Flash Cards. If your score is 15 (75%) correct or greater, click Print on the File menu to print your results. If your score is less than 15 (75%) correct, then redo this exercise by clicking the Replay button.

3 Practice Test

Below Dreamweaver Project 2, click the Practice Test link. Answer each question, enter your first and last name at the bottom of the page, and then click the Grade Test button. When the graded practice test is displayed on your screen, click Print on the File menu to print a hard copy. Continue to take practice tests until you score 80% or better.

4 Who Wants To Be a Computer Genius?

Below Dreamweaver Project 2, click the Computer Genius link. Read the instructions, enter your first and last name at the bottom of the page, and then click the PLAY button. When your score is displayed, click the PRINT RESULTS link to print a hard copy.

5 Wheel of Terms

Below Dreamweaver Project 2, click the Wheel of Terms link. Read the instructions, and then enter your first and last name and your school name. Click the PLAY button. When your score is displayed, right-click the score and then click Print on the shortcut menu to print a hard copy.

6 Crossword Puzzle Challenge

Below Dreamweaver Project 2, click the Crossword Puzzle Challenge link. Read the instructions, and then enter your first and last name. Click the SUBMIT button. Work the crossword puzzle. When you are finished, click the Submit button. When the crossword puzzle is redisplayed, click the Print Puzzle button to print a hard copy.

7 Tips and Tricks

Below Dreamweaver Project 2, click the Tips and Tricks link. Click a topic that pertains to Project 2. Right-click the information and then click Print on the shortcut menu. Construct a brief example of what the information relates to in Dreamweaver to confirm you understand how to use the tip or trick.

8 Newsgroups

Below Dreamweaver Project 2, click the Newsgroups link. Click a topic that pertains to Project 2. Print three comments.

9 Expanding Your Horizons

Below Dreamweaver Project 2, click the Expanding Your Horizons link. Click a topic that pertains to Project 2. Print the information. Construct a brief example of what the information relates to in Dreamweaver to confirm you understand the contents of the article.

10 Search Sleuth

Below Dreamweaver Project 2, click the Search Sleuth link. To search for a term that pertains to this project, select a term below the Project 2 title and then use the Google search engine at google.com (or any major search engine) to display and print two Web pages that present information on the term.

Apply Your Knowledge

1 Modifying the B & B Lawn Service Web Site

Instructions: Start Dreamweaver. Data and image files for the B & B Lawn Service Web site are included on the Data Disk. See the inside back cover of this book for instructions for downloading the Data Disk or see your instructor for information on accessing the files in this book.

You add three new pages to the B & B Lawn Service Web site: a services page, an employment page, and a references page. In this exercise, you add relative and absolute links to each page. You also add a background image to the new pages. Next, you insert images on all pages and use the settings in Table 2-4 on page DW 186 to align the images and enter the Alt text. You then add an e-mail link to the home page and relative links from the three new pages to the home page. The pages for the Web site are shown in Figures 2-90a through 2-90d on pages DW 184 through DW 186.

Software and hardware settings determine how a Web page is displayed in a browser. Your Web pages may display differently in your browser than those in the figures do.

(a) Lawn Services Index (Home) Page

FIGURE 2-90 (*continued*)

Apply Your Knowledge

(b) Lawn Services –
Services Page

(c) Lawn Services – Employment Opportunities Pages

FIGURE 2-90 (continued)

(continued)

Apply Your Knowledge

Modifying the B & B Lawn Service Web Site *(continued)*

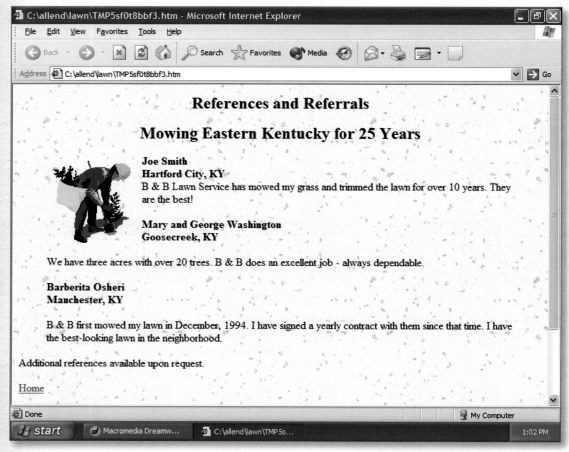

(d) References and Referrals Page

FIGURE 2-90 (*continued*)

Table 2-4 Image Property Settings for the B & B Lawn Service Web Site						
IMAGE NAME	W	H	V SPACE	H SPACE	ALIGN	ALT
trimming2.gif	174	193	6	6	Right	Tree trimming
shovel.gif	124	166	6	8	Left	Shovel
mowing.gif	120	135	None	20	Left	Grass mowing
shakehands.gif	200	170	None	150	Right	Shaking hands
planting.gif	186	165	6	None	Right	Tree planting
planting2.gif	122	125	8	8	Left	Tree planting

Apply Your Knowledge

Perform the following tasks:

1. Use the Windows My Computer option to copy the data files and images to your lawn folder.
2. If necessary, display the panel groups. Select Lawn Service on the Files pop-up menu in the Files panel. Double-click the index.htm file in the Files panel. If necessary, click the expander arrow to expand the Property inspector. If necessary, display the Standard toolbar.
3. Click index.htm in the Files panel to select it. Right-click index.htm and then click Set as Home Page on the context menu.
4. Position the insertion point to the left of the first line of the first paragraph. Drag the trimming2.gif image to the insertion point and then select the image. Apply the settings in Table 2-4 on the previous page to align the image and enter the Alt text. If necessary, scroll down. Position the insertion point to the left of the last sentence on the Web page. Drag the shovel.gif image to the insertion point and then select the image. Apply the settings in Table 2-4.
5. If necessary, scroll up. Select Services (the first bulleted item heading). Use the drag-and-drop file method to create a link to the Services page. Repeat this process to add links from Employment Opportunities and References (the second and third bulleted item headings) to their respective Web pages. Select your name. Use the Insert menu to create an e-mail link using your name. Save the index page (Figure 2-90a on page DW 184).
6. Open services.htm. Click Modify on the menu bar and click Page Properties. Click the Background image Browse button to add the background image (lawnbg.gif) to the services.htm page.
7. Position the insertion point to the left of the page heading, drag the mowing.gif image to the insertion point, and then select the image. Apply the settings in Table 2-4 and then click the Resample button. Position the insertion point to the right of the first bulleted item and then drag the shakehands.gif image to the insertion point. Select the image. Apply the settings in Table 2-4.
8. If necessary, scroll down. Select Home and then create a relative link to the index page. Title the page B&B Lawn Service - Services. Save the Services page (Figure 2-90b on page DW 185).
9. Open employment.htm. Add the background image to the employment.htm page as you did in Step 6 to the services.htm page.
10. Position the insertion point to the right of the heading and then drag the planting.gif image to the insertion point. Select the image. Apply the settings in Table 2-4.
11. Scroll to the bottom of the page. Select the words —To contact us, click here!. Use the Insert menu to create an e-mail link using your e-mail address. Select Home at the bottom of the page and then drag index.htm to the Link box in the Property inspector to create a relative link to the index.htm file. Title the page B&B Lawn Service - Employment. Save the Employment page (Figure 2-90c on page DW 185).
12. Open references.htm. Apply the same background image you applied to the other pages in this Web site.
13. Create a link from Home to the index page.
14. Position the insertion point to the left of the text, Joe Smith. Drag the planting2.gif image to the insertion point. Select the image. Apply the settings in Table 2-4. Title the page B & B Lawn Service - References. Save the References page (Figure 2-90d on the previous page).
15. View the Web site in your browser. Check each link to verify that it works. Print a copy of each page if required and hand the copies in to your instructor. Close the browser. Quit Dreamweaver.

1 Modifying the CandleDust Web Site

Problem: Mary Stewart, for whom you created the CandleDust Web site and Web page, is very pleased with the response she has received. She has asked you to create a second page with links and images added to the index page. Mary wants the new page to include information about her company's history. The revised Web site is shown in Figures 2-91a and 2-91b. Table 2-5 on the next page includes the settings and Alt text for the images. Software and hardware settings determine how a Web page displays in a browser. Your Web pages may display differently in your browser than those in the figures do.

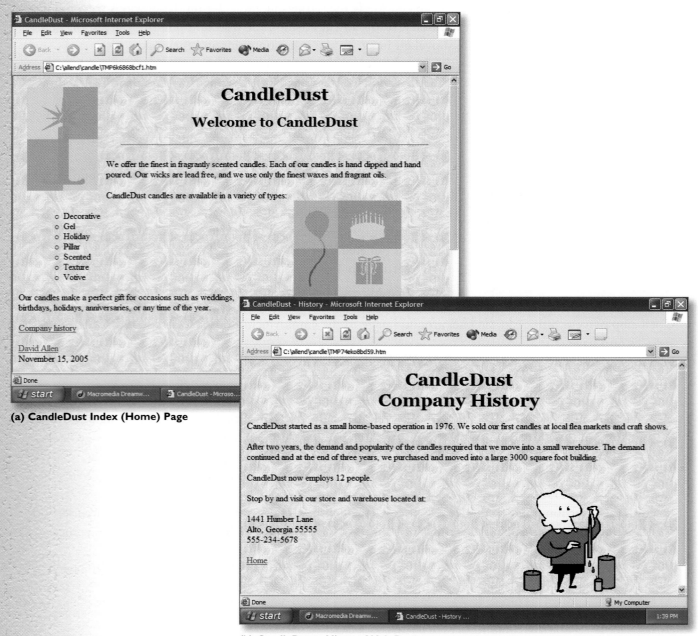

(a) CandleDust Index (Home) Page

(b) CandleDust - History Web Page

FIGURE 2-91

In the Lab

Table 2-5 Image Property Settings for the CandleDust Web Site

IMAGE NAME	W	H	V SPACE	H SPACE	ALIGN	ALT
candle1.gif	126	192	6	15	Left	Logo
candle2.gif	192	178	None	75	Right	Candles
candle_dip.gif	164	191	10	100	Right	Candle dipping

Instructions: Perform the following tasks:

1. Use the Windows My Computer option to copy the data files and images to your candle folder.
2. Start Dreamweaver. Display the panel groups. Select CandleDust on the Files pop-up menu in the Files panel. Double-click the index.htm file in the Files panel. If necessary, click the expander arrow to expand the Property inspector. If necessary, display the Standard toolbar.
3. Click index.htm in the Files panel to select it. Right-click index.htm and then click Set as Home Page on the context menu.
4. Position the insertion point to the left of the heading and then drag the candle1.gif image to the insertion point. Select the image. Apply the settings in Table 2-5 to align the image and enter the Alt text.
5. Position the insertion point to the right of the text, CandleDust candles are available in a variety of types:, and then drag the candle2.gif image to the insertion point. Select the image and then apply the settings in Table 2-5.
6. Position the insertion point to the right of the text, Our candles make a perfect gift for occasions such as weddings, birthdays, holidays, anniversaries, or any time of the year, and then press the ENTER key. Type Company history. Select the Company history text and use the drag-and-drop method to create a link to the history.htm page. Select your name. Use the Insert menu to create an e-mail link using your e-mail address. Save the index page (Figure 2-91a on the previous page).
7. Open history.htm. Apply the background image to the history.htm page. Click Modify on the menu bar and then click Page Properties. Click the Browse button in the Page Properties dialog box, click the images folder, and then select the candlebg.gif image. Click the OK button in the Select Image Source dialog box and in the Page Properties dialog box.
8. Position the insertion point at the end of the sentence – CandleDust now employs 12 people – and then drag the candle_dip.gif image to the insertion point. Select the image and then apply the settings in Table 2-5. Title the page CandleDust - History.
9. Select Home and then create a relative link to the index page. Save the History page (Figure 2-91b on the previous page).
10. View your pages in your browser and verify that your links work. Print a copy of each page if required and hand the copies in to your instructor. Close your browser. Quit Dreamweaver.

2 Modifying the Credit Protection Web Site

Problem: Marcy Cantu has received favorable comments about the Web page and site you created about credit information. Her law firm wants to utilize the Web site to provide additional information to its clients. Marcy

(continued)

Modifying the Credit Protection Web Site *(continued)*

has asked you if you would be willing to work with her and another intern at the firm to create two more Web pages to add to the site. They want one of the pages to discuss credit protection and the other page to contain information about identity theft. The revised Web site is shown in Figures 2-92a, 2-92b, and 2-92c (on the next page). Table 2-6 includes the settings and Alt text for the images. Software and hardware settings determine how a Web page displays in a browser. Your Web pages may display differently in your browser than those in the figures do.

(a) Credit Protection Index (Home) Page

(b) Credit Protection - Identity Theft Web Page

FIGURE 2-92

In the Lab

(c) Credit Protection - Questions and Answers Web Page

FIGURE 2-92 (*continued*)

Table 2-6 Image Property Settings for the Credit Protection Web Site						
IMAGE NAME	W	H	V SPACE	H SPACE	ALIGN	ALT
money1.gif	174	110	None	20	Absolute Middle	Money
answer.gif	202	176	None	100	Right	Reporting options
protection.gif	240	170	14	20	Left	Identity theft
theft.gif	172	169	20	None	Right	Protect personal information
question.gif	148	366	None	15	Right	Questions?

(continued)

In the Lab

Modifying the Credit Protection Web Site *(continued)*

Instructions: Perform the following tasks:

1. Use the Windows My Computer option to copy the data files to your credit folder. The data files consist of five image files and two data files, questions.htm and theft.htm.

2. Start Dreamweaver. Display the panel groups. Select Credit Protection on the Files pop-up menu in the Files panel. Open index.htm.

3. If necessary, display the Property inspector and the Standard toolbar. Expand the Property inspector.

4. Right-click the index.htm file and set the page as the home page.

5. Position the insertion point to the right of the heading and then drag the money1.gif image to the insertion point. Select the image and then apply the settings in Table 2-6 on the previous page. Position the insertion point to the right of the text, Equifax Information Services, LLC. Drag the answer.gif image to the insertion point and then select the image. Apply the settings in Table 2-6.

6. Select the text, financial tool, located in the first sentence of the first paragraph. Create a relative link from the selected text to questions.htm. Select the name of the company in the first bulleted list item (Equifax Information Services, LLC) and create an absolute link using http://www.equifax.com. Create a link from the other two company names, using http://www.experian.com and http://www.transunion.com.

7. Position the insertion point at the end of the second paragraph. Press the SPACEBAR. Type Credit card and identity theft can be a major issue when applying for credit. Select the text you just typed and then create a relative link to the theft.htm file. Add an e-mail link to your name. Save the index page (Figure 2-92a on page DW 190).

8. Open theft.htm and apply the background image (creditbg.htm) to the theft.htm page.

9. Position the insertion point to the left of the second line and then drag the protection.gif image to the insertion point. Select the image. Apply the settings in Table 2-6 on the previous page. Position the insertion point after the first sentence in the second bulleted point and then drag the theft.gif image to the insertion point. Select the image. Apply the settings in Table 2-6.

10. Drag to select the text, Identity theft, at the beginning of the first sentence and then create an absolute link using http://www.consumer.gov/idtheft/ as the URL. Create an absolute link from the protection.gif image using the same URL. Select the image and then type the URL in the Link box. Select Home and then create a relative link to the index.htm page. Title the page Credit Protection - Identity Theft. Save the Theft page (Figure 2-92b on page DW 190).

11. Open questions.htm. Apply the background image that you added to the theft.htm page in Step 8. Create a relative link to the index page.

12. Position the insertion point to the right of the first line of text (Questions to consider about your credit:) and then drag the question.gif image to the insertion point. Select the image. Apply the settings in Table 2-6.

13. Create an absolute link from the Fair Credit Billing Act text in question 3. Use http://www.ftc.gov/bcp/conline/pubs/credit/fcb.htm as the URL. Title the page Credit Protection - Questions and Answers. Save the Questions page (Figure 2-92c on the previous page).

14. View the site in the Site Map. Then view the Web site in your browser and verify that your external and relative links work. *Hint:* Click the image on the theft.htm page. Print a copy of each page if required and hand the copies in to your instructor. Close your browser and quit Dreamweaver.

In the Lab

3 Modifying the Plant City Web Page

Problem: Juan Benito recently became a member of a marketing group promoting Plant City's strawberry history. He wants to expand the Web site you created for him by adding two new Web pages that will highlight other features of Plant City, Florida. You inform Juan that you can create the new pages. The revised Web site is displayed in Figures 2-93a, 2-93b, and 2-93c (on pages DW 193–194). Table 2-7 on the next page includes the settings and Alt text for the images. Software and hardware settings determine how a Web page displays in a browser. Your Web pages may display differently in your browser than those in the figures do.

(a) Plant City, Florida Index (Home) Page

(b) Plant City, Florida - Strawberry Facts Web Page

FIGURE 2-93 (*continued*)

(*continued*)

Modifying the Plant City Web Page *(continued)*

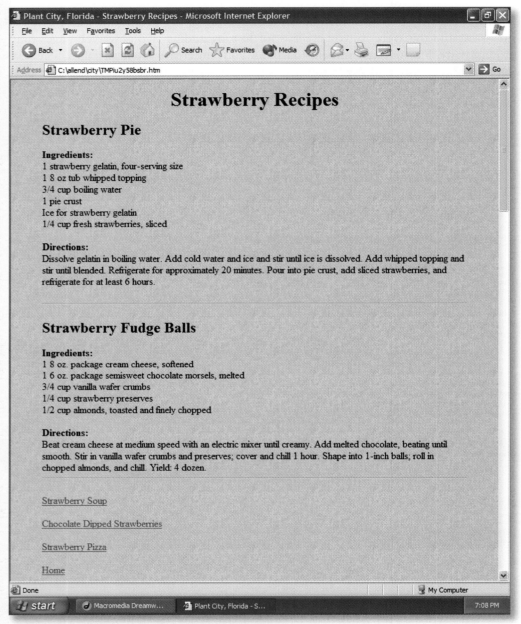

(c) Plant City, Florida - Strawberry Recipes Web Page

FIGURE 2-93 (*continued*)

Table 2-7 Image Property Settings for the Plant City Web Site						
IMAGE NAME	W	H	V SPACE	H SPACE	ALIGN	ALT
strawberry01.gif	77	75	None	80	Right	Strawberry
train.gif	225	140	6	8	Right	Train
strawberry02.gif	200	145	None	25	Right	Strawberry

Instructions: Perform the following tasks:

1. Use the Windows My Computer option to copy the data files. The data files consist of three images and two Web pages, facts.htm and recipes.htm.
2. Start Dreamweaver. Display the panel groups. Select Plant City on the Files pop-up menu.
3. Open index.htm. If necessary, display the Property inspector and the Standard toolbar. Expand the Property inspector.
4. Select the index.htm file and set the index.htm page as the home page.
5. Position the insertion point after the last numbered item (6) on the page and then press the ENTER key. Click the Ordered List button to deselect the numbered list. Type `Facts | Recipes` as the link text.
6. Create a relative link from the text, Facts, to the facts.htm page and then create a relative link from the text, Recipes, to the recipes.htm page.
7. Position the insertion point to the right of the first line of the first paragraph and then drag the strawberry01.gif image to the insertion point. Select the image. Apply the settings in Table 2-7 on the previous page.
8. Insert the train.gif image to the right of the first numbered item. Apply the settings in Table 2-7. Insert an e-mail link. Save the index page (Figure 2-93a on page DW 193).
9. Open facts.htm and apply the citybg.gif image to the background.
10. Position the insertion point to the left of the heading and then drag the strawberry02.gif image to the insertion point. Select the image. Apply the settings in Table 2-7.
11. Scroll to the bottom of the page and then select Home. Create a relative link to the index.htm page. Click to the right of Home. Press the ENTER key and then type `Strawberry Varieties`. Select the text and create an absolute link to http://www.extension.umn.edu/extensionnews/2002/New StrawberryVarieties.html. Title the page Plant City, Florida - Strawberry Facts. Save the Facts page (Figure 2-93b on page DW 193).
12. Open recipes.htm. Apply the citybg.gif image to the background.
13. Position the insertion point at the end of the second horizontal rule and then press the ENTER key. Type the following text. Press the ENTER key after typing each line of text:
    `Strawberry Soup`
    `Chocolate Dipped Strawberries`
    `Strawberry Pizza`
    Add absolute links to these three items as follows:
    For Strawberry Soup, type `http://www.sweettechnology.com/straw1.htm` as the URL; for Chocolate Dipped Strawberries, type `http://momo.essortment.com/recipestrawberr_pwh.htm` as the URL; and for Strawberry Pizza, type `http://www.recipesource.com/main-dishes/pizza/strawberry01.html` as the URL.
14. Use a search engine and find another Web site with strawberry recipes. Select a recipe you like and make a note of the URL. Position the insertion point at the end of the text, Strawberry Pizza, and then press the ENTER key. Type the name of the recipe you selected and then create an absolute link to the Web site.
15. Create a relative link to the index page. Title the page Plant City, Florida - Strawberry Recipes. Save the Recipes page (Figure 2-93c on the previous page).
16. View the Web site in your browser and verify the links. Print a copy of each page if required and hand in the copies to your instructor. Close your browser and quit Dreamweaver.

Cases and Places

The difficulty of these case studies varies:
■ are the least difficult and ■■ are the most difficult. The last exercise is a group exercise.

1 ■ In Project 1, you created a Web site and a Web page listing your favorite sport. Now, you want to add another page to the site. Create and format the page. The page should include general information about your selected sport. Create a relative link from the home page to the new page and from the new page to the home page. Add a background image to the new page and insert an image on one of the pages. Include an appropriate title for the page. Save the page in the sports subfolder. For a selection of images and backgrounds, visit the Dreamweaver MX 2004 Media Web page (scsite.com/ dreamweavermx04/media) and then click Media below Project 2.

2 ■ Several friends of yours were impressed with the Web page and Web site you created about your favorite hobby in Project 1. They have given you some topics they think you should include on the site. You decide to create an additional page that will consist of details about your hobby and the topics. Format the page. Add an absolute link to a related Web site and a relative link from the home page to the new page and from the new page to the home page. Add a background image to the new page. Create an e-mail link on the index page. Title the page the name of the selected hobby. Save the page in the hobby subfolder. For a selection of images and backgrounds, visit the Dreamweaver MX 2004 Media Web page (scsite.com/dreamweavermx04/media) and then click Media below Project 2.

3 ■■ Modify the favorite type of music Web site you created in Project 1 by creating a new page. Format the page. Discuss your favorite artist or band on the new page. Add a background image to the new page. On the index page, align the image to the right, and on the new page, align the image to the left. Position each image appropriately on the page by adding H Space and V Space. Add appropriate Alt text for each image. Add an e-mail link on the index page, and add text and a relative link from the new page to the index page. View your Web pages in your browser. Give the page a meaningful title and then save the page in your music subfolder. For a selection of images and backgrounds, visit the Dreamweaver MX 2004 Media Web page (scsite.com/dreamweavermx04/media) and then click Media below Project 2.

Cases and Places

4 ■■ In Project 1, you created a Web site and a Web page to publicize your running for office campaign. Develop two additional pages to add to the site. Apply a background image to the new pages. Apply appropriate formatting to the two new pages. Scan a picture of yourself or make a picture with a digital camera and include the picture on the index page. Add a second image illustrating one of your campaign promises. Include at least two images on one of the new pages and one image on the other new page. Add appropriate H Space and V Space to position the images, and add Alt text for all images. Create e-mail links on all three pages and create relative links from the home page to both pages and from each of the pages to the home page. Create an absolute link to a related site on one of the pages. Set the index page as the home page. Give each page a meaningful title and then save the pages in the office subfolder. For a selection of images and backgrounds, visit the Dreamweaver MX 2004 Media Web page (scsite.com/dreamweavermx04/media) and then click Media below Project 2.

5 ■■ **Working Together** The student trips Web site you and your classmates created in Project 1 is a success. Everyone loves it. The dean is so impressed that she asks the group to continue with the project. Your team creates and formats three additional Web pages, one for each of three possible locations for the trip. Add a background image to all new pages. Add two images to each of the pages, including the index page, and set the index page as the home page. Resize one of the images. Add appropriate H Space and V Space to position each image, and then add Alt text for each image. Create a link from the index page to each of the three new pages and a link from each page to the index page. Create an absolute link to a related informational Web site on each of the three new pages. Add an appropriate title to each page. Preview in a browser to verify the links. Save the pages in your trips subfolder. For a selection of images and backgrounds, visit the Dreamweaver MX 2004 Media Web page (scsite.com/dreamweavermx04/media) and then click Media below Project 2.

Tables and Page Layout

CASE PERSPECTIVE

The Florida Parks Web site has been very successful thus far. David has received several e-mail messages asking for additional information about the three national parks. Joan suggests that a separate page on each park would be a good addition to the Web site. Both David and you agree this is a good idea. The two of you volunteer to research various sources and to create the content for the three new pages.

Joan further suggests that, in addition to adding the same background to these pages as that on the rest of the site, the three new pages also should have some consistency in the displayed information. The team decides that each page should include a header with the name of the park, that the information contained in the body content should describe the location and contain some interesting facts, and that each page should list the park's address, including an e-mail link. The footer will contain links to the home page and to the other two national parks pages. You all are eager to get started on this new addition to the Florida Parks Web site.

As you read through this project, you will learn how to plan and design Web pages and how to create pages using tables. You also will learn how to modify and delete tables.

MACROMEDIA

Dreamweaver MX 2004

Tables and Page Layout

PROJECT

3

Objectives

You will have mastered the material in this project when you can:

- Understand and plan page layout
- Describe Standard mode and Layout mode
- Design a Web page using tables in Standard mode
- Design a Web page using tables in Layout mode
- Describe visual guides
- Modify a table structure
- Describe HTML table tags
- Add content to a table
- Format table content
- Format a table
- Create head content

Introduction

Project 3 introduces the use of tables for page layout and the addition of head content elements. Page layout is an important part of Web design. Page layout refers to the way your page will display in the browser, which is one of the major challenges for any Web designer.

Dreamweaver's table feature is a great tool for designing a Web page. The table feature is very similar to the table feature in word processing programs such as Microsoft Word. A table allows you to add vertical and horizontal structure to a Web page. Using a table, you can put just about anything on your page and have it display in a specific location. You can lay out tabular data. You can create columns of text or navigation bars. You can delete, split, and merge rows and columns; modify table, row, or cell properties to add color and alignment; and copy and paste cells.

Dreamweaver provides two views, or ways, to use the table feature: Standard mode and Layout mode. Standard mode uses the Insert Table dialog box, and Layout mode is a free-form process in which you draw the table and the individual cells. This project discusses both views and the advantages and disadvantages of each.

The second part of the project discusses the addition and value of head content. When you create a Web page, the underlying HTML code is made up of two main sections: the head section and the body section. The body section contains the page content that displays in the browser. In Projects 1 and 2, you created your Web pages in the body section. The head section contains a variety of information. With the exception of the page title, all head content is invisible when viewed in the

Dreamweaver Document window or in a browser. Some head content is accessed by other programs, such as search engines, and some content is accessed by the browser. This project discusses the head content options and the importance of this content.

Project Three Florida Parks Page Layout —

In this project, you continue with the creation of the Florida Parks Web site. You use tables to create three new Web pages focusing on Florida's three national parks. You then add these new pages to the parks Web site and link to them from the national.htm Web page (Figures 3-1a, 3-1b, and 3-1c on pages DW 202 through 203). When you complete your Web page additions, you will add keywords and a description as the head content.

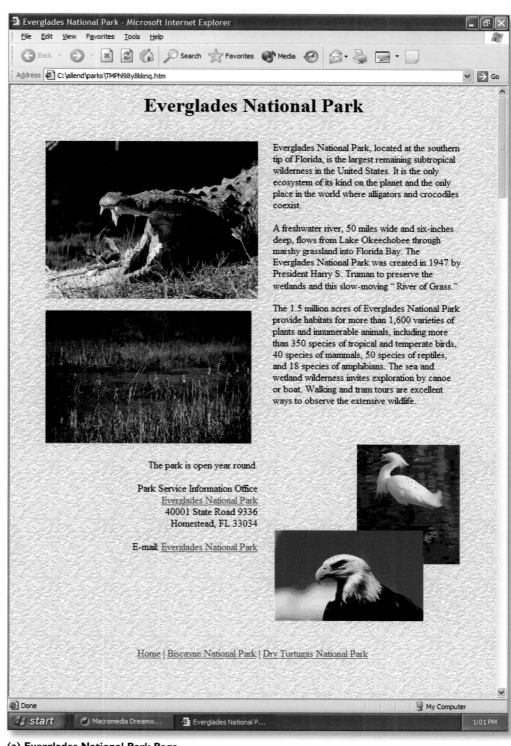

(a) Everglades National Park Page

FIGURE 3-1 (continued)

(b) Biscayne National Park Page

(c) Dry Tortugas National Park Page

FIGURE 3-1

This project uses a hierarchical structure. The structure now is expanded to include the three new pages (Figure 3-2).

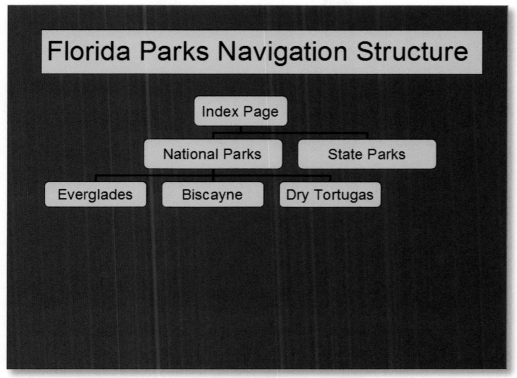

FIGURE 3-2

Understanding and Planning Page Layout

Page layout is the process of arranging the text, images, and other elements on the page. The basic rules of page layout are that your site should be easy to navigate, easy to read, and quick to download. Studies indicate that visitors will lose interest quickly in your Web site if the majority of a page does not download within 15 seconds. One popular design element that downloads quickly is tables.

Tables download very fast because they are created with HTML code. They can be used anywhere — for the home page, menus, images, navigation bars, frames, and so on. Tables originally were intended for use in presenting data arranged by rows and columns, such as tabular data within a spreadsheet. Web designers, however, quickly seized upon the use of tables to produce specific layout effects. You can produce good designs by using tables creatively. Tables provide the ability to position elements on a Web page with much greater accuracy. Using tables for layout provides the Web page author with endless design possibilities.

A typical Web page is composed of three sections: the header, the body, and the footer (Figure 3-3). The **header**, generally located at the top of the page, can contain logos, images, or text that identifies the Web site. The header also may contain hyperlinks to other pages within the Web site.

The **body** of the Web page contains informational content about your site. This content may be in the form of text, graphics, animation, video, and audio.

The **footer** provides hyperlinks for contact information. Many Web designers also include navigational controls in the footer. This may be in addition to the navigation controls in the header. Other common items contained within a footer are the name and e-mail address of the author or of the Webmaster. Sometimes, hyperlinks to other resources or to Help information are part of the footer. A typical Web page structure is displayed in Figure 3-3.

FIGURE 3-3

It is easy to create this header/body/footer structure with tables or to create any other layout structure applicable to your specific Web page needs. The entire structure can be contained within one table or a combination of multiple and nested tables. You will use a structure similar to that in Figure 3-3 to create the three new pages for the Florida Parks Web site.

Standard Mode and Layout Mode

Dreamweaver provides two options for creating tables: Standard mode and Layout mode. In **Standard mode**, a table is presented as a grid of rows and columns. This view is similar to a Microsoft Excel spreadsheet or a table created in a word processing program such as Microsoft Word. In **Layout mode**, you can draw, resize, and move boxes on the page while Dreamweaver still uses tables for the underlying structure. If you have used a desktop publishing program such as Microsoft Publisher or Adobe PageMaker, then you are familiar with the format in which layout tables are created. Using Layout mode, you can place content at any location in the Document window.

Copying Data Files to the Local Web Site

Your Data Disk contains images for Project 3. These images are in an images folder. You use the Windows My Computer option to copy the Project 3 images to your parks images folder. See the inside back cover for instructions for downloading the Data Disk or see your instructor for information about accessing the files required for this book.

The DataFiles folder for this project is stored on Local Disk (C:). The location on your computer may be different. If necessary, verify with your instructor the location of the DataFiles folder. The following steps illustrate how to copy the files to the parks local root folder.

To Copy Data Files to the Parks Web Site

1 Click the Start button on the Windows taskbar and then click My Computer.

2 Double-click Local Disk (C:) and then navigate to the location of the data files for Project 3.

3 Double-click the DataFiles folder and then double-click the Proj03 folder.

4 Double-click the parks folder and then double-click the images folder.

5 Click the birds.gif image file or the first file name in the list.

6 Hold down the SHIFT key and then click the turtle.jpg image file (or the last file name in the list) to select the ten image files.

7 Right-click the selected files to display the context menu.

8 Click the Copy command and then click the My Computer Back button the number of times necessary to navigate to the your name folder.

9 Double-click the your name folder, double-click the parks folder, and then double-click the images folder.

10 Right-click anywhere in the open window to display the context menu, and then click Paste (Figure 3-4).

11 Click the images window Close button.

The 10 new image files are pasted into the Florida Parks Web site images folder (Figure 3-4).

FIGURE 3-4

Starting Dreamweaver and Opening a Web Site

Each time you start Dreamweaver, it opens to the last site displayed when you closed the program. It, therefore, may be necessary for you to open the parks Web site. The **Files pop-up menu** in the Files panel lists sites you have defined. When you open the site, a list of pages and subfolders within the site displays. The following steps show how to start Dreamweaver and open the Florida Parks Web site.

To Start Dreamweaver and Open the Florida Parks Web Site

1 Click the Start button on the Windows taskbar.

2 Point to All Programs on the Start menu, point to Macromedia on the All Programs submenu, and then click Macromedia Dreamweaver MX 2004 on the Macromedia submenu.

3 Click the Files panel box arrow and point to Florida Parks on the Files panel pop-up menu.

4 Click Florida Parks.

The Florida Parks Web site hierarchy displays in the Files panel (Figure 3-5).

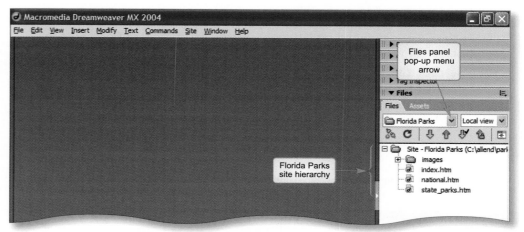

FIGURE 3-5

Adding Pages to a Web Site

You copied the images necessary to begin creating your new Web pages to the parks local root folder in the Files panel. You will add three additional pages to the Web site: Everglades, Biscayne, and Dry Tortugas national parks. You first create the Everglades National Park Web page. You then add the background image and a heading to the new page. Next, you use Dreamweaver's Standard mode to insert tables and add text, images, and links into the cells within the table.

Opening a New Document Window

The next step is to open a new Document window. This will become the Everglades National Park page. The following steps illustrate how into open a new Document window and save the page as everglades.

To Open a New Document Window

1 Click File on the menu bar and then point to New.

2 Click New. If necessary, click the General tab and then click Basic page in the Category list.

3 If necessary, click HTML in the Basic page list.

4 Click the Create button.

5 Click the Save button on the Standard toolbar.

6 Type everglades as the file name. If necessary, select the parks folder, and then click the Save button.

The everglades.htm page is saved in the parks local folder and displays in Dreamweaver's Files panel. The path and file name (parks/everglades.htm) appear on the Dreamweaver title bar (Figure 3-6).

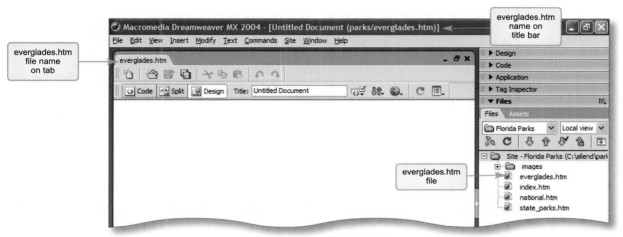

FIGURE 3-6

Creating the Everglades National Park Web Page

You start creating the Everglades National Park page by applying a background image. This is the same background image you used for the Florida Parks Web site pages in Projects 1 and 2. To provide additional space in the Document window, you hide the panel groups. You expand the Property inspector to display the additional table options. The following steps illustrate how to apply the background image.

To Add a Background Image to the Everglades National Park Web Page

1 Click the panel groups expand/collapse arrow to hide the panel groups.

2 If necessary, click the Property inspector expander arrow to display both the top and lower sections.

3 Click Modify on the menu bar and then click Page Properties.

4 Click the Browse button to the right of the Background image box.

5 If necessary, navigate to the parks\images folder.

6 Click **parksbg.gif** and then click the **OK** button in the Select Image Source dialog box.

7 Click the **OK** button in the Page Properties dialog box.

The background image is applied to the Everglades National Park page. The panel groups is hidden, and the Property inspector is expanded. The insertion point is aligned at the left (Figure 3-7).

FIGURE 3-7

Next, you add and format the heading. The following steps show how to add the heading and apply the Heading 1 format.

To Insert and Format the Heading

1 Click the Document window. **Type** Everglades National Park **as the heading.**

2 Apply Heading 1, click the Align Center button in the Property inspector, and then press the ENTER key.

3 Click the Align Left button.

4 Title the page Everglades National Park.

5 Click the Save button on the Standard toolbar.

The heading is centered and formatted, and the title is added (Figure 3-8).

FIGURE 3-8

Understanding Tables

Tables have many uses in HTML design. The most obvious is a table of data, but, as already mentioned, tables also are used for page layout, such as to place text and graphics on a page at just the right location. Tables provide Web designers with a method to add vertical and horizontal structure to a page. A **table** consists of three basic components: rows, columns, and cells. A **row** is a horizontal collection of cells, and a **column** is a vertical collection of cells. A **cell** is the container created when the row and column intersect. Each cell within the table can contain any standard element you use on a Web page. This includes text, images, and other objects.

Q&A

Q: Need Help?

A: Click the F1 key for comprehensive information about all Dreamweaver features.

Inserting a Table into the Everglades National Park Page

You will add two tables to the Everglades National Park page and then add text and images to the cells within the tables. The first table will consist of three rows and two columns with a cell padding of 2 and cell spacing of 20. The border is set to 0. When the table displays in Dreamweaver, a border outline is displayed around the table. When the table's border is set to 0 and the table is viewed in a browser, however, this outline does not display.

The table width is 90 percent. When specifying the width, you can select percent or pixels. A table with the width specified as a **percent** expands with the width of the window and monitor size in which it is being viewed. A table with the width specified as **pixels** will remain the same size regardless of the window and monitor size. If you select percent and an image is larger than the selected percent, the cell and table will expand to accommodate the image. Likewise, if the **No Wrap** property is enabled and the text will not fit within the cell, the cell and table will expand to accommodate the text. It is not necessary to declare a table width. When no value is specified, the table is displayed as small as possible and then expands as content is added. If modifications are necessary to the original specified table values, these values can be changed in the Property inspector.

The second table is a one-cell table, consisting of one row and one column. This table will contain links to the Home page and to the other two national parks pages. You use the Insert bar with the Layout category and the Property inspector to control and format the tables.

The Insert Bar

The Insert bar is considered to be a panel, but is quite different from other Dreamweaver panels. It displays at the top of the window below the menu bar. This panel group contains buttons for creating and inserting objects such as tables, layers, and images. The Insert bar contains eight separate categories, and is fully customizable through the Favorites category. When the current document contains server-side code, additional categories display.

Some categories have buttons with pop-up menus. When you select an option from a pop-up menu, it becomes the default action for the button. Any time you select a new option from the pop-up menu, the default action for the button changes. You can hide or display the Insert bar as necessary.

Category Types

The default Insert bar contains the following categories:

COMMON CATEGORY The **Common category** contains buttons for the most frequently used Web publishing tasks.

LAYOUT CATEGORY The **Layout category** contains buttons pertaining to the design modes for Web publishing and enables you to insert tables, div tags, layers, and frames. You also can choose from among three table modes: Standard (default), Expanded Tables, and Layout. When you select Layout mode, you can use the Dreamweaver layout tools: Draw Layout Cell and Layout Table.

FORMS CATEGORY The **Forms category** contains buttons for creating forms and inserting form elements.

TEXT CATEGORY The **Text category** contains buttons for text formatting.

HTML CATEGORY The **HTML category** contains buttons related to HTML code for head content, horizontal rules, tables, scripts, and frames.

SERVER-CODE CATEGORIES **Server-code categories** display only for pages that use a particular server language, including ASP, ASP.NET, CFML Basic, CFML Flow, CFML Advanced, JSP, and PHP. Each of these categories provides server-code objects that you can insert in Code view.

APPLICATION CATEGORY The **Application category** contains buttons relating to records, dynamic data, and other database elements.

FLASH ELEMENTS CATEGORY The **Flash elements** category contains a button allowing you to insert Flash elements.

FAVORITES CATEGORY The **Favorites category** enables you to group and organize the Insert bar buttons you use the most in one common place.

You use the Layout category to assist with the page design and insert tables. The following steps illustrate how to display the Insert bar and select the Layout category.

To Display the Insert Bar and Select the Layout Category

1

• **If necessary, click Window on the menu bar and then point to Insert.**

The Window menu is displayed, and the Insert command is highlighted (Figure 3-9).

FIGURE 3-9

2

• **Click the Insert command.**

The Insert bar is displayed at the top of the screen below the menu bar and the Common category also is displayed (Figure 3-10). The category last displayed becomes the default category, so your screen may display a different category.

FIGURE 3-10

• **Click the arrow to the right of the Common category, and then point to Layout on the Common category pop-up menu.**

The Common category pop-up menu is displayed (Figure 3-11).

FIGURE 3-11

4

• **Click the Layout command.**

The Layout category is displayed (Figure 3-12).

FIGURE 3-12

Layout Category

The Layout category (Figure 3-13) enables you to work with tables and layers. Dreamweaver provides two ways to create tables — Standard mode and Layout mode. In Standard mode, a table displays as a grid and expands as you add text and images. You define the structure of the table using the Insert Table dialog box. In Layout mode, you create tables and cells by drawing them. The Layout category also contains a button for Expanded Tables mode. This mode enables you to select items in tables and to place the insertion point precisely. Use this mode as a temporary visual aid for insertion point placement. After placing the insertion point, return to Standard mode to make your edits and to provide a better visualization of your changes.

You will work with Layout mode later in this project. Table 3-1 on the next page lists the button names and descriptions available in the Insert bar Layout category.

FIGURE 3-13

Table 3-1 Buttons on the Layout Insert Bar	
BUTTON NAME	**DESCRIPTION**
Table	Places a table at the insertion point
Insert Div Tag	Inserts a <div> tag
Draw Layer	Creates a layer
Standard mode	Displays a table as a grid of lines
Expanded Tables mode	Temporarily adds cell padding and spacing
Layout mode	Displays a table as boxes that can be drawn, dragged, and resized
Layout Table	Used to draw a layout table in the Design view of the Document window
Draw Layout Cell	Used to draw individual table cells in the Design view of the Document window
Insert Row Above	Used to insert a row above the selected row
Insert Row Below	Used to insert a row below the selected row
Insert Column to the Left	Used to insert a column to the left of the selected column
Insert Column to the Right	Used to insert a column to the right of the selected column
Frames	Displays Frames pop-up menu
Tabular Data	Import tabular data

More About

Dreamweaver Table Views

For more information about Dreamweaver MX 2004 table views, visit the Dreamweaver MX 2004 More About Web page (scsite.com/dreamweavermx04/more.htm) and then click Dreamweaver MX 2004 Tables.

Table Defaults and Accessibility

When you insert a table, the Table dialog box displays and contains default settings for each of the table attributes. The Table dialog box in Figure 3-14 contains the values shown in Table 3-2 on the next page. After you have created a table, however, and made changes to these defaults, the settings displayed are the settings from the last table created.

FIGURE 3-14

Table 3-2 Table Dialog Box Default Values

ATTRIBUTE	DEFAULT	DESCRIPTION
Rows	3	Determines the number of rows in the table
Columns	3	Determines the number of columns in the table
Table width	200 pixels	Specifies the width of the table as a percentage of the browser window's width or in pixels
Border	0 pixels	Specifies the border width in pixels or percent
Cell padding	0	Specifies the number of pixels between a cell's border and its contents
Cell spacing	0	Specifies the number of pixels between adjacent table cells
Header	None	Specifies if the top row and/or column is designated as a header cell
Caption	None	Provides a brief description of the table
Align caption	default	Specifies where the table caption appears in relation to the table
Summary	None	Provides a table description; used by screen readers

Q&A

Q: What is the Web site address for Macromedia online support?

A: You can find Macromedia online support at www. macromedia. com/support/ dreamweaver/.

It is advisable to use headers for tables when the table presents tabular information. Screen readers read table headings and help screen-reader users keep track of table information. Additionally, the Caption option provides a table title that displays outside of the table, the Align caption option specifies where the table caption appears in relation to the table, and the Summary option provides a table description. Screen readers read the summary text, but the text does not appear in the user's browser. Summary text is similar to the Alt text you added for images in Project 2.

Standard Mode

When using a table for layout, however, other options apply. Structurally and graphically, the elements in a table used for layout should be invisible in the browser. For instance, when using a table for layout, use the None option for headers. The None option prevents the header tags <th> and <\th> from being added to the table. Because the table does not contain tabular data, a header would be of no benefit to the screen-reader user. Screen readers read table content from left to right and top to bottom. It, therefore, is important to structure the content in a linear arrangement.

The following steps illustrate how to insert a table using Standard mode with three rows and two columns into the Everglades National Park Web page.

To Insert a Table Using Standard Mode

1

• **Click the Standard button on the Insert bar and then click the Table button.**

The Table dialog box is displayed (Figure 3-15). The settings displayed are the default settings from the last table created, so your dialog box may contain different values.

2

• **If necessary, type** 3 **and then press the TAB key to move to the Columns box.**

• **Type** 2 **as the new value in the Columns box and then press the TAB key.**

• **Type** 90 **as the new value in the Table width box and then click the Table width arrow.**

• **Select percent and then press the TAB key.**

• **Type** 0 **in the Border thickness box and then press the TAB key.**

• **Type** 2 **in the Cell padding box and then press the TAB key.**

• **Type** 20 **in the Cell spacing box and then press the TAB key.**

• **If necessary, select None for the Header.**

• **Click the Summary text box and type** Table layout for Everglades National Park Web page. The table contains three rows and two columns with images and text in the table cells.

The Table dialog box displays with the new settings, as shown in Figure 3-16.

FIGURE 3-15

FIGURE 3-16

3

• **Click the OK button.**

The table is inserted into the Document window (Figure 3-17). The dark border around the table and the three handles on the lower and right borders indicate the table is selected. The `<table>` tag displays as highlighted in the tag selector, also indicating the table is selected. The cell spacing between each cell is 20 pixels. The default alignment for the table is left. The border is set to 0 and displays as an outline when the table is viewed in Dreamweaver. When the table is viewed in a browser, however, no border is displayed.

FIGURE 3-17

Other Ways

1. On Insert menu click Table, select table properties, click OK button
2. Press CTRL+ALT+T

Property Inspector Table Features

As you have seen, the Property inspector options change depending on the selected object. You use the Property inspector to modify and add table attributes. When a table is selected, the Property inspector displays table properties in both panels. When another table element — a row, column, or cell — is selected, the displayed properties change and are determined by the selected element. The following section describes the table-related features of the Property inspector shown in Figure 3-18.

FIGURE 3-18

TABLE ID An identifier used for Cascading Style Sheets, scripting, and accessibility. A table ID does not need to be assigned.

ROWS AND COLS The number of rows and columns in the table.

W Used to specify the minimum width of the table in either pixels or percent. If a size is not specified, the size can vary depending on the monitor and browser settings. A table width specified in pixels is displayed at the same size in all browsers. A table width specified in percent is altered in appearance based on the user's monitor resolution and browser window size.

H Used to specify the height of the table in either pixels or percent. Generally, the height of a table consists of the height of the collective rows and is not specified.

CELLPAD The number of pixels between the cell border and the cell content.

CELLSPACE The number of pixels between adjacent table cells.

ALIGN Determines where the table appears, relative to other elements in the same paragraph, such as text or images. The default alignment is to the left.

BORDER Specifies the border width in pixels.

CLEAR COLUMN WIDTHS AND CLEAR ROW HEIGHTS Deletes all specified row height or column width values from the table.

CONVERT TABLE WIDTHS TO PIXELS AND CONVERT TABLE HEIGHTS TO PIXELS Sets the width or height of each column in the table to its current width expressed as pixels.

CONVERT TABLE WIDTHS TO PERCENT AND CONVERT TABLE HEIGHTS TO PERCENT Sets the width or height of each column in the table to its current width expressed as a percentage of the Document window's width and also sets the width of the whole table to its current width as a percentage of the Document window's width.

BG COLOR The table background color.

BRDR COLOR The table border color.

BG IMAGE The table background image.

CLASS An attribute used with Cascading Style Sheets.

Cell, Row, and Column Properties

When a cell, row, or column is selected, the properties in the upper pane of the Property inspector are the same as the standard ones for text. You can use these properties to incorporate standard HTML formatting tags within a cell, row, or column. The part of the table selected determines which properties display in the lower pane of the Property inspector. The properties for all three features (cell, row, and column) are the same, except for one element—the icon displayed in the lower-left pane of the Property inspector. The section beginning on the next page describes the row-related features (Figure 3-19), cell-related features (Figure 3-20), and column-related features (Figure 3-21) of the Property inspector.

FIGURE 3-19

FIGURE 3-20

FIGURE 3-21

HORZ Specifies the horizontal alignment of the contents of a cell, row, or column. The contents can be aligned to the left, right, or center of the cells.

VERT Specifies the vertical alignment of the contents of a cell, row, or column. The contents can be aligned to the top, middle, bottom, or baseline of the cells.

W AND H Specifies the width and height of selected cells in pixels or as a percentage of the entire table's width or height.

BG (UPPER TEXT FIELD)   The file name of the background image for a cell, column, or row.

BG (LOWER COLOR BOX AND TEXT FIELD)   The background color of a cell, column, or row, using the color picker.

BRDR   The border color for the cells.

NO WRAP   Prevents line wrapping, keeping all text in a given cell on a single line. If No Wrap is enabled, cells widen to accommodate all data as it is typed or pasted into a cell.

HEADER   Formats the selected cells as table header cells. The contents of table header cells are bold and centered by default.

MERGE CELLS   Combines selected cells, rows, or columns into one cell (available when rows or columns are selected).

SPLIT CELLS   Divides a cell, creating two or more cells (available when a single cell is selected).

Table Formatting Conflicts

When formatting tables in Standard mode, you can set properties for the entire table or for selected rows, columns, or cells in the table. When you are applying these properties, however, a potential for conflict exists. To resolve this potential conflict, HTML assigns levels of precedence. The order of precedence for table formatting is cells, rows, and table. When a property, such as background color or alignment, is set to one value for the whole table and another value for individual cells, cell formatting takes precedence over row formatting, which in turn takes precedence over table formatting.

If you set the background color for a single cell to green, and then set the background color of the entire table to red, for example, the green cell does not change to red, because cell formatting takes precedence over table formatting. Dreamweaver, however, does not always follow the precedence. The program will override the settings for a cell if you change the settings for the row that contains the cell. To eliminate this problem, you should change the cell settings last.

Understanding HTML Structure within a Table

As you work with and become more familiar with tables, it is helpful to have an understanding of the HTML structure within a table. Suppose, for example, you have a table with two rows and two columns, displaying a total of four cells, such as the following:

First cell	Second cell
Third cell	Fourth cell

More About

Table Formatting Conflicts

For more information about Dreamweaver MX 2004 table formatting conflicts, visit the Dreamweaver MX More About Web page (scsite.com/dreamweavermx04/more.htm) and then click Dreamweaver MX 2004 Tables.

The general syntax of the table is:

```
<table>
<tr>
    <td> First cell </td>
    <td> Second cell </td>
</tr>
<tr>
    <td> Third cell </td>
    <td> Fourth cell </td>
</tr>
</table>
```

When you view your table in Dreamweaver, the tag selector displays the <table>, <td>, and <tr> tags. The <table> tag indicates the whole table. Clicking the <table> tag in the tag selector selects the whole table. The <td> indicates table data. Clicking the <td> tag in the tag selector selects the cell containing the insertion point. The <tr> tag indicates table row. Clicking the <tr> tag in the tag selector selects the row containing the insertion point.

Selecting the Table and Selecting Cells

The Property inspector displays table attributes only if the entire table is selected. To select the entire table, click the upper-left corner of the table, anywhere on the top or bottom edge of the table, or on a row or column's border. When you move the pointer over the border, the pointer changes to a table grid icon, indicating that when the mouse button is clicked, the table is selected (Figure 3-22).

FIGURE 3-22

As discussed previously, another method for selecting a table is to click anywhere in the table and then click the <table> tag in the tag selector. When selected, the table will display with a dark border and selection handles on the table's lower and right edges (Figure 3-23 on the next page).

FIGURE 3-23

Selecting a row, column, or cell is easier than selecting the entire table. When a cell, row, or column is selected, the selected item has a dark border. To select a cell, click inside the cell. To select a row or column, click inside one of the cells in the row or column and drag to select the other cells. A second method for selecting a row or column is to point to the left edge of a row or the top edge of a column. When the pointer changes to a selection arrow, click to select the row or column. In Figure 3-24, the selection arrow is pointing to a row and the row is selected.

FIGURE 3-24

Centering a Table

When a table is inserted into the Document window with a specified width, it defaults to the left. Using the Property inspector, you can center the table by selecting it and then applying the Center command. The following steps illustrate how to select and center the table.

To Select and Center a Table

1

• **Click row 1, column 1.**

The insertion point is in the first cell of the first row and the first column (Figure 3-25).

FIGURE 3-25

2

• **Click <table> in the tag selector.**

• **Click the Align box arrow in the Property inspector and then point to Center.**

The table is selected, and handles are displayed on the lower and right borders of the table. The <table> tag is bold, indicating it is selected. Center is highlighted in the Align pop-up menu (Figure 3-26).

FIGURE 3-26

3

- **Click Center.**

The table is centered in the Document window (Figure 3-27).

FIGURE 3-27

Changing the Default Cell Alignment

The default horizontal cell alignment is left. When you enter text or add an image to a cell, it defaults to the left margin of the cell. You can change the left alignment through the Property inspector by clicking the cell and then changing the default to center or right. The default vertical cell alignment is middle, which aligns the cell content in the middle of the cell. Other vertical alignment options include the following:

Top — aligns the cell content at the top of the cell.
Bottom — aligns the cell content at the bottom of the cell.
Baseline — aligns the cell content at the bottom of the cell (same as Bottom).

You can change the vertical alignment through the Property inspector by clicking the cell and then selecting another vertical alignment option.

The following steps show how to select the cells and change the default vertical alignment from middle to top.

To Change Vertical Alignment from Middle to Top

1

• **Click in row 1, column 1 and then drag to the right and down to select the three rows and two columns in the table.**

• **Click the Vert box arrow and then point to Top in the Vert pop-up menu.**

The three rows in the table are selected. The Property inspector changes to reflect the properties for a row. The Vert pop-up menu is displayed, and Top is highlighted (Figure 3-28).

FIGURE 3-28

2

• **Click Top.**

The vertical alignment is changed to top (Figure 3-29). This change does not display in the Document window.

FIGURE 3-29

Specifying Column Width

When a table width is specified as a percentage, each column's width expands to accommodate the text or image. When you add content to the table, this expansion can distort the table appearance and make it difficult to visualize how the final page will display. You can control this expansion by setting the column width. The objective for the Everglades National Park page is to display the page in two columns of equal width of 50 percent. The following step shows how to specify column width.

To Specify Column Width

1

• **Click the cell in row 1, column 1 and then drag to select all cells in column 1.**

• **Click the W box in the Property inspector. Type** 50% **and then press the** ENTER **key.**

• **Click the cell in row 1, column 2 and then drag to select all cells in column 2.**

• **Click the W box in the Property inspector. Type** 50% **and then press the** ENTER **key.**

FIGURE 3-30

The width for column 1 and column 2 is specified as 50% at the top of the table (Figure 3-30). The W box in the Property inspector shows only a portion of the 50% value.

Table ID and Accessibility

Earlier in this project, the accessibility options available through the Table dialog box were discussed. The Property inspector for tables contains another accessibility option — table ID. For accessibility purposes, it is recommended that you add a table ID. This provides a name for the table within the HTML code. The table ID is similar to the alternate text for an image, identifying the object to devices that read browser screens. You must select the table to display the Table Id text box. The following step illustrates how to add a table ID to the Everglades National Park feature table.

To Add a Table ID to the Everglades National Park Feature Table

1

• **Click <table> in the status bar to select the table.**

• **Click the Table Id text box and then type** Everglades National Park feature page **as the table ID text.**

• **Press the** ENTER **key.**

FIGURE 3-31

The table ID is added to the Table Id text box and appears on the status bar (Figure 3-31).

Adding Text to the Everglades National Park Web Page

Next, you will enter and format the text for the Everglades National Park Web page. Table 3-3 on the next page includes the text for the first table. The text is entered into the table cells. If you have not set the width and height of a cell, when you begin to enter text into a table cell, the cell expands to accommodate the text. The other cells may appear to shrink, but they also will expand when you type in the cells or add an image to the cells.

The steps on the next page show how to add text to the Everglades National Park page. Press the ENTER key or insert a line break, <br>, as indicated in the table. Press SHIFT+ENTER to insert a line break. Press the TAB key to move from cell to cell.

Table 3-3 Everglades National Park Web Page Text	
SECTION	TEXT FOR EVERGLADES NATIONAL PARK WEB PAGE
Part 1	Everglades National Park, located at the southern tip of Florida, is the largest remaining subtropical wilderness in the United States. It is the only ecosystem of its kind on the planet and the only place in the world where alligators and crocodiles coexist.\<ENTER\>
	A freshwater river, 50 miles wide and six-inches deep, flows from Lake Okeechobee through marshy grassland into Florida Bay. The Everglades National Park was created in 1947 by President Harry S. Truman to preserve the wetlands and this slow-moving "River of Grass."\<ENTER\>
	The 1.5 million acres of Everglades National Park provide habitats for more than 1,600 varieties of plants and innumerable animals, including more than 350 species of tropical and temperate birds, 40 species of mammals, 50 species of reptiles, and 18 species of amphibians. The sea and wetland wilderness invites exploration by canoe or boat. Walking and tram tours are excellent ways to observe the extensive wildlife.
Part 2	The park is open year round.\<ENTER\>
	Park Service Information Office\<br\>
	Everglades National Park\<br\>
	40001 State Road 9336\<br\>
	Homestead, FL 33034\<ENTER\>
	E-mail: Everglades National Park\<br\>

To Add Everglades National Park Text

1

• **Type the three paragraphs of Part 1 in Table 3-3 in row 1, column 2 of the table in the Document window. Press the ENTER key and insert line breaks <br> as indicated in the table.**

The three paragraphs are entered into row 1, column 2. Figure 3-32 shows the third of the three paragraphs.

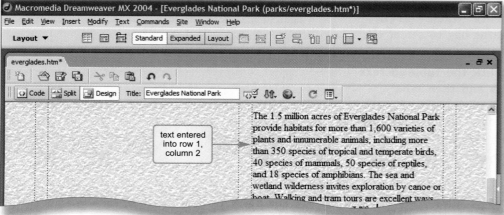

FIGURE 3-32

2

• **If necessary, scroll down to display the rest of the table. Type the text of Part 2, as shown in Table 3-3, into row 3, column 1 of the Document window. Use SHIFT+ENTER to insert the line breaks.**

The text is entered (Figure 3-33). The insertion point still is within the cell and may not display because a line break was added. A line break moves the insertion point to the next line, but does not always create a blank space within a table cell such as when the ENTER key is pressed.

FIGURE 3-33

3

• **Select the text in row 3, column 1.**

• **Click the Align Right button in the Property inspector.**

The text is aligned to the right in the cell (Figure 3-34).

FIGURE 3-34

Other Ways

1. Right-click selected text, point to Align on context menu, click Right on Align submenu

Q&A

Q: Where can I find more information on accessibility?

A: For additional information on making Web content accessible for people with disabilities, visit the Dreamweaver MX 2004 More About Web page (scsite.com/dreamweavermx04/more.htm), then click accessibility guidelines.

Adding a Second Table to the Everglades National Park Web Page

Next, you add a second table to the Everglades National Park Web page. This table will contain one row and one column and will serve as the footer for your Web page. The text is centered in the cell and will contain links to the home page and to the other two national parks Web pages. The following steps show how to add the second table and text.

To Add a Second Table to the Everglades National Park Web Page

1

• **Click outside the right border of the existing table to position the insertion point outside the table.**

The insertion point is located and blinking to the right of the table border (Figure 3-35).

FIGURE 3-35

2

- **Press the ENTER key.**
- **Click the Table button on the Layout Insert bar.**

The Table dialog box is displayed (Figure 3-36). The dialog box retains the settings from the first table. The dialog box on your computer may show different settings.

FIGURE 3-36

3

- **Change the number of rows to 1, the number of columns to 1, the width to 75, the cell padding to 0, and the cell spacing to 10.**
- **Type** Links table **in the Summary text box.**
- **If necessary, change other settings to match the settings shown in Figure 3-37.**

The Table dialog box displays the new table settings, as shown in Figure 3-37.

FIGURE 3-37

4

• **Click the OK button.**

The table is inserted into the Document window (Figure 3-38). The dark border and handles indicate the table is selected. The table contains one cell and is centered. If, however, the table defaults to the left, click the Align box arrow and then click Center.

FIGURE 3-38

5

• **Click the cell in the table. Type** Home **and then press the SPACEBAR. Press SHIFT + | (vertical bar) and then press the SPACEBAR. Type** Biscayne National Park **and then press the SPACEBAR. Press SHIFT + | and then press the SPACEBAR. Type** Dry Tortugas National Park **as the last link text.**

The text is entered into the table (Figure 3-39).

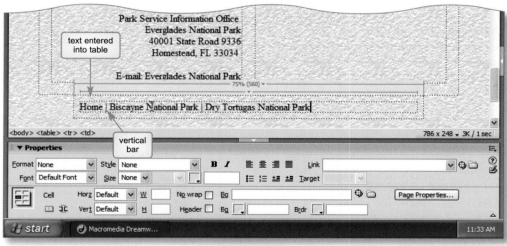

FIGURE 3-39

Adjusting the Table Width

Determining table width is a matter of judgment. You may overestimate or underestimate the table width when first inserting it into the Document window. When this happens, it is easy to make adjustments to the table width through the Property inspector. The table with the names that will contain links is too wide for the text it contains and needs to be adjusted. You adjust the table width by selecting the table and then changing the width in the Property inspector. The following steps illustrate how to adjust the width and add the table ID.

To Adjust the Table Width, Center the Text, and Add the Table ID

1

- **Click the cell in table 2. Click <table> in the tag selector to select the table.**

- **Double-click the W box in the Property inspector.**

- **Type 60 and then press the ENTER key.**

The dark border around the table indicates the table is selected. The Property inspector displays table properties. The table width is decreased (Figure 3-40).

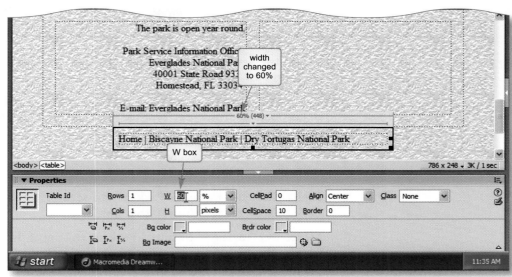

FIGURE 3-40

2

- **If necessary, click <table> in the tag selector to select the table.**

- **Click the cell in the table.**

- **Click the Align Center button in the Property inspector.**

- **Click the Table Id text box, type Everglades links table, and then press the ENTER key.**

- **Click anywhere in the Document window to de-select the table.**

The text is centered in the cell, and the table is named (Figure 3-41). This is a one-cell table, so the text also is centered in the table.

FIGURE 3-41

Next, you add relative, absolute, and e-mail links to the Everglades National Park page. The following steps show how to add the links.

To Add Links to the Everglades National Park Page

1 Select the first instance of **Everglades National Park** located in the first table in **row 3, column 1**.

2 Type http://www.nps.gov/ever/ in the **Link** box to create an absolute link.

3 Select the second instance of **Everglades National Park** located in the first table in **row 3, column 1**.

4 Click **Insert** on the menu bar and then click **Email Link**. When the **Email Link** dialog box is displayed, type everglades@parks.gov as the e-mail address. Click the **OK** button.

5 Select **Home** in the second table. Type index.htm in the **Link** box to create the relative link.

6 Select **Biscayne National Park** in the second table. Type biscayne.htm in the **Link** box to create the relative link.

7 Select **Dry Tortugas National Park** in the second table. Type dry_tortugas. htm in the **Link** box to create the relative link.

8 Click the **SAVE** button on the Standard toolbar.

9 Press the **F12** key to view the Web page. Scroll down to view the links, as shown in Figure 3-42.

10 Click the first **Everglades National Park** link and then click the Browser back button.

11 Close the browser and return to the **Dreamweaver window**.

The links are added to the Web page (Figure 3-42). The links for Biscayne National Park and Dry Tortugas National Park are not active at this point. You will add these two pages later in this project.

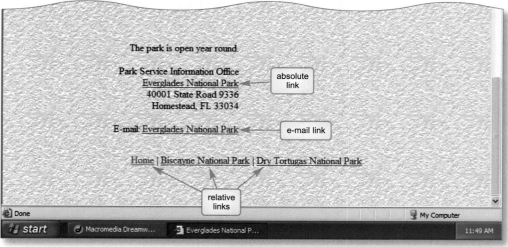

FIGURE 3-42

Editing and Modifying Table Structure

Thus far, you have created two tables and made adjustments in Dreamweaver for the Everglades National Park Web page. For various reasons, as you create and develop Web sites, you will need to edit and modify a table, change the dimensions of a table, add rows and columns, or delete the table and start over. The following section on the next page describes how to accomplish editing, modifying, and deleting table elements within the structure.

DELETE A ROW OR COLUMN Select a row or column and then press the DELETE key. You also can delete a row or column by clicking a cell within the row or column, right-clicking to display the context menu, pointing to Table, and then clicking Delete Row or Delete Column on the Table submenu.

INSERT A ROW OR COLUMN To insert a row or column, click in a cell. Right-click to display the context menu, point to Table, and then click Insert Row or Insert Column on the Table submenu. To insert more than one row or column and to control the row or column insertion point, click in a cell, right-click to display the context menu, point to Table, and then click Insert Rows or Columns on the Table submenu to display the Insert Rows or Columns dialog box (Figure 3-43). Make your selections and then click the OK button. To add a row automatically, press the TAB key in the last cell of a table.

FIGURE 3-43

MERGE AND SPLIT CELLS By merging and splitting cells, you can set alignments more complex than straight rows and columns. To merge two or more cells, select the cells and then click Merge Cells in the Property inspector. The selected cells must be contiguous and in the shape of a line or a rectangle. You can merge any number of adjacent cells as long as the entire selection is a line or a rectangle. To split a cell, click the cell and then click Split Cells in the Property inspector to display the Split Cell dialog box (Figure 3-44). In the Split Cell dialog box, specify how to split the cell and then click the OK button. You can split a cell into any number of rows or columns, regardless of whether it was merged previously. When you split a cell into two rows, the other cells in the same row as the split cell are not split. The same is true if a cell is split into two or more columns — the other cells in the same column are not split. To select a cell quickly, click the cell and then click the <td> tag on the tag selector.

FIGURE 3-44

RESIZE A TABLE, COLUMNS, AND ROWS You can resize an entire table or resize individual rows and columns. To resize the table, select the table and change the W (width) in the Property inspector. A second method is to select the table and then drag one of the table selection handles. When you resize an entire table, all of the cells in the table change size proportionately. If you have assigned explicit widths or heights to a cell or cells within the table, resizing the table changes the visual size of the cells in the Document window but does not change the specified widths and heights of the cells. To resize a column or row, select the column or row and change the properties in the Property inspector. A second method to resize a column is to select the column and then drag the right border of the column. To resize a row, select the row and then drag the lower border of the row.

DELETE A TABLE   You easily can delete a table. Select the table tag in the tag selector and then press the DELETE key. All table content is deleted along with the table.

Merging Cells and Adding Images

The concept of merging cells probably is familiar to you if you have worked with spreadsheets or word processing tables. In HTML, however, merging cells is a complicated process. Dreamweaver makes this easy by hiding some complex HTML table restructuring code behind an easy-to-use interface in the Property inspector. Dreamweaver also makes it easy to add images to a table. When you add and then select an image in a table cell, the Property inspector displays the same properties as were displayed when you added and selected an image in the Document window in Project 2. When the image in the cell is not selected, the Property inspector displays the same properties as it does for any cell. These properties were described earlier in this project.

You will merge two cells (rows 1 and 2, column 1) and add three images to the Everglades National Park page. The first and second images go into the merged cells, and the third image goes in row 3, column 2. The following steps show how to merge two cells.

To Merge Two Cells

1

• **If necessary, scroll up and then click row 1, column 1 in the first table.**

• **Drag to select the cells in rows 1 and 2 in column 1.**

The two cells are selected (Figure 3-45).

FIGURE 3-45

2

- **Click the Merge Cells button.**

The two cells are merged (Figure 3-46).

FIGURE 3-46

Next, you add three images to the table. You then align and modify the size of the images. The following steps illustrate how to display the images in the Assets panel and then add, align, and modify images in a table displayed in Standard mode.

To Add Images to a Standard Mode Table

1

- **Click the panel groups expand/collapse button and then click the Assets tab in the panel groups.**
- **Scroll to the top of the table and then click the cell in row 1, column 1.**
- **Press the ENTER key.**

The insertion point is positioned in the merged cell (Figure 3-47). The gator.jpg image will be inserted at the location of the insertion point.

FIGURE 3-47

2

• **Drag the gator.jpg image from the Assets panel to the insertion point in the merged cell. If necessary, click the Refresh Site List button to view the images.**

The gator.jpg image is inserted in the cell and selected (Figure 3-48). The Property inspector for images displays.

FIGURE 3-48

3

• **Click below the gator.jpg image.**

The insertion point displays below the gator.jpg image (Figure 3-49). The swamp.jpg image will be inserted at the location of the insertion point.

FIGURE 3-49

4

• **Drag the swamp.jpg image to the insertion point.**

The swamp.jpg image is displayed below the gator.jpg image and is selected (Figure 3-50). The image is larger than the cell, and the cell expands to accommodate the image.

FIGURE 3-50

5

• **Scroll up and click the gator.jpg image to select it.**

The gator.jpg image is selected (Figure 3-51). The Property inspector displays image properties.

FIGURE 3-51

6

• **Click the Image text box in the Property inspector and type** Gator **as the image ID.**

• **Press the TAB key and type** 340 **in the W box.**

• **Press the TAB key to move to the H box and then type** 260 **as the new value.**

• **Click the Alt box, type** Florida alligator **as the Alt text, and then press the ENTER key.**

The specified properties are applied to the gator.jpg image (Figure 3-52).

FIGURE 3-52

7

• **Scroll down and then click the swamp.jpg image to select it.**

• **Click the Image text box in the Property inspector and then type** Swamp **as the image ID.**

• **Press the TAB key and then type** 330 **in the W box.**

• **Press the TAB key to move to the H box and then type** 220 **as the new value.**

• **Click the Alt box, type** Florida swamp **as the Alt text, and then press the ENTER key.**

The specified properties are applied to the swamp.jpg image (Figure 3-53).

FIGURE 3-53

8

• **Scroll down and to the right. Click row 3, column 2.**

The insertion point is displayed in the cell (Figure 3-54). The birds.gif image will be inserted at the location of the insertion point.

FIGURE 3-54

9

• **Drag the birds.gif image from the Assets panel to the insertion point in row 3, column 2.**

• **Verify that the birds.gif image is selected, click the Image text box, and type** florida_birds. **Click the Alt box, type** Florida birds **as the Alt text, and then press the ENTER key.**

The birds.gif image is displayed in the cell and is selected (Figure 3-55). The Alt text is entered. The cell expands to accommodate the image.

FIGURE 3-55

10

• **Scroll up. Click the cell in row 2, column 2 and then drag to select this cell and the cell in row 3, column 2.**

The two cells are selected (Figure 3-56).

FIGURE 3-56

11

• **Click the Merge cells button, and then click the Save button.**

The two cells are merged, and the birds.gif image moves to the top of the cell. The page is saved (Figure 3-57).

FIGURE 3-57

12
- **Press the F12 key to view the page in your browser.**
- **The Everglades National Park page displays in the browser (Figure 3-58).**

13
- **Close the browser window.**

Dreamweaver displays.

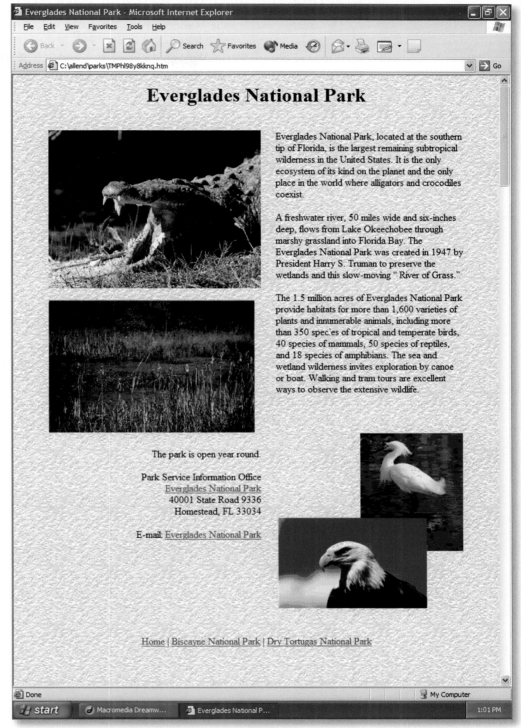

FIGURE 3-58

Creating the Biscayne National Park Web Page

To create the Biscayne National Park Web page, you open a new Document window. You start by applying the background image. This is the same background image you used for the Florida Parks Web site in Projects 1 and 2. The following steps illustrate how to open a new Document window and apply a background image.

To Open a New Document Window and Add a Background Image to the Biscayne National Park Web Page

1 Click File on the menu bar and then click New. If necessary, click the General tab and then click Basic page in the Category list. If necessary, click HTML in the Basic page list.

2 Click the Create button.

3 Click Modify on the menu bar and then click Page Properties.

4 Click the Browse button to the right of the Background image box.

5 If necessary, navigate to the parks\images folder.

6 Click parksbg.gif and then click the OK button in the Select Image Source dialog box.

7 Click the OK button in the Page Properties dialog box. If a warning dialog box displays, click OK.

8 Click the Save button on the Standard toolbar and then type biscayne as the file name. Save the Web page in the parks folder.

The biscayne.htm page is saved in the parks local folder. The path and file name (parks/biscayne.htm) appear on the Dreamweaver title bar (Figure 3-59).

FIGURE 3-59

Next, you insert and center a three-row, two-column table. Then you add the page title to the Biscayne National Park page. You also add three images to the table. One of the images is centered within a cell. The DIV, or page division, element is a tag that defines logical divisions within the content of a page. Primarily you apply this tag when using Cascading Style Sheets (which are discussed in Project 5). In Dreamweaver Code Format preferences, however, the centering default is to add the DIV tag. If this option is selected within Preferences, and you center a single image within the table, then all elements within the table, including text and other images, are centered. The following steps show how to turn off the DIV tag centering option.

To Turn Off the DIV Tag Centering Option

1

• **Click Edit on the menu bar and then click Preferences.**

• **Click the Code Format category and then click the Use CENTER tag option button.**

The Use CENTER tag option button is selected (Figure 3-60).

2

• **Click the OK button.**

• **Collapse the panel groups.**

The settings are applied, but no visible difference is noticeable in the Document window.

FIGURE 3-60

The next step is to insert and center a table and to add a title to the table, as shown in the following steps.

To Insert and Center a Table

1 **Click the Table button.**

2 **In the Table dialog box, change the settings as follows: Rows** 3, **Columns** 2, **W** 90 **Percent, Border** 4, **Cell padding** 0, **and Cell spacing** 2.

3 **Click the Summary text box and then type** Biscayne National Parks feature page **as the summary text.**

4 **Press the OK button to insert the table.**

5 **Title the page Biscayne National Park.**

6 **Click the Table Id text box in the Property inspector and then type**
Biscayne National Park feature page **as the table ID. Click the Align box arrow and then click Center.**

7 **Click the Save button on the Standard toolbar.**

The centered table is added to the Web page (Figure 3-61). The Web page is saved in the parks folder. The <center> tag may not be displayed on your tag selector.

FIGURE 3-61

An understanding of HTML and how it relates to a table and to parts of a table provides you with the ability to select a table and table components and to modify a table through the code. Merging and varying the span of columns (as you did in the Everglades National Park page) and merging and varying the span of rows is helpful for grouping information, adding emphasis, or deleting empty cells. When you merge two cells in a row, you are spanning a column. Continuing with the <table> example on pages DW 195 and 196 and spanning the two cells in row 1, the HTML tags would be <td colspan="2">First cellSecond cell</td>. When you merge two cells in a column, you are spanning a row. The attribute ROWSPAN would replace COLSPAN in the above example. Understanding COLSPAN and ROWSPAN will help you determine when and if two columns or two rows have been merged.

For the Everglades National Park page, you entered a heading outside the table and links to the other pages in a second table. For the Biscayne National Park page, you merge the cells in row 1 and then merge the cells in row 3. You enter a heading in row 1 and then enter text for the links to the home page and other national parks pages in row 3. The steps on the next page illustrate how to merge the cells in row 1 and merge the cells in row 3.

To Merge Cells in Row 1 and in Row 3

1 Click row 1, column 1 and then drag to select all of row 1.

2 Click the Merge Cells button in the Property inspector.

3 Click row 3, column 1 and then drag to select all of row 3.

4 Click the Merge Cells button in the Property inspector.

The cells in row 1 are merged into one column, and the cells in row 3 also are merged into one column (Figure 3-62).

FIGURE 3-62

Next, you add and center a heading in row 1 of the table. The following steps show how to add and center the heading in row 1.

To Add a Heading to Row 1

1

• **Click row 1 and then click the Align Center button in the Property inspector.**

The insertion point is aligned in the middle of the row (Figure 3-63).

FIGURE 3-63

2

• **Type** Biscayne National Park **and then use the Format pop-up menu to apply Heading 1.**

The heading is centered in row 1, and Heading 1 is applied to the text (Figure 3-64).

FIGURE 3-64

3

• **Click row 3 and then click the Align Center button in the Property inspector.**

The insertion point is centered in row 3 (Figure 3-65).

FIGURE 3-65

4

• **Type** Home **and then press the SPACEBAR.**

• **Press SHIFT + | (vertical bar) and then press the SPACEBAR.**

• **Type** Everglades National Park **and then press the SPACEBAR.**

• **Press SHIFT + | and then press the SPACEBAR.**

• **Type** Dry Tortugas National Park **as the last link text.**

The text for the links is centered in the row (Figure 3-66).

FIGURE 3-66

More About

Column Width

In addition to using the Property inspector to change the width or height of a column, you also can change cell widths and heights directly in the HTML code.

Splitting and Merging Cells

Tables in a traditional sense generally are thought of as having an internal **symmetry**; that is, cells of the same size form neatly arranged columns and rows. On a Web page, however, by varying the size of a cell, you can use tables to create an asymmetrical arrangement. This design option allows for more visual variation on a Web page. In a three-column table, for example, you could specify the width of the first column as 20 percent and that of the second and third columns as 40 percent each. Depending on the number of columns, hundreds of percentage variations can be applied. In the Biscayne National Park page, you adjust the width for columns 1 and 2 and then change the vertical alignment to Top within both columns. The following steps show how to adjust the width and change the vertical spacing.

To Adjust the Column Width

1

• **Click row 2, column 1.**

The insertion point is located in row 2, column 1 (Figure 3-67).

FIGURE 3-67

2

• **Click the W box in the Property inspector.**

• **Type** 40% **and then press the ENTER key.**

• **Click row 2, column 2.**

• **Click the W box in the Property inspector.**

• **Type** 60% **and then press the ENTER key.**

Column 1 is decreased in size to reflect the new percentage. and column 2 is increased in size to reflect the new percentage (Figure 3-68).

FIGURE 3-68

3

• **Select row 2, columns 1 and 2.**

• **Click the Vert box arrow in the Property inspector and then select Top from the Vert pop-up menu.**

Top is selected in the Vert box (Figure 3-69). No noticeable differences display in the table. Any image or text in these cells, however, will align to the top.

FIGURE 3-69

Now you add the text and images to row 2, columns 1 and 2. Table 3-4 contains the text for the Biscayne National Park Web page.

Table 3-4 Biscayne National Park Web Page Text	
SECTION	**TEXT FOR BISCAYNE NATIONAL PARK WEB PAGE**
Part 1	Located off the eastern coast of Florida, the 180,000-acre Biscayne National Park is less than an hour's drive from Miami. The park originally was established as a national monument in 1968. It became a national park in 1980, specifically to protect the incredible diversity of mammals, birds, fish, and plants.\<ENTER>\<ENTER>
Part 2	Park Service Information Office:\ Biscayne National Park\ P. O. Box 1369\ Homestead, FL 33090\<ENTER> E-mail: Biscayne National Park\
Part 3	More than 95 percent of the park is underwater and includes mangrove swamps, coral reefs, and the waters of Biscayne Bay. The remaining 5 percent includes 44 islands that form an 18-nautical mile north-south chain. In this watery paradise, one can find more than 200 varieties of fish, which inhabit the coral reefs. Starfish, sponges, soft corals, and other marine plants and animals live and thrive in Biscayne Bay.\<ENTER>\<ENTER>
Part 4	Biscayne National Park is best explored with snorkels or scuba gear. For those not quite so adventurous, glass-bottom boat trips and canoe rentals are available.\<ENTER>

More About

Inserting Images into a Table

In Macromedia Dreamweaver MX 2004, you can work in Design view or Code view to insert images in a document.

To Add Text and Images to the Biscayne National Park Web Page

1

• **Click row 2, column 1.**

• **Press the ENTER key and then type the text of Part 1 as shown in Table 3-4.**

• **When typing the text, press the ENTER key as indicated in Part 1, Table 3-4.**

The text is entered as shown in Figure 3-70.

FIGURE 3-70

2

• **Type the text of Part 2 as shown in Table 3-4 on the previous page.**

• **Insert line breaks and then press the ENTER key as indicated in Table 3-4.**

The text is entered as shown in Figure 3-71.

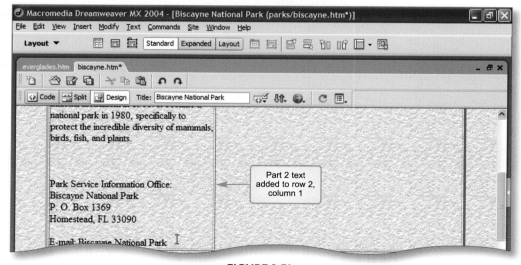

FIGURE 3-71

3

• **Scroll up and click row 2, column 2.**

The insertion point is positioned in row 2, column 2 (Figure 3-72).

FIGURE 3-72

4

• **Type the text of Part 3 as shown in Table 3-4.**

• **Press the ENTER key as indicated in Table 3-4.**

The text is entered as shown in Figure 3-73.

FIGURE 3-73

5

• **Type the text of Part 4 as shown in Table 3-4.**

• **Press the ENTER key as indicated in Table 3-4.**

The text is entered as shown in Figure 3-74.

FIGURE 3-74

6

- **Click the panel groups expand/collapse arrow to display the panel groups. If necessary, click the Assets tab.**

- **Click row 2, column 1 above the text you typed in Part 1.**

- **Drag the island.gif image to the insertion point in row 2, column 1.**

- **Click the Image text box and then type** scubadiving **as the image ID.**

- **Click the Alt box and then type** Scuba diving **as the Alt text. Press the ENTER key.**

The island.gif image displays in row 2, column 1, and the image is selected (Figure 3-75).

FIGURE 3-75

7

- **Click row 2, column 2 below the text you typed in Part 3.**

- **Drag the palmtree.gif image to the insertion point.**

- **Click the Image text box and then type** palmtree **as the image ID.**

- **Click the Alt text box and then type** Palm tree **as the Alt text.**

- **Press the ENTER key.**

The palmtree.gif image displays in row 2, column 2. The image is selected (Figure 3-76).

FIGURE 3-76

8

- **Click row 2, column 2 below the text you typed in Part 4.**
- **Drag the island2.gif image to the insertion point.**
- **Double-click the W box in the Property inspector and then type** 375 **as the new value.**
- **Press the TAB key and type** 220 **as the new value in the H box.**
- **Click the Align Center button.**
- **Click the Image text box and then type** island **as the image ID.**
- **Type** Island **as the Alt text and then press the ENTER key.**

FIGURE 3-77

The image is inserted into the cell, resized, and centered (Figure 3-77).

Adding a Border and a Border Color

A **border** is the width, in pixels, of the table border. The purpose of most tables in a Web page is to provide a structure for the positioning of text and images. When a table is created within Dreamweaver, therefore, the default border is 0 (zero), or no border. Adding a border to a Web page, however, transforms the table into a graphical element itself. Depending on the content, a border can become a visual cue for the reader by separating content. For the Biscayne National Park page, a border is applied to the full table. You cannot apply a border to an individual cell unless the table consists of only one cell.

When you created the table for the Biscayne National Park Web page, you specified a border size of 4. By default, borders are gray, but the border color can be changed. Using the color picker, you can apply a color of your choice. You can apply a border color to a single cell or to a range of cells.

Background images and background color work the same for a table as they do for a Web page. The image or color, however, is contained within the table and does not affect the rest of the page. Background color and images can be applied to a single cell or to a range of cells. The steps on the next page illustrate how to add a border color to the table and a background color to a merged cell.

More About

Borders

A border can help separate content within a table. Borders are especially useful if the table includes information that contains data that must be read across a row or down a column.

To Add Border Color and Cell Background Color

1

• **Click <table#Biscayne National Park feature page> in the tag selector and then click the Brdr Color box arrow in the Property inspector. Point to row 9, column 2.**

The table is selected, and the Continuous Tone color palette is displayed (Figure 3-78).

FIGURE 3-78

2

• **Click row 9, column 2 to select the blue color, hexadecimal #0000FF. Press the TAB key.**

A shade of blue is applied to the border (Figure 3-79).

FIGURE 3-79

3

• **If necessary, scroll up and left. Click anywhere in row 1.**

• **Click the Bg Color box arrow. If necessary, select the Color Cubes palette and then point to the second column from the right and fourth row from the bottom — hexadecimal color #FFCC66.**

The color palette displays the selected background color (Figure 3-80).

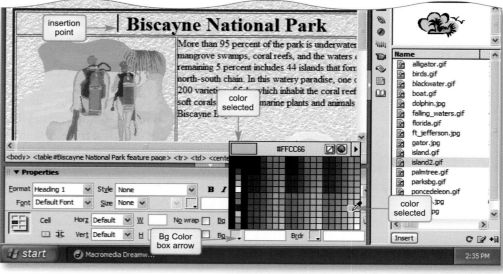

FIGURE 3-80

4

• **Click the mouse pointer.**

The palette is closed, and the background color is applied to the row (Figure 3-81).

FIGURE 3-81

Your last tasks for the Biscayne National Park page are to add links, spell check, and save the page. The following steps illustrate how to spell check; add the absolute, relative, and e-mail links to the Biscayne National Park page; and then save the Web page.

To Add Links To and Spell Check the Biscayne National Park Page

1 Click the panel groups expand/collapse button to hide the panel groups.

2 Scroll down and select the first instance of Biscayne National Park in the address in row 2, column 1. Type http://www.nps.gov/bisc/ in the Link box and then press the ENTER key.

3 Select the second instance of Biscayne National Park. Click Insert on the menu bar and then click Email Link. Type biscayne@parks.gov in the E-Mail text box. Click the OK button in the Email Link dialog box.

4 Select the text, Home, in row 3, type index.htm in the Link box, and then press the ENTER key.

5 Select the text, Everglades National Park, type everglades.htm in the Link box, and then press the ENTER key.

6 Select the text, Dry Tortugas National Park, type dry_tortugas.htm in the Link box, and then press the ENTER key.

7 Click Text on the menu bar and then select the Check Spelling command. Check the spelling.

8 Click the Save button on the Document toolbar.

9 Press the F12 key to view the Web page in your browser, as shown in Figure 3-82. If necessary, save any changes. Close the browser and then close the Web page.

In the browser, the Biscayne National Park page is displayed (Figure 3-82).

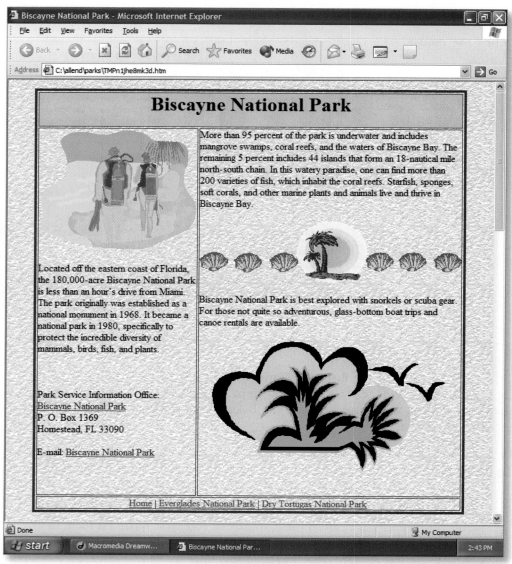

FIGURE 3-82

Layout Mode

Tables created in Standard mode are useful for creating Web pages that are simple in format or contain tabular data. A second option for creating tables in Dreamweaver is the Layout mode. Layout mode provides more flexibility than Standard mode. In Layout mode, you draw your own table and cells. When using Layout mode, you are creating the framework for the entire table. The layout can be as simple or as complex as you want.

Layout mode is a tool unique to Dreamweaver. Terms such as Layout mode and layout cell do not exist in HTML. When you draw a **layout table**, Dreamweaver creates an HTML table. When you draw a **layout cell**, Dreamweaver creates a tag (<td>) in the table. The <td> tag is a container for the content rendered inside one cell of a table element. When a cell is drawn in a layout table, it stays within the row-and-column grid as it does in Standard mode. Cells cannot overlap, but they can span rows and columns. When you draw cells of different widths and different heights, Dreamweaver creates additional cells in the HTML table to fill in the empty spots. These cells display with a gray background.

You can use Layout mode to modify the structure of an existing page created in Standard mode. Layout mode, however, provides the greatest advantage when you are designing the page from the start. As you draw the table and/or cells in Layout mode, Dreamweaver creates the code. If you draw a layout cell first, a layout table is inserted automatically to serve as a container for the layout cell. A layout cell cannot exist outside of a layout table. You can create your page using one layout table with several layout cells contained within the table or you can have multiple layout tables. For uncomplicated pages, use one layout table. For a more complicated layout, use multiple tables. Using multiple layout tables isolates parts of your layout so one section does not affect another. For example, the cell size within a table can affect the other cells in the same row and column. Multiple tables eliminate this problem, especially for pages with numerous elements.

When you draw a table in Layout mode, Dreamweaver outlines the table in green. A tab labeled Layout Table displays at the top of each table. Clicking the tab selects the table. When you complete your page design for the Dry Tortugas National Park, it will look similar to the page shown in Figure 3-83 on the next page.

The steps on the next page show how to add a new page, add a background image, and prepare the work area of the page. This page contains one layout table and 10 layout cells.

Q&A

Q: Does Dreamweaver support nested layout tables?

A: Yes — you can draw a layout table inside another layout table.

Dry Tortugas National Park

The Dry Tortugas National Park is located about 70 nautical miles west of Key West, Florida. This cluster of seven coral reefs and sand islands, along with surrounding shoals and waters, make up the Dry Tortugas National Park. Ponce de Leon discovered these islands in 1513. He named them Dry Tortugas for their absence of fresh water and abundance of tortoises.

Dominating the Garden Key Island is Fort Jefferson. This fort is the largest of the nineteenth-century American coastal forts. Fort Jefferson's construction began on Garden Key in 1846 and continued for 30 years, but was never finished.

In 1935, President Franklin D. Roosevelt declared Fort Jefferson and the surrounding waters a national monument. In 1992, the area was designated as the Dry Tortugas National Park to protect the natural and historical qualities. Dry Tortugas is one of the country's more inaccessible national parks. Of the park's 64,657 acres, 99 percent is water and submerged islands.

Park Service Information Office
Dry Tortugas National Park
P. O. Box 6208
Key West, FL 33041

E-mail: Dry Tortugas National Park

Home | Everglades National Park | Biscayne National Park

FIGURE 3-83

To Add a New Page and Add a Background Image to the Dry Tortugas National Park Web Page

1 Click File on the menu bar and then click New. If necessary, click the General tab and then click Basic page in the Category list. If necessary, click HTML in the Basic page list.

2 Click the Create button.

3 Click Modify on the menu bar and then click Page Properties.

4 Click the Browse button to the right of the Background image box.

5 If necessary, navigate to the parks\images folder.

6 Click parksbg.gif and then click the OK button in the Select Image Source dialog box.

7 Click the OK button in the Page Properties dialog box. If a Macromedia alert dialog box appears, click OK.

8 Type Dry Tortugas National Park as the title.

9 Click the expand/collapse button in the panel groups to hide the panels.

10 Click the Save button on the Standard toolbar and save the Web page in the parks folder. Type dry_tortugas as the file name.

FIGURE 3-84

Using Visual Guides

Dreamweaver provides three types of visual guides to help you design documents and project how the page will appear in a browser: rulers, tracing image, and grid.

RULERS Provide a visual cue for positioning and resizing layers or tables.

TRACING IMAGE Used as the page background to duplicate a design.

GRID Provides precise positioning and resizing of layers.

You can use the rulers to help approximate cell width and height and cell location within a table or you can use the pixel measurements that display in the right corner of the status bar. Then, if necessary, you can make final adjustments to the cells and table using the settings in the Property inspector. The steps on the next page illustrate how to display the rulers in the Document window.

To Display the Rulers

1

• **Click View on the menu bar, point to Rulers, and then point to Show on the Rulers submenu.**

Dreamweaver displays the View menu and the Rulers submenu (Figure 3-85).

FIGURE 3-85

2

• **Click Show.**

• **If necessary, select the Layout category in the Insert bar.**

• **Click the Property inspector expander button.**

The Layout category is selected, and the rulers are displayed at the top and left margins of the Document window (Figure 3-86). The rulers' measurements are in pixels. The lower pane of the Property inspector collapses.

FIGURE 3-86

Creating a Layout Table for the Dry Tortugas National Park Web Page

You begin creating the Dry Tortugas National Park page by drawing a table. In the table, you create ten cells: one cell to hold the heading, four cells to hold text content, four cells to hold images, and one cell to contain links to the home page and the other two national park pages.

Your next task is to draw the layout table. This table has an approximate width of 650 pixels and an approximate height of 925 pixels. The following steps illustrate how to create the layout table. Figure 3-83 on page DW 257 provides a good visual guide for cell locations.

To Create the Layout Table

1

• **Click the Layout Mode button.**

Layout mode, with an exit option, displays at the top of the screen (Figure 3-87). If a Getting Started in Layout Mode dialog box displays, read the information and click OK. The dialog box may not display if the Don't show me this message again check box was checked previously.

FIGURE 3-87

2

• **Click the Layout Table button.**

• **Position the mouse pointer at the insertion point in the upper-left corner of the Document window.**

The mouse pointer changes to a plus sign, which indicates you can draw a table (Figure 3-88).

FIGURE 3-88

3

• **Use the rulers and pixel measurements in the right corner of the status bar as a guide and drag to draw a table with a width of approximately 650 pixels and a height of approximately 925 pixels.**

• **If necessary, make any adjustments in the Property inspector Width and Height boxes.**

The table is added to the Document window and is outlined in green. The Property inspector changes to reflect the table in Layout mode (Figure 3-89). The Layout Table tab is displayed at the top of the table, and the table displays with a gray background.

FIGURE 3-89

Layout Table and Layout Cell Properties

When a layout table is selected, the Property inspector displays properties related to the layout table. Some properties, such as width and height, background color, cell padding, and cell spacing, are the same as those for a table in Standard mode. The following describes the properties unique to the table in Layout mode (Figure 3-90).

FIXED Sets the table to a fixed width.

AUTOSTRETCH The rightmost column of the table stretches to fill the browser window width. The column header area for an autostretch column displays a wavy line instead of a number. If the layout includes an autostretch column, the layout always fills the entire width of the browser window.

FIGURE 3-90

If the table is not the correct width or height or needs other modifications, adjustments can be made through the Width, Height, and other properties of the Property inspector.

For maximum flexibility, you should draw each cell as you are ready to add content to the cell. This method leaves blank space in the table, making it easier to move or resize cells. The next step is to add a cell that will contain the table heading. Once the cell is added, you type and format the heading within the layout cell. The heading is aligned to the left at the top of the table. The following steps illustrate how to add a layout cell and to enter and format a left-aligned heading.

To Add a Layout Cell and Heading

1

• **Click the Draw Layout Cell button on the Layout tab.**

The status bar indicates the function of the button (Figure 3-91).

FIGURE 3-91

2

• **Click the upper-left corner of the layout table and drag to draw a cell with an approximate width of 425 and an approximate height of 50.**

• **Click the cell outline or the <td> in the tag selector to select the cell and make any necessary width and height adjustments in the Property inspector Width and Height boxes.**

A layout cell is created in the upper-left corner of the layout table. The cell displays in the table with a blue outline (Figure 3-92). The handles on the borders indicate the cell is selected.

FIGURE 3-92

3

• **Click the cell and type** Dry Tortugas National Park **as the heading.**

• **Apply Heading 1 to the text.**

The heading is inserted into the cell, and Heading 1 is applied to the text (Figure 3-93). Text properties are displayed in the Property inspector.

FIGURE 3-93

Adding Content and Images to the Cells

In the previous steps, you added content to a layout cell. Adding text content and images to layout cells is similar to adding content and images to cells in a Standard mode table. The only place content can be inserted in a layout table is in a layout cell. When Dreamweaver creates a layout cell, it automatically assigns a vertical alignment of Top. You have the same options as you did in Standard mode to change the alignment to Middle, Bottom, or Baseline. When you insert an image into a layout cell, all the properties in the Property inspector that were available for images in Standard mode also are available in Layout mode. If you need to move a layout cell, click the outline of the cell to select it. Hold down the mouse button and drag the cell to a new location. To move the cell in small increments, select the cell and then press the Up, Down, Left, or Right Arrow keys.

Next, you draw a layout cell directly below the heading cell. This cell will hold text. You enter the text into the layout cells just as you entered it in the cells in the Standard mode table. Table 3-5 contains the text for the Dry Tortugas National Park Web page. If necessary, refer to Figure 3-83 on page DW 257 for a visual guide on the layout cell's placement.

Table 3-5 Dry Tortugas National Park Web Page Text	
SECTION	**TEXT FOR DRY TORTUGAS NATIONAL PARK WEB PAGE**
Part 1	The Dry Tortugas National Park is located about 70 nautical miles west of Key West, Florida. This cluster of seven coral reefs and sand islands, along with surrounding shoals and waters, make up the Dry Tortugas National Park. Ponce de Leon discovered these islands in 1513. He named them Dry Tortugas for their absence of fresh water and abundance of tortoises.
Part 2	Dominating the Garden Key Island is Fort Jefferson. This fort is the largest of the nineteenth-century American coastal forts. Fort Jefferson's construction began on Garden Key in 1846 and continued for 30 years, but was never finished.
Part 3	In 1935, President Franklin D. Roosevelt declared Fort Jefferson and the surrounding waters a national monument. In 1992, the area was designated as the Dry Tortugas National Park to protect the natural and historical qualities. Dry Tortugas is one of the country's more inaccessible national parks. Of the park's 64,657 acres, 99 percent is water and submerged islands.
Part 4	Park Service Information Office:\<br\> Dry Tortugas National Park\<br\> P. O. Box 6208\<br\> Key West, FL 33041\<ENTER\> E-mail: Dry Tortugas National Park\<ENTER\>
Part 5	Home | Everglades National Park | Biscayne National Park

To Add Text to a Layout Cell for the Dry Tortugas National Park Web Page

1

• **Click the Draw Layout Cell button.**

• **Click about 50 pixels to the right of and below the first cell, and then draw a cell with an approximate width of 250 and an approximate height of 190, as shown in Figure 3-94.**

• **Click the cell to select it and make any necessary width and height adjustments in the Property inspector Width and Height boxes.**

• **If necessary, select and drag the cell or use the keyboard arrow keys for placement.**

The second cell is added to the table and is selected (Figure 3-94). This cell will contain text.

FIGURE 3-94

2

• **Click in the cell and type the text of Part 1 as shown in Table 3-5 on page DW 265.**

The text is entered into the second cell (Figure 3-95).

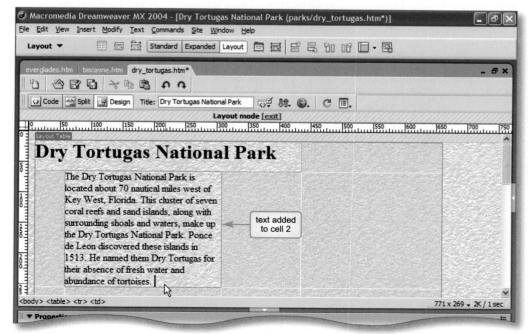

FIGURE 3-95

The third cell you draw will contain an image. You draw this cell to the right of the second cell. You add images to the layout cells just as you added images to the cells in the Standard mode table — by dragging the image from the Assets panel to the cell. The steps on the next page show how to draw the third cell and insert an image into the cell.

To Add an Image to a Layout Cell

1

• **Click the Draw Layout Cell button and then draw a cell to the right of and about 25 pixels below the second cell, with an approximate width of 290 and an approximate height of 200, as shown in Figure 3-96.**

• **Click the cell outline to select it and make any necessary width and height adjustments in the Property inspector Width and Height boxes.**

• **Click the panel groups expand/collapse button and then, if necessary, click the Assets tab.**

• **If necessary, scroll to view the entire cell.**

FIGURE 3-96

The third cell is added to the table and is selected, and the Assets panel displays (Figure 3-96). This third cell will contain an image.

2

• **Drag the ft_jefferson.jpg file from the Assets panel to the insertion point.**

• **Click the Alt text box in the Property inspector and then type** Ft. Jefferson **as the Alt text.**

• **Click the Image text box and type** ftjefferson **as the image ID. Press the ENTER key.**

The image is selected and displays in the third cell, and the Alt text and image ID display in the Property inspector (Figure 3-97).

FIGURE 3-97

3

• **If necessary, deselect the image, scroll down and to the left, and then click the Draw Layout Cell button.**

• **Click approximately 20 pixels below the second cell and about 20 pixels to the right of the table border.**

• **Draw a cell with a width of approximately 180 and a height of approximately 275, as shown in Figure 3-98.**

• **Click the outline of the cell to select it and make any necessary width and height adjustments in the Property inspector Width and Height boxes.**

FIGURE 3-98

The fourth cell is added to the table and is selected (Figure 3-98). The cell will contain an image.

4

• **Drag the turtle.jpg image from the Assets panel to the cell.**

• **Click the Alt text box in the Property inspector and type** Florida Turtle **as the Alt text.**

• **Click the Image text box and type** turtle **as the image ID. Press the ENTER key.**

The image is selected and displays in the fourth cell, and the Alt text and image ID display in the Property inspector (Figure 3-99).

5

• **Click anywhere on the page to deselect the image.**

FIGURE 3-99

So far, you have added four cells to the layout table — one containing the heading, one containing text, and two containing images. Now you add five more cells. Two of the cells will contain images and three will contain text. The following steps show how to add the additional five cells.

To Add Five Additional Cells to the Dry Tortugas National Park Web Page

1

• **Click the panel groups expand/collapse button to hide the panel groups.**

• **Click the Draw Layout Cell button.**

• **Click 20 pixels below and 50 pixels to the left of the third cell, and draw a cell with a width of approximately 325 and a height of approximately 100.**

• **Click the outline of the cell to select it and make any necessary width and height adjustments in the Property inspector Width and Height boxes.**

• **Click in the cell and type the text of Part 2 as shown in Table 3-5 on page DW 265.**

FIGURE 3-100

The fifth cell is added to the table. The cell contains text (Figure 3-100).

2

• **Click the Draw Layout Cell button.**

• **Click about 20 pixels below and about 50 pixels to the right of the fifth cell, and draw a cell with a width of approximately 185 and a height of approximately 135, as shown in Figure 3-101.**

• **Click the cell outline to select it and then make any necessary width and height adjustments in the Property inspector Width and Height boxes.**

• **Click the panel groups expand/collapse button. If necessary, scroll to view the cell.**

• **Click in the sixth cell and then drag the dolphin.jpg image to the cell.**

• **Click the Alt text box in the Property inspector and then type** Florida dolphin **as the Alt text.**

• **Click the Image text box and type** dolphin **as the image ID.**

• **Click the Save button on the Standard toolbar.**

The sixth cell is added to the table and contains the dolphin.jpg image (Figure 3-101).

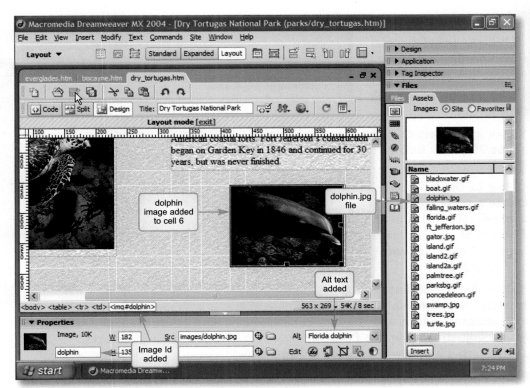

FIGURE 3-101

3

• Click the panel groups expand/collapse button to hide the panels.

• Click the Draw Layout Cell button.

• Click at the left margin about 20 pixels below the sixth cell.

• Drag to the left to create a table with an approximate width of 620 and an approximate height of 85, as shown in Figure 3-102.

• Click the cell outline to select it and make any necessary width and height adjustments in the Property inspector Width and Height boxes.

• Click in the cell and then type the text of Part 3 as shown in Table 3-5 on page DW 265.

The seventh cell is inserted, and the text displays (Figure 3-102).

FIGURE 3-102

4

• Click the Draw Layout Cell button and draw an eighth cell about 5 to 10 pixels below the seventh cell, with an approximate width of 250 and an approximate height of 150.

• Select the cell and make any necessary adjustments to the width and height in the Property inspector.

• Click in cell 8 and type the text of Part 4 as shown in Table 3-5 into the cell.

• Align the text to the right.

The eighth cell is inserted, and the text displays centered in the cell (Figure 3-103).

FIGURE 3-103

5

- Click the Draw Layout Cell button and draw the ninth cell to the right of the eighth cell and about 5 to 10 pixels below cell 8, with an approximate width of 275 and an approximate height of 130.

- Select the cell and make any necessary adjustments to the width and height in the Property inspector.

- Display the Assets panel and then drag the trees.jpg image to the ninth cell.

- Type Palm trees as the Alt text and palmtrees as the image ID.

FIGURE 3-104

The ninth cell is inserted, and the trees.jpg image displays (Figure 3-104).

6

- Hide the panel groups.

- Scroll down and then click the Draw Layout Cell button.

- Draw the tenth cell about 10 pixels below cells 8 and 9 and about 100 pixels from the left border, with an approximate width of 425 and an approximate height of 35.

- Select the cell and make any necessary adjustments to the width and height in the Property inspector.

FIGURE 3-105

- Click in cell 10 and then type the text of Part 5 as shown in Table 3-5 into the cell.

- Click the Align Center button in the Property inspector.

- Click the Save button.

The text for the links displays centered in cell 10, and the page is saved (Figure 3-105).

Next, you add absolute, e-mail, and relative links to the Dry Tortugas National Park page. The following steps show how to add the links.

To Add Absolute, E-Mail, and Relative Links

1

• **Select the first instance of Dry Tortugas National Park in cell 8. Type** http://www. nps.gov/dry_tort/ **in the Link box to create an absolute link.**

• **Select the second instance of Dry Tortugas National Park. Click Insert on the menu bar and then click Email Link. When the Email Link dialog box is displayed, type** dry_tortugas@parks. gov **as the e-mail address. Click the OK button.**

• **Select Home in cell 10 (the last cell in the table). Type** index.htm **in the Link box to create the relative link.**

FIGURE 3-106

• **Select Everglades National Park in cell 10. Type** everglades.htm **in the Link box to create the relative link.**

• **Select Biscayne National Park in cell 10. Type** biscayne.htm **in the Link box to create the relative link.**

• **Click the Save button on the Standard toolbar.**

The page is saved, and the links are added, as shown in Figure 3-106.

Centering the Table in Standard Mode

Layout mode does not provide all the features that are provided for a table in Standard mode. For example, you cannot select a number of rows or select a number of columns when creating Web pages in Layout mode, and you cannot center a table when in Layout mode. To access these features requires that the table be displayed in Standard mode. Your next task is to center the table. The following steps illustrate how to display the Web page in Standard mode, to center the table, and to turn off the rulers.

To Center a Table Created in Layout Mode

1

• **Click the Standard Mode button on the Layout tab. Click any cell in the table and then click the <table> tag in the tag selector.**

The table displays in Standard mode and is selected (Figure 3-107).

FIGURE 3-107

2

• **Click the Align box arrow in the Property inspector, press the ENTER key, and then click Center.**

The table is selected and centered in the Document window (Figure 3-108).

FIGURE 3-108

• **Click the Save button on the Standard toolbar and then press the F12 key to view the page in your browser.**

The Web page displays centered in the browser (Figure 3-109).

• **Close the browser.**

5

• **Click View on the menu bar, click Rulers, and then click the Show command to deselect it.**

More About

Layout Tables

For more information about Dreamweaver MX 2004 layout tables, visit the Dreamweaver MX 2004 More About Web page (scsite.com/dreamweavermx04/more.htm) and then click Dreamweaver MX 2004 Layout Tables.

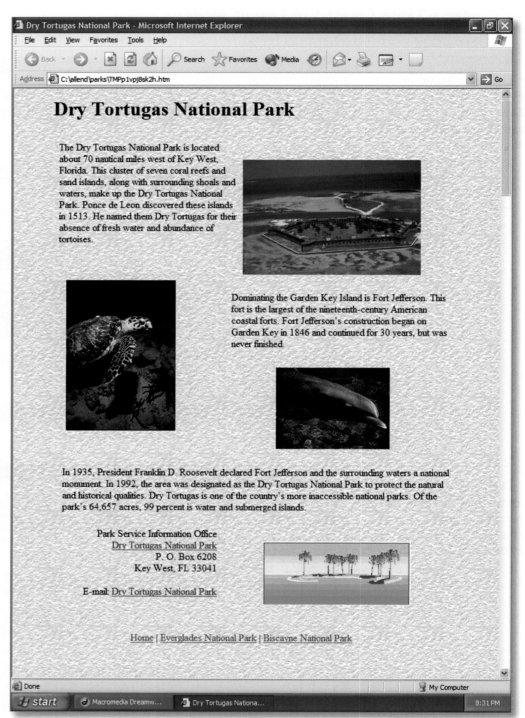

FIGURE 3-109

The Web site has expanded to include pages on the three national parks located in Florida. To integrate the page within the Web site, you add links from the national.htm page. The following steps show how to add the links.

To Add Links to the National Parks Web Page

1

• **Click File on the menu bar, select Open, and then open the national.htm page in the parks folder.**

The national.htm page displays (Figure 3-110).

FIGURE 3-110

2

• **Select the Everglades National Park heading and then type** everglades.htm **in the Link box.**

• **Select the Biscayne National Park heading and then type** biscayne.htm **in the Link box.**

• **Select the Dry Tortugas National Park heading and then type** dry_tortugas.htm **in the Link box.**

The links are added to the three parks (Figure 3-111).

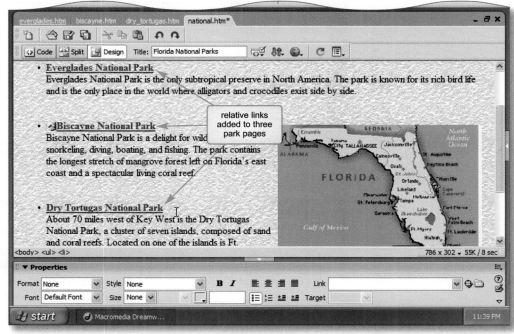

FIGURE 3-111

3

• **Press the F12 key to view the page in your browser. Test each link and then close the browser.**

• **Save the national.htm page and then close the page.**

• **Close the other three pages — everglades.htm, biscayne.htm, and dry_tortugas.htm.**

Q&A

Q: Can I change the color of the table outline when in layout mode?

A: Yes — click Edit, select Preferences, and then select the Layout Mode category. Click the Table Outline Color box and then select a color of your choice.

Head Content

HTML files consist of two main sections: the head section and the body section. The head section is one of the more important sections of a Web page. A standard HTML page contains a <head> tag and a <body> tag. Contained within the head section is site and page information. With the exception of the title, the information contained in the head does not display in the browser. Some of the information contained in the head is accessed by the browser, and other information is accessed by other programs such as search engines and server software. In Figure 3-112, the head content of the index page is displayed. The title and the default meta tag are the only pieces of information currently contained between the start <head> and end </head> tags.

FIGURE 3-112

Head Content Elements

Dreamweaver makes it easy to add content to the head section by providing a pop-up menu in the Insert bar HTML category. The Head pop-up menu contains the following elements that can be added to your Web page.

META A <meta> tag contains information about the current document. This information is used by servers, browsers, and search engines. HTML documents can have as many <meta> tags as needed, but each item uses a different set of tags.

KEYWORDS Keywords are a list of words that someone would type into a search engine search field.

DESCRIPTION The description contains a sentence or two that can be used in a search engine's results page.

REFRESH The <refresh> tag is processed by the browser to reload the page or load a new page after a specified amount of time has elapsed.

BASE The base tag sets the base URL to provide an absolute link and/or a link target that the browser can use to resolve link conflicts.

LINK The link element defines a relationship between the current document and another file. This is not the same as a link in the Document window.

Keywords, descriptions, and refresh settings are special-use cases of the meta tag. The following steps show how to add keywords and a description to the index.htm page.

> *More About*
>
> **Head Content**
>
> Meta tags are information inserted into the head content area of Web pages. The meta description tag allows you to influence the description of a page in the search engines that support the tag. For more information about meta tags, visit the Dreamweaver MX 2004 More About Web page (scsite.com/dreamweavermx04/more.htm) and then click Dreamweaver MX 2004 Meta Tags.

To Add Keywords and a Description

1

• **Open the index.htm file.**

• **Click the Insert box arrow and then select HTML from the pop-up menu. Point to the Head button (Figure 3-113).**

FIGURE 3-113

2

• **Click the Head button and then point to Keywords on the pop-up menu.**

The pop-up menu displays, and Keywords is highlighted (Figure 3-114).

FIGURE 3-114

3

• **Click Keywords on the Head pop-up menu. Type the following keywords in the Keywords text box, separating each keyword with a comma:** parks, Florida, national parks, state parks.

Keywords are added to the Keywords dialog box (Figure 3-115). When a search is done with a search engine for any of the keywords, the Web site address will be displayed in the browser search results.

FIGURE 3-115

4

• **Click the OK button, click the Head pop-up menu, and then click Description. Type** A Web site featuring Florida state and national parks **in the Description text box.**

The Description dialog box is displayed as shown in Figure 3-116.

FIGURE 3-116

5

• **Click the OK button and then click the Code button on the Document toolbar.**

The keywords and description that you entered are displayed in Code view (Figure 3-117).

6

• **Click the Design button on the Document toolbar and then click the Save button on the Standard toolbar.**

The Web page is saved.

FIGURE 3-117

Other Ways

1. Click Code button on Document toolbar, type keywords code in code window

Publishing a Web Site

In Project 1 you defined a local site, and in Projects 1, 2, and 3, you added Web pages to the local site. This local site resides on your computer's hard disk, a network drive, or possibly a Zip disk. You can view the organization of all files and folders in your site through the Files panel.

To prepare a Web site and make it available for others to view requires that you **publish** your site by putting it on a Web server for public access. A **Web server** is an Internet- or intranet-connected computer that delivers, or *serves up*, Web pages. You **upload** files to a folder on a server and **download** files to a folder in the Files panel on your computer. Generally, when Web site designers publish to a folder on a Web site, they do so by using a file transfer (FTP) program such as WS_FTP or Cute FTP, or Windows XP Web Folders. Dreamweaver, however, includes built-in support that enables you to connect and transfer your local site to a Web server without requiring an additional program. To publish to a Web server requires that you have access to a Web server.

Publishing and maintaining your site using Dreamweaver involves the following steps:

1. Use the Site Definition Wizard to enter the FTP information.
2. Specify the Web server to which you want to publish your Web site.
3. Connect to the Web server and upload the files.
4. Synchronize the local and remote sites.

Your school or company may have a server that you can use to upload your Web site. Free Web hosting services such as those provided by Angelfire, Tripod, or GeoCities are other options. These services, as well as many other hosting services, also offer low-cost Web hosting from approximately $3.95 to $9.95 a month. The FreeSite.com contains a list of free and inexpensive hosting services, and FreeWebspace.net provides a PowerSearch form for free and low-cost hosting.

Table 3-6 contains a list of Web hosting services. Appendix C contains step-by-step instructions on publishing a Web site to a remote folder.

Table 3-6 Web Site Hosting Services		
NAME	**WEB SITE**	**COST**
Angelfire®	angelfire.lycos.com	Free (ad-supported); starting at $4.95 monthly ad-free
Yahoo! GeoCities	geocities.yahoo.com	Free (ad-supported); starting at $4.95 monthly ad-free
Tripod®	tripod.lycos.com/	Free (ad-supported); starting at $4.95 monthly ad-free
The FreeSite.com	thefreesite.com/Free_Web_Space	A list of free and inexpensive hosting sites
FreeWebspace.net	freewebspace.net	A searchable guide for free Web space

For an updated list of Web site hosting services, visit the Macromedia Dreamweaver MX 2004 Web page (scsite.com/dreamweavermx04) and then click Web Hosting. If required by your instructor, publish the Florida Parks Web site to a remote server by following the steps in Appendix C.

With your work completed, you are ready to quit Dreamweaver.

More About

Publishing Your Florida Parks Web Site

Appendix C contains step-by-step instructions on publishing the Florida Parks Web site.

Quitting Dreamweaver

After you add pages to your Web site and add the head content, Project 3 is complete. The following step illustrates how to close the Web site, quit Dreamweaver MX 2004, and return control to Windows.

To Close the Web Site and Quit Dreamweaver

1 **Click the Close button on the right corner of the Dreamweaver title bar.**

The Dreamweaver window, the Document window, and the Florida Parks Web site all close. If you have unsaved changes, Dreamweaver will prompt you to save the changes. Clicking the Yes button in the Dreamweaver MX 2004 dialog box saves the changes.

Project Summary

Project 3 introduced you to tables and to Web page design using tables. You created three Web pages, using the Standard mode for two pages and the Layout mode for the third page. You merged and split cells and learned how to add text and images to the tables. Next, you added a border color and cell background color. Finally, you added head content to one of the Web pages.

What You Should Know

Having completed this project, you should be able to perform the tasks below. The tasks are listed in the same order they were presented in the project. For a list of the buttons, menus, toolbars, and commands introduced in this project, see the Quick Reference Summary at the back of this book and refer to the Page Number column.

1. Copy Data Files to the Parks Web Site (DW 205)
2. Start Dreamweaver and Open the Florida Parks Web Site (DW 206)
3. Open a New Document Window (DW 207)
4. Add a Background Image to the Everglades National Park Web Page (DW 207)
5. Inset and Format the Heading (DW 208)
6. Display the Insert Bar and Select the Layout Category (DW 211)
7. Insert a Table Using Standard Mode (DW 215)
8. Select and Center a Table (DW 222)
9. Change Vertical Alignment from Middle to Top (DW 224)
10. Specify Column Width (DW 225)
11. Add a Table ID to the Everglades National Park Feature Table (DW 225)
12. Add Everglades National Park Text (DW 226)
13. Add a Second Table to the Everglades National Park Web Page (DW 228)
14. Adjust the Table Width, Center the Text, and Add the Table ID (DW 231)
15. Add Links to the Everglades National Parks Page (DW 232)
16. Merge Two Cells (DW 234)
17. Add Images to a Standard Mode Table (DW 235)

18. Open a New Document Window and Add a Background Image to the Biscayne National Park Web Page (DW 242)

19. Turn Off the DIV Tag Centering Option (DW 243)

20. Insert and Center a Table (DW 243)

21. Merge Cells in Row 1 and in Row 3 (DW 245)

22. Add a Heading to Row 1 (DW 246)

23. Adjust the Column Width (DW 248)

24. Add Text and Images to the Biscayne National Park Web Page (DW 250)

25. Add Border Color and Cell Background Color (DW 254)

26. Add Links To and Spell Check the Biscayne National Park Page (DW 255)

27. Add a New Page and Add a Background Image to the Dry Tortugas National Park Web Page (DW 258)

28. Display the Rulers (DW 259)

29. Create the Layout Table (DW 261)

30. Add a Layout Cell and Heading (DW 263)

31. Add Text to a Layout Cell for the Dry Tortugas National Park Web Page (DW 266)

32. Add an Image to a Layout Cell (DW 267)

33. Add Five Additional Cells to the Dry Tortugas National Park Web Page (DW 270)

34. Add Absolute, E-Mail, and Relative Links (DW 274)

35. Center a Table Created in Layout Mode (DW 275)

36. Add Links to the National Parks Web Page (DW 277)

37. Add Keywords and a Description (DW 279)

38. Close the Web Site and Quit Dreamweaver (DW 283)

Learn It Online

Instructions: To complete the Learn It Online exercises, start your browser, click the Address bar, and then enter the Web address scsite.com/dreamweavermx2004/learn. When the Dreamweaver MX 2004 Learn It Online page is displayed, follow the instructions in the exercises below. Each exercise has instructions for printing your results, either for your own records or for submission to your instructor.

1 Project Reinforcement TF, MC, and SA

Below Dreamweaver Project 3, click the Project Reinforcement link. Print the quiz by clicking Print on the File menu for each page. Answer each question.

2 Flash Cards

Below Dreamweaver Project 3, click the Flash Cards link and read the instructions. Type 20 (or a number specified by your instructor) in the Number of playing cards text box, type your name in the Enter your Name text box, and then click the Flip Card button. When the flash card is displayed, read the question and then click the ANSWER box arrow to select an answer. Flip through Flash Cards. If your score is 15 (75%) correct or greater, click Print on the File menu to print your results. If your score is less than 15 (75%) correct, then redo this exercise by clicking the Replay button.

3 Practice Test

Below Dreamweaver Project 3, click the Practice Test link. Answer each question, enter your first and last name at the bottom of the page, and then click the Grade Test button. When the graded practice test is displayed on your screen, click Print on the File menu to print a hard copy. Continue to take practice tests until you score 80% or better.

4 Who Wants To Be a Computer Genius?

Below Dreamweaver Project 3, click the Computer Genius link. Read the instructions, enter your first and last name at the bottom of the page, and then click the PLAY button. When your score is displayed, click the PRINT RESULTS link to print a hard copy.

5 Wheel of Terms

Below Dreamweaver Project 3, click the Wheel of Terms link. Read the instructions, and then enter your first and last name and your school name. Click the PLAY button. When your score is displayed, right-click the score and then click Print on the shortcut menu to print a hard copy.

6 Crossword Puzzle Challenge

Below Dreamweaver Project 3, click the Crossword Puzzle Challenge link. Read the instructions, and then enter your first and last name. Click the SUBMIT button. Work the crossword puzzle. When you are finished, click the Submit button. When the crossword puzzle is redisplayed, click the Print Puzzle button to print a hard copy.

7 Tips and Tricks

Below Dreamweaver Project 3, click the Tips and Tricks link. Click a topic that pertains to Project 3. Right-click the information and then click Print on the shortcut menu. Construct a brief example of what the information relates to in Dreamweaver to confirm you understand how to use the tip or trick.

8 Newsgroups

Below Dreamweaver Project 3, click the Newsgroups link. Click a topic that pertains to Project 3. Print three comments.

9 Expanding Your Horizons

Below Dreamweaver Project 3, click the Expanding Your Horizons link. Click a topic that pertains to Project 3. Print the information. Construct a brief example of what the information relates to in Dreamweaver to confirm you understand the contents of the article.

10 Search Sleuth

Below Dreamweaver Project 3, click the Search Sleuth link. To search for a term that pertains to this project, select a term below the Project 3 title and then use the Google search engine at google.com (or any major search engine) to display and print two Web pages that present information on the term.

Apply Your Knowledge

1 Modifying the B & B Lawn Service Web

Instructions: Start Dreamweaver. See the inside back cover of this book for instructions for downloading the Data Disk or see your instructor for information on accessing the files in this book.

The B & B Lawn Service Web site currently contains four pages. You will add a fifth page with a table created using Standard mode. The new Web page will include a seven-row, three-column centered table with a list of services, how often the services are scheduled, and the price of each service. You merge one of the rows and then add and center an image in the row. A border color is applied to the entire table, and the first row has a background color applied. Keywords and a description are added. You then add a link to the home page, save the page, and upload the Web site to a Web server. The new page added to the Web site is shown in Figure 3-118. Software and hardware settings determine how a Web page is displayed in a browser. Your Web page may display differently than the one shown in Figure 3-118.

Appendix C contains instructions for uploading your local site to a remote site.

FIGURE 3-118

Apply Your Knowledge

1. Use the Windows My Computer option to copy the triming.gif image from the DataFiles folder to your /lawn/images folder.

2. Select Lawn Service from the Site pop-up menu in the Files panel. Click File on the menu bar and then click New. If necessary, click the General tab and then click Basic page in the Category list. Click the Create button. Save the page as prices.

3. Use the Page Properties dialog box to apply the lawnbg.gif image to the new page.

4. If necessary, display the Insert bar. Click the upper-left corner of the Document window. Type Services Price Chart and then apply Heading 1 to the text. Press the ENTER key and then click the Layout category on the Insert bar. If necessary, click the Standard Mode button and then click the Table button in the Layout category. Type the following data in the Table dialog box: 7 for Rows, 5 for Cell padding, 3 for Columns, 2 for Cell spacing, 70 for Width, and 3 for Border.

5. Type the text as shown in Table 3-7. Press the TAB key to move from cell to cell.

Table 3-7 Lawn Services Price Chart

Services	Schedule	Yearly Price
Mowing/trimming	Weekly	$1,200
Pruning	Monthly	$600
Fertilizing	Quarterly	$600
Irrigation	As needed	Price varies
Weed and insect control	As needed	Price varies

6. Click anywhere in row 1 and then click the <tr> tag in the tag selector to select row 1. Apply Heading 2 and center the heading. Click the Bg box in the Property inspector and apply background color #FFCC99 (Color Cubes palette, row 3 from the bottom and column 2 from the right).

7. Click anywhere in row 7 in the table and then click the <tr> tag in the tag selector to select row 7. Click the Merge Cells button and then click the Align Center button in the Property inspector. If necessary, display the Assets panel. With the insertion point in the middle of the merged row 7, drag the triming.gif image to the insertion point. Select the image and then type Tree trimming as the Alt text.

8. Click the <table> tag in the tag selector and then apply border color #FF9900 (Color Cubes palette, row 7 from the top and column 3 from the right). Center the table.

9. Position the insertion point outside the table by clicking to the right of the table. Press the ENTER key and then click the Text Indent button two times. Type Home and then create a relative link to the index.htm file.

10. Click the HTML category on the Insert bar, click the Head pop-up menu, and then click the Keywords command. When the Keywords dialog box is displayed, type lawn service, price schedule, your name in the Keywords text box and then click the OK button. Click the Head pop-up menu and select click the Description command. When the Description dialog box is displayed, type B & B Lawn Service price schedule in the Description text box and then click the OK button.

11. Title the page B & B Lawn Service - Prices. Check spelling. Save the Web page.

12. Open the index.htm page and then scroll to the end of the page. Click above your name and then press the ENTER key. Type Check our Prices and then create a link from the word, Prices, to the prices.htm page.

13. Print a copy of the page if required by your instructor. If required by your instructor, publish the Lawn Service Web site to a remote server by following the steps in Appendix C. Close the Lawn Service Web site. Close Dreamweaver.

In the Lab

1 Adding a Page with a Table to the CandleDust Web Site

Problem: Publicity from the Web site has generated several requests for examples of Mary Stewart's candles. Mary has asked you to add a page to the site that shows some of her creations and the price of each candle. The Web page will have a link to the home page and will be named products. The new page is shown in Figure 3-119. Appendix C contains instructions for uploading your local site to a remote site.

FIGURE 3-119

Instructions: Perform the following tasks:

1. Use the Windows My Computer option to copy the six images (candle3.gif through candle8.gif) from the DataFiles folder to your /candle/images folder.

2. Start Dreamweaver. Select CandleDust from the Files pop-up menu in the Files panel. Click File on the menu bar and then click New. If necessary, click the General tab and then click Basic page in the Category list. Click the Create button. Save the page as products.

3. Use the Page Properties dialog box to add the background.gif image. Title the page CandleDust Specialty Candles.

4. Click the upper-left corner of the page and then press the ENTER key.

5. If necessary, click the Insert bar's Layout category, the Standard Mode button, and then the Table button. Enter the following data in the Table dialog box: 6 for Rows, 3 for Cell padding, 3 for Columns, 3 for Cell spacing, 80 for Width, and 3 for Border. Center the table.

6. Merge the three cells in row 1 into one cell. Click the Align Center button in the Property inspector and then type CandleDust Specialty Candles as the heading. Apply Heading 1 to the text heading.

7. Click column 1, row 2 and then drag to select all cells in rows 2 through 6. Click the Align Center button, click the Vert box arrow, and then select Middle. Select column 1, rows 2 through 6. Click the Width box and type 33% as the new width. Repeat this step for column 2, rows 2 through 6, and column 3, rows 2 through 6.

8. Display the Assets panel. Click column 1, row 2 and drag candle3.gif to the insertion point. Repeat this step, dragging candle4.gif to column 2, row 2, and candle5.gif to column 3, row 2.

9. Type the following information in row 3: $3.75 in column 1, $4.50 in column 2, and $7.25 in column 3.

10. Merge the three cells in row 4.

11. Click column 1, row 5 and drag candle6.gif to the insertion point. Repeat this step, dragging candle7.gif to column 2, row 5, and candle8.gif to column 3, row 5.

12. Type the following information in row 6: $4.50 in column 1, $7.00 in column 2, and $7.25 in column 3.

13. Click outside of the table to the right and then press the ENTER key. Type Home and create a link from the products.htm page to the index.htm page.

14. Open the index.htm page and click below the Company History link. Type Products and then create a link to the products.htm page. Save the index.htm page.

15. Save the products.htm page and then view your page in your browser. Verify that your link works. Print a copy of the Web page if required and hand it in to your instructor. If required by your instructor, publish the CandleDust Web site to a remote server by following the steps in Appendix C. Close your browser. Close Dreamweaver.

2 Adding a Table Page to the Credit Web Site

Problem: The Credit Protection Web site has become very popular. Marcy receives numerous e-mail messages requesting that the Web site be expanded. Several messages have included a request to provide some hints and tips about how to save money. Marcy asks you to create a new page for the Web site so she can share some of this information. Figure 3-120a on the next page shows the table layout, and Figure 3-120b on page DW 271 shows the Web page. Appendix C contains instructions for uploading your local site to a remote site.

(continued)

Adding a Table Page to the Credit Web Site *(continued)*

(a) Table Layout

(b) Web Page

FIGURE 3-120

In the Lab

Instructions: Perform the following tasks:

1. Use the Windows My Computer option to copy the three images (car.gif, check.gif, and credit_card.gif) from the DataFiles folder to your /credit/images folder. Start Dreamweaver. Select Credit Protection from the Site pop-up menu in the Files panel.
2. Add a new Web page and name it saving. Add the creditbg.gif image. Title the page Tips and Hints.
3. Display the rulers. Click the Insert bar's Layout category and then click the Layout button.
4. Click the Draw Layout Table button on the Layout tab and then create a table with a fixed width of approximately 600 pixels and a height of approximately 615 pixels.
5. Use Figure 3-120a on page DW 295 as a guide and draw the five layout cells. Use the information in Table 3-8 for the widths and heights.

Table 3-8	Credit Protection Cell Layout Guide					
NUMBER	CELL NAME	W	H	IMAGE ALT TEXT	IMAGE NAME
1	Heading	285	75	None	None
2	Checking	325	210	Checking Account	check.gif
3	Automobiles	250	235	Car	car.gif
4	Credit Cards	600	105	Credit Cards	credit_card.gif
5	Links	295	40	None	None

6. Use Figure 3-120b on the previous page as a reference and type the text into each of the layout cells. Apply Heading 1 to the text in the first cell. Apply Heading 3 to the headings in cells 2 through 4 and then underline the headings.
7. Insert the images into the cells. Refer to the invisible element marker in Figure 3-120b as the insertion point for the images in cells 2 and 4. For cell 3, press the ENTER key after item 2 and then click the Align Center button in the Property inspector. Drag the car.gif to the insertion point.
8. Add relative links to the three text items in cell 5.
9. Click the Standard mode button on the Layout tab, select the table, and then center the table.
10. Click the Head button in the HTML category of the Insert bar. Click the Keywords button in the pop-up menu and then type credit, money, tips, checking, saving, [your name] in the Keywords dialog box. Click the Description button and then type Tips and hints on how to save money in the Description dialog box. Save the Web page.
11. Open the index.htm page and click below the last bulleted item. Type Tips on Saving and create a link from this text to the saving.htm page. Save the index.htm page.
12. View the Web site in your browser and verify that your links work. Close the browser. If required, print a copy for your instructor. If required by your instructor, publish the Credit Protection Web site to a remote server by following the steps in Appendix C.

3 Adding a Table Page to the Plant City Web Site

Problem: In his job as a member of the Plant City marketing group, Juan Benito has been exploring the city's history. On a recent tour, Juan discovered that the city contains many well-preserved historic homes. He would like to feature some of these homes on the Web site and has requested that you add a new page to the Plant City Web site. You elect to use a layout table to create this page. The Web page is displayed in Figure 3-121. Appendix C contains instructions for uploading your local site to a remote site.

FIGURE 3-121

Instructions: Perform the following tasks:

1. Use the Windows My Computer option to copy the four images (house01.gif through house04.gif) from the DataFiles folder to your /city/images folder. Start Dreamweaver. Select Plant City from the Site pop-up menu in the Files panel.
2. Add a new page and then add the background image you added in Project 1. Title the page Plant City, Florida - Historic Homes and then save the page with the file name homes.
3. Display the rulers. Click the Insert bar's Layout category and then click the Layout button.
4. Create a layout table with a fixed width of approximately 650 pixels and a height of approximately 675 pixels.
5. Use Figure 3-121 on the previous page as a guide and draw the 10 layout cells. Use the information in Table 3-9 for the widths, heights, and file names.

Table 3-9 Plant City Cell Layout Guide

NUMBER	CELL NAME	W	H	IMAGE ALT TEXT	FILE NAME
1	Heading	390	85	None	None
2	Victorian House	220	160	Victorian House	house01.gif
3	Text	220	50	None	None
4	Atkinson House	225	190	Atkinson House	house02.gif
5	Text	160	70	None	None
6	Lowry/Allen House	245	160	Lowry/Allen House	house03.gif
7	Text	245	50	None	None
8	Text	245	90	None	None
9	Nyberg House	300	170	Nyberg House	house04.gif
10	Text	300	40	None	None

6. Type the text into each of the layout cells as indicated. Apply Heading 1 to the first line of text in the first cell and Heading 3 to the second line of text.
7. Insert the images into the cells. Refer to Table 3-9 for the image file names.
8. Click the Standard mode button on the Layout category, select the table, and then center the table. Add a link at the bottom of the page to the Home page.
9. Click the Keywords button, and then type Plant City, Florida, homes, history, your name in the Keywords dialog box. Click the Description button and then type A tour of Plant City, Florida historic homes in the Description dialog box.
10. Open the index.htm page. Click to the right of the Recipes link. Add a vertical line and then type Historic Homes. Create a link from the Historic Homes text to the homes.htm page.
11. View the Web site in your browser. Close the browser. If required by your instructor, publish the Plant City Web site to a remote server by following the steps in Appendix C. If required, print a copy for your instructor.

Cases and Places

The difficulty of these case studies varies:
■ are the least difficult and ■■ are the most difficult. The last exercise is a group exercise.

1 ■ The sports Web site has become very popular. Several of your friends have suggested that you add a statistics page. You agree that this is a good idea. Create the new page. Using the Internet or other resources, find statistics about your selected sport. Add a background image to the page and use Standard mode to insert a table that contains your statistical information. Add an appropriate heading to the table and an appropriate title for the page. Create a link to the home page. Save the page in your sports Web site. For a selection of images and backgrounds, visit the Dreamweaver MX 2004 Media Web page (scsite.com/dreamweavermx04/media) and then click Media below Project 3.

2 ■ Modify your hobby Web site. Expand the topic and add an additional page with a table created in Standard mode. The table should contain a minimum of three rows and three columns, and a 2-pixel border. Include information in the table about your hobby. Include a minimum of two images in the table. Merge one of the rows or one of the columns and add a border color. Add a background image to the page and give your page a title. Create a link to the home page. Save the page in your hobby Web site. For a selection of images and backgrounds, visit the Dreamweaver MX 2004 Media Web page (scsite.com/dreamweavermx04/media) and then click Media below Project 3.

3 ■■ Modify your favorite type of music Web site by adding a new page. The new page should contain a table with three columns and four rows created in Standard mode. Merge one of the rows and add a background color to the row. Add at least two images to your table. Center the images in the cell. View your Web pages in your browser. Give your page a title and save the page in your music subfolder. Appendix C contains instructions for uploading your local site to a remote site. For a selection of images and backgrounds, visit the Dreamweaver MX 2004 Media Web page (scsite.com/dreamweavermx04/media) and then click Media below Project 3.

Cases and Places

4 ■■ Your running for office campaign is going well. You want to add a new page to the Web site to include pictures and text listing some of your outstanding achievements. Apply a color scheme and a background image to the page. Draw a layout table with a minimum of four layout cells. Include your picture in one of the cells. Add an appropriate title, keywords, and a description to the page. Center the table. Save the page in the office subfolder and then view the page in your browser. Appendix C contains instructions for uploading your local site to a remote site. For a selection of images and backgrounds, visit the Dreamweaver MX 2004 Media Web page (scsite.com/dreamweavermx04/media) and then click Media below Project 3.

5 ■■ **Working Together** The students at your school are requesting more information about the student trips. To accommodate the request, the members of your team decide to add another page to the Web site. Each team member is responsible for researching possible destinations and developing content for the selected destination. Add a heading to the new page and format it appropriately. Draw a layout table with a minimum of six layout cells. Each member adds at least one image and text content to a cell. One member formats the page — including the text and images. Add a title, keywords, meta tags, and a description. Save the page and view it in your browser. Appendix C contains instructions for uploading your local site to a remote site. For a selection of images and backgrounds, visit the Dreamweaver MX 2004 Media Web page (scsite.com/dreamweavermx04/media) and then click Media below Project 3.

MACROMEDIA
Dreamweaver MX 2004

Forms

PROJECT

4

CASE PERSPECTIVE

Each day the Florida Parks Web site receives increasingly more hits. Even though the Web site has been expanded, David is receiving numerous e-mail messages asking questions about the parks. Many of the messages request information about hotel accommodations, especially for the national parks. David meets with you and Joan and asks for suggestions. Joan is involved with a group of friends who coordinate the Florida National Parks Volunteer Association. The members suggest to Joan that adding a form to the Web site could provide access to hotel information for the three national parks. The volunteer group also distributes a daily, weekly, and monthly newsletter. They suggest that the form contain an option for requesting the newsletter. David and Joan like this idea and further suggest that both forms contain a link to the Florida National Parks page and to the Home page.

The team agrees that this is a good idea and that interactive forms with links to the Florida National Parks page and the Home page will enhance and add significantly to their effort to share their affection for Florida's great outdoors.

As you read through this project, you will learn about form processing and how to design and create a form, add behaviors to a form, and review form accessibility options.

Dreamweaver MX 2004

Forms

PROJECT

4

Objectives

You will have mastered the material in this project when you can:

- Discuss form processing
- Describe the difference between client-side and server-side form processing
- Create a form
- Discuss form design
- Insert a table into a form
- Describe form objects
- Describe and add text fields and text areas to a form

- Describe and add check boxes and radio buttons to a form
- Describe and add lists and menus to a form
- Describe and add form buttons to a form
- Describe form accessibility options
- Apply behaviors to a form
- View and test a form

Introduction

Forms enable the Web page designer to provide visitors with dynamic information and to obtain and process information and feedback from the people viewing the Web page. Web forms are a highly versatile tool that can be used for tasks such as surveys, guest books, order forms, tests, automated responses, user questions, and reservations. As you complete the activities in this project, you will find that forms are one of the more important sources of interactivity on the Web and are one of the standard tools for the Web page designer.

Project Four — Creating and Using Interactive Forms

In this project, you learn to create forms and to add form fields to the forms. You add forms and modify two Web pages — a general information page and a hotel reservations form page. The general information page, sponsored by the Florida National Parks Volunteer Association, is shown in Figure 4-1a. This Web page contains a small form at the bottom of the page that provides the viewer with an opportunity to subscribe to a free newsletter. Contained on the page are two relative links — one to the Florida Parks index page and one to the Florida National Parks Web page. The Hotel Reservations Form, shown in Figure 4-1b on the next page, also contains a relative link to the Florida Parks index page and a relative link to the Florida National Parks Web page. The hotel reservations form page contains a request for a hotel reservation at one of the three national parks and provides a jump menu with an absolute link to the Web site for each of the three parks.

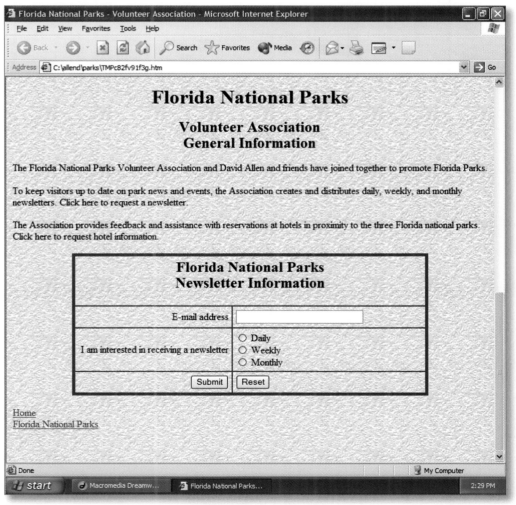

FIGURE 4-1a (continued)

FIGURE 4-1b (*continued*)

Understanding How Forms Work

Forms are interactive elements that provide a way for the Web site visitor to interact with the site. A form provides a method for a user to give feedback, submit an order for merchandise or services, request information, and so on. Forms are created using HTML tags. Each form must have a beginning <form> tag and an ending </form> tag. You cannot nest forms. Each HTML document, however, may contain multiple forms.

Form Processing

A form provides a popular way to collect data from a Web site visitor. Forms, however, do not process data. Forms require a script in order for the form input data to be processed. Such a script generally is a text file that is executed within an application and usually is written in Perl, VBScript, JavaScript, Java, or C++. These scripts reside on a server. Therefore, they are called **server-side scripts**. Other server-side technologies include Macromedia ColdFusion, ASP, ASP.NET, PHP, and JavaServer Pages (JSP). Some type of database application typically supports these technologies.

A common way to process form data is through a **Common Gateway Interface** (**CGI**) script. When a browser collects data, the data is sent to a Hypertext Transfer Protocol (HTTP) server (gateway) specified in the HTML form. The server then starts a program (which also is specified in the HTML form) that can process the collected data. The gateway can process the input however you choose. It may return customized HTML based on the user's input, log the input to a file, or e-mail the input to someone.

The **<form> tag** includes parameters that allow you to specify a path to the server-side script or application that processes the form data and indicate which HTTP method to use when transmitting data from the browser to the server. The two HTTP methods are GET and POST, and both of these methods are attributes of the <form> tag. The **GET method** sends the data with a URL. This method is not widely used because it places a limitation on the amount and format of the data that is transmitted to the application. Another limitation of the GET method is that the information being sent is visible in the browser's Address bar. The **POST method** is more efficient because it sends the data to the application as standard input with no limits. The POST method can send much more information than the typical GET method. With POST, the information is not sent with the URL, so the data is invisible to the site visitor.

As an example of form data processing, when a user enters information into a form and clicks the Submit button, the information is sent to the server, where the server-side script or application processes it. The server then responds by sending the requested information back to the user, or performing some other action based on the content of the form.

The specifics of setting up scripts and database applications are beyond the scope of this book. Another option for form data processing exists, however, in which a form can be set up to send data to an e-mail address. The e-mail action is not 100 percent reliable and may not work if your Internet connection has extensive security parameters. In some instances, submitting a mailto form results in just a blank mail message being displayed. Nothing is harmed when this happens, but no data is attached and sent with the message. Additionally, some browsers display a warning message whenever a form button using mailto is processed. This book uses the e-mail action, however, because this is the action more widely available for most students and users. On the other hand, your instructor may have server-side scripting available. Verify with your instructor the action you are to use.

Between the <form> and </form> tags are the tags that create the body of the form and collect the data. These tags are <input>, <select>, and <textarea>. The most widely used is the **<input> tag**, which collects data from check boxes, radio buttons, single-line text fields, form/image buttons, and passwords. The **<select> tag** is used with list and pop-up menu boxes. The **<textarea>** tag collects the data from multiline text fields.

If you are using Internet Explorer with Windows XP Service Pack 2 (SP2), Internet Explorer automatically blocks content such as form elements. Thus, for all instances in this project where pages containing forms are displayed in Internet Explorer, you must choose to "allow blocked content" by right-clicking the Information Bar and selecting the Allow Blocked Content command from the context menu, or modify the Internet Explorer security settings to allow form elements to display.

More About

Form Processing

Forms can contain form objects that enable user interaction and allow the Web page designer to interact with or gather information from visitors to a Web site. After the data is collected from a user, it is submitted to a server for processing or e-mailed to a designated e-mail address. For more information about form processing, visit the Dreamweaver MX 2004 More About Web page (scsite.com/dreamweavermx04/more.htm) and then click Form Processing.

More About

Windows Service Pack 2 (SP2)

There are some changes to the operating system and to Internet Explorer that may affect Macromedia Dreamweaver if you are using Windows SP2. For more information about Windows SP2, visit the Dreamweaver MX 2004 More About Web page (scsite.com/dreamweavermx04/more.htm) and then click Windows Service Pack 2.

More About

The GET Method

Do not use the GET method to send long forms. URLs are limited to 8,192 characters. If the amount of data sent is too large, data will be truncated, leading to unexpected or failed processing results.

Copying Data Files to the Local Web Site

Your Data Disk contains files and images for Project 4. You use the Windows My Computer option to copy the Project 4 data files to your parks folder. The data files consist of two .htm files and one image file. You first copy and paste the image file to the parks images folder and then you copy and paste the two .htm files to the parks folder. See the inside back cover for instructions for downloading the Data Disk or see your instructor for information about accessing the files required for this book.

The DataFiles folder for this project is stored on Local Disk (C:). The location on your computer may be different. If necessary, verify with your instructor the location of the DataFiles folder. The following steps show how to copy the project data files to the parks local root folder.

To Copy Data Files to the Parks Web Site

1 Click the Start button on the Windows taskbar and then click My Computer.

2 Double-click Local Disk (C:) and then navigate to the location of the data files for Project 4.

3 Double-click the DataFiles folder and then double-click the Proj04 folder.

4 Double-click the parks folder and then double-click the images folder.

5 Click the line.gif image file.

6 Right-click the selected file to display the context menu.

7 Click the Copy command and then click the My Computer Back button the number of times necessary to navigate to the your name folder.

8 Double-click the your name folder, double-click the parks folder, and then double-click the images folder.

9 Right-click anywhere in the open window to display the context menu.

10 Click the Paste command to paste the line.gif image file into the images folder.

11 Click the My Computer Back button the number of times necessary to navigate to the Proj04 parks folder. Hold down the SHIFT key and select the two data files. Right-click and click the Copy command.

12 Click the My Computer Back button the number of times necessary to navigate to the your name folder. Paste the two data files into the parks folder. Close the My Computer window.

The image file and data files are pasted into the Florida Parks Web site images folder (Figure 4-2).

Q&A

Q: Why would I use the <label> tag?

A: Use the <label> tag to associate any form element with specific text to make it available for screen readers.

FIGURE 4-2

Starting Dreamweaver and Opening a Web Site

Each time you start Dreamweaver, it opens to the last site displayed when you closed the program. It, therefore, may be necessary for you to open the parks Web site. The **Files pop-up menu** in the Files panel lists sites you have defined. When you open the site, a list of the pages and subfolders within the site displays. The following steps illustrate how to start Dreamweaver and open the Florida Parks Web site.

To Start Dreamweaver and Open the Florida Parks Web Site

1 Click the Start button on the Windows taskbar.

2 Point to All Programs on the Start menu, point to Macromedia on the All Programs submenu, and then click Macromedia Dreamweaver MX 2004 on the Macromedia submenu.

3 If necessary, display the panel groups.

4 Click the Files panel box arrow and then point to Florida Parks on the Files pop-up menu.

5 Click Florida Parks.

The Florida Parks Web site hierarchy displays in the Files panel (Figure 4-3 on the next page). The two new data files — volunteer.htm and hotel_form.htm — display in the list of files.

More About

File Order Display

The order in which files are displayed in the Files panel is determined by the View selected in Windows Explorer.

FIGURE 4-3

More About

Form Design

When designing a form, keep the form simple and to the point. Before you create the form, sketch it on paper. The layout should be uncomplicated and clear. For more information about form design, visit the Dreamweaver MX 2004 More About Web page (scsite.com/dreamweavermx04/more.htm) and then click Form Design.

Form Design

Consistency in Web pages ties a Web site together. Using the same background image on all pages within the site is one way to achieve consistency. The background that has been used for the Florida Parks Web site already has been added to the two HTML documents you copied from the DataFiles folder.

You open the hotel_form.htm document and then insert, center, and format a page heading. Then you add a page title and save the Web page. The following steps show how to open the document and to insert and format the heading.

To Insert and Format the Heading

1. Double-click hotel_form.htm in the Files panel.

2. Click the Title text box and title the page Florida Parks - Hotel Reservations.

3. Click the Document window and then type Florida National Parks as the first line of the heading and then press SHIFT+ENTER to insert a line break. Type Hotel Reservations Form as the second heading line.

4. Drag to select both lines of text, apply Heading 1, and then click the Align Center button in the Property inspector.

5. Click outside the selected text and then press the ENTER key.

6. Drag the line.gif image from the Files panel Images folder to the insertion point in the Document window and then press the ENTER key.

7. Click the Align Left button.

8 Click View on the menu bar, point to Visual Aids, and then, if necessary, click to enable Invisible Elements.

9 Click the Save button on the Standard toolbar.

10 Hide the panel groups.

The title is added, the heading is centered and formatted, and the line.gif image is inserted (Figure 4-4). The Web page is saved in the parks folder, and the panel groups are hidden.

FIGURE 4-4

Forms and Web Pages

Web page designers create forms consisting of a collection of input fields so users can obtain useful information and can enter data. When a user clicks the form Send or Submit button, the data is processed with a server-side script or is sent to a specified e-mail address. A typical form, such as the one created in this project, is composed of form objects. A **form object** can be a text box, check box, radio button, list, menu, or other buttons. Form objects are discussed in more detail later in this project.

Inserting a Form

Inserting a form is accomplished in the same manner as inserting a table or any other object in Dreamweaver. Simply position the insertion point where you want the form to start and then click the Form button on the Forms category. Dreamweaver inserts the <form> and </form> tags into the source code and then displays a dotted red outline to represent the form in Design view. You cannot resize a form by dragging the borders. Rather, the form expands as objects are inserted into the form.

More About

Dreamweaver and Forms

Dreamweaver makes it easy to add forms to your Web pages. The Forms category on the Insert bar contains all of the traditional form objects. When the object is entered into the form, Dreamweaver creates the JavaScript necessary for processing the form. For more information about Dreamweaver and forms, visit the Dreamweaver MX 2004 More About Web page (scsite.com/ dreamweavermx04/more.htm) and then click Dreamweaver and Forms.

When viewed in a browser, the form outline does not display; therefore, no visible border exists to turn on or off. The following steps illustrate how to insert a form into the hotel_form.htm page.

To Insert a Form

1

• **If necessary, display the Insert bar. Click the arrow to the right of the display category on the Insert bar and then point to Forms on the Insert bar pop-up menu.**

The Insert bar pop-up menu displays, and Forms is highlighted (Figure 4-5).

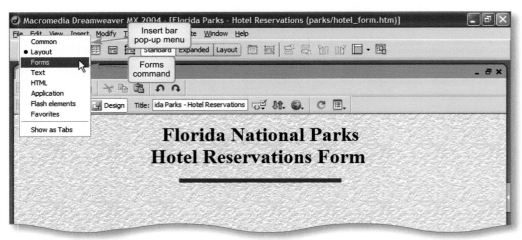

FIGURE 4-5

2

• **Click Forms and then click the Form button.**

The form is inserted into the Document window and is indicated by a dotted red outline. The Form Property inspector is displayed (Figure 4-6). The insertion point is blinking inside the dotted red outline.

FIGURE 4-6

Other Ways

1. On Insert menu, click Form, click Form on submenu

Property Inspector Form Properties

As you have seen, the Property inspector options change depending on the selected object. The following section describes the form-related features of the Property inspector shown in Figure 4-7. When you insert and select a form, in some instances, the Class box may be displayed in the Property inspector.

FIGURE 4-7

FORM NAME Naming a form makes it possible to reference or control the form with a scripting language, such as JavaScript or VBScript.

ACTION Contains the mailto address or specifies the URL to the dynamic page or script that will process the form.

TARGET Specifies the window or frame in which to display the data after processing if a script specifies that a new page displays. The four targets are _blank, _parent, _self, and _top. The **_blank** target opens the referenced link (or processed data) in a new browser window, leaving the current window untouched. The _blank target is the one most often used with a jump menu, which is discussed later in this project. The **_self** target opens the destination document in the same window as the one in which the form was submitted. The two other targets mostly are used with frames.

METHOD Indicates the method by which the form data is transferred to the server. The three options are **POST**, which embeds the form data in the HTTP request; **GET**, which appends the form data to the URL requesting the page; and **Default**, which uses the browser's default setting to send the form data to the server. Generally, the default is the GET method. The POST and GET methods were discussed earlier in this project.

ENCTYPE Specifies a **MIME (Multipurpose Internet Mail Extensions)** type for the data being submitted to the server so the server software will know how to interpret the data. The default is application/x-www-form-urlencode and typically is used in conjunction with the POST method. This default automatically encodes the form response with non-alphanumeric characters in hexadecimal format. The multipart/form-data MIME type is used with a form object that enables the user to upload a file. You can select one of these two values from the Enctype list box or manually enter a value in the Enctype list box. The text/plain value is useful for e-mail replies, but is not an option in the Enctype list box and must be entered manually. This value enables the data to be transmitted in a readable format instead of as one long string of data.

When naming the form and the form elements (discussed later in this project), use names that identify the form or form element. Be consistent with your naming conventions and do not use spaces or other special characters, except the underscore. This project uses lowercase letters to name the form and form elements. If you are using server-side scripting, be aware of and avoid reserved words that exist in the scripting language.

The following steps illustrate how to name the form and to set the other form properties, including using the mailto: action. Verify with your instructor that this is the correct action and that the form data is not to be processed with a server-side script.

To Set the Form Properties

1

• **Double-click the Form name text box in the Property inspector. Type** hotel_form **and then press the TAB key.**

The form is named (Figure 4-8). The insertion point is blinking in the Action text box.

FIGURE 4-8

2

• **Type** mailto:dallen@parks. com **(use your own e-mail address).**

Your e-mail address displays in the Action text box (Figure 4-9).

FIGURE 4-9

3

• **Click the Target box arrow, select _self, and then press the TAB key.**

The insertion point moves to the Enctype box (Figure 4-10).

FIGURE 4-10

4

• **Type** text/plain **and then press the ENTER key.**

The Enctype box displays the text, text/plain (Figure 4-11).

FIGURE 4-11

More About

Naming Forms

A form does not need a name
to work, but a name is helpful
if you use a Dreamweaver
behavior or JavaScript to
interact with the form.

Inserting a Table into a Form

Adding and lining up labels within a form sometimes can be a problem. The text field width for labels is measured in **monospace**, meaning that each character has the same width. Most regular fonts, however, are not monospaced; they are proportional. Two options to solve this problem are preformatted text and tables. To align labels properly using preformatted text requires the insertion of extra spaces. Using tables and text alignment, therefore, is a faster and easier method to use when creating a form.

The following steps show how to add an 11-row, 2-column table to the form.

To Insert a Table into a Form

1

• **Click inside the form
(the dotted red outline).**

• **Click Insert on the
menu bar and then
point to Table.**

*The Insert menu displays,
and Table is highlighted
(Figure 4-12).*

FIGURE 4-12

2

• **Click Table.**

The Table dialog box displays (Figure 4-13). The Table dialog box on your computer most likely will display different values than those contained in Figure 4-13.

FIGURE 4-13

3

• **Type the following values in the table: Rows –** 11, **Columns –** 2, **Table Width –** 75 **percent, Border thickness –** 4, **Cell padding –** 5, **Cell spacing –** 0, **and** Hotel reservation form for Florida's three national parks **as the Summary text.**

The Table dialog box displays the new values (Figure 4-14).

FIGURE 4-14

Macromedia
Dreamweaver MX 2004

4

• **Click the OK button.**

*The table is inserted into the
form outline (Figure 4-15). The
<table> tag is selected in the
tag selector, and the table
properties are displayed in the
Property inspector.*

FIGURE 4-15

5

• **Click the Align box
arrow in the Property
inspector and then
select Center.**

*The table is centered within
the form outline (Figure 4-16).*

FIGURE 4-16

Formatting the Table within the Form

Adding formatting to a form creates a more attractive page. In this instance, formatting includes changing the column width, aligning the text for the labels in column 1 to the right, and changing the border color. The following steps show how to add these formatting changes.

To Format the Form

1

• **If necessary, scroll up, click row 1, column 1, and then drag to select all of column 1. Click the W text box, type 35%, and then press the ENTER key.**

The column width is set to 35% (Figure 4-17).

2

• **Click the Align Right button in the Property inspector.**

No noticeable changes display in the column. When text is entered into the table cells in column 1, however, the text aligns to the right.

FIGURE 4-17

3

• **Click the <table> tag in the tag selector. Click the Brdr color hexadecimal text box. Type** #336666 **and then press the ENTER key.**

The table is selected, the Table Property inspector is displayed, and the form border color is changed (Figure 4-18).

4

• **Click the Save button on the Standard toolbar.**

The form is saved.

FIGURE 4-18

Form Objects

In Dreamweaver, data is entered through form input types called form objects. After you add a form to your Web page, you begin creating the form by adding form objects. Forms can contain various objects that enable user interaction and are the mechanisms that allow users to input data. Examples of form objects are text fields, check boxes, and radio buttons. Each form object should have a unique name, except the radio buttons within the same group. In that case, the radio buttons should share the same name.

The two steps used to insert a form field in a Web page are (1) to add the form field and any accompanying descriptive labels, and (2) to modify the properties of the form object. All Dreamweaver form objects are available through the Forms category on the Insert bar. Table 4-1 on the next page lists the button names and descriptions available on the Forms category (Figure 4-19 on the next page).

Table 4-1	**Buttons on the Insert Bar Forms Category**
BUTTON NAME	**DESCRIPTION**
Form	Inserts a form into the Document window
Text Field	Accepts any type of alphanumeric text entry
Hidden Field	Stores information entered by a user and then uses that data within the site database
Textarea	Provides a multiline text entry field
Checkbox	Allows multiple responses within a single group of options and permits the user to select as many options as apply
Radio Button	Represents an exclusive choice; only one item in a group of buttons can be selected
Radio Group	Represents a group of radio buttons
List/Menu	List displays option values within a scrolling list that allows users to select multiple options; Menu displays the option values in a pop-up menu that allows users to select only a single item
Jump Menu	Special form of a pop-up menu that lets the viewer link to another document or file
Image Field	Creates a custom, graphical button
File Field	Allows users to browse to a file on their computers and upload the file as form data
Button	Performs actions when clicked; standard Submit and Reset buttons send data to the server and clear the form fields
Label	Provides a way to associate the text label for a field with the field structurally
Fieldset	Inserts a container tag for a logical group of form elements

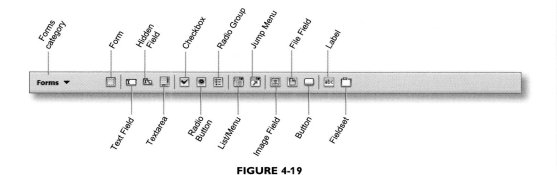

FIGURE 4-19

More About

Adding Form Tags

If you attempt to insert a form object without first creating the form, Dreamweaver will display the message, Add form tags? Choose Yes to let Dreamweaver create form tags for the object.

Text Fields

A **text field** is a form object in which users enter a response. Forms support three types of text fields: single-line, multiple-line, and password. Input into a text field can consist of alphanumeric and punctuation characters. When you insert a text field into a form, the TextField Property inspector is displayed (Figure 4-20 on the next page).

FIGURE 4-20

The following section describes the text field attributes for a single-line and password form. The multiple-line attributes are described later in this project.

TEXTFIELD Assigns a unique name to the form object.

CHAR WIDTH Specifies the maximum number of characters that can be displayed in the field.

MAX CHAR Specifies the maximum number of characters that can be entered into the field.

TYPE Designates the field as a single-line, multiple-line, or password field.

INIT VAL Assigns the value that is displayed in the field when the form first loads.

CLASS An attribute used with Cascading Style Sheets.

Typically, a **single-line text field** provides for a single word or short phrase response. A **password text field** is a single-line text box that contains special characters. When a user types in a password field, asterisks or bullets replace the text as a security precaution. Note, however, that passwords sent to a server using a password field are not encrypted and can be intercepted and read as alphanumeric text. For this reason, you always should provide encryption for data you want to keep secure. A **multiple-line text field** provides a larger text area in which to enter a response. The Property inspector for a multiple-line text field contains some minor differences than that shown in Figure 4-20. A multiple-line text field is discussed later in this project.

Inserting Text in a Form

You will notice as you insert form objects in a Web page that typically they contain no text label. **Labels** identify the type of data to be entered into the text field form object. Adding a descriptive label to the form that indicates the type of information requested provides a visual cue to the Web site visitors about the type of data they should type into the text box. Inserting text in a form is as simple as positioning the insertion point and then typing.

Q&A

Q: Why would I use a hidden field?

A: You can use a hidden field to store information entered by a user, such as a name, e-mail address, or viewing preference, and then use that data when the user next visits the site.

Q&A

Q: How can I create a password field?

A: Easy — just insert a TextField form object and then select the Password option in the TextField Property inspector.

Single-Line Text Fields

Use single-line text fields for short, concise answers such as a word or phrase. In the TextField Property inspector, you enter a unique name for each text field in the form. Server-side scripts use this name to process the data. If you use the mailto option, the name is contained within the data in the e-mail that is sent to your e-mail address. Form object names are case sensitive and cannot contain spaces or special characters other than an underscore.

The Char width field default setting is 20 characters. You can change the default, however, by typing in another number. If the Char width is left as the 20-character default and a user enters 50 characters, the text scrolls to the right and only the last 20 of those characters are displayed in the text field. Even though the characters are not displayed, they are recognized by the form field object and will be sent to the server for processing or contained within the data if mailto is used.

Entering a value into the Max Chars field defines the size limit of the text field and is used to validate the form. If a user tries to exceed the limit, an alert is sounded. If the Max Chars field is left blank, users can enter any amount of text.

To display a default text value in a field, type the default text in the Init val text box. When the form displays in the browser, this text displays.

The following steps show how to add name, address, and e-mail single-line text boxes to the Hotel Reservations form.

To Add Descriptive Labels and Single-Line Text Fields to the Hotel Reservations Form

1

• **If necessary, scroll up and then click row 1, column 1.**

The insertion point aligns to the right in the cell (Figure 4-21).

FIGURE 4-21

2

• **Type** Name **as the descriptive label and then press the TAB key.**

The insertion point displays in row 1, column 2 (Figure 4-22).

FIGURE 4-22

3

• **Click the Text Field button.**

A text field form object is inserted into the table (Figure 4-23). The Property inspector displays properties relative to the text field.

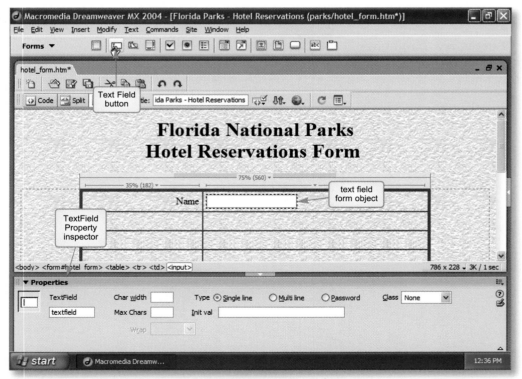

FIGURE 4-23

4

• **Double-click the TextField text box in the Property inspector, type** name**, and then press the TAB key.**

• **Type** 50 **in the Char width text box and then press the TAB key. If necessary, click Single line.**

The text field expands to a character width of 50 (Figure 4-24).

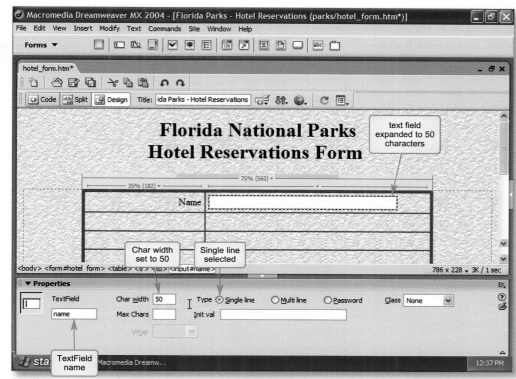

FIGURE 4-24

5

• **Click row 2, column 1, type** Address**, and then press the TAB key.**

• **Click the Text Field button on the Forms category.**

The Address label displays in row 2, column 1, and the text field form object is inserted into the table (Figure 4-25). The Property inspector displays TextField properties.

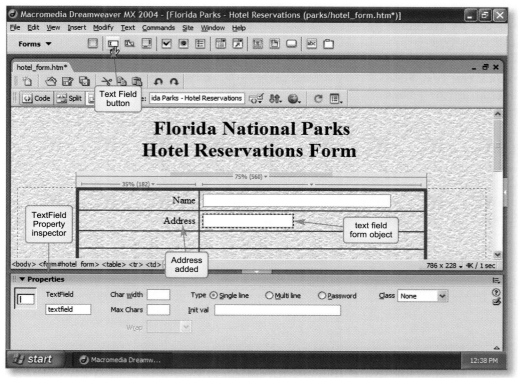

FIGURE 4-25

6

• **If necessary, scroll down. Double-click the TextField text box in the Property inspector, type** address**, and then press the TAB key.**

• **Type** 50 **in the Char width text box and then press the TAB key. If necessary, click Single line.**

The text field expands to a character width of 50 (Figure 4-26).

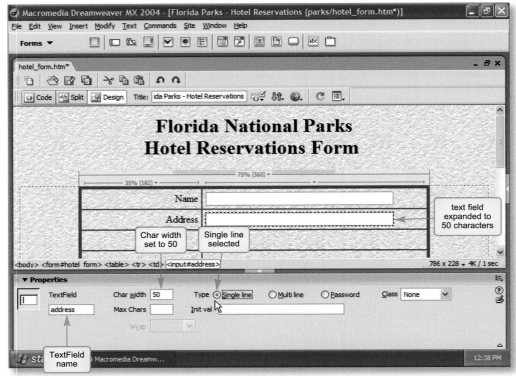

FIGURE 4-26

7

• **Click row 3, column 1, and then type** City**. Press the TAB key.**

• **Click the Text Field button on the Forms category.**

• **Type** city **as the TextField name.**

• **Type** 50 **in the Char width text box and then press the TAB key. Ensure Single line is selected.**

The label, City, displays in row 3, column 1. The text field expands to a character width of 50 (Figure 4-27).

FIGURE 4-27

8

• **Click row 4, column 1. Type** State/Zip Code **as the label and then press the TAB key.**

The label, State/Zip Code, displays in row 4, column 1, and the insertion point is blinking in row 4, column 2 (Figure 4-28).

FIGURE 4-28

9

• **Type** State **and then press the SPACEBAR.**

The descriptive label for State displays (Figure 4-29).

FIGURE 4-29

10

• **Click the Text Field button. Type** state **as the TextField name.**

• **Type** 2 **for the Char width and Max Chars values. Ensure Single line is selected.**

The TextField name displays as state, and the Char width and Max Chars values are set to 2 (Figure 4-30).

FIGURE 4-30

11

• **Click to the right of the State form object and then press the SPACEBAR. Type** Zip Code **and then press the SPACEBAR.**

• **Click the Text Field button.**

• **Type** zip **as the TextField name.**

• **Type** 10 **for the Char width and Max Chars values and then press the TAB key. Ensure Single line is selected.**

Zip Code displays as the descriptive label. The Char width and Max Chars values are set to 10 (Figure 4-31).

FIGURE 4-31

12

• **If necessary, scroll down. Click row 5, column 1, and then type** E-mail address.

• **Press the TAB key and then click the Text Field button.**

The descriptive label for the e-mail address displays, and the text field form object is added to the document (Figure 4-32).

FIGURE 4-32

13

• **Type** email **as the TextField name.**

• **Type** 45 **for the Char width value and then press the ENTER key. Ensure Single line is selected.**

The text field is named, and the size of the text box form object is adjusted (Figure 4-33).

• **Press CTRL+S to save the page.**

FIGURE 4-33

Other Ways

1. On Insert menu point to Form, click Text Field

Check Boxes

Check boxes allow the Web user to click a box to toggle a value to either yes or no. They frequently are used to enable the visitor to select as many of the listed options as desired. Figure 4-34 displays the Property inspector for a check box. Just like a text field, each check box should have a unique name. The Checked value text box contains the information you want to send to the script or to include in the mailto information to identify the data. For the Initial state, the default is Unchecked. Click Checked if you want an option to appear selected when the form first loads in the browser. The following steps illustrate how to add three check boxes to the Hotel Reservations form.

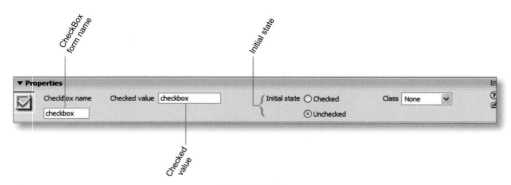

FIGURE 4-34

To Add Check Boxes

1

• **Click row 6, column 1, type** Hotels, **and then press the TAB key.**

• **Click the Checkbox button on the Forms category.**

Hotels is displayed as the descriptive label, and a check box is added to the form (Figure 4-35). The Property inspector changes to display the Checkbox properties.

FIGURE 4-35

2

• **Type** hotel1 **as the CheckBox name.**

• **Press the TAB key and then type** biscayne **in the Checked value text box.**

The properties for the first check box are displayed (Figure 4-36).

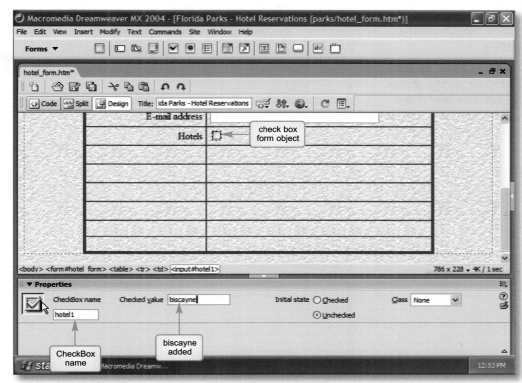

FIGURE 4-36

3

• **Click to the right of the check box form object and then press SHIFT+ENTER to add a line break.**

The insertion point is positioned below the first check box (Figure 4-37).

FIGURE 4-37

4

• **Click the Checkbox button.**

• **Type** hotel2 **as the CheckBox name. Press the TAB key and then type** everglades **in the Checked value text box.**

The second check box is added to the form, and the properties for the second check box are displayed (Figure 4-38).

FIGURE 4-38

5

• **Click to the right of the second check box, press SHIFT+ENTER to add a line break, and then click the Checkbox button on the Forms category.**

The third check box is added (Figure 4-39).

FIGURE 4-39

6

• **Type** hotel3 **as the CheckBox name.**

• **Press the TAB key and then type** dry_tortugas **in the Checked value text box.**

The properties for the third check box display (Figure 4-40).

FIGURE 4-40

7

• **Click to the right of the first check box.**

• **Type** Biscayne Royale **and then press the Down Arrow key.**

• **Type** Everglades Station **as the descriptive label for the second check box, press the Down Arrow key, and then type** Dry Tortugas Beach Club **as the label for the third check box.**

The descriptive labels are entered for all three check boxes (Figure 4-41).

8

• **Click the Save button on the Standard toolbar.**

FIGURE 4-41

List/Menu

Another way to provide form field options to your Web site visitor is with lists and menus. These options provide many choices within a limited space. A **list** provides a scroll bar with up and down arrows that lets a user scroll the list, whereas a menu contains a pop-up list. Multiple selections can be made from a list, while users can select only one item from a menu. The menu option is discussed later in this project. Figure 4-42 illustrates the Property inspector for a list.

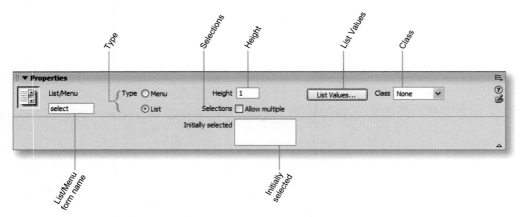

FIGURE 4-42

LIST/MENU Assigns a name to the list or menu.

TYPE Designates if the form object is a pop-up menu or a scrolling list.

HEIGHT Specifies the number of lines that display in the form; the default is 1.

SELECTIONS Designates if the user can select more than one option; not available with the menu option.

LIST VALUES Opens the List Values dialog box.

INITIALLY SELECTED Contains a list of available items from which the user can select.

CLASS An attribute used with Cascading Style Sheets.

As with all other form objects, the list should be named. You control the height of the list by specifying a number in the Height box. You can elect to show one item at a time or show the entire list. If you display the entire list, the scroll bar does not display. Selecting the Selections check box allows the user to make multiple selections. Clicking the List Values button opens the List Values dialog box so you can add items to a list or pop-up menu, or remove them. These added items are displayed in the Initially selected box. Each item in the list has a label and a value. The label represents the text that appears in the list, and the value is sent to the processing application if the item is selected. If no value is specified, the label is sent to the processing application instead.

The following steps show how to add a scrolling list to the Hotel Reservations form.

To Create a Scrolling List

• **Click row 7, column 1.**
Type Accommodations
and then press the TAB
key. Click the List/Menu
button on the Forms
category.

The label, Accommodations, is
entered, and the List/Menu
form object is inserted. The
Property inspector displays
the List/Menu properties
(Figure 4-43).

FIGURE 4-43

2

• **Type** accommodations
as the List/Menu name.

• **Click List in the Type**
options.

• **Type** 2 **in the**
Height box.

• **Click the Selections**
check box to allow
multiple selections.

The list is named, the height
is set to 2, and Allow multiple
selections is selected
(Figure 4-44).

FIGURE 4-44

3

• **Click the List Values button.**

The List Values dialog box displays (Figure 4-45). The insertion point is blinking in the Item Label column.

FIGURE 4-45

4

• **Type** Single **as the first Item Label, press the TAB key, and then type** single **as the Value.**

• **Press the TAB key.**

A second line is added to the Item Label list (Figure 4-46).

FIGURE 4-46

5

• **Type** Double **as the second Item Label.**

• **Type** double **as the Value and then press the TAB key.**

• **Type** Suite **as the third Item Label.**

• **Type** suite **as the Value and then press the TAB key.**

• **Type** Luxury Suite **as the fourth Item Label.**

• **Type** luxury_suite **as the Value.**

The items for the list are added to the List Values dialog box (Figure 4-47).

FIGURE 4-47

6

• **Click the OK button.**

The list displays in the Initially selected box in the Property inspector (Figure 4-48).

FIGURE 4-48

7

• **Click Single in the Initially selected box in the Property inspector.**

Single is designated as the default item in the list (Figure 4-49).

8

• **Click the Save button on the Standard toolbar.**

FIGURE 4-49

Pop-Up Menus

You can offer your Web site visitors a range of choices by using a pop-up menu. This type of menu (also called a drop-down menu) lets a user select a single item from a list of many options. A **pop-up menu** is useful when you have a limited amount of space because it occupies only a single line of vertical space in the form. Only one option choice is visible when the menu form object displays in the browser. Clicking a down arrow displays the entire list. The user then clicks one of the menu items to make a choice. The following steps illustrate how to create a pop-up menu.

To Create a Pop-Up Menu

1

• **If necessary, scroll down and then click row 8, column 1.**

• **Type** Number of nights **and then press the TAB key.**

• **Click the List/Menu button on the Forms category.**

The descriptive label for the pop-up menu is added to the form, and the List/Menu form object is displayed. The Property inspector changes to reflect the selected form object (Figure 4-50).

FIGURE 4-50

2

• **Type** nights **in the List/Menu text box to name the pop-up menu.**

The pop-up menu is named (Figure 4-51).

FIGURE 4-51

3

• **Click the List Values button. In the List Values dialog box, type** 1 **as the Item Label, press the TAB key, and then type** 1 **for the Value.**

• **Press the TAB key.**

The List Values dialog box displays (Figure 4-52). The Item Label and Value are entered.

FIGURE 4-52

4

• **Repeat Step 3 in the List Values dialog box, incrementing the number each time by 1 in the Item Label and Value fields, until the number 7 is added to the Item Label field and the Value field.**

The List Values dialog box displays Item Label and Value field numbers 1 through 7 (Figure 4-53).

FIGURE 4-53

5

• **Click the OK button.**

The numbers display in the Initially selected box (Figure 4-54).

FIGURE 4-54

6

• **Click the number 1 in the Initially selected box in the Property inspector.**

The number 1 displays in the List/Menu form object as the default value (Figure 4-55).

FIGURE 4-55

Jump Menus

A **jump menu** is a special type of pop-up menu that provides options that link to documents or files. You can create links to documents on your Web site, links to documents on other Web sites, e-mail links, links to graphics, or links to any other file type that can be opened in a browser. A jump menu can contain three basic components:

- An optional menu selection prompt: This could be a category description for the menu items or instructions, such as Choose one.
- A required list of linked menu items: When the user chooses an option, a linked document or file is opened.
- An optional Go button: With a Go button, the user makes a selection from the menu, and the new page loads when the Go button is clicked. Without a Go button, the new page loads as soon as the user makes a selection from the menu.

The following steps illustrate how to add a jump menu with a link to a Web site for each of the three national parks. The menu will contain a Choose one selection prompt, and the linked Web site will open in the main window.

To Insert a Jump Menu

1

- **Click row 9, column 1, type** Links, **and then press the TAB key.**

The label for the jump menu is inserted in the form (Figure 4-56).

FIGURE 4-56

2

• **Click the Jump Menu button.**

• **Type** Choose one **in the Text text box and then point to the plus (+) button.**

The Insert Jump Menu dialog box displays (Figure 4-57). The text, Choose one, is added as the first menu item in the Text text box.

FIGURE 4-57

3

• **Click the plus button and then double-click the Text text box.**

• **Type** Biscayne National Park **as the text for the second menu item and then press the TAB key.**

Biscayne National Park is added as the text for the second menu item (Figure 4-58). The insertion point is blinking in the When selected, go to URL text box.

FIGURE 4-58

4

• **Type** http://www.nps. gov/bisc/index.htm **and then point to the plus button.**

The URL for the Biscayne National Park Web site is added to the Insert Jump Menu dialog box (Figure 4-59).

FIGURE 4-59

5

• **Click the plus button, double-click the Text text box, type** Dry Tortugas National Park **as the entry, and then press the TAB key.**

• **Type** http://www.nps. gov/drto/index.htm **and then point to the plus button.**

Dry Tortugas National Park is added as the third menu item, and the URL for the Dry Tortugas National Park Web site is added to the Insert Jump Menu dialog box (Figure 4-60).

FIGURE 4-60

6

• **Click the plus button, double-click the Text text box, type** Everglades National Park **as the entry, and then press the TAB key.**

• **Type** http://www.nps. gov/ever/index.htm **and then click Select first item after URL change to select the check box.**

• **Click the OK button.**

Everglades National Park is added as the fourth menu item, and the URL for the Everglades National Park Web site is added to the Insert Jump Menu dialog box (Figure 4-61). The Select first item after URL change check box is selected.

FIGURE 4-61

7

• **Click Choose one in the Initially selected box in the Property inspector.**

The jump menu is added to the form and is completed (Figure 4-62).

8

• **Click the Save button on the Standard toolbar.**

FIGURE 4-62

Other Ways

1. On Insert menu point to Form, click Jump Menu

Textarea Text Fields

Earlier in this project, you added several single-line text field form objects to the Hotel Reservations form. A second type of text field is the textarea form object, which supports multiline objects. The Property inspector settings for the textarea text field are similar to those for single-line text fields except you can specify the maximum number of lines the user can enter and can specify the wrap attributes. The Property inspector for a textarea text field is shown in Figure 4-63.

FIGURE 4-63

The Wrap pop-up menu in the Property inspector enables the Web page designer to select one of four options: Off, Default, Virtual, or Physical. Selecting **Off** or **Default** prevents the text from wrapping to the next line and requires the user to press the ENTER key to move the insertion point to the next line. **Virtual** limits word wrap to the text area. If the user's input exceeds the right boundary of the text area, the text wraps to the next line. When data is submitted for processing, however, it is submitted as one string of data. **Physical** sets word wrap in the text area and applies it to the data when it is submitted for processing.

An initial value can be added to the Init val box. When the user clicks the textarea text field, this initial value is highlighted and then deleted when the user begins to enter text. The following steps illustrate how to add a multiline text field to create a comments text area in your Hotel Reservations form.

To Add a Textarea Text Field

1

- **If necessary, scroll down. Click row 10, column 1.**

- **Type** Comments **and then press the TAB key.**

- **Click the Textarea button on the Forms category.**

The label is inserted, and the textarea form object is added to the Document window (Figure 4-64).

FIGURE 4-64

2

- **Type** comments **as the name for the textarea.**

- **Press the TAB key and type** 50 **for the Char width value. Press the TAB key and type** 4 **for the Num Lines value.**

- **Click the Init val box, type** Please add your comments **as the entry.**

The form is named, the character width and number of lines are set, and an initial value is entered (Figure 4-65).

- **Click the Save button on the Standard toolbar.**

Other Ways

1. On Insert menu point to Form, click Textarea

FIGURE 4-65

Form Buttons

Form buttons control form operations. HTML provides three basic types of form buttons: Submit, Reset, and Command. Submit and Reset buttons are standard features of almost every form. When the user presses the **Submit button,** the data entered into a form is sent to a server for processing or forwarded to an e-mail address. In some instances, the data is edited by JavaScript or other code prior to processing. The **Reset button** clears all the fields in the form. You also can assign to a **Command button** other processing tasks that you have defined in a script. For example, a Command button might calculate the total cost of a hotel room for a week. Command buttons require that additional code be added using Code view. The Button name Property inspector is displayed in Figure 4-66.

FIGURE 4-66

BUTTON NAME Assigns a name to the button. Submit and Reset are reserved names.

SUBMIT BUTTON Tells the form to submit the form data to the processing application or script or to send the data to an e-mail address.

RESET BUTTON Tells the form to reset all the form fields to their original values.

LABEL Determines the text that appears on the button.

ACTION Determines what happens when the button is clicked and how the data is to be processed. Form processing was discussed earlier in this project. The three processing options are to submit the contents of the form, to clear the contents of the form, or to do nothing.

CLASS An attribute used with Cascading Style Sheets.

The following steps illustrate how to add the Submit and Reset buttons to the Hotel Reservations form.

To Add the Submit and Reset Buttons

1

• **If necessary, scroll down and then click row 11, column 1. (Figure 4-67).**

FIGURE 4-67

2

• **Click the Button button on the Forms category.**

The Submit button form object is added to the form, and the Property inspector displays the Submit button attributes (Figure 4-68).

FIGURE 4-68

3

• **Click row 11, column 2, and then click the Button button on the Forms category.**

The Submit button form object is added to the form, and the Property inspector displays the Submit button attributes (Figure 4-69).

FIGURE 4-69

4

• **Type** Reset **in the Button name text box and then press the TAB key.**

• **Type** Reset **in the Label text box and then click Reset form in the Action area.**

The button is renamed Reset, and Reset form is selected (Figure 4-70).

5

• **Click the Save button on the Standard toolbar.**

FIGURE 4-70

Other Ways

1. On Insert menu point to Form, click Button

Radio Buttons and Radio Button Groups

Radio buttons provide a set of options from which the user can select only one button. Clicking a second button automatically deselects the first choice. Each button in a form consists of a radio button and a corresponding descriptive label. In Dreamweaver, you can insert radio buttons one at a time or insert a radio button group. When you insert an individual radio button, the Property inspector shown in Figure 4-71 is displayed. In the Property inspector's Radio Button text box, type a descriptive name. If you are inserting individual radio buttons to create a group, you must label each button. In the Checked value text box, enter the value you want sent to the server-side script or application when a user selects this radio button. For the Initial state, click Checked if you want an option to appear selected when the form first loads in the browser.

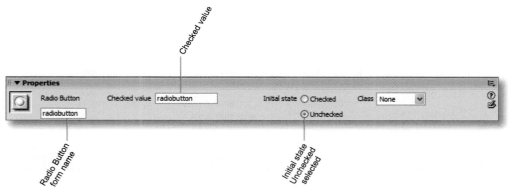

FIGURE 4-71

A radio button group is a commonly used option. If you are adding multiple radio buttons to a form, each set of radio buttons must have a unique name. When you click the Radio Group button on the Forms category, the Radio Group dialog box is displayed. Radio button groups will be discussed later in this project.

Form Objects, the Label Button, and Accessibility

So far, when you added a form object to a page, you also added a descriptive label to identify the object. Traditionally, this is the way most Web page authors label form objects. The current HTML specifications, however, provide the <label> tag. This tag adds functionality to the form object by associating the descriptive label for the form object directly with that object. This is particularly helpful for the users of speech-based browsers.

The Insert bar Forms category contains a Label button. To add a label, select the specific form object to which you want to associate the label, and then click the Label button. When you click a radio button, for instance, and then click the Label button, Code view is displayed. You then manually type the descriptive text between the <label> and </label> tags. Similarly, Dreamweaver does not provide a Property inspector for labels, so any editing of labels is done in Code view.

Manual editing of the <label> tag can be time-consuming and error-prone, but Dreamweaver provides an alternative with the Accessibility options for form objects. When the Accessibility option for form objects is enabled, Dreamweaver displays the Input Tag Accessibility Attributes dialog box (Figure 4-72 on the next page). Table 4-2 on the next page contains a description of the options in this dialog box. Recall that

Accessibility options are turned on by clicking Edit on the menu bar and then selecting Preferences. In the Preferences dialog box, click the Accessibility category and then click the check box for Form objects. Appendix B contains an expanded discussion of accessibility options.

FIGURE 4-72

Table 4-2 Input Tag Accessibility Attributes	
ATTRIBUTE NAME	**DESCRIPTION**
Label	The descriptive text that identifies the form object.
Style	Provides three options for the <label> tag: *Wrap with label tag* wraps a label tag around the form item. *Attach label tag using 'for' attribute* allows the user to associate a label with a form element, even if the two are in different table cells. *No label tag* turns off the Accessibility option.
Position	Determines the placement of the label text in relation to the form object — before or after the form object.
Access key	Selects the form object in the browser using a keyboard shortcut (one letter). This key is used in combination with the CTRL key (Windows) to access the object.
Tab Index	Specifies the order in which the form objects are selected when pressing the TAB key. The tab order goes from the lowest to highest numbers.

Adding a Form to the Volunteer.htm Web Page

The next step is to add a form and radio button group form field to the volunteer.htm Web page. Informational text already has been added and the background image applied to this data file. You open the file and then add a form containing an e-mail form object and a radio button group.

The following steps illustrate how to open the volunteer.htm Web page.

To Open the Volunteer.htm Web Page

1 Click the expand/collapse arrow to display the panel groups.

2 Double-click volunteer.htm in the Files panel.

3 Click the expand/collapse arrow to hide the panel groups.

The volunteer.htm file is displayed in the Document window (Figure 4-73).

FIGURE 4-73

The following steps show how to add a form and a table to the volunteer.htm Web page.

To Add a Form and Table to the Volunteer.htm Web Page

1 If necessary, scroll down and then position the insertion point at the end of the last line of text. Press the ENTER key.

2 Click the Form button on the Forms category.

3 In the Property inspector, type newsletter as the form name.

4 Type mailto:dallen@parks.com (use your e-mail address) in the Action text box.

5 Select _self on the Target pop-up menu, type text/plain in the Enctype box, and then press the ENTER key.

6 Click inside the form in the Document window. Click Insert on the menu bar and then click the Table command.

7 Create a four-row, two-column table, with a cell padding of 5, a width of 75%, and a border thickness of 4. Type `Florida National Parks newsletter` in the Summary text box. Click the OK button.

8 Select column 1 and then set the column width to 35%.

9 Select the table, click the Align pop-up menu in the Property inspector, and then center the table.

10 Enter #336666 in the Brdr color hexadecimal text box and then press the ENTER key.

11 Select row 1 and then merge the cells.

12 Click row 1, type `Florida National Parks` as the entry, and then press SHIFT+ENTER to insert a line break.

13 Type `Newsletter Information` and then select the two lines of text.

14 Apply Heading 2 and then center the heading.

15 Select rows 2 through 4, column 1, and then click the Align Right button in the Property inspector.

16 Click the Save button on the Standard toolbar.

The form and table are added to the volunteer.htm Web page (Figure 4-74).

FIGURE 4-74

Inserting an E-Mail Address Text Box

Next, you add descriptive text for the e-mail address and a single-line text field for user input to row 2. The following steps illustrate how to add the e-mail address and single-line text form object.

To Insert a Single-Line Text Box

1 Click row 2, column 1, type E-mail address as the entry, and then press the TAB key.

2 Click the Text Field button on the Forms category.

3 Double-click the TextField text box in the Property inspector. Type email and then press the TAB key.

4 Type 30 and then press the TAB key.

The descriptive text and text form object for the e-mail address are added to the form (Figure 4-75). A character width of 30 is set.

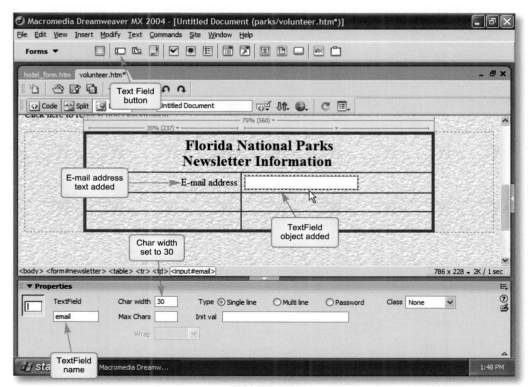

FIGURE 4-75

Radio Groups

When you are adding multiple radio buttons to a form, the **Radio Group** form object is the fastest and easiest method to use. The steps on the next page show how to add descriptive text and a radio group to the Newsletter Information form.

To Add a Radio Group

1

• **Click row 3, column 1. Type** I am interested in receiving a newsletter **and then press the TAB key.**

• **Point to the Radio Group button on the Forms category.**

The descriptive text is added (Figure 4-76).

FIGURE 4-76

2

• **Click the Radio Group button.**

The Radio Group dialog box displays (Figure 4-77). The insertion point is blinking in the Name text box.

FIGURE 4-77

3

• **Type** newsletter **and then click the first instance of Radio in the Label field.**

The Radio Label is selected (Figure 4-78).

FIGURE 4-78

4

• **Type** Daily **as the Label and then press the TAB key.**

• **Type** daily **as the Value.**

The Label and Value are entered (Figure 4-79).

FIGURE 4-79

5

• **Press the TAB key, type** Weekly **in the Label field, and then press the TAB key.**

• **Type** weekly.

The Label and Value are entered (Figure 4-80).

FIGURE 4-80

6

• **Click the Plus button, type** Monthly **in the Label field, and then press the TAB key.**

• **Type** monthly **and then, if necessary, click the Lay out using Line breaks (
 tags) radio button.**

*The text, Monthly, is entered for the Label, and monthly is entered for the Value. The Lay out using Line breaks (
 tags) radio button is selected (Figure 4-81).*

FIGURE 4-81

7

• **Click the OK button.**

The radio group and labels are inserted into the form (Figure 4-82).

FIGURE 4-82

Other Ways

1. On Insert menu point to Form, click Radio Group

The final step is to add the Submit and Reset buttons to the form. The following steps show how to add these two buttons.

To Add the Submit and Reset Buttons to the Volunteer.htm Form

1 If necessary, scroll down. Click row 4, column 1, and then click the Button button on the Forms category.

2 Click row 4, column 2, and then click the Button button on the Forms category.

3 Type Reset as the Button name and then press the TAB key.

4 Type Reset in the Label text box and then click Reset form in the Action area.

5 Title the page Florida National Parks - Volunteer Association.

6 Click the Save button on the Standard toolbar.

The properties are set, and the Submit and Reset buttons are added to the form (Figure 4-83 on the next page).

FIGURE 4-83

Adding Links

Project 2 discussed the different types of links, including relative links, absolute links, named anchors, and e-mail links. The following steps illustrate how to add links to the volunteer.htm and hotel_form.htm Web pages and to add links from the national.htm Web page to the volunteer.htm and hotel_form.htm Web pages.

To Add Links to the Volunteer.htm, Hotel_Form.htm, and National.htm Web Pages

1 Display the panel groups and open the national.htm Web page.

2 Scroll to the end of the Web page and then add a line break after the Home link. Press the END key.

3 Type Florida National Parks Volunteer Association. **Add a line break, and then type** Florida National Parks Hotel Reservations.

4 Select the text Florida National Parks Volunteer Association and create a link to the volunteer.htm Web page. Select the text Florida National Parks Hotel Reservations and create a link to the hotel_form.htm Web page.

5 Save the national.htm Web page and then press the F12 key to display the page in your browser (Figure 4-84a on the next page). Verify that the links work and close the browser. Close the national.htm Web page.

6 Click the volunteer.htm tab and then scroll to the bottom of the page. Type Home **and then add a line break.**

7 Type Florida National Parks **as the entry.**

8 Select the Florida National Parks text and then create a link to the national.htm Web page.

9 Select the Home text and then create a link to the index.htm Web page.

10 Save the volunteer.htm Web page.

11 Press the F12 key to display the Web page in your browser and then verify that the links work (Figure 4-84b on the next page). Close the browser.

12 Click the hotel_form.htm tab and then, if necessary, scroll to the bottom of the page. Type Home and then add a line break.

13 Type Florida National Parks as the entry.

14 Select the Florida National Parks text and then create a link to the national.htm Web page.

15 Select the Home text and then create a link to the index.htm Web page.

16 Save the hotel_form.htm Web page.

17 Press the F12 key to display the Web page in your browser and then verify that the links work (Figure 4-84c on the next page). Close the browser.

FIGURE 4-84a (*continued*)

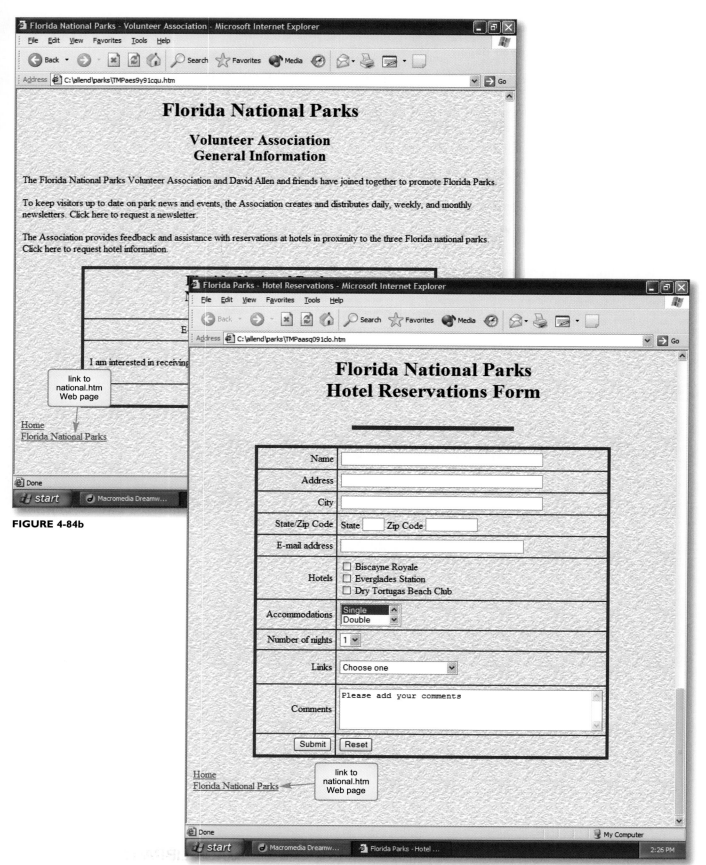

FIGURE 4-84b

FIGURE 4-84c

Behaviors

A **behavior** is a combination of an event and an action. Behaviors are attached to a specific element on the Web page. The element can be a table, an image, a link, a form, a form object, and so on. When a behavior is initiated, Dreamweaver uses JavaScript to write the code. **JavaScript** is a scripting language written as a text file. After a behavior is attached to a page element, and when the event specified occurs for that element, the browser calls the action (the JavaScript code) that is associated with that event. A scripting language, such as JavaScript, provides flexibility, interaction, and power to any Web site.

Using Behaviors with Forms

To create this type of user interaction with almost any other software program requires that you write the JavaScript. When you attach a behavior in Dreamweaver, however, the JavaScript is produced and inserted into the code for you. Dreamweaver provides two form-related behaviors: the Validate Form and Set Text of Text Field. These behaviors are available only if a text field has been inserted into the form.

The **Validate Form** behavior verifies that the user has entered data into each designated field. The form is checked when the user clicks the Submit button. If omissions or other errors occur, a Microsoft Internet Explorer (or other browser) dialog box is displayed. The errors then must be corrected before the form can be submitted successfully.

The **Set Text of Text Field** action replaces the content of a form's text field with the content you specify when creating the behavior. For example, this behavior could be used to insert the current date. The Behaviors panel is displayed in Figure 4-85. The steps on the next page show how to add the Validate Form behavior to the Hotel Reservations form.

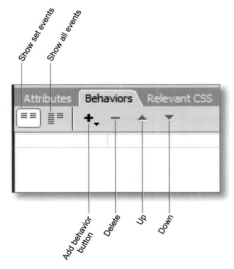

FIGURE 4-85

To Add the Validate Form Behavior

1

• **Display the panel groups and hide the Property inspector.**

• **If necessary, click the hotel_form.htm tab.**

• **Click Window on the menu bar and then point to Behaviors.**

The Window menu is displayed (Figure 4-86).

FIGURE 4-86

2

• **Click Behaviors.**

The Behaviors panel is displayed (Figure 4-87).

FIGURE 4-87

3

• **Click <form#hotel_form> in the tag selector. Click the Add Behavior button in the Behaviors panel and then point to Validate Form on the pop-up menu.**

The form is selected (Figure 4-88). If form#hotel_form does not display in the tag selector, verify that the insertion point is in the form and not in the table.

FIGURE 4-88

4

• **Click Validate Form.**

The Validate Form dialog box is displayed (Figure 4-89). Each of the text fields in the hotel_form.htm document is listed in the Named fields list. The text "name" in form "hotel_form" field is highlighted, and the Anything radio button is selected.

FIGURE 4-89

5

• **Click the Value Required check box.**

The Value Required check box is selected for the "name" field. An (R) is inserted to the right of the field name (Figure 4-90).

FIGURE 4-90

6

• **Click the text "address" in form "hotel_form" field and then click Value Required for the "address" field.**

The Value Required check box is selected for the "address" field. An (R) is inserted to the right of the field name (Figure 4-91).

FIGURE 4-91

7

• **Repeat Step 6 for the city, state, and zip fields.**

The Value Required check box is selected for the "city", "state", and "zip" fields. An (R) is inserted to the right of each of the field names (Figure 4-92).

FIGURE 4-92

8

• **Click the text "email" in the form "hotel_form" field. Click the Value Required check box and the Email address radio button.**

The Value Required check box and the Email address radio button are selected (Figure 4-93).

FIGURE 4-93

9

• **Click the OK button. Click the Save button on the Standard toolbar.**

The Event and Action are displayed in the Behaviors panel. No visible changes are evident in the Document window (Figure 4-94).

FIGURE 4-94

Q: When you are using form validation, what is the difference between the onBlur event and the onSubmit event?

A: Use the onBlur event to validate the fields as the user is filling out the form, and use the onSubmit event to validate several text fields at once when the user clicks the Submit button.

Viewing and Testing the Forms

To ensure that the forms objects work correctly, they are viewed through the browser and each of the form objects is tested. The following steps illustrate how to view and test the hotel_form.htm and volunteer.htm forms.

To View and Test the Hotel_Form.htm Form

1

• **Press the F12 key.**

The hotel_form.htm page is displayed in the browser (Figure 4-95).

FIGURE 4-95

2

• **Complete the form, typing data in each field, and then click the Submit button.**

A Microsoft Internet Explorer dialog box is displayed (Figure 4-96).

3

• **Read the information in the dialog box, and then click the OK button.**

The form is processed, and the data is e-mailed to you. In some instances, your e-mail message may not include the data attachment. This is determined by the e-mail program, server, and security set up on your computer.

FIGURE 4-96

4

• **Close the browser and return to Dreamweaver.**

The steps below illustrate how to add behaviors and to view and test the volunteer.htm form.

To Add Behaviors, View, and Test the Volunteer.htm Form

1 Click the **volunteer.htm** tab. Click inside the form, but not in the table, and then click the **<form#newsletter>** in the tag selector. Verify that **form#newsletter** displays in the tag selector.

2 Click the **Add behavior** button on the Behaviors panel and then click **Validate Form** on the pop-up menu.

3 Click the **Value Required** check box and the **Email address** radio button and then click the **OK** button.

4 Save the form.

5 Press the **F12** key to display the form in your browser (Figure 4-97 on the next page).

6 Click the **E-mail address** form object and then type your e-mail address.

7 Click the **Weekly** radio button and then click the **Submit** button.

8 Click the **OK** button in the Microsoft Internet Explorer dialog box to e-mail the data.

9 Close the browser and return to Dreamweaver.

10 If instructed to do so, upload your Web site to a remote server. Appendix C contains information on uploading to a remote server. A remote folder is required before you can upload to a remote server. Generally, the remote folder is defined by the Web server administrator or your instructor.

Figure 4-97 shows the Volunteer Association Web page as it displays in the browser in Step 5.

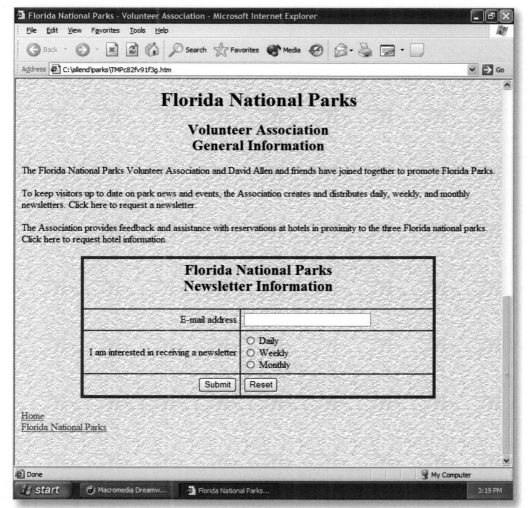

FIGURE 4-97

Quitting Dreamweaver

After you have created your forms, tested and verified that the forms work, and uploaded the Web site to a remote server, Project 4 is complete. The step on the next page shows how to close the Web site, quit Dreamweaver MX 2004, and return control to Windows.

To Close the Web Site and Quit Dreamweaver

1 **Click the Close button on the upper-right corner of the Dreamweaver title bar.**

The Dreamweaver window, the Document windows, and the parks Web site all close. If you have unsaved changes, Dreamweaver will prompt you to save the changes. Clicking the Yes button in the Dreamweaver MX 2004 dialog box saves the changes.

Project Summary

Project 4 introduced you to forms and to Web page design using forms. You created two forms and added a table to each of the forms to format them. In the Hotel Reservations form, you added the following form objects: text fields, check boxes, a list and pop-up menu, a jump menu, a text area, and Submit and Reset buttons. You added a text field, radio group buttons, and Submit and Reset buttons to the Newsletter Information form. You then used the Behaviors panel to attach the Validate Form behavior to both forms. Finally, you viewed and tested the forms in your browser.

What You Should Know

Having completed this project, you now should be able to perform the tasks below. The tasks are listed in the same order they were presented in the project. For a list of keyboard commands for topics introduced in this project, see the Quick Reference for Windows at the back of this book and refer to the Shortcut column.

Learn It Online

Instructions: To complete the Learn It Online exercises, start your browser, click the Address bar, and then enter the Web address scsite.com/dreamweavermx2004/learn. When the Dreamweaver MX 2004 Learn It Online page is displayed, follow the instructions in the exercises below. Each exercise has instructions for printing your results, either for your own records or for submission to your instructor.

1 Project Reinforcement TF, MC, and SA

Below Dreamweaver Project 4, click the Project Reinforcement link. Print the quiz by clicking Print on the File menu for each page. Answer each question.

2 Flash Cards

Below Dreamweaver Project 4, click the Flash Cards link and read the instructions. Type 20 (or a number specified by your instructor) in the Number of playing cards text box, type your name in the Enter your Name text box, and then click the Flip Card button. When the flash card is displayed, read the question and then click the ANSWER box arrow to select an answer. Flip through Flash Cards. If your score is 15 (75%) correct or greater, click Print on the File menu to print your results. If your score is less than 15 (75%) correct, then redo this exercise by clicking the Replay button.

3 Practice Test

Below Dreamweaver Project 4, click the Practice Test link. Answer each question, enter your first and last name at the bottom of the page, and then click the Grade Test button. When the graded practice test is displayed on your screen, click Print on the File menu to print a hard copy. Continue to take practice tests until you score 80% or better.

4 Who Wants To Be a Computer Genius?

Below Dreamweaver Project 4, click the Computer Genius link. Read the instructions, enter your first and last name at the bottom of the page, and then click the PLAY button. When your score is displayed, click the PRINT RESULTS link to print a hard copy.

5 Wheel of Terms

Below Dreamweaver Project 4, click the Wheel of Terms link. Read the instructions, and then enter your first and last name and your school name. Click the PLAY button. When your score is displayed, right-click the score and then click Print on the shortcut menu to print a hard copy.

6 Crossword Puzzle Challenge

Below Dreamweaver Project 4, click the Crossword Puzzle Challenge link. Read the instructions, and then enter your first and last name. Click the SUBMIT button. Work the crossword puzzle. When you are finished, click the Submit button. When the crossword puzzle is redisplayed, click the Print Puzzle button to print a hard copy.

7 Tips and Tricks

Below Dreamweaver Project 4, click the Tips and Tricks link. Click a topic that pertains to Project 4. Right-click the information and then click Print on the shortcut menu. Construct a brief example of what the information relates to in Dreamweaver to confirm you understand how to use the tip or trick.

8 Newsgroups

Below Dreamweaver Project 4, click the Newsgroups link. Click a topic that pertains to Project 4. Print three comments.

9 Expanding Your Horizons

Below Dreamweaver Project 4, click the Expanding Your Horizons link. Click a topic that pertains to Project 4. Print the information. Construct a brief example of what the information relates to in Dreamweaver to confirm you understand the contents of the article.

10 Search Sleuth

Below Dreamweaver Project 4, click the Search Sleuth link. To search for a term that pertains to this project, select a term below the Project 4 title and then use the Google search engine at google.com (or any major search engine) to display and print two Web pages that present information on the term.

1 Creating a Form for B & B Lawn Service

Instructions: Start Dreamweaver. See the inside back cover of this book for instructions for downloading the Data Disk or see your instructor for information on accessing the files in this book.

The B & B Lawn Service Web site currently contains five pages. You will add a sixth page with a form containing a table. You copy a data file that contains the background image. Then you add to this page a heading and a form with single-line text fields and textarea fields, a list, Submit and Reset buttons, and a link to and from the B & B Lawn Service services page. The new page added to the Web site is shown in Figure 4-98. Software and hardware settings determine how a Web page is displayed in a browser. Your Web page may display differently than the one shown in Figure 4-98. Appendix C contains instructions for uploading your local site to a remote server.

FIGURE 4-98

Apply Your Knowledge

Table 4-3 Lawn Services List Values

ITEM LABEL	VALUE
Brush cutting	brush
Edging	edging
Fertilization	fertilize
Mowing/Trimming	mowing
Irrigation	irrigate
Landscaping	landscape
Mulching	mulching
Pruning	pruning
Weed/Insect control	weed

1. Use the Windows My Computer option to copy the data file (services_form.htm) from the DataFiles folder to your lawn folder.
2. Start Dreamweaver. Select Lawn Service from the Files pop-up menu in the Files panel and open the services_form.htm file.
3. Hide the panel groups. Display the Insert bar and then click the Forms category.
4. Click the upper-left corner of the Document window. Type B & B Lawn Service and then press SHIFT+ENTER. Type Service Request and then press the ENTER key.
5. Select both lines. Apply Heading 2 and then center the two lines of text.
6. Click below the heading. Click the Form button on the Forms category. Double-click the Form name text box in the Property inspector and then type services as the form name. Click the Action text box and then type mailto:dallen@parks.com (use your e-mail address). Click the Target box arrow and then select _self. Click the Enctype box and then type text/plain as the entry.
7. Click inside the form. Click Insert on the menu bar and then click Table. Insert a seven-row, two-column table with a width of 80%, a cell padding of 5, and a border of 4.
8. If necessary, select the table. Click the Align box arrow in the Property inspector and then click Center.
9. Select column 1 and then click the Align Right button. Set the column W (width) to 30%. Select the table. Click the Brdr color hexadecimal text box and then type #663333 as the border color.
10. Click row 1, column 1, type Name as the entry, and then press the TAB key.
11. Click the Text Field button on the Forms category. In the Property inspector, type name as the form object name. Press the TAB key and then type 50 as the Char width.
12. Click row 2, column 1, type Address as the entry, and then press the TAB key. Insert a TextField form object in row 2, column 2. Type address as the form object name, and then specify a Char width of 50.
13. Click row 3, column 1, type City/State/Zip Code as the entry, and then press the TAB key.
14. Type City and then press the SPACEBAR. Insert a TextField form object named city with a Char width of 30. Click to the right of the text field and then press the SPACEBAR.
15. Type State and then press the SPACEBAR. Insert a TextField form object named state with a Char width of 2. Click to the right of the text field and then press the SPACEBAR.
16. Type Zip and then press the SPACEBAR. Insert a TextField form object named zip with a Char width of 5.

(continued)

Creating a Form for B & B Lawn Service *(continued)*

17. Click row 4, column 1, type Service as the entry, and then press SHIFT+ENTER. Type (Hold down CTRL key to select multiple items) as the entry.

18. Click row 4, column 2, and then click the List/Menu button on the Forms category. Type service as the List/Menu form object name, click the List radio button in the Property inspector Type area, specify a height of 3, click the Selections Allow multiple check box, and then click the List Values button. Type each Item Label and Value as shown in Table 4-3 on the previous page. Press the TAB key to move from field to field.

19. Click the OK button, click row 5, column 1, type Comments as the entry, and then press the TAB key. Insert a textarea form object named comments, with a Char width of 40. Type 4 for the Num Lines value.

20. Click row 6, column 1, type E-mail address as the entry, and then press the TAB key. Insert a TextField form object named email, with a Char width of 35.

21. Click row 7, column 1, and then insert a Submit button. Click row 7, column 2 and then insert a button named Reset. Type Reset in the Label text box, and then click the Reset form radio button in the Action area.

22. If necessary, display the panel groups and the Behaviors panel. Click form#services in the tag selector and then click the Add behavior button in the Behaviors panel. Click Validate Form on the Action menu.

23. In the Validate Form dialog box, click Value Required for all fields. In the Accept area, click Anything for all fields except the email field. For the email field, click Email address. Click the OK button in the Validate Form dialog box and then close the Behaviors panel.

24. Click below the form. Type Services as the entry, select the text, and then create a link to the services.htm Web page. Click the Save button on the Standard toolbar.

25. Open the services.htm Web page and then scroll down to the bottom of the page. Type Services Request Form and then create a link to the services_form.htm Web page. Save the Web page.

26. Press F12 to display the services.htm Web page in your browser. Click the Services Request Form link to display the services_form.htm Web page. Input data into the form and then click the Submit button to test the form. Then test the link to the services.htm Web page. Close the browser.

27. Print a copy of the form if instructed to do so. Upload the services_form.htm and services.htm Web pages to the lawn Web site on a remote server if instructed to do so. Close Dreamweaver.

1 Creating a Web Form for the CandleDust Web Site

Problem: Mary has decided she would like to conduct a survey to determine which candles her Web site visitors like best and their favorite location to burn the candles. She wants to include a comments section and provide a copy of the results to those visitors who are interested. To do the survey, she has requested that you add a form to the CandleDust site. The data file contains the Web site background. The completed form is shown in Figure 4-99 on the next page. Appendix C contains instructions for uploading your local site to a remote server.

In the Lab

FIGURE 4-99

Table 4-4 CandleDust List Values

ITEM LABEL	VALUE
Decorative	decorative
Gel	gel
Holiday	holiday
Pillar	pillar
Scented	scented
Texture	texture
Votive	votive

(continued)

Creating a Web Form for the CandleDust Web Site *(continued)*

Instructions: Perform the following tasks:

1. Use the Windows My Computer option to copy the file (survey_form.htm) from the DataFiles folder to your candle folder.
2. Start Dreamweaver. If necessary, display the panel groups. Select CandleDust from the Files pop-up menu in the Files panel.
3. Double-click survey_form.htm to open the data file and then hide the panel groups.
4. Click the upper-left corner of the Document window. Add and center the two-line heading, CandleDust Visitor Survey, as shown in Figure 4-99 on the previous page. Apply Heading 1 and then click below the heading.
5. If necessary, click the Forms category on the Insert bar and then click the Form button. Type `survey` as the form name. Type `mailto:dallen@parks.com` (use your e-mail address) in the Action text box and then select _self in the Target box. Click the Enctype box and then type `text/plain` as the entry.
6. Click inside the form and then insert a table with the following attributes: 6 rows, 2 columns, width of 75%, cell padding of 7, cell spacing of 3, and a border of 6. Center the table in the form and then specify a width of 45% for column 1.
7. Select the table and click the Brdr color hexadecimal text box and then type `#000000` as the border color. Select column 1 and then click the Align Right button.
8. Click row 1, column 1, type `Favorite type of candle` as the entry, and then enter a line break. Type `To select more than one, hold down the CTRL key.` and then press the TAB key.
9. Click the List/Menu button on the Forms category. Type `favorite` as the List/Menu name, click List in the Type area, type 3 in the Height box, and then click Selections to select Allow multiple.
10. Click the List Values button. Type each Item Label and Value as shown in Table 4-4 on the previous page. Press the TAB key to move from field to field.
11. Click row 2, column 1. Type `Favorite room to burn candle` and then click the TAB key. Click the List/Menu button on the Forms category. Type `burn` as the menu name. If necessary, click Menu in the Type area, and then click the List Values button. Type each Item Label and Value as shown in Table 4-5. Press the TAB key to move from field to field. Selected Bedroom in the initially selected text box.

Table 4-5 CandleDust Menu Values	
ITEM LABEL	**VALUE**
Bedroom	bedroom
Dining room	dining room
Bathroom	bathroom
Kitchen	kitchen

12. Click row 3, column 1, type `Comments` as the entry, and then press the TAB key. Insert a Textarea form object named comments, with a Char width of 40 and Num Lines of 6.
13. Click row 4, column 1. Type `Would you like to receive a copy of the survey results?` and then press the TAB key.

In the Lab

14. Insert a Radio Group form object named group results. Click the first instance of Radio below Label, type Yes as the Label, and then press the TAB key. Type yes for the Value and then press the TAB key. Type No for the second Label field, press the TAB key, and then type no for the second Value. Click the OK button.

15. Position the insertion point to the right of No and then insert a line break. Type If yes, please enter your e-mail address below and then press the TAB key.

16. Type E-mail address and then press the TAB key. Insert a TextField form object named email and then set a Char width of 35.

17. Click row 6, column 1, and then insert a Button form object named send. Type Send in the Label text box.

18. Click row 6, column 2, and then insert a Button form object named clear. Type Clear Form in the Label text box, and then click Reset form in the Action area.

19. Click below the form. Type Home as the entry, select the text, and then add a link to the index.htm Web page. Click the Save button on the Standard toolbar. Press the F12 key to view the form in your browser. Input data into the form and then click the Submit button to test the form.

20. Open the index.htm Web page and then scroll down to the bottom of the page. Create a link to the survey_form.htm Web page. Save the Web page and then test the link in your browser. Print a copy of the form if instructed to do so. Upload the survey_form.htm and index.htm Web pages to the candle Web site on a remote server if instructed to do so.

2 Creating a Form Web Page for the Credit Protection Web Site

Problem: Marcy recently received several e-mails asking for suggestions on how to spend money wisely. She has created three informational articles and would like to provide these articles to her Web site visitors. Marcy asks you to create a form so she can provide this information. The form is shown in Figure 4-100. Appendix C contains instructions for uploading your local site to a remote server.

FIGURE 4-100

(continued)

In the Lab

Creating a Form Web Page for the Credit Protection Web Site *(continued)*

Table 4-6 Credit Protection List Values	
ITEM LABEL	**VALUE**
Saving Secrets	saving
Frugal Living	frugal
Budgeting	budget

Instructions: Perform the following tasks:

1. Use the Windows My Computer option to copy the data file from the DataFiles folder to your credit folder.
2. Start Dreamweaver. Display the credit site in the Files panel.
3. Double-click tips_form.htm to open the data file.
4. Click to the right of the last sentence and then press the ENTER key. If necessary, click the Forms category on the Insert bar and then click the Form button. Name the form guest_comments. Type `mailto:dallen@parks.com` (use your e-mail address) in the Action text box and then select _self in the Target box. Click the Enctype box and then type `text/plain` as the entry.
5. Click inside the form and then insert a table with the following attributes: 5 rows, 2 columns, width of 75%, cell padding of 7, cell spacing of 3, and a border of 0. Center the table in the form and specify a width of 30% for column 1.
6. Select column 1 and then click the Align Right button.
7. Click row 1, column 1, type `Name` as the entry, and then press the TAB key. Add a single-line text field named name, with a Char width of 40.
8. Click row 2, column 1, type `E-mail address` as the entry, and then press the TAB key. Add a TextField form object named email, with a Char width of 40.
9. Click row 3, column 1, type `Money-saving tips` as the entry, and then press the TAB key. Insert a List/Menu form object named saving, with a Type of List and a Height of 3. Click Selections to select Allow multiple.
10. In the List Values box, type each Item Label and Value as shown in Table 4-6. Press the TAB key to move from field to field.
11. Click row 4, column 1. Type `Rate this Site: 1 for Excellent and 3 for Poor` and then press the TAB key. Type 1 and then press the SPACEBAR. Insert a Radio Button form object and then click to the right of the object. Press the SPACEBAR. Type 2 and then press the SPACEBAR. Insert a Radio Button form object and then click to the right of the object. Press the SPACEBAR. Type 3 and then press the SPACEBAR. Insert a Radio Button form object. In the Property inspector, name each button and the Checked value with the related number, that is, 1, 2, and 3. The initial state should be unchecked.
12. Click row 5, column 1. Insert the Submit button and change the Label to Submit form. Click Row 5, column 2. Insert another button, type `Reset Form` as the Label, and then click Reset form in the Action area.
13. Add a link to the index.htm Web page.
14. Display the panel groups and then press SHIFT+F4 to display the Behaviors panel. Select the form. Click the Add behavior button and then apply the Validate form command.
15. Save the form and then view the form in your browser. Input data into the form and then click the Submit button to test the form. Close the browser.

16. Open the index.htm Web page and then scroll down to the bottom of the page. Type Information Request as the entry, select the text, and then create a link to the tips_form.htm Web page. Print a copy of the form if instructed to do so. Upload the tips_form.htm and index.htm Web pages to the credit Web site on a remote server if instructed to do so.

3 Creating a Guest Book Form for the Plant City Web Site

Problem: The Plant City Web site provides information about the city, but does not provide a means of response from your visitors. The mayor would like visitors to comment on the Web site and the city and asks that you add a guest book to the site. The Web page is shown in Figure 4-101. Appendix C contains instructions for uploading your local site to a remote server.

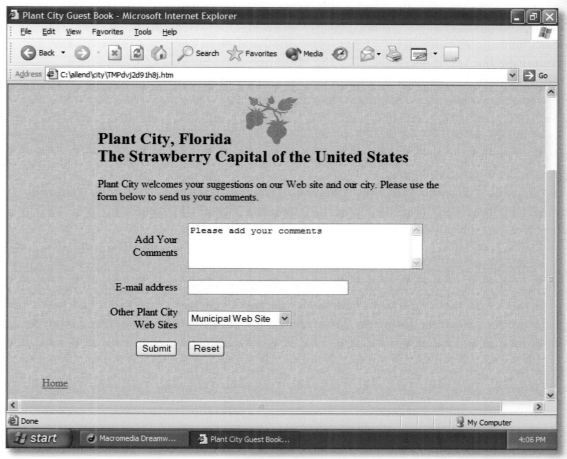

FIGURE 4-101

Table 4-7 Text and URLs	
TEXT	**WHEN SELECTED, GO TO URL**
Municipal Web Site	http://www.ci.plant-city.fl.us/
Community Directory	http://www.plantcity.com/
Dinosaur World	http://www.dinoworld.net/florida.htm

(continued)

Creating a Guest Book Form for the Plant City Web Site *(continued)*

Instructions: Perform the following tasks:

1. Use the Windows My Computer option to copy the file from the DataFiles folder to your city folder.
2. Start Dreamweaver. Open the Plant City Web site.
3. Double-click guest_form.htm to open the data file.
4. If necessary, click the Forms category on the Insert bar. Insert a form named guests. Type `mailto:dallen@parks.com` (use your e-mail address) in the Action text box and then select _self in the Target box. Click the Enctype box and then type `text/plain` as the entry.
5. Click inside the form and then insert a table with the following attributes: 4 rows, 2 columns, width of 75%, cell padding of 5, cell spacing of 5, and a border of 0. Center the table in the form.
6. Select column 1 and then click the Align Right button.
7. Click row 1, column 1, type `Add Your Comments` as the entry, and then press the TAB key. Insert a textarea form object named comments, with a Char width of 40 and Num Lines of 4. Type `Please add your comments` for the Init val. If necessary, click the Multi line radio button.
8. Click row 2, column 1, type `E-mail address` as the entry, and then press the TAB key. Insert a TextField form object named email, with a Char width of 35.
9. Click row 3, column 1, type `Other Plant City Web Sites`, and then press the TAB key. Insert a Jump Menu form object. Type the Text and URL values as shown in Table 4-7 on the previous page. Press the TAB key to move from field to field and click the Plus button to add additional menu items.
10. Type `city` as the jump menu name.
11. Click row 4, column 1, and then insert the Submit button form object. Click row 4, column 2 and then insert a button named Reset. Type `Reset` as the Label, and then click Reset form.
12. Add a link to the Plant City Web site index.htm page.
13. Click SHIFT+F4 to display the Behaviors panel. Click the Add behavior button and validate the form.
14. Save the form and then view the form in your browser. Input data into the form and then click the Submit button to test the form. Open the index.htm Web page and then scroll down to the bottom of the page. Insert a vertical bar to the right of the Historic Homes link. Type `Comments` as the entry, select the text, and then create a link to the guest_form.htm Web page. Print a copy of the form if instructed to do so. Upload the guest_form.htm and index.htm Web pages to the city Web site on a remote server if instructed to do so.

Cases and Places

The difficulty of these case studies varies:
■ are the least difficult and ■■ are the most difficult. The last exercise is a group exercise.

1 ■ Your sports Web site is receiving more hits each day. You have received many e-mails asking for statistics and other information. You decide to start a weekly newsletter and want to add a form so your visitors can subscribe to the newsletter. Add a background image to the page and add a title to the page. Insert a form and name the form appropriately. Next, add a table to your form. Include text fields for name and e-mail address and a text area for comments. Add descriptive text asking if the visitor would like to subscribe to the newsletter and then include a radio group with Yes and No options. Add Submit and Reset buttons. Create a link to and from the home page. Save the page in your sports Web site. For a selection of images and backgrounds, visit the Dreamweaver MX 2004 Media Web page (scsite.com/dreamweavermx04/media) and then click Media below Project 4.

2 ■ You would like to add some interactivity to your hobby Web site. You decide to do this by adding a survey. First, add a background image to the page and then add an appropriate title. Insert a form and then add a table to your form. Add a four-pixel border to the form. Add a list form object that contains a list of hobbies. Ask your viewers to select their favorite hobby. Create an e-mail text field for those visitors who would like a copy of your survey results. Add Submit and Reset buttons. Create a link to and from the home page. Upload the page to a remote site if instructed to do so. For a selection of images and backgrounds, visit the Dreamweaver MX 2004 Media Web page (scsite.com/dreamweavermx04/media) and then click Media below Project 4.

3 ■■ Add an informational form to your music hobby Web site and then add a background to the page. Insert a form and a table. Include form objects for name, address, telephone number, and e-mail address. Include a menu with at least five choices and then add the Submit and Reset buttons. Rename the buttons. Fill in all relevant attributes in the Property inspector for each object. Create a link to and from the home page. Upload the page to a remote site. For a selection of images and backgrounds, visit the Dreamweaver MX 2004 Media Web page (scsite.com/dreamweavermx04/media) and then click Media below Project 4.

Cases and Places

4 ■■ Your campaign for political office is progressing well. Create a new Web site and name it office_form. Add two pages with forms to the new site. The first page should contain a form asking for opinions and comments about your political views. The second form should contain form objects requesting donations and campaign volunteers. Create a link to and from the home page. Upload the office_form Web site to a remote server. For a selection of images and backgrounds, visit the Dreamweaver MX 2004 Media Web page (scsite.com/dreamweavermx04/media) and then click Media below Project 4.

5 ■■ **Working Together** Last week, the student government officers selected three possible vacation sites to visit. Now they would like to have a form page for students to provide feedback about each of the three sites. Each student in your group creates a page with introductory text and a form listing each of the three student trip locations. Provide form objects so the Web site visitors can vote on which trip they would like to take and provide feedback regarding the number of days, minimum and maximum costs, and other related information. Integrate the three pages into one. Create a link to and from the home page. For a selection of images and backgrounds, visit the Dreamweaver MX 2004 Media Web page (scsite.com/dreamweavermx04/media) and then click Media below Project 4.

Templates and Style Sheets

PROJECT

5

CASE PERSPECTIVE

The Florida Parks Web site offers visitors many interesting and informative Web pages. David, however, would like to add additional enhancements to the site. He asks you and Joan for ideas and suggestions. After numerous discussions and the exchange of ideas, several proposals are put forward. One idea is to do a photo album page containing various images from several of the state parks. To add variety to the Web site, however, Joan suggests that a new Web page be developed that will spotlight a different park each month. David expresses concern that changing this page each month will become quite a chore.

Joan explains that instead of redeveloping the entire page each month, the team can use a template. She also explains that style sheet attributes can be added to the template to provide consistency in the heading, park description, and display of images and links. All team members agree to add the Web page and develop a template.

As you read through this project, you will learn about templates and style sheets, how to create a cascading style sheet (CSS), and how to apply CSS attributes to a template. In addition, you will learn how to create a Web page from a template and how to use the Assets panel.

MACROMEDIA
Dreamweaver MX 2004

Templates and Style Sheets

5

Objectives

You will have mastered the material in this project when you can:

- Describe a template
- Create a template
- Describe the different types of style sheets
- Create a Cascading Style Sheet
- Apply Cascading Style Sheet attributes to a template
- Create a Web page from a template
- Describe and use the Assets panel

Introduction

Project 5 introduces the addition of a Dreamweaver template to the Florida Parks Web site. Designing a Web site is a complex process that requires the author to make decisions about the structure of the site and the appearance and content of each Web page within the site. Templates are an important element of many Web sites and are used in a variety of ways. For example, a Web site developer can use a template to provide a basic framework for the structured organization of the entire Web site. Or an educational institution could have a template for student home pages. The student supplies the content for the Web page. The template then takes care of the rest of the job and displays the page in a format that promotes consistency between the student Web pages. Another example is the content within an e-commerce catalog page. Using a template, the content developer easily can add and delete new products, change prices, and make other modifications.

Project Five — Creating Templates and Style Sheets

In this project, you learn how to create a Dreamweaver template, create a style sheet, and apply styles to the template. Using the template, you then create a Web page highlighting one of Florida's state parks.

First, you create a single page that has all the elements you want to include in your Web page and then you save the page as a template. After creating the template, you create the style sheet and then apply the style sheet attributes to the template. Next, you use the template, containing the style sheet attributes, to create a Web page featuring one of Florida's state parks — Bahia Honda State Park — shown in Figure 5-1. This Web page contains a logo and four designated regions that can be edited. These editable regions are as follows: a heading, a short description, and two tables. You use styles to apply font and color attributes to the heading and description and to apply fonts, font color attributes, a background, and a border to the two tables. The first table contains template cells for park images. You also will add a short description of each image. The second table contains cells for links. In this project, you add a relative link to the Florida Parks home page and an absolute link to the Bahia Honda State Park Web site.

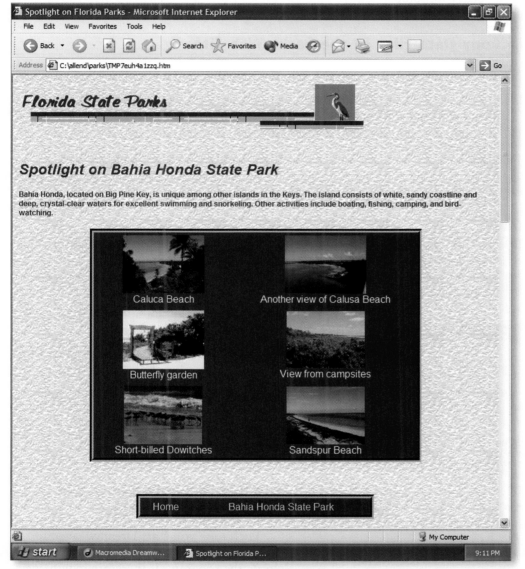

FIGURE 5-1

Workspace Organization

Organization and preparation lead to a more productive work setting. Successful Web developers prepare their Dreamweaver workspace to provide an effective work environment. As you learn to use additional Dreamweaver tools, including templates and style sheets, you will become even more proficient working in the Dreamweaver environment.

Copying Data Files to the Local Web Site

Your Data Disk contains images for Project 5. You use the Windows My Computer option to copy the Project 5 images to your parks\images folder. See the inside back cover for instructions for downloading the Data Disk or see your instructor for information about accessing the files required for this book.

The DataFiles folder for this project is stored on Local Disk (C:). The location on your computer may be different. If necessary, verify with your instructor the location of the DataFiles folder. The following sections show how to copy the files to the parks local root folder.

To Copy Data Files to the Parks Web Site

1 Click the Start button on the Windows taskbar and then click My Computer.

2 Double-click Local Disk (C:) and then navigate to the location of the data files for Project 5.

3 Double-click the DataFiles folder and then double-click the Proj05 folder.

4 Double-click the parks folder and then double-click the images folder.

5 Click the first image file in the list, hold down the SHIFT key, and then click the last image file in the list.

6 Right-click the selected files to display the context menu.

7 Click the Copy command and then click the My Computer Back button the number of times necessary to navigate to the your name folder.

8 Double-click the your name folder, double-click the parks folder, and then double-click the images folder.

9 Right-click in the open window to display the context menu.

10 Click the Paste command to paste the image files into the images folder.

11 Click the images window Close button.

FIGURE 5-2

The image files are pasted into the Florida Parks Web site images folder (Figure 5-2).

Starting Dreamweaver and Closing Open Panels

Each time you start Dreamweaver, it opens to the last site displayed when you closed the program. It therefore may be necessary that you open the parks Web site. The **Files pop-up menu** in the Files panel lists sites you have defined. When you open the site, a list of pages and subfolders within the site displays. The following section illustrates how to start Dreamweaver and open the Florida Parks Web site.

To Start Dreamweaver and Open the Florida Parks Web Site

1 Click the Start button on the Windows taskbar.

2 Point to All Programs on the Start menu, point to Macromedia on the All Programs submenu, and then click Macromedia Dreamweaver MX 2004 on the Macromedia submenu.

3 If necessary, display the panel groups and expand the Property inspector.

4 Click the Files panel box arrow and then point to Florida Parks on the Files pop-up menu.

5 Click Florida Parks.

Dreamweaver opens, and the Florida Parks Web site hierarchy displays in the Files panel (Figure 5-3). In Figure 5-3, the Insert bar displays. If the Insert bar does not display on your screen, you will open it later in this project.

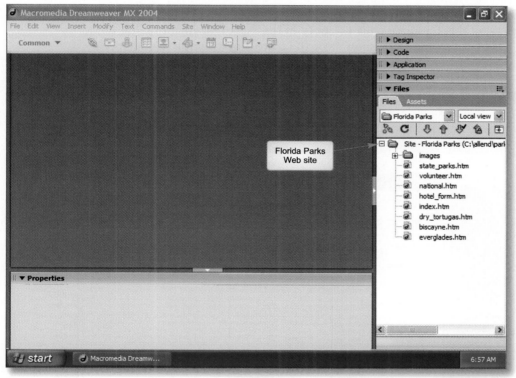

FIGURE 5-3

Understanding Templates

Templates exist in many forms. A stencil, for instance, is a type of template. Or you may have used a template in Microsoft Office or other software applications to create documents with a repeated design. In Web site development with Dreamweaver, a **template** is a predesigned Web page that contains the definition of the appearance of the page, including items such as the default font, font size, logos and images, and backgrounds. A template provides an alternative to separately creating similar-type pages on your Web site. Instead, you create a basic layout and navigation system and use it as a template for each similar page. A template page can function as a pattern for other pages, can save time, and can guarantee a consistent and standardized design.

Planning is an important element in creating a template. Organizing the information and deciding how to structure the template will make the template user-friendly and a more effective site-design tool. The first step is to determine the look of the page, including backgrounds, fonts, and logos. Other elements to consider are heading styles and the inclusion of links, tables, graphics, and other media.

Creating a Template

Dreamweaver provides three methods to create a template: (1) create a template from an existing file, (2) create a template from a new document Basic page, or (3) use the File menu New command and select the Template page category in the New Document dialog box. To create a template from an existing file, you open the file, use the Save as Template command on the File menu, and then define the editable regions. To create a template from a new document Basic page, use the Save as Template command on the File menu. In this project, you use the third method — selecting the Template page category in the New Document dialog box.

The following steps show how to create a new template document.

To Create a New Template Document

1

• **Click New on the File menu.**

The New Document dialog box displays (Figure 5-4).

FIGURE 5-4

2

• **Click Template page in the Category list and then click HTML template in the Template page list.**

Template page is selected in the Category list, and HTML template is highlighted in the Template page list (Figure 5-5).

FIGURE 5-5

3

• **Click the Create button.**

A template document window displays, and [<<Template>> (Untitled-1)] displays on the title bar (Figure 5-6).

FIGURE 5-6

You have created a new template document. The next step is to save the template.

Saving a Template

When the first template for a Web site is saved, Dreamweaver automatically creates a Templates folder in the Web site local root folder and then saves the template with a **.dwt extension** within that folder. Any additional templates added to the Web site automatically are saved in the Templates folder.

The following section illustrates how to save the Web page as a template and to have Dreamweaver create the Templates folder.

To Save the Web Page as a Template

1

• **Click File on the menu bar and then click Save.**

A Dreamweaver Warning box displays.

2

• **Click OK.**

The Save As Template dialog box displays (Figure 5-7). Untitled-1 is highlighted in the Save as text box.

FIGURE 5-7

3

• **Type** spotlight_parks **in the Save as text box.**

The spotlight_parks name is displayed in the Save as text box (Figure 5-8).

FIGURE 5-8

4

• **Click the Save button.**

The template is saved. A Templates folder is created automatically in the Florida Parks Files panel (Figure 5-9). If the Templates folder does not display, click the Files panel Refresh button.

FIGURE 5-9

5

• **Click the plus sign to the left of the Templates folder.**

The folder expands. The template name, spotlight_parks.dwt, is displayed in the Templates folder (Figure 5-10). The .dwt extension indicates it is a template file.

FIGURE 5-10

The Dreamweaver Template

A **Dreamweaver template** is a special type of HTML document. When you create a template, Dreamweaver inserts special code into the template. A **template instance**, which is a Web page based on a template, looks identical to the template. The difference, however, is that you can make changes only to designated parts of the template instance. The sections of the page to which you can make changes are called **editable regions**. An editable region can be any part of a page: a heading, a paragraph, a table, a table cell, and so on. You designate the editable regions when you design the template. Other parts of the page are locked.

One of the more powerful benefits templates provide to the developer within Dreamweaver is the ability to update multiple pages at once. After a new document is created from a template, the document remains attached to the original template unless it specifically is separated. Therefore, you can modify a template and immediately update the design in all of the documents based on it.

The purpose of the template created in this project is to use it as a foundation to spotlight a different park each month. The next section shows how to begin the creation of the spotlight template page.

To Add a Background Image and Title to the Template Page

1 Click Modify on the menu bar and then click Page Properties.

2 Click the Browse button to the right of the Background image box.

3 If necessary, navigate to the images folder. Click parksbg.gif and then click the OK button in the Select Image Source dialog box.

4 Click the OK button in the Page Properties dialog box.

5 Click the Title text box, delete Untitled Document, and type Spotlight on Florida Parks as the entry.

6 Press the ENTER key and then click the Document window.

The background image and title are applied to the Spotlight template page (Figure 5-11). The insertion point is blinking at the top of the page.

FIGURE 5-11

Editable and Noneditable Regions

When a template first is created, Dreamweaver automatically locks most parts of the template document. The title, however, is not locked. The template author defines which regions of a template-based document will be editable by inserting editable regions or editable parameters in the template. Dreamweaver supports four different types of regions in a template: editable regions, repeating regions, optional regions, and editable tag attributes. The following section describes these four regions.

EDITABLE REGION An **editable region** is the basic building block of a template and is an unlocked region. A template author can define any area of a template as editable. This is a section a content developer can edit, and it can be a heading, a paragraph, a table, and so on. A template can have, and usually does contain, multiple editable regions. For a template to be functional, it should contain at least one editable region; otherwise, pages based on the template cannot be edited.

REPEATING REGION A **repeating region** is a section in a document that is set to repeat. Repeating regions enable the template author to control the layout of regions that are repeated on a page. The two types of repeating template objects are repeating table and repeating region. For instance, a list of catalog products may include a name, description, price, and picture in a single row. You can repeat the table row to allow the content developer to create an expanding list, while still enabling the template author to keep the design under his or her control. A repeating region is a section of a template that can be duplicated as often as desired in a template-based page. By default, the repeating region does not include an editable region, but the template author can insert an editable region into the repeating region. A repeating region generally is used with a table, but also can be defined for other page elements.

OPTIONAL REGION An **optional region** lets the content developer show or hide content on a page-by-page basis. For example, the template author may want to include an optional region that would contain special promotional products.

EDITABLE TAG ATTRIBUTE An **editable tag attribute** lets the content developer unlock a tag attribute in a template and edit the tag in a template-based page. For instance, the template developer could unlock the table border attribute, but keep locked other table attributes such as padding, spacing, and alignment.

The steps on the next page show how to add a logo image to the template. This logo is part of the template and is a noneditable item. When a content developer uses this template, the logo image will remain as is and cannot be deleted or aligned to another position.

To Add the Logo Image to the Template

1

• **Click the Assets tab in the panel groups. If necessary, click the Images icon. Scroll down and click the logo.gif file.**

The Assets panel displays, and logo.gif is highlighted (Figure 5-12).

FIGURE 5-12

2

• **Drag the logo.gif image to the top-left corner of the Document window.**

• **Click the Alt text box and type** Florida Parks logo **as the entry.**

• **Click to the right of the image to deselect it and then press the ENTER key two times.**

The logo.gif image displays in the Document window, and the insertion point is at the left margin below the image (Figure 5-13).

FIGURE 5-13

Designing the Template

When you are creating a template, one of the best methods to use is to finalize a single page that includes all the elements you want in the template. Next, save the document as a template and then mark all of the editable regions. Consider the following when designing your template page:

- Include as much content as possible. Structure and design will enable the content developer to produce a Web page based on the template more quickly.
- Use prompts in the editable regions to inform the content developer as to the type of content to be added to a particular region.
- Give your editable regions meaningful names.
- Use placeholders if possible, particularly for images.

The following steps show how to add prompts for two editable regions in the template page. The prompt for the first editable region is the heading and includes instructions to add the park name; the prompt for the second editable region is the instruction to add a short description of the park.

More About

Template Editing

Using the Assets panel, you can edit, rename, or delete a template. Select the template name and then right-click to display the context menu. Choose Edit and then select the Rename or Delete command. For more information about revising templates, visit the Dreamweaver MX 2004 More About Web page (scsite.com/dreamweavermx04/more.htm) and then click Revising Templates.

To Add the Park Name and Park Description Prompts for the First Two Editable Regions

1

- **Collapse the panel groups.**

- **Type** Spotlight on [name of state park] **as the heading prompt.**

The heading text, Spotlight on [name of state park], appears in the Document window below the logo image (Figure 5-14).

FIGURE 5-14

2

• **Click the Format box arrow in the Property inspector and apply Heading 2 to the spotlight prompt.**

Heading 2 is applied to the heading text prompt (Figure 5-15).

FIGURE 5-15

3

• **Press the ENTER key.**

The insertion point is blinking at the left below the prompt (Figure 5-16).

FIGURE 5-16

4

• **Type** Add short description of park **as the prompt for the second editable region and then press the ENTER key.**

The insertion point is blinking at the left below the description prompt (Figure 5-17).

FIGURE 5-17

Adding Tables for Images and Links

The third editable region will consist of a one-row, two-column centered table that will contain centered images and a short image description immediately below each image. The table is editable, so depending on the park to be spotlighted and the number of available images, additional rows and columns can be added to the table as needed.

A second table will become the fourth editable region. This one-row, two-column centered table will contain cells for a relative link to the Florida Parks index page and an absolute link to the Florida Department of Parks Bahia Honda State Park Web page. This second table also is editable, which will permit the content developer to add additional links as needed.

The section on the next page illustrates how to add the first table as the third editable region.

More About

Editable Tables

You can define an individual cell or an entire table as an editable region. You cannot, however, select several individual cells and define them as one editable region.

To Add and Center a Table as the Third Editable Region

1

• **Click Insert on the menu bar and then click Table.**

• **Enter the following data in the Insert Table dialog box: 1 for Rows, 2 for Columns, 70 percent for Table width, 0 for Border thickness, 5 for Cell padding, and 0 for Cell spacing. Type** Spotlight on Florida Parks **as the Summary text.**

The table data is entered (Figure 5-18).

FIGURE 5-18

2

• **Click the OK button.**

• **Click the Align box arrow in the Property inspector, and then click Center to center the table.**

The table is centered in the Document window (Figure 5-19).

FIGURE 5-19

3

• **Click the left cell in the table and then drag to select both cells in the table.**

Both cells are selected (Figure 5-20).

FIGURE 5-20

4

• **Click the Horz box arrow in the Property inspector and then click Center. Click the Vert box arrow and then click Middle.**

The specified attributes are applied to the table cells (Figure 5-21). No changes are evident in the Document window at this time.

FIGURE 5-21

5

• **Click the left cell in the table and then type** Add additional columns and rows as necessary. Add images and short descriptions of image to each cell in the table **as the prompt.**

The prompt is entered into the left cell (Figure 5-22).

FIGURE 5-22

6

• **Click the right cell. Click Insert on the menu bar, point to Image Objects, and then point to Image Placeholder.**

The Insert menu and Image Objects submenu are displayed, and Image Placeholder is highlighted (Figure 5-23).

FIGURE 5-23

7

• **Click Image Placeholder.**

• **When the Image Placeholder dialog box is displayed, type** add_image **in the Name text box as the prompt.**

• **Press the TAB key. Type** 64 **for the Width.**

• **Press the TAB key two times, type** #006600 **for the Color, and then press the TAB key.**

The Image Placeholder dialog box displays. The width is changed to 64, and the color is entered as #006600 (Figure 5-24). Alternate text will be added when the image is inserted into the cell.

FIGURE 5-24

8

• **Click the OK button.**

The image placeholder is added to the table cell (Figure 5-25).

FIGURE 5-25

9

• **Click to the right of the table and then press the ENTER key two times.**

The insertion point is blinking at the left margin below the table (Figure 5-26).

FIGURE 5-26

The second table will serve as a table for links. The following steps show how to add the link table as the fourth editable region.

To Add and Center a Table as the Fourth Editable Region

1 Click Insert on the menu bar and then click Table to display the Insert Table dialog box.

2 Enter the following data in the Insert Table dialog box: 1 for Rows, 2 for Columns, 50 percent for Table width, 0 for Border thickness, 5 for Cell padding, and 0 for Cell spacing. Type Web site links as the Summary text. Click the OK button.

3 Click the Align box arrow in the Property inspector, and then center the table.

4 Click the left cell and then drag to select both cells in the table.

5 Click the Horz box arrow in the Property inspector and then click Center. Click the Vert box arrow and then click Middle.

6 Click the left cell and then type Add additional columns as necessary for links as the prompt. Press CTRL+S to save the file. If a Dreamweaver warning box appears, click the OK button.

The second table is added and centered, and a prompt is added to the table (Figure 5-27 on the next page).

FIGURE 5-27

More About

Detaching a Page from a Template

To detach a page from a template, click Modify on the menu bar, point to Templates, and then click Detach from Template on the Templates submenu. The page becomes a regular document, and locked regions become editable.

Adding Editable Regions

As previously discussed on page DW 389, Dreamweaver supports four different regions in a template: editable regions, repeating regions, optional regions, and editable tag attributes. All Dreamweaver region objects, along with other template-related objects, are available through the Templates pop-up menu on the Common category of the Insert bar. Figure 5-28 shows the Templates pop-up menu. Table 5-1 lists the commands and descriptions on the Templates pop-up menu.

FIGURE 5-28

Table 5-1 Commands on the Templates Pop-Up Menu	
COMMAND NAME	**DESCRIPTION**
Make Template	Displays the Save As Template dialog box; features in the dialog box include selecting a Web site in which to save the template, a list of existing templates, and a Save As box to name the template.
Make Nested Template	Creates a template whose design and editable regions are based on another template; useful for sites in which all pages share certain elements and subsections of those pages share a subset of page elements.
Editable Region	Creates an unlocked region; the basic building block of a template.
Optional Region	Designates a region that can be used to show or hide content on a page-by-page basis; use an optional region to set conditions for displaying content in a document.

Table 5-1 Commands on the Templates Pop-Up Menu (*continued*)	
COMMAND NAME	**DESCRIPTION**
Repeating Region	Creates a section of a template that can be duplicated as often as desired in a template-based page.
Editable Optional Region	Designates a region that can be used to show or hide content on a page-by-page basis.
Repeating Table	Defines a table and then defines the location of editable regions in each cell in the table.

Displaying the Insert Bar Templates Commands

The Templates pop-up menu is located on the Insert bar Common category. Commands on this menu are helpful when creating editable regions. The following step shows how to display the Insert bar and Common category.

To Display the Insert Bar and Common Category

1

• **If necessary, click Window on the menu bar and then click Insert.**

• **If the Common category is not displayed, click the arrow to the right of the displayed category on the Insert bar and then click Common on the Insert bar pop-up menu.**

• **Click the Property inspector expand/ collapse arrow to hide the Property inspector.**

The Insert bar is displayed, and the Common category selected. The Property inspector is hidden (Figure 5-29).

FIGURE 5-29

Marking Existing Content as an Editable Region

As discussed previously, an editable region is one that the content developer can change. Editable template regions control which areas of a template-based page can be edited. Each editable region must have a unique name. Dreamweaver uses the name to identify the editable region when new content is entered or the template is applied. The next section shows how to make the heading an editable region.

To Create the First Editable Region

1

• **If necessary, scroll to the top and then click to the left of the heading prompt.**

The insertion point is blinking to the left of the heading text prompt (Figure 5-30).

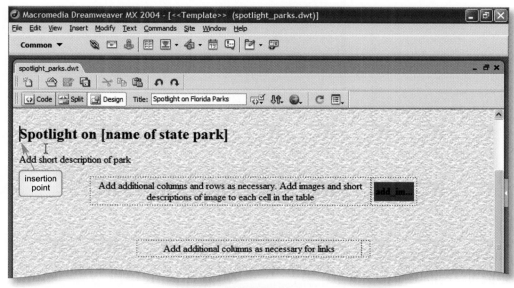

FIGURE 5-30

2

• **Click the <h2> tag in the Tag selector.**

The prompt for the title is highlighted, and the <h2> tag is selected (Figure 5-31).

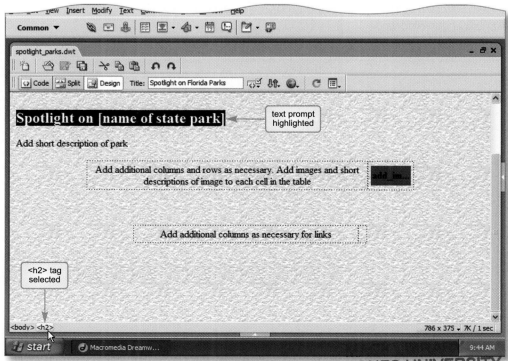

FIGURE 5-31

3

• **Click the Templates pop-up menu and point to Editable Region.**

The Templates pop-up menu displays, and Editable Region is highlighted (Figure 5-32).

FIGURE 5-32

4

• **Click Editable Region.**
• **Type** park_name **in the Name text box.**

The New Editable Region dialog box is displayed, and park_name is typed in the Name text box (Figure 5-33).

FIGURE 5-33

5

• **Click the OK button.**

The editable region name is added. The editable region is enclosed in a highlighted rectangular outline in the template (Figure 5-34).

FIGURE 5-34

The second editable region that needs to be identified and given a name is the text area that will provide a short description of the featured park. The following steps illustrate how to make the park description section an editable region.

To Create the Second Editable Region

1

• **Click to the left of the prompt, Add short description of park, in the Document window.**

The insertion point is blinking to the left of the prompt (Figure 5-35).

FIGURE 5-35

Other Ways

1. Click Document window, select content, on Insert menu point to Template Objects, click Editable Region on Template Objects submenu
2. Click Document window, select content, right-click selected content, click Templates, click New Editable Region on the Templates submenu

2

• **Click the <p> tag in the tag selector. Click the Templates pop-up menu and then click Editable Region.**

The New Editable Region dialog box is displayed (Figure 5-36).

FIGURE 5-36

3

• **Type** park_ description **in the Name text box and then click the OK button.**

The editable region name, park_description, is added. The editable region is enclosed in a highlighted rectangular outline in the template (Figure 5-37).

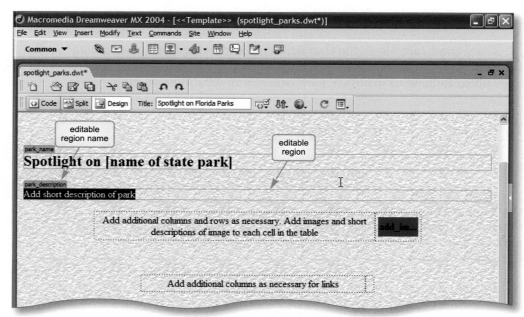

FIGURE 5-37

The third and fourth editable regions are the two tables that were added to the template. The following steps show how to make both tables editable regions.

To Create the Third and Fourth Editable Regions

1

• **Click in the left cell of the first table and then click the <table> tag in the tag selector.**

The table is selected (Figure 5-38).

FIGURE 5-38

2

• **Click the Editable Region command on the Templates pop-up menu.**

• **Type** parks_images **in the Name text box, and then click the OK button.**

The editable region name, parks_images, is added. The editable region is enclosed in a highlighted rectangular outline in the template (Figure 5-39).

FIGURE 5-39

3

• **If necessary, scroll down to display the second table, click in the left cell of the second table, click the `<table>` tag in the tag selector, and then click the Editable Region command on the Templates pop-up menu.**

The table is selected, and the New Editable Region dialog box is displayed (Figure 5-40).

FIGURE 5-40

4

• **Type** links **in the Name text box and then click the OK button.**

The editable region name, links, is added. The editable region is enclosed in a highlighted rectangular outline in the template (Figure 5-41). If a warning dialog box displays indicating you have placed an editable region inside a `<p>` tag, click OK to continue.

5

• **Click the Save button.**

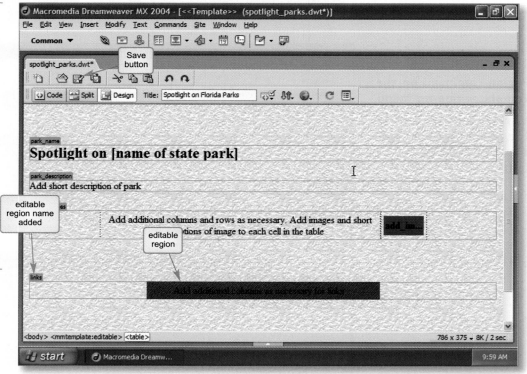

FIGURE 5-41

You have completed adding the editable regions to the template. Next, you create a style sheet and apply the style attributes to the text and tables contained within the template.

Introduction to Style Sheets

If you have used styles in a word processing program such as Microsoft Word, then the concept of styles within HTML and Dreamweaver will be familiar. A **style** is a rule describing how a specific object is formatted. A style sheet (discussed later in this section) is a file that contains a collection of these rules or styles.

Dreamweaver supports two types of styles: HTML styles and Cascading Style Sheets.

HTML Styles

Thus far, when you have formatted text, you have selected the text in the Document window and then applied font attributes using the Property inspector. You selected and then formatted each text element individually: the heading, character, word, paragraph, and so on. **HTML styles**, however, are a feature within Dreamweaver that a Web page developer can use to apply formatting options quickly and easily to text in a Web page. HTML styles use HTML tags such as the <font> and <b> tags to apply the formatting. Once you have created and saved an HTML style, you can apply it to any document in the Web site.

One advantage of HTML styles is that they consist only of font tags, and therefore display in just about all browsers, including Internet Explorer 3.0 and earlier versions. One of the main disadvantages of HTML styles, however, is that changes made to an HTML style are not updated automatically in the document. If a style is applied and then the style is modified, the style must be reapplied to the text to update the formatting. To use HTML styles, you must deselect the Use CSS Instead of HTML Tags option in the General category of the Preferences dialog box.

The HTML 4.0 specification released by the World Wide Web Consortium (W3C) in early 1998 discourages the use of HTML formatting tags in favor of Cascading Style Sheets (CSS). This project, therefore, focuses on Cascading Style Sheets.

Cascading Style Sheets

Cascading Style Sheets, also called **CSS** and **style sheets**, are a collection of formatting rules that control the appearance of content in a Web page. Cascading Style Sheets are the cornerstone of Dynamic HTML (DHTML). **DHTML** is an extension to HTML that enables a Web page to respond to user input without sending a request to the Web server. Compared with HTML styles, style sheets provide the Web site developer with more precision and control over many aspects of page design. After creating a style, you can apply it instantly to text, margins, images, and other Web page elements. Some of the advantages of style sheets include the following:

- Precise layout control
- Smaller, faster downloading pages
- Browser-friendly — nonsupporting CSS browsers ignore the code
- All attached Web pages can be updated at one time

The capability of updating every element with a certain style simultaneously is one of the main benefits of style sheets. For example, suppose you create a text style defined as 24-point Times New Roman bold. Later, you decide to change the text color to red. All elements formatted with that style instantly are changed and display in red.

More About

HTML Styles

Use the HTML Styles panel to record the HTML styles you use in your Web site, and then you can share them with other users, local sites, or remote sites. For more information about HTML styles, visit the Dreamweaver MX 2004 More About Web page (scsite.com/ dreamweavermx04/more.htm) and then click HTML Styles.

More About

External Style Sheets

External style sheets are separate files and exist independently of any HTML pages within the Web site. Any and all Web pages within a Web site can access a common set of properties by linking to the same external style sheet. For more information about external style sheets, visit the Dreamweaver MX 2004 More About Web page (scsite.com/ dreamweavermx04/more.htm) and then click Style Sheets.

A CSS style rule contains two parts: the **selector,** which is the name of the style, and the **declaration,** which defines the style elements. An example of a selector is h2 (defining the HTML h2 tag) and an example of a declaration is 24pt Courier, defining the font size and type to apply to the h2 tag.

Conflicting Styles

The term, **cascading,** refers to the capability of applying multiple style sheets to the same Web page. When more than one style is applied to the same Web page, an order of preference is involved. Styles are used as described and applied in the following preference order:

- An **external style sheet** is a single style sheet that is used to create uniform formatting and contains no HTML code. An external style sheet can be linked to any page within the Web site or imported into a Web site. Using the Import command creates a @import tag in the HTML code and references the URL where the published style sheet is located. This method does not work with Netscape Navigator.
- An **internal style sheet,** or **embedded style sheet,** contains styles that apply to a specific page. The styles that apply to the page are embedded in the <HEAD> portion of the Web page.
- A specified element within a page can have its own style.

In some instances, two styles will be applied to the same element. When this occurs, the browser displays all attributes of both styles unless an attribute conflict exists. For example, one style may specify Arial as the font and the other style may specify Times New Roman. When this happens, the browser displays the attribute of the style closest to the text within the HTML code.

The CSS Styles Panel

To develop a style sheet, you start with the **CSS Styles panel** (Figure 5-42), which is part of the Design panel group. Styles are created and controlled through the CSS Styles panel. A **custom style** is a style you can create and name and specify all the attributes you want the style to include. The name of a custom style always begins with a period.

At the bottom of the CSS Styles panel are four buttons. These buttons are used for the following tasks:

- The **Attach Style Sheet** button opens the Link External Style Sheet dialog box. Select an external style sheet to link to or import into your current document.
- The **New CSS Style** button opens the New CSS Style dialog box. You use the New CSS Style dialog box to define a type of style.
- The **Edit Style Sheet** button opens the CSS Style Definition dialog box. Edit any of the styles in the current document or in an external style sheet.
- The **Delete CSS Style** button removes the selected style from the CSS Styles panel, and removes the formatting from any element to which it was applied.

FIGURE 5-42

The following steps show how to display the Design panel group and the CSS Styles panel.

To Display the Design Panel Group

1

• **Scroll up in the Document window. Click the expand/collapse arrow to expand the panel groups.**

The panel groups are expanded (Figure 5-43).

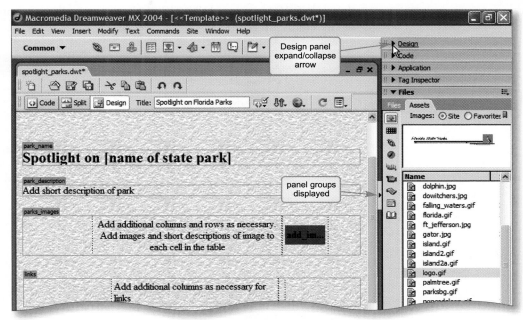

FIGURE 5-43

2

• **Click the Design panel expand/collapse arrow. If necessary, click the CSS Styles tab.**

The Design panel group expands, and the CSS Styles panel displays (Figure 5-44).

FIGURE 5-44

Other Ways

1. Press SHIFT+F11

Defining Style Attributes

Dreamweaver makes it easy to add style attributes to the style sheet. This is done through the CSS Style Definition dialog box (Figure 5-45). The CSS Style Definition dialog box contains eight categories with more than 70 different CSS attributes. As you are defining a style, select a category to access the attributes for that category. Styles from more than one category can be applied to the same element. Tables 5-3 through 5-10 on pages DW 439–441 contain a description of each attribute in each of the eight categories.

FIGURE 5-45

Adding a Style and Saving the Style Sheet

Recall that styles and style sheets are applied in a variety of formats: an external style sheet can be linked or imported to any number of Web pages, an embedded style sheet is contained within one Web page, or you can apply a style to a specific element within a Web page. The spotlight style sheet you create in the following steps is an external style sheet that is linked to the template page. When you apply the first style, a Document window with a .css extension opens behind the original Document window. This window contains the code for the applied styles; it does not display in Design view. When you complete adding styles, you also save and close the .css window.

In this project, the original Document window is a template. The Document window, however, does not have to be a template. It also can be a basic page or a frame to which you can apply styles. The following steps show how to create the heading style and then save the style sheet.

To Add a Style and Save the Style Sheet

1

• **Click the Files panel tab.**

• **Click to the left of the text, Spotlight on [name of state park], in the park_name editable region and then click the <h2> tag in the tag selector.**

The heading prompt is selected in the Document window, and the <h2> tag is selected in the tag selector (Figure 5-46).

FIGURE 5-46

2

• **Click the New CSS Style button.**

• **Click the Tag (redefines the look of a specific tag) radio button to select it.**

• **Click the Tag box and type h2 as the tag name.**

• **Verify that (New Style Sheet File) is selected in the Define in: section.**

The New CSS Style dialog box displays. The Tag (redefines the look of a specific tag) and Define in (New Style Sheet File) radio buttons are selected. The h2 tag name displays in the Tag box (Figure 5-47).

FIGURE 5-47

3

• **Click the OK button.**

The Save Style Sheet File As dialog box displays (Figure 5-48). The Templates folder is displayed in the Save in box.

FIGURE 5-48

4

• **Click the Save in box arrow and then click the parks folder name. Click the File name text box and then type** spotlight **as the style sheet name.**

The parks folder is selected and is displayed in the Save in text box (Figure 5-49). The style sheet name, spotlight, is displayed in the File name text box.

FIGURE 5-49

5

• **Click the Save button.**

The CSS Style Definition for h2 in spotlight.css dialog box is displayed. The Type category is highlighted (Figure 5-50). In some instances, the spotlight.css tab may not display.

FIGURE 5-50

6

• **Click the Font box arrow, click Arial, Helvetica, sans-serif in the Font list, and then press the TAB key.**

• **Click the Size box arrow, click 24 in the Size list, and then press the TAB key two times.**

• **Click the Weight box arrow, click bolder, and then press the TAB key.**

• **Click the Style box arrow and then click italic.**

• **Click the Color text box, type #0029DE, and then press the TAB key.**

The style definitions are entered as shown in Figure 5-51. The shade of blue in the Color box matches the blue color in the logo.

FIGURE 5-51

7

• **Click the OK button and then click anywhere in an editable region on the page to deselect the heading prompt.**

The heading prompt in the Document window changes to reflect the new style of the applied attributes. The spotlight.css tab displays in the Document wndow. The new CSS style is displayed as h2 in the left column of the CSS Styles panel, and the style attributes display in the right column (Figure 5-52).

FIGURE 5-52

Next, you create a style for the paragraph text. The following section illustrates how to redefine the HTML paragraph tag for the park_description editable region.

To Create a Style for the Paragraph Text

1

• **Click to the left of the prompt, Add short description of park, and then click the <p> tag in the tag selector.**

The prompt is selected (Figure 5-53).

FIGURE 5-53

2

• **Click the New CSS Style button in the CSS Styles panel.**

The New CSS Style dialog box displays. The p tag is highlighted in the Tag box, and spotlight.css is displayed in the Define in box (Figure 5-54).

FIGURE 5-54

3

• **Click the OK button.**

The CSS Style Definition for p in spotlight.css dialog box displays (Figure 5-55).

FIGURE 5-55

4

• **Click the Font box arrow and then click Arial, Helvetica, sans-serif.**

• **Click the Size box arrow and then click 12.**

• **Click the Weight box arrow and then click bold.**

• **Click the Color text box and then type #0029DE for the color. Press the TAB key.**

The CSS Style Definition attributes for Type are added (Figure 5-56).

FIGURE 5-56

5

• **Click the OK button.**

• **Click to the right of the paragraph to deselect it.**

The text changes to reflect the new attributes. The new style is displayed as p in the CSS Styles panel (Figure 5-57).

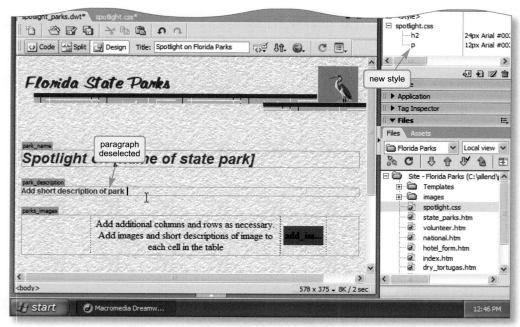

FIGURE 5-57

Other Ways

1. Select content, right-click selected content, point to CSS Styles on context menu, click New on CSS Style submenu

Adding a background, border, and text color to the tables is your next goal. To accomplish this, you use the Type, Background, and Border categories in the CSS Style Definition dialog box. The following steps show how to select a font, a background color of blue, and a shade of green for the border to match the green color in the logo image.

To Add a Background, Border, and Text Color to a Table

1

- **Click in the first cell of the parks_images table.**
- **Click the <table> tag in the tag selector.**

The parks_images table is selected (Figure 5-58).

FIGURE 5-58

2

- **Click the New CSS Style button in the CSS Styles panel.**

The New CSS Style dialog box is displayed (Figure 5-59). The table tag is highlighted in the Tag box, the Tag (redefines the look of a specific tag) radio button is selected, and spotlight.css is displayed in the Define in box.

FIGURE 5-59

3

• **Click the OK button.**

The CSS Style Definition for table in spotlight.css dialog box is displayed (Figure 5-60). The Type category is highlighted.

FIGURE 5-60

4

• **Click the Font box arrow and then click Arial, Helvetica, sans-serif.**

• **Click the Color text box, type #FFFFFF, and then press the TAB key.**

The font is displayed as Arial, Helvetica, sans-serif, and the hexadecimal #FFFFFF is displayed in the Color text box (Figure 5-61). The color is white.

FIGURE 5-61

5

• **Click Background in the Category list.**

The Background category is highlighted, and background attributes are displayed (Figure 5-62).

FIGURE 5-62

6

• **Click the Background color text box, type #000099 as the color and then press the TAB key.**

The background color is displayed in the Background color box (Figure 5-63).

FIGURE 5-63

7

• **Click Border in the Category list.**

• **Verify that the Same for all check boxes are selected for Style, Width, and Color.**

The Border category is highlighted, and border attributes are displayed (Figure 5-64).

FIGURE 5-64

8

• **Click the Top box arrow and then click groove in the Top pop-up menu.**

• **Click the Width box arrow and then click thick in the Width pop-up menu.**

• **Click the top text box in the Color area and then type** #9CCE9C **for the border color. Press the TAB key.**

The attributes are defined and will apply to both tables (Figure 5-65).

FIGURE 5-65

9

• **Click the OK button and then, if necessary, scroll down in the Document window to display both tables.**

The attributes are added to both tables, and the table style is added to the spotlight.css style sheet in the CSS Styles panel (Figure 5-66).

color and borders added to both tables

FIGURE 5-66

Style Sheets and Links

When you selected the <table> tag for the parks_images table and applied the attributes, these attributes were added to all tables in the template. Now you will add two links to the table — a relative link to the Florida Parks index Web page and an absolute link to the Bahia Honda State Park page. Style sheets provide new ways to display links, which enable the content developer to match the style of the links with that of the rest of the Web page. For example, all of the attributes available in the Selector Type category in the New CSS Style dialog box also can be applied to links. When you are defining the style for links, four attributes are available: a:link, a:visited, a:hover, and a:active.

- **a:link** defines the style of an unvisited link.
- **a:visited** defines the style of a link to a Web site that you have visited.
- **a:hover** defines the style of a link when the mouse pointer moves over the link.
- **a:active** defines the style of a clicked link.

Using the Advanced Selector Type and attributes from the Selector pop-up menu, you specify that the links will use white for the text color and will not contain an underline when displayed in the browser. The check boxes within the **Decoration** attribute in the CSS Style Definition dialog box provide options to add an underline, an overline, or a line through the text, or to make the text blink. The default setting for regular text is none. The default setting for links is underline. When you set the link attribute to none, you remove the underline from links. You also specify that when the mouse pointer moves over a link, the underline is displayed. This indicates to the Web page visitor that the link is available. The Decoration attribute is supported by both Microsoft Internet Explorer and Netscape Navigator. The steps on the next page show how to add the attributes for links as they will display in a browser.

To Modify the A:Link Attribute

1

• **Select the links table.**

• **Click the New CSS Style button in the CSS Styles panel.**

• **Click the Advanced (IDs, contextual selectors, etc) radio button.**

• **Click the Selector box arrow, and then point to a:link.**

The New CSS Style dialog box is displayed, and a:link is highlighted in the pop-up menu (Figure 5-67).

FIGURE 5-67

2

• **Click a:link.**

The a:link attribute is displayed in the Selector box (Figure 5-68).

FIGURE 5-68

3

• **Click the OK button.**

The CSS Style Definition for a:link in spotlight.css dialog box is displayed (Figure 5-69).

FIGURE 5-69

4

• **Click none to select the none Decoration attribute.**

• **Click the Color text box, type #FFFFFF, press the TAB key.**

The a:link style is added to the spotlight.css style sheet (Figure 5-70). The link color is white.

• **Click the OK button.**

FIGURE 5-70

More About

Modifying Links

To make a link look like it is highlighted, use the Background category in the CSS Style Definition dialog box and define a bright background color for the link. For more information about modifying links, visit the Dreamweaver MX 2004 More About Web page (scsite.com/ dreamweavermx04/more.htm) and then click Modifying Links.

Q & A

Q: How can I remove a style?

A: To remove a style from an element on a Web page, select the element and then click the Delete CSS Style button in the CSS Styles panel.

The link attribute is added to the template, and the next step is to add the visited attribute. After a Web site visitor clicks a link, it will display as yellow.

To Add the A:Visited Attribute

1 Verify that the links table is selected.

2 Click the New CSS Style button in the CSS Styles panel to display the New CSS Style dialog box.

3 Click the Advanced (IDs, contextual selectors, etc) radio button.

4 Click the Selector box arrow and then click a:visited.

5 Click the OK button to display the CSS Style Definition for a:visited in spotlight.css dialog box.

6 Click the none check box to select the none Decoration attribute.

7 Type #FFFF00 in the Color text box and then press the TAB key (Figure 5-71).

8 Click the OK button.

The a:visited style is added to the spotlight.css style sheet, and the visited link color is yellow (Figure 5-71).

FIGURE 5-71

The final attribute to be added is the a:hover attribute. Many Web site visitors are accustomed to having links identified by underlines. Because the links in this template are designed to not include underlines, the **a:hover attribute** is applied to the links. Thus, when the mouse pointer moves over a link, an underline is displayed. Note, however, that the hover attribute is not displayed by all browsers. The following steps illustrate how to add the a:hover attribute.

To Add the A:Hover Attribute

1 Verify that the links table is selected.

2 Click the New CSS Style button in the CSS Styles panel to display the New CSS Style dialog box.

3 If necessary, click the Advanced (IDs, contextual selectors, etc) radio button.

4 Click the Selector box arrow and then click a:hover.

5 Click the OK button to display the CSS Style Definition for a:hover in spotlight.css dialog box.

6 Type #FFFF00 in the Color text box and then press the TAB key. Click the none check box to select the None Decoration attribute.

7 Click the OK button and then click the Save button on the Standard toolbar (Figure 5-72). If a Dreamweaver warning dialog box appears, click No. At this point, the template is not attached to any documents.

8 Close the spotlight_parks template.

9 Click the Save button on the spotlight.css document and then close the style sheet.

The CSS styles are defined for the spotlight_parks template, as shown in Figure 5-72, before the template and style sheet are closed.

FIGURE 5-72

Style and Style Sheet Maintenance

After a style is created, it can be edited, deleted, or duplicated. You apply these commands through the CSS Styles panel. To edit a style sheet, right-click the style sheet name in the CSS Styles panel and then select the Edit command on the context menu. You also can click the style sheet name and then click the Edit Style Sheet button. To delete a style sheet, select the style sheet name and then click the Delete CSS Style button in the CSS Styles panel.

Detaching a Page from a Template

To detach a page from a template, click Modify on the menu bar, point to Templates, and then click Detach from Template on the Templates submenu. The page becomes a regular document, and locked regions become editable.

Creating the Web Page for the Bahia Honda State Park

The template has been created, and styles have been added to the template. The following steps show how to open a basic page and then save the page as an HTML document.

To Create the Bahia Honda State Park Spotlight Web Page

1 Click the Design panel expand/collapse arrow to collapse the panel.

2 Click File on the menu bar and then click New.

3 Click Basic Page in the New Document dialog box and then click the Create button.

4 Click the Save button on the Standard toolbar and then save the page in the parks folder. Use bahia_park.htm as the file name.

The bahia_park document is saved in the parks folder (Figure 5-73).

FIGURE 5-73

To apply a template to a document, you use the Assets panel. The following steps illustrate how to display the Assets panel and apply the template to the Bahia Honda State Park Web page.

To Apply a Template to the Bahia Honda State Park Web Page

1

• **Click the Assets panel tab in the Files group panel.**

• **If necessary, click the Templates icon in the Assets panel.**

• **Click spotlight_parks.**

The Assets panel is displayed, and the template is selected in the Assets panel (Figure 5-74).

FIGURE 5-74

2

• **Click the Apply button.**

• **Collapse the panel groups.**

The template is applied to the bahia_park document. The template name, Template:spotlight_parks, is displayed in the upper-right corner of the Document window (Figure 5-75). The panel groups are collapsed.

Other Ways

1. Click Document window, on Modify menu point to Templates, click Apply Template to Page on Templates submenu, select a template from list, click Select button
2. Click Document window, from Assets panel drag template to Document window

FIGURE 5-75

Now you use the template to create the Bahia Honda State Park Web page. You first add the name of the park and then add a short description of the park. The following steps show how to add the park name and park description.

To Add the Park Name and Park Description to the Bahia Honda State Park Web Page

1

• **Select the text and brackets, [name of state park], in the park_name editable region.**

The text and brackets, [name of state park], are highlighted (Figure 5-76).

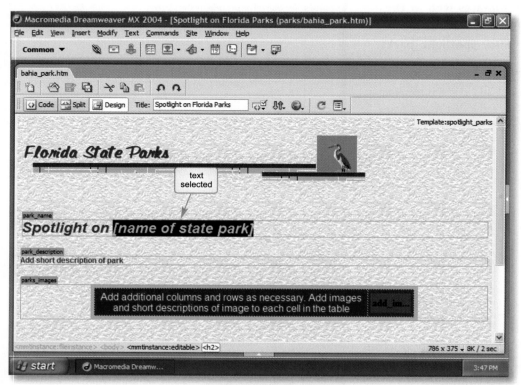

FIGURE 5-76

2

• **Type** Bahia Honda State Park **as the park name.**

The park name, Bahia Honda State Park. is added to the bahia_park.htm Web page (Figure 5-77).

FIGURE 5-77

3

• **Select the prompt, Add short description of park, in the park_description editable region. Type the following text:** Bahia Honda, located on Big Pine Key, is unique among other islands in the Keys. The island consists of white, sandy coastline and deep, crystal-clear waters for excellent swimming and snorkeling. Other activities include boating, fishing, camping, and bird-watching.

The description is added to the park_description editable region (Figure 5-78).

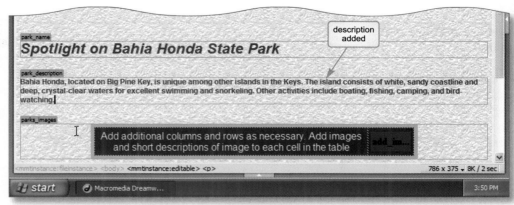

FIGURE 5-78

The Bahia Honda State Park Web page table will contain six images, in three rows and two columns. The parks_images editable table currently contains only one row and two columns. The following steps show how to add two additional rows.

To Add Rows to the Parks_Images Table

1

• **Click in the left cell of the parks_images table. Click Modify on the menu bar, point to Table, and then point to Insert Rows or Columns.**

The Modify menu and Table submenu are displayed (Figure 5-79).

FIGURE 5-79

2

• **Click Insert Rows or Columns.**

The Insert Rows or Columns dialog box is displayed (Figure 5-80). The number of rows displayed may be different on your screen.

FIGURE 5-80

3

• **Double-click the Number of rows text box and then type 2 for the number of rows.**

The number of rows is changed to 2 (Figure 5-81).

FIGURE 5-81

4

• **Click the OK button.**

The additional two rows are added to the parks_images table (Figure 5-82).

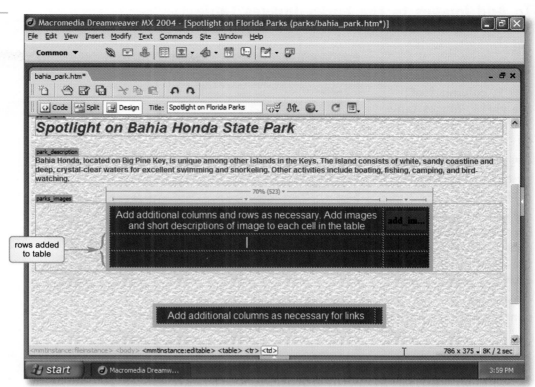

FIGURE 5-82

Expanded Tables Mode

Inserting an image into a table cell and then clicking to the right or left of the image is somewhat awkward in Dreamweaver. **Expanded Tables mode** temporarily adds cell padding and spacing to all tables in a document and increases the tables' borders to make editing easier. This mode enables you to select items in tables or precisely place the insertion point. You return to Standard mode when you complete adding images and text to the table.

The steps on the next page illustrate how to add the six images and a short description of each image. To add an image, you drag the image from the Files panel to a table cell. You use Expanded Tables mode to assist with insertion point placement. You add a <br> tag by holding down the SHIFT key and pressing the ENTER key. Then you type the image description.

Table 5-2 Park Images File Names and Descriptions			
CELL	**IMAGE**	**IMAGE DESCRIPTION**	**ALT TEXT**
Row 2, Column 1	butterfly_garden.jpg	Butterfly Garden	Bahia Honda butterfly garden
Row 2, Column 2	campsites.jpg	View from campsites	Bahia Honda campground
Row 3, Column 1	dowitchers.jpg	Short-billed Dowitches	Bahia Honda Dowitches
Row 3, Column 2	sandspur_beach.jpg	Sandspur Beach	Bahia Honda Sandspur Beach

To Add Images to the Parks_Images Table

1

• **Select the text in row 1, column 1 of the parks_images table and then press the** DELETE **key.**

• **Press the** F6 **key to switch to Expanded Tables mode.**

• **If a Getting Started in Expanded Tables Mode dialog box displays, read the information and then click the OK button.**

• **Display the panel groups.**

The table displays in Expanded Tables mode, and the prompt is deleted from the first cell (Figure 5-83).

FIGURE 5-83

2

• **Click the Assets tab in the panel groups, and then click the Images icon.**

• **Drag the calusa_beach01.jpg image to row 1, column 1 of the parks_images table.**

• **Click to the right of the image.**

The image is displayed in the cell. The insertion point is blinking to the right of the image (Figure 5-84).

FIGURE 5-84

3

• **Hold down the SHIFT key and then press the ENTER key.**

• **Type** Calusa Beach **as the description.**

The text, Calusa Beach, is added to the cell (Figure 5-85).

FIGURE 5-85

4

• **Press the TAB key to move the insertion point to row 1, column 2.**

The image placeholder is selected (Figure 5-86).

FIGURE 5-86

5

• **Press the DELETE key to delete the image placeholder and then drag the calusa_beach02. jpg image to the cell.**

• **Click to the right of the image.**

• **Hold down the SHIFT key and then press the ENTER key.**

• **Type** Another view of Calusa Beach **as the description.**

The image is displayed in the cell, and the description is added below the image (Figure 5-87).

FIGURE 5-87

6

• **Add the four other images and descriptions to the parks_images table as indicated in Table 5-2 on page DW 431.**

• **Drag each image to the appropriate table cell, click to the right of the image, hold down SHIFT and press the ENTER key, and then type the description.**

• **Press the TAB key to move from cell to cell.**

• **Press the F6 key to exit from Expanded Tables mode.**

The images and descriptions are added to the park_image table (Figure 5-88).

FIGURE 5-88

7

• **Hide the panel groups.**

• **Display the Property inspector.**

• **Select the first image in the table and type** Bahia Honda Calusa Beach **as the Alt text.**

• **Select the second image in the table and type** Another view of Bahia Honda Calusa Beach **as the Alt text.**

• **Use the Alt Text column in Table 5-2 on page DW 431 to add the Alt text for the other four images.**

Alt text is added for all six images. No visible changes display in the Document window.

To complete the Bahia Honda State Park Web page, you add two links in the links table. The first link is a relative link to the Florida Parks index page. The second link is an absolute link to the Florida Department of State Parks Bahia Honda State Park Web page. Thus far, when creating links, you used the default and did not specify a target. The target for your links, therefore, has been to open the linked document in the same browser window.

When you create the link to the Bahia Honda State Park Web page, however, the page opens in a new browser window. Recall from Project 2 that the Target option in the Property inspector specifies the frame or window in which the linked page displays. When the _blank target is specified, the linked document opens in a new browser window. The other three choices in the Target option are _parent, _self, and _top. These options are discussed in detail in Project 7, when you create a framed Web site. The following steps show how to add the two links to the links table.

To Add Links to the Links Table

1

• **Scroll down to display the links table. Select the text in the left cell of the links table and then press the DELETE key.**

The text is deleted from the cell (Figure 5-89).

FIGURE 5-89

2

• **Type** Home **as the text link in the left cell and then select the text.**

• **Click the Link text box in the Property inspector, type** index.htm **as the link text, and then press the TAB key.**

The link to the home page is added and centered in the cell (Figure 5-90). The link is not underlined because the selected Decoration style is None.

FIGURE 5-90

3

• **Click the right cell in the links table. Type** Bahia Honda State Park **as the text for the link and then select the text.**

• **Click the Link text box in the Property inspector and then type** http://www. floridastateparks. org/bahiahonda **as the link text.**

• **Click the Target box arrow and select _blank.**

The text is displayed in the table, and the link is added to the Link text box (Figure 5-91). The linked page will open in a new window when the link is clicked.

4

• **Click the Save button on the Standard toolbar.**

The bahia_park.htm Web page is saved.

FIGURE 5-91

The following steps illustrate how to complete the updating of the Florida Parks Web site by adding a link from the State Parks page to the Bahia Honda State Park page.

To Add a Link from the State Parks Page to the Bahia Honda State Park Page

1 Expand the panel groups and open the state_parks page. If necessary, click the Files tab.

2 Scroll to the bottom of the page and then click to the right of the Home link. Press the END key.

3 Hold down the SHIFT key and then press the ENTER key.

4 Type Featured Park as the link text.

5 Select the text and then drag bahia_park.htm from the Files panel to the Property inspector Link text box.

6 Click the Save button on the Standard toolbar.

7 Press the F12 key to preview the state_parks.htm page in your browser. Scroll down and then click the Featured Park link to view the Bahia Honda State Park Web page, as shown in Figure 5-92 on the next page.

8 Verify that the Bahia Honda State Park Web page links work.

9 If instructed to do so, print a copy of the Bahia Honda State Park Web page and hand it in to your instructor.

10 If instructed to do so, upload your Web site to a remote server. Appendix C contains information on uploading to a remote server. A remote folder is required before you can upload to a remote server. Generally, the remote folder is defined by the Web server administrator or your instructor.

11 Close the browser.

The Bahia Honda State Park Web page is displayed in the browser after you complete step 7 (Figure 5-92).

Quitting Dreamweaver

After you have created your Web page based on a template with applied styles, and tested and verified that the links work, Project 5 is complete. The following steps show how to close the Web site, quit Dreamweaver MX 2004, and return control to Windows.

To Close the Web Site and Quit Dreamweaver

1 Click the Close button on the upper-right corner of the Dreamweaver title bar.

The Dreamweaver window, the Document window, and the Florida Parks Web site all close. If you have unsaved changes, Dreamweaver will prompt you to save the changes. Clicking the Yes button in the Dreamweaver MX 2004 dialog box saves the changes.

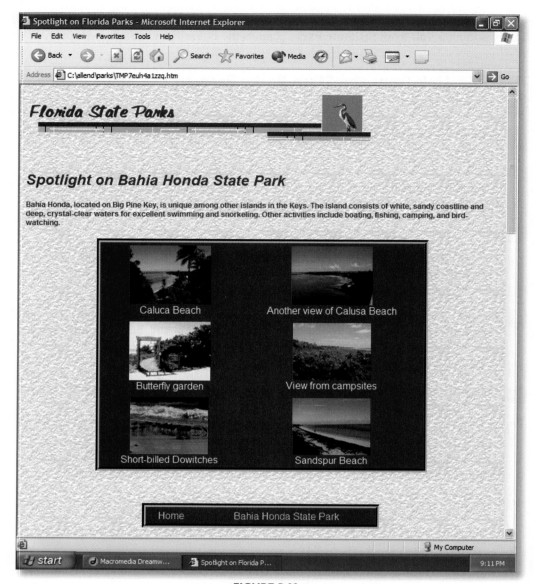

FIGURE 5-92

CSS Style Definition Category Descriptions

The following tables list the attributes and descriptions of the eight categories available through the CSS Style Definition dialog box. Not all browsers support all properties; browser support is indicated in the Description column. The phrase, both browsers, refers to Microsoft Internet Explorer and Netscape Navigator.

Table 5-3 Type Style Properties

ATTRIBUTES	DESCRIPTION
Font	Sets the font family for the style; supported by both browsers.
Size	Defines the size of the text. Enter or select a number and then select a unit of measurement. Selecting pixels prevents Web site visitors from adjusting the text size in their Web browsers. Supported by both browsers.
Weight	Defines the thickness of the font. Thirteen different choices are available; normal and bold are the most common and work in all browsers that support CSS.
Style	Specifies normal, italic, or oblique as the font style; supported by both browsers.
Variant	Specifies small-caps or normal. Dreamweaver does not display this attribute in the Document window. Not supported by Netscape Navigator.
Line Height	Refers to the amount of space between lines of text; also called leading. Normal allows the line height for the font size to be calculated automatically. Supported by both browsers.
Case	Capitalizes the first letter of each word in the selection or sets the text to all uppercase or lowercase; supported by both browsers.
Decoration	Adds an underline, overline, or line-through to the text, or makes the text blink; supported by both browsers.
Color	Sets the text color; supported by both browsers.

Table 5-4 Background Style Properties

ATTRIBUTES	DESCRIPTION
Background Color	Sets the background color for an element — a character, a word, a paragraph, or even the Web page itself; supported by both browsers.
Background Image	Adds a background image to either a Web page or a table; supported by both browsers.
Repeat	Repeats the background image; supported by both browsers.
Attachment	Determines whether the background image is fixed at its original position or scrolls along with the content; not supported by Netscape Navigator.
Horizontal and Vertical Positions	Specifies a position for selected text or other Web page elements; can be used to align a background image to the center of the page, both vertically and horizontally, or to align the element relative to the Document window; not supported by Netscape Navigator.

Table 5-5 Block Style Properties

ATTRIBUTES	DESCRIPTION
Word Spacing	Sets the spacing between words; not displayed in the Document window. The bigger the number, the more space between the words. Supported by both browsers.
Letter Spacing	Sets the spacing between letters or characters; supported by both browsers.
Vertical Alignment	Specifies the vertical alignment of the element to which it is applied; displayed in Document window only when applied to an image; supported by both browsers.
Text Align	Sets the text alignment within the element; supported by both browsers.
Text Indent	Specifies the amount of space the first line of text is indented; supported by both browsers.
Whitespace	Determines how the browser displays extra white space; supported by Netscape Navigator and Internet Explorer 5.5 and higher.
Display	Specifies whether an element is displayed, and, if so, how it is displayed; supported by both browsers.

Table 5-6 Box Style Properties

ATTRIBUTES	DESCRIPTION
Width and Height	Sets the width and height of an element; supported by both browsers.
Float	Sets on which side other elements, such as text, layers, and tables, will float around an element; supported by both browsers.
Clear	Prevents an element from wrapping around an object with a right or left float; supported by both browsers.
Padding	Specifies the amount of space between the content of an element and its border or margin if there is no border; supported by both browsers.
Margin	Specifies the amount of space between the border of an element or the padding if there is no border and another element; supported by both browsers.
Same for All (Padding and Margin)	Sets the same padding or margin attributes to the Top, Right, Bottom, and Left of the element to which it is applied; supported by both browsers.

Table 5-7 Border Style Properties

ATTRIBUTES	DESCRIPTION
Style	Sets the style appearance of the border. Appearance may be rendered differently in different browsers. Supported by both browsers.
Width	Sets the thickness of the element; supported by both browsers.
Color	Sets the color of the border; supported by both browsers.
Same For All	Applies the same style, thickness, or color to the Top, Bottom, Right and Left of the element to which is it is applied; supported by both browsers.

Table 5-8 List Style Properties

ATTRIBUTES	DESCRIPTION
Type	Sets the appearance of bullets or numbers; supported by both browsers.
Bullet Image	Specifies a custom image for the bullet; supported by both browsers.
Position	Sets whether list item text wraps and indents (outside) or whether the text wraps to the left margin (inside); supported by both browsers.

Table 5-9 Positioning Style Properties (Used with Layers)

ATTRIBUTES	DESCRIPTION
Type	Determines how the browser should position the element (absolute, relative, or static); supported by both browsers.
Visibility	Determines the initial display condition of the layer; supported by both browsers.
Width	Sets the width of the layer; supported by both browsers.
Z-Index	Determines the stacking order of the layer; supported by both browsers.
Height	Sets the height of the layer; supported by both browsers.
Placement	Specifies the location and size of the layer (Left, Top, Right, or Bottom); supported by both browsers.
Clip	Defines the part of the layer that is visible (Left, Top, Right, or Bottom); supported by both browsers.

Table 5-10 Extensions Style Properties

ATTRIBUTES	DESCRIPTION
Page Break	Creates a page break during printing either before or after the object controlled by the style; supported by both browsers.
Visual Effect (Cursor and Filter)	Cursor changes the pointer image when the pointer is over the object controlled by the style; supported by both browsers. Filter applies special effects to the object controlled by the style; supported by both browsers.

Project Summary

Project 5 introduced you to templates and style sheets. You created a template, added editable regions, applied styles to the template, and then saved the template. Next, you applied the template to a blank document and added text and images. You used the Assets panel and the CSS Styles panel to complete these tasks.

What You Should Know

Having completed this project, you now should be able to perform the tasks below. The tasks are listed in the same order they were presented in the project. For a list of keyboard commands for topics introduced in this project, see the Quick Reference for Windows at the back of this book and refer to the Shortcut column.

1. Copy Data Files to the Parks Web Site (DW 382)
2. Start Dreamweaver and Open the Florida Parks Web Site (DW 383)
3. Create a New Template Document (DW 384)
4. Save the Web Page as a Template (DW 386)
5. Add a Background Image and Title to the Template Page (DW 388)
6. Add the Logo Image to the Template (DW 390)
7. Add the Park Name and Park Description Prompts for the First Two Editable Regions (DW 391)
8. Add and Center a Table as the Third Editable Region (DW 394)
9. Add and Center a Table as the Fourth Editable Region (DW 398)
10. Display the Insert Bar and Common Category (DW 400)
11. Create the First Editable Region (DW 401)
12. Create the Second Editable Region (DW 403)
13. Create the Third and Fourth Editable Regions (DW 405)
14. Display the Design Panel Group (DW 409)
15. Add a Style and Save the Style Sheet (DW 411)
16. Create a Style for the Paragraph Text (DW 414)
17. Add a Background, Border, and Text Color to a Table (DW 417)
18. Modify the A:Link Attribute (DW 422)
19. Add the A:Visited Attribute (DW 424)
20. Add the A:Hover Attribute (DW 425)
21. Create the Bahia Honda State Park Spotlight Web Page (DW 426)
22. Apply a Template to the Bahia Honda State Park Web Page (DW 427)
23. Add the Park Name and Park Description to the Bahia Honda State Park Web Page (DW 428)
24. Add Rows to the Parks_Images Table (DW 429)
25. Add Images to the Parks_Images Table (DW 432)
26. Add Links to the Links Table (DW 435)
27. Add a Link from the State Parks Page to the Bahia Honda State Park Page (DW 437)
28. Close the Web Site and Quit Dreamweaver (DW 437)

Learn It Online

Instructions: To complete the Learn It Online exercises, start your browser, click the Address bar, and then enter the Web address scsite.com/dreamweavermx2004/learn. When the Dreamweaver MX 2004 Learn It Online page is displayed, follow the instructions in the exercises below. Each exercise has instructions for printing your results, either for your own records or for submission to your instructor.

1 Project Reinforcement TF, MC, and SA

Below Dreamweaver Project 5, click the Project Reinforcement link. Print the quiz by clicking Print on the File menu for each page. Answer each question.

Flash Cards

Below Dreamweaver Project 5, click the Flash Cards link and read the instructions. Type 20 (or a number specified by your instructor) in the Number of playing cards text box, type your name in the Enter your Name text box, and then click the Flip Card button. When the flash card is displayed, read the question and then click the ANSWER box arrow to select an answer. Flip through Flash Cards. If your score is 15 (75%) correct or greater, click Print on the File menu to print your results. If your score is less than 15 (75%) correct, then redo this exercise by clicking the Replay button.

3 Practice Test

Below Dreamweaver Project 5, click the Practice Test link. Answer each question, enter your first and last name at the bottom of the page, and then click the Grade Test button. When the graded practice test is displayed on your screen, click Print on the File menu to print a hard copy. Continue to take practice tests until you score 80% or better.

4 Who Wants To Be a Computer Genius?

Below Dreamweaver Project 5, click the Computer Genius link. Read the instructions, enter your first and last name at the bottom of the page, and then click the PLAY button. When your score is displayed, click the PRINT RESULTS link to print a hard copy.

5 Wheel of Terms

Below Dreamweaver Project 5, click the Wheel of Terms link. Read the instructions, and then enter your first and last name and your school name. Click the PLAY button. When your score is displayed, right-click the score and then click Print on the shortcut menu to print a hard copy.

6 Crossword Puzzle Challenge

Below Dreamweaver Project 5, click the Crossword Puzzle Challenge link. Read the instructions, and then enter your first and last name. Click the SUBMIT button. Work the crossword puzzle. When you are finished, click the Submit button. When the crossword puzzle is redisplayed, click the Print Puzzle button to print a hard copy.

7 Tips and Tricks

Below Dreamweaver Project 5, click the Tips and Tricks link. Click a topic that pertains to Project 5. Right-click the information and then click Print on the shortcut menu. Construct a brief example of what the information relates to in Dreamweaver to confirm you understand how to use the tip or trick.

8 Newsgroups

Below Dreamweaver Project 5, click the Newsgroups link. Click a topic that pertains to Project 5. Print three comments.

9 Expanding Your Horizons

Below Dreamweaver Project 5, click the Expanding Your Horizons link. Click a topic that pertains to Project 5. Print the information. Construct a brief example of what the information relates to in Dreamweaver to confirm you understand the contents of the article.

10 Search Sleuth

Below Dreamweaver Project 5, click the Search Sleuth link. To search for a term that pertains to this project, select a term below the Project 5 title and then use the Google search engine at google.com (or any major search engine) to display and print two Web pages that present information on the term.

Apply Your Knowledge

1 Creating a Template and Style Sheet for B & B Lawn Service

Instructions: Start Dreamweaver. See the inside back cover of this book for instructions for downloading the Data Disk or see your instructor for information on accessing the files in this book.

The proprietors of B & B Lawn Service would like to add a page to their Web site that features native plants for different areas of the country. They want something that is modified easily, so a template is used. To create this template and then add styles, you copy six images from the DataFiles folder to the Lawn Service Web site images folder. You begin the process by creating a template, then define styles. When this is completed, you apply this template to a new blank page and then create a page for Florida native plants. Finally, you add a link to and from the B & B Lawn Service home page. When you create this template, you select the This document only option in the New CSS Style dialog box. Because this template is applied to one document, an external style sheet is not created.

The template is shown in Figure 5-93a and the Web page in Figure 5-93b on the next page. Software and hardware settings determine how a Web page is displayed in a browser. Your Web page may display differently than the ones shown in Figures 5-93a and 5-93b. Appendix C contains instructions for uploading your local site to a remote server.

FIGURE 5-93(a) *(continued)*

(continued)

Creating a Template and Style Sheet for B & B Lawn Service *(continued)*

FIGURE 5-93(b) *(continued)*

Table 5-11 B & B Lawn Service Editable Regions	
REGION TEXT	**REGION NAME**
Landscaping with Natural Plants in [NAME OF STATE]	subtitle
Introductory paragraph	introductory_paragraph
Some [NAME OF STATE] native plant examples:	example
The table	table_images
Index	links

1. Use the Windows My Computer option to copy the data files from the DataFiles folder to your lawn/images folder. Start Dreamweaver.
2. Display the panel groups. Select Lawn Service from the Files pop-up menu in the Files panel. Click File on the menu bar and then click New. Select Template page in the New Document dialog box General category and HTML template in the Template page column. Click Save on the menu bar and type plants for the file name.
3. To begin creating the template, click Modify on the menu bar and then click Page Properties. Apply the lawnbg.gif background image. Type B & B Lawn Service as the Web page title.
4. In the Document window, type B & B Lawn Service as the entry. Apply Heading 1 and then press the ENTER key.
5. Type Landscaping with Natural Plants in [NAME OF STATE] as the entry. Apply Heading 3 and then press the ENTER key.
6. Type Introductory paragraph: and then press the ENTER key.
7. Type Some [NAME OF STATE] native plant examples: and then press the ENTER key.
8. Insert a one-row, two-column table with a width of 50 percent, and cell padding of 5. Type Landscaping with natural plants as the Summary text, and then center-align the table.
9. If necessary, click the Property inspector expander arrow to expand the Property inspector. Drag the background_table.gif file to the Bg Image text box. Click to the right of the table in the Document window and then press the ENTER key.
10. Type Index and then select the text. Drag the index.htm file name to the Property inspector Link box.
11. Drag the logo.gif image to the right of the heading and then select the image. Set a V Space of 4 and H Space of 50. Type Landscaping as the Alt text. Right-align the logo.gif image. Press the ENTER key.
12. Use the Editable Regions button on the Templates tab to create the five editable regions as indicated in Table 5-11 on the previous page.
13. Click the Design panel arrow to display the CSS Styles panel.
14. Click anywhere in the heading, B & B Lawn Service, and then click the <h1> tag in the tag selector. Click the New CSS Style button in the CSS Styles panel. In the New CSS Style dialog box, verify that h1 is selected in the Tag box and that Tag (redefines the look of a specific tag) and Define in This document only are selected, and then click the OK button. In the CSS Style Definition dialog box, set the following values in the Type category: Verdana, Arial, Helvetica, sans-serif for the Font; 36 pixels for the Size; bolder for the Weight; oblique for the Style; and #996600 for the Color. Click the OK button.
15. Click anywhere in the first paragraph prompt, Landscaping with Natural Plants in [NAME OF STATE], and then click the <h3> tag in the tag selector. Click the New CSS Style button in the CSS Styles panel. In the New CSS Style dialog box, verify that h3 is selected in the Tag box and that Tag (redefines the look of a specific tag) and Define in This document only are selected, and then click the OK button. Set the following values in the Type category: Verdana, Arial, Helvetica, sans-serif for the Font; 14 pixels for the Size; 600 for the Weight; and #996633 for the Color. Click the OK button.

(continued)

Apply Your Knowledge

Creating a Template and Style Sheet for B & B Lawn Service *(continued)*

16. Click anywhere in the table and then click the <table> tag in the tag selector. Click the New CSS Style button in the CSS Styles panel. In the New CSS Style dialog box, verify that table is selected in the Tag box and that Tag (redefines the look of a specific tag) and Define in This document only are selected, and then click the OK button. Set the following values in the Type category: Verdana, Arial, Helvetica, sans-serif for the Font; 14 pixels for the Size; #996600 for the Color; and none for the Decoration. Set the following values in the Border category: Outset for the Style and #996633 for the Color. Click the OK button. Click row 1, column 1, and then type Add additional rows/columns as needed as the entry. Then click row 1, column 2, and type Add images to table as the entry.

17. Select the text, Index, and then click the New CSS Style button in the CSS Styles panel. In the New CSS Style dialog box, click Advanced (IDs, contextual selectors, etc), and Define in This document only. Click the Selector arrow and then click a:link. Set the following values in the Type category: Verdana, Arial, Helvetica, sans-serif for the Font; 16 pixels for the Size; and #996633 for the Color. Click the OK button, and then save and close the template.

18. Open a new Basic Page Document window and save the page as native_plants.htm in the lawn folder.

19. Click the Assets tab in the Files panel group and then click the Templates button. Click the Apply button to apply the template to the native_plants.htm page.

20. Use Table 5-12 as a guide to add content to each of the editable regions as shown in this table. Title the document Native Plants.

21. Save the document. Open the services.htm file. Scroll to the bottom of the page and then click to the right of the Services Form Request link. Press the END key, insert a line break, and then type Native Plants as the link text. Add a link to the native_plants.htm page. Save the services.htm page.

22. Press the F12 key to view the page in your browser. Click the Native Plants link. Print a copy of the template and Web page if instructed to do so. Upload the page to the lawn Web site on a remote server if instructed to do so.

Table 5-12 B & B Lawn Service Page Content

REGION TEXT	REGION NAME
Landscaping with Natural Plants in Florida	subtitle
Native plants are plants that are indigenous to a specific area. Some people believe native plants to be weeds, but native plants are beautiful and hardy. Once established, they require less maintenance than conventional plants.	introductory_paragraph
Some Florida native plant examples:	examples
(Note: Press TAB to move from cell to cell) Row 1, column 1: plant01.gif Row 1, column 2: plant02.gif Row 2, column 1: plant03.gif Row 2, column 2: plant04.gif	table_images

In the Lab

1 Creating a Template for the CandleDust Web Site

Problem: The CandleDust Web site is receiving a large number of hits every day, and Mary is receiving increasingly more orders each day. She foresees a time when she will need to expand the Web site and is considering a standard design for her pages. Mary is not sure exactly how a template works within a Web site and has requested that you put together an example. You know that she has been considering beeswax for candle making, so you decide to create the page using this topic. The template is shown in Figure 5-94a and the example in Figure 5-94b on the next page. The template contains five tables — one non-editable table and four editable tables. Your Web page may display differently than the ones shown in Figures 5-94a and 5-94b. Appendix C contains instructions for uploading your local site to a remote server.

FIGURE 5-94(a) *(continued)*

(continued)

Creating a Template for the CandleDust Web Site *(continued)*

FIGURE 5-94(b) (continued)

In the Lab

Instructions: Perform the following tasks:

1. Use the Windows My Computer option to copy the data files from the DataFiles folder to your candle/images folder.

2. Start Dreamweaver. Display the panel groups. Select CandleDust from the Files pop-up menu in the Files panel. Click File on the menu bar and then click New. Select Template page in the New Document dialog box General category and HTML template in the Template Page column. Click Save on the menu bar and type `primary` for the file name.

3. Use the Page Properties dialog box to add the candlebg.gif background image to the page.

4. Create a one-row, two-column table with a table width of 60 percent and cell padding of 5. Type `CandleDust logo table` as the Summary text. This is a noneditable table. Select the table cells and set Vert to Middle. Drag the candle1.gif image to the first cell and then type `logo_image` as the Alt text. Drag the logo.gif image to the second cell and type `logo` as the Alt text.

5. Click to the right of the table and then press the ENTER key. Add a one-row, one-column table with a width of 90 percent. Type `Table heading` as the Summary text. Click in the table and type `Heading goes here` as the prompt. Apply Heading 1 to the text. Click the Bg color hexadecimal text box and type `#CC9966` as the entry. Click to the right of the table and press the ENTER key.

6. Add a one-row, two-column table with a width of 60 percent and cell padding of 5. Type `General information` as the Summary text. Align the table to the right. Select the table cells and set Vert to Middle. In the first cell, type `Image or text goes here` as the text prompt, and in the second cell, type `Add as many additional columns/rows as necessary` as the text prompt. Click to the right of the table and then press the ENTER key two times.

7. Add a third editable table with one row and three columns. Use a width of 80 percent and cell padding of 5. Center the table. In the first cell, type `Image or text here` as the prompt, and in the second cell, type `Add as many additional columns/rows as necessary` as the prompt. Drag the candle2.gif image to the third cell. Click outside the table and then press the ENTER key.

8. Insert a fourth editable table — a one-row, one-column table with a width of 60 percent and cell padding of 5. Select the cell and set Horz to Center and Vert to Middle. Type `Links go here` in the table cell.

9. Create four editable regions in the template — the first with the heading and then the three tables. Name the heading editable region heading, name the first table text_image01, the second table text_image02, and the third table links.

10. Click anywhere in the heading prompt and then click the <table> tag in the tag selector. Click the New CSS Style button in the CSS Styles panel. In the New CSS Style dialog box, verify that table is selected in the Tag box and that Tag (redefines the look of a specific tag) and Define in (New Style Sheet File) are selected, and then click the OK button. Name the style sheet primary.css. In the CSS Style Definition dialog box, set the font to Georgia, Times New Roman, Times, serif; the size to 14; the style to italic; and the weight to bolder. Save the template and style sheet.

11. Open a new Document window and save it as beeswax.htm. Click the Assets tab in the Files panel group. Apply the template to the new Document window.

12. Type `Beeswax -- The Original Wax` in the heading editable region.

13. Drag the bee.gif image to the left cell in the first editable table — text_image01. Type `bee` as the image Alt text. In the right cell of the first table, type `Beeswax is naturally fragrant. It burns cleaner and longer than petroleum-based waxes, so there is no smoke coming from the candle.`

(continued)

Creating a Template for the CandleDust Web Site *(continued)*

14. Click the left cell of the text_image02 table and then type Beeswax candles produce a brighter flame than paraffin candles and create a warm glow. A beeswax candle is something that every candle lover should experience. A beeswax candle smells sweetly of honey without the addition of any fragrance. Click the center cell of the second table and then type Beeswax is all natural and chemical and particle free. It is perfect for making soaps, painting fabric, or creating specialty furniture polish.

15. Click the Links table, type Index as the entry, and then drag the index.htm file to the Link text box in the Property inspector. Save the page.

16. Open the index.htm file. Scroll to the bottom of the page and then click to the right of the Survey link. Insert a line break and then type Candlemaking as the link text. Create a link to the beeswax.htm page. Save the index page.

17. Press the F12 key to view the page in your browser. Click the Candlemaking link. Print a copy of the template and Web page if instructed to do so. Upload the page to the candle Web site on a remote server if instructed to do so.

2 Creating a Template for the Credit Protection Web Site

Problem:
Marcy has decided to add additional Web pages emphasizing the ABCs of Credit. She would like to have a uniform format for these pages and has asked you to create a template. She has provided you with content for the first one of these pages. The template is shown in Figure 5-95a and the Web page in Figure 5-95b. Appendix C contains instructions for uploading your local site to a remote server.

FIGURE 5-95(a) *(continued)*

FIGURE 5-95(b) (*continued*)

Instructions: Perform the following tasks:

1. Use the Windows My Computer option to copy the data files from the DataFiles folder to your credit/ images folder.

2. Start Dreamweaver. Select Credit Protection from the Files pop-up menu in the Files panel. Click File on the menu bar and then click New. Select Template page in the New Document dialog box General category and HTML template in the Template page column. Click Save on the menu bar and type credit for the file name. Display the panel groups. Title the template Credit Protection. Use the Page Properties dialog box to add the creditbg.gif background image to the page.

3. Insert a seven-row, three-column table with a width of 90 percent, cell padding of 5, Summary text of ABCs of Credit. Center the table. Drag the logo.gif image to the first cell in the first row. Merge the last two cells in row 1. Type The ABCs of Credit in the merged cells.

(continued)

Creating a Template for the Credit Protection Web Site *(continued)*

4. Merge all three cells in row 2. Drag the line.gif image to the merged row.

5. Merge all three cells in row 4 and then type Leave this row blank in those merged cells. Repeat this instruction in row 6.

6. Click row 3, column 1, type Add heading as the entry, and then apply Heading 2 to this text. Repeat this instruction in column 1 of rows 5 and 7.

7. Click row 3, column 2, type Add text or image as the entry, and then copy this text. Paste the text into row 3, column 3; row 5, columns 2 and 3; and row 7, columns 2 and 3.

8. Click outside of the table, press the ENTER key, and then type Index as the entry. Create a link from this text to the index.htm page.

9. Click anywhere in the table and then click the <table> tag in the tag selector. Click the Editable Region button on the Template pop-up menu. Name the editable region table_credit.

10. Open the CSS Styles panel and then click the Add CSS Style button. In the New CSS Style dialog box, verify that table is selected in the Tag box and that Tag (redefines the look of a specific tag) and Define in (New Style Sheet File) are selected, and then click the OK button. Name the style sheet credit_info.css and save it in your credit folder. Apply the following attributes in the Type category: Georgia, Times New Roman, Times, serif for the Font; 14 for the Size; and bold for the Weight. Click the Save button and close the template.

11. Open a new Document window and save it as credit_info.htm. Click the Assets panel tab and then click the Apply button. Delete the text, Leave this row blank, from all cells.

12. Click row 3, column 1, type Cleaning up Your Credit as the entry, and then click row 3, column 3. Type The first step is to get a copy of your merged credit report, which shows all three of the major bureaus. The Index page contains contact information. Select the text Index page and add a link to the index.htm page. Click row 3, column 2, and drag the credit_card.gif image to the cell.

13. Select the text in row 5, column 1, type Credit Report Mistakes as the entry, and then click row 5, column 2. Type Most likely, almost every item on your credit report will have some mistake, even if only slight. Make a note of all inaccuracies, and send a letter to the credit bureaus. Click row 5, column 3 and then drag the money3.gif image to the cell.

14. Click row 7, column 1, type Rebuild Your Credit as the entry, and then click row 7, column 2. Type Obtain a credit card and use it a little each month to charge normal purchases such as gasoline or food. Pay the card balance in full each month. Click row 7, column 3, and then drag the rebuild.gif image to the cell.

15. Save the document and the credit_info.css page. Open the index.htm file. Scroll to the bottom of the page, click to the right of the Information Request link, and then press the END key. Insert a line break and then type Credit Information as the link text. Create a link to the credit_info.htm page. Press the ENTER key and save the page.

16. Press the F12 key to view the page in your browser. Click the Credit Information link. Print a copy of the template and Web page if instructed to do so. Upload the page to the credit Web site on a remote server if instructed to do so.

3 Creating a Template for the Plant City Web Site

Problem: The Plant City Web site provides information about the city, but provides very little information about activities. The mayor wants to let visitors know about upcoming attractions and events. She wants the page to have a structured format and would like it to be changed easily. You will use a template to accomplish this task. The template is shown in Figure 5-96a, and the Web page is shown in Figure 5-96b.

FIGURE 5-96(a) *(continued)*

(continued)

Creating a Template for the Plant City Web Site *(continued)*

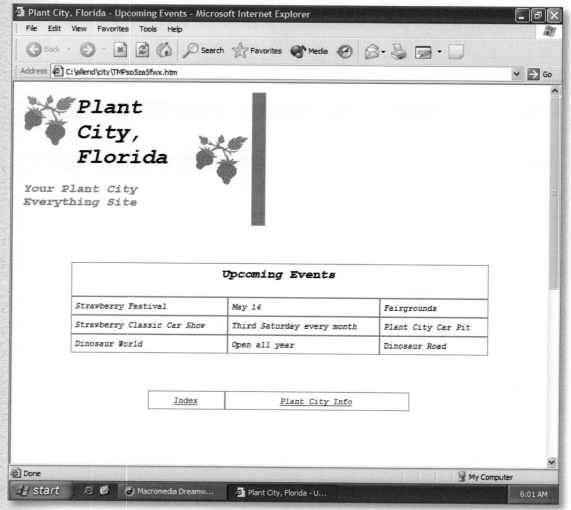

FIGURE 5-96(b) *(continued)*

Table 5-13 Plant City Upcoming Events Text		
LEFT CELL	MIDDLE CELL	RIGHT CELL
Strawberry Festival	May 14	Fairgrounds
Strawberry Classic Car Show	Third Saturday every month	Plant City Car Pit
Dinosaur World	Open all year	Dinosaur Road

Instructions: Perform the following tasks:

1. Start Dreamweaver. No data files are required for this exercise.
2. Display the panel groups. Select Plant City from the Files pop-up menu in the Files panel. Title the page Plant City, Florida - Upcoming Events. Click File on the menu bar and then click New. Select Template page in the New Document dialog box General category and HTML template in the Template Page column. Click Save on the menu bar and type events for the file name.

3. Add a one-row, three-column table with a width of 50 percent and cell padding of 5. Click column 1 and type Plant City, Florida as the heading. Apply Heading 1 to the text. Press the ENTER key and type Your Plant City Everything Site and then apply Heading 3 to the text. Select the text and then type #FF0000 in the Text Color hexadecimal text box.

4. Drag the strawberry01.gif image to the left of the text, Plant City, Florida. Select the image and align it to the left. Drag the strawberry01.gif image to column 2. Align the image to the right. Click column 3. Type #FF0000 in the Bg hexadecimal text box. Click to the right of the table and then press the ENTER key two times.

5. Add a second table, with four rows and three columns. Use a width of 80 percent and cell padding of 5. Center align the table.

6. Click row 1, column 1 in the second table and then merge all three cells in row 1. Type Upcoming Events and then center the text. Apply Heading 3 to the text.

7. Click row 2, column 1, type Add Event Name as the entry, and then add this same text to rows 3 and 4, column 1.

8. Click row 2, column 2, type Add Date as the entry, and add this same text to rows 3 and 4, column 2.

9. Click row 2, column 3, type Add Location as the entry, and add this same text to rows 3 and 4, column 3.

10. Click to the right of the second table and then press the ENTER key two times. Add a third table with one row and two columns, with a width of 50 percent and cell padding of 5. Center the table. Select the row and then select Center in the Horz box.

11. Click anywhere in the second table and then select the <table> tag in the tag selector. Click the Templates pop-up menu and then click the Editable Region command. Name the new editable region event_table.

12. Click anywhere in the second table. Click <table> in the tag selector and then click the New CSS Style button. Verify that the table is selected in the Tag box and that Tag (redefines the look of a specific tag) and Define in (New Style Sheet File) are selected. Click the OK button and name the style sheet events.css. Add the following attributes: Courier New, Courier, mono for the Font; 14 for the Size; normal for the Weight; and oblique for the Style. Click the OK button.

13. Click the first cell in the third table and then type Index as the entry. Select the text, Index, and create a link to the Plant City Web site index.htm page. Click the second cell and then type Plant City Info as the entry. Create an absolute link from this text to www.plantcity.org.

14. Click anywhere in the third table and then click the <table> tag in the tag selector. Click the Templates pop-up menu and then click the Editable Region command. Name the new editable region links.

15. Click the <table> tag in the tag selector. Click the New CSS Style button and then click the Advanced (IDs, contextual selectors, etc) radio button. Add the following attributes for the a:link: Courier New, Courier, mono for the Font; 12 for the Size; normal for the Weight; and oblique for the Style. Click the Decoration attribute none check box.

16. For the a:visited link, apply the same attributes, but add #FF0066 for the Color and none for the Decoration. Save and close the template.

17. Open a new Document window and save it as events.htm. Apply the template. Add the data in Table 5-13 to the second table as the Upcoming Events.

18. Save the document. Open the index.htm file. Scroll to the bottom of the page and then click to the right of the Comments link. Type a vertical line, and then type Upcoming Events as the link text. Create a link to the events.htm page.

19. Press the F12 key to view the page in your browser. Click the Upcoming Events link. Print a copy of the template and Web page if instructed to do so. Upload the page to the city Web Site on a remote server if instructed to do so.

Cases and Places

The difficulty of these case studies varies:
■ are the least difficult and ■■ are the most difficult. The last exercise is a group exercise.

1 ■ Your sports Web site has become very popular. You have received many e-mails asking for statistics and other information. You decide to add a Web page that will contain statistics and will be updated on a weekly basis. Add a background image to the page and add a title to the page. Create the template using tables. Add descriptive prompts and then create editable regions. Add styles to the headings and text. Then create a page, apply the template, and save the page in your sports Web site. Create a link to and from the home page. For a selection of images and backgrounds, visit the Dreamweaver MX 2004 Media Web page (scsite.com/dreamweavermx04/media) and then click Media below Project 5.

2 ■ You have decided to add a do-it-yourself section to your hobby Web site and want to use a consistent format and look for the page. You decide to use a template to create this new section. Create the template using a logo, tables, and links. Add descriptive prompts to the editable regions and apply styles to enhance the text and text size. Create the first do-it-yourself Web page and apply the template. Create a link to and from the home page. Upload the pages to a remote server if instructed to do so. For a selection of images and backgrounds, visit the Dreamweaver MX 2004 Media Web page (scsite.com/dreamweavermx04/media) and then click Media below Project 5.

3 ■■ Create a template for your music hobby Web site and then add a background to the page. Insert logos, tables, and other appropriate elements. Add a background image to a table. Apply a border to the table. Use the CSS Styles panel and apply styles to the elements on the page. Create a new Web page featuring a new topic for your Web site and apply the template. Create a link to and from the home page. Upload the page to a remote server if instructed to do so. For a selection of images and backgrounds, visit the Dreamweaver MX 2004 Media Web page (scsite.com/dreamweavermx04/media) and then click Media below Project 5.

Cases and Places

4 ■■ Your campaign for political office is progressing well, and you are one of the top two candidates. You have decided to add a new section to your Web site featuring your campaign supporters. To provide consistency and control, you use a template for this site. After completing the template, attach styles. Next, create two new pages for the site and then apply the template. Create a link to and from the home page. Upload the new pages to a remote server if instructed to do so. For a selection of images and backgrounds, visit the Dreamweaver MX 2004 Media Web page (scsite.com/dreamweavermx04/media) and then click Media below Project 5.

5 ■■ **Working Together** Each member of the group decides to create a template for the three vacation sites previously selected. Include on the templates headings, tables, links, and graphics. Present the three templates to the group and determine which one best meets the needs of the Web site. Next, add appropriate styles, including styles from the Type, Background, and Border categories. Include at least two images and a logo on the template. Create the three vacation site Web pages and apply the template. Then create links to and from the home page. Upload the new pages to a remote server if instructed to do so. For a selection of images and backgrounds, visit the Dreamweaver MX 2004 Media Web page (scsite.com/dreamweavermx04/media) and then click Media below Project 5.

Layers, Image Maps, and Navigation Bars

PROJECT

6

CASE PERSPECTIVE

David Allen recently attended a business workshop and was fascinated by some of the Web sites demonstrated by other workshop attendees. He particularly was impressed with some of the options offered through the use of layers and behaviors. He describes to you and Joan some of the features of layers, including flexibility and precise positioning. The concept that impressed David the most, however, was that of adding behaviors to show and hide different objects on a Web page.

Another feature that David specifically liked on some of the demonstrated Web sites was a navigation bar. He felt this gave the Web page a more professional look. You and Joan both agree that layers, behaviors, and a navigation bar would be good additions to the Web site.

Web page visitors have been inquiring about some of the more popular parks throughout the state. Therefore, Joan thinks that a new page could be added to the Web site using layers to display some of the parks that receive large numbers of visitors. She further suggests that you develop a navigation bar and add it to the index page. Everyone agrees that these are both good suggestions, and you are eager to get started with these modifications and additions.

As you read through this project, you will learn about layers and how to use layers to design a Web page. You also learn how to create an image map and a navigation bar, add a date object, and control various elements through Dreamweaver's Behaviors panel.

Layers, Image Maps, and Navigation Bars

Objectives

You will have mastered the material in this project when you can:

- Explain the concept of layers
- Insert, select, resize, and move a layer
- Name a layer
- Align layers
- Describe an image map
- Create an image map
- Add and edit behaviors
- Describe a navigation bar
- Create a navigation bar
- Insert a Date object

Introduction

Project 6 introduces three unique Dreamweaver features: layers, image maps, and navigation bars. Web developers have long dreamed of being able to position graphics, text, and other HTML objects at specific pixel coordinates. Tables provide some placement control, but not absolute precision. Layers, however, can be positioned anywhere on the page. They remain in the same position relative to the top and left margins of the window regardless of how a user resizes the browser window.

An image map is the second feature discussed in this project. An image map is an image that is divided into regions, called hotspots. When a user clicks a hotspot, an assigned action occurs. You can create multiple hotspots in an image, and you can have more than one image map on a single Web page.

The third feature introduced in this project is the navigation bar. Navigation bars often provide an easy way to move among the pages and files on a site. The linking elements within a navigation bar can consist of text, images, and/or a combination of text and images. To complement the Florida Parks Web site with these new elements, you modify the index page by adding an interactive navigation bar. As you complete the activities in this project, you will find that adding these features to a Web page provide interactivity and excitement.

If you are using Internet Explorer with Windows XP Service Pack 2 (SP2), Internet Explorer automatically blocks active content such as that contained in this and other projects. Thus, for all instances where Web pages containing active content are displayed in Internet Explorer, you must choose to "allow blocked content" by right-clicking the Information Bar and selecting the Allow Blocked Content command from the context menu, or modify the Internet Explorer security settings to allow elements such as image maps and layers to be displayed.

Project Six — Layers, Image Maps, and Navigation Bars

In this project, you learn how to use and apply three favorite Dreamweaver tools to the Florida Parks Web site. You begin the project by adding a new page to the Web site containing interactive layers and an image map (Figure 6-1a). Four separate layers are added to the page, and images then are embedded in each of the layers. One of the layers contains a Florida map, which serves as the image map. Clicking different spots on the image map displays a list of some of the favorite state parks in north, central, and south Florida. Next, you revise the index page by deleting the existing links and adding a navigation bar (Figure 6-1b on the next page). The navigation bar adds a more professional look by bringing all of the links together in one location at the top of the Web page. When the mouse pointer moves over an image link within the navigation bar, the image changes color to indicate that this is an active link. Each image also has alternate text to address accessibility issues.

FIGURE 6-1a (*continued*)

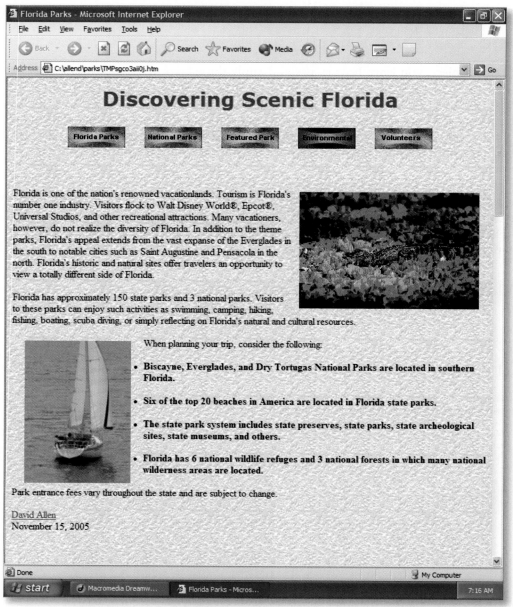

FIGURE 6-1b (continued)

Workspace Organization

Organization and preparation lead to a more productive work setting. Successful Web developers prepare their Dreamweaver workspace to provide an effective work environment. As you learn to use additional Dreamweaver tools, including layers, image maps, and navigation bars, you will become even more proficient working in the Dreamweaver environment.

Copying Data Files to the Local Web Site

Your Data Disk contains images for Project 6. You use the Windows My Computer option to copy the Project 6 images to your parks/images folder. See the inside back cover for instructions for downloading the Data Disk or see your instructor for information about accessing the files required for this book.

The DataFiles folder for this project is stored on Local Disk (C:). The location on your computer may be different. If necessary, verify with your instructor the location of the DataFiles folder. The following steps show how to copy the files to the parks local root folder.

To Copy Data Files to the Parks Web Site

1 Click the Start button on the Windows taskbar and then click My Computer.

2 Double-click Local Disk (C:) and then navigate to the location of the data files for Project 6.

3 Double-click the DataFiles folder and then double-click the Proj06 folder.

4 Double-click the parks folder and then double-click the images folder.

5 Click the first image file in the list, hold down the SHIFT key, and then click the last image file in the list.

6 Right-click the selected files to display the context menu.

7 Click the Copy command and then click the My Computer Back button the number of times necessary to navigate to the your name folder.

8 Double-click the your name folder, double-click the parks folder, and then double-click the images folder.

9 Right-click in the open window to display the context menu.

10 Click the Paste command to paste the image files into the images folder (Figure 6-2).

11 Navigate to the Proj06 parks folder. Double-click the parks folder.

12 Click the state_parks_activities.htm file, and then right-click to display the context menu.

13 Click the Copy command and then navigate to the your name folder.

14 Double-click the your name folder, double-click the parks folder, and then right-click to display the context menu.

15 Click the Paste command to paste the data file into the parks folder.

16 Close the My Computer window.

The image files are pasted into the Florida Parks Web site images folder (Figure 6-2).

FIGURE 6-2

Starting Dreamweaver and Closing Open Panels

Each time you start Dreamweaver, it opens to the last site displayed when you closed the program. It, therefore, may be necessary for you to open the parks Web site. The **Files pop-up menu** in the Files panel lists sites you have defined. When you open the site, a list of pages and subfolders within the site displays. The next steps illustrate how to start Dreamweaver and open the Florida Parks Web site.

To Start Dreamweaver and Open the Florida Parks Web Site

1 Click the Start button on the Windows taskbar.

2 Point to All Programs on the Start menu, point to Macromedia on the All Programs submenu, and then click Macromedia Dreamweaver MX 2004 on the Macromedia submenu.

3 If necessary, display the panel groups and expand the Property inspector.

4 Click the Files panel box arrow and point to Florida Parks on the Files pop-up menu.

5 Click Florida Parks.

Dreamweaver opens, and the Florida Parks Web site hierarchy displays in the Files panel (Figure 6-3). Note that the Insert bar displays in Figure 6-3. If the Insert bar does not display on your screen, you will open it later in this project.

FIGURE 6-3

Understanding Layers

A **layer** is similar to a table — it is a container that holds other types of content, such as images, text, form objects, and even other layers (nested layers). Anything you can put in an HTML document, you also can put in a layer. Layers can be stacked on top of one another, placed side by side, or overlapped. They easily can be moved, dragged, or resized. Web site developers use layers for page layout much as they use tables for page layout. A layer, however, provides more flexibility than a table because it can be placed in an exact spot anywhere on the page with pixel-perfect precision. It remains in this position (relative to the top and left margins of the page) regardless of how the Web page visitor resizes the browser window or views the text size. This is called **absolute positioning** and is possible because layers are positioned using a standard x-, y-, and z-coordinate system, similar to what you would use to create a graph on graph paper. Instead of having the point of origin be in the bottom-left corner, however, the x- and y-coordinates correspond to a layer's top and left positions within the page. The z-coordinate, also called the **z-index**, determines a layer's stacking order when more than one layer is added to a page.

Netscape does not fully support layers. If designing for Netscape, it is best to convert the layers to tables. To convert layers to tables, click the Modify menu, point to Convert, and then select the Layers to Table command.

Q&A

Q: How would I change the stacking order of several layers?

A: Press the F2 key to open the Layers panel. Drag a layer up or down to the desired stacking order.

Layers and DHTML

Layers are a component of dynamic HTML. **Dynamic HTML** (**DHTML**) is an extension of HTML that gives Web page developers the capability of precisely positioning objects on the Web page. DHTML combines layers, Cascading Style Sheets (CSS), and JavaScript coding, enabling the creation of dynamic page elements. Additionally, because a layer uses both DHTML and CSS, it offers a wide range of flexibility and control. Some possible effects you can accomplish using DHTML are as follows:

- Add images that are hidden from view initially and then display them when a user clicks a button or hotspot
- Create pop-up menus
- Position objects side by side
- Drag and drop objects
- Create animations
- Provide feedback to right and wrong answers

A disadvantage of using layers is that older browsers do not support them. Internet Explorer 4.0 and Netscape Navigator 4.0 (and later) support layers under the original W3C **Cascading Style Sheets-Positioning** (**CSS-P**) specifications. Browsers older than version 4.0, however, ignore the layer code and display the content in the normal flow of the page (no absolute positioning). Also, even though current browsers support layers, Internet Explorer and Netscape Navigator implement DHTML differently, and, therefore, some discrepancy in the display of layers exists. Navigator 4.0 in particular has a difficult time with layers and often displays them incorrectly. Dreamweaver, however, contains a Netscape 4 Resize Fix option, which is available through the Layers category in the Preferences dialog box.

Dreamweaver provides two options for creating layers: the Draw Layer button located on the Layout category in the Insert bar, and the layer option available through the Design panel group. In this project, you use the Draw Layer button on the Layout category on the Insert bar and modify attributes through the Layer Property inspector. Displaying Dreamweaver's layout tools such as the rulers or the grid helps with precise positioning. In this project, you use the rulers.

The steps on the next page show how to open the state_park_activities.htm page and to display the rulers.

To Open the Florida State Park Activities Page and Display the Rulers

1

• **If necessary, click the Files tab in the panel groups.**

• **Double-click the state_park_activities.htm file.**

The state_park_activities.htm file opens in the Document window (Figure 6-4). The insertion point is blinking at the top of the page, to the left of the heading.

FIGURE 6-4

2

• **Click View on the menu bar, point to Rulers, and then point to Show on the Rulers submenu.**

The View menu and Rulers submenu are displayed (Figure 6-5).

FIGURE 6-5

3

• **Click Show.**

Dreamweaver displays the rulers in the Document window (Figure 6-6). The ruler-origin icon is displayed in the upper-left corner where the rulers meet in the Document window.

FIGURE 6-6

Layer Property Inspector

When you insert a layer into a Web page and the layer is selected, Dreamweaver displays the Layer Property inspector (Figure 6-7). The following section describes the layer properties that are available through the Layer Property inspector.

FIGURE 6-7

LAYER ID Assigns a unique name to identify the layer in the Layers panel and in JavaScript code. Layer names must start with a letter and can contain only standard alphanumeric characters.

Q: Can layers be converted to tables?

A: Yes — select Modify on the menu bar and then select the Layers to Table command on the Convert submenu.

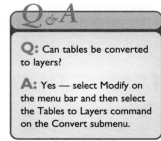

Q: Can tables be converted to layers?

A: Yes — select Modify on the menu bar and then select the Tables to Layers command on the Convert submenu.

L AND T Specifies the position of the layer's top-left corner relative to the top-left corner of the page, or of the parent layer if the layer is nested. A nested layer, or child layer, is a layer whose code is contained in another layer. Nesting often is used to group layers together. A nested layer moves with its parent layer and can be set to inherit visibility from its parent. Parent and child layers are discussed in more detail in the section on nesting, overlapping, and stacking layers later in this project.

W AND H Specifies the width and height of the layer in Design view. In Design view, if the content of the layer exceeds the specified size, the bottom edge of the layer stretches to accommodate the content. When the layer appears in a browser, however, the bottom edge does not stretch unless the Overflow property is set to visible. The default unit for position and size is pixels (px). Other units include pc (picas), pt (points), in (inches), mm (millimeters), cm (centimeters), and % (percentage of the parent layer's corresponding value). The abbreviations must follow the value without a space: for example, 3mm indicates 3 millimeters.

Z-INDEX Determines the stacking order of the layer. In a browser, higher-numbered layers appear in front of lower-numbered ones. The z-index values can be positive or negative. The stacking order can be changed through the Layers panel.

VIS Specifies whether the layer is visible initially or not. The following options are available:

- **default** does not specify a visibility property. When no visibility is specified, most browsers default to inherit.
- **inherit** uses the visibility property of the layer's parent.
- **visible** displays the layer contents, regardless of the parent's value.
- **hidden** hides the layer contents, regardless of the parent's value. Note that hidden layers created with ilayer (a tag unique to Netscape Navigator) still take up the same space as if they were visible.

BG IMAGE Specifies a background image for the layer.

BG COLOR Specifies a background color for the layer. Leave this option blank to specify a transparent background.

CLASS Lets you apply CSS rules to the selected object.

OVERFLOW Works only with the <div> and <span> tags and controls how layers appear in a browser when the content exceeds the layer's specified size. The following options are available:

- **visible** indicates that the extra content appears in the layer.
- **hidden** specifies that the extra content is not displayed in the browser.
- **scroll** specifies that the browser should add scroll bars to the layer whether or not they are needed.
- **auto** causes the browser to display scroll bars for the layer only when the layer's contents exceed its boundaries.

CLIP Defines the visible area of a layer. Specify left, top, right, and bottom coordinates to define a rectangle in the coordinate space of the layer (counting from the top-left corner of the layer). The layer is *clipped* so only the specified rectangle is visible.

In Project 3, you learned how to display and use the rulers. Now you use the rulers as a visual guide and create a layer that will be a container for the Florida map image. When you draw the layer in the Document window, a rectangular image appears, representing the layer. (If the layer borders do not display in the Document window, they can be turned on through the View menu.) The rectangular image, however, does not display when the page is viewed in a browser. Instead, only the content of what is contained within the layer is displayed in the browser.

The default rulers appear on the left and top borders of the Document window, marked in pixels. The **ruler origin** is the 0 point, or the location on the page where the horizontal and vertical lines meet and read 0. The 0 point is represented by the **ruler-origin icon**, which is located in the Document window when the page is displayed in Design view and the rulers are displayed (see Figure 6-6 on page DW 467). Generally, this location is the upper-left corner of the Document window.

Using the rulers as a drawing guideline can be somewhat difficult to manage. To make measuring easier, you can move the 0 point anywhere within the Document window. To move the 0 point, move the mouse pointer to the upper-left corner where the vertical and horizontal lines meet, and then click and drag the cross hairs to the desired location. When you move the 0 point, the cross hairs are displayed in the Document window and follow the mouse pointer. The mouse pointer position is indicated with a dotted line on both the vertical and horizontal ruler lines.

Relocating the 0 point does not affect the page content. You can relocate the 0 point as many times as necessary. You also can reset the ruler origin by right-clicking anywhere on the rulers and then selecting Reset Origin on the context menu. The following steps illustrate how to create, select, and drag a layer.

Q&A

Q: Can layers be prevented from overlapping?

A: Yes — click the Prevent overlaps check box in the Layers panel.

To Create, Select, and Drag a Layer for the Florida Map Image

1

• **If necessary, display the Insert bar and then select the Layout category from the Insert bar pop-up menu.**

• **Click below the last line of text in the Document window.**

• **Click the ruler-origin icon and drag it to the insertion point.**

The insertion point is blinking below the last line of text in the Document window. Notice that the cross hair increases in size as you drag the ruler. The vertical ruler 0 point now is to the left of the insertion point (Figure 6-8).

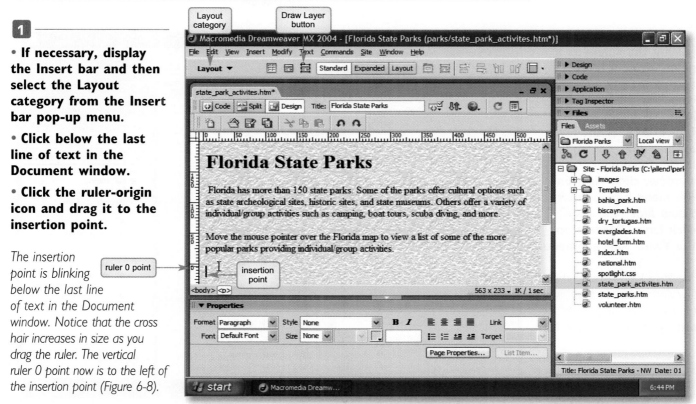

FIGURE 6-8

2

• **Click the Draw Layer button on the Insert bar Layout category and then move the pointer to the insertion point.**

The layer pointer is displayed in the Document window (Figure 6-9).

FIGURE 6-9

3

• **Using the rulers as a guide, draw a layer approximately 315 pixels wide and 285 pixels high, as shown in Figure 6-10. If the layer outline does not appear in the Document window, click View on the menu bar, point to Visual Aids, and then click Layer Borders on the Visual Aids submenu.**

The layer is displayed in the Document window. Most likely, the layer overlaps some of the text, as shown in Figure 6-10.

FIGURE 6-10

4

• **Move the mouse pointer over any border of the layer outline and then click the border.**

The layer is selected, as indicated by the resize handles that appear around the layer (Figure 6-11). The mouse pointer changes to a four-headed arrow when positioned on a border, indicating that the layer can be selected and moved. Dreamweaver displays the Layer Property inspector. The L (left) and T (top) attributes indicate the position of the layer's top-left corner relative to the top-left corner of the page.

FIGURE 6-11

Your measurements and layer position are approximate and most likely will not match those in Figure 6-11. You will have an opportunity to adjust the size and position later in this project.

5

• **Using the rulers as a visual guide, move the mouse pointer over a border and drag the top border of the layer until it is about 25 pixels below the text.**

The layer is displayed in its new position (Figure 6-12). The L and T attributes indicate the layer's new position. Your measurements and layer position are approximate and most likely will not match those in Figure 6-12. You will have an opportunity to adjust the size and position later in this project.

FIGURE 6-12

6

• **Right-click anywhere on the rulers and select Reset Origin on the context menu.**

The vertical 0 point returns to its original position.

Other Ways

1. On Insert menu click Layout Objects, click Layer

In addition to moving a layer by positioning the mouse pointer on a layer border, you also can drag the **selection handle** that appears above the layer in the upper-left corner (see Figure 6-11 on the previous page).

The Layer-Code Marker

When you insert a layer, a **layer-code marker** appears in the Document window. This small yellow square indicates that a layer is on the page. For the layer-code marker to display, the Anchor points for layers check box must be selected through the Invisible Elements category in the Preferences dialog box. When the Invisible Elements option is turned on, the markers may cause the elements on the page in the Document window to appear to shift position. These markers, however, are not displayed in the browser. When you view the page in your browser, the layers and other objects are displayed in the correct positions.

The layer-code marker is similar in appearance to the invisible element marker that displayed when you inserted images into a Web page in Project 2. In Project 2, dragging the image marker to another position in the Document window also moved the image to another position. Normally, the position of HTML objects in the Document window and in the browser is determined by their order in the HTML source code. They are displayed in a top-to-bottom sequence that mirrors their order in the source code.

Dragging or moving the layer-code marker, however, generally does not reposition the layer and has no effect on the way a Web page displays the layer in a browser. When you move a layer-code marker, you are not moving the layer; instead, you are repositioning the layer's code in the HTML of the page. Moving a layer-code marker, therefore, can affect how the code is interpreted and the order in which the layer content is loaded. It is possible to have a layer's content displayed at the top of the Web page while the source code is at the end of the page.

If your Web page contains tables, do not drag the layer-code marker into a table cell. This can cause display problems in some browsers. You can drag a layer, however, to overlap a table or make a label display so it appears to be inside the table cell as long as the layer-code marker itself is not in the table cell. When you use the Draw Layer button to create the layer, Dreamweaver will not put the code into a table cell. The following steps illustrate how to view and move the layer-code marker.

To View and Move the Layer-Code Marker

1

• **If necessary, click Edit on the menu bar, select Preferences, click the Invisible Elements category, and then click the Anchor points for layers check box. Scroll to the top of the Document window.**

The layer-code marker is selected because the layer is selected (Figure 6-13).

FIGURE 6-13

2

• **Drag the layer-code marker to the top of the layer. If the paragraph splits when you are moving the layer-code marker, click the Undo button on the Standard toolbar and then move the layer-code marker again. If necessary, drag the layer.**

The layer-code marker is moved so it appears above the layer. The layer still is in the same position, as indicated by the L and T attributes in the Property inspector (Figure 6-14). The position on your screen and the L and T attributes most likely will be different from those in Figure 6-14. You will adjust these later in this project.

FIGURE 6-14

The Layers Panel

The **Layers panel**, part of the Advanced Layout group, is helpful in managing the layers in your document. Use the Layers panel to prevent overlaps, to change the visibility of layers, to nest or stack layers, and to select one or more layers. All of the layers on a Web page are listed in the panel. The panel contains three columns: Visibility, Name, and Z-Index. The Visibility column uses eye icons. A **closed-eye icon** indicates a layer is hidden; an **open-eye icon** indicates the layer is visible. The absence of an eye icon indicates that the layer is in its default state — that it is showing, but not defined as showing in the HTML code. The middle column displays the names of the layers. Clicking a layer name in the Layers panel is another way to select a layer. In the Z-Index column, layers are displayed in order of their z-index values. The first-created layer appears at the bottom of the list, and the most recently created layer at the top of the list. Nested layers are displayed as indented names connected to parent layers (as discussed later in this project). The Prevent overlaps check box, when clicked, prevents layers from overlapping. When the Prevent overlaps option is on, a layer cannot be created in front of, moved or resized over, or nested within an existing layer.

The following step illustrates how to display the Layers panel.

To Display the Layers Panel

1

• **Press the F2 key to display the Layers panel.**

The Layers panel is displayed and is part of the Design group panel (Figure 6-15). The Layers panel on your screen may be in a different location.

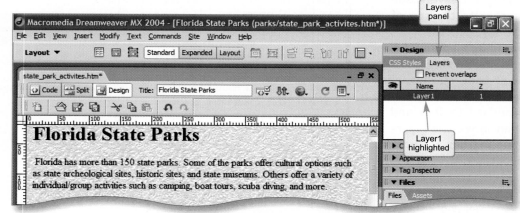

FIGURE 6-15

The next step is to rename the layer, to adjust the layer width and height properties, and to specify the layer visibility using the Property inspector.

To Name the Layer and Adjust the Layer Properties

1

• **Click the Layer ID text box in the Property inspector and then type** flmap **as the layer name. If necessary, double-click the W box and change the width to 315px. Then double-click the H box and change the height to 285px. Click the Vis box arrow and then click visible.**

• **Click the Overflow box arrow and then click hidden.**

• **Press the TAB key.**

The property changes for the flmap layer are made in the Property inspector. The flmap name appears in the Layers panel with the open-eye icon

FIGURE 6-16

indicating the layer is visible (Figure 6-16). Your measurements and layer position are approximate and most likely will not match those in Figure 6-16. Later in this project, you will adjust the L and T attributes.

Adding Objects to Layers

As indicated previously, a layer is a container that can hold objects. The objects can be anything that can be added to an HTML page and include such items as images, text, form objects, and even other layers (nested layers). Objects, including images, can be inserted onto layers through the Insert menu. Images also can be dragged from the Files panel onto the layer. The following steps show how to add the Florida map image to the flmap layer.

Other Ways

1. Double-click layer name in Layers panel

To Add an Image to the Flmap Layer

1

• **Scroll down in the Document window. Click the Assets panel tab and, if necessary, click the Images icon.**

• **Locate and click the florida_map.jpg image (Figure 6-17). If the florida_map.jpg file does not appear in the Assets panel, click the Refresh button.**

FIGURE 6-17

2

• **Drag the florida_map.jpg image onto the layer.**

• **Click the SAVE button on the Standard toolbar.**

The Florida map image is selected and displayed in the layer. The Property inspector displays image properties (Figure 6-18).

FIGURE 6-18

Other Ways

1. On Insert menu click Image, select file name in the Select Image Source dialog box, click OK button

More About

Absolute Positioning

Absolute positioning is the more common and widely used CSS positioning method. Dreamweaver uses this method. Two other methods, however, also are available: static positioning and relative positioning. Relative positioning places the layer using the coordinates entered in the Placement boxes relative to the object's position in the text flow of the document. This option is not displayed in the Document window. Static positioning places the layer at its location in the text flow.

More About

Z-Index

The term, z-index, comes from the coordinate system used in algebra. The z-index is the third coordinate that works with x and y and is required to describe three-dimensional space.

Nesting, Overlapping, and Stacking Layers

Several methods are available to manage and manipulate layers. As noted previously, layers can be nested, overlapped, or stacked one on top of another.

Nesting is used to group layers. This process also is referred to as creating a parent-child relation. A nested layer, also called a **child layer**, is similar in concept to a nested table or a nested frame. Having a nested layer, however, does not necessarily mean that one layer resides within another layer. Rather, it means that the HTML code for one layer is written inside the code for another layer. The nested layer can be displayed anywhere on the page. It does not even have to touch the **parent layer**, which is the layer containing the code for the other layers. The primary advantage of nested layers is that the parent layer controls the behavior of its child layers. If the parent layer is moved on the screen, the nested layers move with it. Additionally, if you hide the parent layer, you also hide the nested layers. In the Layers panel, nested layers are indented below the parent layer.

To create a nested layer, draw the layer inside an existing layer while holding down the CTRL key. To unnest a nested layer, drag the layer-code marker to a different location in the Document window, or, in the Layers panel, drag the nested layer to an empty spot.

Layers also can overlap and/or be stacked one on top of another. Layers that float on top of each other have a **stacking order**. In the HTML source code, the stacking order, or z-index, of the layers is determined by the order in which they are created. The first layer you draw is 1, the second is 2, and so on. The layer with the highest number appears on top or in front of layers with lower numbers. Stacking layers provides opportunities for techniques such as hiding and displaying layers and/or parts of a layer, creating draggable layers, and creating animation.

Two different methods are available through the Layers panel to change the z-index for a layer and set which layer appears in front of or behind another layer. First, you can click the layer name and then drag it up or down in the list. A line appears, indicating where the layer will be placed. The second method is to click the number of the layer you want to change in the Z column and then type a higher number to move the layer up or a lower number to move the layer down in the stacking order. After you change the z-index, Dreamweaver automatically rearranges the layers from highest to lowest, with the highest number on top. You also can turn off the overlapping feature in the Layers panel. When the Prevent overlaps check box is selected, layers cannot be overlapped or stacked.

The steps on the next page illustrate how to draw three stacked layers, one on top of the other. The placement of the layers in Figures 6-19 through 6-28 on pages DW 477–DW 482 is approximate. Later in this project, you align and position the layers.

To Create Stacked Layers

1

• **Click the expand/collapse arrow to collapse the panel groups.**

The panel groups are collapsed (Figure 6-19).

FIGURE 6-19

2

• **Click the ruler-origin icon and drag it about 25 pixels to the right of the flmap layer.**

• **Click the Draw Layer button on the Insert bar and then use the rulers as a visual guide to draw a layer measuring approximately 350px in width and 325px in height to the right of the flmap layer.**

The layer is drawn and appears to the right of the flmap layer (Figure 6-20).

FIGURE 6-20

3

• **Right-click anywhere on the rulers and then click Reset Origin on the context menu.**

• **Move the mouse pointer over any border of the layer outline and then click the border.**

• **Click the Layer ID text box and then type** northfl **as the layer name. If necessary, change the W to 350px and the H to 325px in the Property inspector. Click the Vis box arrow and then click hidden. Click the Overflow box arrow and then click hidden.**

• **Press the TAB key.**

FIGURE 6-21

The properties for the northfl layer are added and are displayed in the Property inspector. The 0 origin point for the rulers is reset to 0 (Figure 6-21). You will align the T and L properties later in this project. Pressing the TAB key activates the action for the selected box.

4

• **Scroll up to see the top of the layer. Click the Draw Layer button on the Insert bar and then draw a second layer directly on top of the northfl layer.**

• **Select the layer. Add and modify the following properties in the Property inspector: Layer ID – cenfl, W – 350px, H – 325px, Vis – hidden, and Overflow – hidden.**

• **Press the TAB key.**

The properties are modified and added for the cenfl layer, and are displayed in the Property inspector (Figure 6-22). You will align the T and L properties later in this project.

FIGURE 6-22

5

• **Scroll up. Click the Draw Layer button in the Insert bar and then draw a third layer on top of the cenfl layer.**

• **Select the layer. Add and modify the following attributes in the Property inspector: Layer ID – southfl, W – 350px, H – 325px, Vis – hidden, and Overflow - hidden.**

• **Press the TAB key.**

The properties are added and modified for the southfl layer, and are displayed in the Property inspector (Figure 6-23). You will align the T and L properties later in this project.

FIGURE 6-23

Selecting Stacked Layers

The next step is to add images to each of the layers, but before you add the images, you first must select the correct layer. Dreamweaver provides the following options for selecting layers:

- Click the name of the desired layer in the Layers panel.
- Click a layer's selection handle. If the selection handle is not visible, click anywhere inside the layer to make the handle visible.
- Click a layer's border.
- Press CTRL+SHIFT. If multiple layers are selected, this deselects all other layers and selects only the one that you clicked.
- Click the layer-code marker (in Design view) that represents the layer's location in the HTML code.

When layers are stacked, the easiest way to select a layer is to click the name in the Layers panel. The next steps illustrate how to select layers and add images to each layer.

To Select Layers and Add Images

1

• **Click the expand/collapse arrow to expand the panel groups. Collapse the Property inspector.**

The southfl layer is highlighted in the Layers panel and selected in the Document window. Closed-eye icons are displayed to the left of the three hidden layers. An open-eye icon displays to the left of the flmap layer (Figure 6-24).

FIGURE 6-24

2

• **Scroll to the right in the Document window.**

• **Scroll in the Assets panel and locate the southern.jpg file. Drag the southern.jpg image onto the southfl layer.**

The southern.jpg image is displayed in the southfl layer (Figure 6-25).

FIGURE 6-25

3

• **Click cenfl in the Layers panel.**

The cenfl layer is highlighted in the Layers panel and selected in the Document window (Figure 6-26).

FIGURE 6-26

4

• **If necessary, scroll up in the Assets panel and locate the central.jpg file. Drag the central.jpg image into the cenfl layer.**

The central.jpg image is displayed in the cenfl layer (Figure 6-27).

FIGURE 6-27

5

- **Click northfl in the Layers panel.**

- **Locate the northern.jpg image in the Assets panel and drag the image onto the northfl layer.**

The northern.jpg image is displayed in the northfl layer (Figure 6-28).

FIGURE 6-28

Image Maps

Image maps are an exciting and interesting way to liven up your Web site. An **image map** is an image that has one or more hotspots placed on top of it. A **hotspot** is a designated area on an image map that the user clicks to cause an action to occur. You can create a hotspot on an image map to link to different parts of the same Web page, to link to other Web pages within the Web site or outside the Web site, or to display content within a hidden layer.

Two types of image maps exist: server-side and client-side. The way in which **map data** is stored and interpreted depends on the type of map. Map data is the description in HTML code of the mapped regions or hotspots within the image. A Web server interprets the code or map data for **server-side maps**. When a visitor to a Web page clicks a hotspot in a server-side image map, the browser transfers data to a program running on a Web server for processing. The code for **client-side maps** is stored as part of the Web page HTML code. The Web browser, therefore, interprets the code for client-side maps. When a visitor to a Web page clicks a hotspot in a client-side image map, the browser processes the HTML code without interacting with the Web server. The code for client-side maps is processed faster because it does not have to be sent to a server.

You can add both client-side image maps and server-side image maps to the same document in Dreamweaver. Browsers that support both types of image maps give priority to client-side image maps. When you create an image map in the Document window, Dreamweaver automatically creates the code for client-side image maps. To include a server-side image map in a document, you must write the appropriate HTML code in Code view. In this project, you create a client-side image map.

Creating a Client-Side Image Map

The first step in creating the image map is to place the image on the Web page. In this project, the image is the Florida map. Earlier in this project, you placed the image on the flmap layer. It is not necessary to place an image on a layer to create an image map. You can insert the image anywhere on the page just as you previously have inserted images in earlier projects. Placing the image in a layer, however, provides absolute positioning. Using this method, you can be assured that the image map will display properly in all browsers supporting CSS-P.

When you create an image map and add a hotspot, you are creating an area that is clickable on the image. To define a hotspot, use one of three shapes: a rectangle, a circle (or oval), or a polygon. Select the tool you want to use and then drag the pointer over the image to create the hotspot. Use the **Rectangular Hotspot Tool** to create a rectangular-shaped hotspot. Use the **Oval Hotspot Tool** to define an oval or circular hotspot area. Use the **Polygon Hotspot Tool** to define an irregularly shaped hotspot. Click the **Pointer Hotspot Tool** (arrow) to close the polygon shape.

When an image is selected, the Property inspector for images is displayed. The Map name text box and hotpot tools are available in the lower portion of the Property inspector (Figure 6-29a).

FIGURE 6-29a

FIGURE 6-29b

The **Map name** and the **hotspot tools** allow you to label and create a client-side image map. The other properties in the Image Property inspector are described in Project 2 on page DW 143.

After you create a hotspot, Dreamweaver displays the Property inspector for a hotspot (Figure 6-29b). If you are linking to other locations within the same Web page or to Web pages outside of your existing Web site, the link or URL is inserted into the Link text box. On the Target pop-up menu, choose the window in which the file should open in the Target field. If the Web site contains frames, a list of the frame names is contained on the pop-up menu. You also can select from the reserved target names: _blank, _parent, _self, and _top. See page DW 558 in Project 7 for a discussion about these target names. The target option is not available unless the selected hotspot contains a link.

In this image map, you will not link to another Web site or Web page. Instead, you add behaviors to the hotspots to link to and to display hidden layers. Behaviors are discussed later in this project. Clicking the top third of the Florida map displays an image listing some of the more popular parks in north Florida, clicking the middle portion of the map displays an image listing some of the more popular parks in central Florida, and clicking the lower third of the map displays an image listing some of the more popular parks in south Florida.

If Windows SP2 is installed on your computer, the Internet Explorer security settings can prevent the display of active content such as the layers associated with the hotspots. To display the content, right-click the information bar at the top of the Internet Explorer window, and choose to allow blocked content.

Earlier in this project, you used the View menu to select Visual Aids, and then verified that Layer Borders was selected. This same menu also contains an Image Maps command. To see a visual of the hotspot on the image, the Image Maps command must be active. The following steps illustrate how to verify that the Image Maps command is selected and how to create three rectangular hotspots on the Florida map image.

To Create Hotspots on the Florida Map Image

1

• **Expand the Property inspector and collapse the panel groups.**

• **If necessary, scroll up to display the top of the flmap layer. Click the florida_map.jpg image in the flmap layer.**

The florida_map.jpg image is selected. The Image Property inspector is displayed and the panel groups are hidden (Figure 6-30).

FIGURE 6-30

2

• **Click the Rectangular Hotspot Tool and then move the cross hair pointer to the upper-left corner of the florida_map.jpg image.**

The cross hair pointer is located in the upper-left corner of the florida_map.jpg image (Figure 6-31).

FIGURE 6-31

3

• **Drag to draw a rectangle encompassing approximately the top third of the florida_map.jpg image. If the rectangular hotspot does not appear, click View on the menu bar, point to Visual Aids, and then click Image Maps on the Visual Aids submenu.**

A rectangular hotspot is drawn on the florida_map.jpg image (Figure 6-32). Dreamweaver displays the Hotspot Property inspector.

FIGURE 6-32

4

• **Draw two more hotspots on the florida_map.jpg image by dragging the cross hair pointer over the middle third of the image and then over the lower third of the image.**

• **Click anywhere in the window to cancel the cross hair pointer, and then, if necessary, scroll down.**

The second and third hotspots are drawn in the middle and lower thirds of the florida_map.jpg image (Figure 6-33). The cross hair pointer is canceled.

FIGURE 6-33

More About

Behaviors

Use Dreamweaver behaviors to allow visitors to interact with a Web page. Simply specify the action and the event that triggers that action. For more information about behaviors, visit the Dreamweaver MX 2004 More About Web page (scsite.com/dreamweavermx04/more.htm) and then click Behaviors.

Behaviors

In Project 4, you learned about the Behaviors panel and about using behaviors with forms. Recall that a **behavior** is a combination of an event and an action. Behaviors are attached to a specific element on a Web page. The element can be a table, an image, a link, a form, a form object, and even a hotspot on an image map. Some of the actions you can attach to hotspots (or other elements) include Show Pop-Up Menu, Play Sound, Drag Layer, Swap Image, and Show-Hide Layers.

Dreamweaver contains three standard events designed expressly for working with layers: Drag Layer, Set Text of Layer, and Show-Hide Layers. **Drag Layer** is used to set up an interactive process in which the user can drag or rearrange elements of the design. **Set Text of Layer** is used to change a layer's content dynamically; using this action, the user can swap the content of one layer for new content. **Show-Hide Layers** is used to make visible and to hide a layer and the layer's content.

Actions to invoke these events are **onMouseOut**, which initiates whatever action is associated with the event when the mouse is moved out of an object; **onMouseOver**, which initiates whatever action is associated with the event when the mouse is moved over the object; **onClick**, which initiates whatever action is associated with the event when the object is clicked; and **onDblClick**, which initiates whatever action is associated with the event when the object is double-clicked. These actions are selected through the Behaviors panel. The default is onMouseOver. To change the action for an event, click the existing event in the Behaviors panel. An arrow then is displayed to the right of the event, listing the four actions. Click the arrow to display a pop-up menu and to select another action: onClick, onDblClick, onMouseOut, or onMouseOver. Note that the arrow for the pop-up menu does not display until the existing event is clicked.

Adding Behaviors

Selecting a hotspot and then clicking the Actions (+) pop-up menu in the Behaviors panel displays a menu of actions that can be attached to the hotspot. When you choose an action on this menu, Dreamweaver displays a dialog box in which you can specify the parameters for the action. In this project, you use the Show-Hide Layers action.

The following steps show how to attach the Show-Hide Layers action to each of the three image map hotspots.

To Add the Show-Hide Layers Action to the Image Map Hotspots

1

• **Display the panel groups and collapse the Property inspector.**

• **Press SHIFT+F4 to display the Behaviors panel. If necessary, collapse the Files panel.**

The Behaviors panel displays and is part of the Tag panel group (Figure 6-34). Your panel may display in a different location on your screen.

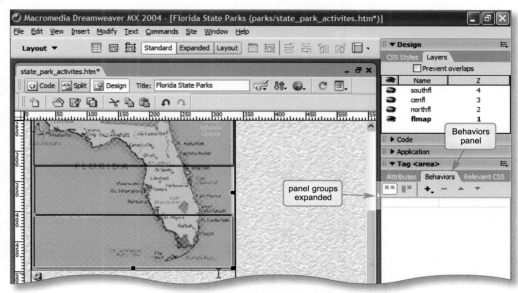

FIGURE 6-34

2

• **If necessary, scroll up and then click the top rectangular hotspot on the florida_map.jpg image.**

The top rectangular hotspot is selected on the florida_map.jpg image (Figure 6-35).

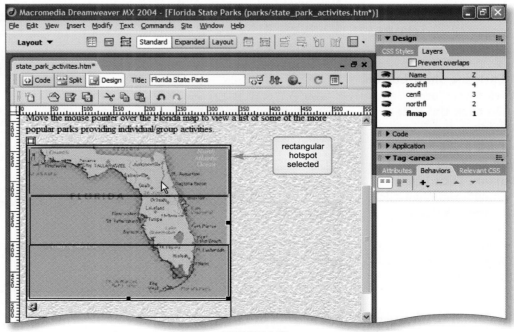

FIGURE 6-35

3

• **Click the Actions (+) button to display the Actions pop-up menu in the Behaviors panel. Point to Show-Hide Layers.**

Dreamweaver displays the Actions pop-up menu, and the Show-Hide Layers command is highlighted (Figure 6-36).

FIGURE 6-36

4

• **Click Show-Hide Layers. If necessary, click layer "northfl" in the Named layers list.**

Dreamweaver displays the Show-Hide Layers dialog box (Figure 6-37). The order of the layers in your dialog box may be different.

FIGURE 6-37

5

• **Click the Show button. Click layer "cenfl" and then click the Hide button.**

• **Click layer "southfl" and then click the Hide button. Click layer "flmap" and then click the Show button.**

The selected Show-Hide Layers behaviors are added to each of the layers (Figure 6-38).

FIGURE 6-38

6

- **Click the OK button.**

- **Click the middle hotspot on the florida_map.jpg image, click the Actions (+) button in the Behaviors panel, and then click Show-Hide Layers on the Actions pop-up menu.**

The middle hotspot is selected in the florida_map.jpg image. Dreamweaver displays the Show-Hide Layers dialog box (Figure 6-39). The order of the layers in your dialog box may be different.

FIGURE 6-39

7

- **If necessary, click layer "northfl" and then click the Hide button. Click layer "cenfl" and then click the Show button. Click layer "southfl" and then click the Hide button. Click layer "flmap" and then click the Show button.**

The selected Show-Hide Layers behaviors are added to each of the layers (Figure 6-40).

FIGURE 6-40

8

- **Click the OK button.**

- **If necessary, scroll down in the Document window and then click the bottom hotspot on the florida_map.jpg image.**

- **Click the Actions (+) button in the Behaviors panel, and then click Show-Hide Layers on the Actions pop-up menu.**

FIGURE 6-41

The bottom hotspot is selected in the florida_map.jpg image. Dreamweaver displays the Show-Hide Layers dialog box (Figure 6-41). The order of the layers in your dialog box may be different.

9

• **If necessary, click layer "northfl" and then click the Hide button. Click layer "cenfl" and then click the Hide button. Click layer "southfl" and then click the Show button. Click layer "flmap" and then click the Show button.**

The selected Show-Hide Layers behaviors are added to each of the layers (Figure 6-42).

FIGURE 6-42

10

• **Click the OK button.**

• **Click the SAVE button on the Standard toolbar and then press the F12 key to display the Web page in your browser.**

• **If necessary, maximize the browser window.**

• **Move the mouse pointer over the hotspots on the florida_map.jpg image to display each of the hidden layers.**

As you move the mouse pointer over each hotspot on the Florida map image, the images appear to the right. The layer with the image for Northern Florida State Parks is displayed in Figure 6-43.

FIGURE 6-43

11

• **Close the browser window and return to Dreamweaver.**

Positioning Layers

When you displayed the Florida map image and the images in the browser, you may have noticed that quite a bit of space appeared between the images and the paragraph above the images. You can position a layer anywhere on the page. In some instances, to eliminate extra space, it is necessary to drag the image over existing text. Even though the text is covered in the Document window, it is displayed correctly in the browser.

This sometimes can be a trial-and-error process. You can select and drag the layer by the selection handle or you can move the layer pixel by pixel by selecting the image, holding down the SHIFT key, and then pressing one of the arrow keys.

The following steps show how to adjust the position of the flmap layer.

To Adjust Layer Placement

1

• **Display the Property inspector. If necessary, click flmap in the Layers panel and then scroll up in the Document window to display the top of the flmap layer.**

• **Click the T text box in the Property inspector and type** 200 **as the pixel number.**

The Layer Property inspector is displayed. The flmap layer is highlighted in the Layers panel (Figure 6-44). Some of the Layer properties may be different on your screen than those in Figure 6-44. You will adjust other properties later in this project.

FIGURE 6-44

2

• **Press the TAB key and then click anywhere in the Document window.**

The flmap layer is moved up in the Document window and overlaps part of the text (Figure 6-45). The text will not be overlapped when displayed in the browser.

FIGURE 6-45

3

• **Press the F12 key to view the Web page in your browser. Verify that none of the text is covered and that the image is positioned nicely within the Web page.**

• **Close the browser to return to Dreamweaver.**

• **Make any necessary adjustments in the Document window to adjust the placement of the flmap layer.**

More About

Positioning Layers

Control the absolute positioning of layers on a Web page by setting five attributes: Left, Top, Width, Height, and Z-Index. For more information about positioning layers, visit the Dreamweaver MX 2004 More About Web page (scsite.com/ dreamweavermx04/more.htm) and then click Positioning Layers.

More About

Resizing Layers

To resize a layer one pixel at a time, hold down the CTRL key while pressing an arrow key.

Selecting, Aligning, and Resizing Multiple Layers

Dreamweaver contains yet another command that you can use to lay out your Web page: the **Align command**. This command, which is accessed through the Modify menu, lets you align layers to their left, right, top, or bottom edges. The Align command also provides an option to make the width and/or height of selected layers the same. When you are using the Align command, the layer you select last controls the alignment selection. For instance, if you first select northfl, then cenfl, and finally southfl, the alignment placement is determined by southfl. Likewise, if you select the option to make the width and/or height of selected layers the same, the last layer selected is the one whose values are used as the values for the other layers.

To align two or more layers, you first must select the layers. To select multiple layers in the Layers panel, you select one layer, hold down the SHIFT key, and then click the other layers you want to align. A second method for selecting multiple layers is to click the border of one layer, hold down the SHIFT key, and then click the border of any other layers. When multiple layers are selected, the handles of the last selected layer are highlighted in black. The resize handles of the other layers are highlighted in white.

Layers do not have to be stacked or overlapped to be aligned. The three layers you are going to align, however, are stacked one on top of the other. Thus, the best method for selecting the three layers is through the Layers panel.

The final steps for this Web page are to use the Align command to align the tops of the three hidden layers with the flmap layer, make the three hidden layers the same height and width, and then align the three layers to the left. Finally, you add a link from the state_parks.htm Web page to this new state_parks_activities.htm page. The next steps illustrate how to complete the alignment options and to add the link.

To Select and Align Multiple Layers

1

• **Select the southfl layer in the Layers panel. Hold down the SHIFT key and then select the cenfl, northfl, and flmap layers.**

All four layers are selected in the Layers panel. The flmap layer should be the last one selected. The Property inspector for Multiple Layers is displayed (Figure 6-46).

FIGURE 6-46

2

• **Click Modify on the menu bar, point to Align, and then point to Top on the Align submenu.**

The Modify menu and Align submenu are displayed (Figure 6-47).

FIGURE 6-47

3

• **Click Top. If necessary, scroll down in the Document window.**

All four layers are aligned at the top (Figure 6-48).

FIGURE 6-48

4

• **Hold down the SHIFT key and then click flmap in the Layers panel.**

The flmap layer is deselected (Figure 6-49). The other three layers still are selected.

FIGURE 6-49

5

• **Click Modify on the menu bar, point to Align, and then click Left on the Align submenu.**

• **Click Modify on the menu bar, point to Align, and then click Make Same Width on the Align submenu.**

• **Click Modify on the menu bar, point to Align, and then click Make Same Height on the Align submenu.**

The three stacked layers are aligned at the left and are now the same width and height. No apparent changes appear in the Document window.

6

• **Press the F12 key to view the Web page in your browser. Move the mouse pointer over the Florida map to verify that the images display and that they are aligned properly.**

The browser is displayed (Figure 6-50). In Figure 6-50, the mouse pointer is over the middle portion of the Florida map, and the image for Central Florida is displayed.

7

• **Close the browser and return to Dreamweaver.**

• **Click View on the menu bar, point to Rulers, and then click Show on the Rulers submenu to hide the rulers.**

FIGURE 6-50

• **Press F2 to collapse the Design group and then press SHIFT+F4 to collapse the Tag Inspector group.**

• **Press F8 to display the Files pane. Open the state_parks.htm file and scroll to the bottom of the page. Click below the Featured Park link. Type** Popular state parks **as the entry, create a link to the state_park_activities.htm page, and then save the state_parks.htm file.**

• **Press F12 to view the Web page and test the link. Close the browser and then close the state_parks.htm page.**

The Netscape Resize Fix

The Netscape 4 browser has a known compatibility problem that causes layers to lose their positioning coordinates when a visitor resizes a browser window.

Dreamweaver provides a fix for this through the Preferences dialog box by adding JavaScript code that forces the page to reload each time the browser window is resized, thus reassigning the layers to the correct positions. This option may be activated on your system. If not, the following steps show how to set the fix.

To Set the Netscape Resize Fix

1

• **Click Edit on the menu bar and then click Preferences.**

• **Click the Layers category and then click the Netscape 4 compatibility Add resize fix when inserting layer check box to select it. If necessary, click the Nesting Nest when created within a layer check box to select it.**

The Netscape 4 compatibility Add resize fix when inserting layer check box is selected (Figure 6-51).

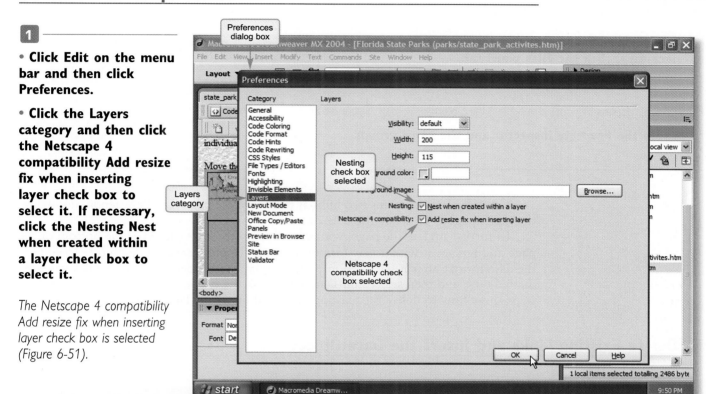

FIGURE 6-51

2

• **Click the OK button. Click the Save button on the Standard toolbar and then close the state_park_activities.htm page.**

The Navigation Bar and Date Object

In earlier projects, you used text to add links to your Web pages. Dreamweaver provides another quick-and-easy method to provide navigation: a navigation bar. A **navigation bar** (or **nav bar**) is a set of interactive buttons that the Web site visitor uses as links to other Web pages or Web sites or other frames. The Insert Navigation Bar dialog boxes provide an option to insert the navigation bar horizontally or vertically. Many Web site developers consider a navigation bar to be a convenient, customized alternative to a browser's Back and Forward buttons.

Dreamweaver also provides the **Date object**, which inserts the current date in a format of your preference and provides the option of updating the date (with or without the time) whenever you save the file.

You add these two objects (navigation bar and Date object) to the index page. You open the existing index.htm page, delete the existing links, and then insert a

More About

Navigation Bar

Dreamweaver's navigation bar feature provides a visually interesting option that allows visitors to navigate the Web site easily. A navigation bar often extends along the top or side of a Web page and can include text, images, or animations that link to other sections or pages in the site. For more information about navigation bars, visit the Dreamweaver MX 2004 More About Web page (scsite.com/ dreamweavermx04/more.htm) and then click Navigation Bars.

navigation bar to replace these links. Additionally, you delete the static date and replace it with the Date object.

The following step illustrates how to open and prepare the index.htm page for the navigation bar and Date object.

To Open and Prepare the Index.htm Page

1

• **If necessary, click the Files panel tab.**

• **Double-click index.htm in the Files panel to open the index.htm file.**

Dreamweaver displays the index.htm page in the Document window (Figure 6-52).

• **Collapse the Property inspector and the panel groups.**

The index page contains two links at the top of the page. The first step in modifying the index page is to delete these links.

To further update the page, you remove the static date placed at the bottom of the page and replace it with a new format using the Dreamweaver Date object. To edit the date format after it has been inserted, display the Property inspector, click the formatted text, and then select Edit Date Format in the Property inspector. The next steps show how to delete the existing links and insert the Date object.

To Delete Existing Links and Insert the Date Object

1

• **Move the insertion point to the left of the two links at the top of the index.htm page and then drag to select the links.**

The two links are selected (Figure 6-52).

Q: I inserted the Date object and selected the Update automatically on save option. Now I want to edit the format of the date. How do I do this?

A: You can edit the date format after it has been inserted into the document by clicking the formatted text and selecting Edit Date Format in the Property inspector.

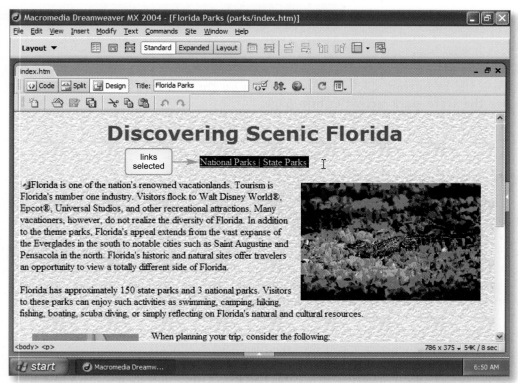

FIGURE 6-52

2

• **Press the DELETE key to remove the two links.**

The links are deleted (Figure 6-53).

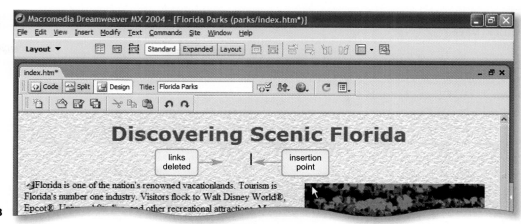

FIGURE 6-53

3

• **Scroll to the bottom of the page.**

• **Select the date below your e-mail address link and then press the DELETE key.**

The date is deleted. The insertion point is blinking below your linked e-mail address (Figure 6-54).

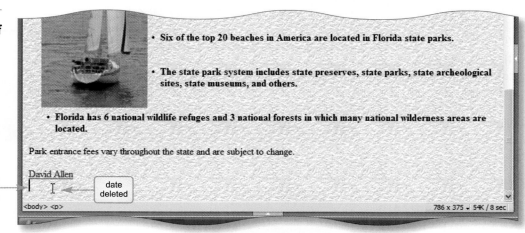

FIGURE 6-54

4

• **Click Insert on the menu bar and then point to Date.**

The Insert menu is displayed (Figure 6-55).

FIGURE 6-55

5

• **Click Date.**

Dreamweaver displays the Insert Date dialog box. The March 7, 1974 Date format is selected, which is the one you will use (Figure 6-56). The dates and times shown in the Insert Date dialog box neither are the current date nor reflect the dates/times that visitors will see when they display your site. They are examples of the ways in which you can display this information.

• **Click the Update automatically on save check box.**

The Update automatically on save check box is selected (Figure 6-56).

FIGURE 6-56

6

• **Click the OK button. Click the SAVE button on the Standard toolbar.**

The current date is inserted (Figure 6-57). The date on your Web page will be different from that displayed in Figure 6-57.

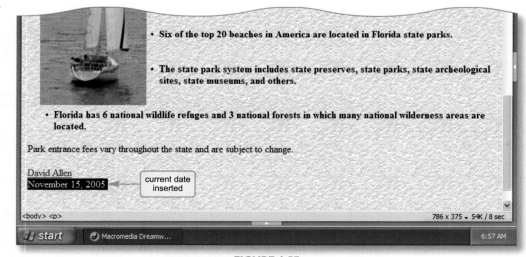

FIGURE 6-57

Other Ways

1. Click Common category in Insert bar, click the Date button on Common category, select Date format in Insert Date dialog box, click OK button

Creating a Navigation Bar

You create a navigation bar using icon or button elements. Each element is a little different shape or a different color. An element in a navigation bar is called a **rollover** if animation takes place when you move the mouse pointer over the element or click the element. The original image is swapped out for a different one, thus creating a simple animation.

Each element in a Dreamweaver navigation bar can have up to four different states. It is not necessary, however, to include images for all four states. The four possible images and states are as follows:

- **Up**: the image that displays when the visitor has not clicked or interacted with the element.
- **Over**: the image that appears when the mouse pointer is moved over the Up image.
- **Down**: the image that appears after the element is clicked.
- **Over While Down**: the image that appears when the pointer is rolled over the Down image after the element is clicked.

Dreamweaver also provides several features that contribute to the versatility of the navigation bar. Some of these features are:

- The navigation bar can be placed within a table or directly integrated into the HTML code.
- An Alternate text text box is available for use with nongraphical browsers and as an accessibility option.
- You can copy the navigation bar to other Web pages.
- A Preload images check box is available; select Preload images to download the images when the page loads.
- Check the Show "Down image" check box to display the selected element initially in its Down state when the page is displayed, instead of in its default Up state.

Modifying a navigation bar is easy. After you create the navigation bar, you can add images to it or remove them from it by using the Navigation Bar command on the Modify menu. You can use this command to change an image or set of images, to change which file opens when an element is clicked, to select a different window or frame in which to open a file, and to reorder the images.

The Florida Parks navigation bar contains five links. You specify three different states for each link — Up, Over, and Down. The same image is used for the Over and Down states. The following steps illustrate how to create the navigation bar.

Q: If I create a navigation bar, are the button images part of the Dreamweaver program?

A: No — you must create a set of images for the display states of each navigation element.

Q: Why do I need to add alternate text for each button in a navigation bar?

A: Alternate text appears in place of images for text-only browsers or for browsers that have been set to download images manually. Screen readers read alternate text, and some browsers display alternate text when the user mouses over the navigation bar element.

To Create the Navigation Bar

1

• **Scroll up to the top of the page in the Document window and then click below the heading. Click Insert on the menu bar, point to Image Objects, and then point to Navigation Bar on the Image Objects submenu.**

The Insert menu and Image Objects submenu are displayed (Figure 6-58).

FIGURE 6-58

2

• **Click Navigation Bar.**

Dreamweaver displays the Insert Navigation Bar dialog box (Figure 6-59). The insertion point is blinking in the Element name text box.

FIGURE 6-59

3

• **Type** FloridaParks **in the Element name text box. If necessary, click the Use tables check box to select it, and then point to the Browse button for the Up image text box.**

FloridaParks is displayed in the Element name text box and the Use tables check box is selected (Figure 6-60).

FIGURE 6-60

4

• **Click the Browse button to the right of the Up image text box. If necessary, double-click the images folder in the Select image source dialog box.**

Dreamweaver displays the Select image source dialog box (Figure 6-61).

FIGURE 6-61

5

• **Click the flaparksbutton01 file.**

The flaparksbutton01 image is highlighted (Figure 6-62). The Image preview area shows how the button will look.

FIGURE 6-62

6

• **Click the OK button in the Select image source dialog box and then point to the Browse button to the right of the Over image text box.**

The path to the flaparksbutton01.gif image is inserted into the Up image text box (Figure 6-63).

FIGURE 6-63

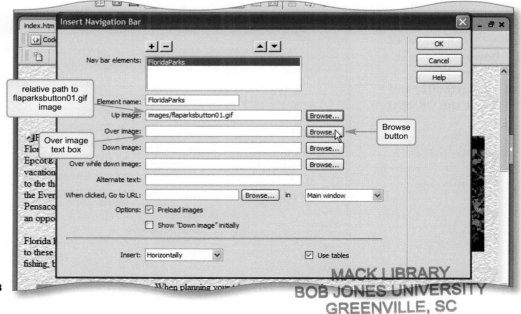

7

• **Click the Browse button to the right of the Over image text box and then click flaparksbutton02.**

The flaparksbutton02 file is selected (Figure 6-64).

FIGURE 6-64

8

• **Click the OK button. Point to the Browse button to the right of the Down image text box.**

The path to the flaparksbutton02.gif image is inserted into the Over image text box (Figure 6-65).

FIGURE 6-65

9

• **Click the Browse button to the right of the Down image text box. Click flaparksbutton02, and then click the OK button.**

The path to the flaparksbutton02.gif image is inserted into the Down image text box (Figure 6-66).

FIGURE 6-66

10

• **Click the Alternate text text box and then type** Florida Parks **as the alternate text. Point to the Browse button to the right of the When clicked, Go to URL text box.**

Florida Parks is displayed in the Alternate text text box (Figure 6-67).

FIGURE 6-67

11

• **Click the Browse button. If necessary, navigate to the parks folder. Click the state_parks file and then point to the OK button in the Select HTML file dialog box.**

Dreamweaver displays the Select HTML file dialog box (Figure 6-68). The state_parks.htm file is highlighted.

FIGURE 6-68

12

• **Click the OK button in the Select HTML file dialog box. Point to the Add Item button.**

The link to the state_parks.htm file is displayed in the When clicked, Go to URL text box (Figure 6-69).

FIGURE 6-69

13

• **Click the Add Item button.**

The data for the first button for the navigation bar is added, and the Insert Navigation Bar dialog box is ready for the next button (Figure 6-70).

FIGURE 6-70

14

• **Repeat Steps 3 through 13 to add the other four buttons, using the data shown in Table 6-1 on the next page.**

• **If necessary, display the Property inspector and then click the <table> tag in the tag selector. Center the table that contains the navigation bar.**

The navigation bar is created and is inserted into the Document window. It displays within a table (Figure 6-71).

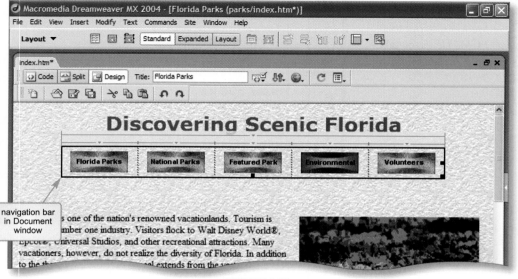

FIGURE 6-71

15
- Press the F12 key to view the navigation bar in your browser, and test each one of the links.

The navigation bar displays in the browser window (Figure 6-72).

16
- If instructed to do so, print a copy of the state_parks_activities.htm page and the revised index.htm page, hand them in to your instructor, and upload the revised Web pages to a server. Close the browser and then click the Save All button on the Standard toolbar.

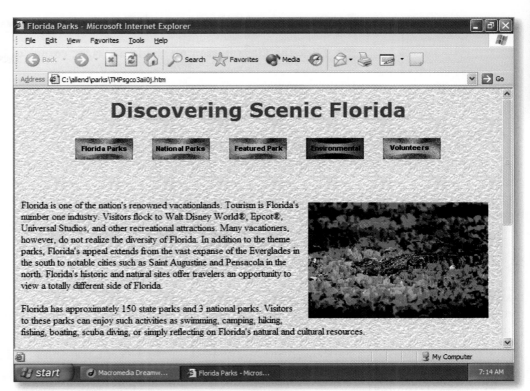

FIGURE 6-72

ELEMENT NAME	UP IMAGE	OVER IMAGE	DOWN IMAGE	ALTERNATE TEXT	URL
NationalParks	natparksbutton01.gif	natparksbutton02.gif	natparksbutton02.gif	National Parks	national.htm
FeaturedPark	featurebutton01.gif	featurebutton02.gif	featurebutton02.gif	Featured Park	bahia_park.htm
EnvironInfo	environbutton01.gif	environbutton02.gif	environbutton02.gif	Environmental	http://www.dep.state.fl.us/
Volunteer	volunbutton01.gif	volunbutton02.gif	volunbutton02.gif	Volunteer Information	volunteer.htm

Table 6-1   Navigation Bar Buttons

Quitting Dreamweaver

After you added a new page with layers and an image map and modified the index page by adding a Date object and a navigation bar, Project 6 is complete. The following step shows how to close the Web site, quit Dreamweaver MX 2004, and return control to Windows.

To Close the Web Site and Quit Dreamweaver

1 **Click the Close button on the upper-right corner of the Dreamweaver title bar.**

The Dreamweaver window, the Document window, and the Florida Parks Web site all close.

Project Summary

Project 6 introduced you to layers, image maps, navigation bars, and the Date object. You added single layers and stacked layers. You selected and aligned several layers. Next, you created an image map and then added hotspots that displayed hidden layers. Then, you modified the existing index page by deleting links and replacing those links with a navigation bar. You also inserted a Date object on the index page.

What You Should Know

Having completed this project, you now should be able to perform the tasks below. The tasks are listed in the same order they were presented in the project. For a list of keyboard commands for topics introduced in this project, see the Quick Reference for Windows at the back of this book and refer to the Shortcut column.

1. Copy Data Files to the Parks Web Site (DW 463)
2. Start Dreamweaver and Open the Florida Parks Web Site (DW 464)
3. Open the Florida State Park Activities Page and Display the Rulers (DW 466)
4. Create, Select, and Drag a Layer for the Florida Map Image (DW 469)
5. View and Move the Layer-Code Marker (DW 472)
6. Display the Layers Panel (DW 474)
7. Name the Layer and Adjust the Layer Properties (DW 474)
8. Add an Image to the Flmap Layer (DW 475)
9. Create Stacked Layers (DW 477)
10. Select Layers and Add Images (DW 480)
11. Create Hotspots on the Florida Map Image (DW 484)
12. Add the Show-Hide Layers Action to the Image Map Hotspots (DW 487)
13. Adjust Layer Placement (DW 491)
14. Select and Align Multiple Layers (DW 492)
15. Set the Netscape Resize Fix (DW 495)
16. Open and Prepare the Index.htm Page (DW 496)
17. Delete Existing Links and Insert the Date Object (DW 496)
18. Create the Navigation Bar (DW 499)
19. Close the Web Site and Quit Dreamweaver (DW 506)

Learn It Online

Instructions: To complete the Learn It Online exercises, start your browser, click the Address bar, and then enter the Web address scsite.com/dreamweavermx2004/learn. When the Dreamweaver MX 2004 Learn It Online page is displayed, follow the instructions in the exercises below. Each exercise has instructions for printing your results, either for your own records or for submission to your instructor.

1 Project Reinforcement TF, MC, and SA

Below Dreamweaver Project 6, click the Project Reinforcement link. Print the quiz by clicking Print on the File menu for each page. Answer each question.

2 Flash Cards

Below Dreamweaver Project 6, click the Flash Cards link and read the instructions. Type 20 (or a number specified by your instructor) in the Number of playing cards text box, type your name in the Enter your Name text box, and then click the Flip Card button. When the flash card is displayed, read the question and then click the ANSWER box arrow to select an answer. Flip through Flash Cards. If your score is 15 (75%) correct or greater, click Print on the File menu to print your results. If your score is less than 15 (75%) correct, then redo this exercise by clicking the Replay button.

3 Practice Test

Below Dreamweaver Project 6, click the Practice Test link. Answer each question, enter your first and last name at the bottom of the page, and then click the Grade Test button. When the graded practice test is displayed on your screen, click Print on the File menu to print a hard copy. Continue to take practice tests until you score 80% or better.

4 Who Wants To Be a Computer Genius?

Below Dreamweaver Project 6, click the Computer Genius link. Read the instructions, enter your first and last name at the bottom of the page, and then click the PLAY button. When your score is displayed, click the PRINT RESULTS link to print a hard copy.

5 Wheel of Terms

Below Dreamweaver Project 6, click the Wheel of Terms link. Read the instructions, and then enter your first and last name and your school name. Click the PLAY button. When your score is displayed, right-click the score and then click Print on the shortcut menu to print a hard copy.

6 Crossword Puzzle Challenge

Below Dreamweaver Project 6, click the Crossword Puzzle Challenge link. Read the instructions, and then enter your first and last name. Click the SUBMIT button. Work the crossword puzzle. When you are finished, click the Submit button. When the crossword puzzle is redisplayed, click the Print Puzzle button to print a hard copy.

7 Tips and Tricks

Below Dreamweaver Project 6, click the Tips and Tricks link. Click a topic that pertains to Project 6. Right-click the information and then click Print on the shortcut menu. Construct a brief example of what the information relates to in Dreamweaver to confirm you understand how to use the tip or trick.

8 Newsgroups

Below Dreamweaver Project 6, click the Newsgroups link. Click a topic that pertains to Project 6. Print three comments.

9 Expanding Your Horizons

Below Dreamweaver Project 6, click the Expanding Your Horizons link. Click a topic that pertains to Project 6. Print the information. Construct a brief example of what the information relates to in Dreamweaver to confirm you understand the contents of the article.

10 Search Sleuth

Below Dreamweaver Project 6, click the Search Sleuth link. To search for a term that pertains to this project, select a term below the Project 6 title and then use the Google search engine at google.com (or any major search engine) to display and print two Web pages that present information on the term.

Apply Your Knowledge

1 Adding Layers to the B & B Lawn Service

Instructions: Start Dreamweaver. See the inside back cover of this book for instructions for downloading the Data Disk or see your instructor for information on accessing the files in this book.

The proprietors of B & B Lawn Service would like to make some additions to their Web site. First, they would like to add a navigation bar to the main page. Second, they would like to have an additional informational page that provides tree-pruning tips. You begin the process by adding a navigation bar to the index.htm page. Next, you open a data file and add layers to show some tree-pruning procedures. The modified index.htm page and the new tree-pruning page are shown in Figures 6-73a and 6-73b on the next page. Software and hardware settings determine how a Web page is displayed in a browser. Your Web page may display differently than the ones shown in Figures 6-73a and 6-73b. Appendix C contains instructions for uploading your local site to a remote server.

FIGURE 6-73a (*continued*)

Apply Your Knowledge

FIGURE 6-73b (*continued*)

1. Display the Property inspector, Standard toolbar, and panel groups. Select Lawn Service on the Files pop-up menu in the Files panel.
2. Delete the services.htm page from the Lawn Service Web site (you will replace this page). Use the Windows My Computer option to copy the data files and the images from the DataFiles folder to your lawn folder and lawn/images folder. The new services.htm file is contained within the data files. This is simply an updated page with a link to the new tree-pruning page. You will not need to make any changes to this page.
3. Open the index.htm page. Scroll to the top of the page and delete the horizontal rule. If you delete the extra line space, press the ENTER key. Display the rulers.
4. Click Insert on the menu bar, point to Image Objects, and then click Navigation Bar on the Image Objects submenu. Verify that Preload images is selected, that Horizontally is selected, and that the Use tables check box is selected in the Insert Navigation Bar dialog box.
5. Type Ecology as the element name. Click the Browse button to the right of the Up image text box. Navigate to the yourname/lawn/images folder, click ecol01.gif, and then click the OK button. Click the Browse button to the right of the Over image text box. Click ecol02.gif, and then click the OK button. Click the Browse button to the right of the Down image text box, click ecol02.gif, and then click the OK button. Click the Alternate text text box and then type Ecological Information as the entry. Click the When clicked, Go to URL text box and then type http://www.eap.mcgill.ca/Publications/EAP68.htm as the linked text.

(*continued*)

Adding Layers to the B & B Lawn Service *(continued)*

6. Click the Add Item button. Type References as the element name. Click the Browse button to the right of the Up image text box, click refer01.gif, and then click the OK button. Click the Browse button to the right of the Over image text box, click refer02.gif, and then click the OK button. Click the Browse button to the right of the Down image text box, click refer02.gif, and then click the OK button. Type References in the Alternate text text box. Click the When clicked, Go to URL text box and then type references.htm (or the appropriate path in your Web site).

7. Click the Add Item button. Type NativePlants as the element name. Click the Browse button to the right of the Up image text box and then click plants01.gif. Click the Browse button to the right of the Over image text box and then click plants02.gif. Click the Browse button to the right of the Down image text box and then click plants02.gif. Type Native Plants in the Alternate text text box. Click the When clicked, Go to URL text box and then type native_plants.htm (or the appropriate path in your Web site). Click the OK button.

8. If necessary, select and center the table. Press the F12 key, and test each link. Save and close the index.htm page.

9. Open the tree_pruning.htm page. Click the ruler-origin icon and drag it about 25 pixels below the last paragraph. Click the Draw Layer button on the Layout category on the Insert bar and draw a layer approximately 150 by 150 pixels in size. Make any necessary W and H adjustments in the Property inspector. Type map in the Layer ID text box. Press the TAB key and change the L property to 100px. Press the TAB key again and change the T property to 200px. Click the Overflow box arrow and then click hidden. Drag the trees.gif image onto the layer.

10. Add three more layers. Use the rulers to approximate the L and T positions on the page as indicated in Table 6-2. Name the layers and drag images onto each layer, using the data as indicated in the table. Make any other necessary adjustments in the Property inspector.

Table 6-2 Layer Properties					
LAYER ID	L AND T PROPERTIES	W AND H PROPERTIES	VIS PROPERTY	OVERFLOW PROPERTY	IMAGE
before	380px, 200px	160px, 170px	hidden	hidden	before.gif
after	500px, 250px	180px, 200px	hidden	hidden	after.gif
topping	550px, 165px	175px, 170px	hidden	hidden	topping.gif

11. Add three rectangular hotspots to the trees.gif image. Each hotspot should cover about one-third of the image. Display the Behaviors panel. Select the first hotspot, click the Actions button in the Behaviors panel, and then click Show-Hide Layers on the Actions pop-up menu. In the Show-Hide Layers dialog box, show layer "map" and layer "before." Hide layer "after" and layer "topping." Click the second hotspot and then click the Actions button in the Behaviors panel. Click Show-Hide Layers on the Actions pop-up menu. Show layer "map" and layer "after." Hide layer "before" and layer "topping." Click the third hotspot, click the Actions button in the Behaviors panel, and then click Show-Hide Layers on the Add pop-up menu. Show layer "map" and layer "topping." Hide layer "before" and layer "after."

12. Click the Save button and then press the F12 key to view the Web page in your browser. Move the mouse pointer over the map image and verify that each layer is displayed in its proper spot. Close the browser to return to Dreamweaver.

13. Print a copy of the index and tree-pruning Web pages if instructed to do so. Upload the pages to the lawn Web site on a remote server if instructed to do so.

In the Lab

1 Creating a New Index Page for the CandleDust Web Site

Problem: The CandleDust Web site has become very popular. Mary would like to redesign the index page and give it a more professional look. She has requested that you help her with this project by adding a navigation bar, rearranging some of the text by using layers, adding an automatic Date object so the current date is displayed on the page, and aligning existing layers. You agree to help her. The revised Web page is shown in Figure 6-74. Appendix C contains instructions for uploading your local site to a remote server.

FIGURE 6-74

(continued)

In the Lab

Creating a New Index Page for the CandleDust Web Site *(continued)*

Instructions: Perform the following tasks:

1. Use the Windows My Computer option to copy the images from the DataFiles folder to your candle/images folder.

2. Select CandleDust on the Files pop-up menu in the Files panel. Display the panel groups and the Insert bar Layout category.

3. Open a new file and name it index01.htm. Later in this project, you will save this as index.htm so that it will replace the current index.htm page. Add the candlebg.gif image to the background. The insertion point is blinking at the top left of the page. Press the ENTER key two times.

4. The first task is to add a vertical navigation bar with four links. Click Insert on the menu bar, point to Image Objects, then click Navigation Bar on the Image Objects submenu. Verify that Preload images and Use tables check boxes are selected and that Vertically is selected in the Insert box.

5. Use the data in Table 6-3 to complete the Insert Navigation Bar dialog box.

Table 6-3	Navigation Bar Data				
ELEMENT NAME	UP IMAGE	OVER IMAGE	DOWN IMAGE	ALTERNATE TEXT	WHEN CLICKED, GO TO URL
History	history01.gif	history02.gif	history02.gif	Company history	history.htm
Links	links01.gif	links02.gif	links02.gif	Instruction links	http://www.candleandsoap.about.com/cs/candlemaking1/
Products	products01.gif	products02.gif	products02.gif	Products for sale	products.htm
Survey	survey01.gif	survey02.gif	survey02.gif	Survey	survey_form.htm

6. After all data is entered, click the OK button to insert the navigation bar.

7. Now, you add a layer for the logo. Display the rulers and then move the ruler-origin point about 150px to the right and approximately 50px from the top. Click the Draw Layer button on the Insert bar and then draw a layer with an approximate width of 120px and height of 150px. Make any necessary size adjustments in the Property inspector. Name the layer logo. Click the Vis box arrow and then click visible. Drag the candle1.gif image onto the layer. Right-click anywhere on the rulers and select Reset Origin on the context menu.

8. Next, you add five new layers: one for the heading and three for the text data contained on the original index page and a layer for your e-mail address and date at the end of the page. Open the original index.htm page to use as a guide.

9. Using the data from Table 6-4 on the next page, draw the heading layer. Make any L and T and W and H adjustments in the Property inspector. Click the index.htm page tab and copy the heading text. Click the index01.htm page tab and paste the heading text onto the headinglayer.

10. Using the data from Table 6-4, repeat Step 9 to add the four remaining layers and to copy and paste the text from the index page.

11. Delete the existing date in the date layer. Click Insert on the menu bar and then click Date. Select the first option in the Insert Date dialog box. Click the Update automatically on save check box and then click the OK button.

In the Lab

12. Select the text02 layer in the Layers panel. Hold down the SHIFT key and select the text03 layer. Click Modify on the menu bar, click Align, and then click Left to align both layers to the left.

13. Close the index.htm file. If prompted to save the file, click No. Save the index01.htm file as index.htm by clicking the File menu and then click Save As. Type index.htm in the File name text box of the Save As dialog box, then click Save. Click the Yes button in response to the Macromedia alert dialog box. The Web page is saved as index.htm.

14. Right-click the index01.htm file in the Files panel to display the context menu. Point to Edit and then click Delete. Click the Yes button in response to the Macromedia alert dialog box.

15. Press the F12 key to view the page in your browser. Click each of the links in the navigation bar to verify that they work. Print a copy of the Web page if instructed to do so. Upload the page to the candle Web site on a remote server if instructed to do so.

Table 6-4 Layer Properties

LAYER ID	L AND T PROPERTIES	W AND H PROPERTIES	VIS PROPERTY	OVERFLOW PROPERTY	IMAGE/TEXT
heading	340px, 75px	275px, 100px	Visible	Visible	CandleDust Welcome to CandleDust
text01	320px, 200px	325px, 90px	visible	visible	We offer the finest in fragrantly scented candles. Each of our candles is hand dipped and hand poured. Our wicks are lead free, and we use only the finest waxes and fragrant oils.
text02	250px, 325px	350px, 80px	visible	visible	CandleDust candles are available in a variety of types: • Decorative • Gel • Holiday • Pillar • Scented • Texture • Votive
text03	250px, 600px	350px, 65px	visible	visible	Our candles make a perfect gift for occasions such as weddings, birthdays, holidays, anniversaries, or any time of the year.
date	35px, 675px	130px, 50px	visible	visible	Your name and Date object

2 Modifying the Questions Web Page for the Credit Protection Web Site

Problem: Marcy would like to add more interaction to the Credit Protection Web site and has asked you for ideas. You suggest that the questions.htm page could be revised so when a question is clicked, the answer to the question is displayed. Marcy likes your suggestion, and you agree to revise the page. The revised page is shown in Figure 6-75 and shows one of the answers after the question is clicked. Appendix C contains instructions for uploading your local site to a remote server.

(continued)

In the Lab

Modifying the Questions Web Page for the Credit Protection Web Site *(continued)*

FIGURE 6-75

Instructions: Perform the following tasks:

1. Use the Windows My Computer option to copy the data files and the images from the DataFiles folder to your credit folder and credit/images folder. The data files contain a questions.htm file, which will replace the existing questions.htm file. Click the Yes button in response to the Confirm File Replace dialog box.

2. Start Dreamweaver. Select Credit on the Files pop-up menu in the Files panel. Display the panel groups and the Insert bar Layout category.

3. Open the questions.htm file. Display the rulers. Position the insertion point below the horizontal line and type Wondering about your credit? Click any of the following questions to find some answers. Press the ENTER key two times.

4. Click the Draw Layer button on the Insert bar and use the rulers as a guide to draw a layer with the following properties: Layer ID - questions, L 25px, T 225px, W 305px, H 220px, Vis - visible. Drag the questions.gif from the Files panel onto the questions layer.

5. Draw three more layers. Use the rulers as a guide to draw the layers. Use Table 6-5 on the next page for the properties for each layer. After you create each layer, type the text as listed in the Text column.

6. Select the questions layer and then draw a rectangular hotspot over the first question. With the hotspot selected, click the Actions button in the Behaviors panel and then click Show-Hide Layers on the Actions pop-up menu. Show layer "questions" and layer "quest01." Hide layers "quest02" and "quest03."

7. Draw a second rectangular hotspot over the second question. With the hotspot selected, click the Actions button in the Behaviors panel and then click Show-Hide Layers on the Actions pop-up menu. Show layer "questions" and layer "quest02." Hide layers "quest01" and "quest03."

8. Draw a third rectangular hotspot over the third question. With the hotspot selected, click the Actions button in the Behaviors panel and then click Show-Hide Layers on the Actions pop-up menu. Show layer "questions" and layer "quest03." Hide layers "quest01" and "quest02."

9. Press CTRL+S to save the questions.htm Web page.

10. Press the F12 key to view the page in your browser. Click each of the hotspots to verify that they work correctly. Print a copy of the Web page if instructed to do so. Upload the page to the credit Web site on a remote server if instructed to do so.

Table 6-5 Layer Properties				
LAYER ID	**L/T IN PX**	**W/H IN PX**	**VIS**	**TEXT**
quest01	400/200	280/205	hidden	Consider how you will use the card. Do you pay the entire balance at the end of every month? Or, do you make minimum payments? For those individuals who pay the entire balance each month, interest rate is not a priority. Most likely, you will not have to pay finance charges. Instead, look for a company that does not charge an annual fee. If you tend to carry an outstanding balance, search for a card issuer that charges very low interest rates.
quest02	400/255	275/145	hidden	Credit disability insurance pays off your credit card bills if you become unable to work. Many credit card and direct mail companies offer this type of insurance. The insurance is generally very expensive. If you are in good health, a broader policy would probably be a better option.
quest03	400/300	285/160	hidden	The Fair Credit Billing Act is a federal law that determines how billing errors and disputes involving credit and charge cards are handled. If you check the back of your monthly statement, generally you will find information about this process. If the company violates any provision of the law, you can sue to recover any damages.

3 Creating a Layered Page for the Plant City Web Site

Problem: Juan wants to add some interactivity to the Plant City Web site. You suggest to Juan that a navigation bar on the index page would be a good addition and that a different layout for the recipes page would enhance the overall site. Juan likes your ideas, and you are ready to get started. The revised pages are shown in Figures 6-76a and 6-76b.

(continued)

Creating a Layered Page for the Plant City Web Site *(continued)*

FIGURE 6-76a *(continued)*

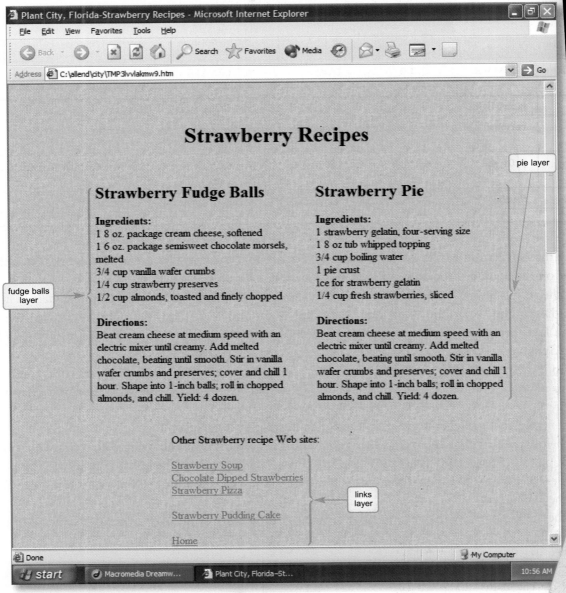

FIGURE 6-76b

Instructions: Perform the following tasks:

1. Use the Windows My Computer option to copy the images from the DataFiles folder to your/images folder.
2. Display the panel groups. Select City on the Files pop-up menu in the Files panel.
3. Open the index.htm page. Display the rulers. Delete the links at the end of the page. Delete the horizontal rule at the top of the page and then press the ENTER key. Click below heading 2, The Strawberry Capital of the United States. If necessary, center the insertion point.
4. Click the Insert menu, point to Image Objects, and then click Navigation Bar on the Image Objects submenu. In the Insert Navigation Bar dialog box, verify that Horizontally and Use table are selected. Use the data in Table 6-6 to create the navigation bar.

(continued)

In the Lab

...ge for the Plant City Web Site *(continued)*

...gation Bar

	OVER IMAGE	DOWN IMAGE	ALTERNATE TEXT	WHEN CLICKED, GO TO URL
	facts02.gif	facts02.gif	Plant City facts	facts.htm
...1.gif	recipes02.gif	recipes02.gif	Strawberry recipes	recipes.htm
...f	pc02.gif	pc02.gif	Plant City city Web site	http://www.ci.plant-city.fl.us/
...back01.gif	feedback02.gif	feedback02.gif	feedback form	guest_form.htm

...avigation bar. Press the F12 key, and verify that the navigation bar links work. Click the Save ...ie Standard toolbar and then close the index.htm page.

...ecipes.htm Web page. Delete the two horizontal rules. Select and cut the Strawberry Fudge Balls ...play the rulers and then move the origin point about 125px to the right and down about 150px. ...iyer with the following properties: Layer ID – fudgeballs, L – 125px, T – 150px, W – 295px, ...px, Vis – visible.

...e the layer and then click the Paste button on the Standard toolbar to paste the recipe onto the layer. 8... the right of the fudgeballs layer and draw a second layer with the following properties: Layer ID – pie, ...5px, T – 150px, W – 295px, H – 335px, Vis – visible.

...t and cut the Strawberry Pie recipe and then paste it into the layer.

...below the first two layers and then draw a third layer with the following properties: Layer ID – links, ...0px, T – 525px, W – 295px, H – 335px, Vis – visible. Click in the links layer. Type Other ...erry recipe sites and then press the ENTER key. Cut and paste the links into this layer. Save and

11. ...F Web page.

Us... F12 key to view the page in your browser. Print a copy of the Web pages if instructed to do so. ...ie page to the city Web site on a remote server if instructed to do so.

Cases and Places

The difficulty of these case studies varies:
■ are the least difficult and ■■ are the most difficult. The last exercise is a group exercise.

1 ■ You would like to add some interactivity to your sports Web site. You have looked at some other Web sites and are impressed with navigation bars. You decide to modify the index page and add a navigation bar to your sports Web site. You also decide to add the Date object so the date will be updated automatically when you save the page. Create a navigation bar for your sports site. Determine if a vertical or horizontal bar will best fit your needs. Then insert the Date object at the end of the page. For a selection of images and backgrounds, visit the Dreamweaver MX 2004 Media Web page (scsite.com/dreamweavermx04/media) and then click Media below Project 6.

2 ■ Your hobby Web page has become very popular and you want to give it a more professional look. One object you can add is a navigation bar. Determine if a vertical or horizontal bar will best suit your particular Web page. Next, use layers to create a new layout for one of your pages. Determine which page in your Web site you will revise and then add at least four layers to the page. Name each layer and place it appropriately on the page. Add images and/or text to the layers. Upload the page to a remote site if instructed to do so. For a selection of images and backgrounds, visit the Dreamweaver MX 2004 Media Web page (scsite.com/dreamweavermx04/media) and then click Media below Project 6.

3 ■■ You are receiving a lot of e-mail about what a great Web site you have for your music hobby. You decide to make it more interactive by adding a navigation bar on the index page, adding a layer with an image map, and then adding two additional layers. Create the navigation bar and then create the three layers — the first one with the image map and the other two displaying images related to your music site. Add hotspots to your image map to show and hide the two images. Upload the revised pages to a remote site. For a selection of images and backgrounds, visit the Dreamweaver MX 2004 Media Web page (scsite.com/dreamweavermx04/media) and then click Media below Project 6.

4 ■■ Polls indicate that you are the favorite to win your political campaign. You want to add a new page to the site that will provide some interactivity and give the page a professional look. Add a navigation bar to the index page. Next, add another page with additional text information and then add a layer for an image map. Add at least two additional layers with pictures of yourself campaigning. Add hotspots to the image map to hide and show the pictures. Upload the revised and new pages to a remote server. For a selection of images and backgrounds, visit the Dreamweaver MX 2004 Media Web page (scsite.com/dreamweavermx04/media) and then click Media below Project 6.

5 **Working Together** The student trips Web site still is receiving numerous hits, and the debate about which location to pick for the trip is continuing. Add a new page to the Web site. Include a navigation bar that will link to various Web sites providing information about three different possible vacation spots. Then, add at least four layers to the Web site. The first layer will contain a map of the United States. The other three layers will contain pictures of possible trip locations. Add hotspots to the image map on the individual states and then add the Show-Hide Layers action. Upload the new pages to a remote server. For a selection of images and backgrounds, visit the Dreamweaver MX 2004 Media Web page (scsite.com/dreamweavermx04/media) and then click Media below Project 6.

MACROMEDIA
Dreamweaver MX 2004

Page Layout with Frames

PROJECT

7

CASE PERSPECTIVE

The Florida Parks Web site is very popular and is receiving numerous hits each day. David received 43 e-mail messages last week asking for more general information about Florida State Parks. The messages included questions such as the cost to visit a park, accessibility options, and whether pets are allowed. David shares the e-mail messages with you and Joan and explains that answering these messages is very time-consuming. He asks if either of you have any suggestions or solutions for how he can respond in a more efficient way.

Joan suggests that adding additional pages to the existing Web site could be one solution. Everyone agrees that this is a good idea, but David expresses concern that the main Web site focuses on different parks and this is a more general topic. You suggest that a new Web site be created and that it be linked to/from the main Web site. Joan further suggests that frames be used to keep this Web site compact and easy to navigate. The team agrees that this is the best solution and that a framed Web site containing general information about Florida parks is a good addition.

As you read through this project, you will learn about the advantages and disadvantages of frames, the difference between a frame and a frameset, how to create a frameset and frames, and how to add a navigation bar using Flash buttons.

Page Layout with Frames

Objectives

You will have mastered the material in this project when you can:

- Describe the advantages and disadvantages of using frames on a Web page
- Describe frameset layout and properties
- Create a frameset and frames
- Define frames and describe how they work
- Delete a frame

- Set the properties for a frame and for a frameset
- Apply and modify the properties of a frame
- Add static content to a frame using the main content frame
- Add Flash buttons as navigation elements
- Save the frame and frameset

Introduction

You learned in Projects 3 and 6 that you can use tables and layers to control the arrangement or layout of items on a Web page. Frames are another layout option and a unique way to design the presentation of your Web pages and Web sites. This project focuses on creating a Web site using frames and examines the advantages and disadvantages of using a framed Web site.

Web designers use frames to present information in a more flexible and useful fashion. A **frame** is an area that acts as an independent browser window and acts independently of other regions in the window. Using frames, a Web page is divided into multiple, scrollable regions, or panes. Each frame contains its own source document. For instance, you could have four different HTML documents displaying in a single window.

When the pages in a Web site share many of the same links and images, creating and maintaining these links for each page involves considerable duplication. With frames, you can create a Web page to display the common links in one frame and display the linked target Web pages in another frame. Some typical uses of frames include displaying a navigation bar consisting of links in one frame and displaying the corresponding Web pages in another; placing a number of images in one frame and displaying the accompanying descriptions and details in another; and placing a list of vocabulary words in one frame and displaying their definitions in another.

With frames, a Web page designer can place elements the user always should see, such as navigation buttons and title graphics, in static frames that do not change. As the user navigates the site, the static frame's contents remain fixed, even as new pages display in adjoining frames. Another example is a side-by-side frame design that allows a user to enter a query and view the answer in the same browser window. One frame contains the query and the other one displays the results.

Although most Web browsers support frames, some Web site visitors may have older browsers that do not support frames or may prefer a no-frames version. Dreamweaver lets you add a <noframes> tag to specify the content to display in text-based browsers and in older graphical browsers that do not support frames. When a browser that does not support frames loads the frameset file, the browser displays only the content enclosed by the <noframes> tag.

Project Seven — Florida Parks Web Page Layout with Frames

In this project, you learn to use frames to create and display general information for a new local site that will be linked to the main Florida Parks Web site.

The frameset, which is an HTML file that defines the layout and properties of a set of frames, will display three frames. The top frame is a single-row, single-column static frame that contains a title image or logo. The second row contains two columns with a left frame and a right frame. The left frame is the navigation frame, or navigate_frame, and contains Flash buttons that link to content files. The right frame is the main frame, which will display the linked content files. When a visitor clicks one of the buttons in the left frame, related park information is displayed in the right frame. The navigate_frame contains five Flash buttons. Clicking any of the first four buttons displays the associated page in the right frame (Figures 7-1a and 7-1b on the next page and Figures 7-1c and 7-1d on page DW 525). The Home button breaks out of the frames and returns the visitor to the main Florida Parks Web site index page.

Borders separate the frames. The right frame is scrollable and contains a scroll bar when the content extends beyond the screen. Each button in the navigate_frame contains text to meet Web design accessibility standards.

If you are using Internet Explorer with Windows XP Service Pack 2 (SP2), Internet Explorer automatically blocks content such as Flash buttons. Thus, for all instances in this project where pages containing Flash buttons are displayed in Internet Explorer, you must either choose to allow blocked content by right-clicking the Information Bar and choosing the Allow Block Content command from the context menu or modify the Internet Explorer security settings to allow Flash elements to display.

More About

Windows Service Pack 2 (SP2)

There are some changes to the operating system and to Internet Explorer that may affect Macromedia Dreamweaver if you are using Windows SP2. For more information about Windows SP2, visit the Dreamweaver MX 2004 More About Web page (scsite.com/dreamweavermx04/more.htm) and then click Windows Service Pack 2.

FIGURE 7-1a

FIGURE 7-1b

FIGURE 7-1c

FIGURE 7-1d

Workspace Organization

Creating a separate local site is the best way to organize and control the number of pages within the Florida Parks Web site. This new, local site, named Parks_Frames, will be linked to the main Florida Parks Web site. After creating your local site, you use the My Computer option to copy Project 7 data files to the site. The following steps show how to create a local site.

To Use Site Definition to Create a Local Web Site

1 Click Site on the menu bar and then click Manage Sites.

2 Click the New button.

3 Click Site on the pop-up menu.

4 If necessary, click the Advanced tab. Verify that Local Info is selected in the Category column.

5 Type Parks_Frames as the site name.

6 Click the folder icon to the right of the Local root folder text box.

7 Navigate to the your name folder and then double-click the your name folder.

8 Click the Create New Folder icon.

9 Type frames as the name of the new folder and then press the ENTER key.

10 Double-click the frames folder name.

11 Click the Select button.

12 Click the folder icon to the right of the Default images folder text box.

13 Navigate to the your name folder and then double-click the frames folder.

14 Click the Create New Folder icon.

15 Type images as the name of the new folder and then press the ENTER key.

16 Double-click the images folder name.

17 Click the Select button.

18 Verify that the Refresh local file list automatically and the Enable cache check boxes are selected in the Site Definition dialog box (Figure 7-2).

19 Click the OK button.

20 Click the Done button.

The Site Definition dialog box displays (Figure 7-2). The path for the frames displays in the Local root folder text box, and the path for the default images folder displays in the Default images folder text box. The Dreamweaver window displays, and the Parks_Frames site displays in the Files panel.

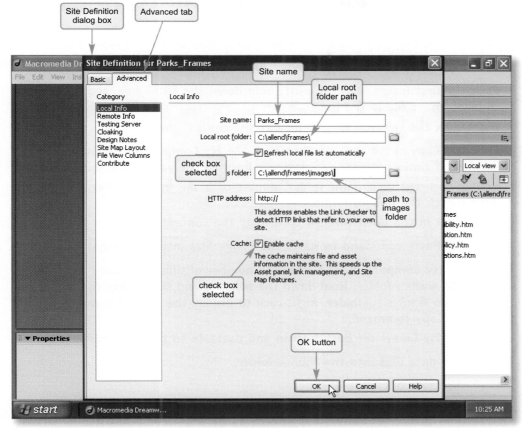

FIGURE 7-2

The Parks_Frames Web site you create in this project requires additional HTML documents and images. These documents and images need to be copied from the DataFiles folder to the Parks_Frames Web site.

Copying Data Files to the Local Web Site

Your Data Disk contains data files and images for Project 7. You use the Windows My Computer option to copy the Project 7 images to your frames\images folder. See the inside back cover for instructions for downloading the Data Disk or see your instructor for information about accessing the files required for this book.

The DataFiles folder for this project is stored on Local Disk (C:). The location on your computer may be different. If necessary, verify with your instructor the location of the DataFiles folder. The steps on the next page illustrate how to copy the files to the frames\images folder.

To Copy Data Files to the Parks_Frames Web Site

1 Click the Start button on the Windows taskbar and then click My Computer.

2 Double-click Local Disk (C:) and then navigate to the location of the data files for Project 7.

3 Double-click the DataFiles folder and then double-click the Proj07 folder.

4 Double-click the parks_frames folder and then double-click the images folder.

5 Click the first image file in the list, hold down the SHIFT key, and then click the last image file in the list.

6 Right-click the selected files to display the context menu.

7 Click the Copy command and then click the My Computer Back button the number of times necessary to navigate back to the your name folder.

8 Double-click the your name folder, double-click the frames folder, and then double-click the images folder.

9 Right-click in the open window to display the context menu.

10 Click the Paste command to paste the image files into the images folder.

11 Click the My Computer Back button the number of times necessary to return to the parks_frames folder. Hold down the SHIFT key and then select the data files and the no_frames subfolder. Right-click to display the context menu, and then click the Copy command.

12 Click the My Computer Back button and navigate to the your name folder.

13 Paste the data files into the frames folder.

14 Click the Close button.

The data files are pasted into the Parks_Frames Web site root folder (Figure 7-3).

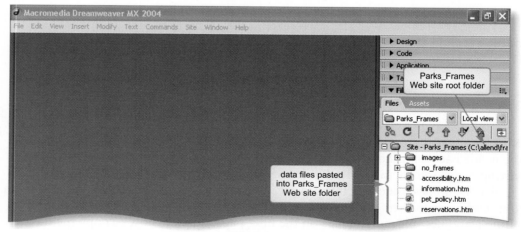

FIGURE 7-3

Advantages and Disadvantages of Frames

Frames became a standard on Web pages with the release of Netscape Navigator 2.0 and were added to the HTML specification with HTML 4.0. After being added to the specification, they experienced immediate popularity and became widely used as a design tool. Designing with frames, however, can be difficult. The complexity of designing with frames is particularly challenging for inexperienced Web site authors. As a result, poorly designed frame-based Web sites became fairly common. This resulted in a controversy among Web site developers and users regarding the value and use of frames for Web site development.

When frames are well designed and used for specific purposes, however, they can be very useful. Some advantages of using frames include the following:

- Navigation-related graphics do not have to be reloaded for every page in the Web site.
- Each frame can have its own scroll bar, permitting the visitor to scroll the frames independently.
- Static content remains fixed.
- Content and navigation can be separated from each other in a clear way.

Users who dislike frames generally have encountered sites that use frames poorly or unnecessarily. Or they may dislike frames because of the following disadvantages:

- Some browsers, and Netscape in particular, do not support the file:// protocol. The link to the home or index page in this project, therefore, will not work in Netscape unless modified in the code.
- Frames may be difficult to navigate for visitors with disabilities.
- Printing pages with frames may be a problem.
- Pages that are displayed in the main frame are displayed in a smaller window than they would be if they were displayed in a full browser window, and are difficult to bookmark or to add to favorites.

Several of the disadvantages, however, are compensated for in the more recent versions of the major browsers. For example, when a user views a frame-based site in a browser, right-clicking in a particular frame displays a context menu with a number of commands, including Add to Favorites, View Source, and Print. Selecting the Print command displays the Print dialog box, which includes options to print just the selected frame, to print all frames individually, to print the page as laid out on the screen, to print all linked documents, and to print a table of links.

Frameset and Frame Basics

Creating a framed Web site is more complex than creating a Web page without frames. The <body> tag is not used to create a framed page. Instead, a **frameset** defines the layout of the frames when displayed on the screen. A frameset requires a combination of two HTML tags: <frameset> and <frame>. When the frameset is created, Dreamweaver automatically includes the <noframes> tag for those viewers using browser versions that do not support frames. Most Web site developers also include a no-frames option link for those users whose browsers do not support frames or for those who prefer a no-frames version.

Frameset Layout

Frames on a page function independently of one another. A separate HTML document is loaded into each frame. As discussed above, creating a framed Web page requires an accompanying file called a frameset. The frameset is an underlying HTML document that defines the layout and properties of a set of frames and then displays navigation elements, title graphics, content documents, and so on inside the defined frames.

The frameset can be compared to a sectioned box, such as a desk drawer organizer. Each section of the box is designed to hold a specific item, such as pens, pencils, or paper clips. The design of each section of the box determines what should be

---

More About

Designing with Frames

Many Web sites consist of a narrow left frame and a wide right frame. The navigation links are displayed in the left frame, and the site's main content is displayed in the right. Other site designs may split the window vertically. In these cases, the site's title and navigation links typically appear in a narrow top frame and the main content appears in a wider lower frame. For more information about frame design, visit the Dreamweaver MX 2004 More About Web page (scsite.com/ dreamweavermx04/more.htm) and then click Frame Design.

placed within that section. The frameset works in a similar way. The <frame> tags within a frameset provide information to the browser about what the frameset's set of frames displays and what documents are displayed in the frames. Some frames may contain static documents such as title graphics, while the content in other frames changes based on the provided navigation options.

Creating the Frameset

Dreamweaver provides two methods for creating a frameset: you can design it yourself or you can use a predefined frameset. You design a frameset in the following way:

- Display a new Document window.
- Click Modify on the menu bar, select Frameset, and then select Split Frame Left, Split Frame Right, Split Frame Up, or Split Frame Down on the Frameset submenu.

To split the frame into smaller sections, use one of the following methods:

- Click the frame and then select Split Frame Left, Split Frame Right, Split Frame Up, or Split Frame Down on the Frameset submenu.
- To split a frame or set of frames vertically or horizontally, drag a frame border from the edge of the Design view into the middle of the Design view.
- To split a frame using a frame border that is not at the edge of the Design view, press the ALT key and then drag the desired frame border.
- To divide a frame into four frames, drag a frame border from one of the corners of the Design view into the middle of a frame.

The second method for creating a frameset in Dreamweaver is to use a predefined frameset. A **predefined frameset** provides a visual representation of how the framed window will display. You can use a predefined frameset without modifications or you can use the predefined frameset as a starting point and then modify the frameset using one or more of the options listed previously for splitting frames.

Dreamweaver provides two methods to create a predefined frameset: the Frames pop-up menu in the Layout category of the Insert bar and the New Document dialog box. The Insert bar Frames pop-up menu generally is used to create a predefined frameset and, at the same time, display an existing document in one of the frames. The New Document dialog box is used to create a new empty predefined frameset.

In this project, you use the New Document dialog box to create a predefined nested frameset, such as the one shown in the expanded Frames panel in Figure 7-4. Notice, in Figure 7-4, that Dreamweaver names the frames in the Frames panel: topFrame, leftFrame, and mainFrame. The primary frameset is selected as indicated by the <frameset> tag in the tag selector, and the dark border surrounding the frame in the Frames panel. In the Property inspector, Row is selected.

A frameset inside another frameset is called a **nested frameset**. Most framesets contain nested framesets, and most Web pages that use frames use nested frames. The majority of the predefined framesets in Dreamweaver also use nesting. A single frameset file can contain multiple nested framesets. Any set of frames in which different numbers of frames are in different rows or columns creates a nested frameset.

FIGURE 7-4

The most common frame layout has one frame in the top row and two frames in the second row. Generally, the top frame contains a title graphic or logo. The left frame in the second row usually is a navigation frame, and the right frame generally is the main frame that displays the linked content. In this case, the second row is the nested frameset. As shown in Figure 7-5, the tag selector displays a second or nested <frameset> tag, a dark border surrounds the frame's second row in the Frames panel, and a dotted border surrounds the nested frameset. In the Property inspector, Column is selected.

You copied the images and files necessary to begin creating the new framed Web site to the frames local root folder. You begin the project by using a visual aid to make the frame borders visible in the Document window. Then you create, name, and save the frameset. The steps on the next page illustrate how to create the frameset.

FIGURE 7-5

To Create the Frameset

1

• **Click File on the menu bar and then click New. Point to Framesets in the Category list.**

The New Document dialog box is displayed (Figure 7-6).

FIGURE 7-6

2

• **Click Framesets. Point to Fixed Top, Nested Left in the Framesets column.**

The Framesets category is displayed within the New Document dialog box. The Framesets category contains 15 predefined framesets. The Fixed Bottom frameset is selected, as indicated by the preview and description displayed in the right pane (Figure 7-7). Your selection might be different.

FIGURE 7-7

3

• **Click Fixed Top, Nested Left in the Framesets column. Point to the Create button.**

The Fixed Top, Nested Left frameset is selected. A preview and description of the selected frameset are displayed in the right pane (Figure 7-8).

FIGURE 7-8

4

• **Click the Create button. If necessary, expand the Property inspector.**

• **If the frame borders do not display, click View on the menu bar, point to Visual Aids, and then click Frame Borders on the Visual Aids submenu. If the Property inspector is not expanded so both panes display, hide the panel groups, click the Property inspector expander arrow, and then redisplay the panel groups.**

The UntitledFrameset-1 displays in the Document window (Figure 7-9). The dotted border around the frameset indicates that the

FIGURE 7-9

frameset is selected. The Property inspector displays attributes relevant to the frameset in both panes. The tag selector displays the <frameset> tag. The number of the untitled frameset may be different on your computer.

Other Ways

1. On Insert bar click Layout category, click Frames button, select frameset

More About

**Inserting
a Predefined
Frameset**

Dreamweaver's predefined
framesets make it easy for
you to select the type of
frameset you want to create.
For a predefined frameset to
be inserted, the Dreamweaver
Document window must be
open in Design view.

Frameset Properties

Just as many other objects in Dreamweaver do, the frameset has its own Property inspector that displays a frameset's properties when that frameset is selected in the Document window. Clicking the expander arrow in the lower-right corner expands the Property inspector to show additional attributes.

Dreamweaver determines the default attributes used for each predefined frameset. These default attributes are applied automatically to each frame. In the Fixed Top, Nested Left example, the mainFrame default is no borders, no scroll bars, and no resizing of frames in the browser. Using the Property inspector, however, these attributes can be changed easily and additional attributes can be applied. The following section describes the frameset-related features of the Property inspector (Figure 7-10). The Property inspector for frames is discussed later in this project.

FIGURE 7-10

FRAMESET VISUAL A visual representation of a frameset is displayed in the upper-left corner of the Property inspector. This visual is generated automatically and cannot be altered through the Property inspector.

BORDERS Borders determines if borders should appear around the frames when the document is viewed in a browser. Clicking the Borders box arrow to the right of the Borders box displays three options: Yes, No, and Default. Selecting Yes causes borders to display around the frames when the Web page is viewed in a browser. Selecting No causes borders not to display in the browser. Selecting Default allows the user's browser to determine how borders are displayed.

BORDER WIDTH In the **Border width** box, a number specifies a width for all the borders in the frameset.

BORDER COLOR Use the color box to select a Border Color, or type the hexadecimal value for a color in the related text box.

FRAMESET COLUMN SIZES AND ROW SIZES The **RowCol Selection** box on the right side of the Property inspector is a visual representation of the frameset. On the top and left sides of the box are tabs. Click a tab on the left side of the RowCol Selection area to select a row, or click a tab on the top to select a column. When the row is selected, you can enter a height for the selected row. When a column is selected, you can enter a width for the selected column. When you click the **Units** box arrow, three options are displayed: Pixels, Percent, and Relative. Table 7-1 on the next page contains information about these three size options.

In Figures 7-9 on page DW 533 and 7-10 on the previous page, the RowCol Selection in the Property inspector contains columns. Recall that this frameset contains a nested frameset. If the nested frameset is selected, then the Property inspector displays two columns instead of two rows in the RowCol Selection area.

Table 7-1 Frameset Row and Column Size Measurements	
UNIT	**RESULT**
Pixels	Sets the size of the row or column to an absolute value. This option is the best choice for a frame that always should be the same size, such as a title frame or navigation frame.
Percent	A percentage-based frame stretches and shrinks based on the width of the browser window. Frames with Units set to Percent are allocated space after frames with Units set to Pixels, but before frames with Units set to Relative.
Relative	Relative specifies that the selected column or row be allocated the leftover space after pixels and percent frames have had space allocated; the remaining space is divided proportionally among the frames with sizes set to Relative.

Selecting and Naming Frames and the Frameset

Selecting framesets and frames can be somewhat complex. Dreamweaver provides two basic ways to select a frame or frameset: select the frame or frameset directly in the Document window or use the Frames panel.

Displaying the Frames Panel

The easiest method to select a frame or frameset is to use the Frames panel. In the Frames panel, clicking within a frame or on a frame border selects that frame. Clicking the frameset border selects the frameset. The step on the next page shows how to display the Frames panel.

More About

Selecting Framesets and Frames in the Document Window

In the Document window, clicking a frame border selects the frameset that contains the frame. When a frameset is selected, all the borders of the frames within the frameset are outlined with a dotted border. To select a frame in the Document window, hold down the ALT key and then click inside the frame. When a frame is selected, its borders are outlined with a dotted border.

To Display the Frames Panel

1

If necessary, expand the panel groups. Click Window on the menu bar and then click Frames (Figure 7-11).

The Frames panel is displayed (Figure 7-11). A dark border appears around the frameset in the Frames panel. The <frameset> tag is displayed in the tag selector, indicating the frameset is selected. Each frameset within the Frames panel has a name: topFrame, leftFrame, and mainFrame. Dreamweaver automatically names these frames. To view the leftFrame name fully, the panel groups must be expanded.

FIGURE 7-11

More About

Defining Row and Column Size

You can mix pixel, percent, and relative point sizes when defining row and column size measurements. Deciding which to use, however, is a hotly contended issue. For more information about pixels versus points, visit the Dreamweaver MX 2004 More About Web page (scsite.com/ dreamweavermx04/more.htm) and then click Pixels versus Points.

Frames and Framesets

The frameset and the frame documents must be saved before you can preview framed pages in a browser. When you use visual aids in Dreamweaver to create a set of frames, each new document that appears in a frame is given a default file name. As indicated earlier in this project, when you create a frameset using a predefined frameset, the frames are given names such as topFrame and leftFrame in the Frames panel. These are not the default names Dreamweaver uses, however, when you select one of the Save commands. Instead, the first frameset file is named UntitledFrameset-1, while the first document in a frame is named UntitledFrame-1, and so on. You can use the default names to save the frameset and frames, but you might find it less confusing if you give meaningful names to the frameset and the frames. Frames and framesets also should be given titles. You add a title to a frame or frameset the same way you added a title to previous HTML documents: by typing the title in the Title text box on the Document toolbar. In this project, you use the same title for all the framesets and frames: Florida Parks - General Information.

Dreamweaver provides several options for saving your documents. You can save the frameset file and each framed document individually, or you can save the frameset file and all documents appearing in the frames at once. In this project, you save the frameset and each frame separately.

Selecting a Frame

To save a frame or to make changes to the properties of a frame, you first select the frame. You can select a frame by clicking the frame border in the Document window or by using the Frames panel. When you select a frame, a dotted border appears around the frame in both the Frames panel and the Document window's Design view. Placing the insertion point in a document that is displayed in a frame is not the same as selecting a frame.

Frames Properties

Like other objects in Dreamweaver, a frame has a specific Property inspector. When you select a frame within the Document window or in the Frames panel, the Property inspector displays the frame's properties. Clicking the expander arrow in the lower-right corner expands the Property inspector to show additional attributes.

When a frame is created, the default attributes are applied automatically. Using the Property inspector, however, you easily can change these attributes and apply additional attributes. The following section describes the frame-related features of the Property inspector (Figure 7-12).

FIGURE 7-12

FRAME NAME The **Frame name** is used by a link's target attribute or by a script to refer to the frame. A frame name must be a single word and must start with a letter (not a numeral). An underscore (_) is allowed, but hyphens (-), periods (.), and spaces cannot be used. Frame names are case-sensitive.

SRC The **Src** box specifies the source document to display in the frame.

SCROLL The **Scroll** box specifies whether scroll bars appear in the frame. Setting this option to Default allows each browser to use its default value of Auto. This causes scroll bars to display only when needed to display the full contents of the current frame.

NO RESIZE The **No resize** check box specifies whether the user can change the frame size by dragging the frame borders.

BORDERS The Borders box displays or hides the borders of the current frame when it is viewed in a browser. Choosing a Borders option for a frame overrides the frameset border settings. Most browsers default to showing borders unless the parent frameset has Borders set to No.

BORDER COLOR The **Border color** box specifies a color for the frame borders. The selected color applies to all borders that touch the frame, and overrides the specified border color of the frameset.

MARGIN WIDTH The **Margin width** box sets the width in pixels of the space between the frame borders and the content.

MARGIN HEIGHT The **Margin height** box sets the height in pixels of the space between the frame borders and the content.

Naming and Saving the Frames

The frameset that you created contains three frames. These three frames need to be named and saved. When naming and saving a frame, remember that a frame is not a data file and is considered a holder for a content document. A frame contains a document. You can use the default name of UntitledFrame-xx.htm to save the frame, but providing meaningful names to frames causes less confusion. In this project, the topFrame is named title_frame, the leftFrame is named navigate_frame, and the rightFrame is named content_frame. Frames are saved with an .htm extension. The following steps show how to name and save the three frames.

To Name and Save the Three Frames

1

• **Click the topFrame in the Document window.**

The insertion point is displayed in the topFrame (Figure 7-13). The UntitledFrame number may be different on your computer.

FIGURE 7-13

2

• **Click File on the menu bar and then point to Save Frame As (Figure 7-14).**

FIGURE 7-14

3

• **Click Save Frame As.**

The Save As dialog box is displayed (Figure 7-15). The root folder, frames, is displayed in the Save in box. The default name is displayed in the File name text box. The number in the file name on your computer may be different.

FIGURE 7-15

4

• **Type** `title_frame` **in the File name text box (Figure 7-16).**

FIGURE 7-16

5

• **Click the Save button and then scroll down in the Files panel.**

The frame is saved as title_frame.htm and is displayed in the Files panel (Figure 7-17). The file name also is displayed on the frame tab and the title bar.

FIGURE 7-17

You save the other two frames the same way in which you saved the title frame. The following steps illustrate how to save the other two frames: navigate and main.

To Save the Navigate and Main Frames

1 Click the left frame in row 2, click File on the menu bar, and then click Save Frame As.

2 In the Save As dialog box, type `navigate_frame` in the File name text box and then click the Save button.

3 Click the right frame in row 2. Click File on the menu bar and then click Save Frame As.

4 In the Save As dialog box, type `content_frame` in the File name text box and then click the Save button. If necessary, scroll down in the Files panel.

The navigate_frame.htm and content_frame.htm file names are displayed in the Files panel (Figure 7-18).

FIGURE 7-18

Deleting a Frame

Deleting a frame is simple. Drag a frame border off the page or to the edge of the frameset. If a document in a frame that is being removed contains unsaved content, Dreamweaver prompts you to save the document. After a frame is deleted, you will not be able to undo the deletion.

Naming and Saving the Frameset

Just as you named the frames, you also must save and name the frameset. The steps on the next page show how to name and save the frameset.

To Name and Save the Frameset

1

• **Click the outside border of the frameset in the Frames panel. Verify that <frameset> is selected in the tag selector. Select Untitled Document in the Title text box on the Document toolbar and then type** Florida Parks - General Information **as the title.**

The Florida Parks - General Information title is displayed in the Title text box, and the frameset is selected (Figure 7-19).

FIGURE 7-19

2

• **Click File on the menu bar and then point to Save Frameset As (Figure 7-20).**

FIGURE 7-20

3

• **Click Save Frameset As.**

The Save As dialog box is displayed (Figure 7-21). If necessary, navigate to the root folder, frames, so it is displayed in the Save in box. The default file name, UntitledFrameset-1, is displayed in the File name text box, and the insertion point is blinking at the end of the file name. The number in the file name on your computer may be a number other than 1.

FIGURE 7-21

4

• **Type** parks_frameset **as the frameset name.**

The parks_frameset file name is displayed in the File name text box (Figure 7-22).

FIGURE 7-22

5

• **Click the Save button. If necessary, scroll in the Files panel.**

The frameset is saved in the frames root folder (Figure 7-23).

FIGURE 7-23

More About

Removing and Deleting a Frameset

You can remove a frame by dragging its borders. You cannot, however, remove a frameset entirely by dragging its borders. To remove a frameset, close the Document window in which it is displayed. If the frameset file has been saved, delete the file.

Formatting the Frames

Backgrounds, text, tables, images, and other elements can be added to a frame in a manner similar to the way in which they are added to a regular Document window. To each of the frames you add the same background that you used in the main Florida Parks Web site you developed in Projects 1 through 3. The title_frame also contains a title graphic, and the navigate_frame contains buttons to load content into the main frame.

The Title_Frame

One of the advantages of frames is that they can reduce the amount of duplicate information on each page, thus saving download time. A title image, for instance, can be inserted into a frame and remains static as new content is viewed in the main frame. The steps on the next page illustrate how to apply a background image to the title frame and to give the frame a title.

To Add a Background Image to the Title_Frame

1

• **Click in the title_frame (topFrame) in the Document window. Click Modify on the menu bar and then click Page Properties. Point to the Browse button.**

The Page Properties dialog box is displayed (Figure 7-24).

FIGURE 7-24

2

• **Click the Browse button. If necessary, double-click the images folder and then click the parksbg.gif file.**

The Select Image Source dialog box is displayed (Figure 7-25). The parksbg.gif file is highlighted.

FIGURE 7-25

3

• **Click the OK button.**

The path and parksbg.gif file name are displayed in the Background image text box in the Page Properties dialog box (Figure 7-26).

FIGURE 7-26

4

• **Click the OK button.**

The background image is applied to the frame (Figure 7-27).

FIGURE 7-27

5

• **Type** Florida Parks - General Information **in the Title text box and then click the Save button.**

The title is displayed in the Title text box on the Document toolbar and on the title bar (Figure 7-28).

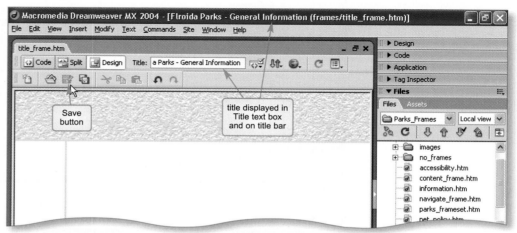

FIGURE 7-28

Adding an Image to the Title_Frame.htm File

The next step is to add an image to the title_frame and then adjust the margin height so the image will display correctly when viewed in a browser. Placing a 0 in the Margin height box assures that the image will display properly in a browser. After making these changes, you will need to resave the frame.

To Add a Title Image to the Title_Frame

1

• **Click the Assets tab in the panel groups. If necessary, click the Images icon, scroll down, and then click the logo.gif image. If necessary, click the Reset button in the Assets panel to display the logo.gif file.**

The logo.gif image is selected (Figure 7-29).

FIGURE 7-29

2

• **Drag the logo.gif image to the title_frame.**

The logo.gif image is selected and displayed in the title_frame.htm frame (Figure 7-30).

More About

Inserting an Image into a Frame

Regular images, as well as background images, also can be inserted into a frame. If the image is smaller than the frame, a blank space appears around the image. For more information about images and frames, visit the Dreamweaver MX 2004 More About Web page (scsite.com/dreamweavermx04/more.htm) and then click Frames and Images.

FIGURE 7-30

3

• **Click the Save button and then click the topFrame in the Frames panel.**

The title_frame.htm (topFrame) frame is selected and a dotted border surrounds the frame. The Property inspector displays frame attributes (Figure 7-31).

FIGURE 7-31

4

• **Click the Margin height box in the Property inspector. Type 0 and then press the TAB key.**

The Margin height value is changed to 0 (Figure 7-32). No changes are evident in the Document window. Changing the margin height affects how the image is displayed in the browser.

5

• **Click the Save button.**

The title_frame.htm file is saved.

FIGURE 7-32

The Navigate_Frame

In the navigate_frame (leftFrame), buttons provide links to each of the four content pages and to the Florida Parks main Web site. The content_frame (mainFrame) uses most of the display area and shows the content of the page. To display another page in the content_frame.htm frame, simply click another button in the navigate_frame.htm frame. Displaying the content in the content_frame.htm frame requires that text or image links be added to one of the frames. Image links with text in the form of Flash buttons will be inserted into the navigate_frame.htm frame. First, however, you add the background image and title to the navigate_frame.htm frame.

To Add a Background Image and a Frame Title to the Navigate_Frame

1 Click in the navigate_frame (leftFrame) in the Document window.

2 Click Modify on the menu bar and then click Page Properties.

3 Click the Browse button, select the parksbg.gif image, and then click the OK button in the Select Image Source dialog box.

4 Click the OK button.

5 Type `Florida Parks - General Information` **as the title in the Title text box (Figure 7-33).**

6 Click the Save button.

The title is added and the background image is applied to the navigate_frame.htm frame (Figure 7-33).

FIGURE 7-33

Flash Buttons

In Project 6, you added a navigation bar, which contained Flash buttons. The Macromedia Flash program is used to develop vector-based graphics and animations. In most instances, creating these graphics and animations requires that the Flash program be installed on your computer. Dreamweaver, however, comes with Flash objects that you can use without having the Flash program.

You can use the Flash objects to create and insert Flash buttons in your documents while working in Design view or in Code view. You also can use the objects to create Flash text. You must save your document before inserting a Flash button or text object.

Flash can generate three different file types, as follows:

FLASH FILE (.FLA) This is the source file for any project and is created in the Flash program. Opening a .fla file requires the Flash program. Using Flash, you then can export the .fla file as a .swf or .swt file, which can be viewed in a browser.

FLASH MOVIE FILE (.SWF) This is a compressed version of the Flash (.fla) file, optimized for viewing on the Web. The .swf file can be played back in browsers and previewed in Dreamweaver, but cannot be edited in Flash. This is the type of file you create when using the Flash button and text objects in Dreamweaver.

FLASH TEMPLATE FILE (.SWT) This file type enables you to modify and replace information in a Flash movie file. The Flash button object uses .swt files.

The Flash Player is available as both a Netscape Navigator plug-in and an ActiveX control for Microsoft Internet Explorer, and it is incorporated in the latest versions of Netscape Navigator, Microsoft Internet Explorer, and the America Online browser.

When a Flash button is saved in Dreamweaver, it has a .swf extension. This file can be played back in browsers and previewed in Dreamweaver. When a Flash object is selected, the Property inspector displays properties specific to the Flash object. The following section describes the Flash-related features of the Property inspector (Figure 7-34).

FIGURE 7-34

NAME The **Name** box specifies the Flash button name that identifies the button for scripting. It is not necessary to enter a name.

W AND H The **W** and **H** boxes indicate the width and height of the Flash object in pixels. You also can specify the width and height as a percentage. In that case, the % sign must follow the value without a space (for example, 3%).

FILE The **File** box contains the path to the Flash object file and the file name.

EDIT Clicking the **Edit** button displays the Insert Flash Button dialog box, or a related dialog box if the object is other than a button.

RESET SIZE The **Reset size** button resets the selected button to its original size.

V SPACE AND H SPACE The **V space** and **H space** boxes specify the number of pixels of white space above, below, and on both sides of the button.

QUALITY The **Quality** box contains options that set the quality parameter for the object and embed tags that define the button. The options are High, Low, Auto Low, and Auto High. **Low** emphasizes speed over appearance, whereas **High** favors appearance over speed. **Auto Low** emphasizes speed at first, but improves appearance when possible. **Auto High** emphasizes both qualities at first, but sacrifices appearance for speed, if necessary.

SCALE The **Scale** box options define how the button (movie) is displayed within the area defined for the movie by the width and height values. The options are Default (Show all), No Border, and Exact Fit.

ALIGN The **Align** box options define how the object is aligned on the page. The align options are the same as those for images discussed in Project 2.

BG The **Bg** box contains a palette of colors you can use to specify a background color for the object. The color also is represented by the hexadecimal value in the adjacent box.

PLAY/STOP The **Play/Stop** button lets you preview the Flash object in the Document window. Click the green Play button to see the object in Play mode; click the red Stop button to stop the movie.

PARAMETERS The **Parameters** button opens a dialog box for entering additional parameters. These values are for special parameters that can be defined for Shockwave and Flash movies, ActiveX controls, Navigator plug-ins, and Java applets.

CLASS Class styles are a type of CSS style that can be applied to any text in a document, regardless of which tags control the text.

Inserting Flash Buttons into the Navigate_Frame

You insert five Flash buttons into the navigate_frame. The first four of these buttons display content in the content_frame. This content is generated from the four HTML documents you copied from the Data Files folder. The four documents (information, accessibility, pet_policy, and reservations) already are formatted and the background image has been added to each one. The steps on the next page illustrate how to insert the first Flash button into the navigate_frame (leftFrame).

To Insert a Flash Button into the Navigate_Frame

1

• **Collapse the panel groups.**

• **Click Insert on the menu bar, point to Media, and then point to Flash Button on the Media submenu.**

The Insert menu is displayed, and Flash Button is highlighted on the Media submenu (Figure 7-35).

FIGURE 7-35

2

• **Click Flash Button. Point to Blue Warper in the Style list.**

The Insert Flash Button dialog box is displayed (Figure 7-36).

FIGURE 7-36

3

• **Click Blue Warper. Click the Button text text box and then type** Information **as the text to display on the first button. Double-click the Size box and then type** 12 **as the new value. Point to the Browse button to the right of the Link box.**

The Blue Warper button sample is displayed in the Sample area, Information is displayed in the Button text text box, and the font size is changed to 12 (Figure 7-37).

FIGURE 7-37

4

• **Click the Browse button. When the Select file dialog box is displayed, click information.htm in the Look in list. Click the Relative to box arrow and then select Document.**

The Select file dialog box is displayed (Figure 7-38). The frames folder is displayed in the Look in box. The information.htm file is selected, information is displayed in the File name text box, and information.htm is displayed in the URL box.

FIGURE 7-38

5

• **Click the OK button in the Select file dialog box. Point to the Target box arrow.**

The information.htm link is displayed in the Link box in the Insert Flash Button dialog box (Figure 7-39).

FIGURE 7-39

6

• **Click the Target box arrow and then point to mainFrame.**

The mainFrame target is highlighted (Figure 7-40).

FIGURE 7-40

7

• **Click mainFrame and then point to the OK button.**

The mainFrame frame is selected as the target frame (Figure 7-41).

FIGURE 7-41

8

• **Click the OK button to insert the Flash button.**

The Flash button is inserted into the navigate_frame and is selected (Figure 7-42). The navigate_frame currently is not wide enough to display the entire button. Later in this project, you will learn how to adjust the width of the frame so the whole button is displayed.

FIGURE 7-42

9

• **Click below the button to deselect it and then press the ENTER key.**

A blank line space is inserted between the button and the insertion point (Figure 7-43).

FIGURE 7-43

Inserting the Remaining Buttons

You insert the Accessibility, Pet Policy, and Reservations buttons using the same steps you used to add the Information button. The next steps show how to insert the Accessibility button.

To Insert the Accessibility Button

1 Click Insert on the menu bar, point to Media, and then click Flash Button on the Media submenu.

2 Click Blue Warper.

3 Click the Button text text box. Type Accessibility as the button text.

4 Change the font size to 12.

5 Click the Link Browse button, click accessibility.htm, and then click the OK button in the Select file dialog box.

6 Click the Target box arrow and then select mainFrame.

7 Click the OK button to insert the Accessibility button into the navigate_frame.

8 Click below the button and then press the ENTER key.

The Accessibility button is inserted into the navigate_frame, and a blank line is inserted below the button (Figure 7-44 on the next page).

FIGURE 7-44

The following steps illustrate how to add the Pet Policy button.

To Insert the Pet Policy Button

1 Click Insert on the menu bar, point to Media, and then click Flash Button on the Media submenu.

2 Click Blue Warper. Click the Button text text box. Type Pet Policy as the button name. Change the font size to 12.

3 Click the Link Browse button, click pet_policy.htm, and then click the OK button in the Select file dialog box.

4 Click the Target box arrow and then select mainFrame.

5 Click the OK button to insert the Pet Policy button into the navigate_frame.

6 Click below the button and then press the ENTER key.

You have inserted the first three buttons. The following steps show how to insert the Reservations button.

To Insert the Reservations Button

1 Click Insert on the menu bar, point to Media, and then click Flash Button on the Media submenu.

2 Click Blue Warper. Click the Button text text box. Type Reservations as the button text. Change the font size to 12.

3 Click the Link Browse button, click reservations.htm, and then click the OK button in the Select file dialog box.

4 Click the Target box arrow and then select mainFrame.

5 Click the OK button to insert the Reservations button into the navigate_frame.

6 Click below the button and then press the ENTER key.

7 Click the Save button on the Standard toolbar.

The first four buttons are inserted (Figure 7-45). The navigate_frame.htm frame is saved.

FIGURE 7-45

Thus far, the target for your links has been the mainFrame. The last button to be added to the navigate_frame is the Home button. When clicked, this button will cause the main index page of the Florida Parks Web site to display on the screen. Other possible targets within the same frameset include leftFrame and topFrame. Targets outside the frameset include _blank, _parent, _self, and _top. The following section describes these targets.

- The **_blank** target opens the linked document in a new browser window, leaving the current window untouched.
- The **_parent** target opens the linked document in the parent frameset of the frame the link appears in, replacing the entire frameset.
- The **_self** target opens the link in the current frame, replacing the content in that frame.
- The **_top** target opens the linked document in the current browser window, replacing all frames.

To create the Home button, you use an absolute link. If you published the main Florida Parks Web site to a remote server in a previous project, use the remote server Web site address for the index page as the link. Otherwise, use the path to the location of the C:/yourname/parks/index.htm folder. To further create this link, you select _blank as the target. Selecting this option opens the linked document in a new browser window, leaving the current window untouched. The following steps illustrate how to create a link to the main Web site index page.

To Insert the Home Button

1

• **Click Insert on the menu bar, point to Media, and then click Flash Button on the Media submenu. Click Blue Warper. Click the Button text text box and then type** Home **as the button text. Change the font size to 12.**

Home is displayed in the Button text text box, and the font size is changed to 12 (Figure 7-46).

FIGURE 7-46

2

• **If you are linking to a remote server, copy and paste the URL to the main Florida Parks Web site into the Link box. If you are linking to the C:/yourname/parks/index.htm folder, type that path in the Link box.**

The path to the index.htm file for the main Florida Parks Web site appears in the Link box (Figure 7-47).

FIGURE 7-47

3

• **Click the Target box arrow and then select _blank in the list.**

The Target box displays _blank (Figure 7-48).

FIGURE 7-48

4

• **Click the OK button and then click the Save button on the Standard toolbar.**

The five buttons are added to the navigate_frame (Figure 7-49), and the navigate_frame is saved.

FIGURE 7-49

Adjusting Column Width

The Flash buttons are only partially displayed in the navigate_frame. You can adjust the size of the buttons or you can adjust the column width. In this project, you adjust the column width and use pixels as the measurement for the width. Using pixels ensures that the column width does not change when displayed in a browser. The navigate_frame is in the nested frameset. You can adjust the column width by dragging the right border of the frame or you can adjust the column width through the Property inspector. To adjust the column width through the Property inspector, first you must select the nested frameset. The following steps show how to select the nested frameset and to adjust the column width of the navigate_frame.

To Adjust the Column Width of the Navigate_Frame

1

• **Display the panel groups.**

• **Click the border surrounding the leftFrame and the mainFrame in the Frames panel.**

The nested frameset is selected. A second <frameset> tag is selected in the tag selector. The Property inspector for the frameset is displayed. A dotted border surrounds the selected frames (Figure 7-50).

FIGURE 7-50

2

• **If necessary, click the tab on the first column in the Property inspector. Double-click the Column Value box, type** 120 **as the entry, and then press the ENTER key.**

The column width is expanded to 120 pixels (Figure 7-51).

3

• **Click the Save button on the Standard toolbar to save the navigate_frame.htm file and the changes to the frameset.**

FIGURE 7-51

The Content_Frame

The content_frame is where the content is displayed when one of the Flash navigation buttons is clicked. The four content pages are information, accessibility, pet policy, and reservations. The following steps illustrate how to add the background image and title to the content_frame page.

To Add a Background Image and Frame Title to the Content_Frame

1 Click the content_frame (mainFrame) in the Document window.

2 Click Modify on the menu bar and then click Page Properties.

3 Click the Browse button to the right of the Background Image box, navigate to and select the parksbg.gif image, and then click the OK button in the Select Image Source dialog box.

4 Click the OK button in the Page Properties dialog box.

5 Type Florida Parks - General Information **as the title.**

6 Click the Save button on the Standard toolbar.

The background image is applied to the content_frame, and the title is added. The insertion point is blinking in the main frame (Figure 7-52 on the next page).

FIGURE 7-52

Linking and Targeting

You created the links and targets for the navigation buttons when you created the buttons. To display default content in the content_frame, however, requires that content be added in a manner similar to adding the title graphic and navigate_frame content. The default content is the information.htm file. The next steps show how to add the default content to the content_frame.

More About

Editing Framesets

Frame names appear only in the Target pop-up menu when you are editing a document within a frameset. When you edit a document in its own Document window, outside of the frameset, frame names do not appear in the Target pop-up menu.

To Link and Target the Default Content

1

• **Click the mainFrame in the Frames panel.**

A dotted border appears around the mainFrame in the Document window. The Frames Property inspector is displayed (Figure 7-53).

FIGURE 7-53

2

• **Double-click content_frame.htm in the Src box in the Property inspector.**

The text, /content_frame.htm, is highlighted in the Src box (Figure 7-54).

FIGURE 7-54

3

• **Type information.htm and then press the ENTER key.**

• **If a Dreamweaver Warning box displays, click the Yes button.**

The contents of the information.htm file are displayed in the mainFrame (Figure 7-55). Vertical and horizontal scroll bars also are displayed in the mainFrame. If your screen setting is greater than 800 × 600, the scroll bars may not display.

4

• **Click File on the menu bar and then click Save All.**

All the framesets and frames are saved.

FIGURE 7-55

Adding a Border and Border Color to the Framesets

The Borders feature in the Property inspector determines whether borders should appear around the frames when a document is viewed in a browser. You can add a border to an individual frame or to the frameset. If the frameset contains one or more nested framesets, then each nested frameset must be selected and the border added to it. The Border width specifies a width for all the borders in the frameset, and the Border Color sets a color for the borders. Border colors and widths selected for an individual frame override the border color and border width of the frameset properties. Use the color picker to select a color, or type the hexadecimal value for a color. The following steps illustrate how to add a border and border color to the main frameset. If your screen setting is greater than 800 × 600, the scroll bars may not display.

To Add a Border and Border Color to the Frameset

1

• **Click the border around the outer frameset in the Frames panel.**

A dark border surrounds the entire frame in the Frames panel, and a dotted border surrounds the frameset and frames in the Document window (Figure 7-56). The Property inspector for the frameset is displayed, and <frameset> is selected in the tag selector.

FIGURE 7-56

2

• **Click the Borders box arrow and then point to Yes in the Borders list.**

The Borders list is displayed, and the mouse pointer points to Yes (Figure 7-57).

FIGURE 7-57

3

• **Click Yes. Double-click the Border width box. Type** 4 **and then press the ENTER key.**

The Yes option is selected in the Borders box, and the border width is changed to 4 (Figure 7-58).

FIGURE 7-58

4

- **Click the Border color hexadecimal box, type #0000FF for the border color, and then press the ENTER key.**

The hexadecimal number #0000FF displays. The border color is applied to the frameset (Figure 7-59). The border color, however, is not applied to the nested frameset.

FIGURE 7-59

5

- **Click the border surrounding the leftFrame and the mainFrame in the Frames panel.**

The nested frameset is selected (Figure 7-60). The nested <frameset> tag is highlighted in the tag selector.

FIGURE 7-60

Q&A

Q: What are some of the pros and cons of using frames?

A: Frames have advantages and disadvantages. Web designers and Web site visitors generally love or hate frames. For more information about this controversy, visit the Dreamweaver MX 2004 More About Web page (scsite.com/ dreamweavermx04/more.htm) and then click Pros and Cons of Using Frames.

Applying the Border and Border Color to the Nested Frameset

The steps to apply the border color to the border of the nested frameset are the same as those to apply the border color to the outside frameset. The following steps show how to apply the border color to the nested frameset.

To Apply the Border and Border Color to the Nested Frameset

1 Click the Borders box arrow in the Property inspector and then click Yes in the Borders list.

2 Double-click the Border width box. Type 4 and then press the ENTER key.

3 Click the Border color hexadecimal box, type #0000FF as the entry, and then press the ENTER key.

4 Click the File menu and then click Save All.

The border color is applied to the nested frameset in Step 3 (Figure 7-61). The frames and the framesets for the Web site are saved.

FIGURE 7-61

Adding a No-Frames Link to the Information Page

When you created the predefined frameset at the beginning of this project, Dreamweaver automatically included a <noframes> tag within the HTML code. If a visitor accesses the Web site with a browser that does not support frames, then the <noframes> code takes him or her out of the framed Web site into a non-framed version of the Web site. Other visitors, who have browsers that do support frames, also may prefer a no-frames version. A no-frames version was included in the Project 7 data files you copied to the Parks_Frames Web site. Accessing the no-frames version requires that a link be created to and a target designated for the no-frames version. This link is added to the information.htm page. The following steps illustrate how to add a no-frames link.

To Add a No-Frames Link

1

• **Position the insertion point at the end of the Information heading and then press the ENTER key.**

A blank line is inserted below the heading (Figure 7-62).

FIGURE 7-62

2

• **Type** No frames version **as the text for the link.**

The text, No frames version, is displayed in the information.htm Document window (Figure 7-63).

FIGURE 7-63

3

• **Select the text, No frames version.**

The text, No frames version, is selected (Figure 7-64).

FIGURE 7-64

4

• **If necessary, scroll in the Files panel to display the no_frames folder. Click the plus sign to the left of the no_frames folder and then click the information.htm file in that folder.**

The no_frames folder is open, and the information.htm file is selected (Figure 7-65).

FIGURE 7-65

5

• **Drag the information.htm file to the Link box in the Property inspector and then press the ENTER key.**

The link, no_frames/information.htm, is displayed in the Link box (Figure 7-66). Note that the entire link name may not be visible.

FIGURE 7-66

6

• **Click the Target box arrow and then select _top. Click the Save button on the Standard toolbar.**

The _top option is selected in the Target box, and the file is saved (Figure 7-67).

FIGURE 7-67

The last step is to view the Web site and verify that the links work. The next steps show how to display the pages in your browser.

To View the Web Site and Verify Links

1 Press the F12 key to preview the Parks_Frames Web site.

2 Click each of the navigation buttons to verify that they work (Figures 7-68a through 7-68d on pages DW 572 and DW 573).

3 Click the No frames version link and then click the browser Back button to return to the framed version.

4 If instructed to do so, upload the Web site to a remote server.

5 If instructed to do so, right-click in each frame, print a copy of each frame, and hand in the copies to your instructor.

6 Close the browser.

FIGURE 7-68a

FIGURE 7-68b

FIGURE 7-68c

FIGURE 7-68d

Adding a Link to the Florida Parks Web Site Index Page

To connect the Florida Parks Web site to the Parks_Frames Web site, you add a link to the Florida Parks index page. This link will display at the end of the page. The following steps illustrate how to add the link.

To Add a Link from the Florida Parks Web Site to the Parks_Frames Web Site

1 **Open the Florida Parks Web site and then open the index.htm page.**

2 **Scroll to the bottom of the page and then click to the right of last sentence on the page. Press the ENTER key.**

3 **Type** General Information **and then create an absolute link from the text, General Information, to the information.htm file in the Parks_Frames Web site frames folder. If a warning box displays, click No to proceed.**

4 **If you are publishing to a remote site, copy and paste the Florida Parks Web site address into the Link box.**

5 **If you are saving your work to a local computer or server, use the Browse for File icon in the Property inspector to create the link path.**

6 **Click the Save button on the Standard toolbar.**

7 **Press F12 to preview the file in your browser. Click the General Information link.**

8 **Close the browser.**

Quitting Dreamweaver

After you have created your framed Web site, verified that the navigation works, and uploaded it to a remote server, Project 7 is complete. The following step shows how to close the Web site, quit Dreamweaver MX, and return control to Windows.

To Close the Web Site and Quit Dreamweaver

1 **Click the Close button on the right corner of the Dreamweaver title bar.**

The Dreamweaver window, the Document window, and the Parks_Frames Web site all close. If you have unsaved changes, Dreamweaver prompts you to save the changes. Clicking the Yes button in the Dreamweaver MX 2004 dialog box saves the changes.

Project Summary

Project 7 introduced you to frames and to Web page design using frames. You created a framed Web site that included two framesets — one a nested frameset. You named the framesets and the frames and modified the frameset and frame properties. You added navigation links in the form of Flash buttons to display content in the main frame. Finally, you added a link for a no-frames version of the Web site for those visitors who do not want to use frames.

What You Should Know

Having completed this project, you now should be able to perform the tasks below. The tasks are listed in the same order they were presented in the project. For a list of keyboard commands for topics introduced in this project, see the Quick Reference for Windows at the back of this book and refer to the Shortcut column.

1. Use Site Definition to Create a Local Web Site (DW 526)
2. Copy Data Files to the Parks_Frames Web Site (DW 528)
3. Create the Frameset (DW 532)
4. Display the Frames Panel (DW 536)
5. Name and Save the Three Frames (DW 538)
6. Save the Navigate and Main Frames (DW 541)
7. Name and Save the Frameset (DW 542)
8. Add a Background Image to the Title_Frame (DW 545)
9. Add a Title Image to the Title_Frame (DW 547)
10. Add a Background Image and a Frame Title to the Navigate_Frame (DW 549)
11. Insert a Flash Button into the Navigate_Frame (DW 552)
12. Insert the Accessibility Button (DW 556)
13. Insert the Pet Policy Button (DW 557)
14. Insert the Reservations Button (DW 557)
15. Insert the Home Button (DW 559)
16. Adjust the Column Width of the Navigate_Frame (DW 561)
17. Add a Background Image and Frame Title to the Content_Frame (DW 562)
18. Link and Target the Default Content (DW 563)
19. Add a Border and Border Color to the Frameset (DW 565)
20. Apply the Border and Border Color to the Nested Frameset (DW 568)
21. Add a No-Frames Link (DW 569)
22. View the Web Site and Verify Links (DW 571)
23. Add a Link from the Florida Parks Web Site to the Parks_Frames Web Site (DW 574)
24. Close the Web Site and Quit Dreamweaver (DW 574)

Learn It Online

Instructions: To complete the Learn It Online exercises, start your browser, click the Address bar, and then enter the Web address scsite.com/dreamweavermx2004/learn. When the Dreamweaver MX 2004 Learn It Online page is displayed, follow the instructions in the exercises below. Each exercise has instructions for printing your results, either for your own records or for submission to your instructor.

1 Project Reinforcement TF, MC, and SA

Below Dreamweaver Project 7, click the Project Reinforcement link. Print the quiz by clicking Print on the File menu for each page. Answer each question.

Flash Cards

Below Dreamweaver Project 7, click the Flash Cards link and read the instructions. Type 20 (or a number specified by your instructor) in the Number of playing cards text box, type your name in the Enter your Name text box, and then click the Flip Card button. When the flash card is displayed, read the question and then click the ANSWER box arrow to select an answer. Flip through Flash Cards. If your score is 15 (75%) correct or greater, click Print on the File menu to print your results. If your score is less than 15 (75%) correct, then redo this exercise by clicking the Replay button.

3 Practice Test

Below Dreamweaver Project 7, click the Practice Test link. Answer each question, enter your first and last name at the bottom of the page, and then click the Grade Test button. When the graded practice test is displayed on your screen, click Print on the File menu to print a hard copy. Continue to take practice tests until you score 80% or better.

4 Who Wants To Be a Computer Genius?

Below Dreamweaver Project 7, click the Computer Genius link. Read the instructions, enter your first and last name at the bottom of the page, and then click the PLAY button. When your score is displayed, click the PRINT RESULTS link to print a hard copy.

5 Wheel of Terms

Below Dreamweaver Project 7, click the Wheel of Terms link. Read the instructions, and then enter your first and last name and your school name. Click the PLAY button. When your score is displayed, right-click the score and then click Print on the shortcut menu to print a hard copy.

6 Crossword Puzzle Challenge

Below Dreamweaver Project 7, click the Crossword Puzzle Challenge link. Read the instructions, and then enter your first and last name. Click the SUBMIT button. Work the crossword puzzle. When you are finished, click the Submit button. When the crossword puzzle is redisplayed, click the Print Puzzle button to print a hard copy.

7 Tips and Tricks

Below Dreamweaver Project 7, click the Tips and Tricks link. Click a topic that pertains to Project 7. Right-click the information and then click Print on the shortcut menu. Construct a brief example of what the information relates to in Dreamweaver to confirm you understand how to use the tip or trick.

8 Newsgroups

Below Dreamweaver Project 7, click the Newsgroups link. Click a topic that pertains to Project 7. Print three comments.

9 Expanding Your Horizons

Below Dreamweaver Project 7, click the Expanding Your Horizons link. Click a topic that pertains to Project 7. Print the information. Construct a brief example of what the information relates to in Dreamweaver to confirm you understand the contents of the article.

10 Search Sleuth

Below Dreamweaver Project 7, click the Search Sleuth link. To search for a term that pertains to this project, select a term below the Project 7 title and then use the Google search engine at google.com (or any major search engine) to display and print two Web pages that present information on the term.

Apply Your Knowledge

1 Creating a Framed Web Site for B & B Lawn Service

Instructions: Start Dreamweaver. See the inside back cover of this book for instructions for downloading the Data Disk or see your instructor for information on accessing the files in this book.

    B & B Lawn Service recently started selling lawn mowers and other lawn equipment and would like to investigate the possibility of selling this equipment on the Internet. Its goal is to start with a framed Web site displaying four of the more popular lawn mowers. The Web site will contain five pages: the index page and a page describing each of the four lawn mowers. The frameset will contain three frames: topFrame, mainFrame, and bottomFrame. The top frame (named title) displays the title, the middle frame displays the linked content, and the bottom frame contains the navigation text, as shown in Figures 7-69a through 7-69e on page DW 579. Appendix C contains instructions for uploading your local site to a remote server.

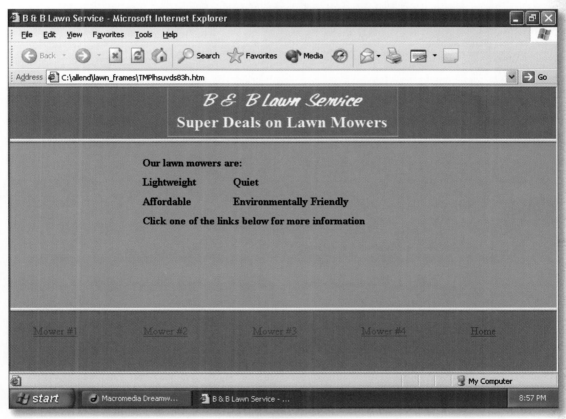

FIGURE 7-69a

(continued)

Apply Your Knowledge

Creating a Framed Web Site for B & B Lawn Service *(continued)*

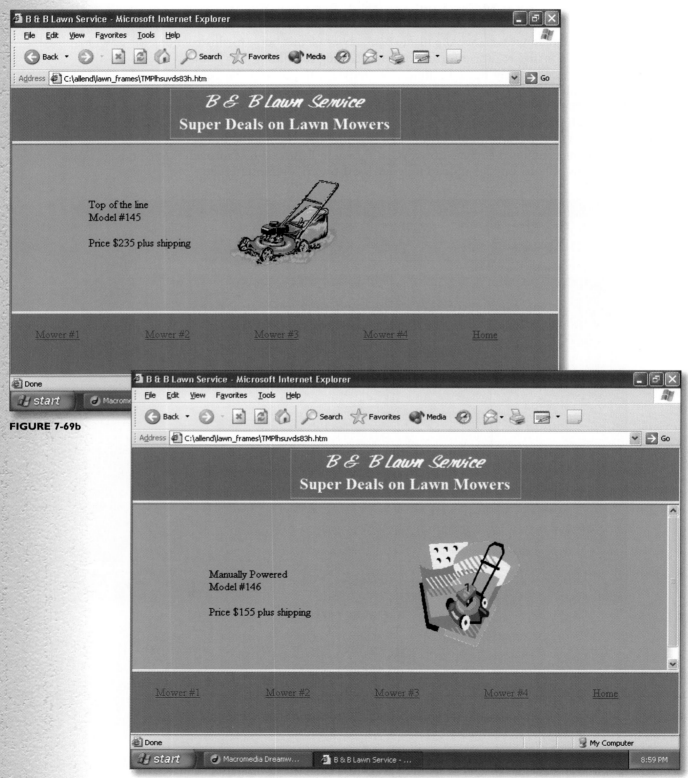

FIGURE 7-69b

FIGURE 7-69c

Apply Your Knowledge

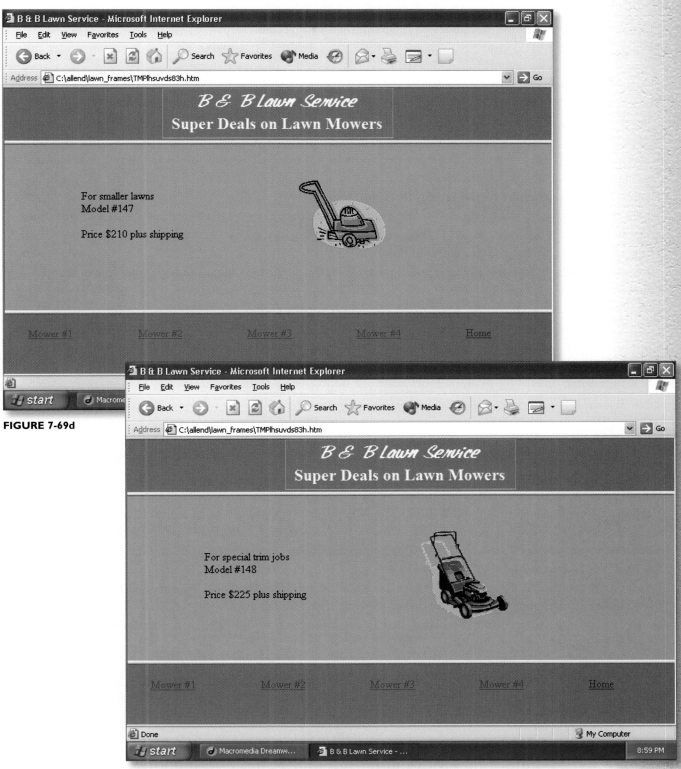

FIGURE 7-69d

FIGURE 7-69e

(continued)

Creating a Framed Web Site for B & B Lawn Service *(continued)*

1. Start Dreamweaver, display the panel groups, and then display the Frames panel.
2. Create a new Web site. Name the Web site Lawn Service Frames. Store your Web site in a new folder called lawn_frames. Add an images folder. The path will be C:/yourname/lawn_frames.
3. Use the Windows My Computer option to copy the data files and the images from the Data Files to your lawn_frames local root folder.
4. Click File on the menu bar, click New, and then click Framesets in the General column on the New Document dialog box. Select Fixed Top, Fixed Bottom and then click the Create button to create the frameset.
5. If necessary, select the frameset by clicking the frameset border in the frames panel. Drag to select Untitled Document in the Title text box on the Document menu bar. Type B & B Lawn Service as the title. Save the frameset as index.htm in the lawn_frames local root folder.
6. Click in the topFrame, click Modify on the menu bar, and then click Page Properties. In the Background color hexadecimal box, type #3399FF and then press the TAB key. Click the OK button. Type B & B Lawn Service in the Title text box for the topFrame.
7. Drag the title.gif file to the topFrame and then center the title.gif file. Click the topFrame in the Frames panel to display the Frames Property inspector. Click the Margin height box and then type 0 as the entry. Click in the topFrame in the Document window and then save the topFrame. Use title.htm as the frame name.
8. Click in the mainFrame in the Document window. Type B & B Lawn Service in the Title text box. Click the Page Properties button in the Property inspector. In the Background color hexadecimal box, type #66CCFF and then click the OK button. Save the mainFrame. Use main.htm as the file name.
9. Click the mainFrame in the Frames panel and then double-click main.htm in the Src box in the Property inspector.
10. Type content.htm as the entry, press the ENTER key, and then click the Save button.
11. Click in the bottomFrame. Type B & B Lawn Service in the Title text box. Click the Page Properties button, type #3399FF in the Background color hexadecimal box, and then click the OK button. Save the frame as navigate.htm in the lawn_frames local root folder.
12. Create a one-row, five-column table in the navigate frame. Use 0 for the Cell Padding, Cell Spacing, and Border, and use 95 Percent for the Width. Center the table. Type Mower #1 in column 1, type Mower #2 in column 2, type Mower #3 in column 3, type Mower #4 in column 4, and type Home in column 5.
13. Select the text, Mower #1, in column 1. Drag the file, mower01.htm, from the Files panel to the Link box in the Property inspector and then press the ENTER key. Click the Target box arrow and then select mainFrame.
14. Repeat Step 13 for columns 2, 3, and 4, dragging the related files (mower02.htm through mower04.htm) to the Link box. Select mainFrame as the target for each of these.
15. Select Home in the fifth column and then drag content.htm to the Link box. Select mainFrame as the target. Save the navigate frame.
16. Select the frameset in the Frames panel.
17. Click the Borders arrow in the Property inspector and then set the Borders attribute to Yes. Double-click the Border width box and then type 2 as the entry. Click File on the menu bar and then click Save All. If instructed to do so, upload your Web sites to a remote server.

Apply Your Knowledge

18. Open the Lawn Service Web site, open the index.htm page, scroll to the bottom of the page, and then click to the right of the last bulleted item. Press the ENTER key. Type Lawn mowers for sale and then insert two line breaks between the two bulleted items. Create an absolute link from the text, Lawn mowers for sale, to the index.htm file in the Lawn Service Frames Web site. Set the Target to _blank. If you are publishing to a remote site, copy and paste the Lawn Service Frames Web site address into the Link box. If you are saving your work to a local computer or server, use the Browse for File icon in the Property inspector to create the link path. Click the Save button on the Standard toolbar. If instructed to do so, upload your Web site changes to a remote server.

19. Press the F12 key to view the Lawn Service index.htm page in your browser. Click the Lawn mowers for sale link to display the Lawn Service Frames Web site. Click each of the navigation buttons to verify that they work. Print copies of each frame if instructed to do so.

In the Lab

1 Adding a Framed Web Page to CandleDust

Problem: Mary has received several e-mails asking how to make candles. She has some specialty recipes for votive and pillar candles and would like to put these online. Mary has requested that you add a left and right framed page to the CandleDust site. The navigation will be Flash buttons in the left frame. The recipe formulas will be displayed in the right frame. The left frame also will contain a link to the CandleDust home page. The framed Web site is shown in Figures 7-70a, and 7-70b and 7-70c on the next page.

FIGURE 7-70a

(continued)

Adding a Framed Web Page to CandleDust *(continued)*

FIGURE 7-70b

FIGURE 7-70c

Instructions: Perform the following tasks:

1. Use the Windows My Computer option to copy the images and the data files to your candle folder.
2. Start Dreamweaver. Display the panel groups. Select CandleDust from the Files pop-up menu in the Files panel.
3. Create a predefined frameset. Use the Split Vertical frameset. Add the title, Candle Formulas, to the frameset. Save the frameset as recipes.htm in the candle root folder.
4. Click the leftFrame and then save the frame as navigate.htm in the candle root folder. Add the candlebg.gif image as the background image. Add the title, Candle Formulas, to the frame.
5. Click the mainFrame and then save the frame as main.htm. Add the candlebg.gif as the background image. Title the frame Candle Formulas.
6. Click the mainFrame in the Frames panel.
7. Double-click main.htm in the Src box in the Property inspector, type content.htm as the entry, press the TAB key, and then click the Save All button.
8. Click the leftFrame. Type Menu and then center the text. Apply Heading 2. Press the ENTER key.
9. Click Insert on the menu bar, point to Media, and then click Flash Button on the Media submenu. Select the Beveled Rect-bronze button.
10. Type Votive Candles as the button text. Select votive.htm as the link and mainFrame as the target.
11. Click to the right of the first button and then press the ENTER key. Repeat Step 9 to create another button.
12. Type Pillar Candles as the button text and then select pillar.htm as the link and mainFrame as the target.
13. Click to the right of the second button and then press the ENTER key. Repeat Step 9 to create another button.
14. Type Main as the button text and then select content.htm as the link and mainFrame as the target.
15. Click to the right of the third button and then press the ENTER key. Repeat Step 9 to create another button.
16. Type Home as the button text and then select index.htm as the link and _blank as the target.
17. Select the frameset in the Frames panel to display the Property inspector for the frameset. Type 25 as the value in the Column text box and then change the Units to Percent.
18. Click the Borders pop-up menu and then select Yes. Type 3 as the border width and #CC9999 in the Border color hexadecimal box.
19. Click File on the menu bar and then click Save All.
20. Open the index.htm page. Click after the Votive bullet point, press ENTER, and then click the Unordered List button. Type Candle Recipes and then create a link to recipes.htm. Change the target to _blank. Click the Save button.
21. Press the F12 key to view the index page and then click the Candle Recipes link. Test each button. Print copies of each frame if instructed to do so. Upload the Web site to a remote server if instructed to do so.

2 Creating a Framed Layout for the Credit Protection Web Site

Problem: The Credit Protection Web site has become very popular. Marcy recently received several e-mails asking for suggestions on how to spend money wisely. Marcy asks you to create a new Web site with frames so she can share some of this information. The framed Web site is shown in Figures 7-71a on the next page through 7-71d on page DW 585.

(continued)

Creating a Framed Layout for the Credit Protection Web Site *(continued)*

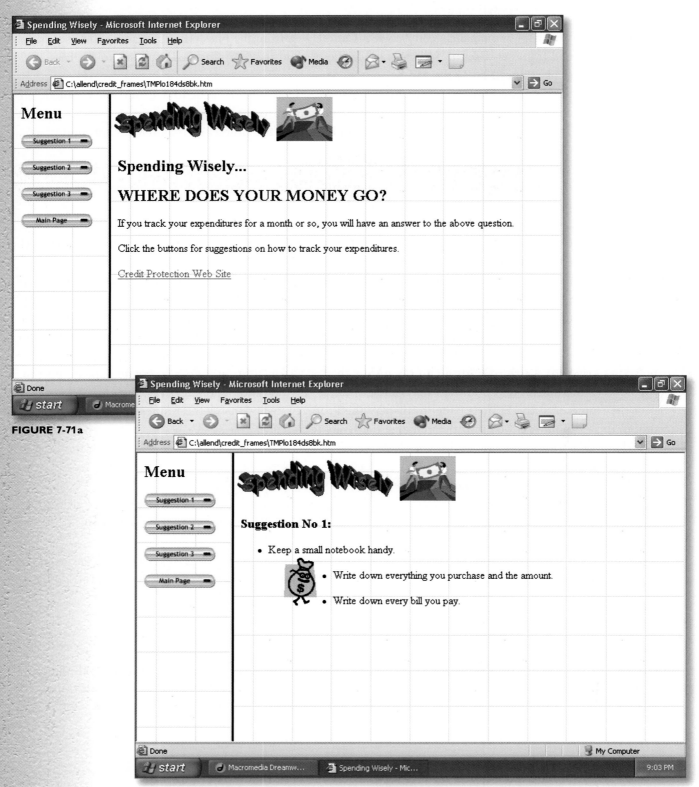

FIGURE 7-71a

FIGURE 7-71b

In the Lab

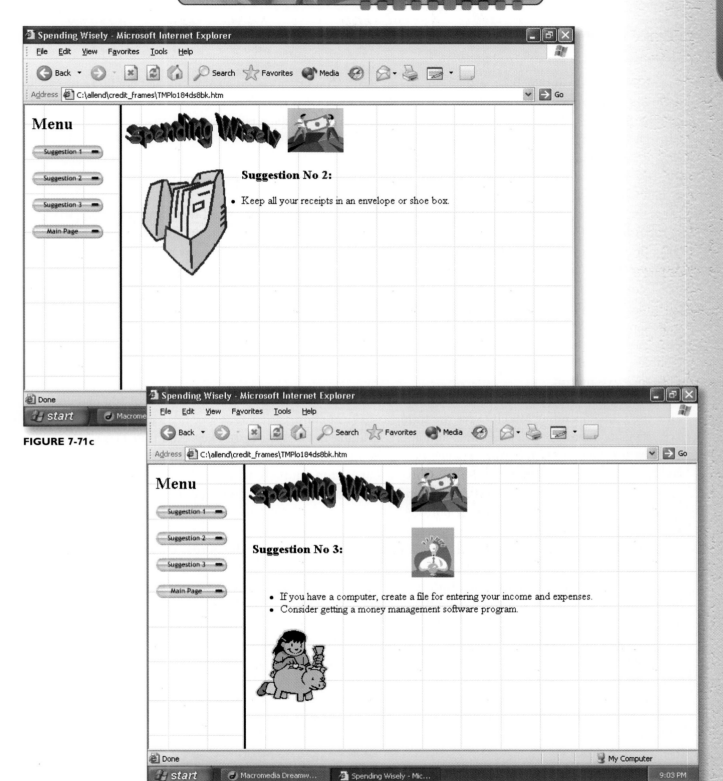

FIGURE 7-71c

FIGURE 7-71d

(continued)

In the Lab

Creating a Framed Layout for the Credit Protection Web Site *(continued)*

Instructions: Perform the following tasks:

1. Create a new Web site. Name the Web site Credit Frames and then create a folder named credit_frames. The path will be C:/yourname/credit_frames. Create a default images folder for the site.

2. Use the Windows My Computer option to copy the data files to the credit_frames Web site.

3. Start Dreamweaver. Display the panel groups.

4. Create a predefined frameset. Use the Fixed Left, Nested Top frameset. Drag to select Untitled Document in the Title text box on the Document toolbar and then type Spending Wisely as the entry. Save the frameset as index.htm in the credit_frames local root folder.

5. Click the topFrame. Apply the creditbg.gif image as the background image and then type Spending Wisely as the title. Save the frame as title.htm. Create a one-row, two-column table in the title frame (topFrame). Drag title01.gif to the first column and title02.gif to the second column. Adjust the table size so the images display proportionally. Select the topFrame in the frames panel and then add a margin height of 0. Save the title frame.

6. Click the mainFrame. Apply the same background to the mainFrame as you did to the title frame. Title the frame Spending Wisely and save the frame as main.htm.

7. Click the mainFrame in the Frames panel.

8. Double-click main.htm in the Src box in the Property inspector, type content.htm as the entry, and then click the Save button.

9. Click the leftFrame. Apply the same background to the leftFrame as you did to the topFrame and mainFrame. Title the frame Spending Wisely. Save the frame as navigate.htm.

10. Type Menu at the top of the leftFrame, and apply Heading 2. Press the ENTER key. Add four Flash buttons. The text for the first Flash button is Suggestion 1, for the second is Suggestion 2, for the third is Suggestion 3, and for the fourth is Main Page. Use the Chrome Bar button with a font size of 10. The links for buttons 1, 2, and 3 are money01.htm, money02.htm, and money03.htm, respectively. The link for the Main Page button is content.htm. The target for all four buttons is the mainFrame. Adjust the width of the leftFrame to accommodate the button size and then press CTRL+S to save the frame.

11. Add a three-pixel border to the frameset. Use hexadecimal #330000 for the border color. Click File on the menu bar and then click Save All. If instructed to do so, upload your Web site to a remote server.

12. Open the Credit Protection Web site, open the index.htm page, and then scroll to the bottom of the page. Insert a blank line above your name and then type Spending Wisely as the entry. Create a link from the text, Spending Wisely, to the index.htm file in the Credit Frames Web site. Set the Target to _blank. If you are publishing to a remote site, copy and paste the Credit Frames Web site address into the Link box. If you are saving your work to a local computer or server, use the Browse for File icon in the Property inspector to create the link path. Click the Save button on the Standard toolbar.

13. If instructed to do so, upload your Web site changes to a remote server. Press the F12 key to view the Credit Protection index.htm page in your browser. Click the Spending Wisely link to display the Credit Frames Web site. Click each of the navigation buttons to verify that they work. Print copies of each frame if instructed to do so.

3 Adding a Framed Page to the Plant City Web Site

Problem: The mayor has requested that Juan Benito further enhance the Plant City Web site and has suggested that an employment section be added. Juan agrees that this is an excellent idea and meets with you to discuss this new addition. You suggest that a framed-based section be added to the main Web site. Juan supports the idea and provides you with the information to begin creating the site. The Web site is displayed in Figures 7-72a through 7-72d on page DW 590.

FIGURE 7-72a

(continued)

In the Lab

Adding a Framed Page to the Plant City Web Site *(continued)*

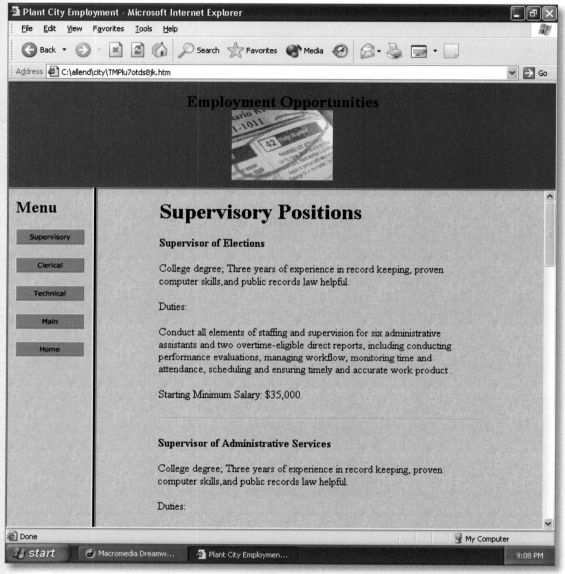

FIGURE 7-72b

In the Lab

FIGURE 7-72c

(continued)

Adding a Framed Page to the Plant City Web Site *(continued)*

FIGURE 7-72d

Instructions: Perform the following tasks:

1. Use the Windows My Computer option to copy the data files to the /yourname/city folder.
2. Start Dreamweaver. Display the panel groups. Select Plant City in the Files pop-up menu in the Files panel.
3. Create a predefined frameset. Use the Fixed Top, Nested Left frameset. Type `Employment Opportunities` in the Title text box on the Document toolbar. Save the frameset as employment.htm in the city local root folder.
4. Click the topFrame. Type `Employment Opportunities` and then center the text. Apply Heading 2 as the style. Add a line break and then drag the help_wanted.gif to the center point under the Employment Opportunities text. Select the topFrame and then add a margin height of 0. Apply a background color using hexadecimal #993333 as the color. Save the topFrame as title.htm.
5. Click the mainFrame. Add the citybg.gif background image to the mainframe. Save the frame as main.htm.
6. Click the mainFrame in the Frames panel.
7. Drag content.htm to the Src box. Click the File menu and then click Save.
8. Click the leftFrame. Type `Menu` at the top of the leftFrame and then apply Heading 2. Press the ENTER key. Add the citybg.gif image. Save the frame as navigate.htm.

9. Add five Flash buttons. The text for the first Flash button is Supervisory, for the second is Clerical, for the third is Technical, for the fourth is Main, and for the fifth is Home. Use the Generic-Ruby button with a font size of 10. The document links for the first three buttons are the same names as those for the buttons (supervisory.htm, etc.). The document link for the Main button is content.htm. The target for all of the buttons, except for the Home button, is the mainFrame. The link for the Home button is index.htm, and the target is _blank. Adjust the width and height of the frames to accommodate the text and images.

10. Select the nested frameset and then apply a three-pixel black border. Click File on the menu bar and then click Save All.

11. Open the index.htm page. Scroll to the bottom of the page and then click to the right of the Comments link. Add a vertical line, press SPACEBAR, type Employment, then create a relative link to employment.htm. Select _blank in the Target pop-up menu. Click the Save button.

12. Press the F12 key to view the Web site in your browser. Click the Employment link. Test each button. Print copies of each frame if instructed to do so. If instructed to do so, upload your Web site changes to a remote server.

Cases and Places

The difficulty of these case studies varies:
■ are the least difficult and ■■ are the most difficult. The last exercise is a group exercise.

1 ■ Your sports Web site has become very popular. You have decided to add two pages showing uniform types for football and baseball. To show these, you will use a right and left frame. The left frame will contain the name, or the link. When the user clicks the link, a picture of the uniform type will display in the right frame. Add a background image to the pages and add a title to each page. Create a link to the home page. Save the page in your sports Web site. For a selection of images and backgrounds, visit the Dreamweaver MX 2004 Media Web page (scsite.com/dreamweavermx04/media) and then click Media below Project 7.

2 ■ Modify your hobby Web site by adding a two-framed Web page. The left frame should contain three navigation links. Use buttons or text. The first link loads general information about your hobby into the content frame. The second link loads a page with an introductory paragraph and a minimum of three links to other related Web sites. The third link displays the index page in a separate window. Create a link to your home page. Add a four-pixel border to the frame. Upload the Web site changes to a remote site if instructed to do so. For a selection of images and backgrounds, visit the Dreamweaver MX 2004 Media Web page (scsite.com/dreamweavermx04/media) and then click Media below Project 7.

3 ■■ Create a new site for your music hobby. Name the site music_frames. Select one of the predefined framesets. Add three pages of content and a title graphic. Use buttons or text in the navigate_frame to access and display the content pages in the main frame. Name your frames and framesets and add titles to all frames. Add a background to all frames. Upload the entire Web site to a remote site. For a selection of images and backgrounds, visit the Dreamweaver MX 2004 Media Web page (scsite.com/dreamweavermx04/media) and then click Media below Project 7.

Cases and Places

4 ■■ Your campaign for political office is doing terrific. Create a new Web site and name it office_frames. Use a predefined frameset. Create three content pages with information highlighting at least three major accomplishments over the past 12 months. Create a static title frame and add your logo to this frame. Create a navigate_frame using Flash buttons — one of each for the content pages. Add a three-pixel border to the frame. Upload the framed Web site to a remote server. For a selection of images and backgrounds, visit the Dreamweaver MX 2004 Media Web page (scsite.com/ dreamweavermx04/media) and then click Media below Project 7.

5 ■■ **Working Together** The student trips Web site is receiving hundreds of hits each day, and the student government officers have selected three possible sites to visit. Create a trip_frames Web site using a predefined frameset. Create four content pages: one with general information and the other three highlighting the three possible student trip locations. Include at least one image on each of the content pages. Create a static title frame and a navigate_frame. Add a background image to all frames. Create a link to the home page to break out of the framed Web site. Upload the framed Web site to a remote server. For a selection of images and backgrounds, visit the Dreamweaver MX 2004 Media Web page (scsite.com/dreamweavermx04/media) and then click Media below Project 7.

Animation and Behaviors

PROJECT

8

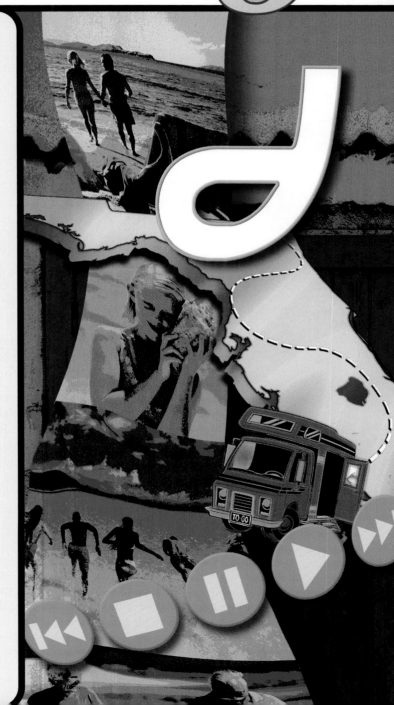

CASE PERSPECTIVE

Adding interactivity to Web pages makes visiting and surfing Web sites interesting. David Allen thinks it would be a good idea to add some animation to the Florida Parks Web site. Now that he understands how to use layers and behaviors, he wants to add animation using these Dreamweaver features. He comes to you for help in utilizing these more advanced concepts. You explain that Dreamweaver provides the capability of adding animation by using layers through the Timelines panel.

The next decision is where within the Web site to add the animation and what will be the focus of the animated page. Joan suggests that this be a project similar to the spotlight page previously added to the site. Instead of a static page, however, this Web page will contain a slide show where the viewer controls the display of images of various state parks. Joan further suggests that a second page be added to the site. The second page would contain a map focused on one part of the state and include the names and locations of the parks. The map would contain an image such as a motor home that would move across the northwest part of the state from park to park. Everyone on the team agrees that both of these pages would be a great addition to the site.

As you read through this project, you will learn about timelines and how to use timelines to create linear and nonlinear animations. You also will learn to control timelines by applying different behaviors.

Animation and Behaviors

Objectives

You will have mastered the material in this project when you can:

- Describe a timeline
- Describe the Timelines panel
- Create a nonlinear timeline
- Add a behavior to a layer
- Add a play button to a timeline
- Create a linear timeline
- Add a layer to a timeline
- Show and hide a layer
- Play an animation

Introduction

In Project 6, you applied some simple animation techniques when you learned about layers and behaviors and how to show and hide layers. Project 8 continues with the layer feature and introduces the integration of layers and timelines using the Dreamweaver Timelines panel. You can use timelines in three ways:

- To alter a layer's position, size, visibility, and depth
- To apply Dreamweaver's JavaScript behaviors
- To change the source for any image and replace it with another

Using this feature, the layers and images can be manipulated over time. Thus, adding layers and applying behaviors to the layers within a timeline provide the Web site designer the ability to add interactivity and animation to a Web site.

A timeline is similar to a strip of movie film. Just like movies, animation requires movement and time. A timeline is made up of frames. Each frame represents a moment in time, similar to that in a movie or video. A collection of frames makes a timeline. The Web site developer also can control the speed of the timeline or how fast the frames play. The default is 15 **fps**, or frames per second. If you decrease the number of fps, the animation takes longer to play; increase the number of fps and the animation plays faster.

Because timelines depend on layers, they require version 4 or later browsers. In addition, some features work only in Microsoft Internet Explorer. Only layers and images can be added to a Dreamweaver timeline, and only layers can be positioned. Using the timeline feature to add animation is a valuable tool that captures the interest of Web site visitors.

Project Eight — Creating Timeline Animation

In this project, you learn how to use Dreamweaver's Timelines panel and how to add animation to the Florida Parks Web site. You begin the project by adding a new page to the Web site, a page containing a map of northwest Florida (Figure 8-1a). A layer then is added to the page, and an image of a motor coach is embedded in the layer. Clicking a Forward button on the page moves the motor coach image over the map from one park location to another. This animation is created by dragging the image to create a nonlinear **animation path**. Dreamweaver automatically records the path, but does not record the timing of the drag operation. You specify these movements through the Timelines panel. Therefore, when you are creating the animation path, you can take your time to make sure that the path is what you want.

The second page added to the Web site is a slide show presentation (Figure 8-1b on the next page). The Web site visitor controls the display of the slide show by clicking a Forward button. The six slides within the slide show correspond to the park names displayed on the northwest Florida map and the motor coach path you create for the first page. You create this second animation using a linear, or straight-line, animation technique.

Exercises in this project use **active content**, which is content in a Web page that is interactive or dynamic. This type of content can be a security risk. In Windows XP SP2, Microsoft introduced a set of security technologies for protection from viruses and worms. When previewing a file, therefore, before Internet Explorer runs active content, the Information Bar displays, informing users about the potential security risk of running active content. Macromedia has worked with Microsoft to ensure security within Macromedia Flash, Shockwave, and Authorware Players, so users can acknowledge the warning and run content by clicking through the Information Bar prompts. If your computer uses a different operating system or does not use SP2, the Information Bar will not display.

FIGURE 8-1(a)

FIGURE 8-1(b)

Workspace Organization

Organization and preparation lead to a more productive work setting. Successful Web developers prepare their Dreamweaver workspace to provide an effective work environment. As you learn to use additional Dreamweaver tools, including timelines and behaviors, you will become even more proficient working in the Dreamweaver environment.

Copying Data Files to the Local Web Site

Your Data Disk contains data files and images for Project 8. You use the Windows My Computer option to copy the Project 8 files to your parks folder. See the inside back cover for instructions for downloading the Data Disk or see your instructor for information about accessing the files required for this book.

The DataFiles folder for this project is stored on Local Disk (C:). The location on your computer may be different. If necessary, verify with your instructor the location of the DataFiles folder. The following steps show how to copy the files to the parks local root folder.

To Copy Data Files to the Florida Parks Web Site

1. Click the Start button on the Windows taskbar and then click My Computer.

2. Double-click Local Disk (C:) and then navigate to the location of the data files for Project 8.

3 Double-click the DataFiles folder and then double-click the Proj08 folder.

4 Double-click the parks folder and then double-click the images folder.

5 Click the first image file in the list, hold down the SHIFT key, and then click the last image file in the list.

6 Right-click the selected files to display the context menu.

7 Click the Copy command and then click the My Computer Back button to navigate to the your name folder.

8 Double-click the your name folder, double-click the parks folder, and then double-click the images folder.

9 Right-click in the open window to display the context menu.

10 Click the Paste command to paste the image files into the images folder.

11 Navigate to the Proj08 parks folder. Double-click the parks folder.

12 Click the first file in the list, hold down the SHIFT key, and then click the last file in the list.

13 Right-click the selected files to display the context menu. Click the Copy command and then navigate to the your name folder.

14 Double-click the your name folder, double-click the parks folder, and then right-click to display the context menu. Click the Paste command to paste the data files into the parks folder.

15 Close the My Computer window.

Starting Dreamweaver and Closing Open Panels

Each time you start Dreamweaver, it opens to the last site displayed when you closed the program. It, therefore, may be necessary for you to open the Florida Parks Web site. The **Files pop-up menu** in the Files panel lists sites you have defined. When you open the site, a list of pages and subfolders within that site displays. The following steps illustrate how to start Dreamweaver and open the Florida Parks Web site.

To Start Dreamweaver and Open the Florida Parks Web Site

1 Click the Start button on the Windows taskbar.

2 Point to All Programs on the Start menu, point to Macromedia on the All Programs submenu, and then click Macromedia Dreamweaver MX 2004 on the Macromedia submenu.

3 If necessary, display the panel groups and expand the Property inspector.

4 Click the Files panel box arrow on the Files pop-up menu, and then click Florida Parks.

Dreamweaver opens, and the Florida Parks Web site hierarchy displays in the Files panel (Figure 8-2 on the next page).

Preparing the Web Page

Creating an animation in Dreamweaver requires some Document window preparation before you create the actual animation. To prepare the Web page requires that you add images and a layer.

To begin the preparation for the tour.htm page, you first add a map of northwest Florida. The map contains the name and location of each park. Highways and roadways are marked on the map and will provide a guideline for creating a non-linear animation path. Creating the animation path is discussed later in this project. Animations are built around images and layers, which requires that a layer be added to the map and that an image of a motor coach be added within that layer. The layer and image move along the highways and roadways from park to park.

Florida Parks Web site hierarchy

FIGURE 8-2

To Add the NW Florida Map Image and Layer

1

- **Double-click tour.htm in the Files panel. If necessary, click below the introductory paragraph. If necessary, press CTRL+F2 to close the Insert bar.**

The tour.htm page is displayed in the Document window, and the insertion point is centered below the introductory paragraph (Figure 8-3).

FIGURE 8-3

• **Click the Assets panel tab, scroll down if necessary, and then drag the nw_map.gif image to the Document window insertion point.**

• **Click the Alt box in the Image Property inspector and then type NW Florida map as the alternate text.**

The nw_map.gif image is displayed and selected. The Property inspector for images is displayed. The Alt box contains the text, NW Florida map (Figure 8-4). If the nw_map.gif image does not appear in the Assets panel, click the Files panel tab, and then click the Refresh button.

FIGURE 8-4

• **Close the Property inspector.**

• **Click Insert on the menu bar, click Layout Objects, and then click Layer. If necessary, use the Document window horizontal and vertical scroll bars to display the layer.**

• **Press F2 to display the Layers panel.**

A layer is added to the Document window, and Layer1 is displayed in the Layers panel (Figure 8-5).

FIGURE 8-5

4

• **Double-click the Layer1 name in the Layers panel. Type** motortour **as the layer name and then press the ENTER key.**

Layer1 is now named motortour, and the layer is selected (Figure 8-6).

FIGURE 8-6

5

• **Click the motortour layer selection handle and then drag the layer so it is located above Big Lagoon on the map.**

The motortour layer is displayed on the map (Figure 8-7).

FIGURE 8-7

6

• **Click inside the motortour layer and then drag the motorhome.jpg image from the Assets panel onto the layer.**

The motorhome.jpg image is displayed in the layer (Figure 8-8).

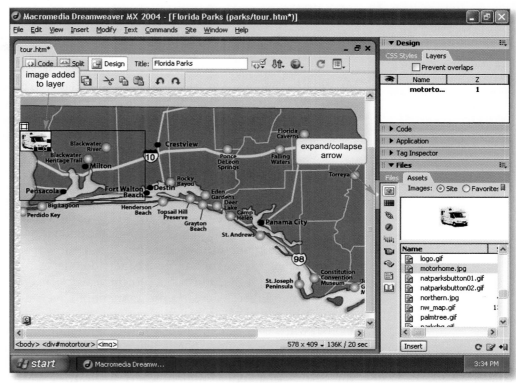

FIGURE 8-8

7

• **Click the expand/ collapse arrow to collapse the panel groups.**

• **Select the motortour layer, click a resize handle, and then resize the layer to fit the motorhome.jpg image.**

• **Click the layer selection handle and then drag the layer so it is placed above and in close proximity to the Big Lagoon park name.**

The panel groups are collapsed, and the layer is resized and placed close to the Big Lagoon park name (Figure 8-9).

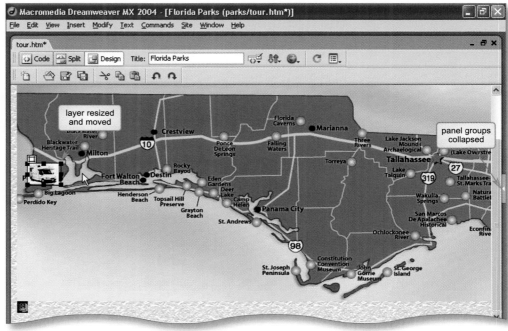

FIGURE 8-9

Other Ways

1. On Window menu click Insert, click Draw Layer button on Layout category

Introduction to Timelines

More About

Timelines

To display a list of commands that can be applied to timelines, click the Timelines panel menu button. For more information about timelines, visit the Dreamweaver MX 2004 More About Web page (scsite.com/dreamweavermx04/more.htm) and then click Timelines.

Timelines use dynamic HTML (DHTML) to change the position of a layer or the source of an image over time or to call behavior actions automatically after the page has loaded. (See page DW 407 for a detailed discussion of DHTML.) The timeline is the critical component for creating animation on a Web page. This Dreamweaver feature lets the Web site developer create animations that do not require plug-ins, ActiveX controls, or Java applets. As the Web site developer, you can choose to control the animation or you can add controls that let the Web site visitor control the animation.

Timeline Features

A timeline is composed of a series of frames. A **frame** is one cell or one point of time in a timeline. The total number of frames in the timeline determines the length of the presentation. You can create multiple animations on a Web page. The animations all can be contained within one timeline or spread out over several timelines. A single timeline can contain up to 32 individual layers.

As you create the animation, Dreamweaver converts the timeline commands into JavaScript and thereby creates the animation. Layers and images are the only objects that can be added to a timeline. Anything you add to a layer, however, can be animated, whether it is text, images, forms, tables, or other objects. A basic animation moves from one point on the timeline to another. Any animation created in the timeline must have a start and stop point. These start and stop points are marked on the timeline by small circles and are called **keyframes**. Keyframes are discussed in more detail throughout this project.

The Timelines Panel

The Web site developer uses the **Timelines panel** to create animation. The Timelines panel resembles a spreadsheet somewhat, showing units of time as columns and animated objects as rows. Figure 8-10a shows an overall view of the Timelines panel, and Figure 8-10b on the next page shows a view of the playback options and command buttons for viewing an animation.

The following section describes the Timelines panel (Figure 8-10a).

FIGURE 8-10a

ANIMATION BAR The animation bar shows the duration of each object's animation. A single row can include multiple bars representing different objects. Different bars cannot control the same object in the same frame.

ANIMATION CHANNEL The animation channel contains the bars for animating layers and images.

BEHAVIORS CHANNEL The behaviors channel executes behaviors along a channel at a particular frame in the timeline.

FRAME A frame is one cell or one point of time in a timeline. The total number of frames in the timeline determines the length of the presentation.

FRAME NUMBERS The frame numbers indicate the sequential numbering of frames. The number between the Back and Play buttons is the current frame number. The Web site developer controls the duration of an animation by setting the total number of frames and the number of frames per second (fps). The default setting is 15 fps.

KEYFRAME A keyframe contains specific properties (such as position) for an object; small circles indicate keyframes.

PLAYBACK HEAD The playback head indicates which frame of the timeline currently is displayed in the Document window.

TIMELINE POP-UP MENU The Timeline pop-up menu contains the names of a document's recent timelines; the Timeline pop-up menu text box displays which of the document's timelines currently appears in the Timelines panel.

The timeline contains several playback options and command buttons. You can use the command buttons to preview and control an animation in the Document window. The following section describes the playback options and command buttons (Figure 8-10b) within the Timelines panel. The buttons are similar to the controls on a VCR.

FIGURE 8-10b

AUTOPLAY When Autoplay is checked, a timeline begins playing automatically when the current page loads in a browser. Autoplay attaches a behavior to the page's body tag that executes the Play Timeline action when the page loads.

BACK The Back button moves the playback head one frame to the left. You can play the timeline backward by clicking the Back button and holding down the mouse button.

LOOP When the Loop check box is selected, the current timeline loops indefinitely while the page is open in a browser. Loop inserts the Go to Timeline Frame behavior in the behaviors channel after the last frame of the animation.

PLAY/FORWARD The Play/Forward button moves the playback head one frame to the right. You can play the timeline forward by clicking the Play button and holding down the mouse button.

REWIND The Rewind button moves the playback head to the first frame in the timeline.

Nonlinear Animations

The most common kind of timeline animation involves moving a layer along a path. Using layers and the Timelines panel, you can create linear, or straight-line, animations and nonlinear animations. A **nonlinear animation** is one that does not follow a straight path. Creating a linear, or straight-line, animation is discussed later in this project.

To create a layer with a complex path for a nonlinear animation, it is easier to drag the layer rather than to create individual keyframes. Earlier in this project, you added a NW Florida map image to the tour.htm Web page, added and resized a layer, and then added the motorhome image to the layer. The object of the animation is to create a path where the motorhome image moves to the right across the page via the path, then up and then back to the left to its original position. The roadways and highways are used as guidelines for this animated movement.

To create this animation, you drag the layer containing the motorhome image. This is a freeform exercise, so the path on which you drag the image will vary somewhat from the path shown in Figures 8-16a through 8-16c.

The next steps show how to add the nonlinear animation path to the tour.htm Web page. As you are creating this animation, you will find it necessary to expand and collapse the Timelines panel and the panel groups to provide maximum Document window visibility. You also will find that at times you will have to scroll horizontally and vertically within the Document window to redisplay the motorhome image. When you are dragging this image, a thin grey line will indicate the path you are creating. Recall that Dreamweaver automatically records the path, but does not record the timing of the drag operation. You control the timing through the Timelines panel.

To Create a Nonlinear Animation

1

• **Press ALT+F9 to display the Timelines panel. If necessary, expand the Timelines panel.**

The Timelines panel is displayed (Figure 8-11).

FIGURE 8-11

2

• **Double-click the Timeline pop-up menu text box.**

• **Type** tour **as the timeline name and then press the TAB key.**

The timeline is renamed tour (Figure 8-12).

FIGURE 8-12

3

• **If necessary, select the motortour layer or click the motortour layer selection handle in the Document window and then right-click the selected motortour layer or motortour selection handle.**

• **Point to Record Path on the context menu.**

The motortour layer is selected, and the context menu is displayed (Figure 8-13).

FIGURE 8-13

4

• **Click Record Path and then point to the Timelines panel expand/collapse arrow.**

The motortour layer is selected, and the Record Path command is active (Figure 8-14).

FIGURE 8-14

5

• **Click the Timelines panel expand/collapse arrow. If necessary, scroll to view the map.**

The Timelines panel is collapsed (Figure 8-15).

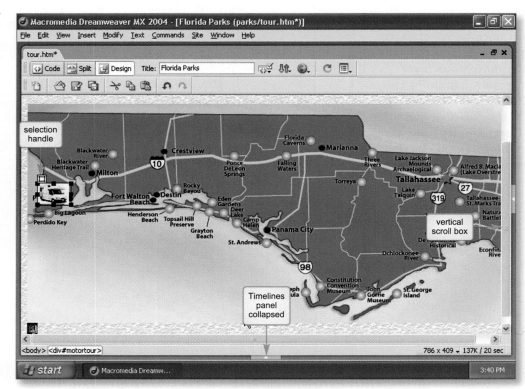

FIGURE 8-15

6

• **Click the motortour layer selection handle and then drag it east (right) on Highway 98 to Rocky Bayou (Figure 8-16a), then to St. George Island (Figure 8-16b), east (right), then north (up) to Highway 319 and Wakulla Springs, north and then west (left) on Highway 10 to Three Rivers, continuing west to Ponce DeLeon Springs, and ending back at Big Lagoon. Do not release the mouse button while dragging.**

• **If a Dreamweaver dialog box displays, read the information and then click the OK button.**

Figure 8-16a shows the motortour layer and the line created as the layer was dragged to the first stop. A red line is displayed in Figure 8-16a for visibility purposes. The line you create will be a thin grey line. Figure 8-16b shows the motor coach after it is dragged to the second stop. Figure 8-16c on the next page is for illustration purposes only and displays all the stops along the route.

FIGURE 8-16a

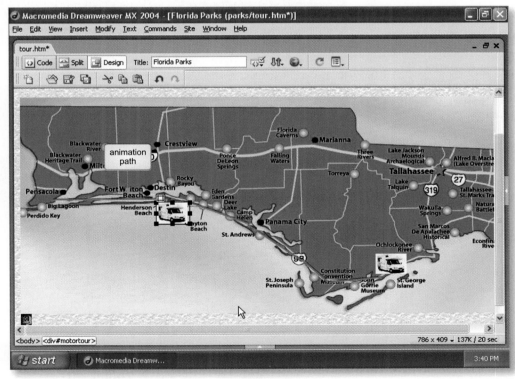

FIGURE 8-16b

Your screen will not show the red line or multiple motor coaches as displayed in Figure 8-16c. The path on which the motor coach is dragged is freeform; your line will not be identical to the one shown here.

FIGURE 8-16c

7

• **Click the Timelines panel expand/collapse arrow to expand the Timelines panel. If necessary, scroll to display the map and timeline.**

A timeline has been added to the animation channel in the Timelines panel. A thin grey line on the image map shows the image drag path (Figure 8-17). The timeline is selected in the animation channel. Several keyframes are shown on the timeline. These keyframes are added when you hesitate or drag the timeline in a nonlinear line. The timeline on your screen will be somewhat different from the one shown here, and the keyframes will be in different frames. Viewing the entire timeline requires that you scroll to the right in the Timelines panel.

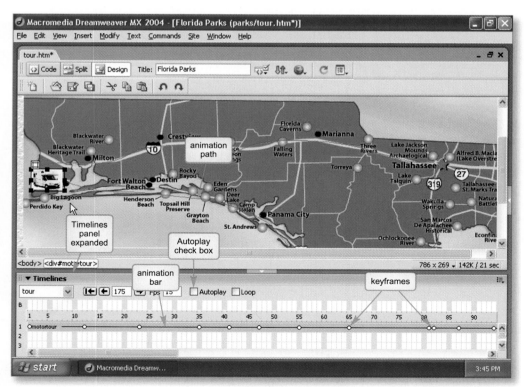

FIGURE 8-17

8

• **Click the Autoplay check box in the Timelines panel.**

• **If a Dreamweaver dialog box is displayed, read the information, and then click the OK button.**

• **Click the Save button on the Standard toolbar.**

• **Press the F12 key to view the animation in your browser. Close the browser and return to Dreamweaver.**

The motorhome image travels across the map and returns to its original position.

Editing a Timeline

As you are creating a timeline, occasionally you will need to edit different features. The following provides editing information for frames, timelines, behaviors, and animation channels.

- To add or remove a frame in the timeline, click the frame, right-click the timeline, and then click Remove Frame or Add Frame on the context menu.
- To remove or rename a timeline, click the timeline to select it, right-click the timeline, and then click Remove Timeline or Rename Timeline on the context menu.
- To remove a behavior from the Timelines panel, right-click the behavior in the behaviors channel and then click Remove Behavior on the context menu.
- To remove a keyframe, select the keyframe, right-click the keyframe, and select Remove Keyframe on the context menu.
- To remove an animation channel, select it in the Timelines panel, right-click the animation channel, and then click Delete on the context menu.

In addition to using the context menu, you also can select the object in the timeline, and then click the Timelines Options pop-up menu.

Adding Behaviors to the Timeline

In Project 6, you learned about behaviors and how to add behaviors to show and hide objects. These behaviors are ready-to-use Dreamweaver-created JavaScript functions. The available functions vary based on the selected object. You also can add behaviors to your timeline animations. Examples of behaviors you can add to a timeline include playing sound, showing pop-up messages, showing and hiding layers, starting and stopping timelines, and other events. To add a pop-up message, for example, select the object, click the Add behavior (+) button in the Behaviors panel, and then click Popup Message. Type the message in the Popup Message dialog box and then click the OK button.

The steps on the next page show how to add Stop Timeline behaviors to the tour timeline. You add a Stop Timeline behavior at each of the six parks listed in the previous steps. Keep in mind that this is a freeform exercise and that the frame numbers in the Timelines panel in the following figures most likely will not match those on your screen.

To Add the Stop Timeline Behavior

1

• **If necessary, scroll down in the Document window so the Rocky Bayou park name is displayed.**

• **If necessary, click the motortour layer so the selection handle is displayed.**

• **Click a frame in the animation channel that moves the motortour layer close to the Rocky Bayou park name. In Figure 8-18, this is frame 25, but your frame number may be different.**

• **Use the Document window vertical scroll bar as necessary to reposition the image so the motortour layer is displayed.**

FIGURE 8-18

The motortour layer moves based on the selected frame number and is positioned in close proximity to the Rocky Bayou park name. The playback head is in frame 25 in the animation channel (Figure 8-18). The location of the motortour layer and the frame number on your screen most likely will be different.

2

• **Click the panel groups expand/collapse arrow and then press SHIFT+F4 to display the Behaviors panel. If necessary, collapse the Files panel.**

• **Point to the frame number in the timeline behaviors channel that is the same number as the one in the animation channel on your screen. In Figure 8-19, this is frame 25. Most likely the frame number on your screen will be a different number.**

FIGURE 8-19

The panel groups are expanded, and the Behaviors panel is displayed (Figure 8-19). When expanding and collapsing panels, it may appear that the motortour layer changes positions. Recall, however, that a layer enables absolute positioning of objects and elements on a page. The repositioning most likely is caused by the movement of the nw_map image. When the panel groups are collapsed, the motortour layer will return to its correct position.

3

• **Click your selected frame in the behaviors channel and then point to the Add behavior (+) button in the Behaviors panel.**

Frame 25 is selected in the behaviors channel (Figure 8-20). Most likely the frame number on your screen will be different.

FIGURE 8-20

4

• **Click the Add behavior (+) button, point to Timeline on the Add behavior pop-up menu, and then point to Stop Timeline on the Timeline submenu.**

The Add behavior pop-up menu is displayed, and the Stop Timeline command is highlighted (Figure 8-21).

FIGURE 8-21

5

• **Click Stop Timeline.**

• **In the Stop Timeline dialog box, click the Stop Timeline box arrow and then point to tour.**

The Stop Timeline dialog box is displayed, and tour is highlighted (Figure 8-22).

FIGURE 8-22

6

• **Click tour and then click the OK button.**

The Stop Timeline behavior is added to the Behaviors panel, and a minus sign is displayed in frame 25 in the behaviors channel. The event and action are displayed in the Behaviors panel (Figure 8-23). Most likely the frame number for the behaviors channel on your screen will be different.

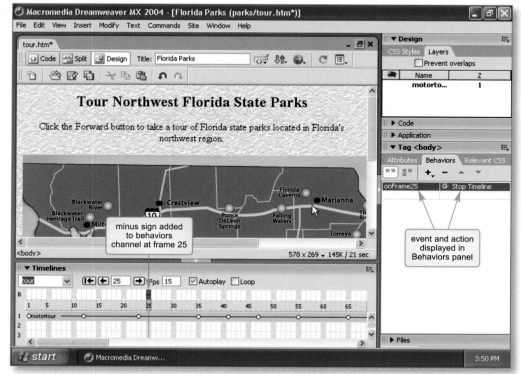

FIGURE 8-23

7

- **Click the panel groups expand/collapse arrow to collapse the panels.**

- **Scroll down in the Document window to display the motortour layer and the St. George Island park name.**

- **Click a frame in the animation channel that moves the motortour layer so it is close to the St. George Island park name. In Figure 8-24, this is frame 68, but your frame number may be different. Use the vertical scroll bar as needed to reposition the image so that the motortour layer and St. George Island park name are displayed.**

- **If necessary, click other frame numbers until the motortour layer is in close proximity to the St. George Island park name on your screen.**

FIGURE 8-24

The motortour layer is positioned in close proximity to the St. George Island park name (Figure 8-24). The playback head is located at frame 68. Most likely the frame number of your screen will be different.

8

- **Click the panel groups expand/collapse arrow.**

- **If necessary, scroll to the right in the Timelines panel.**

- **Click your selected frame in the behaviors channel. In Figure 8-25, this is frame 68, but your frame number most likely will be different.**

- **Click the Add behavior (+) button in the Behaviors panel.**

- **Point to Timeline and then click Stop Timeline.**

- **Click the Stop Timeline box arrow in the Stop Timeline dialog box, click tour, and then click the OK button.**

FIGURE 8-25

The Stop Timeline behavior is added to the Behaviors panel, and a minus sign is displayed in frame 68 (or your selected frame) in the behaviors channel (Figure 8-25).

9

• **Repeat Steps 7 and 8 using Table 8-1 for the list of the other four park names and the approximate frame numbers to stop the motortour layer. The frame numbers listed in the table are example values. Modify the frame numbers to fit your timeline. Use the horizontal and vertical scroll boxes as needed to scroll to display the rest of the animation bar in the animation channel.**

The Stop Timeline behavior is added to each frame close to one of the designated park names.

Table 8-1 Park Names and Frame Numbers	
PARK NAMES	**APPROXIMATE FRAME NUMBER***
Wakulla Springs	Frame 96
Three Rivers	Frame 111
Ponce DeLeon Springs	Frame 130
Big Lagoon	Frame 175

*Your frame numbers most likely will be different.

Controlling the Timeline

In Project 6, you learned about the onMouseOver event. In addition to the onMouseOver event, Dreamweaver provides access to several other events that you can assign as animation controls. These events include onClick, onDblClick, onKeyDown, onKeyPress, onKeyUp, onMouseDown, onMouseOut, onMouseUp, onAbort, onError, and onLoad.

When you add an event and then click the event name in the Behaviors panel, a pop-up menu appears when you click the arrow button next to the selected event name. This pop-up menu contains a list of all the events that can trigger the action. This menu is visible only when an event in the behavior list is selected. Different events appear depending on the object selected.

With the Stop Timeline behaviors added to the timeline, a method is needed to start the timeline and move from park to park. This is done by adding another layer, adding an image to that layer, and then adding the Start Timeline behavior to the image. To control the Start Timeline behavior, the user clicks the image. The default event for the selected object is onLoad. The goal here, however, is to allow the user to control the timeline by clicking the mouse. You, therefore, change the event from onLoad to onClick. The following steps illustrate how to add the Forward button and the Start Timeline behavior to the tour.htm Web page.

To Add a Forward Button

1

• Use the vertical and horizontal scroll bars to scroll as necessary in the Document window.

• Click to the right of the layer-code marker, click Insert on the menu bar, point to Layout Objects, and then click Layer.

A new layer and new layer code-marker are inserted in the Document window (Figure 8-26).

FIGURE 8-26

2

• Double-click the Layer1 name in the Layers panel and rename the layer forward.

• Click the forward layer selection handle and then drag the layer up and onto the nw_map.gif image as shown in Figure 8-27.

The layer is renamed forward and is displayed on the nw_map.gif image.

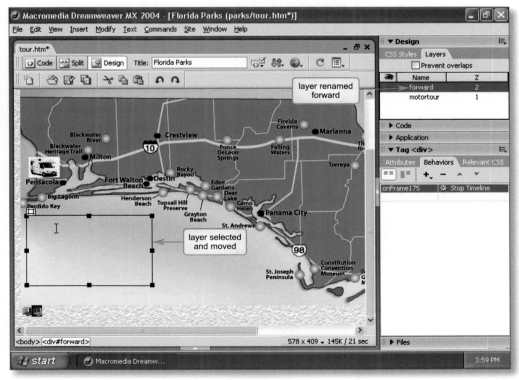

FIGURE 8-27

Macromedia
Dreamweaver MX 2004

3

• **Double-click the Files panel title bar and then click the Assets tab.**

• **Drag the forward.gif image onto the forward layer. Click to the right of the forward.gif image.**

• **Hold down the SHIFT key and then press the ENTER key.**

• **Type** Forward **as the text.**

The forward image is displayed in the forward layer, and the text, Forward, is added (Figure 8-28).

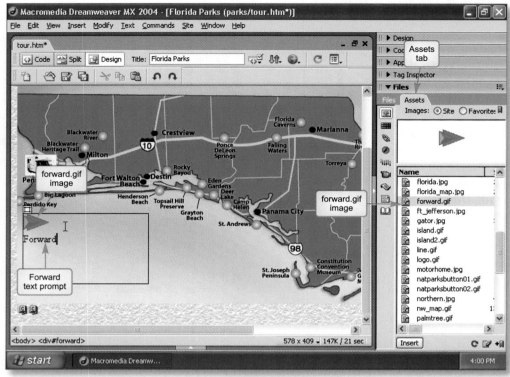

FIGURE 8-28

4

• **Select the forward layer.**

• **Click a resize handle on the forward layer and then resize the layer around the image.**

• **Press CTRL+F3 to display the Property inspector. Set L at 50 and T at 330.**

• **Close the Property inspector.**

• **If necessary, scroll down to view the forward layer and image.**

The forward layer is resized and selected, and left and top attributes are set for the forward image layer (Figure 8-29). The Property inspector is closed.

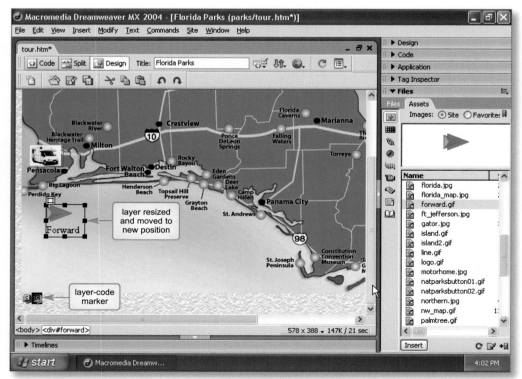

FIGURE 8-29

5

• **Expand the Timeline. Click anywhere in the animation channel 2 (or any empty frame) to deselect the behavior in the Behaviors panel.**

• **Double-click the Tag Inspector panel title bar in the panel groups.**

• **Click the forward image (not the layer).**

• **Click the Add behavior (+) button in the Behaviors panel, point to Timeline, and then click Play Timeline.**

• **Click the OK button in the Play Timeline dialog box.**

The onLoad event and the Play Timeline action are added to the Behaviors panel (Figure 8-30).

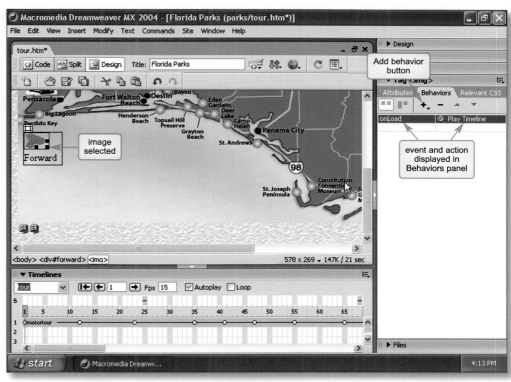

FIGURE 8-30

6

• **Click to the right of onLoad in the Behaviors panel to display the pop-up menu arrow.**

• **Click the pop-up menu arrow that displays to the right of onLoad.**

• **If necessary, scroll up and then point to onClick.**

The Events pop-up menu to the right of onLoad displays, and onClick is highlighted (Figure 8-31).

FIGURE 8-31

7

• **Click the onClick command.**

The onClick command displays in the Behaviors panel (Figure 8-32).

FIGURE 8-32

8

• **Click the Loop check box. If a warning dialog box displays, read the information, and then click the OK button.**

• **Deselect the Autoplay check box.**

The behavior for the Loop action is added to the Behaviors panel, and the Autoplay check box is deselected (Figure 8-33). Most likely, the Events frame number in the Behaviors panel on your screen will be different.

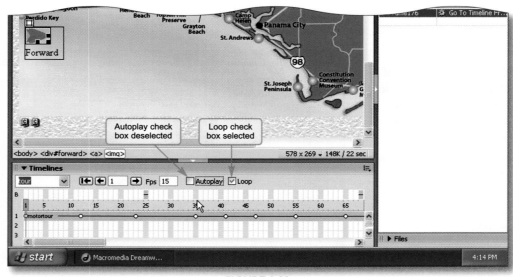

FIGURE 8-33

9

• **Press the F12 key to view the animation in your browser. Click the Forward button to move the motorhome image along the animation path. Close the browser and return to Dreamweaver.**

The motorhome image moves along the animation path and returns to the Big Lagoon starting point.

• **Save and then close the tour Web page.**

To integrate the Web page into the Florida Parks Web site, later in this project you create a link to the state_parks.htm page. You also create a link from the state_parks.htm to this page (tour.htm) and to the slideshow.htm page you create next.

Linear, or Straight-Line, Path Animations

With the animation using a nonlinear path created, your next objective is to create a slide show using a **linear**, or **straight-line**, **path animation**. You accomplish this primarily through the Timelines panel, by adding keyframes at various points along the timelines. As discussed previously, keyframes are marked on the timeline by small circles. A keyframe is the main tool for controlling an animation. Using a keyframe, you can change the properties of an object in a timeline. In this exercise, you change the Show-Hide properties.

The slide show will contain six layers, one for each image of the six state parks the motor home visits on its tour of northwest Florida. You use the Show-Hide behavior to display and hide the park images, or slides. All images are the same size and use absolute positioning. The Web site visitor cycles through the images by clicking a Forward button. The image sequence loops, and, at the end of the loop, the Forward button returns the visitor to the beginning slide.

To begin creating your slide show, you add six layers and six images. The images are positioned on top of each other, and each is aligned to the same coordinates. Using same-sized images and absolute positioning provides for a smooth transition between slides and keeps the user's attention focused on a single spot. The following steps show how to create the layers and add images to each layer.

More About

Creating Simple Animations

Do not create animations that demand more than current browsers can provide. Browsers always play every frame in a timeline animation, even when system or Internet performance decreases. Therefore, create simple animations.

To Add the First Layer and Image

1

• **Close the Timelines panel.**

• **Double-click the Files panel title bar, and expand the Design Panel title bar. If necessary, click the Layers tab.**

• **If necessary, click the Files panel tab. Open slideshow.htm.**

• **Press CTRL+F3 to display the Property inspector. If necessary, click below the heading and then click the Align Left button in the Property inspector.**

The slideshow.htm page is displayed in the Document window. The insertion point is at the left in the Document window (Figure 8-34).

FIGURE 8-34

2

• **Click Insert on the menu bar, point to Layout Objects, and then click Layer.**

A layer is inserted into the Document window. The layer-code marker is displayed in the upper-left corner, and the insertion point is blinking inside the layer (Figure 8-35).

FIGURE 8-35

3

• **Click the Assets tab. Drag the big_lagoon.jpg image onto the layer.**

The Big Lagoon image is displayed in Layer1 (Figure 8-36).

FIGURE 8-36

4

• **Click the Layer1 name in the Layers panel.**

The Layer1 name is selected in the Layers panel, and the Property inspector for layers is displayed (Figure 8-37).

FIGURE 8-37

5

• **In the Property inspector, add the following attributes: Layer ID biglagoon, L 150, and T 60.**

The properties are added for the biglagoon layer, and the Layer1 name changes to biglagoon in the Layers panel (Figure 8-38).

FIGURE 8-38

6

• **Click the Visibility column to the left of the biglagoon layer in the Layers panel until the closed-eye icon is displayed.**

• **If necessary, click the Document window to hide the layer and image.**

The closed-eye icon is displayed (Figure 8-39). Later in this project, you will change this closed-eye icon to the open-eye icon.

FIGURE 8-39

The first layer and image for the slide show have been added to the Document window. Next, you add five more layers, add an image to each layer, and then change the properties for each of the layers.

More About

Slide Shows

When creating a slide show, make all the images the same size in order to create smooth transitions. Most browsers running on average computer systems cannot display animations at rates faster than 15 fps. For more information about slide shows, visit the Dreamweaver MX 2004 More About Web page (scsite.com/dreamweavermx04/more.htm) and then click Slide Shows.

To Add the Next Five Layers and Images

1

• **Click Insert on the menu bar, point to Layout Objects, and then click Layer.**

• **Drag the rocky_bayou.jpg image onto the layer.**

Layer1 is added to the Layers panel. The Rocky Bayou image is displayed in the Document window (Figure 8-40).

FIGURE 8-40

2

• **Select the Layer1 name in the Layers panel. Add the following attributes in the Layer Property inspector: Layer ID rockybayou, L 150, and T 60.**

The properties are added for the Rocky Bayou layer, and the layer name changes to rockybayou in the Layers panel (Figure 8-41).

FIGURE 8-41

3

• **Click the Visibility column to the left of the rockybayou layer in the Layers panel until the closed-eye icon is displayed. If necessary, click the Document window to hide the layer and image.**

The closed-eye icon is displayed for the rockybayou layer in the Layers panel. The rockybayou image no longer appears in the Document window.

4

• **Four more layers must be added to prepare for the slide show. Repeat Steps 1 through 3 to add the next four layers. Table 8-2 contains the attributes for each layer. Apply the closed-eye icon to all of the layers. Move the mouse pointer over the horizontal line below the Layers panel until the pointer turns into a two-headed arrow. Drag the mouse pointer down until all six layers display.**

All six layers are added and are hidden (Figure 8-42).

FIGURE 8-42

5

• **Click the Save button on the Standard toolbar.**

The slideshow.htm file is saved.

Table 8-2 Layer Attributes

IMAGE NAME	LAYER ID	L AND T
st_george.jpg	stgeorge	150 and 60
wakulla.jpg	wakulla	150 and 60
three_rivers.jpg	threerivers	150 and 60
ponce.jpg	poncedeleon	150 and 60

Next, you display the Timelines panel and then name the timeline. Recall that the Timelines panel shows how the properties of layers and images change over time. The following steps show how to accomplish this task.

To Display and Name the Timeline

1

• **Close the Property inspector. Press ALT+F9 to display the Timelines panel.**

The Timelines panel is displayed, and the Property inspector is closed (Figure 8-43).

FIGURE 8-43

2

• **Click the Timelines pop-up menu text box. Delete the default text entry, type** slideshow, **and then press the TAB key.**

The timeline is named, and the name is displayed in the Timelines pop-up menu text box (Figure 8-44).

FIGURE 8-44

Adding Layers to a Timeline

The next step is to add the six layers to the timeline. The timeline for each layer is on a separate animation channel. The steps on the next page illustrate how to add the six layers to the timeline.

To Add the Layers to the Timeline

1

• **Scroll as necessary in the Layers panel. Click the biglagoon layer.**

The biglagoon layer is selected in the Layers panel, and its layer-code marker in the Document window is highlighted. The Big Lagoon image is displayed in the Document window (Figure 8-45).

FIGURE 8-45

2

• **Drag the biglagoon layer-code marker to animation channel 1, frame 1, in the Timelines panel. If a Dreamweaver dialog box is displayed, read the information and then click the OK button.**

The biglagoon layer is displayed and highlighted in animation channel 1 (Figure 8-46).

FIGURE 8-46

3

• **Click the rockybayou layer in the Layers panel.**

The rockybayou layer is selected in the Layers panel, and the rockybayou layer-code marker is selected in the Document window (Figure 8-47).

FIGURE 8-47

4

• **Drag the rockybayou layer-code marker to animation channel 2, frame 1, in the Timelines panel. If a Dreamweaver dialog box is displayed, click the OK button.**

The rockybayou layer is displayed and highlighted in animation channel 2 (Figure 8-48).

FIGURE 8-48

5

• **Move the mouse pointer over the Timelines horizontal bar until the pointer turns into a two-headed arrow. Drag the horizontal bar up until six animation channels are displayed.**

• **Repeat Steps 3 and 4, selecting and dragging the remaining four layers to the Timelines panel: the stgeorge layer to animation channel 3, the wakulla layer to animation channel 4, the threerivers layer to animation channel 5, and the poncedeleon layer to animation channel 6.**

The poncedeleon timeline is highlighted (Figure 8-49).

FIGURE 8-49

Adjusting the Number of Frames

The slide show is not a self-running animation. Instead, the Web site user controls the slide show by clicking a button. Thus, the time, or fps, is not relevant. The number of frames within each of the timelines, therefore, can be set to a minimum. Keyframes are added to the timeline to show and hide each layer, and a pause is added between the show and hide events. The pause is added through the behaviors channel. Because fps are not relevant and because you want to create the most efficient slide show, the number of frames for each timeline is set to the lowest number required to create the slide show.

As discussed previously, a keyframe is required to hide and then show each of the six images within the layers. Keyframe number 3, for instance, is used to hide the biglagoon layer and to display the rockybayou layer. Another keyframe is required to stop the display of each of the layers, and an ending keyframe is required. Therefore, to determine the minimum number of frames, multiply the number of images in your sequence by 2 and then add 1. In this instance, the slide show contains six slides, which makes the number of required frames 13. You adjust the number of frames by dragging the last keyframe for each of the timelines to the left. The following steps illustrate how to adjust the number of keyframes for each timeline.

To Adjust the Number of Keyframes

1

• **Click the keyframe at frame 15 in the biglagoon animation bar in the Timelines panel.**

The playback head moves to frame 15, and the keyframe circle is highlighted (Figure 8-50).

FIGURE 8-50

2

• **Drag the keyframe to frame 13.**

The playback head moves to frame 13 (Figure 8-51).

FIGURE 8-51

3

• **Repeat Steps 1 and 2 for the other five layers.**

All six timelines are adjusted to 13 frames (Figure 8-52).

FIGURE 8-52

More About

Animation Sequences

After you have an animation sequence that you like, you can copy it and paste it into another area of the current timeline, into another timeline in the same document, or into a timeline in another document. You also can copy and paste multiple sequences at once.

Adding Keyframes to Show and Hide Layers

Recall that you use a keyframe to define the properties of an object in a timeline. A start keyframe and a stop keyframe automatically are added to the beginning and end of each timeline. You can use keyframes to change an object's position or to show and hide layers. As the slide show plays, for instance, the layers are displayed and then hidden.

When using keyframes to show and hide layers, as within a slide show, visualize the keyframes as a stairstep process. To display the slide show, a layer is turned on and then turned off. When the layer is turned off, the next layer is turned on, and so on. The slide show starts with the biglagoon layer displayed at frame 1 and the other five layers hidden. Showing and hiding layers is accomplished through the Visibility column in the Layers panel, using the open-eye and closed-eye icons. Therefore, for the biglagoon timeline, the keyframe at frame 1 shows the layer (the open-eye icon in the Layers panel). The keyframes at frame 1 for the other five layers show closed-eye icons. To hide the biglagoon layer and to show the rockybayou layer, the keyframe at frame 3 for the biglagoon layer is a closed-eye icon (i.e., the layer is hidden) and the keyframe at frame 3 for the rockybayou layer is an open-eye icon. When the biglagoon layer is hidden, the next layer (the rockybayou layer) is displayed. Continuing with the slide show, the keyframe at frame 5 for the rockybayou layer is a closed-eye icon and the keyframe at frame 5 for the stgeorge layer is an open-eye icon, and so on. When one layer is hidden, the next one is turned on. In between layers being shown and hidden, a behavior is added to the even-numbered frames to stop the slide show. Clicking the Play button resumes the slide show presentation.

In the following steps, keyframes are added to the timeline to show and hide layers. When the timeline is executed and a keyframe is encountered, then the visibility of the selected layer is turned on or off. The next steps show how to add keyframes to show or hide a selected layer. The keyframes are added at odd-numbered frames for each of the timelines.

To Add Keyframes to Show and Hide Layers

1

• **Click the biglagoon timeline in the Timelines panel at frame 1.**

• **If necessary, drag the playback head to frame 1 and then click the Visibility column for the biglagoon layer in the Layers panel until the open-eye icon is displayed.**

The playback head is in frame 1 and the open-eye icon appears for the big lagoon layer (Figure 8-53). The open-eye icon for keyframe 1 displays the first slide when the slide show opens in the browser window.

FIGURE 8-53

2

• **Drag the playback head to frame 3.**

The playback head is at frame 3, and the biglagoon timeline is selected (Figure 8-54).

FIGURE 8-54

3

• **Click and then right-click the biglagoon timeline at frame 3. Point to Add Keyframe on the context menu.**

The context menu displays, and Add Keyframe is highlighted (Figure 8-55).

FIGURE 8-55

4

• **Click Add Keyframe.**

• **Click the Visibility column for the biglagoon layer in the Layers panel until the closed-eye icon is displayed.**

A keyframe is added to the biglagoon layer at frame 3. This keyframe setting hides the biglagoon layer when the animation plays and the layer advances to frame 3 (Figure 8-56).

FIGURE 8-56

5

• **Click the rockybayou timeline at frame 3 in the Timelines panel. Right-click to display the context menu and then click Add Keyframe.**

• **Click the Visibility column for the rockybayou layer in the Layers panel until the open-eye icon displays.**

The open-eye icon is displayed to the left of the rockybayou layer in the Layers panel. A keyframe is added to the rockybayou timeline at frame 3 (Figure 8-57). This keyframe setting displays the Rocky Bayou image during the slide show presentation.

FIGURE 8-57

6

• **Drag the playback head to frame 5.**

• **Click the rockybayou timeline at frame 5 in the Timelines panel.**

The rockybayou timeline is selected in the Timelines panel (Figure 8-58).

FIGURE 8-58

7

• **Right-click the rockybayou frame 5 and then click Add Keyframe.**

• **Click the Visibility column for the rockybayou layer in the Layers panel until the closed-eye icon is displayed.**

A keyframe is added to the rockybayou timeline at frame 5 (Figure 8-59). This keyframe setting hides the image during the slide show presentation.

FIGURE 8-59

8

• **Click the stgeorge timeline at frame 5 in the Timelines panel.**

The stgeorge timeline is selected at frame 5 (Figure 8-60).

FIGURE 8-60

9

• **Right-click the stgeorge timeline and then click Add Keyframe.**

• **Click the Visibility column for the stgeorge layer in the Layers panel until the open-eye icon is displayed.**

A keyframe is added to the stgeorge timeline at frame 5 (Figure 8-61). This keyframe setting shows the image during the slide show presentation.

FIGURE 8-61

10

• **Click frame 7 in the stgeorge timeline in the Timelines panel, right-click, and then click Add Keyframe.**

• **Click the Visibility column for the stgeorge layer in the Layers panel until the closed-eye icon is displayed.**

A keyframe is added to the stgeorge timeline at frame 7 (Figure 8-62). This keyframe setting hides the image during the slide show presentation.

FIGURE 8-62

11

• **Click frame 7 in the wakulla timeline in the Timelines panel, right-click, and then click Add Keyframe.**

• **Click the Visibility column in the wakulla layer in the Layers panel until the open-eye icon is displayed.**

A keyframe is added to the wakulla timeline at frame 7 (Figure 8-63). This keyframe setting shows the image during the slide show presentation.

FIGURE 8-63

12

• **Click the wakulla timeline at frame 9 in the Timelines panel, right-click, and then click Add Keyframe.**

• **Click the Visibility column in the wakulla layer in the Layers panel until the closed-eye icon is displayed.**

A keyframe is added to the wakulla timeline at frame 9 (Figure 8-64). This keyframe setting hides the image during the slide show presentation.

FIGURE 8-64

13

- **Click the threerivers timeline in the Timelines panel at frame 9, right-click, and then click Add Keyframe.**
- **Click the Visibility column in the threerivers layer in the Layers panel until the open-eye icon is displayed.**

A keyframe is added to the threerivers layer at frame 9 (Figure 8-65). This keyframe setting shows the image during the slide show presentation.

FIGURE 8-65

14

- **Click the threerivers timeline at frame 11 in the Timelines panel, right-click, and then click Add Keyframe.**
- **Click the Visibility column in the threerivers layer in the Layers panel until the closed-eye icon is displayed.**

A keyframe is added to the threerivers layer at frame 11 (Figure 8-66). This keyframe setting hides the image during the slide show presentation.

FIGURE 8-66

15

• **Click the poncedeleon timeline at frame 11 in the Timelines panel, right-click, and then click Add Keyframe.**

• **Click the Visibility column in the poncedeleon layer in the Layers panel until the open-eye icon is displayed.**

A keyframe is added to the poncedeleon layer at frame 11 (Figure 8-67). This keyframe setting shows the image during the slide show presentation.

FIGURE 8-67

16

• **Click the poncedeleon timeline at frame 13 in the Timelines panel.**

• **If necessary, click the Visibility column in the poncedeleon layer in the Layers panel until the closed-eye icon is displayed.**

This keyframe setting hides the image during the slide show presentation (Figure 8-68). The closed-eye icon is displayed for all six layers at this point.

FIGURE 8-68

17

• **Click the keyframe in frame 13 in the biglagoon timeline in the Timelines panel.**

• **Click the Visibility column in the biglagoon layer in the Layers panel until the open-eye icon is displayed.**

The visibility setting is added to keyframe 13 of the biglagoon layer (Figure 8-69). This keyframe setting redisplays the first image at the end of the slide show presentation so the viewer is not left with a blank screen.

FIGURE 8-69

18

• **Click the Autoplay check box in the Timelines panel. If a Dreamweaver dialog box is displayed, read the information and then click the OK button.**

• **Click the Save button on the Standard toolbar.**

• **Press the F12 key to view the presentation in your browser.**

The presentation cycles through quickly. It ends with the first image, Big Lagoon (Figure 8-70).

FIGURE 8-70

19

• **Close the browser window and return to Dreamweaver.**

Other Ways

1. Click a frame, on Modify menu point to Timeline, click Add Keyframe on Timeline submenu

Using Behaviors to Pause the Slides

The next step is to add a pause between each slide. Adding a pause stops the timeline from playing. Adding pauses between slides is accomplished through the Timelines panel behaviors channel. Simply click the desired frame number in the behaviors channel and apply the Stop Timeline behavior. The Stop Timeline behavior is added to even-numbered frames for this timeline. The Play Timeline behavior is added through the Forward button. You add the Forward button later in this project. The following steps show how to add the pauses.

To Use Behaviors to Pause between Slides

1

• **Press SHIFT+F4 to display the Behaviors panel. If necessary, collapse the Files panel.**

• **Click frame 2 in the behaviors channel in the Timelines panel.**

The Behaviors panel is displayed, and frame 2 in the behaviors channel is highlighted (Figure 8-71).

FIGURE 8-71

2

• **Click the Add behavior (+) button in the Behaviors panel, point to Timeline, and then point to Stop Timeline.**

The Add behavior pop-up menu is displayed (Figure 8-72).

FIGURE 8-72

3

• **Click Stop Timeline. In the Stop Timeline dialog box, click the Stop Timeline box arrow, click slideshow, and then click the OK button.**

The Stop Timeline behavior is added to frame 2 in the behaviors channel. The event and action are displayed in the Behaviors panel (Figure 8-73).

FIGURE 8-73

4

• **Click frame 4 in the behaviors channel. Click the Add behavior (+) button in the Behaviors panel, point to Timeline, and then click Stop Timeline.**

• **Click the Stop Timeline box arrow, click slideshow, and then click the OK button.**

The Stop Timeline behavior is added to frame 4 in the behaviors channel. The event and action are displayed in the Behaviors panel for frame 4 (Figure 8-74).

FIGURE 8-74

5

• **Repeat Step 4 to add the Stop Timeline behavior to frames 6, 8, 10, and 12 in the Timelines panel behaviors channel.**

The Stop Timeline behavior is added to frames 6, 8, 10, and 12 (Figure 8-75).

FIGURE 8-75

Previewing a Timeline in the Timelines Panel

After creating a timeline, you can preview it in Dreamweaver by using the Timelines panel playback options (see page DW 605). Recall that the Rewind button moves the playback head to the first frame in the timeline. The Back button moves the playback head one frame to the left. Clicking the Back button and holding down the mouse button plays the timeline backward. The Play/Forward button moves the playback head one frame to the right. Clicking the Play/Forward button and holding down the mouse button plays the timeline forward. The following step illustrates how to preview your timeline in Dreamweaver.

To Preview a Timeline in the Timelines Panel

1 In the Timelines panel, click the Rewind button to move the playback head to the first frame. Click the Play/Forward button in the Timelines panel. As you click forward to each frame, verify in the Layers panel that the eye icon is appropriately closed or opened for each of the layers and that the minus sign displays for the Stop Timeline action in the correct frames.

Adding a Play Button

To provide the Web site visitor with the ability to control the slide show requires that a Play button be added to the Web page. Clicking the button the first time starts the image sequence. Clicking the button again advances the sequence to the next image. Adding a Play button requires that a layer be added to the Web page and that the button be contained within the layer. The following steps show how to add the layer and then add the Play button.

To Add a Play Button

1

• **Click the Loop check box in the Timelines panel. If necessary, click the OK button in the Dreamweaver dialog box.**

• **Click frame 1 on the animation bar. Close the Timelines panel.**

• **Click to the right of the poncedeleon layer-code marker.**

• **Click Insert on the menu bar, point to Layout Objects, and then click Layer.**

A layer is added and displays (Figure 8-76).

Q: How are animations created within Dreamweaver?

A: Dreamweaver uses JavaScript to create animations. Behaviors place JavaScript code in documents to allow visitors to interact with a Web page to change the page in various ways, or to cause certain tasks to be performed.

FIGURE 8-76

2

• **Double-click the Files panel title bar. Drag the forward.gif image onto the layer.**

• **Press CTRL+F3 to display the Property inspector.**

• **If necessary, display the Layers panel. Select the layer. Name the layer forward, and set L at 350 and T at 400.**

• **Click the Visibility column for the forward layer in the Layers panel until the open-eye icon is displayed.**

• **Press CTRL+F3 to hide the Property inspector and then scroll down to view the layer and image.**

The layer with the forward.gif image is placed on the Web page at the designated location and is selected (Figure 8-77).

FIGURE 8-77

3

• **Resize the layer to fit the image.**

• **Double-click the Tag Inspector panel title bar to display the Behaviors panel.**

• **Click the image within the forward layer, click the Add behavior (+) button in the Behaviors panel, point to Timeline, and then click Play Timeline.**

• **Click the OK button in the Play Timeline dialog box.**

The forward layer is resized to fit the image, and the onLoad event and Play Timeline action are added to the Behaviors panel (Figure 8-78).

FIGURE 8-78

Change Behavior from onLoad to onClick

The default setting for the Forward button behavior is onLoad. Earlier in this project, you changed the Forward button action for the motortour animation to onClick. The following steps illustrate how to change the Forward button action to onClick for the slideshow animation.

To Change from onLoad to onClick

1 Click to the right of onLoad in the Behaviors panel.

2 Click the pop-up menu arrow that displays to the right of onLoad.

3 If necessary, scroll up and then point to <A> onClick (Figure 8-79).

4 Click the onClick command.

5 Save your file and then press the F12 key to view the slide show.

6 Click the Forward button to advance from slide to slide.

The onClick action is highlighted as shown in Step 3 (Figure 8-79).

Behaviors

Use Dreamweaver's Show-Hide Layers and Drag Layer behaviors to create interactive events or games. For more information about Dreamweaver behaviors, visit the Dreamweaver MX 2004 More About Web page (scsite.com/dreamweavermx04/more.htm) and then click Behaviors.

More About

FIGURE 8-79

Next, you add a link from the motortour page and from the slide show page to the Florida State Parks page. The steps on the next page show how to add the first link, from the slide show page to the Florida State Parks page.

To Add a Link from the Slideshow.htm Page to the State_Parks.htm Page

1 Display the Property inspector.

2 Click to the right of the forward layer-code marker.

3 Press the ENTER key 10 times, type Florida State Parks as the link text, and then select the text you just typed.

4 Double-click the Files panel title bar and then click the Files tab.

5 Drag the state_parks.htm file to the Link box and then press the ENTER key (Figure 8-80).

6 Save the slideshow.htm page.

7 Press the F12 key and then check the link to verify that it works.

8 Close the browser to return to Dreamweaver and then close the slideshow.htm page.

The link is added to the Florida State Parks page as shown in Step 5 (Figure 8-80).

FIGURE 8-80

The following steps show how to add a link from the motortour page to the Florida State Parks page.

To Add a Link from the Tour.htm Page to the State_Parks.htm Page

1 Open the tour.htm page.

2 Scroll to the bottom of the Document window and then click to the right of the second layer marker.

3 Press the ENTER key two times, type Florida State Parks as the link text, and then select the text you just typed.

4 Drag the state_parks.htm file to the Link box and then press the ENTER key (Figure 8-81).

5 Save the tour.htm page.

6 Press the F12 key and then check the link to verify that it works.

7 Close the browser to return to Dreamweaver and then close the tour.htm page.

The link is added to the Florida State Parks page, as shown in Step 4 (Figure 8-81).

FIGURE 8-81

Linking to the Tour and Slide Show Pages

To add the two new pages to the Florida Parks Web site, a link is created from the Florida State Parks page to the two new pages, tour.htm and slideshow.htm. The steps on the next page show how to create the links.

To Add Links from the State_Parks.htm Web Page

1 **Open the state_parks.htm page.**

2 **Scroll to the bottom of the page, click to the right of the link, Popular state parks, press the END key, and then press SHIFT+ENTER.**

3 **Type** Florida Parks Slide Show **as the entry, press the END key, and then press SHIFT+ENTER.**

4 **Type** Northwest Florida Tour **as the entry.**

5 **Select the text, Florida Parks Slide Show, and then drag the slideshow.htm file from the Files panel to the Property inspector Link text box.**

6 **Select the text, Northwest Florida Tour, and then drag the tour.htm file from the Files panel to the Property inspector Link text box (Figure 8-82).**

7 **Save the state_parks.htm page and then press the F12 key. Test the links and then close the browser.**

Links are added to the two new Web pages, as shown in Step 6 (Figure 8-82).

FIGURE 8-82

Quitting Dreamweaver

After you have created your animated Web pages containing a slide show and a tour of northwest Florida, and tested and verified that the animations and links work, Project 8 is complete. The following step shows how to close the Web site, quit Dreamweaver MX 2004, and return control to Windows.

To Close the Web Site and Quit Dreamweaver

1 **Click the Close button on the upper-right corner of the Dreamweaver title bar.**

The Dreamweaver window, the Document window, and the Florida Parks Web site all close. If you have unsaved changes, Dreamweaver will prompt you to save the changes. Clicking the Yes button in the Dreamweaver MX 2004 dialog box saves the changes.

Project Summary

Project 8 introduced you to animation using Dreamweaver's Timelines panel. You created two animations: the first one a tour of northwest Florida parks and the second a slide show depicting images of some of the parks located in northwest Florida. Next, you added behaviors to start and stop the animations and events to show and hide objects. You then added a Play button to both pages to provide the Web site visitor with user control.

What You Should Know

Having completed this project, you now should be able to perform the tasks below. The tasks are listed in the same order they were presented in the project. For a list of keyboard commands for topics introduced in this project, see the Quick Reference for Windows at the back of this book and refer to the Shortcut column.

1. Copy Data Files to the Florida Parks Web Site (DW 598)
2. Start Dreamweaver and Open the Florida Parks Web Site (DW 599)
3. Add the NW Florida Map Image and Layer (DW 600)
4. Create a Nonlinear Animation (DW 606)
5. Add the Stop Timeline Behavior (DW 612)
6. Add a Forward Button (DW 617)
7. Add the First Layer and Image (DW 621)
8. Add the Next Five Layers and Images (DW 625)
9. Display and Name the Timeline (DW 627)
10. Add the Layers to the Timeline (DW 628)
11. Adjust the Number of Keyframes (DW 631)
12. Add Keyframes to Show and Hide Layers (DW 633)
13. Use Behaviors to Pause between Slides (DW 642)
14. Preview a Timeline in the Timelines Panel (DW 645)
15. Add a Play Button (DW 645)
16. Change from onLoad to onClick (DW 647)
17. Add a Link from the Slideshow.htm Page to the State_Parks.htm Page (DW 648)
18. Add a Link from the Tour.htm Page to the State_Parks.htm Page (DW 649)
19. Add Links from the State_Parks.htm Web Page (DW 650)
20. Close the Web Site and Quit Dreamweaver (DW 651)

Learn It Online

Instructions: To complete the Learn It Online exercises, start your browser, click the Address bar, and then enter the Web address scsite.com/dreamweavermx2004/learn. When the Dreamweaver MX 2004 Learn It Online page is displayed, follow the instructions in the exercises below. Each exercise has instructions for printing your results, either for your own records or for submission to your instructor.

1 Project Reinforcement TF, MC, and SA

Below Dreamweaver Project 8, click the Project Reinforcement link. Print the quiz by clicking Print on the File menu for each page. Answer each question.

Flash Cards

Below Dreamweaver Project 8, click the Flash Cards link and read the instructions. Type 20 (or a number specified by your instructor) in the Number of playing cards text box, type your name in the Enter your Name text box, and then click the Flip Card button. When the flash card is displayed, read the question and then click the ANSWER box arrow to select an answer. Flip through Flash Cards. If your score is 15 (75%) correct or greater, click Print on the File menu to print your results. If your score is less than 15 (75%) correct, then redo this exercise by clicking the Replay button.

3 Practice Test

Below Dreamweaver Project 8, click the Practice Test link. Answer each question, enter your first and last name at the bottom of the page, and then click the Grade Test button. When the graded practice test is displayed on your screen, click Print on the File menu to print a hard copy. Continue to take practice tests until you score 80% or better.

4 Who Wants To Be a Computer Genius?

Below Dreamweaver Project 8, click the Computer Genius link. Read the instructions, enter your first and last name at the bottom of the page, and then click the PLAY button. When your score is displayed, click the PRINT RESULTS link to print a hard copy.

5 Wheel of Terms

Below Dreamweaver Project 8, click the Wheel of Terms link. Read the instructions, and then enter your first and last name and your school name. Click the PLAY button. When your score is displayed, right-click the score and then click Print on the shortcut menu to print a hard copy.

6 Crossword Puzzle Challenge

Below Dreamweaver Project 8, click the Crossword Puzzle Challenge link. Read the instructions, and then enter your first and last name. Click the SUBMIT button. Work the crossword puzzle. When you are finished, click the Submit button. When the crossword puzzle is redisplayed, click the Print Puzzle button to print a hard copy.

7 Tips and Tricks

Below Dreamweaver Project 8, click the Tips and Tricks link. Click a topic that pertains to Project 8. Right-click the information and then click Print on the shortcut menu. Construct a brief example of what the information relates to in Dreamweaver to confirm you understand how to use the tip or trick.

8 Newsgroups

Below Dreamweaver Project 8, click the Newsgroups link. Click a topic that pertains to Project 8. Print three comments.

9 Expanding Your Horizons

Below Dreamweaver Project 8, click the Expanding Your Horizons link. Click a topic that pertains to Project 8. Print the information. Construct a brief example of what the information relates to in Dreamweaver to confirm you understand the contents of the article.

10 Search Sleuth

Below Dreamweaver Project 8, click the Search Sleuth link. To search for a term that pertains to this project, select a term below the Project 8 title and then use the Google search engine at google.com (or any major search engine) to display and print two Web pages that present information on the term.

Apply Your Knowledge

1 Creating a Slide Show for B & B Lawn Service

Instructions: Start Dreamweaver. If the panels display, press the F4 key to close all panels. See the inside back cover of this book for instructions for downloading the Data Disk or see your instructor for information on accessing the files in this book.

The proprietors of B & B Lawn Service Web site would like to add a slide show to their Web site that shows a variety of plants that they sell. To create this slide show, you copy six images from the DataFiles folder to the Lawn Service Web site images folder and one data file to the lawn folder. You begin the process by creating five layers and adding an image to each layer. When this is completed, you use the Timelines panel to add the start and stop timeline events. Next, you add a Start button. Finally, you add a link to and from the B & B Lawn Service index page. The first slide is shown in Figure 8-83. Software and hardware settings determine how a Web page is displayed in a browser. Your Web page may display differently than the one shown in Figure 8-83. Appendix C contains instructions for uploading your local site to a remote server.

FIGURE 8-83

(continued)

Creating a Slide Show for B & B Lawn Service *(continued)*

Table 8-3 Slide Data				
SLIDE IMAGE	LAYER ID	L	T	EYE ICON
slide02.gif	slide02	250	175	closed
slide03.gif	slide03	250	175	closed
slide04.gif	slide04	250	175	closed
slide05.gif	slide05	250	175	closed

1. Use the Windows My Computer option to copy the six images from the DataFiles lawn/images folder to your lawn/images folder and the data file to your lawn folder.
2. Start Dreamweaver. Select Lawn Service on the Files pop-up menu in the Files panel. Open the slideshow.htm file. Display the Property inspector, Standard toolbar, and panel groups.
3. Click below the introductory paragraph. Click Insert on the menu bar, point to Layout Objects, and then click Layer.
4. Drag the slide01.gif image onto the layer. Click the layer selection handle to select the layer and display the Layer Property inspector. Add the following attributes to the Property inspector: Layer ID slide01, L 250, and T 175.
5. Click the Visibility column for the slide01 layer in the Layers panel until the closed-eye icon is displayed.
6. Using the data in Table 8-3, repeat Steps 3 through 5 to add the next four layers to the Web page and to add images to the layers.
7. Click the Property inspector expand/collapse arrow to close the panel and then press ALT+F9 to display the Timelines panel. Select the text in the Timelines pop-up menu text box and then type flowers to name the timeline.
8. Drag the layer-code marker for the slide01 layer to animation channel 1 in the Timelines panel. Drag the layer-code marker for the slide02 layer to animation channel 2 and so on until all five layers have been added to the Timelines panel. If a Dreamweaver dialog box displays, read the information and then click the OK button.
9. Drag the keyframe at the end of each timeline to change the number of frames to 11.
10. Click keyframe 1 in the slide01 timeline in the Timelines panel and change the closed-eye icon in the Layers panel to the open-eye icon. Click the slide01 timeline at frame 3 in the Timelines panel and right-click to display the context menu. Select Add Keyframe and then click the Visibility column in the Layers panel to display the closed-eye icon.
11. Click the slide02 timeline at frame 3 in the Timelines panel. Right-click to display the context menu and then click Add Keyframe. Click the Visibility column in the Layers panel to display the open-eye icon. Click the slide02 timeline at frame 5 in the Timelines panel. Right-click to display the context menu and then click Add Keyframe. Click the Visibility column in the Layers panel to display the closed-eye icon.
12. Click the slide03 timeline at frame 5 in the Timelines panel. Right-click to display the context menu and then click Add Keyframe. Click the Visibility column in the Layers panel to display the open-eye icon. Click the slide03 timeline at frame 7 in the Timelines panel. Add a keyframe and then click the Visibility column in the Layers panel to display the closed-eye icon.
13. Click the slide04 timeline at frame 7 in the Timelines panel. Add a keyframe and then click the Visibility column in the Layers panel to display the open-eye icon. Click the slide04 timeline at frame 9 in the Timelines panel. Add a keyframe and then click the Visibility column in the Layers panel to display the closed-eye icon.

14. Click the slide05 timeline at frame 9 in the Timelines panel, and add a keyframe. Click the Visibility column in the Layers panel to display the open-eye icon. Click the slide05 timeline at frame 11 in the Timelines panel. Verify that the visibility column in the Layers panel displays the closed-eye icon.

15. Click the slide01 timeline at frame 11 in the Timelines panel. Click the Visibility column in the Layers panel to display the open-eye icon.

16. Use the playback options in the Timelines panel to play the animation in the Document window. Verify that the open and closed-eye icons are correct. When the animation is playing to verify the icons, only one open-eye icon should display and this should be the icon for the layer currently displayed. All other icons in the Layers panel Visibility column should be closed.

17. Press SHIFT+F4 to display the Behaviors panel.

18. Click frame 2 in the behaviors channel, click the Add behavior (+) button in the Behaviors panel, and then add the Stop Timeline behavior.

19. Repeat Step 18 and add the Stop Timeline behavior to frames 4, 6, 8, and 10 in the Timelines panel behaviors channel. Click the Autoplay check box and the Loop check box. Click frame 1 on the animation. Collapse the Timelines panel.

20. Insert another layer in the Document window. Drag the start_button.gif image to the layer and resize the layer around the image.

21. Expand the Property inspector. If necessary, select the layer and then add the following attributes: Layer ID start, L 350, and T 350.

22. Select the start_button.gif image within the layer and then click the Add behavior (+) button in the Behaviors panel. Apply the Play Timeline behavior.

23. Click to the right of onLoad in the Behaviors panel to display the pop-up menu arrow and then click the pop-up menu arrow. If necessary, scroll up and then click onClick. Save the Web page.

24. If necessary, scroll to the bottom of the page. Type Services as the link text and create a link to the services.htm page. Save the document. Press the F12 key to view the slide show in your browser. Click the Start button to move from slide to slide. Close the browser.

25. Open the services.htm page. Select the text, Landscaping, in the bulleted list, and then create a link to the slideshow.htm page. Save the services.htm page.

26. Press the F12 key to view the page in your browser. Click the landscaping link. Print a copy of the slideshow.htm page if instructed to do so. Upload the page to the lawn Web Site on a remote server if instructed to do so.

27. Quit Dreamweaver.

In the Lab

1 The CandleDust Web Site

Problem: Mary would like to add a Web page with some interactivity to the CandleDust Web site. She wants to advertise a sale for some of her special candles. You suggest a page with a nonlinear animation where the special for-sale candles are displayed one by one on the same page (Figure 8-84). The first candle appears in the upper left of the screen, below the heading; the second animates in from the upper right of the screen to the middle of the screen; and the third image animates in from the upper right to the right side of the screen. Mary likes this idea, and you agree to create the page. As you are completing this exercise, expand and collapse the panels as necessary. Because this is a freeform exercise, the placement on your screen is approximate. Appendix C contains instructions for uploading your local site to a remote server.

FIGURE 8-84

Instructions: Perform the following tasks:

1. Use the Windows My Computer option to copy the data file to your candle folder.
2. Start Dreamweaver. Display the panel groups and Standard toolbar. Select CandleDust on the Files pop-up menu in the Files panel. Open the candlesale.htm file.
3. Use the View menu to display the rulers. If necessary, move the insertion point to the left margin below the heading. Click the Insert menu and insert a layer. Drag the candle3.gif image onto the layer and then resize the layer to fit the image.

4. Display the Layers and Timelines panels. In the Timelines panel, name the timeline candlesale. Double-click Layer1 in the Layers panel and then rename the layer sale01. Click the layer-code marker and then drag it to frame 1, animation channel 1, in the Timelines panel. The candle will display in this location, so there is no need to drag it to create a nonlinear animation.

5. Use the Insert menu to add a second layer. This layer will be created on top of the first layer. Drag the candle4.gif image onto the layer. Resize the layer to fit the image. Double-click Layer1 in the Layers panel and then rename the layer sale02.

6. Verify that the playback head is in frame 1 in the Timelines panel. If necessary, select the layer and then right-click the selection handle. Click Record Path on the context menu and then, using the rulers as a guide, drag the layer and image downward about 100 pixels and to the right approximately 300 pixels. The timeline for the sale02 layer is displayed in animation channel 2 of the Timelines panel.

7. If necessary, move the playback head to frame 1. Insert a third layer and then drag the candle5.gif image onto the layer. Resize the layer to fit the image. Double-click Layer1 in the Layers panel and then rename the layer sale03.

8. If necessary, select the layer and then right-click the selection handle. Click Record Path on the context menu and then, using the rulers as a guide, drag the layer and image downward around 100 pixels and to the left approximately 500 pixels. The timeline for the sale03 layer is displayed in animation channel 3 in the Timelines panel.

9. Move the playback head to frame 1 and then click the keyframe for sale01. Click the Visibility column in the Layers panel until the open-eye icon displays. Click the keyframe in frame 1 for the sale02 layer and then click the Visibility column in the Layers panel until the closed-eye icon displays. Click the keyframe in frame 1 for the sale03 layer and then click the Visibility column in the Layers panel until the closed-eye icon displays. For frame 1, sale01 has an open-eye icon and sale02 and sale03 have closed-eye icons.

10. Click the ending keyframe for sale01. The frame number will be somewhere around 15. If necessary, click the Visibility column for sale01 until the open-eye icon is displayed. Click the same frame number (somewhere around 15) in the sale02 animation channel. Right-click to display the context menu and then click Add Keyframe. Click the Visibility column for sale02 until the open-eye icon is displayed.

11. Click the ending keyframe for sale02, and, if necessary, change the eye icon to an open-eye icon.

12. Click the same frame number (somewhere around 20) in the sale03 animation channel. Right-click to display the context menu and then click Add Keyframe. Click the Visibility column for sale03 until the open-eye icon is displayed. Click the ending keyframe for sale03, and, if necessary, change the eye icon to an open-eye icon. All three layers now should display open-eye icons. Click the Autoplay check box in the Timelines panel. Create a link to the Home page.

13. Press the F12 key to view the candlesale page in your browser. The candle02 layer should move down and across the page, followed by the candle03 layer. All three layers should be visible at the end of the animation.

14. Open the products.htm page. Scroll to the end of the page and then create a link following the Home link. Type Special Sale as the link text and link to the candlesale.htm page.

15. Press the F12 key to view the products.htm page in your browser. Verify that the links work. If necessary, close the browser and make any necessary adjustments to your animated Web page. Print a copy of the Web page if instructed to do so. Upload the page to the candle Web site on a remote server if instructed to do so.

In the Lab

2 Creating a Slide Show for the Credit Protection Web Site

Problem: Marcy recently gave a PowerPoint presentation on stock market investing. She has received several requests asking for a copy of her presentation. To accommodate the requests, she would like to add this presentation to the Web site. Marcy saved each slide as a JPEG image and has asked if you can create a Web page with the slide show images. You assure her you can create the slide show. The first screen is shown in Figure 8-85. As you are completing this exercise, expand and collapse the panels as necessary. Appendix C contains instructions for uploading your local site to a remote server.

FIGURE 8-85

Table 8-4 Slide Data				
SLIDE IMAGE	LAYER ID	L	T	EYE ICON
slide2.jpg	stock02	150	80	closed
slide3.jpg	stock03	150	80	closed
slide4.jpg	stock04	150	80	closed

Instructions: Perform the following tasks:

1. Use the Windows My Computer option to copy the data file and images to your credit folder.

In the Lab

2. Start Dreamweaver. Display the panel groups and Standard toolbar. Select Credit Protection on the Files pop-up menu in the Files panel. Open the credit_slides.htm file.

3. If necessary, move the insertion point to the left margin below the heading. Insert a layer. Drag the slide1.jpg image onto the layer.

4. Click Layer1 in the Layers panel to select the layer. Click the Visibility column in the Layers panel until the closed-eye icon is displayed. In the Layer Property inspector, add stock01 as the Layer ID, and set L to 150 and T to 80. Click the layer-code marker and drag it to frame 1, animation channel 1, in the Timelines panel. Name the timeline stockmarket.

5. Insert three more layers. Use the data in Table 8-4 to create the layers and to add the images for each layer.

6. Drag the layer-code marker for the slide2 layer to animation channel 2, the layer-code marker for the slide3 layer to animation channel 3, and the layer-code marker for the slide4 layer to animation channel 4.

7. Drag the keyframe at the end of each timeline to change the number of frames to 9.

8. Click keyframe 1 in the stock01 animation channel of the Timelines panel and then change the eye icon in the Layers panel to the open eye. The closed-eye icon should be displayed in the Layers panel for the other three layers.

9. Click the stock01 animation channel at frame 3. Add a keyframe and then change the eye icon in the Layers panel to the closed eye.

10. Click the stock02 animation channel at frame 3. Add a keyframe and then, if necessary, change the eye icon in the Layers panel to the open eye.

11. Click the stock02 animation channel at frame 5. Add a keyframe and then change the eye icon in the Layers panel to the closed eye.

12. Click the stock03 animation channel at frame 5. Add a keyframe and then change the eye icon in the Layers panel to the open eye. Click the stock03 animation channel at frame 7. Add a keyframe and then change the eye icon in the Layers panel to the closed eye.

13. Click the stock04 animation channel at frame 7. Add a keyframe and then change the eye icon in the Layers panel to the open eye. Click the stock04 animation channel at its frame 9 and verify the eye icon in the Layers panel is closed.

14. Click the stock01 animation channel at frame 9 and then change the eye icon in the Layers panel to the open eye.

15. Click frame 2 in the behaviors channel in the Timelines panel. Click the Add behavior (+) button in the behaviors channel and then add the Stop Timeline behavior.

16. Repeat Step 15 for frames 4, 6, and 8. Click frame 1 on the animation bar.

17. Create another layer and then drag the next.jpg image onto the layer. Resize the layer to fit the image. Set the following properties in the Layer Property inspector: Layer ID next, L 20, T 190. Select the image and then click the Add behavior (+) button in the Behaviors panel. Apply the Play Timeline command. Access Code view in the Document window, and then, if necessary, use the Find and Replace command to change the onLoad behavior to onClick.

18. Click the Autoplay and Loop check boxes. Save the credit_slides.htm file.

19. Open the saving.htm page. Scroll to the bottom of the page and click to the right of the Theft link. Add a vertical line and then a link to the credit_slides.htm page. Type Stock Market Simulation as the linked text. Save the document. Press the F12 key to view the page in your browser. Click the link to display the slide show page. Click the Next button and review the slide show. Print a copy of the Web page if instructed to do so. Upload the page to the credit Web site on a remote server if instructed to do so.

In the Lab

3 Creating an Animation Page for the Plant City Web Site

Problem: Juan wants to add some animation to the Plant City Web site. You suggest to Juan that an animated map through the city and around the outlying areas would enhance the overall site. Juan likes your ideas, and you are ready to get started. As you are completing this exercise, expand and collapse the panels as necessary. The Web page with the map is shown in Figure 8-86. Appendix C contains instructions for uploading your local site to a remote server.

FIGURE 8-86

Instructions: Perform the following tasks:

1. Use the Windows My Computer option to copy the data file and images to your city folder.
2. Start Dreamweaver. Display the panel groups and Standard toolbar. Select Plant City on the Files pop-up menu in the Files panel.
3. Open the tour.htm page. Insert a layer and then drag the map.gif image onto the layer. Select the layer and apply the following properties in the Layer Property inspector: Layer ID map, L 175, T 75.
4. Insert a second layer and then drag the bus.gif image onto the new layer. Resize the layer to accommodate the size of the bus.gif. image. Double-click Layer1 in the Layers panel and then name the layer bus. Drag the bus layer onto the map and place the bus.gif image near the top and to the left of Shilow. Right-click the bus layer and then click Record Path on the context menu.

In the Lab

5. Drag the bus.gif image down and to the left to Highway 92 and then down to Turkey Creek. From Turkey Creek, drag to the right to Beatty's Corner and then to Trapnell. Drag up to Plant City and Baker Street, to the right to Youmans, up to Mount Enon, and then back to Shilow.

6. Name the timeline tour and then add Stop Timeline behaviors at frames near Turkey Creek, Trapnell, Plant City, Mount Enon, and Shilow.

7. Insert another layer. Drag the go.gif button onto the layer and resize the layer to accommodate the image size. Apply the following properties to the layer: Layer ID go, L 85, T 170. Click the image, click the Add behavior (+) button in the Behaviors panel, and then apply the onMouseOver Play Timeline event and action.

8. Click the Loop check box. Save the tour.htm page.

9. Open the index.htm page. Scroll to the bottom and then add a link to the tour.htm page following the Employment link. Type City Tour as the linked text.

10. Press the F12 key to view the tour.htm page in your browser. Move the mouse pointer over the go.gif image to play the animation. Print a copy of the Web page if instructed to do so. Upload the page to the city Web site on a remote server if instructed to do so.

Cases and Places

The difficulty of these case studies varies:
■ are the least difficult and ■■ are the most difficult. The last exercise is a group exercise.

1 ■ Your sports Web site is receiving more hits each day. You decide to add a slide show page highlighting some of the more popular players. Add a background image to the page and then add a title to the page. Insert three layers and then add images to the layers. Use the Timelines panel and Autoplay to create the slide show. Create a link to and from the home page. Save the page in your sports Web site. For a selection of images and backgrounds, visit the Dreamweaver MX Media Web page (scsite.com/dreamweavermx/media) and then click Media below Project 8.

2 ■ You would like to add some interactivity to your hobby Web site. You decide to do this by adding an animation. First, add a background image to the page and then add an appropriate title. Insert four layers and four images. All four images should be the same size. Create a Forward button to advance the slide show from slide to slide. Create a link to and from your home page. Upload the page to a remote site if instructed to do so. For a selection of images and backgrounds, visit the Dreamweaver MX Media Web page (scsite.com/dreamweavermx/media) and then click Media below Project 8.

3 ■■ Add a new page to your music hobby Web site and then add a background to the page. Add a large image that contains images of five musical instruments, musicians, or other applicable musical features. Add a layer and an image that will move from instrument to instrument (or other musical feature). Use Dreamweaver's Record Path command to move the image from instrument to instrument using the Timelines Autoplay feature. Create a link to and from your home page. Upload the page to a remote site. For a selection of images and backgrounds, visit the Dreamweaver MX Media Web page (scsite.com/dreamweavermx/media) and then click Media below Project 8.

4 ■■ Your campaign for political office is doing terrific. Create a new Web page and name it campaign_trail. Add an appropriate background. Next, add a map image showing locations you have visited recently. Add a layer and then add your picture to the layer. Click Dreamweaver's Record Path command and then drag the layer from location to location. Add a Forward button. Add Play Timeline and Stop Timeline behaviors where appropriate. Create a link to and from your index page. Upload the revised Web site to a remote server. For a selection of images and backgrounds, visit the Dreamweaver MX Media Web page (scsite.com/dreamweavermx/media) and then click Media below Project 8.

5 ■■ **Working Together** Recently, the student government officers selected three possible vacation sites to visit. Working with your team, create three slide shows displaying two images from each of these vacation sites. All images should be the same size. Use the T and L properties within the Layer Property inspector to center the layers. Add Stop Timeline and Play Timeline behaviors where appropriate. Add another layer with a Forward button. Create a link to and from the index page. Display the three slide shows and determine which one best suits the needs of your team. Upload the selected slide show to a remote server. For a selection of images and backgrounds, visit the Dreamweaver MX Media Web page (scsite.com/dreamweavermx/media) and then click Media below Project 8.

Media Objects

PROJECT

CASE PERSPECTIVE

After visiting other Web sites for new ideas for the Florida Parks Web site, David Allen has found that many Web sites start with a splash page, which adds visual appeal and interest for visitors. Generally, splash pages contain videos, audio, and/or other media. This is an element that the Florida Parks Web site does not include. David asks how difficult it would be to add a splash page to the Web site. You explain to David that it would involve some technical issues, but that Dreamweaver provides the capability of easily adding these types of features.

David brings the team together to make the next determination: the content of the splash page. Joan suggests that some Flash text, a background sound, and a Flash movie be added and that the state_parks.htm page be modified to contain an embedded sound file and a video file. The video, titled Tracking Kids with GPS, focuses on using technology to keep track of children. This technology is especially useful in areas such as state and national parks.

With the addition of these media objects, the Web site culminates with the best features that Dreamweaver has to offer. David and Joan are grateful to you for your guidance and assistance, which have made the development of their site possible.

As you read through this project, you will learn about media and media objects. You also will learn how to insert Flash text and Flash movies into a Web page, how to add a background sound, and how to embed a sound. Additionally, you will learn how to insert video and Shockwave movies into a Web page and how to insert an applet. Finally, you will use the Dreamweaver Results panel to learn how to validate a Web page, check links, and check target browsers.

Media Objects

Objectives

You will have mastered the material in this project when you can:

- Describe media objects
- Insert Flash text into a Web page
- Insert a Flash movie into a Web page
- Add a background sound to a Web page
- Embed a sound file in a Web page
- Insert a video into a Web page
- Check for plug-ins
- Describe Shockwave and how to insert a Shockwave movie into a Web page
- Describe a Java applet and how to insert an applet into a Web page
- Use the Results panel to validate a Web page, check links, and check target browsers

Introduction

Media objects, also called **multimedia**, are files that can be displayed or executed within HTML documents or in a stand-alone fashion. Examples include graphics such as GIFs and JPEGs, video, audio, Flash objects (SWF), Shockwave objects (DIR or DCR), PDFs (Adobe's Portable Document Format), Java applets, and other objects that can be viewed through a browser using a helper application or using a plug-in. A **helper application** is a program such as the Flash player or Shockwave viewer. These two examples are Macromedia programs and are handled easily through Dreamweaver. A **plug-in** is a program application that is installed on your computer and used to view plug-in programs through the Web browser. Once a plug-in is installed, its functionality is integrated into the HTML file, and the Web browser generally recognizes the plug-in application.

Project Nine — Designing with Interactive Media

In this project, you learn how to add interactive media to a Web page. Interactive media, or multimedia, is not suitable for all Web sites. You most likely have visited Web sites that contained so many bits and pieces of multimedia that, instead of being a constructive part of the site, the multimedia elements were detrimental to the Web experience. Therefore, when adding this type of element to your Web page, you need to consider the value of each element and how it will enhance or detract from your site.

Consider the following guidelines for adding interactive media to your Web site:

- Use it for entertainment
- Assist Web site visitors with navigation
- Direct attention to certain elements
- Provide feedback
- Illustrate and/or demonstrate a particular element or part of the Web page

In Project 9, you learn how to add interactive media to the Florida Parks Web site. You add a splash page that will contain Flash text, a Flash movie, and a background sound. A **splash page** generally consists of a default home page that displays the Web site logo or some other Web site promotion. Many splash pages use various types of interactive media — from Flash movies to animated graphics — and are good mood setters. After one or two visits to the splash page, however, the frequent Web site visitor most likely would prefer to skip the page and move on to the main Web site. Therefore, a link is added that, when clicked, will take the visitor directly to the Web site's index page. The splash page with the link is shown in Figure 9-1a.

Next, you add an embedded sound and a video to the state_parks.htm page (Figure 9-1b on the next page). These two elements use the Windows Media Player as the helper application to display the media within the browser window.

Finally, you use the Results panel to validate a Web page, check links, and check target browsers.

FIGURE 9-1a

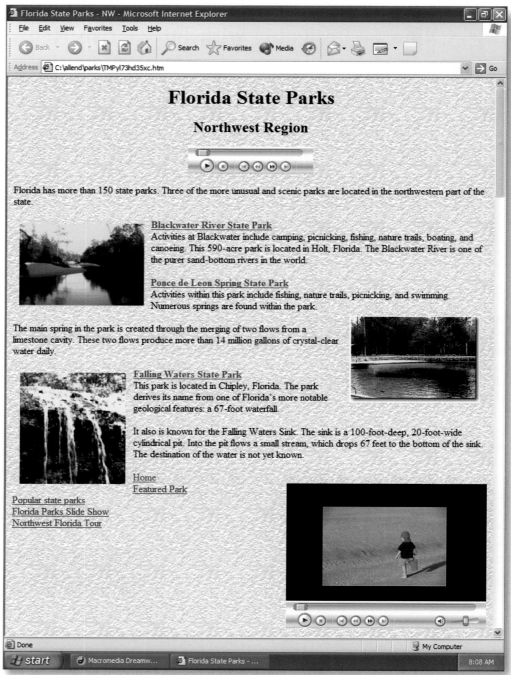

FIGURE 9-1b

Workspace Organization

Organization and preparation lead to a more productive work setting. Successful Web developers prepare their Dreamweaver workspace to provide an effective work environment. As you learn to use additional Dreamweaver tools, including multimedia elements, you will become even more proficient working in the Dreamweaver environment.

Copying Data Files to the Local Web Site

Your Data Disk contains data files and images for Project 9. You use the Windows My Computer option to copy the Project 9 files to your parks folder. See the inside back cover for instructions for downloading the Data Disk or see your instructor for information about accessing the files required for this book.

The DataFiles folder for this project is stored on Local Disk (C:). The location on your computer may be different. If necessary, verify with your instructor the location of the DataFiles folder. The following steps illustrate how to copy the files to the parks local root folder.

To Copy Data Files to the Florida Parks Web Site

1 Click the Start button on the Windows taskbar and then click My Computer.

2 Double-click Local Disk (C:) and then navigate to the location of the data files for Project 9.

3 Double-click the DataFiles folder, double-click the Proj09 folder, and then double-click the parks folder.

4 Right-click the media folder to display the context menu and then copy the media folder to the your name\parks folder using the Copy and Paste commands on the context menu.

5 Click the Back button and navigate to the DataFiles folder. Double-click the DataFiles folder and then double-click the Proj09 folder. Use the context menu to copy the splash.htm file.

6 Navigate to the your name/parks folder and use the context menu to paste the splash.htm file into the folder.

7 Close the My Computer window.

Starting Dreamweaver and Closing Open Panels

Each time you start Dreamweaver, it opens to the last site displayed when you closed the program. It, therefore, may be necessary for you to open the Florida Parks Web site. The **Files pop-up menu** in the Files panel lists sites you have defined. When you open a site, a list of the pages and subfolders within the site displays. The steps below illustrate how to start Dreamweaver and open the Florida Parks Web site.

To Start Dreamweaver and Open the Florida Parks Web Site

1 Click the Start button on the Windows taskbar.

2 Point to All Programs on the Start menu, point to Macromedia on the All Programs submenu, and then click Macromedia Dreamweaver MX 2004 on the Macromedia submenu.

3 If necessary, display the panel groups, and close the Property inspector.

4 Click the Files panel box arrow on the Files pop-up menu and then click Florida Parks.

5 Open the splash.htm page.

6 If necessary, press CTRL+F2 to display the Insert bar and then select the Common category.

Dreamweaver opens, the Florida Parks Web site hierarchy displays in the Files panel, and three tables display in the splash.htm page (Figure 9-2 on the next page).

FIGURE 9-2

Media Objects

Dreamweaver provides two methods to insert media objects: the Media pop-up menu on the Insert bar and the Insert menu. The Media pop-up menu, located on the Insert bar Common category, contains buttons for inserting these special configurable objects (Figure 9-3). You use the Insert bar to complete the steps in this project. Table 9-1 on the next page describes the buttons on the Media pop-up menu on the Insert bar. Recall from Project 1 that when you select an option from a pop-up menu in some categories, that option becomes the default action for the button. The icon displayed for the Media pop-up menu in Figure 9-2 is a default icon. After you select an option from this pop-up menu, the default Media pop-up icon is no longer is available.

FIGURE 9-3

Table 9-1 Commands on the Media Pop-Up Menu	
COMMAND NAME	**DESCRIPTION**
Flash	Places a Flash movie at the insertion point, using the <object> and <embed> tags. A dialog box is displayed in which you can browse to an SWF file. An SWF file is a compressed version of a Flash (.fla) file, and is optimized for viewing on the Web.
Flash Button	Places a Flash button at the insertion point; a Flash button allows a Flash movie to be inserted into the Web page.
Flash Text	Places a Flash Text button at the insertion point; a Flash Text button lets you create and insert a Flash movie that contains just text.
Shockwave	Places a Macromedia Shockwave movie at the insertion point, using the <object> and <embed> tags.
Applet	Places a Java applet at the insertion point. A dialog box is displayed in which you can specify the file that contains the applet's code, or click Cancel to leave the source unspecified. The Java applet is displayed only when the document is viewed in a browser.
param	Inserts a tag that allows you to pass parameters to an applet or object.
ActiveX	Places an ActiveX control at the insertion point. Use the Property inspector to specify a source file and other properties for the ActiveX control.
Plugin	Inserts a file at the insertion point, using an <embed> tag that requires a Netscape Navigator plug-in for playback. A dialog box is displayed in which you can specify the source file.

Macromedia Flash

Macromedia's Flash program is an excellent way to create and add animation and interactivity to a Web page. It is a collection of tools for animating and drawing graphics, adding sound, creating interactive elements, and playing movies. It quickly is becoming a standard for Web animation. Objects within Flash are created using vector graphics. Recall from Project 2 that mathematical formulas are used to describe vector images and produce relatively small file sizes. By contrast, GIF and JPEG graphics use **bitmap technology,** which includes data for every pixel within an object. Bitmap technology therefore produces large file sizes. Thus, vector images are a more efficient method of delivering graphics over the Internet because they are displayed faster on a downloading Web page.

Creating **Flash files** (also called Flash movies) requires that the developer use the Flash program. Learning to use this program and developing Flash movies can be time-consuming. A search of the Internet, however, produces many Web sites with free and/or nominally priced Flash animations that can be downloaded and added to your Dreamweaver Web page.

Most media objects require a helper program or plug-in before they can be displayed in the browser. For instance, the **Flash player** is required to view Flash files. Plug-ins are discussed in more detail later in this project. The Flash player is available as both a plug-in for Netscape Navigator and an ActiveX control for Microsoft Internet Explorer, and it is incorporated in the latest versions of Netscape Navigator, Microsoft Internet Explorer, and America Online. Macromedia also provides this player as a free download at the Macromedia Web site.

Flash Objects

Recall that Dreamweaver comes with two Flash objects you can use without having the Flash program. These two objects are Flash buttons and Flash text. In Project 7, you created a framed Web site and added Flash buttons to the navigation frame. In this project, you add Flash text. Also recall from Project 7 that an object created with the Flash program can generate three different files, as follows:

1. **Flash file (.fla)** This is the source file for any project and is created in the Flash program. To open a .fla file requires the Flash program. Using Flash, you then can export the .fla file as a .swf or .swt file that can be viewed in a browser.

2. **Flash movie file (.swf)** This is a compressed version of the Flash (.fla) file, and is optimized for viewing on the Web. This file can be played back in browsers and previewed in Dreamweaver, but cannot be edited in Flash. This is the type of file you create when using the Flash button and text objects in Dreamweaver.

3. **Flash template file (.swt)** This file type enables you to modify and replace information in a Flash movie file. Flash template files are used in the Flash button object.

Q&A

Q: What is an external editor?

A: You can associate each file type that Dreamweaver does not handle directly with one or more external editors found on your system. The editor that launches when you double-click the file in the Files panel is called the external, primary, editor. You can set which editor is associated with a particular file type in the File Types/Editors preferences.

Flash text is self-contained. Therefore, when creating Flash text, you can use fonts that are not necessarily installed on the Web site visitor's computer. In this project, the Comic Sans MS font is used to create the Flash text file. If this font is not available on your computer, use another one of your own choosing or as directed by your instructor.

Adding Flash Text

To begin creating your splash page, you open the splash.htm data file and then add Flash text. The page includes tables to facilitate page layout and to add borders to the Flash text object and other objects. The splash page contains three tables, each of which is identified with a table ID: table01, table02, and table03. The first table, table01, contains two rows, or two cells. You insert the Flash text into the table cells of table01. The steps below show how to add the Flash text.

To Add Flash Text

1

• Collapse the panel groups. Click the first cell in table01.

The splash.htm file contains three tables: table01, table02, and table03. The alignment for the first cell in table01 is left-aligned and the alignment for the second cell is right-aligned.

FIGURE 9-4

2

• **Click the Media pop-up button on the Insert bar and then point to Flash Text.**

The Flash Text command on the Media pop-up menu is highlighted (Figure 9-5).

FIGURE 9-5

3

• **Click Flash Text.**

The Insert Flash Text dialog box is displayed (Figure 9-6).

FIGURE 9-6

4

• **Click the Font box arrow, scroll down, and then click Comic Sans MS in the Font list. If the Comic Sans MS font is not available on your computer, select another one of your own choosing or as directed by your instructor.**

Comic Sans MS is selected in the Font box (Figure 9-7).

FIGURE 9-7

5

• **If necessary, double-click the Size text box and type** 30 **as the size.**

• **Double-click the Color hexadecimal text box, type** #FFFFFF **as the entry, and then press the TAB key.**

• **In the Rollover color hexadecimal text box, type** #99FF66 **and then press the TAB key. Type** Florida welcomes the world! **in the Text text box.**

6

• **Click the Bg color hexadecimal text box. Type** #000000 **and then press the TAB key.**

• **Type** media/heading01 **in the Save as text box.**

The attributes are added for the Flash text (Figure 9-8).

FIGURE 9-8

7

- **Click the OK button.**

- **Click the second cell in table01 and then click the Flash Text command on the Media pop-up menu.**

The heading01 is saved as a .swf file in the media subfolder. In the second cell of table01, the insertion point is right-aligned, and the Insert Flash Text dialog box is displayed (Figure 9-9).

FIGURE 9-9

8

- **Add the following attributes to the Insert Flash Text dialog box:**
Font: Comic Sans MS;
Size: 20; **Color:** #FFFFFF;
Rollover color: #99FF66;
Text: Visit a Florida park for a vacation of a lifetime!; **Bg color:** #000000; **and Save as:** media/heading02.

The attributes are added to the Insert Flash Text dialog box (Figure 9-10). Note that all of the text in the Text text box may not be visible at the same time.

FIGURE 9-10

9

• **Click the OK button.**

The Flash text is displayed (Figure 9-11).

FIGURE 9-11

Editing Flash Text

You edit Flash text through the Property inspector. If you click Flash text, the Flash Text Property inspector displays Flash attributes (Figure 9-12). The following section describes the Flash Text Property inspector.

FIGURE 9-12

FLASH TEXT NAME The **Flash Text name** is an identifier used to identify the Flash text object for scripting.

W AND H The **W** and **H** boxes indicate the width and height of the object in pixels. You can specify the size in the following units: pc (picas), pt (points), in (inches), mm (millimeters), cm (centimeters), or % (percentage of the parent object's value). The abbreviations must follow the value without a space (for example, 3mm).

FILE The **File** text box allows you to include a file name that specifies the path to the Flash object file. Click the Browse for File icon to browse to a file, or type a path name in the File text box.

EDIT The **Edit** button opens the Flash object dialog box for edits to the selected Flash object. If Flash is not installed on your computer, this button is disabled.

RESET SIZE The **Reset size** button returns the selected object to its original size.

V SPACE AND H SPACE The values entered into the **V space** and **H space** boxes add space, in pixels, along the sides of the object. V space adds space along the top and bottom of the object. H space adds space along the left and right of the object.

QUALITY **Quality** controls antialiasing during playback of the movie. A movie looks better with a Quality setting of High, but that requires a faster processor to render it correctly on the screen. Low emphasizes speed over appearance, whereas High favors appearance over speed. Auto Low emphasizes speed at first, but improves appearance when possible. Auto High emphasizes both qualities at first, but sacrifices appearance for speed if necessary.

SCALE **Scale** determines how the object fits into the dimensions set in the W and H fields. The Default setting displays the entire object. The other options are No border and Exact fit. No border fits the object into the set dimensions so no borders show and so the original aspect ratio is maintained. Exact fit scales the object to the set dimensions, regardless of the aspect ratio.

ALIGN **Align** sets the alignment of the object in relation to other elements on the page.

BG **Bg** specifies a background color for the text area.

PARAMETERS The **Parameters** button opens a dialog box for entering additional parameters to pass to the object. The object must have been designed to receive these additional parameters.

PLAY/STOP The **Play** button plays the object in the Document window. Click the **Stop** button to stop the object from playing. This toggle button is used primarily for Flash or Shockwave movies.

CLASS Used for scripting with cascading style sheets.

Flash Movies

The earliest Web pages were plain, consisting mostly of text with links on a gray or white background. Eventually, typefaces changed, and colors and static images were added. In 1997, Macromedia purchased a software program known as FutureSplash and changed the name to Flash. Flash is a multimedia program developed especially for the Internet and the World Wide Web, and it has changed the look of and added interactivity to Web pages. Today, it is a popular program for creating movies, Web graphics, and other multimedia elements.

Adding a Flash Movie

Dreamweaver makes it easy to insert a Flash movie into a Web page. Simply position the insertion point in the Document window at the location where you would like the movie to display. Then click the Flash button on the Media pop-up menu and select the file name. Flash movies end with .swf extensions. When you insert a movie, Dreamweaver adds the code for the movie. After the movie is inserted into the Document window, a gray rectangle is displayed on the page. This rectangle represents the width and height of the movie. The width and height are determined when the developer creates the movie. The Flash logo is displayed in the center of the gray rectangle.

When a Flash movie is inserted and selected, Dreamweaver displays the Flash Property inspector. Most of the properties for a Flash movie are identical to those for Flash text (described earlier in this project). The following section describes the Flash movie Property inspector properties that are different from those for Flash text (Figure 9-13).

FIGURE 9-13

FLASH MOVIE NAME   The **Flash movie name** is an identifier used to identify the Flash movie object for scripting.

LOOP   When the **Loop** check box is checked, the movie plays continuously; when unchecked, the movie plays once and stops.

AUTOPLAY   When the **Autoplay** check box is checked, the movie plays automatically when the page loads.

BG   **Bg** specifies a background color for the movie area. This color also appears while the movie is not playing (while loading and after playing).

To Add a Flash Movie

1

• **If necessary, scroll down and then click in table02.**

The insertion point is blinking in the center of table02 (Figure 9-14).

FIGURE 9-14

2

• **Display the panel groups and then click the Assets tab. Click the Flash icon and then drag globe.swf to table02.**

The Flash movie is inserted into the table (Figure 9-15).

FIGURE 9-15

3

• **Hide the panel groups and then display the Property inspector.**

• **Click the Flash box in the Property inspector and then type** globe **as the movie name.**

The movie name, globe, appears in the Flash File ID box in the Property inspector (Figure 9-16).

FIGURE 9-16

4

• **Click the Play button in the Property inspector.**

The movie plays in the Document window (Figure 9-17). Notice that the Play button is a toggle button, and as soon as you clicked it, the button became labeled Stop.

5

• **Click the Stop button in the Property inspector.**

The movie stops playing.

FIGURE 9-17

Other Ways

1. On Insert menu point to Media, click Flash
2. Press CTRL+ALT+F

Adding a Link to Go to the Index Page

A splash page adds interest to a Web site, but may annoy frequent visitors. It is always best, therefore, to provide a link for the visitor to go directly to the index and/or home page. The following steps add a link in table03 to the index page.

To Add a Link to Go to the Index Page

1

• **Scroll up in the Document window and then click in table03.**

The insertion point is blinking in the center of table03 (Figure 9-18).

FIGURE 9-18

2

• **Type** Skip Intro **and then select the text.**

The text, Skip Intro, is displayed and selected in table03 (Figure 9-19).

FIGURE 9-19

3

• **Display the panel groups and then click the Files tab. If necessary, scroll down in the Files panel and then drag index.htm to the Link box in the Property inspector. Press the ENTER key.**

The link to the index.htm Web page is added (Figure 9-20).

4

• **Click the Save button on the Standard toolbar and then press the F12 key to view the page in your browser.**

• **Move the mouse pointer over the text in table01 to view the text color change.**

• **Click the link to verify that it works.**

• **Close the browser and return to Dreamweaver.**

FIGURE 9-20

More About

Adding Sound

Some factors to consider before deciding on a format and method for adding sound are the sound's purpose, your audience, the file size, the sound quality you want, and the differences between browsers. For more information about Dreamweaver and adding sound, visit the Dreamweaver MX 2004 More About Web page (scsite.com/dreamweavermx04/more.htm) and then click Adding Sound.

Audio on the Web Page

Adding sound to your Web page can add interest and set a mood. Background music can enhance your theme. Attaching sounds to objects, such as the sound of clicking buttons, can provide valuable feedback to the Web site visitor. Sound, however, can be expensive in terms of the Web site size and download time, particularly for those visitors with baseband access. Another consideration is that adding sound to a Web page can be a challenging and confusing task. Most computers today have some type of sound card and some type of sound-capable plug-in that works with their browser. The difficult part, though, is generating the desirable sounds. As you work with sound, you will discover that the Web supports several popular sound file formats, along with their supporting plug-ins; a standard format does not exist. The trick is to find the one most widely used. Table 9-2 on the next page contains a list and description of the commonly used sound file formats.

Table 9-2 Sound File Formats	
FILE NAME EXTENSION	**DESCRIPTION**
.aif (Audio Interchange File Format, or AIFF)	The AIFF format can be played by most browsers and does not require a plug-in; you also can record AIFF files from a CD, tape, microphone, and so on. The large file size, however, limits the length of sound clips that you can use on your Web pages.
.midi or .mid (Musical Instrument Digital Interface, or MIDI)	The MIDI format is for instrumental music. MIDI files are supported by many browsers and do not require a plug-in. The sound quality is good, but it can vary depending on a visitor's sound card. A small MIDI file can provide a long sound clip. MIDI files cannot be recorded and must be synthesized on a computer with special hardware and software.
.mp3 (Motion Picture Experts Group Audio, or MPEG-Audio Layer-3, or MP3)	The MP3 format is a compressed format that allows for substantially smaller sound files, yet the sound quality is very good. You can stream the file so a visitor does not have to wait for the entire file to download before hearing it. To play MP3 files, visitors must download and install a helper application or plug-in such as QuickTime, Windows Media Player, or RealPlayer.
.ra, .ram, .rpm (RealAudio)	The RealAudio format has a very high degree of compression, with smaller file sizes than the MP3 format. Whole song files can be downloaded in a reasonable amount of time. The files also can be streamed, so visitors can begin listening to the sound before the file has been downloaded completely. The sound quality is poorer than that of MP3 files. Visitors must download and install the RealPlayer helper application or plug-in to play these files.
.wav (Waveform Extension, or WAV)	WAV-formatted files have good sound quality, are supported by many browsers, and do not require a plug-in. The large file size, however, severely limits the length of sound clips that you can use on your Web pages.

ActiveX versus Plug-ins

A Web browser basically is an HTML decoder. Recall that a plug-in is a program that is used to view plug-in applications through the Web browser. A plug-in adds functionality to the browser — it is not a stand-alone program and cannot start and run on its own. To work correctly, plug-in programs must be present in the browser's Plugins folder. Both Internet Explorer and Netscape include Plugins folders within their own application folders. When the browser encounters a file with an extension of .swf, for example, it looks for and attempts to start the Flash player plug-in.

Several years ago, Netscape developed the capability of incorporating plug-ins within the browser by creating the nonstandard HTML tag, <embed>. This tag never was made part of the W3C's official HTML specifications, but it became widely used.

Some of the more popular plug-ins are Adobe's Acrobat Reader, RealAudio and RealVideo, Apple's QuickTime, Macromedia's Flash and Shockwave, and VRML (Virtual Reality Modeling Language). Using these plug-ins, Web site visitors can use their browsers to view specialized content, such as animation, virtual reality, streaming audio and video, and formatted content. These plug-in programs and information are available for download at their related Web sites.

Q: Why should I link to a sound file?

A: Linking to sound files lets visitors choose to listen to the file and makes the file available to the widest audience.

More About

Embed a Sound

When you embed a sound in a Web page, you can set the volume, the way the player looks on the page, and the beginning and ending points of the sound file. For more information about Dreamweaver and embedding sound, visit the Dreamweaver MX 2004 More About Web page (scsite.com/dreamweavermx04/more.htm) and then click Embedding Sound.

More About

ActiveX Controls

ActiveX is a set of rules for how applications should share information. ActiveX controls have full access to the Windows operating system. For more information about ActiveX controls, visit the Dreamweaver MX 2004 More About Web page (scsite.com/dreamweavermx04/more.htm) and then click ActiveX.

In contrast, **ActiveX** is a set of technologies developed by Microsoft and is an outgrowth of OLE (object linking and embedding). An **ActiveX control** is a control that uses ActiveX technologies and currently is limited to Windows environments. ActiveX objects use the <object> tag instead of the <embed> tag. When you insert media using ActiveX, you must specify a ClassID or ActiveX control and, in many instances, add parameters. Parameters are discussed in more detail later in this project.

As a result, two ways exist to insert media content into browsers: as plug-ins using the <embed> tag and as ActiveX objects using the <object> tag. Until recently, both Internet Explorer and Netscape supported Netscape-style plug-ins, but newer versions of Internet Explorer support only ActiveX controls, although Internet Explorer still supports the <embed> tag for ActiveX content.

When adding media to a Web page, the Web page developer must try to predict how Web site visitors will have their browsers configured. One of the more common problems is that a particular plug-in may not be available on a visitor's computer. Fortunately, Dreamweaver helps by offering support for both plug-ins and ActiveX controls.

Windows Media Player is one of the more popular platforms for playing audio and video. This player is Internet Explorer's default multimedia player. This player plays the standard audio formats, including AIFF, AU, MIDI, WAV, and MP3. The WAV format (.wav), for example, is one of the more popular sound formats on the Internet. A compatibility issue exists, however, with the default Netscape installation and the .wav format. If you are using Netscape to view pages that contain the .wav format, most likely you will need to download a compatible plug-in.

Adding Sound to the Splash Page

As with any other technology, you first determine what you want to accomplish by adding a sound. Your sound should serve a clear and useful purpose or have an entertaining or instructional value. Web site developers primarily use one of three methods to add sound to a Web page: linking to an audio file, adding a background sound, or embedding an audio file. The simplest and easiest way to add sound to a Web page is through linking. The link can be any object, such as text, an image, or a table. The object is selected and then a link to a sound file is created. Clicking the link opens the user's designated player, such as Windows Media Player, in a separate window. You might consider using the linking method, for example, to provide instructional enhancement.

If you want to appeal to novelty, a background sound can serve this purpose. A background sound starts to play as soon as the Web page opens in the browser. If you add a background sound, keep the sound short, do not loop the sound, and do provide your visitor with an option to stop the sound.

Embedding a sound file integrates the audio into the Web page. The sound player, along with controls, is inserted directly into the Web page. This process lets Web site visitors choose whether they want to listen to the audio and how many times they want to hear it.

The following steps illustrate how to add the florida.wav background sound to the splash page. When the Web site visitor opens the page, the florida.wav file plays in the background.

To Add a Background Sound and Set Parameters

1

• **Hide the Property inspector. Click below table01.**

The insertion point is blinking at the left margin below the table, and the Property inspector is hidden (Figure 9-21).

FIGURE 9-21

2

• **Click the Media pop-up button arrow and then point to Plugin on the Media pop-up menu.**

The Media pop-up menu displays, and Plugin is highlighted (Figure 9-22).

FIGURE 9-22

3

• **Click Plugin.**

The Select File dialog box displays (Figure 9-23).

FIGURE 9-23

4

• **If necessary, select the media folder and then click florida.wav in the list of files.**

The florida.wav file is selected (Figure 9-24).

FIGURE 9-24

5

• **Click the OK button.**

A 32 x 32 pixel placeholder displays (Figure 9-25). This placeholder indicates the location of the plugin code.

FIGURE 9-25

6

• **Verify that the placeholder is selected. Display the Property inspector and then type** 2 **in the W text box.**

• **Press the TAB key and then type** 2 **in the H text box. Press the ENTER key.**

The placeholder is resized and appears as a dot on the Web page (Figure 9-26).

FIGURE 9-26

7

• **Click the Parameters button.**

The Parameters dialog box displays (Figure 9-27).

FIGURE 9-27

8

• **Type** hidden **in the Parameter column. Press the TAB key two times.**

The hidden parameter is added, and the insertion point is in the Value column (Figure 9-28).

FIGURE 9-28

• **Type** true **in the Value column and then press the TAB key two times.**

The true parameter is added, and the insertion point is in the Parameter column (Figure 9-29).

FIGURE 9-29

• **Type** autoplay **and then press the TAB key two times. Type** true **in the Value column.**

• **Press the TAB key two times. Type** loop **in the Parameter column, press the TAB key two times, and then type** false **in the Value column.**

The autoplay and loop parameters and the true and false values are added to the Parameters dialog box (Figure 9-30).

11

• **Click the OK button.**

• **Save the file.**

• **Press the F12 key to open the browser and to verify that the audio works. A speaker or headphones must be attached to the computer for you to hear the audio. Close the browser.**

• **Close the splash.htm page.**

FIGURE 9-30

Embedding an Audio File

Embedding a sound in a Web page provides the Web site visitor with control over the audio player. The content developer determines the amount of control through parameters. In this project, you embed an audio player into the state_parks.htm page. When the user clicks a control, a bird sound is heard through the Windows Media Player. An ActiveX control is used, thereby requiring specific parameters. A **parameter** defines the characteristics of something. For example, AutoRewind, AutoStart, and font specifications are considered to be parameters. Table 9-3 contains a list of frequently used parameters. This list is an example only, and several other parameters also are available from Microsoft's Web site.

Table 9-3 ActiveX Parameters		
PARAMETER	**DEFAULT**	**DESCRIPTION**
AutoStart	True	Defines whether the player should start automatically
AnimationAtStart	True	Defines whether an animation should show while the file loads
AutoRewind	False	Defines whether the player should rewind automatically
ClickToPlay	True	Defines whether the player should start when the user clicks the play area
DisplayBackColor	False	Shows a background color
EnablePositionControls	True	Provides the user with position controls
EnableFullScreenControls	False	Provides the user with screen controls
Filename	N/A	Indicates the URL of the file to play
InvokeURLs	True	Links to a URL
Mute	False	Mutes the sound
ShowControls	True	Defines whether the player controls should show
ShowAudioControls	True	Defines whether the audio controls should show
ShowDisplay	False	Defines whether the display should show
Volume	-200	Specifies the volume

ActiveX controls also require a ClassID. Dreamweaver uses the ClassID to define the object when generating the code for the ActiveX control. This hexadecimal ID is added through the ActiveX Property inspector. Once added, it will become an option within the ClassID pop-up menu. The following section describes the ActiveX Property inspector (Figure 9-31 on the next page).

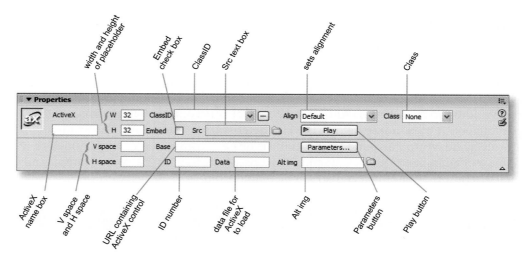

FIGURE 9-31

ACTIVEX NAME BOX The name in the ActiveX name box identifies the ActiveX object for scripting purposes.

W AND H W and H are the width and height, respectively, of the image, in pixels. Dreamweaver automatically inserts the dimensions when a image is inserted into the page. You can specify the image size in the following units: pc (picas), pt (points), in (inches), mm (millimeters), cm (centimeters), and combinations, such as 2in+5mm. Dreamweaver converts the values to pixels in the HTML source code.

CLASSID The **ClassID value** identifies the ActiveX control to the browser. Enter a value or choose one on the pop-up menu. When the page is loaded, the browser uses the ClassID to locate the ActiveX control required for the ActiveX object associated with the page. For all versions of Windows Media Player from version 7 on, use the following ClassID: CLSID:22d6f312-b0f6-11d0-94ab-0080c74c7e95. This number is assigned through the ActiveX Property inspector.

EMBED Checking the **Embed** check box adds an <embed> tag within the <object> tag for the ActiveX control. If the ActiveX control has a Netscape Navigator plug-in equivalent, the <embed> tag activates the plug-in. Dreamweaver assigns the values you entered as ActiveX properties to their Netscape Navigator plug-in equivalents.

ALIGN **Align** sets the alignment of an ActiveX object on the page.

PARAMETERS The **Parameters** button opens a dialog box for entering additional parameters to pass to the ActiveX object.

SRC The **Src** value defines the data file to be used for a Netscape Navigator plug-in if the Embed check box is selected. If a value is not entered, Dreamweaver attempts to determine the value from the ActiveX properties already entered.

V SPACE AND H SPACE The **V space** and **H space** values add space, in pixels, along the sides of the object. V space adds space along the top and bottom of an object. H space adds space along the left and right of an object.

BASE The **Base value** specifies the URL containing the ActiveX control. Internet Explorer downloads the ActiveX control from this location if the control has not been installed already in the visitor's system. If the Base parameter is not specified and if the Web site visitor does not have the relevant ActiveX control installed, the browser cannot display the ActiveX object.

ALT IMG The **Alt img** parameter indicates an image to be displayed if the browser does not support the <object> tag. This option is available only when the Embed check box is not selected.

DATA The **Data** parameter specifies a data file for the ActiveX control to load. Many ActiveX controls, such as Shockwave and RealPlayer, do not use this parameter.

ID This option specifies the data file ID.

PLAY/STOP The Play/Stop button plays and stops the movie in the Document window.

CLASS Used for scripting with cascading style sheets.

To Embed an Audio File

The following steps illustrate how to embed an audio file in the state_parks.htm Web page. A speaker or headphones are required to hear the sound.

To Embed an Audio File

1

• **Open the state_parks.htm page and then hide the panel groups and Property inspector.**

• **Click to the right of the heading text, Northwest Region, and then press the ENTER key.**

• **Click the Media pop-up button arrow and then point to ActiveX.**

The insertion point is centered and below the heading text (Figure 9-32).

FIGURE 9-32

2

- **Click ActiveX. Display the Property inspector.**

A placeholder marks the location where the ActiveX control will appear on the page in Internet Explorer, and the ActiveX Property inspector is displayed (Figure 9-33).

FIGURE 9-33

3

- **Click the ActiveX name box in the Property inspector and then name the ActiveX control** birdsound.

- **Change the W value to** 200 **and the H value to** 45. **Type** CLSID:22d6f312-b0f6-11d0-94ab-0080c74c7e95 **in the ClassID text box.**

- **Press the ENTER key.**

The ActiveX name, W and H values, and ClassID number are added to the ActiveX Property inspector (Figure 9-34). Once you type in the ClassID number, it becomes part of the pop-up menu. It will not be necessary to add the number again.

FIGURE 9-34

4

• **Click the Embed check box and then click the Browse for File icon to the right of the Src text box.**

• **If necessary, when Dreamweaver displays the Select Netscape Plug-In File dialog box, click the Look in box arrow and navigate to the media folder.**

The Select Netscape Plug-In File dialog box is displayed (Figure 9-35).

FIGURE 9-35

5

• **Click the Files of type box arrow and then click All Files. Click the birdsound.au file. Verify that Document is selected in the Relative to box.**

The birdsound.au file is highlighted (Figure 9-36).

FIGURE 9-36

6

• **Click the OK button.**

The link is created to the source file (Figure 9-37). When viewed in a browser, this rectangle will contain the audio controls.

FIGURE 9-37

7

• **Click the Parameters button in the Property inspector.**

• **If necessary, click the Plus (+) button to display the insertion point in the Parameter column.**

The Parameters dialog box is displayed, and the insertion point is in the Parameter column (Figure 9-38).

FIGURE 9-38

8

• **Type** FileName **and then press the TAB key two times. Type** media/birdsound.au **in the Value column.**

The first parameter and value are added to the Parameters dialog box (Figure 9-39).

FIGURE 9-39

9

• **Press the TAB key two times.**

• **Use Table 9-4 on the next page to add the other parameters and values to the Parameters dialog box.**

The parameters are added to the Parameters dialog box (Figure 9-40).

FIGURE 9-40

10

• **Click the OK button and then click the Play button in the Property inspector.**

• **Click the Save button on the Standard toolbar. If a dialog box displays indicating that Dreamweaver is unable to find the plug-in, try previewing in the browser.**

The Media player is displayed in the Document window (Figure 9-41).

FIGURE 9-41

11

• **Click the Stop button in the Property inspector.**

• **Press the F12 key to view the Web page in your browser. Click the Play button to listen to the audio. A speaker or headphones are necessary to hear the sound. If a Dreamweaver dialog box is displayed, read the information and then click the OK button.**

FIGURE 9-42

The Windows Media Player audio control is displayed (Figure 9-42). I If the sound control bar does not display in the browser, see your instructor.

12

• **Close the browser.**

Other Ways

1. On Insert menu point to Media, click ActiveX

Table 9-4 Parameters and Values

PARAMETER	VALUE
AutoStart	false
ShowControls	true
ShowStatusBar	false
ShowDisplay	false
AutoRewind	true

Earlier in this project, you inserted a Flash movie into the splash page. Inserting the Flash movie was a fairly simple process because Flash also is a Macromedia product. Therefore, Dreamweaver comes with built-in controls to display a Flash movie. Movies, however, come in several other formats, and most likely occasions will arise when you will want to insert a movie in another format. Table 9-5 contains a description of video file formats that are used on the Internet. All formats display in both Internet Explorer and Netscape.

More About

Adding Video

When adding video, you can let the user download it or it can be streamed so it plays while downloading. For more information about Dreamweaver and video, visit the Dreamweaver MX 2004 More About Web page (scsite.com/dreamweavermx04/more.htm) and then click Streaming Video.

Table 9-5 Video File Formats

FILE NAME EXTENSION	DESCRIPTION
.avi (Audio Video Interleave, or AVI)	The AVI format is supported by all computers running Windows.
.mpg or .mpeg (Moving Pictures Expert Group, or MPEG)	The MPEG format is one of the more popular formats on the Internet. It is cross-platform, running on Windows and Macintosh computers.
.mov (QuickTime, developed by Apple)	QuickTime is a common format on the Internet for both Windows and Macintosh computers. Playing QuickTime movies on a Windows computer requires the QuickTime Player.
.rm or .ram (RealVideo, developed by RealMedia)	The RealVideo format allows the streaming of video, which reduces downloading time.
.swf (Flash SWF)	The SWF format requires the Macromedia Flash player.
.wmv, .wvx (Windows Media Format, WMV)	The WMF format allows the streaming of video, uses the Windows Media Player, and plays on both Windows and Macintosh computers.

Adding Video to a Web Page

The following steps show how to add a Windows Media Player video file to the state_parks.htm Web page.

To Add Video to a Web Page

1

• **Scroll to the bottom of the page and then click to the right of the Home link.**

The insertion point is blinking to the right of the Home link (Figure 9-43).

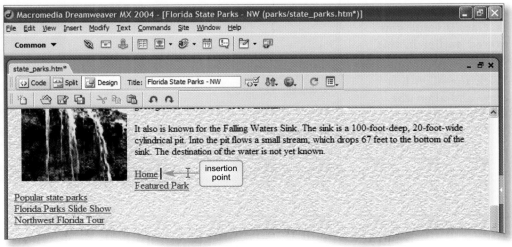

FIGURE 9-43

2

• **Click the ActiveX button on the Common category Insert bar.**

The ActiveX control is displayed and selected in the Document window, and the ActiveX Property inspector is displayed (Figure 9-44).

FIGURE 9-44

3

• **Click the ActiveX name box in the Property inspector and then type** gps **as the name.**

• **Press the TAB key and then change the W value to 320. Press the TAB key and then change the H value to 240.**

• **Click the ClassID box arrow and then select the ClassID value you entered earlier in this project.**

• **Click the Align box arrow and align the ActiveX control to the right.**

The name, W and H, ClassID, and Align properties are added to the Property inspector (Figure 9-45).

FIGURE 9-45

4

• **Click the Embed check box in the Property inspector.**

• **Click the Browse for File icon to the right of the Src text box.**

• **If necessary, navigate to the media folder, click the Files of type box arrow, and then select All Files. Click the Tracking kids with GPS.wmv file.**

The Select Netscape Plug-In File dialog box is displayed (Figure 9-46).

FIGURE 9-46

5

• **Click the OK button.**

The file name and path are added to the Src text box (Figure 9-47).

FIGURE 9-47

6

• **Click the Parameters button in the Property inspector.**

The Parameters dialog box is displayed, and the insertion point is blinking in the Parameter text box (Figure 9-48).

FIGURE 9-48

7

• **Apply the steps you used on pages DW 693 and 694 to add the parameters and values shown in Table 9-6 on the next page to the Parameters dialog box.**

• **Save the page.**

The parameters and values are added to the Parameters dialog box, and the state_parks.htm page is saved (Figure 9-49).

FIGURE 9-49

8

• **Press the F12 key to display the page in your browser. Scroll down to display the video file. Click the Play button.**

The video placeholder is displayed and the video begins to play (Figure 9-50). If you are using Netscape as your browser, most likely the movie starts to play when the page is displayed in the browser.

FIGURE 9-50

9

• **Close the browser to return to Dreamweaver.**

Table 9-6 Parameters and Values	
PARAMETER	**VALUE**
FileName	media/Tracking kids with gps.wmv
AutoStart	false
ShowControls	true
ShowDisplay	false
AutoRewind	true

The Results Panel

Dreamweaver's Results panel (Figure 9-51 on the next page) provides several options to help maintain your site. These options are described below:

- **Search** Use this option to search and replace text, source code, and specific tags for the current document, open documents, selected files in a site, or the entire current local site.

- **Validation** Use this option to locate tag or syntax errors. You can validate the current document or a selected tag.

- **Target Browser Check** The Target Browser Check feature checks the code in your documents to see if any of the tags, attributes, CSS properties, or CSS values are unsupported by your target browser.

- **Link Checker** The Link Checker searches for broken links and unreferenced files in a portion of a local site or throughout an entire local site. External links are not checked.
- **Site Reports** Site reports provide information on workflow or HTML attributes, including accessibility, for the current document, selected files, or the entire site. This option primarily is used by Web teams.
- **FTP Log** This option keeps track of all FTP activity. If an error occurs when you are transferring a file using FTP, the site FTP log can help you determine the problem.
- **Server Debug** This option is a tool to assist with server problems, and is used primarily with dynamic data.

FIGURE 9-51

Using the Link Checker

It is important that you check and verify that your links work. Links are not active within Dreamweaver; that is, you cannot open a linked document by clicking the link in the Document window. You can check any type of link by displaying the page in a browser. Using a browser is the only available validation option for absolute or external and e-mail links. For relative or internal links, Dreamweaver provides the Link Checker feature. Use the Link Checker to check internal links in a document, a folder, or an entire site.

A large Web site can contain hundreds of links that can change over time. Dreamweaver's **Link Checker** searches for broken links and unreferenced files in a portion of a local site or throughout an entire local site. This feature is limited, however, because it verifies internal links only. A list of external links is compiled, but not verified. As previously discussed, external links must be checked through a browser.

The Link Checker does have advantages, however. When you use this feature, the Link Checker displays a statistical report that includes information about broken links, orphaned files, and external links. An **orphaned file** is a file that is not connected to any page within the Web site. The orphaned file option is for informational purposes only. The orphaned file report, however, is particularly valuable for a large site, because it displays a list of all files that are not part of the Web site. Deleting unused files from a Web site increases disk space and streamlines your site. You can use the Link Checker to check links throughout your entire site from any Web page within your site.

The steps on the next page show how to use the Link Checker to verify the internal links for the state_parks.htm page. The link to the Florida Parks Slide Show is changed from slideshow.htm to slide_show.htm intentionally to illustrate how the Link Checker works and how to make corrections. Most likely, your results will be different from the ones shown. The steps on the next page illustrate how to change a file name and to verify internal links using the Link Checker.

To Verify Internal Links with the Link Checker

1

• **Display the panel group, click slideshow.htm, and then press the F2 key.**

• **Type slide_show.htm to rename the file and then press the ENTER key.**

• **If the Update Files dialog box displays, click the Don't Update button.**

• **Hide the panel groups.**

• **Click File on the menu bar, point to Check Page, and then point to Check Links.**

The File menu is displayed, and Check Links is highlighted (Figure 9-52).

FIGURE 9-52

2

• **Click Check Links.**

The Results panel group is displayed, and the Link Checker panel is selected. The statistical report shows information about the links in the site, including 1 Total, 1 HTML, 14 All links, 10 OK, 1 Broken, and 3 External (Figure 9-53). External links are not verified. Your report may include different results.

FIGURE 9-53

3

• **Double-click state_parks.htm in the Results panel.**

The Florida Parks Slide Show linked text is selected, and slideshow.htm is displayed in the Link box. The statistical report indicates 1 Broken link (Figure 9-54).

FIGURE 9-54

4

• **Double-click the Link box and type** slide_show.htm **as the new link.**

• **Click the Save button.**

The link is modified to slide_show.htm in the Property inspector. The broken link is removed from the Link Checker panel, and the statistical report is updated automatically (Figure 9-55).

FIGURE 9-55

Other Ways

1. Press SHIFT+F8

In the previous steps, you used the Check Links command on the Check Page submenu of the File menu to check the links. The Check Page submenu also contains Check Accessibility, Check Target Browsers, Validate Markup, and Validate XML commands. These options all are for a single page.

Dreamweaver also provides another option to check links sitewide or to change a link sitewide. The Check Links Sitewide and Change Link Sitewide commands are accessed through the Site menu.

Checking for Plug-ins

If a visitor accesses a Web page and does not have the appropriate plug-in, it is helpful to provide a link where the visitor can download the plug-in. This is done through the Check Plugin behavior. This is particularly helpful for RealMedia, RealAudio, and other media applications that are not part of a standard Windows installation. The following steps provide information on how to add the Check Plugin behavior.

1. Select an object in the Document window and then open the Behaviors panel.
2. Click the Action (+) button in the Behaviors panel and then click Check Plugin on the Actions pop-up menu.
3. Select a plug-in in the Plugin list in the Check Plugin dialog box or click the Enter option button and then type the exact name of the plug-in in the adjacent text box.
4. In the If Found, Go To URL text box, specify a URL for visitors who have the plug-in.
5. In the Otherwise, Go to URL text box, specify an alternative URL for visitors who do not have the plug-in.
6. Click the Always go to first URL if detection is not possible check box to select it. Click the OK button.

Shockwave

Another popular media type is **Shockwave**. Macromedia's Director program is used to create Shockwave files. Director often is referred to as an authoring tool or development platform. A developer can use a combination of graphics, video, sound, text, animation, and other elements to create interactive multimedia. After the developer creates the multimedia, it can be compressed into a Shockwave file and then added to a Web page. To play Shockwave content within your browser, the Shockwave player must be installed on your computer. You can download the latest version of the player from the Macromedia Web site. Information on Macromedia's Web site indicates that more than 280 million users have the Shockwave player installed.

Several file formats associated with Director and Shockwave are described below.

- **.dcr (Shockwave)** The .dcr file is a compressed file that can be previewed in Dreamweaver and viewed in your browser.
- **.dir** The .dir file is the source file created by Director. These files usually are exported through Director as .dcr files.
- **.dxr** The .dxr file is a locked Director file.
- **.cst** The .cst file contains additional information that is used in a .dxr or .dir file.
- **.cxt** The .cxt file is a file locked for distribution purposes.

The software that plays Shockwave movies is available both as a Netscape Navigator plug-in and as an ActiveX control. When you insert a Shockwave movie into a Web page, Dreamweaver uses both the <object> tag (for the ActiveX control) and the <embed> tag (for the plug-in) to get the best results in all browsers. When you make changes in the Property inspector for the movie, Dreamweaver maps your entries to the appropriate parameters for both the <object> and <embed> tags.

Inserting a Shockwave file is similar to inserting a Flash movie. The following steps explain how to insert a Shockwave file into the Dreamweaver Document window.

1. Click in the Document window where you want to insert the movie.
2. Click the Shockwave command on the Media pop-up menu on the Insert bar.
3. Select a movie file in the Select File dialog box.
4. Enter the W and H values of the movie in the W and H text boxes in the Property inspector.
5. Add any necessary parameters.

Java Applets

An **applet** is a small program written in **Java**, which is a programming language for the Web. The applet can be downloaded by any computer. The applet also runs in HTML and usually is embedded in an HTML page on a Web site. Thus, it can be executed from within a browser. Hundreds, or even thousands, of applets are available on the Internet — many of them for free. Some general categories of applets include text effects, audio effects, visual effects, navigation, games, and utilities. Inserting a Java applet is similar to inserting a Flash or Shockwave movie. The following steps explain how to insert a Java applet into the Dreamweaver Document window.

1. Click in the Document window where you want to insert the applet.
2. Click the Applet command on the Media pop-up menu on the Insert bar.
3. Select an applet file in the Select File dialog box.
4. Set all necessary properties in the Property inspector.
5. Add any necessary parameters.

Quitting Dreamweaver

After you have added the Flash text, Flash movie, audio, and video, and verified that the media objects work, Project 9 is complete. To close the Web site, quit Dreamweaver MX 2004, and return control to Windows, complete the following step.

To Close the Web Site and Quit Dreamweaver

1 **Click the Close button on the upper-right corner of the Dreamweaver title bar.**

The Dreamweaver window, the Document window, and the Florida Parks Web site are closed. If you have unsaved changes, Dreamweaver will prompt you to save the changes. Clicking the Yes button in the Dreamweaver MX 2004 dialog box saves the changes.

Project Summary

Project 9 introduced you to Dreamweaver's media objects. You added a splash page with Flash text, a Flash movie, and a link to an audio file. Then you added a link to the index page from the splash page. Next, you opened the state_parks.htm page and embedded an audio file with controls. Then you added a video to the page. You also learned about the Results panel group and how to use the Link Checker. Finally, you learned the general procedure for adding Shockwave movies and Java applets to Web pages.

What You Should Know

Having completed this project, you now should be able to perform the tasks below. The tasks are listed in the same order they were presented in the project. For a list of keyboard commands for topics introduced in this project, see the Quick Reference for Windows at the back of this book and refer to the Shortcut column.

1. Copy Data Files to the Florida Parks Web Site (DW 667)
2. Start Dreamweaver and Open the Florida Parks Web Site (DW 667)
3. Add Flash Text (DW 670)
4. Add a Flash Movie (DW 677)
5. Add a Link to Go to the Index Page (DW 679)
6. Add a Background Sound and Set Parameters (DW 683)
7. Embed an Audio File (DW 689)
8. Add Video to a Web Page (DW 695)
9. Verify Internal Links with the Link Checker (DW 700)
10. Close the Web Site and Quit Dreamweaver (DW 703)

Learn It Online

Instructions: To complete the Learn It Online exercises, start your browser, click the Address bar, and then enter the Web address scsite.com/dreamweavermx2004/learn. When the Dreamweaver MX 2004 Learn It Online page is displayed, follow the instructions in the exercises below. Each exercise has instructions for printing your results, either for your own records or for submission to your instructor.

1 Project Reinforcement TF, MC, and SA

Below Dreamweaver Project 9, click the Project Reinforcement link. Print the quiz by clicking Print on the File menu for each page. Answer each question.

2 Flash Cards

Below Dreamweaver Project 9, click the Flash Cards link and read the instructions. Type 20 (or a number specified by your instructor) in the Number of playing cards text box, type your name in the Enter your Name text box, and then click the Flip Card button. When the flash card is displayed, read the question and then click the ANSWER box arrow to select an answer. Flip through Flash Cards. If your score is 15 (75%) correct or greater, click Print on the File menu to print your results. If your score is less than 15 (75%) correct, then redo this exercise by clicking the Replay button.

3 Practice Test

Below Dreamweaver Project 9, click the Practice Test link. Answer each question, enter your first and last name at the bottom of the page, and then click the Grade Test button. When the graded practice test is displayed on your screen, click Print on the File menu to print a hard copy. Continue to take practice tests until you score 80% or better.

4 Who Wants To Be a Computer Genius?

Below Dreamweaver Project 9, click the Computer Genius link. Read the instructions, enter your first and last name at the bottom of the page, and then click the PLAY button. When your score is displayed, click the PRINT RESULTS link to print a hard copy.

5 Wheel of Terms

Below Dreamweaver Project 9, click the Wheel of Terms link. Read the instructions, and then enter your first and last name and your school name. Click the PLAY button. When your score is displayed, right-click the score and then click Print on the shortcut menu to print a hard copy.

6 Crossword Puzzle Challenge

Below Dreamweaver Project 9, click the Crossword Puzzle Challenge link. Read the instructions, and then enter your first and last name. Click the SUBMIT button. Work the crossword puzzle. When you are finished, click the Submit button. When the crossword puzzle is redisplayed, click the Print Puzzle button to print a hard copy.

7 Tips and Tricks

Below Dreamweaver Project 9, click the Tips and Tricks link. Click a topic that pertains to Project 9. Right-click the information and then click Print on the shortcut menu. Construct a brief example of what the information relates to in Dreamweaver to confirm you understand how to use the tip or trick.

8 Newsgroups

Below Dreamweaver Project 9, click the Newsgroups link. Click a topic that pertains to Project 9. Print three comments.

9 Expanding Your Horizons

Below Dreamweaver Project 9, click the Expanding Your Horizons link. Click a topic that pertains to Project 9. Print the information. Construct a brief example of what the information relates to in Dreamweaver to confirm you understand the contents of the article.

10 Search Sleuth

Below Dreamweaver Project 9, click the Search Sleuth link. To search for a term that pertains to this project, select a term below the Project 9 title and then use the Google search engine at google.com (or any major search engine) to display and print two Web pages that present information on the term.

Apply Your Knowledge

1 Creating a Splash Page for B & B Lawn Service

Problem: B & B Lawn Service would like to add a splash page to its Web site. The management prefers something attractive and interesting, but somewhat conservative. You decide to copy a data file that contains five layers and images and then add Flash text for the page title. Next, you add a Flash movie, a link to the index.htm page, and a background song. The splash page is shown in Figure 9-56. Appendix C contains instructions for uploading your local site to a remote server.

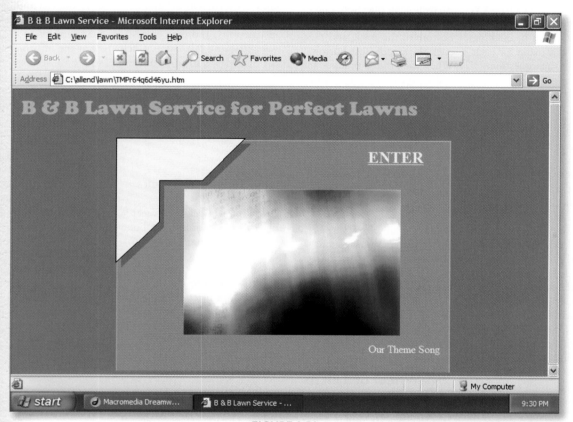

FIGURE 9-56

Instructions: Start Dreamweaver. See the inside back cover of this book for instructions for downloading the Data Disk or see your instructor for information on accessing the files in this book.

1. Use the Windows My Computer option to copy the lawn_splash.htm file, images, and the media folder from the DataFiles folder to your lawn folder.
2. Start Dreamweaver. Display the Property inspector, Standard toolbar, and panel groups. Select Lawn Service on the Files pop-up menu in the Files panel. Open the lawn_splash.htm file.
3. The lawn_splash.htm Web page contains five layers. Click to the right of the layer-code markers in the upper-left corner of the page.
4. Click Flash Text on the Insert bar Media pop-up menu. Change the font to Cooper Black or one of your choice, the color to #CCCC00, the rollover color to #CCFF99, and the background color to #669966. Type B & B Lawn Service for Perfect Lawns in the Text text box. Save the Flash text as media/lawn01.swf.

Apply Your Knowledge

5. Click the fourth layer-code marker from the left. Click in Layer 4 in the Document window. Type enter, change the font color to #FFFFCE, and then select the text. Create a link to the index.htm page.

6. Click the fifth layer-code marker from the left. Scroll down and click in Layer 5 in the Document window. Type Our Theme Song as the entry, and change the font color to #FFFFCE. Click the Media pop-up menu and then click Plugin. In the Select File dialog box, navigate to the media folder and then select the lawn.wav file. Change the plugin placeholder height to 2 and the width to 2. Click the Parameters button and then add the parameters listed in Table 9-7.

Table 9-7 Parameters for Lawn Service Web site	
PARAMETER	**VALUE**
Hidden	true
Autoplay	true
Loop	false

7. Click the third layer-code marker from the left. Click inside Layer 3 and then click the Flash command on the Media pop-up menu. Navigate to the lawn\media folder. Click the lawns.swf file and then click OK.

8. In the Flash Property inspector, change W to 315 and H to 220. If necessary, click the Loop and Autoplay check boxes to select them. Click the Scale box arrow and then click Exact fit. Adjust the size of Layer 3 to fit the Flash movie.

9. Click the Save button on the Standard toolbar.

10. Press the F12 key to view the page in your browser. Click the index link and then click the browser Back button. A speaker or headphones are required to hear the audio.

11. Print a copy of the lawn_splash.htm page if instructed to do so. Upload the page to the lawn Web site on a remote server if instructed to do so.

In the Lab

1 The CandleDust Web Site

Problem: Mary would like a splash page for the CandleDust Web site. She is receiving orders from all over the world and wants to emphasize that her Web site is now an international site. Mary wants to use the same background, but wants a two-row table containing Flash text at the top of the page. She has found a Flash movie that she would like to add to the site. She also wants to add a link to the index page. The splash page is shown in Figure 9-57 on the next page. Appendix C contains instructions for uploading your local site to a remote server.

(continued)

The CandleDust Web Site *(continued)*

FIGURE 9-57

Instructions: Perform the following tasks:

1. Use the Windows My Computer option to copy the media folder from the DataFiles folder to your candle folder.

2. Start Dreamweaver. Select CandleDust on the Files pop-up menu in the Files panel. Open a new Document window. Save the page as candle_splash.htm and then title the page CandleDust. Apply the candlebg.gif image to the background.

3. If necessary, click at the top of the page and then insert a two-row, one-column table with a width of 60 percent and cell padding of 10. Type `Heading for CandleDust Splash page` in the Summary text box. Center-align the table.

4. Click in the first cell (row) in the table and then click Flash Text on the Media pop-up menu of the Insert bar.

5. Add the following attributes to the Insert Flash Text dialog box: Font: Broadway (or a font of your choice); Size: 30; Bold; Color: #660000; Rollover color: #FF9966; Bg color: #FFFFCC. Type `CandleDust` in the Text text box and then save the Flash text as media/heading01.

6. Click in the second cell (row) in the table and then click Flash Text on the Media pop-up menu.

7. Add the following attributes to the Insert Flash Text dialog box: Font: Agency FB; Size: 30; Bold; Color: #660000; Rollover color: #FF9966; Bg color: #FFFFCC. Type `Providing the world with the best in scented candles!` in the Text text box. Save the Flash text as media/heading02.

In the Lab

8. Click to the right of the table (outside the table) and then press the ENTER key. Insert a layer and then add the following properties: Layer ID: world; L: 320px; T: 145px; W: 200px; and H: 115px. Click inside the layer.

9. Click the Flash button on the Media pop-up menu and then insert the candle.swf file located in the CandleDust media folder.

10. Click to the right of the layer code-marker, press ENTER seven times, and then type Visit our Web site as the entry. Select the text and create a link to the index.htm page.

11. Save the candle_splash.htm page and then press the F12 key to view the page in your browser. Note that settings on some computers may display the Flash movie in a different location from that shown in Figure 9-57. Move the mouse pointer over the text heading to view the Flash text animation. Check your link to verify that it works.

12. Print a copy of the Web page if instructed to do so. Upload the page to the candle Web site on a remote server if instructed to do so. Close the browser. Quit Dreamweaver.

2 Adding Video and Sound to the Credit Web Site

Problem: Marcy is interested in identity theft and identity security. She recently read about a proposal requiring that a person's driver's license become part of a national database. She has mixed feelings about this suggestion and has located a video file detailing this proposal. She would like to create a dramatic splash page for her Web site and add this movie to the site. The splash page would contain a title, the movie, and a link to the credit index.htm page. The splash page is shown in Figure 9-58. Appendix C contains instructions for uploading your local site to a remote server.

FIGURE 9-58

(continued)

In the Lab

Adding Video and Sound to the Credit Web Site *(continued)*

Instructions: Perform the following tasks:

1. Use the Windows My Computer option to copy both the bkg.gif image and the media folder from the DataFiles folder to your credit folder.
2. Start Dreamweaver. Select Credit Protection from the Files pop-up menu in the Files panel. Open a new Document window. Save the page as credit_splash.htm in the Credit Web site and then title the page Identity Security.
3. Insert and center a one-row, one-column table with a width of 60 percent at the top of the page.
4. Click in the table cell and then click Flash Text on the Media pop-up menu. Add the following attributes to the Flash Text dialog box: Font: Lucida Calligraphy (or a font of your choice); Size: 45; Color: #FF3300; Rollover color: #CC00FF; and Bg color: #000000.
5. Type What is Identity Theft? in the Text text box. Save the Flash text as media/heading1.swf.
6. Click to the right of the table (outside the table) and then press the ENTER key.
7. Insert a layer and then select the layer. Add the following properties: Layer ID: identity; L: 220px; T: 130px; W: 200px; and H: 115px. Click inside the layer.
8. Click ActiveX on the Media pop-up menu. Add the following properties in the ActiveX Property inspector: ActiveX name: security; W: 320; and H: 240. Click the ClassID box arrow and then click the CLSID number you entered earlier in this project.
9. Click the Embed check box and then click the Browse for File icon located to the right of the Src text box. Navigate to the credit media folder. Click the Files of type arrow and then click All Files. Select the ID security.wmv file from the media folder and then click the OK button.
10. Click the Parameters button and then add the parameters listed in Table 9-8.

Table 9-8 Parameters for Credit Web Site	
PARAMETER	VALUE
FileName	media/ID security.wmv
AutoStart	false
ShowControls	true
ShowDisplay	false
AutoRewind	true

11. Click outside the layer. Press the ENTER key several times or scroll down to move to the end of the document. Type Home Page and then change the text color to blue and bold. Select the text and then create a link to the credit index.htm page.
12. Click the Page Properties command on the Modify menu and then apply the bkg.gif file as the background image. Click the OK button.
13. Save the document. Press the F12 key to view the page in your browser. Note that settings on some computers may display the Flash movie in a different location from that shown in Figure 9-58. Click the Play button to view the movie. Print a copy of the Web pages if instructed to do so. Upload the pages to the credit Web site on a remote server if instructed to do so. Close the browser. Quit Dreamweaver.

In the Lab

3 Creating a Splash Page for the Plant City Web Site

Problem: Juan wants to add some excitement to the Plant City Web site by adding a splash page. You explain to Juan that a splash page can be simple, but effective. You suggest adding some rollover text and a Flash movie. The page also will contain a link to the home page. The splash page is shown in Figure 9-59. Appendix C contains instructions for uploading your local site to a remote server.

Instructions: Perform the following tasks:

1. Use the Windows My Computer option to copy both the city_splash.htm file and the media folder from the DataFiles folder to your city folder.
2. Start Dreamweaver. Select Plant City from the Files pop-up menu in the Files panel. Open the city_splash.htm file.
3. Click in the first cell (row 1) in the table and then click Flash Text on the Media pop-up menu. Apply the following

FIGURE 9-59

attributes: Font: Verdana; Size: 45; Color: #FF0000; Rollover color: #000000; and Bg color: #996666. Type Plant City, Florida in the Text text box. Save the Flash text as media/heading01.swf.
4. Click in the second cell (row 2) in the table and then click Flash Text on the Media pop-up menu. Apply the following attributes: Font: Verdana, Bold; Size: 15; Color: #000000; Rollover color: #FF0000; and Bg color: #996666. Type The Strawberry Capital of the United States in the Text text box. Save the Flash text as media/heading02.swf.
5. Select the layer and name it movie. Click in the layer. Type the following in bold red text: A city without the hustle and bustle and then press the ENTER key.
6. Click Flash on the Media pop-up menu and then navigate to the media folder. Click the city.swf file and then click the OK button to insert the Flash movie into the layer. Save the Web page.
7. Press the F12 key to view the page in your browser. Print a copy of the Web page if instructed to do so. Upload the page to the city Web site on a remote server if instructed to do so. Close the browser. Quit Dreamweaver.

Cases and Places

The difficulty of these case studies varies:
■ are the least difficult and ■■ are the most difficult. The last exercise is a group exercise.

1 ■ You would like to add some pizzazz to your sports Web site. You decide to add a splash page. Add a background image and a title to the page. Add some Flash text and then create a link to an audio file. Create a link to the home page. Save the page in your sports Web site. For a selection of images and backgrounds, visit the Dreamweaver MX 2004 Media Web page (scsite.com/dreamweavermx04/media) and then click Media below Project 9.

2 ■ Your hobby Web site is receiving more and more hits each day. You would like to add some interactivity to your site. You decide to do this by adding a splash page. First, you add a background image to the page and then add an appropriate title. Next, you insert Flash text and Flash buttons. Then you insert a Flash movie. Create a link to your home page. Upload the new page to a remote site if instructed to do so. For a selection of images and backgrounds, visit the Dreamweaver MX 2004 Media Web page (scsite.com/dreamweavermx04/media) and then click Media below Project 9.

3 ■■ Add a new page to your music hobby Web site and then add a background image to the page. Add relevant content and then add Flash text. Add a Flash movie and then embed an audio file. Create a link to and from your home page. Upload the page to a remote site. For a selection of images and backgrounds, visit the Dreamweaver MX 2004 Media Web page (scsite.com/dreamweavermx04/media) and then click Media below Project 9.

4 ■■ Your campaign for political office is doing terrific, and you want to enhance it by adding a splash page to your Web site. Create a new Web page and then add an appropriate background image and title. Add Flash text and Flash buttons. Embed an audio file and then add a video file. Create a link to and from your index page. Upload the revised Web site to a remote server. For a selection of images and backgrounds, visit the Dreamweaver MX 2004 Media Web page (scsite.com/dreamweavermx04/media) and then click Media below Project 9.

5 ■■ **Working Together** The student government Web site has become even more popular. You and your team would like to add a splash page and then add videos to the page that includes various locations that are available for the student trips. Each team member is responsible for locating an appropriate Flash movie. On the splash page, add one of the Flash movies, Flash text, and a link to an audio file. On the page that includes vacation locations, add two or three Flash movies illustrating some of the activities available at the different sites. Create a link to and from the index page. Upload the new pages to a remote server. For a selection of images and backgrounds, visit the Dreamweaver MX 2004 Media Web page (scsite.com/dreamweavermx04/media) and then click Media below Project 9.

Appendix A

Dreamweaver Help

Dreamweaver Help

This appendix shows you how to use the many components of Dreamweaver Help. At any time while you are using Dreamweaver, you can interact with its Help system and display information on any Dreamweaver topic. It is a complete reference manual at your fingertips.

The Using Dreamweaver Help system is viewed through your browser. The Using Dreamweaver MX Help system contains comprehensive HTML-based information about all Dreamweaver features, including the following:

- A table of contents in which the information is organized by subject.
- An alphabetical index that points to important terms and links to related topics.
- A search tool that allows you to find any character string in all topic text.
- A Favorites folder to which you can add frequently accessed topics.

Other Help features include tutorial lessons, context-sensitive help, information on Dreamweaver extensions, help on using Cold Fusion, and 11 online reference manuals, including an HTML reference manual. For additional tutorials and online movies, you can access the Macromedia Dreamweaver Web site at http://www.macromedia.com/software/dreamweaver/productinfo/features/brz_tour/.

The Dreamweaver Help Menu

One of the more commonly used methods to access Dreamweaver's Help features is through the **Help menu** and function keys. Dreamweaver's Help menu provides an easy system to access the available Help options (Figure A-1 on the next page). Table A-1 on the next page summarizes the commands available through the Help menu.

FIGURE A-1

Table A-1 Summary of Help Commands on the Help Menu	
COMMAND ON HELP MENU	**FUNCTION**
Getting Started and Tutorials	The Getting Started and Tutorials command accesses the Getting Started window. This window provides access to several links and tutorials. Each tutorial takes 30 to 45 minutes to complete.
Using Dreamweaver	The Using Dreamweaver command displays the Using Dreamweaver window. This feature is commonly used for locating information. Using Dreamweaver is covered in more detail later in this appendix.
Using ColdFusion	The Using ColdFusion command displays the Using ColdFusion window. ColdFusion MX is a Web application server that lets you create applications that interact with databases.
Reference	When you click the Reference command, the Reference panel displays in the Dreamweaver panel groups. The Reference panel contains the complete text from several reference manuals, including references on HTML, Cascading Style Sheets, JavaScript, and other Web-related features.
Extensions	An **extension** is an add-on piece of software or a plug-in that enhances Dreamweaver's capabilities. Extensions provide the Dreamweaver developer with the capability to customize how Dreamweaver looks and works. Clicking the Extensions command displays a submenu with the following commands: Extending Dreamweaver, API Reference, and Creating and Submitting. Each of these commands opens a related Help window.
Dreamweaver Support Center	The Dreamweaver Support Center command provides access to the online Macromedia Dreamweaver Support Center. This Web site offers a search option, support solutions, support topics, and other support resources.
Macromedia Online Forums	The Macromedia Online Forums command provides access to the Macromedia Online Forums Web page. The forums provide a place for developers of all experience levels to share ideas and techniques.
Activation	The Activation command provides access to product activation, license transfer, online registration, and printing the registration.
About Dreamweaver	The About Dreamweaver command opens a window that provides copyright information and the product license number.

Navigating the Dreamweaver MX 2004 Help System

The Using Dreamweaver command accesses Dreamweaver's primary Help system and provides comprehensive information about all Dreamweaver features. Four options are available: Contents, Index, Search, and Favorites.

Using the Contents Sheet

The **Contents** sheet is useful for displaying Help when you know the general category of the topic in question, but not the specifics. Each topic in the Contents list is preceded by a book icon or question mark icon. A **book icon** indicates subtopics are available. Clicking the book icon (or associated link) displays the list of subtopics below that particular book. A **question mark icon** means information on the topic will display if you click the icon or the associated linked text. The next example shows how to use the Contents sheet to obtain information on how to spell check a Web page.

To Obtain Help Using the Contents Sheet

1

• **Click Help on the menu bar and then click Using Dreamweaver.**

• **Dreamweaver displays the Using Dreamweaver window.**

• **If necessary, double-click the title bar to maximize the window and click the Contents tab.**

• **To display a better view of the text, you can adjust the width of the left pane by moving the mouse pointer over the border separating the two panes.**

• **When the mouse pointer changes to a double-headed arrow, drag to the right or left to adjust the width of the left pane.**

FIGURE A-2

The Using Dreamweaver window displays (Figure A-2). Four options are available: Contents, Index, Search, and Favorites.

2

• **Click the Adding Content to Pages link.**

The Adding Content to Pages book is opened, and the help information is displayed in the right pane (Figure A-3). Additional books are displayed below the chosen topic. Links to these books also are displayed in the right pane.

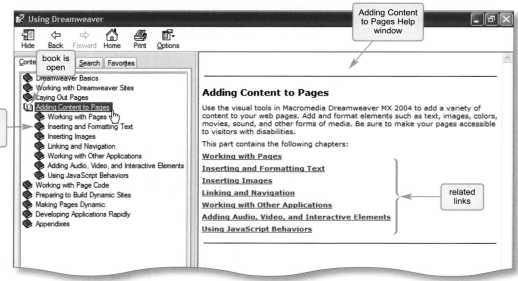

FIGURE A-3

3

• **Click the Inserting and Formatting Text book and then click the Checking spelling link.**

The information on the subtopic displays in the right pane (Figure A-4).

FIGURE A-4

Once the information on the subtopic displays, you can read it, you can click a link contained within the subtopic, or you can click the Print button on the toolbar to obtain a printed copy. Other buttons on the toolbar are Hide, Back, Forward, Home, and Options. The Home button returns you to your original location. The Back and Forward buttons move you back or move you forward to previously accessed screens. The Hide button hides the left pane, and the Options button displays a pop-up menu with all of the displayed buttons, plus Internet options. To view related topics, click the Previous or Next button in the displayed window.

Using the Index Sheet

The second sheet in the Using Dreamweaver window is the Index sheet. Use the **Index** sheet to display Help when you know the keyword or the first few letters of the keyword. The next steps show how to use the Index sheet to obtain help on inserting images.

To Use the Index Sheet

1

• **Click the Index tab.**

The Index sheet is displayed (Figure A-5). The insertion point is blinking in the Type in the keyword to find text box.

FIGURE A-5

2

• **Type** images **in the text box. Point to the inserting subtopic.**

As you type, Dreamweaver scrolls through the list of topics. The topic, images, and subtopics below the images topic display in the left pane (Figure A-6).

FIGURE A-6

3

• **Click the inserting subtopic and then click the Display button.**

Information about inserting an image displays in the right pane (Figure A-7).

FIGURE A-7

Using the Search Sheet

Using the **Search** feature allows you to find any character string, anywhere in the text of the Help system. The next steps show how to use the Search sheet to obtain help about using bold text.

To Use the Search Sheet

- **Click the Search tab.**

- **Type** Bold text **in the Type in the keyword to find text box.**

- **Click the List Topics button.**

- **Click Setting text property options in the Select Topic to display box.**

The Search sheet displays a list of topics containing references to bold and text in the left pane (Figure A-8). All of these topics contain the words bold and text somewhere within the document.

FIGURE A-8

2

- **Click the Display button.**

The Help screen for Setting text property options displays in the right pane. All incidents of the words bold and text are highlighted in the document in the right pane (Figure A-9).

FIGURE A-9

Using the Favorites Sheet

If you find that you search or reference certain topics frequently, you can save these topics in the Favorites sheet. The following steps show how to add the information about the Setting text property options topic to the Favorites sheet.

To Add a Topic to the Favorites Sheet

1

• **Click the Favorites tab. Point to the Add button.**

The Favorites sheet displays in the left pane. The title of the information (Setting text property options) is displayed in the Current topic text box in the left pane. The information on bold text that displayed because of your previous search is displayed in the right pane (Figure A-10).

FIGURE A-10

2

• **Click the Add button.**

The Setting text property options topic is added to the Favorites sheet (Figure A-11).

FIGURE A-11

3

• **Close the Using Dreamweaver Help window and return to Dreamweaver.**

Context-Sensitive Help

Using **context-sensitive help**, you can open a relevant Help topic in panel, inspectors, and most dialog boxes. To view these Help features, click a Help button in a dialog box, choose Help on the Options pop-up menu in a panel group, or click the question mark icon in an inspector.

Using the Question Mark Icon to Display Help

Many of the panels and inspectors within Dreamweaver contain a question mark icon. Clicking this icon displays context-sensitive help. Assume for the following example that you want to know about tables. The following steps show how to use the question mark icon to view context-sensitive help through the Property inspector. In this example, a table is displayed and selected in the Document window and the Property inspector displays table properties.

To Display Context-Sensitive Help on Tables

1

• **Point to the question mark icon in the Property inspector (Figure A-12).**

FIGURE A-12

2

• **Click the question mark icon.**

The Using Dreamweaver window displays and information pertaining to table properties displays in the right pane (Figure A-13). The Favorites tab is selected in the left pane because this was the last tab previously selected.

3

• **Close the Using Dreamweaver window and return to Dreamweaver.**

FIGURE A-13

Using the Options Menu to Display Help

Panels and dialog boxes also contain context-sensitive help. The following steps show how to display context-sensitive help for the Files panel. In this example, the Files panel is open and displayed within the Dreamweaver window.

To Use the Options Menu to Display Context-Sensitive Help for the Files Panel

 1

• **Click the Options button on the Files title bar and then point to Help on the Options pop-up menu.**

The Options pop-up menu is displayed (Figure A-14).

FIGURE A-14

2

• **Click the Help command.**

The Using Dreamweaver window displays, and information pertaining to using the Files panel is displayed in the right pane (Figure A-15). The Favorites tab is selected in the left pane because this was the last tab previously selected.

3

• **Close the Using Dreamweaver window and return to Dreamweaver.**

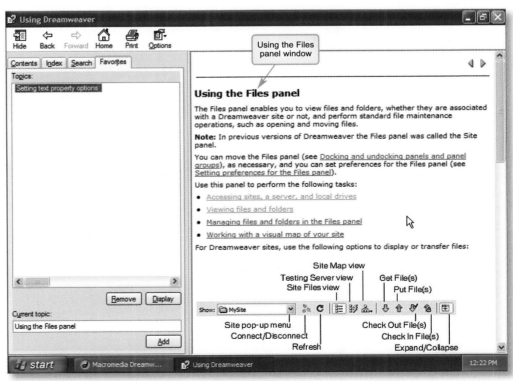

FIGURE A-15

Using the Reference Panel

The Reference panel in the panel groups is another valuable Dreamweaver resource. The Reference panel provides you with a quick reference tool for HTML tags, JavaScript objects, Cascading Style Sheets, and other Dreamweaver features. The next example shows how to access the Reference panel, review the various options, and select and display information on the <body> tag.

To Use the Reference Panel

1

• **Click Window on the menu bar and then point to Reference (Figure A-16).**

FIGURE A-16

2

• **Click Reference, and then click O'REILLY HTML Reference in the Book pop-up menu.**

The Reference panel in the Code panel group displays a welcome message (Figure A-17).

FIGURE A-17

3

• **Click the Tag box arrow and then point to BODY in the tag list.**

BODY is highlighted in the tag list (Figure A-18).

FIGURE A-18

4

• **Click BODY.**

Information on the <body> tag is displayed (Figure A-19).

FIGURE A-19

5

• **Click the Book box arrow and review the list of available reference books.**

A list of 11 reference books displays (Figure A-20). These are complete books and can be accessed in the same way the HTML reference book was accessed.

6

• **Close Dreamweaver.**

• **If the Macromedia Dreamweaver dialog box to save changes is displayed, click the No button.**

FIGURE A-20

Online Help Support

Dreamweaver also provides several support Web sites, including online forums and links to third-party online forums. Examples of these online forums and discussion groups are as follows:

- Dreamweaver — For Dreamweaver users developing Web sites.
- Dreamweaver Application Development — For Dreamweaver users creating dynamic Web sites.
- Dreamweaver Extensibility — For Dreamweaver users interested in extending the functionality of Dreamweaver.
- Dynamic HTML — This group discusses questions and issues regarding Dynamic HTML.
- General Information — This group discusses general information regarding Macromedia products that does not pertain to the other online forums.

For a selection of Help links, visit the Dreamweaver MX 2004 Web page (scsite.com/dreamweavermx04) and then click Appendix Help.

Apply Your Knowledge

1 Viewing the Dreamweaver What's New Features

Instructions: Start Dreamweaver. Perform the following tasks using the Dreamweaver What's New feature.

1. Click Help on the menu bar and then click Getting Started and Tutorials to open the Getting Started window.
2. Click Tutorial: Creating a Static Page and then click Open and Save a new page.
3. Read the information in the right pane.
4. Use a word processing program to write a short overview of what you learned.
5. Print a copy and submit or e-mail your overview to your instructor.

2 Using the Index Sheet

Instructions: Start Dreamweaver. Perform the following tasks using the Index sheet in the Using Dreamweaver Help system.

1. Press the F1 key to display the Using Dreamweaver window.
2. Click the Index tab and then type links in the Type in the keyword to find text box.
3. Click checking in the subtopic list and then click the Display button. Read the information in the right pane.
4. Use a word processing program to write a short overview of what you learned.
5. Print a copy and submit or e-mail your overview to your instructor.

3 Using Context-Sensitive Help

Instructions: Start Dreamweaver. Perform the following tasks using context-sensitive help in the Assets panel.

1. Click the Assets tab in the Files panel group.
2. Click the Options button and then click Help on the Options pop-up menu.
3. Read each of the topics about the Assets panel.
4. Use your word processing program to prepare a report on how to set up a favorite list of assets.
5. Print a copy and submit or e-mail your overview to your instructor.

Appendix B

Dreamweaver and Accessibility

Dreamweaver and Accessibility

Tim Berners-Lee, World Wide Web Consortium (W3C) founder, and inventor of the World Wide Web, indicates that the power of the Web is in its universality. He says that access by everyone regardless of disability is an essential aspect of the Web. In 1997, the W3C launched the **Web Accessibility Initiative** and made a commitment to lead the Web to its full potential. The initiative includes promoting a high degree of usability for people with disabilities. The United States government established a second initiative addressing accessibility and the Web through Section 508 of the Federal Rehabilitation Act.

Dreamweaver includes features that assist you in creating accessible content. To design accessible content requires that you understand accessibility requirements and make subjective decisions as you create a Web site. Dreamweaver supports three accessibility options: screen readers, keyboard navigation, and operating system accessibility features.

Using Screen Readers with Dreamweaver

Screen readers assist the blind and vision-impaired by reading text that is displayed on the screen through a speaker or headphones. The screen reader starts at the top-left corner of the page and reads the page content. If the Web site developer uses accessibility tags or attributes during the creation of the Web site, the screen reader also recites this information and reads non-textual information such as button labels and image descriptions. Dreamweaver makes it easy to add text equivalents for graphical elements and to add HTML tags to tables and forms through the accessibility dialog boxes. Dreamweaver supports two screen readers: JAWS and Window Eyes.

Activating the Accessibility Dialog Boxes

To create accessible pages in Dreamweaver, you associate information, such as labels and descriptions, with your page objects. After you have created this association, the screen reader can recite the label and description information.

You create the association by activating and attaching the accessibility dialog boxes to objects on your page. These dialog boxes appear when you insert an object for which you have activated the corresponding Accessibility dialog box. You activate the Accessibility dialog boxes through the Preferences dialog box. You can activate Accessibility dialog boxes for form objects, frames, images, and media. Accessibility for tables is accomplished by adding Summary text to the Table dialog box and adding image Ids and Alt text through the Property inspector. The steps on the next page use the Florida Parks index page as an example to show how to display the Preferences dialog box and activate the Image Accessibility dialog box.

To Activate the Images Accessibility Dialog Box

1

• **Start Dreamweaver and close all open panels. Click Edit on the menu bar and then point to Preferences (Figure B-1).**

FIGURE B-1

2

• **Click Preferences.**

The Preferences dialog box is displayed (Figure B-2).

FIGURE B-2

3

• **Click Accessibility in the Category list, click Images in the Accessibility area, and then point to the OK button.**

The Accessibility category is highlighted, and the Images check box is selected (Figure B-3). The Accessibility area includes five different options for which you can activate Accessibility dialog boxes: Form objects, Frames, Media, and Images.

4

• **Click the OK button.**

The Preferences dialog box closes, and the Dreamweaver Document window is displayed.

FIGURE B-3

No change is apparent in the Document window, but the Image Tag Accessibility Attributes dialog box is activated.

Inserting Accessible Images

Selecting Images in the Accessibility category activates the Image Tag Accessibility Attributes dialog box. Thus, any time you insert an image into a Web page, this dialog box will display. This dialog box contains two text boxes: Alternate Text and Long Description. The screen reader reads the information you enter in both text boxes. You should limit your Alternate Text entry to about 50 characters. For longer descriptions, provide a link in the Long Description text box to a file that gives more information about the image. It is not required that you enter data into both text boxes. The steps on the next page show how to use the Image Tag Accessibility Attributes dialog box when inserting an image.

To Insert Accessible Images

1

• **Click Insert on the menu bar and then point to Image (Figure B-4).**

FIGURE B-4

2

• **Click Image. If necessary, open the images folder and then click a file name. Point to the OK button.**

The Select Image Source dialog box is displayed (Figure B-5).

FIGURE B-5

• Click the OK button.

The Image Tag Accessibility Attributes dialog box is displayed. The insertion point is blinking in the Alternate text text box (Figure B-6). To display the Image Tag Accessibility Attributes dialog box, you must insert the image by using the Insert menu or by clicking the Image button on the Common tab of the Insert bar. Dragging an image from the Assets or Files panel to the Document window does not activate the Image Tag Accessibility Attributes dialog box.

FIGURE B-6

• Type a brief description of the image in the Alternate text text box.

• Click the folder icon to display the Select File dialog box. Locate and then click the description file name. Click the OK button in the Select File dialog box.

• Point to the OK button.

The image description is displayed in the Alternate text text box, and the long description file location is displayed in the Long description text box (Figure B-7).

FIGURE B-7

• Click the OK button in the Select Image Source dialog box.

No changes are displayed in the Document window. When the page is displayed in the browser, however, the screen reader recites the information you entered in the Image Tag Accessibility Attributes Alternate text text box. If you included a link to a file with additional information in the Long description text box, the screen reader accesses the file and recites the text contained within the file.

6

• Close Dreamweaver. Do not save the changes to the Web page.

Navigating Dreamweaver with the Keyboard

Keyboard navigation is a core aspect of accessibility. This feature also is of particular importance to users who have repetitive strain injuries (RSIs) or other disabilities, and to those users who would prefer to use the keyboard instead of a mouse. You can use the keyboard to navigate the following elements in Dreamweaver: floating panels, the Property inspector, dialog boxes, frames, and tables.

Using the Keyboard to Navigate Panels

When you are working in Dreamweaver, several panels may be open at one time. To move from panel to panel, press CTRL+ALT+TAB. A dotted outline around the panel title bar indicates the panel is selected (Figure B-9). Press CTRL+ALT+SHIFT+TAB to move to the previous panel. If necessary, expand the selected panel by pressing the SPACEBAR. Pressing the SPACEBAR again collapses the panel. Use the arrow keys to scroll the panel choices. Press the SPACEBAR to make a selection.

FIGURE B-8

Using the Keyboard to Navigate the Property Inspector

The following steps use the Florida Parks index page to show how to use the keyboard to navigate the Property inspector.

To Use the Keyboard to Navigate the Property Inspector

1

• **Start Dreamweaver and close all panels. Open a Web page. If necessary, press CTRL+F3 to display the Property inspector and then press CTRL+ALT+TAB until the Property inspector is selected.**

The dotted black outline around the word, Properties, indicates that the focus is on the Property inspector (Figure B-10).

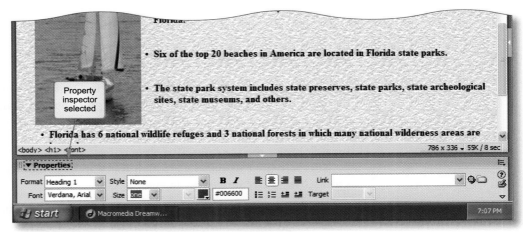

FIGURE B-9

2

• **Press the TAB key to move to the Format box.**

Heading 1 is highlighted in the Format box (Figure B-11).

FIGURE B-10

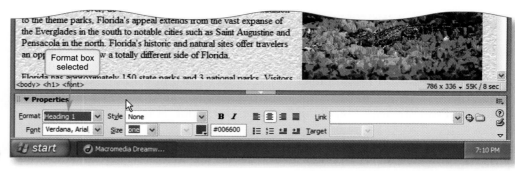

3

• **Use the keyboard Down Arrow key to select Heading 3 and then press the ENTER key.**

A dotted outline is displayed around the Heading 3 selection (Figure B-12). Heading 3 is applied to the text.

4

• **Close Dreamweaver. Do not save any of the changes.**

FIGURE B-11

Operating System Accessibility Features

The third method of accessibility support in Dreamweaver is through the Windows operating system high contrast setting. **High contrast** changes the desktop color themes for individuals who have vision impairment. The color schemes make the screen easier to view by heightening screen contrast with alternative color combinations. Some of the schemes also change font sizes.

You activate this option through the Windows Control Panel. The high contrast setting affects Dreamweaver in two ways:

- The dialog boxes and panels use system color settings.
- Code view syntax color is turned off.

Design view, however, continues to use the background and text colors you set in the Page Properties dialog box. The pages you design, therefore, continue to render colors as they will display in a browser. The steps on the next page show how to turn on high contrast and how to change the current high contrast settings.

To Turn On High Contrast

1

• **In Windows XP, click the Start button on the taskbar and then click Control Panel on the Start menu. If necessary, switch to Classic View and then double-click the Accessibility Options icon.**

The Accessibility Options dialog box is displayed (Figure B-13).

FIGURE B-12

2

• **Click the Display tab and then click Use High Contrast.**

The Display sheet is displayed. A checkmark appears in the Use High Contrast check box (Figure B-14).

FIGURE B-13

**• Click the
Settings button.**

*The Settings for High Contrast
dialog box is displayed
(Figure B-15).*

**• Click the Your current
high contrast scheme is
box arrow.**

*A list of available high
contrast options is displayed
(Figure B-16). High Contrast
Black (large) is selected. The
Web designer, however, would
select the appropriate option
to meet the needs of the
project for which he or she
is designing.*

FIGURE B-14

**• Click the Cancel
button.**

*The settings return to their
original values. To retain these
settings on your computer
would require that you click
the OK button.*

**• Click the Control Panel
Close button.**

*The Control Panel closes, and
the Windows XP desktop
displays.*

FIGURE B-15

Appendix C

Publishing to a Web Server

Publishing to a Remote Site

With Dreamweaver, Web designers usually define a local site and then do the majority of their site designing using the local site. In Project 1 you defined a local site. In creating the projects in this book, you have added Web pages to the local site, which resides on your computer's hard disk, a network drive, or possibly a Zip disk. To prepare a Web site and make it available for others to view requires that you publish your site by putting it on a Web server for public access. A Web server is an Internet- or intranet-connected computer that delivers the Web pages to visitors online. Dreamweaver includes built-in support that enables you to connect and transfer your local site to a Web server. To publish to a Web server requires that you have access to a Web server. Your instructor will provide you with the location, user name, and password information for the Web server on which you will publish your Web site.

After you establish access to a Web server, you will need a remote site folder. The remote folder is the folder that will reside on the Web server and will contain your Web site files. Generally, the remote folder is defined by the Web server administrator or your instructor. The name of your local root folder in this example is your last name and first initial. Most likely, the name of your remote folder also will be your last name and first initial. You upload your local site to the remote folder on the Web server. The remote site connection information must be defined in Dreamweaver through the Site Definition Wizard. You display the Site Definition Wizard and then enter the remote site information. Dreamweaver provides five different protocols for connecting to a remote site. These methods are as follows:

- **FTP** (File Transfer Protocol) This protocol is used on the Internet for sending and receiving files. It is the most widely used method for uploading and downloading pages to and from a Web server.
- **Local/Network** This option is used when the Web server is located on a local area network (LAN) or a company or school intranet. Files on LANs generally are available for internal viewing only.
- **SourceSafe Database, RDS (Remote Development Services), and WebDAV** These three protocols are systems that permit users to edit and manage files collaboratively on remote Web servers.

Most likely, you will use the FTP option to upload your Web site to a remote server.

Defining a Remote Site

You define the remote site by changing some of the settings in the Site Definition dialog box. To allow you to create a remote site using FTP, your instructor will supply you with the following information:

- **FTP host** is the Web address for the remote host of your Web server.
- **Host directory** is the directory name and path on the server where your remote site will be located.
- **Login** is your user name.
- **Password** is the FTP password to authenticate and access your account.

Assume for the following example that you are defining a remote site for the Florida Parks Web site.

To Define a Remote Site

1

• **Click Site on the menu bar and then click Manage Sites.**

• **Click Florida Parks in the Manage Sites dialog box.**

The Manage Sites dialog box displays, and Florida Parks is selected (Figure C-1).

FIGURE C-1

2

• **Click the Edit button. Click the Advanced tab.**

The Site Definition dialog box displays, and Local Info is selected in the Category column (Figure C-2).

FIGURE C-2

 3

• **Click the Remote Info category.**

• **Click the Access box arrow in the Remote Info pane and point to FTP.**

Remote Info is selected, and FTP is highlighted (Figure C-3).

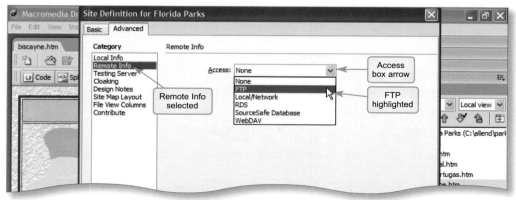

FIGURE C-3

4

• **Click FTP.**

• **Click each of the following boxes and fill in the information as provided by your instructor: FTP host, Host directory, Login, and Password.**

Information for David Allen displays in Figure C-4. Your screen will contain the information provided by your instructor.

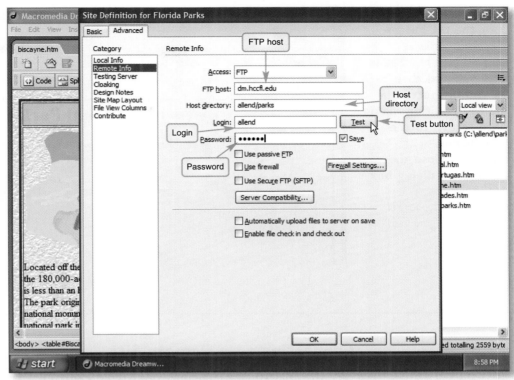

FIGURE C-4

5

• **Click the Test button to test the connection.**

• **If your connection is not successful, review your text box entries and make any necessary corrections. If all entries are correct, check with your instructor.**

Dreamweaver tests the connection and responds with a Macromedia Dreamweaver MX 2004 dialog box (Figure C-5).

FIGURE C-5

6

• **Click the OK button in the Macromedia Dreamweaver MX 2004 dialog box and then click the OK button in the Site Definition dialog box to return to the Dreamweaver workspace. Close the Manage Sites dialog box.**

The Biscayne National Park page displays (Figure C-6).

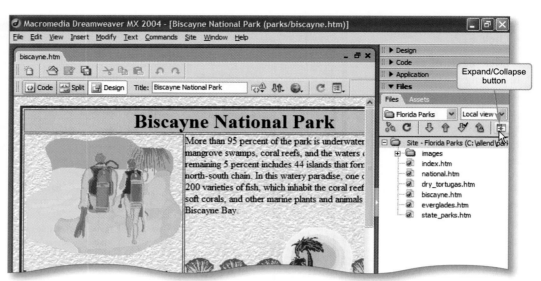

FIGURE C-6

Connecting to a Remote Site

Now that you have completed the remote site information and tested your connection, you can interact with the remote server. The remote site folder on the Web server for your Web site must be established before a connection can be made. This folder, called the **remote site root**, generally is created by the Web server administrator or your instructor. This book uses the last name and the first initial (allend) for the name of the remote site folder. Naming conventions other than your last name and first initial may be used on the Web server to which you are connecting. Your instructor will supply you with this information. If all information is correct, connecting to the remote site is done easily through the Files panel. The following steps illustrate how to connect to the remote site and display your remote site folder.

To Connect to a Remote Site

1

• **Click the Files panel Expand/Collapse button.**

The Site panel expands to show both a right and left pane (Figure C-7). The right pane contains the local site. The left pane contains information for accessing your remote files by clicking the Connects to remote host button.

FIGURE C-7

2

• **Verify that the root folder is selected. Click the Connects to remote host button.**

The connection is made, and the parks root folder displays (Figure C-8). The Connects to remote host/Disconnects from remote host button is a toggle button and changes to indicate that the connection has been made. The root folder on the remote site must be created by your instructor or Web server administrator before a connection can be made.

FIGURE C-8

Uploading Files to a Remote Server

Your next step will be to upload your files to the remote server. **Uploading** is the process of transferring your files from your computer to the remote server. **Downloading** is the process of transferring files from the remote server to your computer. Dreamweaver uses the term **put** for uploading and **get** for downloading.

To Upload Files to a Remote Server

1

• **Click the Put File(s) button. Point to the OK button.**

The Macromedia Dreamweaver MX 2004 dialog box is displayed to verify that you want to upload the entire site (Figure C-9).

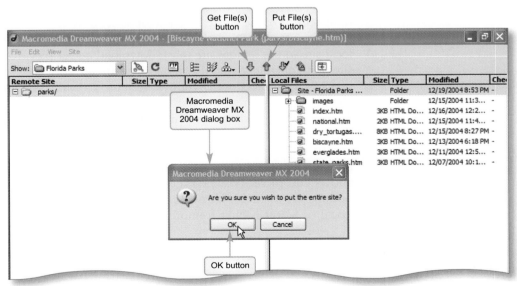

FIGURE C-9

2

• **Click the OK button.**

As the files begin to upload, a Status dialog box displays the progress information. The files are uploaded to the server (Figure C-10). The files may display in a different order from that on the local site. The display order on the server is determined by the settings on that computer.

3

• **Close Dreamweaver.**

FIGURE C-10

Remote Site Maintenance and Site Synchronization

Now that your Web site is on a Web server, you will want to continue to maintain the site. When you are connected to the remote site, you can apply many of the same commands to a folder or file on the remote site as you do to a folder or file on the local site. You can create and delete folders; cut, copy, delete, duplicate, paste, and rename files; and so on. These commands are available through the context menu.

To mirror the local site on the remote site, Dreamweaver provides a synchronization feature. **Synchronizing** is the process of transferring files between the local and remote sites so both sites have an identical set of the most recent files. You can select to synchronize the entire Web site or select only specific files. You also can specify Direction. Within **Direction**, you have three options: upload the newer files from the local site to the remote site (put); download newer files from the remote site to the local site (get); or upload and download files to and from the remote and local sites. Once you specify a direction, Dreamweaver automatically synchronizes files. If the files are already in sync, Dreamweaver lets you know you that no synchronization is necessary. To access the Synchronize command, you first connect to the remote server and then select Synchronize on the Site menu (Figure C-11).

To save the verification information to a local file, click the Save Log button at the completion of the synchronization process. Another feature within Dreamweaver allows you to verify which files are newer on the local site or the remote site. These options are available through the Files panel Edit menu by selecting Select Newer Local or Select Newer Remote.

FIGURE C-11

1 Defining and Uploading the B & B Lawn Service Web to a Remote Server

Instructions: Perform the following steps to define and upload the B & B Lawn Service Web site to a remote server.

1. Click Site on the menu bar, click Manage Sites, and then click Lawn Service. Click the Edit button. When the Site Definition dialog box displays, click the Advanced tab and then click Remote Info. Fill in the information as provided by your instructor, and then test the connection. Click the OK button.
2. Click the Expand/Collapse button on the Files panel toolbar and then click the Connects to remote host button. Click the local file root folder and then click the Put File(s) button on the Site panel toolbar to upload your Web site. Click the OK button in response to the Are you sure you wish to put the entire site? dialog box. Review your files to verify that they were uploaded. The files on the remote server may be displayed in a different order from that on the local site.
3. Click the Disconnects from remote host button on the Files panel toolbar. Click the Expand/Collapse button on the Files panel toolbar to display the local site and the Document window.
4. Close Dreamweaver.

Apply Your Knowledge

2 Defining and Uploading the CandleDust Web Site to a Remote Server

Instructions: Perform the following steps to define and upload the CandleDust Web site to a remote server.

1. Click Site on the menu bar, click Manage Sites, and then click CandleDust. Click the Edit button to display the Site Definition dialog box. Click the Advanced tab and then click Remote Info. Fill in the information as provided by your instructor, and then test the connection. Click the OK button.
2. Click the Expand/Collapse button on the Files panel toolbar and then click the Connects to remote host button. Click the local file root folder and then click the Put File(s) button on the Files panel toolbar to upload your Web site. Click the OK button in response to the Are you sure you wish to put the entire site? dialog box. Review your files to verify that they were uploaded. The files on the remote server may display in a different order from that on the local site.
3. Click the Disconnects from remote host button. Click the Expand/Collapse button on the Files panel toolbar to display the local site and the Document window. Close Dreamweaver.

3 Defining and Uploading the Credit Protection Web Site to a Remote Server

Instructions: Perform the following steps to define and upload the Credit Protection Web site to a remote server.

1. Click Site on the menu bar, click Manage Sites, and then click Credit Protection. Click the Edit button. Click the Advanced tab and then click Remote Info. Fill in the information as provided by your instructor, and then test the connection. Click the OK button.
2. Click the Expand/Collapse button on the Files panel toolbar and then click the Connects to remote host button. Click the local file root folder and then click the Put File(s) button on the Files panel toolbar to upload your Web site. Click the OK button in response to the Are you sure you wish to put the entire site? dialog box. Upload your files to the remote site. Review your files to verify that they were uploaded. The files on the remote server may display in a different order from that on the local site.
3. Disconnect from the site. Click the Expand/Collapse button on the Files panel toolbar to display the local site and the Document window. Close Dreamweaver.

4 Defining and Uploading the Plant City Web Site to a Remote Server

Instructions: Perform the following steps to define and upload the Plant City Web site to a remote server.

1. Click Site on the menu bar, click Manage Sites, and then click Plant City. Click the Edit button. Click the Advanced tab and then click Remote Info. Fill in the information as provided by your instructor, and then test the connection. Click the OK button.
2. Connect to the remote site and then click the local file root folder. Upload your files to the remote site. Disconnect from the site. Click the Expand/Collapse button on the Files panel toolbar to display the local site and the Document window. Close Dreamweaver.

FILE MENU

Action	Shortcut
New Document	Control+N
Open an HTML file	Control+O, or drag the file from the Explorer or Files panel to the Document window
Open in frame	Control+Shift+O
Close	Control+W
Close all	Control+Shift+W
Save	Control+S
Save as	Control+Shift+S
Exit/Quit	Control+Q or Alt+F4

EDIT MENU

Action	Shortcut
Undo	Control+Z or Alt+Backspace
Redo	Control+Y or Control+Shift+Z
Cut	Control+X or Shift+Delete
Copy	Control+C or Control+Insert
Paste	Control+V or Shift+Insert
Clear	Delete
Select all	Control+A
Select parent tag	Control+[
Select child	Control+]
Find and replace	Control+F
Find next	F3
Show code hints	Control+Spacebar
Go to line	Control+G
Indent code	Control+Shift+>
Outdent code	Control+Shift+<
Balance braces	Control+'
Copy HTML (in Design view)	Control+Shift+C
Paste HTML (in Design view)	Control+Shift+V
Preferences	Control+U

PAGE VIEWS

Action	Shortcut
Layout mode	Control+F6
Expanded Tables mode	F6
Live Data mode	Control+R
Live Data	Control+Shift+R
Switch to next document	Control+Tab
Switch to previous document	Control+Shift+Tab
Switch between Design and Code views	Control+`
Server debug	Control+Shift+G
Refresh Design view	F5

VIEWING PAGE ELEMENTS

Action	Shortcut
Visual aids	Control+Shift+I
Show rulers	Control+Alt+R
Show grid	Control+Alt+G
Snap to grid	Control+Alt+Shift+G
Page properties	Control+J

CODE EDITING

Action	Shortcut
Switch to Design view	Control+`
Print code	Control+P
Validate markup	Shift+F6
Edit tag	Control+F5
Open Quick Tag Editor	Control+T
Open Snippets panel	Shift+F9
Show code hints	Control+Spacebar
Insert tag	Control+E
Balance braces	Control+'
Select all	Control+A
Bold	Control+B
Italic	Control+I
Copy	Control+C
Find and replace	Control+F
Find next	F3
Paste	Control+V
Cut	Control+X
Redo	Control+Y
Undo	Control+Z
Toggle breakpoint	Control+Alt+B
Delete word left	Control+Backspace
Delete word right	Control+Delete
Go to line	Control+G
Select line up	Shift+Up
Select line down	Shift+Down
Character select left	Shift+Left
Character select right	Shift+Right
Move to page up	Page Up
Move to page down	Page Down
Select to page up	Shift+Page Up
Select to page down	Shift+Page Down
Move word left	Control+Left
Move word right	Control+Shift+Right
Move to start of line	Home
Move to end of line	End
Select to start of line	Shift+Home
Select to end of line	Shift+End
Move to top of code	Control+Home
Move to end of code	Control+End
Select to top of code	Control+Shift+Home
Select to end of code	Control+Shift+End

EDITING TEXT

Action	Shortcut
Create a new paragraph	Enter
Insert a line break 	Shift+Enter
Insert a nonbreaking space	Control+Shift+Spacebar
Move text or object to another place in the page	Drag selected item to new location
Copy text or object to another place in the page	Control-drag selected item to new location
Select a word	Double-click
Go to next word	Control+Right
Go to previous word	Control+Left
Go to previous paragraph	Control+Up
Open and close the Property inspector	Control+F3
Close window	Control+F4
Check spelling	Shift+F7

FORMATTING TEXT

Action	Shortcut
Indent	Control+Alt+]
Outdent	Control+Alt+[
Format > None	Control+0 (zero)
Paragraph Format	Control+Shift+P
Apply Headings 1 through 6 to a paragraph	Control+1 through 6
Align > Left	Control+Alt+Shift+L
Align > Center	Control+Alt+Shift+C
Align > Right	Control+Alt+Shift+R
Align > Justify	Control+Alt+Shift+J
Make selected text bold	Control+B
Make selected text italic	Control+I
Edit style sheet	Control+Shift+E

FINDING AND REPLACING TEXT

Action	Shortcut
Find	Control+F
Find next/Find again	F3
Replace	Control+H

WORKING IN TABLES

Action	Shortcut
Select table (with insertion point inside the table)	Control+A
Move to the next cell	Tab
Move to the previous cell	Shift+Tab
Insert a row (before current)	Control+M
Add a row at end of table	Tab in the last cell
Delete the current row	Control+Shift+M
Insert a column	Control+Shift+A
Delete a column	Control+Shift+- (hyphen)
Merge selected table cells	Control+Alt+M
Split table cell	Control+Alt+S
Increase column span	Control+Shift+]
Decrease column span	Control+Shift+[

WORKING WITH TEMPLATES

Action	Shortcut
Create new editable region	Control+Alt+V

WORKING IN FRAMES

Action	Shortcut
Select a frame	Alt+click in frame
Select next frame or frameset	Alt+Right Arrow
Select previous frame or frameset	Alt+Left Arrow
Select parent frameset	Alt+Up Arrow
Select first child frame or frameset	Alt+Down Arrow
Add a new frame to frameset	Alt+drag frame border
Add a new frame to to frameset using push method	Alt+Control-drag frame border

WORKING WITH LAYERS

Action	Shortcut
Select a layer	Control+Shift-click
Select and move layer	Shift+Control-drag
Add or remove layer from select	Shift-click layer border
Move select layer by pixels	Arrow keys
Move selected layer by snapping increment	Shift+Arrow keys
Resize selected layer by pixels	Control+Arrow keys
Resize selected layer by snapping increment	Control+Shift+Arrow keys
Toggle the display of the grid	Control+Alt+G
Align layers left	Control+Shift+1
Align layers right	Control+Shift+3
Align layers top	Control+Shift+4
Align layers bottom	Control+Shift+6
Make same width	Control+Shift+7
Make same height	Control+Shift+9

WORKING WITH IMAGES

Action	Shortcut
Change image source attribute	Double-click image
Edit image in external editor	Control-double-click image

GETTING HELP

Action	Shortcut
Using Dreamweaver Help topics	F1
Using ColdFusion Help topics	Control+F1
Reference	Shift+F1

MANAGING HYPERLINKS

Action	Shortcut
Create links	Shift+F8
Create hyperlink (select text)	Control+L
Remove hyperlink	Control+Shift+L
Drag and drop to create a hyperlink from a document	Select the text, image, or object, then Shift-drag the selection to a file in the Files panel
Drag and drop to change a hyperlink using the Property inspector	Select the text, image, or object, then drag the point-to-file icon in the Property inspector to a file in the Files panel
Open the linked to document in Dreamweaver	Control-double-click link
Check links selected	Shift+F8
Check links in the entire site	Control+F8

TARGETING AND PREVIEWING IN BROWSERS

Action	Shortcut
Preview in primary browser	F12
Preview in secondary browser	Shift+F12 or Control+F12

DEBUGGING IN BROWSERS

Action	Shortcut
Debug in primary browser	Alt+F12
Debug in secondary browser	Control+Alt+F12

SITE MANAGEMENT AND FTP

Action	Shortcut
Connect/Disconnect	Control+Alt+Shift+F5
Refresh	F5
Create new file	Control+Shift+N
Create new folder	Control+Alt+Shift+N
Delete file	Control+X
Copy file	Control+C
Paste file	Control+V
Duplicate file	Control+D
Rename file	F2
Get selected files or folders from remote FTP site	Control+Shift+D or drag files from Remote to Local pane in Files panel
Put selected files or folders on remote FTP site	Control+Shift+U or drag files from Local to Remote pane in Files panel
Check out	Control+Alt+Shift+D
Check in	Control+Alt+Shift+U
View site map	Alt+F8
Refresh Local pane	Shift+F5
Refresh remote site	Alt+F5
Cancel FTP	Escape

HISTORY PANEL

Action	Shortcut
Open the History panel	Shift+F10
Start/stop recording command	Control+Shift+X

SITE MAP

Action	Shortcut
View site files	F8
Refresh Local pane	Shift+F5
View as root	Control+Shift+R
Link to new file	Control+Shift+N
Link to existing file	Control+Shift+K
Change link	Control+L
Remove link	Control+Shift+L
Show/Hide link	Control+Shift+Y
Show page titles	Control+Shift+T
Zoom in site map	Control++ (plus)
Zoom out site map	Control+- (hyphen)

RECORDING COMMANDS

Action	Shortcut
Start recording	Control+Shift+X

PLAYING PLUGINS

Action	Shortcut
Play plugin	Control+Alt+P
Stop plugin	Control+Alt+X
Play all plugins	Control+Alt+Shift+P
Stop all plugins	Control+Alt+Shift+X

INSERTING OBJECTS

Action	Shortcut
Any object (image, shockwave movie, and so on)	Drag file from the Explorer or Files panel to the Document window
Image	Control+Alt+I
Table	Control+Alt+T
Flash	Control+Alt+F
Shockwave	Control+Alt+D
Named anchor	Control+Alt+A

OPENING AND CLOSING PANELS

Action	Shortcut
Insert bar	Control+F2
Properties	Control+F3
CSS Styles	Shift+F11
Behaviors	Shift+F3
Tag inspector	F9
Snippets	Shift+F9
Reference	Shift+F1
Databases	Control+Shift+F10
Bindings	Control+F9
Components	Control+F7
Assets	F11
Results	F7
Code inspector	F10
Frames	Shift+F2
History	Shift+F10
Layers	F2
Show/Hide panels	F4